MARKETING HANDBOOK
Third edition

Marketing Handbook

Third edition

Edited by
Professor Michael J Thomas

Gower

Published by
Gower Publishing Company Limited,
Gower House,
Croft Road,
Aldershot
Hants GU11 3HR,
England

Gower Publishing Company,
Old Post Road,
Brookfield,
Vermont 05036,
USA

British Library Cataloguing in Publication Data

Marketing handbook. — 3rd ed.
  1. Marketing
  I. Thomas, M.J. (Michael James)
  658.8

Library of Congress Cataloging-in-Publication Data
Marketing handbook

1. Marketing — Handbooks, manuals, etc.
I. Thomas, Michael J.
HF5415.M2988   1988   658.8   88–5554

ISBN 0–566–02746–1

Printed and bound in Great Britain by
Anchor Press Ltd, Tiptree, Essex

Contents

v

PART V   THE PRACTICE OF MARKETING

List of Illustrations

Figures

Tables

Notes on contributors

Danielle Baillieu *(Franchising)* is Director of Streetwise Franchising and is recognized as a leading authority on franchising. She gained her experience first hand from involvement in the industry, first as a franchisee of the Young's Group, followed by extensive research carried out for her book, *Streetwise Franchising*. In addition to speaking at franchise exhibitions and seminars, Ms Baillieu is actively lobbying for franchise legislation in the UK.

Michael J. Baker *(Developing and launching a new industrial product)* is Deputy Principal (Management) and Professor of Marketing at Strathclyde University. He is the author of numerous books and articles including *Marketing* (4th ed), *Marketing Strategy & Management* and *Market Development* and is editor of *The Marketing Book*. A past Chairman (1987) of the Institute of Marketing, he is active in consultancy and a director of five companies.

Brian Blackshaw *(Market development in the financial services industry)* is Managing Director of Profita Limited, a London-based management consultancy, which provides a range of consulting services to financial institutions and commercial organizations. Mr Blackshaw holds an MA in Marketing, the Diploma in Management Studies and is a member of the British Computer Society. He is also the author of several articles, a frequent presenter at conferences and a fellow of the Royal Society of Arts.

William G. Blyth *(Marketing research)* graduated in Economics and Social Statistics at Exeter University in 1970. He was company statistician at the British Market Research Bureau and group statistician at MIL Research, moving in 1982 to Audits of Great Britain, where he is currently director of research and development. He was recently returned for a second year as chairman of the Market Research Society, and is a fellow of both the Royal Statistical Society and the Institute of Statisticians.

Norman Boakes *(The international dimension* and *Reaching overseas markets)* is Managing Director of Euro Marketors Partnership Limited, a marketing consultancy working on behalf of the food, drink, agriculture and related industries in Europe. A past national chairman of the Institute of Marketing, he started his career as an engineering apprentice and then moved into the agricultural chemical industry as a sales manager before joining Nestlé where he spent thirteen years gaining international sales and marketing experience in the UK, Switzerland and Australia. He was UK export manager for nearly five years before leaving the company to become managing director of an international food broker handling food, drink and toiletries worldwide. He serves on the IM National Marketing Awards Adjudication Panel and is a council member of the Institute of Management Consultants as well as a frequent speaker at international conferences.

Tim Bowles *(Information systems for marketing)* started his market research career in 1970, after six years as a research psychologist. Between 1970 and 1978 he worked with the Schlackman Research Organization where he was a research director, responsible for marketing and social research projects. In 1978 he joined AGB Research as managing director of Research Surveys of Great Britain. In 1981 he moved within AGB to take responsibility for the company's UK market and audience measurement services, as managing director of Audits of Great Britain. In 1986 he joined MRB Group as Managing Director and became Chairman and Chief Executive in February 1987. Tim Bowles has published many papers on marketing research, market information systems and advanced data analysis.

Douglas Brownlie *(Analysing the environment)* worked in management services in the British Steel Corporation, held research and teaching posts in the Department of Marketing, Strathclyde University, before joining the Department of Management Studies of the University of Glasgow where he now teaches marketing and marketing strategy to part-time MBA students. As well as being a senior partner of strategic management consultants Network Associates, he is currently completing a doctoral study of the formation and implementation of marketing strategy. His previous research efforts have included studies of the diffusion of industrial innovation and forecasting of technical developments in offshore engineering.

Patrick Bruce *(Product design)* is currently Managing Director of Conran Design Pacific Limited, a multi-disciplinary sister company of Conran Design Group Limited, servicing the Asia Pacific region. He was formerly commercial director of Conran Design Group Limited. He trained originally as an industrial designer. After thirteen years of design and management experience in industry and education, he graduated from the Cranfield MBA programme prior to moving into a commercial and general management role in the design industry.

Jack Bureau *(Brand management)* a graduate in social studies from Durham University, began his career with five years' experience of market research for several large clients of a prominent London advertising agency. He became market research manager and then group brand manager for shaving and writing products at Gillette Industries and then marketing director of the health and chemical division of Cadbury-Schweppes. Now teaches the Marketing III element of the BA degree course and administers the student counselling scheme for the Strathclyde Business School He is the author of *Brand Management: Planning and Control.* Macmillan, 1981.

Malcolm Carlisle *(The legal framework)* studied history at Cambridge University. He then joined ICI Pharmaceuticals for whom he marketed ethical drugs in Europe. While at ICI he qualified at the Bar and then joined the legal department of Colgate-Palmolive Limited, later becoming deputy group legal adviser. In 1983 he moved to Colgate's affiliate, the Kendall Company, as their European legal counsel.

Charles Channon *(Advertising)* has been successively a researcher, an account director, a creative manager, and a director of account planning, starting at BMRB, moving to JWT on the account side, and then setting up the planning function at Ayer Barker. He was first chairman of the Account Planning Group and has written and spoken widely on advertising and planning. He became Director of Studies at the IPA in 1985.

Martin Christopher *(Physical distribution and logistics management)* is Professor of Marketing and Logistics Systems at Cranfield School of Management where he is head of the Marketing Faculty, one of Europe's largest centres for marketing teaching. His interests in marketing and logistics strategy are reflected in his consultancy and management activities. In this connection, he has worked for major international companies in North America, Europe, the Far East and Australia. As an author, he has written numerous books and articles and is on the editorial advisory board of a number of professional journals in the marketing and logistics area. He has held appointments as Visiting Professor at the Universiy of British Columbia, Canada, and the University of New South Wales, Australia. In addition he is a non-executive director of a number of companies.

Donald Cowell *(Developing and launching a new service)* is Professor of Marketing and Dean of Plymouth Business School at Plymouth Polytechnic, Devon. A graduate of Leeds University, he worked in industry before undertaking postgraduate work at the University of Bradford, Management Centre and then teaching marketing at the University of Loughborough. His current research interests include the marketing of services and he has written a book and a number of papers on this topic.

John A. Dawson *(Wholesaling)* is Fraser of Allander Professor of Distributive Studies at the University of Stirling where he is Director of the Institute for Retail Studies. After graduating in geography from the University of London, he took a Town Planning degree and then completed a doctorate on European retailing. Professor Dawson has held university posts at London, Nottingham and Wales, and visiting research and teaching positions at several American and Australian universities. He was a member of the Distributive Trades Committee of the National Economic Development Council. Current research is focusing on structural change in distribution, particularly in a comparative context, approaches to the introduction of new technology, employment in retailing and public policy approaches to the retail sector.

Bill Donaldson *(Customer service/customer care)* has been a lecturer in the Department of Marketing, University of Strathclyde since 1984. He has over ten years' business experience including a spell in marketing at British Steel followed by working for a UK tool company where he specialized in new product activities later becoming marketing planning manager. More recently he was employed as a marketing manager in the building materials sector.

Martin Duffell *(Recruitment – qualifications and sources* and *Selection – media and methods)* joined Unilever as a graduate marketing trainee in 1960. His career has taken him to four continents and he has managed twenty different brands, from detergents to razor blades. He has also led every size of sales team from six to 600. In 1984 he became the head of management recruitment for Unilever in the UK and he describes his present job as 'marketing Unilever at Britain's universities and polytechnics'.

Gordon Foxall *(Understanding customer behaviour)* is a professor of marketing at the University of Strathclyde. Since graduating in social science and undertaking applied research into the pricing of manufactured products, he has gained wide experience of teaching, research and consultancy. He took a Ph.D. in consumer psychology at the University of Birmingham and has held lectureships in marketing and business policy at the Universities of Newcastle upon Tyne and Birmingham. Subsequently he was Reader in Marketing at Cranfield School of Management. He is author/co-author of nine books on marketing, including the bestselling *Consumer Behaviour,* Croom Helm, 1980.

William Giles *(Marketing planning for maximum growth)* is a director of the Strategic Marketing Development Unit and is the original architect of the 'Marlow method' – a process designed to develop strategic thinking amongst managers in larger organizations. He is also an associate consultant of P-E International and teaches MBA students at the City and Cardiff Business Schools. Prior to joining Stratmar, he held senior marketing positions at 3M and Ciba-Geigy.

Frank Jefkins *(Public relations)* has twenty books in print including his new *International Dictionary of Marketing and Communication.* He is a fellow of the Institute of Public Relations and the British Association of Industrial Editors. In 1986 he was awarded the IPR's

Sir Stephen Tallents medal for his 'exceptional achievement in and contributions to the development of public relations practice'.

Bernard Katz *(Agents* and *Telephone marketing)* graduated in psychology from Edinburgh University. After working with a London export merchant, he subsequently founded his own import–export company and traded round the world for twenty years. Bernard Katz is currently senior lecturer at Missenden Abbey Management Centre. Publications include five marketing books. He conducts seminars regularly in Asia and South America.

John Lidstone *(The art of negotiation)* is Deputy Chairman of Marketing Improvements Group plc, chairman, Management Consultancies Association, 1986–7, non-executive director, Kalamazoo plc and a member of the National Executive Committee of The Institute of Marketing. Internationally recognized for his marketing consultancy and lecturing, author of seven books on marketing, sales management and selling. *Training Salesmen on the Job* and *Negotiating Profitable Sales* were made into widely acclaimed, award-winning films by Rank and Video Arts. In 1981 John Lidstone was elected a member of the British Academy of Film and Television Arts.

Simon Majaro *(Product planning)* is Visiting Professor of Marketing Strategy at the Cranfield School of Management, Director of Strategic Management Learning and also managing director of a firm of international management consultants that bears his name, with offices in London and New York; graduate in law at the University of London; barrister at law; graduate in Business Administration at the IMI, the Geneva-based business school; lectures regularly at Ashridge Management College, and visiting lecturer at a number of US and European business schools. His writings include *International Marketing – A Strategic Approach to World Markets* and *Marketing in Perspective*, both published by Unwin Hyman. He is co-author of *Strategy Search – A Guide to Marketing for Chief Executives and Directors* published by Gower. His book *The Creative Gap – Managing Ideas for Profit*, was launched by Longman in April 1988.

Alan Melkman *(Using new information technology)* is managing director of Marketing Dynamics Ltd, a qualified engineer and a graduate of the London Business School. He started his career in the sales area and obtained his MBA before moving into brand and marketing management in the grocery market. He has been a consultant for more than twenty years. He has gained substantial experience working for many organizations in a wide variety of markets in the UK and overseas and has written a number of marketing articles and books.

Eric Morgan *(Retailing)* was managing director of British American Cosmetics for sixteen years until the business was recently sold to Beecham. BAC included Yardley, Lentheric and a dozen other 'houses' of cosmetics and perfumery, operating in over 140 countries. Previously, he spent eight years with Sterling Drug and ten years with the overseas division of Procter and Gamble. In retirement, he is involved in business strategy, management education and in the encouragement of science and technology in schools.

Rory Morgan *(Pricing as a marketing tool)* joined RBL in 1972 from university with a degree in psychology and physiology. Since then he has worked in a number of consumer groups covering a wide range of product areas, both in the UK and internationally, and in the context of the latter, spent a period of secondment to the research subsidiary in East Africa. He was group head of a consumer group within RBL, with special responsibility for the development of computer modelling techniques and similar areas, in which field he has delivered a number of papers both in Europe and North America. Subsequently appointed technical and development director for the RBL group, part of Research International, with the innovatory role of developing and supporting advanced research techniques, and in particular computer applications. As such, he runs the technical development department within the company.

Nicholas J. O'Shaughnessy *(Direct mail)* is Lecturer in Marketing at Loughborough University of Technology, and a former president of the Oxford Union. As well as his interest in direct mail, he is researching the applications of marketing to politics. He has two manuscripts awaiting publication: *The Phenomenon of Political Marketing*, to be published by Macmillan, and *UK Universities and the Future*, to be published as an Institute of Economics Affairs Hobart Paper.

Stan Paliwoda *(Countertrading)* is lecturer in Marketing and International Business at UMIST (University of Manchester Institute of Science and Technology). He is the author of *Joint East–West Marketing and Production Ventures* (Gower, 1981); *International Marketing* (Heinemann, 1986); and with Peter Turnbull, *Research in International Marketing* (Croom-Helm, 1986). Dr Paliwoda's interests lie in international and industrial marketing. He is a national examiner in marketing for the Institute of Export.

Jerry Parker *(Trade marketing)* has been mainly in sales for fifteen years starting with Kimberly Clark. He moved to Gillette where he was sales planning and promotions manager and general sales manager of one of the UK divisions. A spell as group sales manager for Gallahers' vending operation followed before he joined Cinzano/IDV as sales director. He has held middle management positions in training, marketing, and major account sales. He is now a director of WRPO, a leading trade marketing consultancy.

Pamela Robertson *(Developing and launching a new consumer product)* is an expert in devising development strategies for companies involved in consumer products and services. Ms Robertson has pioneered the development of KAE's trade research operations and is a regular writer and speaker on trade research as well as on business development. She is presently chief executive of KAE Development Limited, and a director of KAE Group.

John Saunders *(Analysing the competition)* is National Westminster Bank Professor of Marketing at the University of Technology, Loughborough. Previously he has worked for Bradford Management Centre, the University of Warwick, the Pacific–Asian Management Institute (Hawaii) and the Hawker Siddeley Group. As a senior consultant he has worked with many companies and institutions. These include Unilever, ICI, TI, THF, Dixons, Woolworth, British Standards Institute, the Asian Development Bank and the Singapore Government.

J. E. Smith *(Financial controls in marketing)* is the Chairman of J. H. Lavender and Co Ltd, aluminium founders of West Bromwich, and the managing partner of Midland Consultants of Sutton Coldfield (who specialize in management accountancy and planning and control procedures). He is also a visiting lecturer at many education establishments including Aston University and on company courses.

Bill Stewart *(Packaging as a marketing tool)* gained M.Inst.Pkg (Dip) in 1970 while working at PIRA. He joined S. Maws & Sons Limited and gained a broad sense of commercial experience. In 1972 he was appointed packaging engineer with 3M UK and during a ten-year working period became manager, packaging engineering. He established a freelance consultancy prior to his appointment as technical packaging manager at Siebert/Head. He is widely experienced in finding economic and technically creative solutions to the many kinds of practical problems encountered in corporate identity and packaging. He was appointed a director of the company in 1985.

Michael J. Thomas *(The marketing function and its organization* and *Customer service/customer care)* having worked for the Metal Box Company in the 1950s, emigrated to the United States where he spent eleven years teaching on postgraduate courses in the School of Management, Syracuse University. He joined the Department of Marketing at Lancaster University in 1972, was appointed a Professor of Marketing at Strathclyde University in January, 1987 and Head of the Marketing Department in 1988. He is on the National Council of the Institute of Marketing, chairman of the Marketing Education Group and is a frequent visitor to overseas markets including Nigeria, Poland and, of course, North America. He is particularly interested in the management of new product development, brand management problems and export marketing. His *Pocket Guide to Marketing* was published by *The Economist*/Basil Blackwell in 1986 and *The Marketing Digest* by Heinemann in 1988.

Stuart Thomson *(Speciality selling)* after much experience 'on the road', in the UK and overseas, has launched, edited and published *Selling* newsletter for speciality salesmen and saleswomen. The newsletter rapidly achieved an international circulation. In March 1986 it was acquired by MCB University Press Limited with Stuart Thomson being retained as its editor. He is a company director.

David Tonks *(Market segmentation)* is a lecturer in the Department of Marketing at the University of Lancaster. He has strong interests in market segmentation and marketing simulations. He also works as a marketing consultant and has been involved in over thirty large assignments for a variety of clients. He was formerly employed as a marketing manager in port services and as a brand manager in food products. He belongs to Acorn Group AO1 and is a light user of brown sauce.

Alan Toop *(Sales promotion)* is president of the sales promotion consultancy, The Sales Machine International, and author of *Choosing the Right Sales Promotion*, and *Only £3.95?!* His early career was in marketing with Unilever, including a spell as Persil brand manager, and in advertising with J Walter Thompson.

David Waterhouse *(Exhibitions)* has been involved in the industry for twenty-seven years – as an exhibitor, as an exhibition designer and, latterly, as managing director of Rapier Design, a member of the Charles Barker Group and one of Britain's leading exhibition design companies. Now retired, he is resident in Queensland, Australia. He is the author of *Making the Most of Exhibitions* (Gower, 1987).

Ian Watson *(Wholesaling)* is a Research Fellow in the Institute for Retail Studies at the University of Stirling. After leaving college he joined James Hall & Co and proceeded to work for the next five years within the food wholesaling industry. He left James Hall to complete his business studies degree. His research interest is structural change within the wholesaling industry.

Jack Wheatley *(Distribution channel management)* is the Chairman and Managing Director of Moores of London Ltd, a company operating internationally in the business forms, business systems and promotional products market areas. His company uses a variety of distribution channels according to the nature of the particular market requirements. He has had a long association with the Institute of Marketing, and was chairman of the Central London and Manchester branches, moving on to national chairman in 1985.

Mike Wilson *(Sales management)* is Chairman of Marketing Improvements Group plc, a leading European marketing consultancy and training organization. Operating out of offices in London and Singapore, MI covers all European markets and languages, with MI Asia Pacific (Pte) Limited servicing the Far East and Australasian markets. Mike Wilson's books, *Managing a Sales Force* and *The Management of Marketing*, are standard texts within many companies and his articles on marketing appear regularly in business publications.

Bernard Wynne *(Staff development and training)* is a consultant advising on management development and training with Cockman, Consultants and Partners Limited, based in London. He was previously Training and Development Manager for Woolwich Building Society.

Jack Zimmerman *(Direct response)* started in the business after leaving school and specialized in direct response advertising at an early age and as he says, there have been tremendous market shifts since those days way back in the 1950s. He regards direct response as the only place you cannot hide. You spend your money and you await the result. It is a business with a very buoyant future.

Preface

The last edition of *Marketing Handbook* appeared in 1981. It was reviewed favourably in both academic journals and publications read by marketing practitioners, hence the publishers felt that it had made a useful contribution. As we approach the end of the 1980s, it has become increasingly clear that, certainly as far as the United Kingdom is concerned, it has been the decade of marketing; that is, a period when marketing as a business discipline has matured, where good marketing practice is a significant discriminator between successful and unsuccessful companies.

It has been my privilege to have been working in the United Kingdom since 1972, and to observe the maturing of the discipline of marketing, the increasing professionalism of marketing managers, the growing stature of the Institute of Marketing, and to see better-qualified students opting for marketing courses in tertiary education, anxious to join a profession that twenty years ago was held in relatively low esteem.

As an academic, part of my responsibility is to monitor new developments in the field and interpret them to both students and practitioners. Marketing academics are denied the privilege(?) of staying within the ivory tower, since they must demonstrate their relevance to their peers in industry and commerce, as well as to their academic colleagues. I have had an opportunity to observe a wide range of contributions to marketing knowledge, and I was delighted therefore, to be asked by Gower to edit a new edition of the Handbook.

As the Notes on Contributors section shows, this new edition draws upon a wide range of talents. Well over half the chapters are written by practitioners, so in no sense is this the world of marketing seen from the ivory tower. Some chapters are considerably longer than others because I have judged that the topics they deal with require in-depth treatment. They are to be used as works of reference as well as sources of enlightenment.

I have organized the book into five main parts. Part I focuses on the need for a strategic view of the marketing task, and provides detailed discussion about marketing information systems, marketing planning, environmental analysis and analysing the competition. It includes a piece on strategic change in a fast-changing environment, that of financial services.

Part II looks at organizing for effective marketing, highlighting such topics as recruiting and selection, development and training, sales management, brand management and controlling the marketing function.

Part III is concerned with developing the product, the term product being used in its broadest sense – new product development, pricing, services marketing and how market research can play a crucial role in the product development process.

Distribution is the subject of Part IV, which examines in detail several aspects of distribution, including marketing to the trade, wholesaling and retailing.

The final Part, 'The practice of marketing', looks at a number of marketing activities where change is rapidly causing knowledge obsolescence; hence my choice of topics reveals where I think marketing managers need to redefine the conventional wisdom. Familiar topics such as advertising, sales promotion and public relations are subjected to scrutiny, newer techniques such as telephone marketing, countertrading and customer care are described in a way that will, I hope, stimulate the reader.

Indeed, my hope is that this entire volume stimulates the reader. We all too easily fall into the trap of thinking we know all we need to know about the problems we deal with in our professional lives. The passage of time is a destroyer, and knowledge gained even five years ago begins to wear thin. Knowledge life-cycles are shortening as fast as product life-cycles. This book is intended to give its readers an update on the multifaceted world of marketing. I hope it succeeds. The ultimate judgement will be made by my customers and you the reader and, if you have critical comments and useful suggestions to make, I hope that you will not hesitate to contact me.

Good marketing, and even better profits and return on investment!

I wish to thank my secretary, Ann Clark, who has borne a responsibility way above the call of duty, managing the complex logistics of meeting both my and my publishers' deadlines with fortitude and good humour. The editor of a work such as this relies very heavily on his authors, and I wish to record my thanks to all the contributors to this book for their ready co-operation and response to my requests.

Michael J Thomas
Professor of Marketing
University of Strathclyde
Glasgow G4 ORQ

Part I
DEVELOPING A MARKETING STRATEGY

1

Information systems for marketing

Tim Bowles

It is now widely accepted that relevant, accurate and timely information is a prerequisite for effective management decisions. The task of management information systems is to provide the right information, at the right time and to the right person. It is also important that this information is presented in a form which can easily be understood and used by its recipients. In marketing management, information can be applied at various levels, including the formulation of strategy, the implementation of strategy, and evaluation and control.

The scope of marketing information systems, and the interest in these systems has certainly grown in the 1980s, driven by the availability of more information and by the development of computer techniques for its manipulation. Much of the available information is, however, still difficult for market management to use effectively, without considerable computer skills. This chapter reviews the types of marketing information available and the tools that can be used to manipulate them.

Readers wanting a more detailed account will find it in Piercy and Evans (1983), *Managing Market Information*, although this useful book pre-dates some of the developments discussed below.

MARKETING DATA SOURCES

A wide variety of types of data can be useful to marketing management. Sources include both textual and statistical material which may originate from inside or from outside the company. The information may be general in nature, with relevance to broad strategic issues, or it may be quite specific and be applied in day-to-day decisions about pricing, distribution and promotional spend.

Some of the main data sources are described in the following paragraphs.

Internal company data

Leading marketing companies now place great emphasis on providing internal data on product performance. The development of internal reporting systems has been greatly assisted by the availability of accounting and spreadsheet systems for analysis and presentation.

The scope of internal marketing information will vary widely both between different industries and between different companies in the same industry. Internal marketing data should in most cases cover at least the following types of report:

1 sales levels – national and by sales territory;
2 revenue, cost and profit performance of product lines or brands;
3 comparison of revenue and costs with budget;
4 seasonal indices of product sales;
5 stock and distribution levels among major customers (both wholesale and retail);
6 product warranty returns;
7 customer complaint analysis;
8 marketing and advertising cost reports.

An analysis of the structure of information systems for marketing management may be found in a 1971 publication from the US National Association of Accountants, entitled *Information for Marketing Management*. It analyses both the types of internal information required and the relationship with various types of management decision. It is a very useful publication for anyone planning or modifying a market information system.

4

Market measurement

Market measurement is perhaps the most vital kind of external information for the marketing department. Whereas internal data can tell us a great deal about the performance of our own products, external data are required to tell us how our own performance measures up against that of our competitors and to give us the clues as to how we might change our performance through product development, distribution, pricing and promotion. There are many sources of market measurement data, each with its own strengths and weaknesses. Each method will provide information on market size, product or brand share, prices paid and retail structure of sales. The information helps manufacturers to monitor their own market performance and the effect of their marketing strategies. It also forms a basis for negotiation between manufacturer and retailer, as manufacturers compete for shelf space in stores.

Retail audits involve the measurement of markets via retail sales. Retail audit interviewers call regularly at a representative sample of retail outlets to record information on consumer sales offtake, retail purchases and stocks, distribution, and retail selling prices. This information can be adjusted statistically to give total market estimates and can be analysed nationally and by region. The strength of retail audit data lies in their coverage of stock and distribution, and the fact that they do not rely upon consumers recording or remembering what they have bought.

In the UK the provision of retail audit information is dominated by the A. C. Nielsen Company which offers retail audit measurements covering groceries, drugs, alcoholic drinks and tobacco products.

Consumer panels are the main alternative method of measuring consumer markets. Groups of consumers keep a diary of their purchases across a number of product fields or retain evidence of these purchases to be collected regularly by interviewers. Panel members are recruited so as to be representative of the total population and the results are used to calculate total market estimates.

A special strength of consumer panels is that the same people are monitored over time. This means that market trends can be tracked very accurately and individual consumer purchasing behaviour can be tracked through time. Analysis of panel data can throw light on such issues as the customer profile for different products and brands, brand share within different retail outlets and the rate at which new products penetrate the buying population. Consumer panel market measurement is carried out in the UK by AGB (Audits of Great Britain). The markets measured by consumer panels include groceries, consumer durables, toiletries, cosmetics, fresh foods and alcoholic drinks.

Industry data pools involve the collection of information on sales volumes via trade associations or other groups of manufacturers. By pooling their internal data on product sales, for analysis by an independent statistical agency, each member of the manufacturing group can compare its own sales volume against that of other members. While such information is useful, it is generally not capable of detailed analysis and is restricted by the level of participation among significant manufacturers. Data pooling arrangements do not normally permit the separate identification of individual manufacturer performance. Each participating manufacturer can therefore compare his own data only against the total market, rather than against individual competitors.

Retail scanning of the bar codes now printed on a wide range of consumer products will become increasingly important in the provision of market measurement information. The introduction of EPOS (electronic point of sale) equipment at supermarket check-outs has opened new possibilities for market measurement, at a level of accuracy which has hitherto been impossible. Access to UK scanner data from retailer check-outs is controlled via the ANA (Article Numbering Association) which represents manufacturers' and retailers' interests. While the penetration of EPOS equipment in UK supermarkets is still growing slowly there is already a commercial service, based on scanner reports from a selected sample of stores, offered by A. C. Nielsen. Such services will become more significant as the retail coverage of scanners increases (Staples, 1986).

The user of market measurement information may be puzzled by

6

multiple sources of what is apparently the same information. In practice, each market measurement source will produce slightly different market estimates because of the data collection method employed. An account of these variations and how they may be reconciled can be found in Bowles and Blyth (1985).

Media audience measurement

Consumer goods manufacturers spend large amounts of money on media advertising and need to evaluate the effectiveness of this spending, in terms of the audience their advertising reaches. Media audience data tend to be handled, on behalf of manufacturers, by their advertising agencies. There is a good reason for this in that the advertising agencies are generally responsible for buying advertising time and space. Information on the audience levels for different media, and the structure of these audiences is essential in media planning and provides a basis on which advertising time and space can be bought and sold.

Marketing departments in some leading manufacturing companies do themselves become involved in the analysis of audience data. In any event, executives concerned in marketing management will need a broad understanding of the source and uses of audience data, even if these data are not incorporated formally in their market information system.

In the UK, audience measurement for the different media is usually controlled by bodies which represent media owners, advertising agencies and the leading manufacturing companies. These bodies lay down the technical specification for audience measurement and act as a channel for sharing the cost of collecting and analysing audience information. The principal audience measurement services are:

1 television – BARB (Broadcasters' Audience Research Board);
2 press and magazines – JICNARS;
3 radio – JICRAR;
4 posters – Outdoor Advertising Association (JICPAR working party);
5 cable TV – JICCAR.

The actual task of audience measurement is awarded, through these joint industry committees, to market research companies which undertake to meet the technical requirements laid down. Access to the data is obtained via subscription to the governing body.

Single-source surveys of markets and media

Single-source surveys of markets and media are also a key source of information for market and media planning. Market measurement services and media audience measurement are normally conducted through quite separate data collection exercises. They offer no facility to relate people's purchasing habits to media exposure. This facility is provided in the UK by the TGI (Target Group Index) single-source survey carried out and marketed by the British Market Research Bureau. It offers a unique opportunity to target media advertising so that it reaches users of particular products or brands. This is possible because people's product usage patterns can be cross-analysed with their TV viewing, reading and radio listening habits, since both kinds of information are collected from the same sample.

While the industry-controlled audience-research studies provide continuous and detailed information on exposure to a single medium, TGI provides less detailed information but covers the whole range of media. It is therefore widely used in the early stages of media selection and planning.

Magazines and the press

Magazines, and the daily and weekly press, are also important sources of marketing information. The trade press, in particular, provides a valuable source of competitive intelligence covering all aspects of marketing activity from brand launches to advertising campaigns for existing brands. The financial press and the financial pages of the daily press provide valuable reports on competitive activity.

In the past, companies have had a choice between maintaining their own press-cutting services or employing one of the commercial services, which will select material relating to particular topics, products or companies. The development of computerized text-retrieval systems has given rise to commercial services which provide on-line access to computerized databanks drawn from the press. Many of these services are too general for detailed marketing application but, in the last two years, a number of database services have been introduced directly aimed at the marketer. These are dealt with at greater length in the section on database services.

Social and economic data

Information on social and economic trends has limited application in the implementation and control of marketing policy. They are much more significant, however, in the stage of strategy development. Important social trends, such as changes in the employment level, increases in the proportion of working housewives and the altering age distribution of the population, all have significant implications for the long-term planning of products and services.

The richest source of such information lies in government statistics and the publications of the Central Statistical Office. A useful overview, which also refers to the major government surveys on which it is based, is the regular HMSO publication *Social Trends*. This is a unique source for those wishing to keep in touch with the changing profile of our population and associated social conditions.

Most of the information published by the government statistical services covers behaviour rather than attitudes and, for information on attitudes and values, the marketer must commission his or her own private surveys or identify a suitable source of syndicated survey information. The MONITOR survey, run by Taylor Nelson Research, is employed by manufacturing and service companies to track changing consumer values and attitudes over time.

Outside the realm of official statistics there is a wide range of other statistical sources which may prove valuable from time to time. A review of such sources has been compiled by the Statistics Service at the University of Warwick and published as *Sources of Unofficial UK Statistics*. These sources include trade associations, professional bodies, local authorities, development corporations and financial and economic forecasting organizations.

Specially commissioned market research

Most of this chapter is concerned with published sources of market information which can be obtained by subscription. The more sophisticated market information systems users will also incorporate their specially commissioned studies in their databanks of information. These privately commissioned studies have a broad coverage which includes product testing, new product development, advertising evaluation and other forms of communication research. They are discussed in detail in Chapter 15. Useful directories of companies offering market research services are published both by the Market Research Society and by AMSO, the Association of Market Survey Organizations.

ACCESSING AND MANIPULATING MARKET INFORMATION

Market information in statistical form, both from internal and external sources, has traditionally been published in the form of detailed printed reports. Since many market and audience measurements are analysed and reported on a weekly or monthly basis, this has meant that the information user would quickly acccumulate large volumes of data which had to be accessed in the manner of a vast telephone directory. Any special analysis required had to be requested via specialist data processing departments, who would then often deliver the analysis long after the management decision, to which the information was relevant, had been taken.

The evolution of computer software in the last twenty years should have changed all that, although, as we shall see, the transformation is far from complete.

On-line data systems

On-line access to market and media information has been an active area for development. In such systems, the user obtains access to a central databank of information, held on a central mainframe computer, via a computer terminal and a special enquiry language. These developments were most rapid for media research because of the large volumes of data generated, particularly from TV audience measurement, and because of the need of media planners to estimate the audience reach and frequency of advertisng exposure achieved by different media schedules. This led to the development of commercial on-line services which offered subscriber access to most of the main media audience databanks. Such on-line systems are offered by IMS, Donovan Data Systems and Telmar in the UK.

On-line access to the market measurement databases has been much slower to develop although several leading manufacturing companies have created their own software for the analysis of market measurement data, the data being delivered in computer tape form, rather than printed form, from the company conducting the source research. Many users of market measurement data, however, remain dependent on printed reports. Decision-support systems provide an alternative for those who have not developed bespoke systems themselves.

Decision-support systems

Decision-support systems are computer systems which enable management to access and manipulate data to help them make better decisions. The term is variously used to describe systems ranging from spreadsheets, such as Lotus 123 or Supercalc, to large integrated modelling programs. There are, however, a number of proprietary decision-support systems which are specially designed to assist marketing management. The more sophisticated examples will provide:

1 terminal or PC access to a central database of internal and external information;
2 menus or enquiry languages for selecting the desired data from the array and transforming it;
3 graphics and presentation facilities;
4 a high level computer language for the development of specific applications;
5 modelling facilities to examine various 'what if' propositions and for forecasting.

ACUSTAR, distributed by MacDonnell Douglas Information Systems, is more directed at marketing decision support than many of the alternatives. It is specifically designed for the interrogation, analysis and reporting of time series data from different marketing information sources. It is, however, more structured and less flexible than two other highly developed decision-support systems which are suitable for marketing application.

Both EXPRESS, distributed by Information Resources, and ACUMEN, distributed by Effem Management Services, offer a very wide range of facilities for data analysis and presentation. Both systems can be used by executives with varying degrees of data processing skill, from those who want to select from a simple menu to those who are familiar with programming personal computers. Both systems also offer an efficient language for the development of tailor-made systems for applications in individual companies.

In the past, decision-support systems of this type have required the storage capacity and power of large minicomputers or mainframe systems. Information Resources has now launched pcEXPRESS, which brings decision support within the reach of a personal-computer user. This is an important development as the mainframe version of EXPRESS has, since its introduction in 1975, been success-fully employed by several leading manufacturing companies to structure their market information requirements.

Expert systems

Most decision-support systems are designed for the retrieval, analysis and reporting of statistical data. To this extent they impose a relatively structured approach upon the user. Perhaps the most promising development for the future arises from the study of artificial intelligence, the attempt to simulate human thinking processes in a computer. Expert systems use techniques of artificial intelligence to support decisions in complex real-life situations which call upon different kinds of expertise. Expert systems are able to reason and infer, rather than simply store and analyse statistics.

These systems work by combining a databank of information in a subject area with rules of thumb which enable conclusions to be drawn. These rules of thumb are normally developed by programming into the computer the views and judgements of recognized experts in the field. This approach allows a company to maximize the value of the experience and judgement of senior executives, by programming the guidelines which they use to make decisions into computer software which can then be used to support decisions by less skilled executives.

Expert systems are distinguished from decision-support systems by their inclusion of rules for decision-making and by the fact that they are interrogated in something approaching natural language, rather than through a structured menu of analyses or a complex computer language. Kastiel (1987) gives some interesting examples of the development of expert systems for various marketing applications, including customer need assessment, financial modelling, direct marketing, pricing and telemarketing. Davis (1986) provides a useful review of how expert systems are assembled and gives concrete examples of two marketing applications.

Past uses of expert systems have tended to be in medicine, computer programming and the physical sciences, but Schwoerer and Frappa (1986) argue that marketing applications will become more common:

Experience strongly suggests that computer applications at marketing and management level stand or fall with their user-friendliness, yet this is the Achilles heel of many systems today. AI (Artificial Intelligence) and ES (Expert Systems) have the potential to make a significant contribution in this precise area of user-friendliness.

GEODEMOGRAPHICS AND MARKET ANALYSIS

Geodemographics and their application in market analysis provide an information source of increasing importance to marketing companies. Market analysis is based upon the very reasonable proposition that people's purchasing and product usage behaviour is strongly related to the kind of neighbourhood in which they live. Geodemographics provide a systematic method of classifying residential neighbourhoods.

Most geodemographic systems are based upon the small-area statistics which are generated from the census and other government surveys. Geodemographics or market analysis involves the manipulation of this information to develop a typology of neighbourhoods, characterized by the type of housing and other characteristics of the area.

13

The best-known, and still the most widely used system is ACORN (a classification of residential neighbourhoods). This system, developed by CACI, clusters neighbourhoods into a series of types, based on the census information.

There are now a number of competing market analysis systems in the UK, the most directly competitive being PINPOINT. A special feature of the PINPOINT system is its computerization of the Ordnance Survey system, which provides a highly accurate geographic location for each individual address within neighbourhood types.

The early applications of geodemographics were in direct mail, where there was an obvious opportunity to improve the efficiency of mailshots by sending only to those addresses where the occupants were likely to be interested in the product being promoted. More recently, the technique has been adopted by retailers, who recurrently face the task of locating new stores in those areas where they have the highest chance of attracting their target customers. The site location potential of market analysis systems has also been exploited by the clearing banks, by local authorities and by public utilities, again using the data to optimize the location of outlets and resources in relation to consuming households. A useful review of ACORN, PINPOINT and alternative market analysis systems has been carried out by Garrett (1987).

The whole subject is dealt with in detail in Chapter 32.

GENERAL MARKETING DATABASES

Decision-support systems, such as EXPRESS and ACUMEN, are primarily designed for the storage, manipulation and presentation of statistical marketing information. Since 1980 there has been a proliferation of on-line database services which offer search and retrieval of information in text form. This information may be drawn from the general or specialist press or from published market research reports. While many database services are extremely general in nature, some are particularly aimed at marketing management.

TEXTLINE, distributed by Finsbury Data Services, began as a general press and magazine database. It now offers a specialist database for marketing, media and retailing. More recently three significant competitors for TEXTLINE have been launched:

MAGIC, distributed by Datasolve, MAID, distributed by Maid Systems and HARVEST, distributed by Harvest Information Services.

MAGIC is targeted at the advertising and marketing business, and claims to contain the complete text of hundreds of newspapers, magazines, research reports and specialist data. Both HARVEST and MAID offer more signposting to the user, the information being structured into a series of report types. MAID is particularly distinguished by its inclusion of Jordan's company profiles and topline market data from A. C. Nielson. All four databases include advertising expenditure analysis from MEAL, the most widely used source of this information.

Bowman (1987) has recently provided a searching review of these four database systems from the advertising agency viewpoint, a review which is nevertheless very relevant to the concerns of market management.

It would be wrong to leave the topic of database systems without referring to the DOMESDAY system which is sponsored by the BBC, in co-operation with Acorn Computers and Philips Electronics. The information is organized into four main groups covering the economy, the environment, society and culture. From the marketer's point of view the appeal of DOMESDAY will lie both in its content and in the method of data storage and presentation.

The information on the DOMESDAY system is stored on laser disk which offers the facility for high resolution graphics and for the presentation of photographs and maps. The system contains a vast amount of data, including information drawn from the census, the General Household Survey, the Family Expenditure Survey and the BBC's Survey on Daily Life in the 1980s. The system also contains the complete Ordnance Survey maps for the UK, arranged on six levels, from the United Kingdom as a whole down to street maps, floor plans and even photographs for special sites. Recently launched, the DOMESDAY system appears to have great potential as an information system to support marketing planning.

SUMMARY

There is no shortage of information for marketing management. The problem is to select the most useful from a diverse array of external data sources and integrate these with internal information to provide support for marketing decisions. The best current way to achieve this integration is to employ one of the proprietary decision-support systems which have been designed with the needs of marketing management in mind. In this way it will be possible to provide a framework to access internal data, market measurement data, media audience data and information on social and economic trends, which can be included in the database. In addition to historic reporting on market data, these systems offer facilities for modelling and forecasting. In the course of strategic market planning it may also be useful to establish a link with one of the commercial database services which offer search and retrieval of press information, and of some published market and company reports.

REFERENCES AND FURTHER READING

Bowles, T. and Blyth, B. (1985), 'How do you like your data: raw, al dente or stewed?' *European Research*, Vol.13, No.4, October, pp.170–178.

Bowman, P. (1987), 'A user guide to on-line information systems', *ADMAP*, March, pp.40–44.

Central Statistical Office (1987), *Social Trends*, No.17, HMSO, London.

Davis, E. J. (1986), 'The use of expert systems in marketing', *ESOMAR*, September, pp.281–298.

Garrett, A. (1987), 'How to home in on the target market', *Marketing Week*, Vol.10, No.14, May, pp.57–60.

Kastiel, D. L. (1987), 'Computerized consultants', *Business Marketing*, March, pp.52–73.

Mort, D. and Siddall, L. (1986), *Sources of Unofficial UK Statistics*, Gower, Aldershot.

National Association of Accountants (1971), 'Research studies in management planning and control', *Information for Marketing Management*, No.3, NAA, New York.

Nijburg, D. A. (1985), 'Microcomputer software for marketing and marketing research', *ESOMAR* (38th Congress Papers), September, pp.37–47.

Piercy, N. and Evans, M. J. (1983), *Managing Marketing Information*, Croom Helm, Beckenham.

Schwoerer, J. and Frappa, J.-P. (1986), 'Artificial intelligence and expert systems: any applications for marketing and marketing research?' *ESOMAR* (39th Congress Papers), September, pp.247–277.

Software Users' Year Book (1988), VNU Business Publications, London.

Staples, N. (1986), 'Scanning – the future', *Survey*, Autumn, pp.15–17.

Vong, J. (1986), 'Information systems for planning and control', *Management Decision*, Vol.24, No.5, pp.17–19.

USEFUL ADDRESSES

Acorn Computers Limited
Cambridge Technopark
645 Newmarket Road
Cambridge
CB5 8PD

ANA (Article Numbering Association)
6 Catherine Street
London WC2B 5JJ

Audits of Great Britain
Research Centre
West Gate
London W5 1UA

BARB (Broadcasters' Audience Research Board Ltd)
Knighton House
52–66 Mortimer Street
London W1N 8AN

British Market Research Bureau Ltd
Saunders House
53 The Mall
Ealing
London W5 3TE

CACI Ltd
59–62 High Holborn
London WC1V 6DX

Central Statistical Office
Great George Street
London SW1P 3AQ

Effem Management Services Ltd
Shoppenhangers Road
Maidenhead
Berkshire
SL6 2PX

Harvest Information Services Ltd
The Mall
359 Upper Street
London N1 OPD

Information Resources
102, Buckingham Avenue
Slough
Berkshire
SL1 4PF

JICNARS (Joint Industry Committee for
   National Readership Surveys)
44 Belgrave Square
London SW1 8QS

JICRAR (Joint Industry Committee for Radio Audience Research)
Knighton House
56 Mortimer Street
London W1N 8AN

MAGIC
Datasolve Ltd
99 Staines Road West
Sunbury-on-Thames
Middlesex
TW16 7AH

Maid Systems Ltd
Maid House
26 Baker Street
London W1M 1DF

A. C. Nielsen Company Ltd
Nielsen House
London Road
Headington
Oxford
OX3 9RX

Outdoor Advertising Association of Great Britain
3 Dean Farrar Street
London SW1H 9JX

Pinpoint Analysis Ltd
Mercury House
Waterloo Road
London SE1

Taylor Nelson Research Ltd
Taylor Nelson House
44–46 Upper High Street
Epsom
Surrey
KT17 5QS

TEXTLINE
Finsbury Data Services Ltd
68–73 Carter Lane
London EC4V 5EA

2

Analysing the environment

Douglas Brownlie

This chapter begins by presenting an argument in favour of formal and systematic environmental analysis. It goes on to describe a general approach to analysing the environment which may be used by corporate and marketing strategist alike; what benefits it brings to practising firms; what management problems are likely to be encountered; and how possibly to surmount them.

BACK TO BASICS

Firms and other commercial organizations owe their existence to the market environment. Like people, they are creatures of their environment and participants, albeit unwilling, in its processes. They, too, spend much of their life learning how to cope with the complexity, hostility, unforeseen traumas, vagaries and opportunities generated by their environment. Indeed, the market environment can be thought of as an ever-changing sum total of the facts of life with which firms must come to terms. Their survival and prosperity is conditioned by the demands imposed by this environment. Thus, in the midst of an environment where frequent and significant change is becoming the rule, they must stay at the forefront of changes which will affect their markets and their positions within them.

The market environment consists of the external forces that directly or indirectly influence the firms' goals, structure, plans, procedures, operations, performance and so on. Environmental analysis is the study of these forces; the relationship among them; and their effects and potential effects on the organization.

The term 'environmental analysis' is often used interchangeably with others such as environmental scanning, environmental forecasting, competitive intelligence gathering, external search, environmental surveillance, strategic marketing information retrieval and so on (Brownlie, 1987). I use the term 'environmental scanning' to encompass the varied information-gathering, analysis and dissemination activities firms pursue to keep up to date with changes in the market environment. Clearly the purpose of these activities is not merely to keep track of environmental changes. Without environmental analysis and forecasting, there is no basis for strategic planning. Environmental scanning involves activities ranging from highly structured and regularly conducted reviews and forecasts of important trends, issues and events in the business environment, to the irregular 'tip' acquired by means of insider access to a network of private and personal contacts, or even by means of espionage.

Environmental scanning is responsible not only for *generating* an up-to-date database of information on the changing business scene. It also has the job of *alerting* management to what is happening in the marketplace, the industry and beyond by *disseminating* important information and analyses to key strategic decision-makers and influencers. However, converting the awareness such dissemination will create into interest, and ultimately to some form of action, is an overtly and covertly political process which can emasculate the most penetrating analyses – particularly where vested interests are threatened and top management support absent. It is widely appreciated that the realization of a marketing orientation is in practice often inhibited, not by failures of the systems, technology or methodologies of marketing, of which environmental analysis is one, but by disabling management attitudes which often express themselves as resistance to change, conservatism, suspicion and prevarication.

The preceding paragraph asks the reader to take a step outside the realm of the environmental analyst and to enter that of the strategic decision-maker. The tasks of gathering, analysing and disseminating information are often organized as discrete activities. The environmental analyst is likely to be a member of the corporate or marketing planning staff, or a top management aide, that is, a decision-influencer, but rarely a decision-maker. Indeed, the 'boffinesque' role in which the analyst often finds himself cast may do little to enhance the credibility and esteem attributed to him by strategic decision-makers. They will be keen to place their own interpretations on what the expert analyst has to say – unless, of course, he has an impeccable track record in which case the expert may find himself being elevated to the status of a 'Delphic oracle'. But, in the absence of any other intelligence-gathering activity, whether systematized or personal, the environmental analyst and forecaster will, by means of the perceived importance of the information he or she generates, be in an enviable position to influence strategic decision-makers' perceptions of the firm's competitive position and the options available to it. Thus, in addition to the technical skills demanded of the environmental scanning staff, political skills could be said to be the hallmark of an effective scanning team.

Management attitudes have a vital role to play in creating an organizational climate that enables an organization not only to operate what should in effect be an 'open window of perception' on the past, present and prospective business scene, but also to act on the insights it provides. Readers will therefore be disappointed if they expect the methodology of environmental scanning to be described here as a panacea for the problems of the current competitive and turbulent environment. Methodology alone will not guarantee success. Indeed, method is less important than the thinking it stimulates. Methodologies can be implanted and replicated with much less difficulty than can ways of thinking.

WHAT CAN ENVIRONMENTAL SCANNING CONTRIBUTE?

Whatever is achieved by environmental scanning will largely depend on the purpose the organization has in mind for it. Small firms may require to be kept up to date with local regulatory and economic trends likely to have an immediate impact on their day-to-day business prospects. Larger organizations will share the requirements of the small firm, but will also expect information which is broader in scope and orientated to the future.

Corporate level environmental scanning is likely to be responsible for monitoring, interpreting and forecasting issues, trends and events which go far beyond the customer, market and competitive analyses most organizations perform as a matter of routine. In this context environmental scanning will be expected to provide a broad but penetrating view of possible future changes in the demographic, social, cultural, political, technological and economic elements of the business environment. In so doing it should seek to arm the strategic decision-makers and influencers with the information, analyses and forecasts they consider pertinent to the formulation of business strategies and plans. It should also provide a basis for questioning the assumptions which underpin the firm's strategic thinking and for generating new assumptions.

In an empirical study of environmental analysis in ninety American corporations, Diffenbach (1983) identified seven types of pay-offs from the activity. These can be summarized as:

1 increased general awareness by management of environmental changes;
2 better strategic planning and decision-making;
3 greater effectiveness in government matters;
4 better industry and market analyses;
5 better results in foreign businesses;
6 improvements in diversifications, acquisitions and in resource allocation;
7 better energy planning.

DEFINING THE MARKET ENVIRONMENT

It has been argued that the ability to exercise control in the firm's current product markets is derived at least partly from a comprehensive and reliable knowledge of customers, suppliers, competitors, regulators and investors. The successful development and upkeep of the knowledge base is thought to be the principal task of formal environmental scanning – one to which the functions of marketing, research and development, purchasing, sales and finance have a significant contribution to make. However, in the long term more is expected of it. For instance, as the firm looks away from its existing product markets for future growth opportunities or acquisition candidates inside and outside its current sphere of operation, knowledge will be required of a new and unfamiliar business environment having its own unique set of technological, economic, political and social trends. In so doing greater demands will be made of environmental analysis.

Churchman (1968) defines the environment of a firm as 'those factors which not only are outside the system's control but which determine, in part, how the system performs'. In theory at least, the market environment is then thought to include all those factors which exert any perceptible direct or indirect influence on the firm. Given such an unbounded definition one could argue that the rest of the world then constitutes the firm's business environment. Clearly, to take such an indiscriminating view has no practical value. The task of environmental scanning can be made manageable only by taking a very selective and carefully considered view of the environment. It must eliminate much of the rest of the world from the firm's immediate attention.

The breadth of the view an organization chooses to take of its business environment has implications for the complexity of the tasks of environmental analysis and forecasting and thus its resource requirements. A broadly defined business mission is associated with a diversified, multi-product, multi-market organization. It would involve environmental scanning in a very broad arena of operation from which a perspective on international political and economic issues, events and trends may be called for by corporate planning. On the other hand, a narrowly defined business mission may focus its environmental scanning more on domestic issues concerning immediate events and trends in proximate product markets. The firm's environmental scanning activities should cover as many relevant aspects of the business environment as the available resources will permit, particularly those aspects having an impact on the assumptions it uses in its strategic planning and decision-making.

The boundaries of the market environment must therefore be structured in such a way to enable the analyst to distinguish important from less important factors and to determine an appropriate time scale for forecasting changes. One would expect there to be factors deserving to be continuously monitored because of their immediate impact on the industry; these would include users, distributors, suppliers, competitors for customers and suppliers, workforce, government regulators, trade unions, product and process developments and so on. The origin of such factors is known as the 'task environment'. It is defined as 'the more specific forces which are relevant to decision-making and transformation processes of the individual organizations' (Dill, 1958).

The concept of the task environment opens the environmental analyst's 'window on the world' on to the organization's immediate product and supply markets; and on to current influences on its position within them. But a wider view would also cast attention towards remote areas where developments could be under way which in the longer term would impinge on the firm's position in its current product and supply markets. For instance, substitute products and processes often originate as spin-offs from technological developments made outside the task environment. Clearly, it is important to look further afield than the task environment. Kast and Rosenzweig (1974) have suggested a framework by means of which the wider market environment can be divided into areas for study and analysis (see Table 2.1). Table 2.2 outlines some of the broad social issues firms might expect to impinge on their European activities in the late 1980s. Environmental scanning would be expected to follow developments of these issues (and others of a technological, political, cultural and economic nature) and evaluate the impact they are thought likely to have on the firm.

THE NEED FOR INFORMATION

Organizations subject themselves to the inconvenience, expense, rigour and pain of strategic planning in order to acquire more control over the outcome of any course of action they choose to pursue. Thus, in accordance with Bacon's dictum that 'knowledge itself is power', it could be argued that *a knowledge of the business environment must precede the acquisition of any degree of control over it.*

The reader is likely to have witnessed the popularization of terms such as espionage, infiltration, moles, security leaks, early warning, electronic surveillance, counter-intelligence, insider dealing and the like. Although evocative of the anxiety and duplicity of our age, the popularization of the vocabulary of the spy lends some credence to the view that the possession of information is itself a factor endowment, and as such it should be treated as a valuable national asset. It is only

Table 2.1   Kast and Rosenzweig's (1974) framework for analysing the wider business environment

Cultural	Including the historical background, ideologies, values and norms of the society. Views on authority relationships, leadership patterns, interpersonal relationships, nationalism, science and technology.
Technological	The level of scientific and technological advancement in society, including the physical base (plant, equipment, facilities) and the knowledge base of technology. Degree to which the scientific and technological community is able to develop new knowledge and apply it.
Educational	The general literacy level of the population. The degree of sophistication and specialization in the educational system. The proportion of the people with a high level of professional and/or specialized training.
Political	The general political climate of society. The degree of concentration of political power. The nature of political organization (degrees of decentralization, diversity of functions, and so on). The political party system.
Legal	Constitutional considerations, nature of legal system, jurisdictions of various governmental units. Specific laws concerning formation, taxation and control of organizations.
Natural resources	The nature, quantity and availability of natural resources, including climatic and other conditions.
Demographic	The nature of human resources available to the society; their number, distribution, age and sex. Concentration or urbanization of population is a characteristic of industrialized societies.
Sociological	Class structure and mobility. Definition of social roles. Nature of social organization and development of social institutions.
Economic	General economic framework, including the type of economic organization – private versus public ownership; the centralization or decentralization of economic planning; the banking system; and fiscal policies. The level of investment in physical resources and consumption.

one small but logical step to argue that since the gathering of information precedes its possession and dissemination, this activity also contributes to the generation of wealth.

To the student of military strategy this view will represent a familiar and even hackneyed line of thought. After all, history offers many examples of battles which could be said to have been fought and won on the basis of 'superior' information. In planning the deployment and employment of their armies' resources, generals rely on the intelligence provided by lines of communication which may have a political origin in their own state, but will certainly infiltrate enemy territory and institutions. Generals expect to use such intelligence to prepare themselves better for the ensuing conflict and to enhance the likelihood of victory – that is, to gain some control over the outcome of the conflict.

Table 2.2   Key European social issues for the 1980s*

Issues	Characteristics
Low growth and uncertainty	Political instability; higher energy prices, lower economic growth; decline of basic industries; protectionism; high levels of inflation; high levels of unemployment; fluctuating financial markets.
Political uncertainty and insecurity	Political stability in Europe; war and revolution in the Third World; international terrorism; urban riots.
Rise of the multinationals	Giant firms; size and diversity; professional management; shareholder power; reform of the board.
Employee participation and trade union power	Works' councils; trade unions; bigness and alienation.
Rise of the organized pressure group	Consumer protection; environmental pollution; women's rights; ethnic minorities; protection health.
Growth of government	Protectionism; growth of public ownership; economic planning; industrial policy.
Social political pressures on business	Lower profits and slower growth in productivity; economic impact of regulation; pressures on top management for the greater disclosure of information, improvement of the working environment; product safety improvement, reduction of environmental pollution, participative decision-making and so on.

*Adapted by the author from Taylor and Ferro (1983).

In the corporate context the tasks of intelligence gathering, surveillance and monitoring are overseen by environmental scanning. It is responsible for managing lines of communication by means of which a flow of information is maintained between important elements of the business environment, the environmental analysts and the organization's strategic decision-makers and influencers. As in the military context, the corporate intelligence service will also provide early warning and careful tracking of possible environmental threats so that a timely response is conceived and executed. Table 2.3 indicates corporate sources of information on the business environment; Table 2.4 comments on their relative importance. Table 2.4 also suggests that to enhance the impact of its work, environmental scanning should not only seek top management support but also its involvement in order to implicate or consult all key decision-makers and influencers at corporate and divisional level.

In recent years the emergence of information technology has encouraged organizations to re-examine carefully the purpose, structure, productivity and accessibility of their management information systems, including those governing elements of the business environ-

Table 2.3 Sources of information on the business environment

Type of infor-mation	Sources of information on business environment
Inside the company	
Written	Internal reports and memos, planning documents, market research, MIS.
Verbal	Researchers, salesforce, marketing, purchasing, advisers, planners, board.
Combination	Formal and informal meetings, for example working parties, advisory committees.
Outside the company	
Written	Annual reports, investment reports, trade association publications, institute yearbooks, textbooks, scientific journals, professional journals, technical magazines, unpublished reports, government reports, unpublished papers, abstracts, newspapers, espionage.
Verbal	Consultants, librarians, government officials, consumers, suppliers, distributors, competitors, academics, market researchers, industry bodies, journalists, spies, bankers, stockbrokers.
Combination	Formal and informal meetings, membership of government working parties and advisory boards, industry bodies, trade associations.

Table 2.4 The relative importance of sources of environmental information

1 Verbal sources of information are much more important than written sources. Seventy-five per cent of information cited by executives was in verbal form.
2 The higher the executive in the organization, the more important verbal sources became.
3 Of the written sources used, the most important were newspapers (two-thirds), followed by trade publications, and internal company reports.
4 Subordinates are the principal source of verbal information, followed by friends in the industry and, very infrequently, superiors.
5 Information received from outside an organization is usually unsolicited.
6 Information received from inside the organization is usually solicited by the executive.
7 Information received from outside tends to have a greater impact on the decision-maker than inside information.
8 The outside sources used varied according to the job of the manager. Thus, marketing managers talked more to customers.
9 The larger the company, the greater the reliance on inside sources of verbal information.

Source: Aguilar (1967)

ment. The outcome has often been to reorganize databases, which involves further systematization of the tasks of collecting, analysing and disseminating information on the business environment. The demanding task of organizing a database governing important elements of the firm's environment is made more so by the character of pertinent information – which, it is safe to assume, will often possess several of the following characteristics:

- poor structure
- irregular availability
- provided by unofficial sources
- qualitative in nature
- questionable credibility
- ambiguous definitions
- opinion-based
- difficult to quantify
- insecure methodology
- likely to change.

THE EVOLUTION OF ENVIRONMENTAL ANALYSIS

Management systems seem to have evolved in response to two trends: the increasing *discontinuity, complexity* and *novelty* of the environmental challenges faced by firms; and the decreasing *visibility* of the future changes in the business environment. The growing impact of these trends is largely responsible for the widespread following which the strategic planning credo has acquired in the wake of the post-1974 trauma. This has led, first, to drawing attention to environmental analysis as an important element of strategic planning and, second, for environmental analysis, or scanning, itself to evolve in response to the challenges confronting the firm and its planning system.

Diffenbach (1983) traces the early evolution of environmental analysis to the mid-1960s, at which time he claims the market environment was generally being studied only for the purpose of making economic forecasts. Only in more recent years does he consider there has been an appreciation of the need to look beyond short-term market conditions to the wider technological, economic, political, social, cultural and demographic elements of the environment. He identifies three distinct evolutionary phases, each of which marks a growth in the scope, systematization, future-orientation and top management recognition of environmental analysis activity. Changes first began during what Diffenbach terms the *appreciation* phase.

A pioneering investigation of environmental analysis was conducted by Aguilar in 1967. In this now classic study the process of
environmental scanning was originally conceptualized. In his research
Aguilar interviewed 137 managers from forty-one chemical firms in
the USA and Europe. He found a lack of a systematic approach to
environmental analysis, which was still being reported in the more
recent research of Thomas (1980), Fahey *et al* (1981) and Stubbart
(1982). The research revealed that the participants collected sixteen
types of information about their business environment: Aguilar
classified them into the five groupings displayed in Table 2.5. He
reported that 52 per cent of environmental information that was
gathered concerned market tidings; 17 per cent and 12 per cent
concerned technical tidings and broad issues respectively.

Aguilar (1967) identified two principal sources of information on
the market environment, ie internal and external to the firm. Table 2.3
classifies sources of information according to Aguilar's scheme. Table
2.4. summarizes his views on the relative importance of several
sources of market information. He found there to be four broad
approaches to the collection of this information:

1 *undirected viewing* (exposure to the elements of the business
   environment without there being a specific purpose in mind);
2 *conditioned viewing* (directed exposure, but without undertaking
   an active search);
3 *informal search* (collection of purpose-orientated information in
   an informal manner); and
4 *formal search* (a structured process for collecting specific information for a designated purpose).

The reader will observe that they differ along the following dimensions: the scope of the environment to be analysed; the impetus for the
analysis; the degree of active search involved; the formality of the
environmental scanning process; and the task-orientation of the
activity.

Aguilar's study concluded that for environmental scanning to make
an effective contribution to the formulation of strategy it must be
conducted in a systematic fashion. He frequently found environmental scanning effort to be fragmented and inhibited by the failure of
participating managers to gather and disseminate information users
considered important; and to make use of accessible information that

Table 2.5 What information do managers need on the business environment?

	Market tidings
Market potential	Supply and demand consideration for market areas of current or potential interest: for example, capacity, consumption, imports, exports.
Structural change	Mergers, acquisitions and joint ventures involving competitors, new entries into the industry.
Competitors and industry	General information about a competitor, industry policy, concerted actions in the industry, and so forth.
Pricing	Effective and proposed prices for products of current and potential interest.
Sales negotiations	Information relating to a specific current or potential sale or contract for the firm.
Customers	General information about current or near-potential customers, their markets, their problems.
	Acquisition leads
Leads for mergers, joint ventures, or acquisitions	Information concerning possibilities for the manager's own company.
	Technical tidings
New products, processes, and technology	Technical information relatively new and unknown to the company.
Product problems	Problems involving existing products.
Costs	Costs for processing, operations, and so forth for current and potential competitors, suppliers, and customers, and for proposed company activities.
Licensing and patents	Products and processes.
	Broad issues
General conditions	Events of a general nature: political, demographic, national, and so forth.
Government actions and policies	Governmental decisions affecting the industry.
	Other tidings
Suppliers and raw materials	Purchasing considerations for products of current or potential interest.
Resources available	Persons, land, and other resources possibly available for the company.
Miscellaneous	Items not elsewhere classified.

Source: Aguilar (1967)

already resided within the firm. His proposals for overcoming the 'fractionalization' of environmental scanning effort called for top management involvement in the definition and execution of analysis activities; greater co-ordination and integration of these activities with strategic planning; and greater support for these activities, not only from top management but also from line managers.

Despite the considerable body of strategic planning literature which addresses environmental scanning, scepticism still surrounds the extent to which organizations apply it. The purpose of Diffenbach's (1983) study was to make some progress towards answering the doubts of the sceptics. The earlier work of Fahey *et al.* (1981) shared this motivation. As a result of their in-depth study of the environmental scanning practices of twelve large American firms, they proposed three broad models of environment analysis systems which represent increasing degress of systematization, sophistication and resource intensity. *Irregular* systems respond to environmentally generated crises. They are found in firms where the strategic planning culture is not well established. Their emphasis is on finding solutions to short-term problems. Little attention is paid to evaluating future environmental changes. The *periodic* model is more sophisticated, systematic, proactive and resource-intensive. It entails a regular review of the task environment and some elements of the wider environment. A forward view is taken. The *continuous* model emphasizes the ongoing monitoring of the business environment, rather than specified issues or events. It draws on the expertise of marketing, sales, purchasing and so on. It operates a clearing house for environmental information and uses regular information systems for analysis and dissemination. A long-term view of environmental change is taken.

Fahey *et al.* (1981) have acknowledged that the models they propose have not found widespread application in US corporations. They have noted a trend towards greater sophistication, but add that the impact so far demonstrated by continuous environmental scanning does not appear to substantiate the major deployment of resources it requires. Of course, the empirical studies of Thomas (1980) and Diffenbach (1983) provide evidence that persuades them to take the opposite view.

The paradox of environmental scanning is that by the time sufficient information has been collected to enable a well-informed environmental analysis to be made, it may be too late for the firm to respond before the threat strikes, or the opportunity passes. Ansoff (1984) proposes an approach to strategic management (see Figure 2.1) which in his view overcomes the paradox by enabling the firm to develop a timely response to partly predictable events which emerge as surprises and develop very quickly. At its heart is the continuous monitoring of the external and internal environment for signals of the evolution of *strategic issues* which the firm considers able to influence its operations. Ansoff's unit of analysis is, then, the strategic issue

32

Environment sector	Event/issue	Threat	Opportunity	Weighting[1]	Importance[2]	Impact on firm's strategies[3]			Σ −	Σ +
						S1	S2	S3		
Technology	1									
	2									
Political										
Economic										
Social										
Etc.										
									Σ −	
									Σ +	

Notes

1 Indicates the degree to which the event is judged to be a threat or opportunity. On an ordinal scale from 1 to 5, 1 represents a weak T/O, and 5 a strong T/O.

2 Indicates the degree to which the weighted event has, or will have, an impact on the firm's strategies. On an ordinal scale from 1 to 5, 1 represents a little impact, 5 a great impact.

3 The impact each event has on each of the firm's strategies is calculated by multiplying the weighted score by the importance score. A large positive (negative) score represents a strong opportunity (threat).

The value in constructing an ETOP profile is largely to be found in the debate that follows the planner's environmental appraisal, when the firm's managers assimilate, debate and develop their own ideas of the organization's threats and opportunities.

In the profile the *row* sums indicate the degree to which each event/issue is thought to *enhance* (+) or *inhibit* (−) the success of the firm's strategies. The *column* sums indicate the degree to which each strategy is itself thought to pose a threat or opportunity to the firm, given its predicted environment.

Figure 2.1 Displaying the firm's environmental threat and opportunity (ETOP profile)

rather than the conventional elements of the business environment. Ansoff's solution to the paradox is a 'graduated response' based on the amplification of and flexible response to weak signals. As he contends, 'instead of waiting for sufficient information to accumulate, the firm should determine what progressive steps in planning and action are feasible as strategic information becomes available in the course of the evolution of a threat or opportunity'.

ANALYSING THE ENVIRONMENT: PROCEDURES AND PROBLEMS

The organization's environmental scanning procedures will evolve over time as its commitment to them and experience of them change. It is unrealistic for a firm about to embrace environmental scanning for the first time to expect to operate a foolproof system from the outset: several technical and managerial constraints will impede progress (see Table 2.6). Of course, the evolutionary period can be shortened by ensuring top management involvement in commissioning the system.

Table 2.6   Diffenbach's (1983) deterrents to effective environmental analysis

Interpretation
The problem is that of interpreting the results of environmental analysis into specific impacts on the company's businesses and into specific responses to be made by the businesses. Included is the problem of the results not being in useful or sufficiently precise form.

- Difficulty of structuring studies in a way that results can be seen to be relevant and meaningful to decision-makers today
- Difficulty of reacting because information from environmental analysis is so intabgible with regard to timing and impact
- Difficulty of assessing the implications of general environmental trends for our specific businesses before they exert themselves
- Difficulty of translating environmental analysis into relevant business terms, e.g. ROI impact
- Difficulty of quantifying the impact of major threats and developing alternatives to these threats
- Difficulty of developing the path from assumption to implication to action, e.g. the tendency to relax or stop after stating the assumption, rather than follow through to an action programme
- Difficulty in seeing the impact of environmental trends on short-range operations, i.e. the gradual, accumulative nature of trends can be deceptive
- Lack of sufficient involvement by top management for them not only to understand the conclusions of environmental analysis but also to internalize them and change behaviour accordingly
- Difficulty of translating potential opportunities into action plans, e.g. conversion of traditional furniture ideas into new lifestyle furniture concepts
- The time and analysis required to apply information to our specific situations, e.g. impact of probable energy shortages or price increases on our market for motor car components

Table 2.6   continued

- Difficulty of institutionalizing environmental planning into the formal planning processes of the company so that division strategies reflect the process
- Difficulty of follow-up planning, e.g. we have pushed ahead on programmes in spite of warning signals that should have alerted us to severe problems
- Identifying impacts on businesses, particularly when negative

Inaccuracy/uncertainty
The problem is that either the output of environmental analysis is inaccurate, too uncertain to be taken seriously, or both

- Uncertainty due to the dynamics of the marketplace
- Inaccurate depicting of environmental events
- So many false predictions
- Inability to predict the future, e.g. past experience revealed inability of experts to predict the extent of inflationary forces
- Difficulty of properly characterizing uncertainties in understandable and meaningful terms
- Difficulty of forecasting the magnitude of the impact of a future trend
- The moving target syndrome, e.g. especially regarding government activity
- Difficulty of predicting social aims, e.g. no-growth versus continuing growth, etc.
- Discontinuities in environmental forecasting for which no company can make satisfactory assessments

Short-term orientation
The problem is that the preoccupation with short-term matters pre-empts attention to environmental analysis

- Pressure of short-term events, which tend to soak up some of the resources nominally or usefully committed to environmental planning
- Dislike for spending money today to help solve a speculative problem tomorrow
- The reluctance to consider more than the short term because that is where the rewards are
- Competition between short and long term, i.e. most environmental problems emerge slowly and require solutions which become effective only over similarly long periods of time
- Organization structures and tasks that force managers to focus on the immediate, short-run elements of their jobs, e.g. budgets are for limited periods of time and encourage concern with this year's results, and maybe next year's

Lack of acceptance
The problem is that environmental analysis is not accepted within the company

- Some degree of scepticism as to the possibility of success with environmental analysis – more so at lower levels than at the top
- Lack of understanding of the usefulness of environmental analysis
- Difficulty of environmental analysts convincing line managers that the former's output is applicable to the latter's problems
- The 'we already know our business' attitude on the part of operating management
- A suspicion in the practical world of business decisions that scenarios and possible occurrences are impractical and somehow dangerous
- The 'we have been successful without it' attitude
- A resistance to change in forecasting methods
- The presumption by too many executives that each of them can be their own expert in assessing environmental impacts upon the company
- Lack of commitment and personal involvement of line executives
- The difficulty of breaking the patterns of thinking in the past.

Diversified businesses
The problem is that diversified businesses mean multiple relevant environments which make environmental analysis too complex

- Difficulty of applying corporate expertise in environmental analysis at the operating level due to the great diversity of our operations

35

Table 2.6   concluded

- Complexity due to multiple and decentralized organization
- Need for too large a corporate staff to keep abreast of environments for decentralized, autonomous businesses, and unwillingness of line managers to support a full-time staff for environmental surveillance at the division level

Misperceptions
The problem is one of narrow, limited or invalid perceptions of the external environment shared by executives

- Tendency of managers to think in non-discontinuous terms
- Unpreparedness of managers, because of education or basic interest, to deal with social, political and cultural aspects of a rapidly changing environment (many managers are knowledge reductionists rather than holistic)
- Traditional inability to think in world market terms (instead of 'plant countries') when considering trends and factors of a social, political, technological and economic origin

---

The provision of top management support throughout the evolutionary period helps ensure that a *viable* system emerges from early efforts, which are likely to be directed towards installing a system modelled on an ideal scanning procedure such as that shown in Table 2.7. An established strategic planning culture should also help expedite matters by providing a receptive organizational climate – but this cannot be guaranteed. Even strategic planners are apt to react to a threatening newcomer in a way that ensures their territorial boundaries and organizational prerogatives are preserved – particularly if the newcomer is to be funded from the existing strategic planning resource base.

Top management involvement in commissioning the environmental scanning system should concentrate on the definition of the following system parameters:

1   the boundaries of both the task and the wider business environment;
2   the appropriate time horizon for future studies;
3   the allocation of responsibility for environmental scanning;
4   the degree of formality circumscribing environmental scanning;
5   the use of environmental analyses in strategy making.

Defining boundaries

To define the boundaries of the firm's environments in terms of concrete measures is an almost impossible task for all but the smallest of one-product firms. Nevertheless, the environmental scanner needs practical guidelines to enable relevant environmental information to

Table 2.7   A typical sequential model of the ideal environmental scanning procedure

1   *Monitor* broad trends, issues and events occurring in the firm's task environment. This can be complemented by means of identifying a core list of relevant publications and assigning them to volunteers who report important articles to environmental analysis for further study. Selected areas of the remote environment should be reviewed from time to time. External consultants may be employed, as they often are in identifying and evaluating candidate diversification or acquisition opportunities within the markets or technologies unfamiliar to the firm.

2   *Identify* trends and the like which may have significance for the firm. An analysis team of senior executives should determine and implement the criteria by means of which *relevance* is established. Weak signals may not be amenable to screening in this way.

3   *Evaluate* the impact of significant trends, etc., on the firm's operations in its current product markets. Those having a significant impact will either be *threats* or *opportunities*. Line managers should participate in the evaluation.

4   *Forecast* the possible future directions of the significant trends, etc., and *examine* the new opportunities and threats they appear more likely to generate. Both analyst and strategist should be involved in making the choice of environmental analysis and forecasting techniques (see Table 2.8).

5   *Evaluate* the impact of these threats and opportunties on the firm's long-term strategies. The output of steps 3, 4 and 5 can be summarized by means of the environmental threat and opportunity profile shown in Figure 2.1.

6   *Report* the progress of specific environmental analysis projects, in addition to the regular monitoring activities, on a periodic basis.

be separated from irrelevant.

Such guidelines should be determined in consultation with members of the top management team responsible for formulating long-term strategies and plans. The user and the analyst can together define the terms of reference and objectives of environmental scanning assignments. In this way an operational definition of a target zone of the environment is a least possible using as a reference point the needs of the strategists for environmental data. Of course, the definition will depend on the position and abilities of the members of the environmental analysis team, their past experience in environmental scanning projects and success in applying the various research and forecasting techniques.

There are no hard and fast rules for making the distinction between relevance and irrelevance. Both Stubbart (1982) and Diffenbach (1983) found that organizations were continuously frustrated in their efforts to arrive at a workable definition of their business environment. The nub of the problem is one of achieving a balanced view of the scope of that environment. To avoid misdirecting effort to peripheral and irrelevant issues it must not be too wide in scope. Neither should it be a narrow, data-dependent, econometric but relevant, if myopic, view. Clearly, the problem will be exacerbated in diversified organizations possessing several relevant environments (see Table 2.6). The opportunity cost of the constricted view of the environment may greatly exceed the actual cost of scanning areas of the wider business environment – particularly where weak signals are to be detected.

Appropriate time horizon

Given the difficulty organizations experience in defining boundaries, it is not surprising that they tend to focus on familiar environments – preferring to study remote environments on an *ad hoc* basis, perhaps with the assistance of consultants. A similarly conservative view is often taken of the appropriate time horizon for the future studies to be conducted by environmental scanning. Diffenbach (1983) found that such studies were considered by divisional management to be more useful the shorter the time horizon they took. Corporate management tended to take a longer view.

The time horizon should in theory be determined by the investment cycle of the industry and the nature of the product or service it provides. For example: in the oil industry a scanning term of twenty-five years is not unusual; in the fashion industry a period of four years is more appropriate. The time horizon of environmental scanning should, then, exceed the duration of the firm's strategic plans. If the firm operates a policy of waiting to see what the industry leaders get up to, environmental scanning activities may be easily resourced. But they will provide a narrow, reactive view which is biased towards the short term. A proactive regime will be more demanding of middle and top management abilities, especially in multi-product or multi-market firms where a variety of time horizons might apply.

Responsibility for environmental scanning

The responsibility for environmental scanning can be allocated in three different ways. First, line managers in functions such as purchasing, sales and marketing can be asked to undertake environmental scanning in addition to their other duties. These managers are likely to be able to provide information on the business environment and should, therefore, contribute in some way to any environmental scanning system. But, this approach suffers from disadvantages: the demotivating resentment line managers may feel towards this additional imposition on their time; the requirement for specialist analytical, research and forecasting skills which line managers are unlikely to possess; the possibly incompatible mentalities of the roles they are asked to play – creative and far-sighted thinker on the one hand, hard-headed operator on the other (see Table 2.6).

The second approach is for environmental scanning to be made part of the strategic planner's job. This division of the strategic planning labour leads to specialization, which may also have some drawbacks. Stubbart (1982) argues that the task of environmental scanning

cannot be easily abdicated to technical specialists at corporate headquarters. Because these specialists do not have to answer for the results of business unit performance, they often do not understand the technical requirements of the unit's business. And, most importantly, these specialists do not have a system for defining, measuring and interpreting a business unit's environment more accurately than the unit's own management can.

It may then be desirable for both planners and line managers to be involved in environmental scanning.

Ansoff (1984) argues that the need for this involvement is seldom more critical than when making the choice of environmental analysis and forecasting techniques. In his view this choice is too important to be left to the environmental analyst, as is often done in practice. He argues that the user of the output of environmental scanning has an overriding duty to exert influence on the choice of technique, if actionable information and understanding are desired. Knowledge of the applicability of a technique is more important to the strategist than knowledge of the details of the technique's execution. The details of environmental analysis and forecasting techniques can readily be found in a voluminous literature on the subject (see Brownlie and Saren, 1983).

Table 2.8 lists a number of the more important techniques and

Table 2.8 Environmental analysis and forecasting techniques*

Technique	Percentage of companies reporting use of techniques (n = 66)	Applicable environmental turbulence level		
		Low	Medium	High
Expert opinion	86	•	•	•
Trend extrapolation	83	•		
Alternate scenarios	68	•	•	•
Single scenarios	55	•		
Simulation models	55	•		
Brainstorming	45		•	•
Causal models	32		•	•
Delphi projections	29			•
Cross-impact analysis	27			•
Input-output analysis	26	•		
Exponential forecasting	21	•		
Signal monitoring	12	•	•	•
Relevance trees	6		•	
Morphological analysis	5		•	

*Adapted by the author from Ansoff (1984) and Diffenbach (1983).

relates them to the environmental condition in which their application could be appropriate. Conventional methodologies such as marketing research, demand forecasting, economic indicators and industry studies are also used.

The third approach is to establish a separate organizational unit responsible for conducting regular and *ad hoc* scanning at all levels, and for channelling results to those for whom they may be relevant. General Electric in the USA is known to operate such a unit and to fund its activities by charging recipients for the environmental information provided by scanning. Where large amounts of data are collected and analysed it has proved useful to establish a special team to make recommendations for action to top management, based on the environmental analysis.

This approach may represent a theoretical ideal. However, combinations of the first two approaches are most popular with all but the very large, diversified organizations which can afford to underwrite a separate unit. Combinations often operate by means of a temporary scanning team, set up on an *ad hoc* basis to oversee the study of the impact a controversial environmental trend, issue or event is thought likely to have on various areas of operations.

The team membership may consist of both line (divisional) and general (corporate) management: line managers consider the product market, top managers scan the wider environment. Line managers may even be temporarily seconded to a staff position for the duration of the study. They will often be closely involved in determining the impact of environmental changes on those areas of operations in which they are experienced. Consultants, either internal or external, may be used where the impact of environmental change is likely to threaten the vested interests of line managers in some way.

There is no clear agreement about the best way to assign responsibilities for environmental scanning. Every organization will experience unique circumstances that merit taking a particular approach which an off-the-shelf environmental scanning system may be incapable of embracing. Attempts to implant an ideal approach to environmental scanning in an off-the-shelf fashion are likely to contribute to inflated and ultimately unfulfilled expectations, and frustration. Researchers agree that firms should involve managers of various levels in environmental scanning activities. It could be argued that only by doing so can environmental scanning hope to become an effective and well-integrated contributor to a strategic decision-making regime.

Clearly, attention should be given to the quality of communications between environmental analysts and managers. Formal management education and training are ways of producing managers with analytical skills, which may serve as a basis for communication with analysts. Conversely, analysts familiar with the needs of managers will be more able to communicate with strategy-makers. Job rotation may also improve communication. The top manager who has previously served as a member of an environmental analysis unit should find it easier to communicate with analysts. But for general managers the range of desired skills is so broad as to make it virtually impossible for one person to acquire them through job rotation in one lifetime. Intermediary advisers or consultants can also be used to improve communications, particularly in organizations where the career of the strategy-maker is very different from that of an analyst – as in the case of a government minister whose analyst is a civil servant.

Whatever the means by which responsibility for environmental analysis is assigned, I argue that those responsible should still undertake the following tasks:

1 monitoring trends, issues and events in the business environment and studying their possible impacts on the firm's operations;
2 developing the forecasts, scenarios and issues analyses which serve as inputs to the firm's strategic decision-making (see Table 8);
3 providing a destination to which environmental intelligence can be sent for interpretation, analysis and storage;
4 constructing a means of organizing environmental information so that a library or database on environmental developments can be easily accessed;
5 providing an internal consulting resource on long-term environmental affairs;
6 disseminating information on the business environment by means of newsletters, reports and lectures;
7 monitoring the performance of environmental analysis activities and improving it by applying new tools and techniques.

Degree of formality

It is not only difficult to decide who is to be responsible for environmental scanning. The degree of formality that should apply is also a matter for top management concern. The view the organization takes will depend on the extent to which top management feels it necessary to be able to exert some control over the day-to-day activities of environmental scanning. Control may be a problem where responsibility for these activities is devolved to line managers whose own day-to-day responsibilites are likely to take precedence over what they may consider to be marginal 'blue sky' and 'ivory tower' exercises. This problem is likely to be worse where no formal system for collecting, analysing and disseminating environmental information has been agreed. The lack of commitment and the scepticism line managers often express about environment analysis can be dealt with only by means of education, training and involvement.

Yet some organizations are content with an informal approach to environmental scanning, relying on key executives in sales, marketing, purchasing and finance to keep abreast of changes in the business environment through newspapers, trade literature, conferences, exhibitions and personal contacts. Others prefer to organize their efforts into a series of structured and planned activities for which specified

Table 2.9 Attributes of a formal approach to environmental scanning

---

1 Environmental trends, events and issues are regularly and systematically reviewed.
2 Explicit criteria have been established which can in turn be used to evaluate the impact of environmental trends.
3 Scanning activities are guided by written procedures.
4 Responsibility for scanning activities has been clearly assigned.
5 Scanning reports, updates, forecasts and analyses are documented in a standardized format.
6 Such documentation is generated on a regular basis and disseminated to predetermined personnel according to a timetable.
7 The application of formal techniques such as delphi studies and multiple scenarios.

(Brownlie, 1987)

staff bear responsibility. The difference is one of degree. Table 2.9 indicates attributes that a formal (informal) approach to environmental scanning is likely to possess to a large (small) extent.

Diffenbach's (1983) research found larger US companies to be more likely to take a formal approach to environmental scanning. This is not surprising given that such companies are also more likely to take a broad view of their business environment, competing as they do in a number of markets with a number of products. But the informal approach is not only the prerogative of the small one-product firm. Diversified companies may prefer to take an informal approach to such scanning activities as long-term forecasting, generating alternative scenarios, issues analyses and the management of weak signals. These activities demand a degree of creative thinking best stimulated in an informal environment – even if the output of the process is subjected to a more formal treatment.

The use of environmental analyses in strategy making

In determining the composition of the environmental scanning unit, top management should also take care to clarify the role of the participating analysts, so as to foster realistic expectations of the contribution they are able to make to strategy formulation. The persistence of unrealistic expectations has a debilitating impact on environmental scanning. Unrealistic expectations are most likely to be held, by analysts and strategists alike, whilst introducing a formal environmental scanning procedure for the first time. Fortunately, experience of environmental scanning puts analysts and strategists in a better position to judge each other's contribution realistically, but some unrealistic expectations may persist. Analysts cannot realistically expect strategy-makers always to make full use of their analyses, or to apply their recommendations completely and without question; they should rarely have the power to prescribe strategy. Yet, where analysts are given to such expectations, as professionals might be, the reality of their participation in strategy making may be one of impotence rather than influence. In such circumstances, the unfulfilled expectations of the analyst can easily become a source of alienation, misunderstanding and ill-feeling. All of which serves only to weaken communications and thereby impede the impact of environmental analysis on strategy formulation – a position made worse by the lack of any demonstrable, direct impact of environmental analyses on strategy formulation. Similarly, top management's desire to delegate strategy-making to the environmental scanning unit should be treated with caution. The careful deflation of these heroic expectations will contribute to improved communications and understanding.

The data and analyses generated by environmental scanning are only one of several inputs to the strategy-making process. Its principal contribution is to identify environmental trends, issues, events or signals that should trigger the reconsideration and, perhaps, revision of the strategic plans. Consequently, there is every chance that environmental scanning will have an important hand in initiating strategy changes. Indeed, where a staff unit for environmental scanning exists, the occurrence of such a trigger is likely to lead to a request from strategists for environmental scanning to conduct a specific study of the related issue or trend.

The indirect use of environmental analyses in strategy-making is at least possible, by virtue of the quality of its work. However, its direct use requires an enabling mechanism directed to the translation of the output of environmental analyses into specific recommendations or even a plan for implementing strategy changes. Communication difficulties must once again be surmounted. The problem is not merely that a thorough understanding of environmental analysis demands skills similar to those of the analysts, which strategy-makers are unlikely to possess. The vocabulary, assumptions, processes and techniques employed by the analysts will also be alien to them. The answer is not to leave the task of translation to environmental analysts alone. They too may be unfamiliar with the arcane terminology, skills, outlook and expectations of the strategists and their peers. The use of specially convened action teams staffed by advisers or consultants is often recommended as a translation mechanism. Care is necessary in the long-term use of this mechanism: if a third party comes between the analysts and the decision-makers, the two principal parties may become further alienated and less likely to co-operate fruitfully. The best solution is one that brings analysts and strategists closer together, as often as possible.

CONCLUSION

Environmental scanning can make an important contribution to the survival and prosperity of the firm. The increasingly turbulent and unpredictable market environment will convince more and more firms of the need to scan and analyse their market environment systematically. It is not an easy task. The firm must expect to encounter many technical and managerial problems, particularly in enabling environmental scanning to contribute fully to the formulation of business strategy. Reading this chapter is no more than a first step.

REFERENCES AND FURTHER READING

Aguilar, F. S. (1967), *Scanning the Business Environment*, Macmillan, New York.

Ansoff, H. I., *Implanting Strategic Management*, Prentice-Hall International, (1984).

Brownlie, D. T. (1987), 'Environmental analysis and forecasting', chapter 6 in M. J. Baker (ed.), *The Marketing Book*, Heinemann, London.

Brownlie, D. T. and Saren, M. A. (1983), 'A review of technology forecasting techniques and their applications', *Management Bibliographies and Reviews*, Vol.9, No.4.

Churchman, C. W. (1968), *The Systems Approach*, Dell Publishing Co., New York.

Diffenbach, J. (1983), 'Corporate environmental analysis in large US corporations', *Long Range Planning*, Vol.16, No.3, pp.107–116.

Dill, W. R. (1958), 'Environment as an influence on management activity', *Administrative Science Quarterly*, Vol.13, March.

Fahey, L., King, W. R. and Narayanan, V. K. (1981), 'Environmental scanning and forecasting in strategic planning – the state of the art', *Long Range Planning*, February, pp.32–39.

Goldsmith, W. and Clutterbuck, D. (1985), *The Winning Streak*, Weidenfeld and Nicolson, London.

Hooley, G.J., West, C. J. and Lynch, J. E. (1983), *Marketing in the UK*, a survey of current practice and performance, *Institute of Marketing*, Cookham.

Kast, F. E. and Rosenzweig, J. E. (1974), *Organisation and Management: A systems Approach*, 2nd ed, McGraw Hill, New York.

Lorenz, C. (1986), *The Design Dimension: Product Strategy and the Challenge of Global Marketing*, Blackwell, Oxford.

McBurnie, T. and Clutterbuck, D. (1987), *The Marketing Edge: Key to Profit and Growth*, Weidenfeld and Nicolson, London.

Ohmae, K. (1983), *The Mind of the Strategies: Business Planning for Competitive Advantage*, Penguin, Harmondsworth.

Peters, T. and Waterman, R. (1982), *In Search of Excellence. Lessons from America's Best Run Companies*, Harper & Row, New York.

Stubbart, C. (1982), 'Are environmental scanning units effective?', *Long Range Planning*, June, pp.139–145.

Taylor, B. and Ferro, L. (1983), 'Key social issues for European business', *Long Range Planning*, Vol.16, No.1, pp.42–69.

Thomas, P. S. (1980), 'Environmental scanning – the state of the art', *Long Range Planning*, February, pp.20–28.

3
Analysing the competition

John Saunders

Competition has created man. Mankind has succeeded because, in the hostile environment in which the species evolved, to survive it had to be superior in some way, somewhere. The same laws now govern the corporate world mankind has created. But, whereas mankind's evolution was unconscious, corporate man hopes to shape organizations so that they succeed.

The analysis of competition has long been part of the assessment of the external environment as practised in strategic management (Pearce and Robinson, 1982). It is part of the capability profile where a company's strengths and weaknesses in dealing with opportunities and threats in the external environment are assessed (SWOT analysis). Within the capability profile competitor analysis has a key role alongside other components of the task environment. Together with customer profiles, the nature of the labour market, suppliers and creditors, competition is one of the immediate factors which provide many of the challenges a company faces when striving to market its goods and services profitably.

So, given the familiar role of competitive analysis in strategic management, why has it recently become such an important issue? The evolutionary analogy helps to explain. Postwar economic growth and the relatively small number of developed countries meant a comparatively benign competitive environment. Burgeoning con-

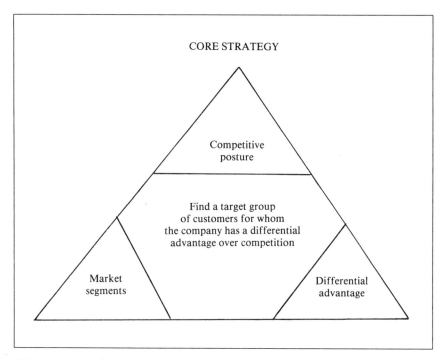

Figure 3.1   Core strategy

sumer demand allowed companies to succeed by understanding their markets and serving them moderately well. Recently, the environment has become more hostile. Economic growth in the developed countries has declined, as has the allegiance of the colonial power's traditional markcts. New competition from south-east Asia has also emerged and, while Western economies were stagnating, has grown at a rate faster than the world has ever known. Whereas in the benign environment, relatively weak corporations – like the dodo – could survive, the current environment requires more adjusted species. With the lower growth and the increased competition, companies have become predators upon one anothers' markets. No longer does a company have to look just at its customers but, to survive, it must be stronger in some domain than its competition. Competitive posture has therefore joined market segmentation and differential advantage at the core of marketing strategy: the task of finding a target group of customers for whom a company has a differential advantage over competiton (see Figure 3.1).

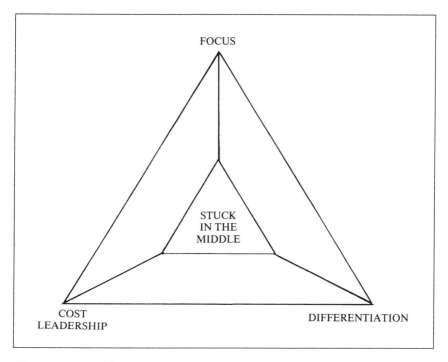

Figure 3.2   The generic strategies
Based on Porter (1980), Figure 2-1.

Having explained the growing importance of competitor analysis, this chapter develops the background for competitor analysis by looking at the alternative competitive strategies and tactics which are available. Once these are understood, a framework for grading competitors is developed and the chapter concludes by describing information systems for gathering competitor information.

COMPETITIVE STRATEGY AND TACTICS

Porter (1980) provides three generic competitive strategies: cost leadership, differentiation and focus. It is supposed, although not proved empirically, that companies succeed competitively by concentrating on one or two of these, and fail by getting confused and so becoming 'stuck in the middle' (see Figure 3.2).

49

Cost leadership

Cost leadership should not be confused with low price. Some cost leaders, such as Amstrad, may use a low price to achieve rapid market penetration, but many operate at the market price or demand a price premium. Boeing, IBM and Toyota are typical of cost leaders who use their low manufacturing costs to generate a high contribution so allowing a large investment in marketing, research and development, and new plant. Cost leaders can, therefore, use their high contribution to fund investments which help maintain their dominant market positions.

In marketing, the cumulative experience accruing from a high market share is the most frequently cited means of achieving low costs. Once a company has the advantage it can use the liberated funds to spend more on marketing or research and development in order to maintain or increase its dominance. Evidence in support of the relationship between experience and cost is strong but the pattern reflects association rather than causality. Making more products does not mean they will become cheaper; it simply provides the opportunity to learn how technology, management techniques and labour can be better used. There are many cases in the engineering industry where the workforce has gained experience at manipulating bonus systems so quickly that manufacturing costs have increased with time. Experience curves depend also upon the company's commitment and ability to take advantage of the available cost-cutting opportunities. Companies and countries have different rates of benefiting from experience. In particular, American companies seem to gain experience faster than European ones, and Japanese companies even faster than the Americans.

Given the limitations of the experience curve, how can a company become a cost leader? Several opportunities depend on large-scale manufacturing. In the steel industry the Japanese and developing countries have been able to undercut the far more experienced Western manufacturers by investing in large-scale modern plant. The globalization of businesses can also help. By marketing global brands companies are able to obtain economies of scale unachievable by multinational companies which allow regional autonomy. Global manufacturing also allows companies to concentrate manufacturing in larger plants in low-cost countries. In reality the expected trend towards offshore manufacturing has not been as great as was once expected since developments in manufacturing technology have allowed some countries with high labour costs to keep their manufacturing costs down.

The rapid price declines in the electronics industry have shown how improved designs using the latest technology can be produced less expensively than the generation they replaced. The same is true of less dynamic industries where new designs can incorporate new materials, electronic rather than electromechanical control systems can be used and new designs use fewer components. Here again, economies are conferred on large-scale manufacturers; they can spend more on perfecting each design and replace products more frequently than their smaller competitors.

Final sources of economy are labour and low overheads. Labour can be made more efficient relatively easily by investing in more productive plant. The labour effectiveness which comes from the workforce's co-operation, flexibility and commitment is not so mechanistically achieved. Neither are the lower overheads that should come from scale and the investment in office automation. A recent American study has shown that, although blue collar workers' productivity has improved significantly over the last ten years, the productivity of white collar workers has actually declined. It would be surprising if the same were not true of the UK.

To achieve cost leadership a company must concentrate upon the tight control of costs. Some of this can be achieved by scale and appropriate manufacturing. It also needs a structured organization to enable costs to be clearly allocated and controlled, and a lean organization motivated by strict quantitative incentives. Experience curves are only a small part of the story.

Differentiation

Success through differentiation demands skills which differ completely from those needed for cost leadership. The differentiator wins by offering a product or service which is unique or superior to competitors'. In the early days of the microcomputer, market competition was based on who could provide the most sophisticated machine with the most facilities. This changed suddenly with the arrival of the IBM PC,

51

which became a dominant design. Differentiators, such as Hewlett Packard and Sinclair, immediately suffered as differentiation became a disadvantage. The new game became low cost and high power but with as little differentiation as possible. It certainly does not follow that differentiation becomes an unsuccessful strategy once markets mature. Until recently 35mm single-lens reflex cameras had become almost standardized; then the electronic cameras launched by Minolta, Canon and others stimulated new differentiation and market growth. In other mature markets design can be used to differentiate products. This approach has been exploited by Bang and Olufsen in hi-fi and by Conran's Habitat chain.

A brand image can be used to differentiate products which are physically indistinguishable. These can be identified by the prominence of the packaging and the manufacturers' labels. Many experiments have shown that in blind tests even loyal consumers are unable to identify their favourite brand of cigarette, soft drink or beer. Without the benefit of the packaging most also find it difficult to distinguish between such seemingly different products as whisky and brandy. The importance of the label and brand image is particularly important among prestige and designer products, where brand names which were once hidden inside the jacket, on the back of a shirt collar, or on the sole of a shoe, are now displayed prominently.

Seemingly identical products can also be differentiated by distribution. For instance, Rington Teas' house-to-house distribution of tea and coffee, Avon Cosmetics' system of agents, and the distribution of some women's magazines through supermarkets or play groups. Perhaps one of the most difficult differentiation tasks is faced by the airlines which, because of bilateral agreements, are all forced to fly the same aeroplanes, to the same destinations and superficially charge the same price. But, as any international traveller will know, there is wide divergence in the services offered by the airlines. Singapore Airlines, Thai Airlines and Japanese Airlines have all gained their high reputation on the basis of the in-flight services they provide. Some of these are based on providing better food with more choice, free movies, many accessories freely available to passengers and slightly more modern aircraft, but it depends largely upon the attentiveness and professionalism of the cabin crews. The power of quality as a differentiating tool extends beyond services. In Britain, Sainsbury and

Marks and Spencer maintain a differential advantage by offering high quality products and good customer service which, although more expensive than competitors', are perceived as being good value for money.

Sir Clive Sinclair's early successes were due to his use of innovation as a means of differentiation. It also caused his fall. A more successful example is Sony, claimed to be world leader in the innovation of new consumer electronics. But even Sony has had to face the reality that innovation is risky. Its Betamax video recorders were first on the market but were eventually pushed out by JVC's VHS format. Its L-cassette audio format sank without trace and its minidiskette system for microcomputers has not yet replaced the traditional floppy disk. However, Sony remains the innovator. Rather than bow to the dominant VHS video technology Sony has introduced its own 16mm system which is well suited for video photography.

The differentiating company clearly needs different skills from the cost leader. Creative people are needed rather than cost controllers. 'Me toos' follow quickly these days, so a differentiator must move quickly to stay ahead of the crowd. This needs close functional co-ordination, and broadly defined performance measures and incentives which encourage innovation.

Focus

Many small companies prosper by pursuing a focus strategy. Without size or resources to achieve cost leadership or overall superiority in a market, they concentrate on providing a product or service tailored to the needs of a well-defined group of customers.

After many British retailers failed by trying to follow Marks and Spencer, success came to Mothercare, Next and Now, which concentrated on providing for distinct market segments. Amstrad, a late entrant into the microcomputer market, was able to gain market share quickly by concentrating on two benefit segments: first, the market for the non-computer literates who wanted a basic machine with all the necessary facilities that they could just plug in and use; and second, the word processor for those with a very specific application in mind but who also needed cheap equipment easy to use. In many ways these two successful Amstrad products were inferior to other microcomputers on the market, but for the target market segments they had clear differential advantages.

To succeed, focused companies must keep close to the customer, and develop the marketing and design skills necessary to serve their particular needs. Also, since the target market is well defined, focused companies often find it beneficial to provide related products that serve the same market. Richard Branson's Virgin Company is a good example of this. Finally,because survival in the long term depends on the identification and exploitation of emerging segments the focused company needs to be entrepreneurial and retain the spirit of the small firm. It needs to follow the dictum 'think small, stay small', in style if not in size.

It is apparent from the examples given that some leading companies have not succeeded by being exclusively cost leaders, differentiators or focused. Many top companies are both cost leaders and differentiators. The buying power and expertise of Marks and Spencer make it a low-cost company but it trades on quality, service and its brand name; IBM is a cost leader which also trades on customer service, and Boeing has lower costs than any other aeroplane manufacturer but the 747, its most profitable product, is unique. Many of the successful low-volume manufacturers complement differentiation with a clear focus. For example, Jaguar, Land Rover and Morgan in the automobile industry, and J. C. Bamford in earth-moving. Lastly, Amstrad's success needs explaining in terms of both cost leadership and focus. Its success in the hi-fi market has been based on integrated systems at the bottom end of the market which the principal Japanese manufacturers were neglecting. Equally, although it was a cost leader, its identification of segment needs enabled it to become a leading supplier with the audacity to challenge IBM.

COMPETITIVE ACTION

Marketing consultants Booz, Allen and Hamilton (Roach, 1981) have identified two classes of successful company in terms of pre-tax return on sales: very large companies which can use their low cost and market dominance to achieve high profitability, and much smaller companies which have found niche markets. Between the two are low performers which have lost their way. Successful competitive strategies have been identified for three classes of company across this size spectrum: the market leader, the number two company and the nicher.

The nicher

The nicher is in fact a common name applied to successful small companies which do not necessarily follow niche strategies. The true nicher provides a unique product or service to a segment neglected by the competitors. Modern examples are the niche retailers such as Tie Rack, Sock Shop and Knobs and Knockers, unique not in terms of the products they sell but in terms of their focus, product range and store locations. They are small and yet can flourish economically because, in the market they serve, they do not face similar competitors. They exemplify three of the basic elements that Hammermesh *et al* (1978) identified as necessary ingredients for successful low-market-share businesses: 'segment, segment, segment', think small, and have a ubiquitous chief executive. They are innovative in terms of their market offering, have grown rapidly, but have kept tightly to their target market.

Other small companies have flourished without being true nichers. These are focused companies which do not occupy a unique position in the marketplace, but have a clear core strategy where they concentrate on a target market for whom they have a differential advantage over competitors. Many of these companies, such as Mercedes or BMW, have a strong brand image with an almost cult-like following. Too large to be niche players, yet too small to have the advantage of leading suppliers in the market, they need a thorough understanding of their market needs and the ability to deliver goods or services which fulfil expectations. So, in addition to their segmentation skills, they must be able to use research and development efficiently to maintain their differentiation through innovation. They must also diversify cautiously and limit their growth so that they can stay close to the target markets they serve. Currently Mercedes is showing signs of having forgotten these rules, with its boardroom battles following its diversification away from its automotive roots into aerospace and consumer electronics.

The strong number two

The benefits of being a strong challenger are epitomized by Doyle, Dane and Bernbach's powerful campaign for Avis which claimed, 'When you are only number two, you try harder. Or else.' This diabolical positioning made life miserable for Hertz, which was number one. Although lower volume can make the number two company in the market less profitable because of its low market share, as a challenger it can have significant combative advantages over the market leader. However, there are major flawed strategies which often lead to the second, third, and lower ranks of industry dissipating their strengths and profits.

As Kotler *et al* (1985) have noticed, challenging strategies lend themselves to a military analogy. There are only two basic ways in which the attacker can approach the defender; directly or indirectly. Of these, in both military and business circles, direct attacks are prone to failure. To challenge a well-established defender, by matching it product by product and expenditure by expenditure, requires resources which challenging companies rarely have. Although direct attacks on markets may be the normal mode of competition and be used to start campaigns, indirect attacks are the means of securing victory.

Whereas direct attacks have the benefit of a crude simplicity, indirect attacks on market have a variety limited only by the creativity of the perpetrators. According to Liddell Hart, the military strategist, history shows that almost all battles have been won by flanking manoeuvres. The same seems to be true for market challenges. In this case the attacker, rather than trying to outspend the defender in established markets, approaches markets which are adjacent to the defender's but where the defender is uncommitted. A classic example of this is Fuji's entry into the photocopier market, against Xerox, by making small machines targeted at the small users neglected by Xerox. Another instance is provided by the Japanese motorcycle industry's attack upon the dominant Western defenders by first marketing small machines in south-east Asia and other markets, then gaining strength as they attacked the market for larger and larger bikes until they were able to swamp the few remaining competitors such as Norton, Triumph and Harley Davidson. Consumer electronics is yet another market in which the Japanese have used indirect attacks. Initially, they made few market share gains against established manufacturers of TV and audio equipment in the West. However, when technological changes occurred – such as colour TV and audio cassettes – a strategic window opened which allowed the attackers to bypass the defenders' established markets and gain a foothold in virgin territory. The aim of the successful strategist, therefore, is to avoid direct confrontation. Gains depend upon the challenger's creativity in identifying market segments which are neglected or emerging; and then having the energy to develop new marketing offerings which destabilize the defender.

Market-leader strategies

Although defenders have a natural advantage, they are most vulnerable when they become myopic in the defence of the markets they dominate. A static defence is as hopeless as a frontal attack. For years Ford tried to defend the dominant market position it gained with its Model T Ford by refining the same model and making it cheaper. This failed against the emerging General Motors which had realized that, with their new-found wealth, the American people wanted something more than a car offering any colour so long as it was black. More recently General Motors is suffering a similar fate, as it tries to defend itself against the Japanese, Ford and Chrysler, by using the same old vertical integration policies on the model changes developed decades ago to defeat Ford.

Static defences do not work. Neither do contracting defences which depend upon retreating into seemingly easily defended market positions: the British motorcycle industry tried this. To succeed, the defender needs the same agility and purpose as the attacker. Like Coca-Cola, the successful defender must use flanking manoeuvres to guard against potential weaknesses. Coca-Cola's launch of Cherry Coke, Diet Coke, New Coke and so on, may have made the company less efficient operationally than if it had stuck to its core product, but the new launches strengthened the company's market position against Pepsi and other challengers. Kellogg's displayed a similarly active defence when faced by the potential challenge of bran products. Rather than waiting until the market had grown to economic proportions, Kellogg's peppered the market with a wide range of bran

57

products in a reactive defence. The key to a successful defence is, therefore, to maintain the energy and initiative that made the company dominant in the first place. It is easy to become lazy once market dominance is achieved, but successful defenders have often avoided such a loss of impetus. Many leading Western fast moving consumer goods companies such as Unilever, Procter and Gamble, and Johnson and Johnson have achieved this, as have many pharmaceutical companies and the Japanese market leaders in consumer durables. Contrast these with several Western companies which have cash mountains and yet are forced to compete with the Japanese by licensing technology from the very companies which are taking their markets from them.

So, although the position of the nicher, the market challenger and the market leader are different, a strong thread runs through the recommended competitive strategies for all three. That is, to create an identification of target markets and to avoid such unsubtle strategies as static defences or direct confrontation. However, there is a difference in the long-term aims of the companies, in terms of the segments they identify. Whereas for the larger companies a shift into flanking segments is a tactical move which they anticipate will give them an advantage in an inevitable strategic confrontation, smaller companies are seeking market positions where they will be left alone with their own moderate ambitions.

ASSESSING COMPETITION

An understanding of competitive alternatives is fundamental to assessing competitors' capabilities. Rather than conducting an abstract analysis of company characteristics, the investigator is looking for evidence of a company's ability to respond and the nature of response that can be expected. This process of competitor analysis can be broken up into two stages. The first looks at the elements which constitute a company's strengths or weaknesses. This can follow closely the competitive position assessment matrix proposed by Hofer and Schenckel (1978). (We have called it the competitor assessment grid.) The second stage then evaluates the likely behaviour of competitors.

The number of issues which could be included in a competitor assessment grid is infinite (see Table 3.1). It is also likely that core issues will change depending on the market and the company being investigated. The use of scales to rate competitors is contentious, so it should not be used in isolation or given too much credibility. The zigzag of ratings given each issue can provide an easily assimilated assessment of each competitor's strengths and weaknesses and draw attention to critical areas, but it needs to be backed by a description of how each of the ratings was derived. Once the limitations of such summary measures are understood, it is safe to go a stage further and provide an overall weighting for a competitor along the lines used in General Electrics' multi-factor portfolio matrix (Hormer, 1982). As Table 3.2 shows, this provides a score for each company by multiplying a rating for each function by a weighting. The weightings are arbitrary and could be changed to fit the perceptions of the users but such tinkering has surprisingly little effect upon final scores.

Competitive imperatives

The competitive imperatives focus upon the key issues of competitor analysis. They add flesh to the abstract competitor profiles and assessment grid. The assessment is essentially subjective but demands statements about competitors' core skills, competitive posture and competitive reflexes.

1 *Core skills* looks at the principal skills of the competitor. These take two forms: internal measures which look at the relative strength of skills across the organization, and comparative measures which look at the competitive strength relative to the industry. It is important to distinguish between the two measures because although one area, such as production, may be seen as the company's dominant strength, when compared with other companies it may appear to be a relative weakness.

2 *Competitive posture* evaluates the stance of the company in terms of its aggressiveness. Is it proactive or reactive? Is it aggressive or complacent when faced with new competition? Is it quick or slow to grasp initiatives?

3 *Competitive reflexes* refers to the competitor's ability to respond quickly to threats. It questions the resource of the company available for deployment in target markets; the company's ability

Table 3.1   Competitor assessment grid

Factor	Issue	Rating* 1 2 3 4 5
Product/technology	Breadth of line	
	Relative quality	
	Modernity	
	New product development skills	
	Core technology	
	Other	
Marketing	Market share	
	Structural advantages	
	Key account strengths	
	Distribution strengths	
	Geographical coverage	
	Price competitiveness	
	Sales competitiveness	
	Promotional competitiveness	
	Other	
Manufacturing	Location	
	Newness	
	Capacity	
	Productivity	
	Cost	
	Flexibility	
	Other	
Financial	Cash resources	
	Risk aversion	
	Access to capital	
	Other	
Organization	Chief Executive Officer (CEO) quality	
	Depth and quality of management	
	Energy	
	Flexibility	
	Other	

*5 = very strong competitive position, 4 = strong, 3 = average, 2 = weak and 1 = very weak.

Table 3.2   Competitor profile

Factor	Weight	Rating*	Weighted score
Product/technology	0.2	3	0.6
Marketing	0.2	2	0.4
Manufacturing	0.2	3	0.6
Financial	0.2	4	0.8
Organization	0.2	4	0.8
			3.2

*5 = very strong competitive position, 4 = strong, 3 = average, 2 = weak and 1 = very weak.

to learn new skills quickly and its energy in terms of its ability to overcome inertia once it is threatened.

The components of the competitor assessment provide a broad picture of competitors and their likely responses to threats. Competitor profiles give an overall grading of each competitor. These are backed by the competitor assessment grid which draws attention to key strengths or weaknesses, and directs attention to supporting background material. The final stage provides an analysis of the core skills of the company and an assessment of how a company is likely to behave when threatened. This last stage is critical since many companies have failed, not because they lack resources and skills but because they lack the commitment to succeed and the energy to pursue new campaigns.

COMPETITOR INTELLIGENCE SYSTEM

It is surprising that, given their importance to long-term survival, the systematic collection and communication of competitive information rarely exist in companies. Marketing executives usually depend upon contacts and reading newspapers to gather information. This can often lead to valuable insights into competitors, yet the system is quite casual, and valuable information can be lost or arrive too late. It is clearly unrealistic to develop a free-standing competitor intelligence system, it is a logical part of a marketing information system. Aguilar (1967) suggested four steps a company should take to improve the quality and quantity of this intelligence.

1   Train and motivate staff to spot and report new developments, particularly sales people, merchandisers, product support and new product development personnel. The importance of this process must be sold to the people concerned and facilitated through a system that makes reporting easy.

2   Motivate distributors, retailers and suppliers to pass on important information about the competition. This often means key managers maintaining close contact with intermediaries and feeding back the intelligence they gather. These initiatives need to be supported by a formalized clippings service which scans literature and maintains an active or passive information system.

3   Purchasing information from outside intelligence suppliers, such as consumer panels and the like.

4   Establishing an information centre to collect and circulate marketing intelligence. The staff can scan leading publications, abstract relevant news, and disseminate a news bulletin to marketing managers. Two communication channels are necessary: an express channel for urgent information and files for the retrieval of background data.

CONCLUSIONS

Increased international competition and limited growth have increased the importance of competitive strategy. It is no longer sufficient to base strategies upon markets, for a company must be able to evaluate its own strengths and weaknesses and compare them with those of its competitors. This ability to identify and establish viable competitive strategies is fundamental to survival. A company must understand these and be able to evaluate its own capability in terms of adopting a strategy of either cost leadership, differentiation, or focus.

To avoid unwinnable battles, companies need to appreciate the tactics that can lead to marketing gains, understand the importance of identifying segments where they can have an advantage over competition, and make them into a platform for further growth or a niche market.

The growing importance of competitive strategy means that competitive intelligence must form an important part of any marketing information system. But, although this has the potential for being an invaluable contributor to marketing decision-making, it will always remain secondary to the exchange of information which should occur in an organization whose culture allows frequent and intensive *ad hoc* communication between its people. Such a flexible organization has advantages in the pursuit of competitive strategy. As in battle, victory does not always go to those with the most resources, but often to those with the best training, the best skills and the will to win.

REFERENCES AND FURTHER READING

Aguilar, F. J. (1967), *Scanning the Business Environment*, Macmillan, New York.

Day, G. S. (1966), *Analysis for Strategic Market Decisions*, West Publishing, New York.

Hammermesh, R. G., Anderson, M. J. and Harris, J. E. (1978), 'Strategies for low market share businesses', *Harvard Business Review*, May–June, pp.95–102.

Hofer, C. W. and Schenckel, D. (1978), *Strategy Formulation: Analytical Concepts*, West Publishing, St. Paul.

Hormer, L. R. T. (1982), *Strategic Management*, Prentice-Hall, Englewood Cliffs, N.J.

Kotler, P., Fahey, L. and Jatusripitak, S. (1985), *The New Competition*, Prentice-Hall, Englewood Cliffs, N.J.

Pearce, J. A. and Robinson, R. B. (1982), *Strategic Management: Strategy Formulation and Implementation*, Irwin, Homewood, Ill.

Porter, M. E. (1980), *Competitive Strategy: Techniques for Analysing Industries and Competitors*, Free Press, London.

Porter, M. E. (1985), *Competitive Advantage: Creating and Sustaining Superior Performances*, Collier Macmillan, London.

Roach, J. D. C. (1981), 'From strategic planning to strategic performance: closing the achievement gap', in *Outlook*, Booz, Allen and Hamilton, New York.

Strategic Planning Institute (The PIMS Program), 1033 Massachusetts Avenue, Cambridge, Mass. 02138.

4

Marketing planning for maximum growth

William Giles

Marketing planning is easy to understand but difficult to execute. Undertaken conscientiously it is a painful yet rewarding process with far wider-reaching implications than the preparation of the plan itself. Despite this, marketing planning is, all too often, reduced to forecasting and budgeting. This neither stretches the capability of the organization nor challenges the inherited wisdom.

This chapter demonstrates how a structured iterative approach to marketing planning can overcome the difficulties experienced using traditional methods. The strategic awareness and understanding it develops amongst managers is discussed in the context of both the process and the marketing orientation of the organization at large.

WHAT IS MARKETING PLANNING?

Marketing planning is the creation of long-term competitive strategies based upon the sound analysis and interpretation of the relationship between an organization, its customers and its competitors. It is, therefore, primarily concerned with viewing the organization and its offerings from a market perspective. The output of the process is measured by the understanding of competitive position. This is neither an alternative nor a replacement to corporate planning – it is the starting point.

Marketing planning by any other name

Marketing planning sits uneasily in the corporate structure. Corporate planning has grown to maturity whilst marketing planning is still generally viewed as an operational function (Lorenz, 1985).

If, as history has shown, the long-term health of companies is determined by the uncertainties of the market place, planning should start here too. That most planning does not is a reflection of the discomfort created by market-based planning.

The traditions of planning lie in accountancy. In contrast, predicting the future of customer needs and competitive activities is fraught with ambiguities. It is a minefield of assumptions. The results do not easily measure up to the precision of the accountant's historically based facts and figures. Finance is measurable, controllable and, above all, engenders a feeling of comfort and reliability.

However, with the continuous acceleration of change in the marketplace, an external dimension has become essential in all types of planning for the future. It cannot be ignored. Already in the more innovative organizations, market criteria are replacing financial parameters as the currency of corporate strategy.

The state of the art

Only since the early 1980s has marketing planning been considered as a subject in its own right. A European survey (Wills *et al*, 1984) commented that

> most companies understand the importance of, and the need for, marketing planning procedures. Of the companies surveyed, 85 per cent professed to have a marketing system. Only 15 per cent had any real procedure other than forecasting and budgeting.

The gap between these two percentages can be explained by managers' inadequate marketing planning skills. More recently, management has been willing to acknowledge these shortcomings and admit that the emphasis is biased heavily towards the financial aspects of business.

Recognition of the need for help with marketing planning is illustrated by the 1987 Institute of Marketing survey of marketing training needs in industry. In this 84 per cent of all executives interviewed expressed a need for assistance with marketing planning. This puts marketing planning well ahead of all other areas of marketing.

Most commercial organizations boast a marketing plan. Closer inspection reveals that attempts at marketing planning are forsaken for the every day pressures of corporate life. Aspirations for the future become reduced to short-term financial goals, which are easier to pursue than the real market gains (Halley *et al*, 1983). Objectives are introvert statements of intent and strategies, where they exist, are bland, catch-all clichés. Strategic plans are budgetary tables with little supporting text and operating plans are tactical in the extreme, often being little more than 'to do' lists.

The need for planning is understood but the concepts of planning are still shrouded in mystery, and its practice is limited. The intellectuals have failed to simplify this complex subject area and so industry, recognizing the need, knows not where to start.

Companies which have mastered the art of marketing planning have achieved it by an intuitive route they guard jealously and are unwilling to intellectualize. It is hard to separate best practice, and difficult to develop their system further. These approaches meet the immediate need of specific business problems well but leave little scope for educating the organization at large.

The answer lies somewhere between intellectual theorizing and practical intuition. As the implementation vehicle of marketing theory, marketing planning should not need to invent a theory of its own. As a practical application tool, it must be intellectualized to the point where its practical nature is capable of transference for others to try.

WHY PLAN MARKETING ANYWAY?

To overcome these very real difficulties, there must be considerable advantages to be gained from the process. These are derived from two areas. The first is in the process itself and its output of the plan. The second is in the strategic skills and positive attitudes it teaches. The overall intention is to make large jumps in long-term performance by breaking the journey into smaller short-term steps. If the benefits are clearly understood, the effort invested should be worthwhile.

The benefits of marketing planning

Obviously the immediate benefits derived from a marketing plan will depend on the specific goals set by the organization. In all cases, however, a sound plan, properly implemented, should improve a company's growth prospects by upgrading its marketing effort from the tactical and operational to the strategic level. Sound marketing plans encourage:

- concentration on specific markets, segments or niches
- efficient use of scarce resources
- competitive strengths focused in areas of opportunity

from which come:

- increased revenue generation
- improved profit levels
- reduced vulnerability to competitive attack
- the confidence to invest in new opportunities

These are not, however, the only benefits of marketing planning. By far the most significant benefits are the strategic awareness and understanding that marketing planning promotes (Porter, 1987). These reach far wider than the authors of the plan and should eventually spread across the entire organization. Furthermore, the skills of thinking strategically which marketing planning instils can be used again in different contexts. They are both more substantial and longer lasting than the prescriptives contained within a single marketing plan.

While marketing planning itself cannot cause change, it is a powerful vehicle for creating an environment in which change takes place. The growing links between organizational behaviour and market knowledge (Piercy, 1985) are becoming apparent although still unde-

67

fined. Involvement in the process of marketing planning provides a forum for exploring new ideas within an objective framework. All organizations need this space to reflect on the broader ramifications of corporate activities. The role of marketing planning, as opposed to any other type of planning, is to set out the issues in their true external context.

Confidence and positiveness come with the deeper understanding of the strategic options provided by marketing planning. It is, though, the human involvement that causes this attitudinal change and not the output of the plan itself. The two should not be confused.

Short-term versus long-term planning

There are inherent dangers in the financially derived planning systems which are commonplace. They rely on comparisons with past performance to set standards for the future. The long term is a crude extrapolation with scant allowance for competitive reaction. There is little room for belief in exceptional results – the staple diet of creative planning.

To achieve real growth the long term cannot be treated as a succession of short terms (Drucker, 1987). This is illustrated in Figure 4.1, which describes the difference in performance and attitude between short-term incremental planning and long-term visionary planning.

The incremental approach of adding year on year will achieve a result relative only to past performance, taking no account of changing customers, competitors or organizational capability. The outcome is a progressive decline in achievement.

The essence of good marketing planning is to view the long term as a continuous evolution from the present. The horizon needs to be a point in time sufficiently far distant to allow substantial change to be effected. This point is the 'visionary goal'. The 'planning gap' is the difference between long-term and short-term planning. The planning process is directed to closing this gap by working back towards the present from the visionary goal. The short term can thus be visualized as a first step in the long term, not as an increment over the previous year. This causes very different actions to be taken.

Marketing planning is a prerequisite for all organizations which

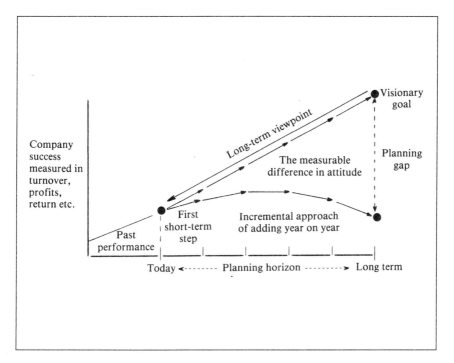

Figure 4.1   The long-term planning horizon

intend both to stay ahead of a changing marketplace and be proactive rather than reactive.

THE DIFFICULTIES OF PLANNING

As one might expect with the emergence of a new discipline, marketing planning has become a fashionable, yet little understood, addition to corporate jargon. The initiative for any serious attempt at marketing planning must come directly from the top of the hierarchy – the ultimate custodians of marketing strategy. If at this level there is difficulty in grasping the significance, there is little hope for the lower echelons. Yet it is not unusual to find the former has least comprehension of the enormity of the planning task. It is also not unusual to find ambiguous goals that provide little guidance to those further down the hierarchy, where the detailed plans are developed in earnest.

Resistance to change

Marketing planning represents a new approach which is not always comfortable. The common objections to marketing planning (McDonald, 1984) may be summarized thus:

1 the company has made good profits without it;
2 planning is time consuming and prevents people from doing their real job;
3 plans are constraining, prevent initiative and create inflexibility to rapid change;
4 plans never come true, valuable time is wasted writing them;
5 companies know their business well, there is no point in writing down the obvious;
6 no one reads the plan when it is written so it becomes simply a traditional annual ritual;
7 some industries are different and do not need plans;
8 long-range plans are full of meaningless numbers;
9 plans are based on unrealistic objectives and prepared without hard market information;
10 departments cannot agree amongst themselves so the plan is never finalized.

Behind these objections lie compelling reasons for a better planning process. They unwittingly reveal the underlying problem. Managers lack the knowledge, skills and confidence to obtain worthwhile results from the time invested.

Shortcomings in the organization

Marketing planning is an onerous process and the time it takes is consistently underestimated (Greenley, 1986). Developing strategies from a mass of data is not an instant activity. Unless the organization can free sufficient time, because the ramifications of not doing so are considered sufficiently important, the changeover to market-focused planning never happens. Superimposed upon the physical demands of time are the creative requirements. For many individuals this is a strain in itself. Creativity is not something that comes spontaneously under the daily pressures of the workplace.

To make the task even more difficult, most organizations are still structured around products, not markets. Despite the insistence on customer orientation, organization structures generally do not reflect this (Foxall, 1981). The choice, therefore, of how best to approach markets using all the company's resources is a difficult one. Furthermore, departmental structures are often parochial in their outlook, compounding the issue still further.

There is no place in marketing planning for company politics. The process demands that an organization see itself through its customers' eyes. Unfortunately, customers pay little attention in their purchasing decisions to the internal politics of their suppliers! Once company politics are allowed to enter the process, objectivity is lost – the plan, and everything that emanates from it, becomes a self-fulfilling prophecy. Marketing planning falls into disrepute and is retained only as a piece of fashionable management science.

Hierarchical power play is a similar defence of the status quo. Senior managers have neither an embargo on valuable experience nor the exclusivity of good ideas. Yet there is a tendency for the solutions carrying the label of seniority to win the day. These are not considerations of our customers, neither should they be the considerations of marketing planners. Company politicians and empire builders are, to marketing planning, what ice was to the *Titanic*!

THE STRUCTURED ITERATIVE APPROACH TO MARKETING PLANNING

It is clear from the difficulties that have been discussed that any marketing planning process likely to succeed will need to be designed very carefully. It must link marketing theory to actual business practice by an easily understood methodology that suppresses neither intuition nor innovation.

The approach described here is a structured iterative method of marketing planning (Giles, 1986), which has overcome many of the difficulties experienced with other planning approaches. This section looks first at the problems associated with traditional methods. It then describes in detail how one particular structured iterative approach, known as the 'Marlow method', overcomes these deficiencies. 'Marlow Method' is the descriptive label applied to the methodology of marketing planning referred to in this chapter.

The organization required to conduct this process is as important as the process itself. It is, however, a subject outside the scope of this chapter, but which, nevertheless, should be investigated carefully before undertaking the process. These considerations are discussed in Giles (1988).

A comparison with traditional methods

The traditional structure starts with corporate goals, progresses through the marketing audit interpreted in a SWOT (strengths, weaknesses, opportunities and threats) analysis, and emerges via a list of stated assumptions into the plan itself. This structure is represented in Figure 4.2, which shows this sequence of steps in diagrammatic form.

It suffers from one serious deficiency which is responsible for most of the mystique that has surrounded the process for so long: the traditional structure is far too logical (Lenz, 1985). The human brain is not sequentially logical in the way in which it releases information and allows it to be used. Managers find it difficult to enter the process by plunging straight into the audit. Familiarization is needed before deeper analysis can be attempted. Planners need to acquaint themselves with the available knowledge and information and also adjust their minds progressively to the methodology to be adopted.

The audit itself is treated as a lengthy information-collection exercise. Interpretation (the ubiquitous SWOT) is held back until it is complete. The time lapse is sufficient to allow many of the valuable nuances that could have been derived to be forgotten. Constant iteration and interpretation, at the time the information is first assembled, will overcome this difficulty and are therefore essential additions to any new methodology.

The plan is written separately from the audit and its interpretation. When faced with this discontinuity, managers compile the ideas for their plan in isolation from the analysis that has taken place. Much of the interpretation is thus lost or reinvented. A process is really needed that can run analysis, interpretation and plan writing in parallel, each depending upon the others to force constant reiteration.

The traditional approach does, however, provide a useful shape for the written plan that emerges at the end of the process. The mistake

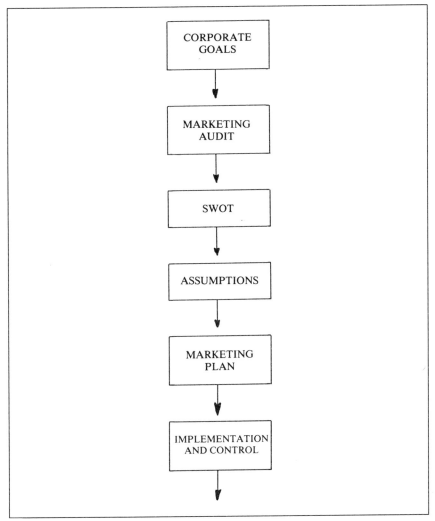

Figure 4.2   The traditional structure of marketing planning

has been to employ a logical output shape as an input structure. Writing objectives followed by strategies and tactics in the correct order is not how the managerial mind works, even though it is how the reader wants the results presented. What has been missing is an input structure which can both capture and interpret information step by step, and interface with the traditional at the end.

These problems explain many of the difficulties practising

managers have faced in preparing their marketing plans. The route taken by the traditional structure has been surrounded by insurmountable difficulties.

The shape of the structured iterative process

The Marlow method is based on a worksheet methodology which promotes iteration, objectivity and self-regulation. The sequence of steps is designed to be in harmony with the mental approach of planners. It differs from the traditional structure in several ways, the most obvious being the nomenclature used to describe each of the steps. Figure 4.3 describes these steps, their sequence, and the titles adopted for each.

Each step has a specific role closely linked to the others. The output from one step is the input to the next. A brief inspection of each shows how this works.

1 *The trigger* is the starting point of the process. Corporate goals are restated here in a way that is specific to the market about to be planned. The goals are framed in a format which the process can use later on. This first step triggers the planning process.
2 *The pencil sketch* gives the planners the opportunity to formulate a broad hypothesis of the plan towards which they are working. It is a pencil sketch of their first ideas of how to meet the challenge in the trigger.
3 *The codebreaker* replaces the conventional audit which traditionally overemphasizes the collection of information to the exclusion of its interpretation. Codebreaking describes the process of assimilating information in a format that is easily analysed and immediately interpreted. The instant decoding of market messages reveals their true significance, at the earliest opportunity.
4 *The blueprint* consolidates the results of the codebreaker into their final form – the strategic plan. Many iterations have been completed in the codebreaker, leaving this stage to blueprint the output.
5 *Action line* is the detailed implementation of the plan. It is the tactical first step towards the future and wholly action-orientated.

Each of these five steps contains worksheets on which the planners

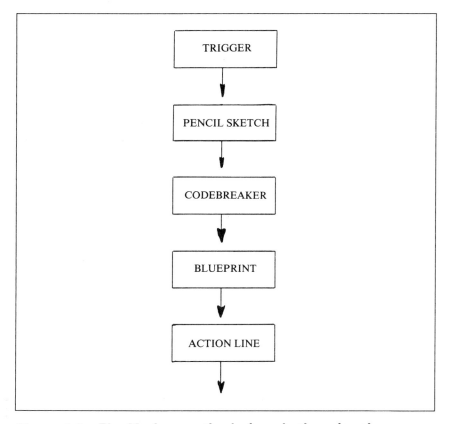

Figure 4.3 The Marlow method of marketing planning

Reproduced with the permission of Strategic Marketing Development Unit.

organize their data, complete their interpretation and draw their conclusions as they progress. This approach breaks each subject area down into smaller manageable tasks. Each worksheet depends upon others to which it is linked and from which it draws information for its own completion. Each builds upon the previous one, pulling different pieces of information together, adding new ideas and opening up the next issue to be tackled.

A particular structure may contain anything up to a hundred worksheets for a specific detailed planning exercise. Different permutations of the worksheet library can be linked together to meet specific planning requirements in different parts of an organization.

The worksheets are deliberately compressed to keep recording areas small. This limits the amount of information that can be used, forcing the planner to concentrate on the important issues. Excessive detail destroys the real purpose of marketing planning, which is to engineer robust strategies to attack significant opportunities. Well-structured worksheets achieve this.

The linkages between the worksheets set standards for self-regulation. Conflicting information is set side by side with proven material, forcing reiteration and preventing self-fulfilling prophecies becoming assumed facts.

The beginning-to-end worksheet methodology is a distinguishing feature of a structured iterative process. Adherence to the concepts involved and an understanding of each worksheet's significance make this a mentally painful but very rewarding exercise. To gain a proper understanding of the structure, each of the five steps will be discussed in detail.

FRAMING USEFUL PLANNING GOALS

The corporate goals of many companies are not sufficiently detailed to be applied to a discrete market. The trigger breaks the overall corporate objective into sets of objectives applicable to each market or business unit. In organizations using several triggers, each for a different market, it is essential that these encompass the total corporate requirement.

One of the common corporate ailments of setting poorly defined goals is overcome at this stage. The trigger must be rigidly defined in terms of customers, products or services, geography and preferred business direction. It must also contain numeric measurements of the targets and the time scale of the planning horizon. The outlook is wholly external, avoiding any possibility of internal politics biasing the picture.

The trigger sets the boundaries of the planners' task without straitjacketing them into a way of doing it. All guidance is helpful. Unambiguous statements keep the planners within the boundaries and time is not wasted by venturing outside. Without the trigger, no planner can hope to plan successfully.

The trigger is the only part of the process that may be subjective. It is a visionary goal reflecting the philosophy described diagramatically

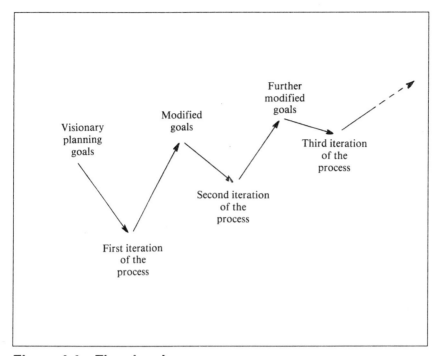

Figure 4.4 The planning consensus
Reproduced with the permission of Strategic Marketing Development Unit.

in Figure 4.1. If goals are set within the immediate comprehension of the planning team, the final output will be unstretching and not achieve real growth. By setting goals that may on first inspection seem impossible, the planning team is forced to look for ways of converting weaknesses into strengths and threats into opportunities. This creates an essential attitude to the task if the conventional wisdom is to be challenged and the dogma brushed aside.

Neither should the trigger be viewed within the process as a 'tablet of stone'. It is the planning team's responsibility to challenge, modify and improve on these goals as they progress. Each iteration within the process modifies the previous stage, as Figure 4.4. demonstrates. Checks are built into the pencil sketch and blueprint to ensure this happens. The dissonance between the aspirations of the goal-setters and the realism of the planners diminishes in time as understanding and consensus are reached. This pattern is upset only by changes in the marketplace or the arrival of senior managers with different visions.

CONSTRUCTING A HYPOTHESIS OF THE MARKETING PLAN

The next stage is the pencil sketch – a step which is absent in traditional models. This is the first opportunity the planning team has to familiarize itself with the process. Pencil sketch is a discrete first iteration within the total process. Customers are split into crude segments and products or services are broadly categorized. Priorities are considered by matching the company's expectations against the likelihood of market success, niche by niche. An initial SWOT analysis leads to a first look at the available strategic options. This generates a financial profile which is checked against the trigger. The output from this iteration is a hypothesis of the marketing plan which will be referred to subsequently as the 'plan hypothesis'.

The pencil sketch provides three bridges between old attitudes and new concepts. The first is to provide a structure in which the trigger can be broken down into meaningful specifics and the viability of each considered in turn. More often than not, the re-aggregation of these specifics into the plan hypothesis meets, or even exceeds, the optimistic vision of the trigger.

Whilst the plan hypothesis is as yet untested and will need to be validated, it simplifies the codebreaker by providing a direction and shape to the analysis. At this stage the formulation of a plan hypothesis that meets the planning goals in the trigger gives planners the necessary impetus to persevere. Alternatively, if the plan hypothesis falls short, this is the first point at which the trigger can be questioned. The interrogation comes now from a positive position (derived from the analysis of pencil sketch) rather than from a position of prejudice and empty rhetoric which may have been prevalent at the outset.

The second bridge the pencil sketch provides is the consensus achieved between members of the planning team. The plan hypothesis is formed directly from the planners' knowledge and, as such, earns their ownership. Frequently, in everyday business life, managers observe the same situation, but through different eyes, and so arrive at different conclusions. Pencil sketch is a forum in which to share these experiences and consolidate the evidence. Opinions can be articulated and given recognition. Bottling them up at this stage can cause havoc with the process later by introducing excessive bias from previously unvoiced instincts.

The third bridge avoids the reinvention of the wheel. However crude, some knowledge and experience is always to hand on almost any market. Traditional models suggest starting with a broad audit that supposes little or no knowledge exists within the organization. This is both wasteful and patronizing. Pencil sketch defines the knowledge base that does exist and identifies the gaps.

The progression into codebreaker is thus a smooth acceleration as the worksheet methodology becomes familiar and the search becomes confined to areas which are recognized as important. In subsequent re-runs of the process the pencil sketch step can be omitted, the previous plan taking the place of this first iteration.

ANALYSING THE MARKET

Codebreaker is the cornerstone of the entire process. It replaces the audit in traditional structures. Being the largest part of the process it is split into five smaller codebreakers each with a specific area to investigate. Figure 4.5 shows how the split is organized. The first, market codebreaker, covers many of the broad market issues and orientates subsequent analysis. The remaining four codebreakers represent the four Ps of the marketing mix. Their contents are roughly equal in size and cover these areas:

1 *Market codebreaker*:
   - Customer needs
   - Buying factors
   - Segmentation
   - Vulnerability analysis
   - Enterers and leavers
   - Market size
   - Competitive shares
2 *Product codebreaker*:
   - Target competitors
   - Product usage
   - Functionality
   - Competitive performance
   - Product attributes
   - Product gaps
3 *Place codebreaker*:

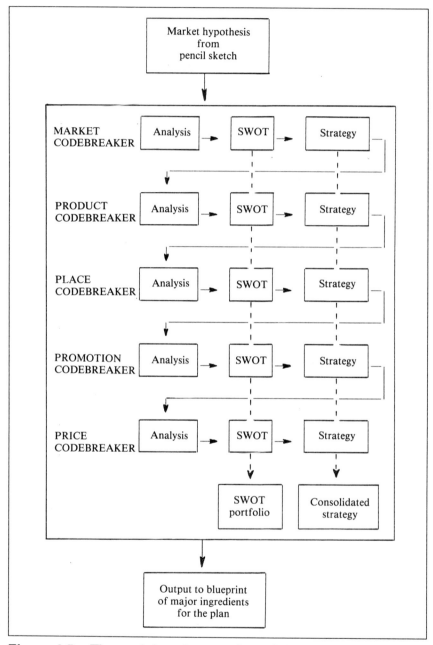

Figure 4.5   The codebreaker section of the process
Reproduced with the permission of Strategic Marketing Development Unit.

- Prime users
- Channel importance
- Channel shares
- Market coverage
- Geographic spread
- Intermediary dependence

4 *Promotion codebreaker*:
  - Competitive positioning
  - Decision-making units
  - Choice of influencers
  - Media effectiveness
  - Share of voice
  - Message styles
  - Customer awareness

5 *Price codebreaker*:
  - End-user pricing
  - Industry pricing
  - Value formulae
  - Price trends
  - Distribution pricing
  - Total cost of ownership

Each of these subject areas has a set of worksheets to structure its analysis.

The order in which the codebreakers are tackled is also important. Market codebreaker comes first to set the scene whilst price codebreaker comes last, after all the other variables have been considered. There is a correlation between those who believe price is the only determining factor and those who suffer from a lack of market knowledge and creative instinct. Placing price codebreaker last provides a better balance of the four Ps and places some objectivity on marketers' obsession with reducing prices.

Some of the special codebreaker techniques

Each of the five codebreakers is split into three distinct stages – analysis, SWOT and strategy. The analysis stage has a common theme running through it. The order of analysis is to identify the customer requirements first, followed by comparing the offerings of competi-

tors against each requirement in turn. Finally, the company introduces its own offering for comparison against all the others. This
order of 'customer–competitors–company' encourages an external
viewpoint to be taken through the customer's own eyes. Industry
norms can be established and the company compared to the other
choices the customer has.

A further sophistication is to rank customers' requirements in order
of importance, weighting them accordingly. Numeric measurements
are used to compare competitive offerings to avoid ambiguity. The
resulting matrices encourage objective discussion on whether
strengths and weaknesses are in areas of high or low customer
preference, thus avoiding the assumption that customers will automatically respond to the company strengths.

The use of the plan hypothesis constructed in pencil sketch is a key
ingredient of codebreaker. First, it is fed into market codebreaker and
the search for information and ideas is dictated by its validation. The
hypothesis emerges from this codebreaker either modified or
enhanced, and is then introduced into the product codebreaker. In this
way, it passes through all the codebreakers and emerges each time
either modified or enhanced until it is finally validated at the end of
the last codebreaker. If at any point the hypothesis fails the test, the
information which disproves it provides the foundations for a new
hypothesis which then passes through the codebreakers in another
iteration.

There are several advantages to this method. Information need not
be collected on a grand scale, it can be specifically aimed at validating
the hypothesis. Considerable time is saved and the process is more
rewarding. In addition, reiteration is encouraged as the hypothesis
changes shape and moves back and forth between the codebreakers.

Traditional processes leave the interpretation to the end. The
richness of much of the information is lost before it is interpreted.
Because each codebreaker has its own SWOT and strategy section,
interpretation of information is immediate. Less irrelevant material is
collected and the shape of the hypothesis can be corrected at an early
stage.

There are those who feel that unless an audit encompasses everything, some opportunities may be missed. Any directed search is
believed to reinforce the self-fulfilling prophecy. In a perfect world
with unlimited resources this would be true. However, for the busy

line manager, the real pressure is to do the job in the most efficient way possible. Codebreaker imposes a strict discipline of objectivity and contains its own self-policing linkages between the worksheets. If the process is adhered to, the leap from undirected to directed search is quite acceptable.

Imposing discipline on interpretation

The method of interpretation is the SWOT analysis. Most managers have attempted this at some time and been disillusioned by its results. The methodology itself is sound, but the application has become ill-disciplined and subjective. The 'Marlow method' uses a variant of SWOT to reinstate objectivity. The differences between the conventional and the variant proposed here are illustrated diagrammatically in Figure 4.6.

The SWOT can be visualized as six boxes in which all information must come to rest, classified under one or other of the six titles marked on the boxes. The contents of each box are described in turn.

1 *Customer perceived strengths and weaknesses* belong to the company, its products or services and its reputation. Any information classified in these two boxes must be perceived by the customer and expressed in language the customer would use. This forces an external market viewpoint to be taken of the company.

2 *Hidden strengths and weaknesses* also belong to the company but are either hidden from the customer or not common knowledge in the marketplace. This imposes a rigid discipline that is often disappointing to the planner. It is not unusual for the hidden boxes to be filled with information long before the perceived ones. When strategy is formulated, hidden strengths must be evidenced in a more positive way than already perceived ones. This is one way in which objectivity is restored to SWOT.

3 *Opportunities and threats* belong to the marketing environment, customers and competitors. These are events that would take place whether or not the organization continued in being. Most traditional SWOT analyses become confused by placing opportunities open to the organization in the first of these two boxes. This is assumptive strategy and not necessarily an opportunity. The 'Marlow method' consciously places a gap between these two

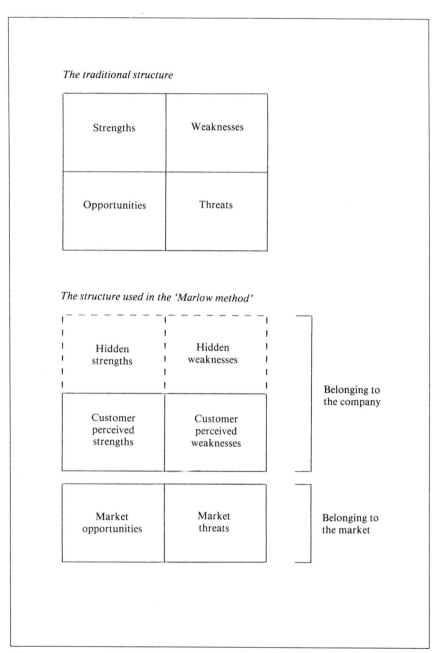

Figure 4.6   The SWOT analysis

Reproduced with the permission of Strategic Marketing Development Unit.

bottom boxes and the rest to accentuate the difference between the market's opportunities and threats from the company's strengths and weaknesses. This is yet another way of restoring objectivity.

Considerable pedantry is needed to keep SWOT objective. For example, a single piece of information cannot be an opportunity and a threat at the same time. Planners have a responsibility to make judgements. Deeper consideration of a situation may lead to one ramification being an opportunity and another being a threat, even though they originate from the same situation. It is the ramifications, not the situation, that need to be recorded.

Motherhood phrases such as 'professional', 'quality' or 'flexible' are unhelpful when it comes to generating strategy. Customers do not phrase their preferences in these loose terms. It is, however, quite permissible to record the ramifications of a situation as both a weakness and a threat. For instance, a customer need may not be satisfied by any of the company's products (weakness) but may be well satisfied by a particular competitor (threat).

Using SWOT as a strategy generator

SWOT is a rich source of strategy ideas which is rarely utilized in conventional processes. The way to extract these ideas starts back at the trigger.

If the visionary goal is appropriately high, situations listed as weaknesses and threats will prevent that goal from being reached. The first step therefore is to formulate a conversion strategy for each item in the three right-hand boxes in Figure 4.6. The idea is to convert hidden and perceived weaknesses into perceived strengths, and threats into opportunities. Some items will only be neutralized and a few will remain unconverted. In the latter case, it is better to know which weaknesses and threats are immovable than to dismiss them completely.

The second step is to match the new list of perceived strengths against the new list of opportunities (assuming the conversion strategies will be successful). It is not surprising to find that some opportunities have no strengths to match them and cannot therefore be good prospects. A more salutary lesson is when some of the company's strengths have no opportunity to chase. This is a warning not to be missed. Industry is littered with corporate corpses which believed that being good at something automatically means that the customer will respond positively towards it (Levitt, 1983). Organizations spend considerable time and resource on improving their skills in areas that do not interest customers. The matching analysis will identify this with uncomfortable ease.

The constant application of this disciplined SWOT analysis to the plan hypothesis throughout the codebreaker is a rigorous process that will challenge the conventional wisdom and produce a robust set of ideas for the next stage.

SHAPING AND IMPLEMENTING THE PLAN

The blueprint acts as a consolidation of the ideas generated in codebreaker into the final plan. Its contents cover the important areas of:

- Strategic situation
- Market summary
- Market priorities
- Critical assumptions
- Information strategy
- Success factors
- Market objectives
- Strategic options
- Competitive reaction
- Key tactics
- Plan costs
- Financial evaluation

Outputs from codebreaker are turned into numeric objectives and checked once again against the trigger. The SWOTs are consolidated into a portfolio. Strategy is organized under the four Ps in each segment and then broken into more detailed tactics. The plan is costed, and a profit statement checked against the trigger finalizes this part of the process.

Most plans suffer from lack of preparation at the conventional audit stage. They are introspectively built on the previous year's activities and results, instead of a thorough inspection of the market-place. No amount of creativity in the blueprint will make up for skimping the earlier stages of the process. On the contrary, even controversial strategies are easily justified if the approach work has been done properly. The blueprint should almost write itself.

The final step in the blueprint is the profit evaluation. This is where the interface is best made with the financial aims of corporate planning. Marketing plans that do not include a financial statement have given some marketers the reputation they deserve – that of head in the clouds and feet off the ground. This step often creates a final iteration. Strategies and tactics chosen may be too costly for the objectives they have to meet. Conversely, it may be possible to apportion some profit back into marketing expenditure and push the objectives still higher. Either way, the financial statement is an arbiter of the value of the plan.

At this point the process departs temporarily from the worksheet methodology to write the long-term strategic plan. The traditional structure described in Figure 4.2 is the best outline for this logical output task. The structured iterative process converts the worksheet contents directly into a written plan. Headings and subheadings are drawn up first based on the traditional structure. Then the contents of each worksheet are found a home under one of these headings. The worksheets themselves, however, should not be used as presentation material. They were not designed for this. Indeed, designing them for both input and output would compromise their layout severely. Instead, the process describes exactly how each worksheet's content can be translated into a succinct part of the report format.

It is not unusual for much of the good work to be nearly lost at this point unless the process is followed closely. It is not always easy to find words to describe the valuable iterations which have taken place or to convey the excitement of some of the more controversial strategies. The process facilitates crisp and unambiguous writing styles – bland catch-all phraseology is excluded. The process is again vulnerable to the creeping paralysis of company politics bastardizing the output. The most difficult task is articulating hard-hitting robust strategies which will survive the ever-changing marketplace.

Robustness and the strategy development loop

Within the blueprint lies the methodology for creating robustness, known as the 'strategy development loop'. Figure 4.7 outlines the steps it follows.

SWOT is a source of strategy generation with its conversion strategies and matching of strengths against opportunities. With this and some creative thinking, it is possible to make a list of strategy options. The object is to create as many strategies as possible without passing judgement on any of them. Once in the strategy development loop they will be severely tested by its rigorous competitive screening which is more powerful than any introspective view.

Each strategy is rephrased in terms of the competitive edge it would give. Those giving no edge are discarded. Simultaneously, competitive SWOTS are completed. They are used to determine each competitor's likely strategies. From the copious information in codebreaker this should be easy to do. These are then pitted against the competitive edge of the company's own strategies and the competitive reaction estimated. At this point, some strategies are discarded and some new ones appear which are fed back into the strategy options to complete the loop. The process is repeated until a set of robust strategies with a sustainable competitive edge emerges. Usually there are relatively few options that will survive this type of testing and these emerge quite quickly.

The output from the loop is a set of chosen strategies and the critical success factors that go with them. Critical success factors, within this process, can be defined as the minimum the company must achieve in the marketplace to be considered a serious competitor. Only now is it worth breaking out the strategies into their detailed tactics which will determine human resources, budgetary requirements and marketing organization.

The need to structure the complexity of this part of the process is essential. Each segment has its own four Ps of the marketing mix and each 'P' has its own strategies. The number of ideas required to be retrieved, compared and sorted at any one time is enormous. The structured worksheet approach allows none of these to be lost.

The big advantage of formulating strategy in this way is competitive comparisons that have to be made. This is a real test of robustness (Giles, 1986). Success is relative only to what the competition can offer, there is no absolute measure. Contrary to expectations strategy rarely emerges the first time around the loop. The first ideas are nearly always tactical. Strategies are commonly formed by grouping tactics

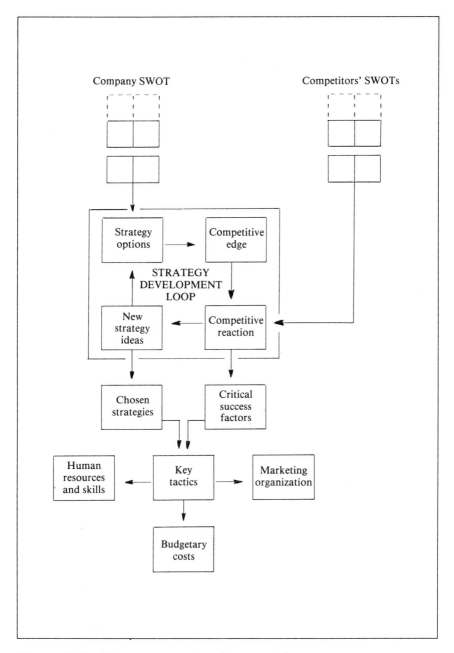

Figure 4.7   The strategy development loop
Reproduced with the permission of Strategic Marketing Development Unit.

that have a common direction and discarding those that do not. Staying in the loop until tactical ideas have matured into strategies means that the real tactics, formulated subsequently, can be geared directly to each strategy, isolating those that do not contribute directly. Thus issues such as marketing organization, a common preoccupation, are left to their rightful place as a tactical issue.

Putting the plan to the final test

Action line is the acid test of the process that turns grandiose strategies and tactics into small steps of reality. It does this with a set of worksheets covering:

- Data completion
- Action tasks
- Implementation diary
- Product sales review
- Internal cost review
- Segment review

Stress is placed on two important areas: delegating specific activities to identifiable people to carry out with a given time scale and prescribed budget; and setting up a monitoring and feedback system.

If the plan is not specific it is extremely difficult to implement. Delegating specific activities will be an impossible task. At this point the whole process may be halted and pushed to one side if the earlier concepts are not well understood (Gray, 1986). It is not the fault of the process, it is the result of superficial content being used to conduct it. The only recourse is to return to some of the earlier stages and reiterate with new knowledge of how the detail will finally be put to use.

The second problem which frequently occurs is that the monitoring system which the process develops is, as would be expected, market-orientated. It uses the customer as the focal point and profit centre. The majority of companies have monitoring and reporting systems based on products, functions or organizational structure. Remodelling the company information system to report by market or segment is often one of the hardest tasks of implementation. Unless a company makes this final leap, it is only paying lip service to market orientation.

This final test of corporate intent ends the process. At least, that is, until another re-run in the following year, by which time both the market and the aspirations of senior management may have changed. A new trigger and another day ...

THE NEED FOR INFORMATION

Lack of information is often given as a reason for not starting to plan. It is, however, a fallacious argument. How can the planner expect to know what information is needed until he or she understands what the planning process requires? This information dilemma faces all marketing planners.

It is true that the structured iterative process does demand a high level of detailed knowledge about the marketplace. Its exhaustive structure investigates all the variables. However, the process also provides a solution by requiring different levels of information to be input at different stages of the process. Figure 4.8 describes this approach. Each of the three levels identified in the diagram will be discussed in turn.

Unlocking human experience

Managers' knowledge is, without doubt, one of the richest sources of information. It is represented by level 1 in Figure 4.8 and is the main input to the pencil sketch. This body of knowledge is the very fabric of an organization. It makes one competitor behave differently from another.

Unlocking the controversial aspects of a manager's knowledge is also the hardest input to which the marketing planning process has to gain access. In many companies a defensive ethic exists that deters managers from committing themselves to public statements unless they reinforce the corporate wisdom fashionable at the time. Controversial, intuitive statements that attack this wisdom must be supported by copious factual evidence. Unfortunately, experience cannot always be voiced in this watertight way. Marketing planning is based on intuitive judgements, best estimates and reasoned opinions. All managers, not just the planners, must learn to live comfortably with ambiguity.

91

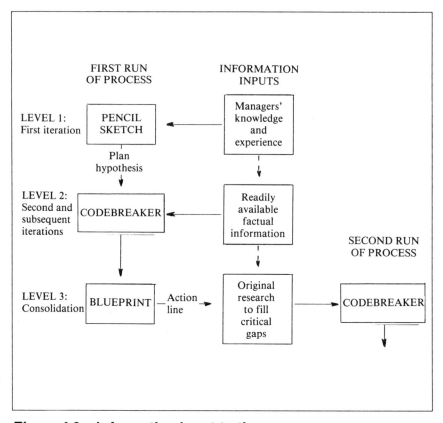

Figure 4.8   Information input to the process
Reproduced with the permission of Strategic Marketing Development Unit.

The way in which the process is structured encourages this trust in sharing experience. The pencil sketch is designed specifically to unlock management experience and blend the disjointed fragments that emerge into a comprehensible picture. The plan hypothesis can be constructed without the aid of external information. There is ample opportunity to input such information to test the hypothesis in the subsequent iterations of codebreaker. The articulation of experience and intuition achieved in pencil sketch is a significant milestone. Almost without exception, planners surprise themselves with the breadth of their own knowledge. Of the gaps that are found, many prove to be unimportant in the later codebreaker validation of the hypothesis. Initial estimates and assumptions made in the pencil sketch are an essential ingredient to getting the process started. A surprisingly substantial picture can be built up quickly at a very early stage. This first iteration introduces the basic concepts of marketing planning and the fundamental skills of strategic undcrstanding using, for its case material, the knowlege, experience and expertise of its participants.

There is one caveat to this approach, but it is important. Where information is employed that is not factual, being based largely on opinion, it must be recorded as such. If assumptions made in this way later prove to be critical, the planners only cheat themselves if they fail to validate them.

Readily available sources of information

The second and subsequent iterations of the process within code-breaker demand a more detailed and factual approach as the plan hypothesis is evaluated. The information gathered for this stage is represented by level 2 in Figure 4.8.

Before embarking on the second iteration of the process in code-breaker a log must be made of the factual material that is readily available. The sources generally fall into three categories:

1 company-held reports from previously commissioned original research surveys;
2 regularly produced company documents such as sales analyses and so on;
3 published information in directories and on-line databases.

The inevitable result of compiling this log is to find that company information is rarely structured by markets. More often, it is based on the product or functional divisions of the organization. When pulled together for the first time with a market focus, large gaps appear. Even organizations with long histories are sometimes surprised to discover how little market information exists within company owner-ship.

The main task during the first run of the process is to establish which are the important gaps to fill. Much time and effort can be saved by establishing priorities. Codebreaker's constant iteration in validating the hypothesis does just that. Priority opportunities emerge as the SWOT analyses throw up the best markets and strategies. The collection of factual information can then focus on these priorities and put to one side the less important areas.

Preoccupation with accuracy is another major hindrance at this stage of the process. Some planners dissipate their entire energies on the search for ultimate accuracy. This is a trap that can be avoided by using a simple yardstick (Giles, 1986) to judge relative accuracy:

> If information was placed at either end of the range of approximation within which it falls, would the decisions taken as a result be different? If the answer is 'no' then sufficient accuracy has been achieved!

Market share measurement is a good example of over-indulgence in accuracy (Majaro, 1982). Results may vary depending upon both the source of the information and the method of collection. But does a share of x per cent or y per cent really matter? No. What really matters is whether market share is growing or declining or whether one competitor is larger or smaller than another. The important question to be asked is how these answers affect the available strategic options. The end result must always be a set of robust strategies which do not rely on the last decimal point. Losing sight of the big picture is the greatest mistake of marketing planning.

The role of original research

Original research within the 'Marlow method' is defined as commissioned research to fill information gaps not filled from the sources of information used in level 2 of the process. Original research is represented by level 3 in Figure 4.8.

It can be seen that original research differs from the other two levels by being an output from the process rather than an input to the process. This is explained by blueprint being the consolidation stage in the process. Assumptions, critical to the success of the plan, must be qualified. Original research is required to establish the strength of these assumptions and the risk they attach to the plan. This task becomes identified in action line as an immediate task.

Original research is very specific. It relates directly to healthy operation of the plan. Non-critical assumptions and information gaps have already been relegated to a lower priority giving very sharp focus and considerable efficiency to the role of original research. The results are subsequently added to the body of factual information that becomes available in level 2 for subsequent re-runs of the process. This way each run of the process builds on a larger base of knowledge than the previous run.

Horizontal and vertical research

Now that the three levels of information have been described, it becomes clearer how the inputs alter as the process progresses. This is easier to understand in the context of 'horizontal' and 'vertical' research. Information gathered early on during the process tends to be of a 'horizontal' nature. Information gathered later in response to validating the plan hypothesis tends to switch progressively from 'horizontal' to 'vertical', with original research being almost entirely 'vertical'. Figure 4.9 describes the difference between these two types of research.

Horizontal research covers broad markets and, because of its scope, can hope to gather only relatively superficial information from generalized investigations. It is inevitable at the pencil sketch stage that there is a desire to find out everything about anything. Research of this nature tends to be of bad value to the planners and unrewarding for the researcher (Wilson, 1985). Responses of 'we know that already', for the parts which accord with corporate wisdom, and 'they asked the wrong questions', for the remainder which do not, are frequent criticisms of horizontal research. Inaccurate and vague research briefings are the norm in the vacuum which exists prior to the formulation of the plan hypothesis. This trap can be avoided by suspending research efforts and using managerial experience to build the plan hypothesis first.

As the process unfolds the information research becomes progressively more refined. At level 2 it is based on finding specific answers to specific questions. The selection of priorities makes this type of research more definite about the sources and the answers. Wastage is eliminated and information that is not directly relevant need not be gathered. Researchers welcome a well-constructed brief. At level 3

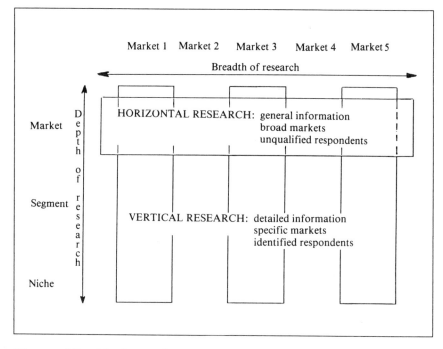

Figure 4.9   Horizontal versus vertical research

where heavy research resource is consumed the situation is even more specific and detailed, delving into the chosen priority segments and niches that published sources do not reach.

Adoption of this disciplined approach to gathering different types of information at different stages of the process, provides the solution to the information dilemma.

CONCLUSION

The structured iterative approach to marketing planning can overcome the difficulties experienced currently by many planners in corporate organizations. If the concepts are rigidly adhered to, the process can raise the growth expectations of an entire organization. The strength of the process is derived from a number of areas which can be summarized as:

1   the mechanism for setting visionary goals (trigger);

2 the unlocking of managerial experience (pencil sketch);
3 constant iteration and interpretation (codebreaker);
4 the generation of robust strategies (blueprint);
5 an action-orientated plan (action line).

The structured iterative approach breaks the highly complex subject of marketing planning into simple realistic steps. However, its start-to-finish worksheet methodology is only as good as those who operate it. Properly organized, it has the power to challenge the conventional wisdom and sweep away the corporate dogma. It engenders a positive attitude to long-term growth in the most competitive of markets. This process makes marketing planning possible and, above all, rewarding.

REFERENCES AND FURTHER READING

Drucker, P. F. (1987), *The Frontiers of Management*, Heinemann, London.

Foxall, G. R. (1981), *Strategic Marketing Management*, Chapter 2, pp.36–44. Croom Helm, London.

Giles, W. D. (1985), 'Marketing planning for maximum growth', *Marketing Intelligence and Planning*, Vol.3, No.3.

Giles, W. D. (1986), 'Marketing planning and customer policy', *Management Decision*, Vol.24, No.3, pp.19–27.

Giles, W. D. (1988) 'Marketing planning and its effect on organisational culture', paper prepared for publication in *European Journal of Marketing*.

Gray, D. H. (1986), 'Uses and misuses of strategic planning', *Harvard Business Review*, January–February, pp.89–97.

Greenley, G. E. (1986), *The Strategic and Operational Planning of Marketing*, McGraw-Hill, London, Chapter 9, pp.143–157.

Halley, C., Kennerley, A. and Brech, E. (1983) *Management Performance and the Board*, Management Research Group, British Institute of Management, Northampton.

Lenz, R. T. (1985), 'Paralysis by analysis', *Long Range Planning*, Vol.18, 4 November, pp.64–72.

Levitt, T. (1983), *The Marketing Imagination*, Macmillan, New York, chapter 7, pp.127–139.

Lorenz, C. (1985), 'Late converts to the gospel of marketing', *Financial Times*, 17 April, p.18.

Majaro, S. (1982), *Marketing in perspective*, Allen & Unwin, London, chapter 8, pp.103–109.

McDonald, H. B. (1984), *Marketing Plans*, Heinemann, London, chapter 3, pp.28–49.

Piercy, N. (1985), *Marketing Organisation*, Allen & Unwin, London.

Porter, M. E. (1987), 'The state of strategic thinking', *The Economist*, 23 May, pp.21–28.

Wills, G., Kennedy, S., Cheese, J. and Rushton, A. (1984), *Introducing Marketing*, Pan, London, chapter 3, p.31.

Wilson, A. (1985), 'Researchers' sorry status', *Marketing*, 18 April, pp.51–52.

5

Market development in the financial services industry

Brian Blackshaw

The United Kingdom is witnessing a revolution in the provision of financial services. Enabling legislation has prompted new products, new services and new entrants to the marketplace. Traditional trading boundaries are being savagely eroded. Such developments are precipitating a marketing response of a fundamental nature, upon which this chapter comments in relation to the marketing of personal financial services.

THE IMPACT OF DEREGULATION

The advent of deregulation, the widening of product and market opportunity through legislation (witness the Building Societies Act 1986 and the Financial Services Act 1986), and the increasingly intrusive and predatory activities of foreign institutions, have all given rise to intense competition in the personal financial sector as institutions seek to build and maintain market share. The trend towards fiscal neutrality, seen by government as essential to the encouragement of free competition, is intended to discourage inefficient trading where this has been sustained by generous operating margins. The Gower Report (Gower, 1984) recommended that, henceforth, taxation policy be applied to the type of product offered rather than the type of institution. Consequently, there is now less scope for institutions to rely upon the promotion of the exclusively tax-efficient features of certain financial products. For example, life assurance companies no longer benefit from the advantage of life assurance premium relief, which was discontinued for policies taken out after 12 March 1984, and are now placing much greater emphasis on their investment expertise and bonus performance in promoting their products.

The belief is that the tighter margins which ensue will restrain any tendencies towards over-aggressive product marketing by hitherto tax-privileged institutions operating a cartel. In order to compete in future, institutions will have to achieve levels of financial return which are much more a direct reflection of their specific abilities and efficiencies. This has important implications for marketing activity and the effective deployment of marketing resources.

COMPETITION FOR THE CUSTOMER

The emergence of financial conglomerates, and the aspirations towards the creation of financial supermarkets, reflect a desire on the part of institutions to provide the customer (and in particular the affluent customer) with products to meet a wide range of financial needs. There is little doubt that the basic strategy of a number of financial institutions is to gain a hold on the assets of up-market households and to serve them as their primary channel to the financial markets, by directing their now disparate transactions towards a single firm. Whatever credence may be placed upon either the wisdom or desirability of endeavouring to provide a 'one-stop' financial service, the ability to undertake superior customer and client management is undoubtedly a key factor upon which such a service is dependent.

In the search for new customers, the pattern of wealth distribution and the penetration levels of financial products sold amongst the various socio-economic groups have provided a basis for assessing the viability of objectives set for product diversification. However, the failure rate of many such product-orientated initiatives is high. This is due to the limited abilities of institutions, as new entrants to a market, to establish a capacity both to reach and influence potential customers. Competing effectively in the deregulated era has proved to depend upon much more than merely increasing the product range.

A knowledge of the considerable extent to which additional business from existing customers can sustain an institution's growth objectives has led to organized cross-selling within the customer bases of many companies. In addition to selling their own products in this way, many institutions have sought collaboration with other organizations. This has enabled them to gain access to wider captive markets which are capable of yielding higher returns of growth and profit (provided that effective methods of market segmentation and communication are employed).

It is perhaps ironic, however, that notwithstanding growing recognition that 'the customer is the business' (Drucker, 1970), many institutions continue to suffer from highly volatile customer movement, with a consequent detrimental impact on business performance. Institutions have thus begun to awaken to the business reality that customer acquisition is one thing, being able to retain and manage the customer another! The ability to identify, attract, secure and manage customers profitably remains a continuing challenge for all institutions.

KNOWING HOW TO TRADE

The redrawing of the traditional battleground trading lines has prompted, among leading financial institutions especially, a requirement to review their development strategies on the most rigorous basis. This is particularly so where institutions are truly national in character and have large decentralized retail networks through which they market their products, either directly to the consumer or through established intermediaries. In developing and serving their customer bases, such institutions have little or no alternative other than to market their products at a level of volume and profit which the economic maintenance of the distribution networks demands. The unacceptable alternative is, of course, to look for reductions in the retail network as a means of maintaining financial performance; a reluctant option which some building societies, for example, are now having to face.

In examining distribution trading performance two significant factors strike hard: first, national institutions do not trade nationally but locally; second, there is a difference between knowing how to trade and knowing how to sell. The unmistakable marketing challenge for any organization is to be able to develop its local markets according to their unique requirements. The corporate view and corporate marketing activity can only go so far to assist branch performance and it is a fallacy to presume that establishing a branch or distribution outlet will lead to markets becoming immediately and wholly accessible. Yet this stereotyped thinking continues to prevail and has resulted in a failure by many institutions to identify and capture specific local markets at branch level. It is therefore understandable that many branch development personnel are frustrated in their present roles, as their organizations lack the methods, systems and techniques to plan, co-ordinate and control their marketing and development activities, both corporately and at regional and branch levels. As a result, marketing activities are dissipated and resources under-used.

THE EFFECTS OF THE NEW COMMERCIAL REALITY

The dual challenge of responding to opportunities to diversify into new products and markets, and achieving higher levels of operational efficiency, has brought about a new commercial reality in the personal financial sector. This is apparent from the more closely defined approaches to market development now being adopted by financial institutions and financial intermediaries alike.

The demand for effective market segmentation techniques is already well established. Competitive strategy depends increasingly upon the ability to identify and quantify markets much more precisely. The capacity to direct all forms of business prospecting much more specifically to individuals and groups, according to priorities established from a stringent analysis of markets and trading situations, is crucial. In this respect, a fundamental opportunity to improve trading performance now lies in being able to build in, and sustain in the sales and distribution system, the ability to trade more effectively. Many competitors will find it difficult to emulate this ability, which is a significant way of improving levels of business production and offsetting the constant threat of price competition. Resources expended on all methods of product distribution and promotion are therefore undergoing close evaluation to avoid waste and to obtain a greater commercial return on monies spent. Today's competitive race is to establish an operational capability to direct products and scarce development resources, through appropriate channels of distribution, to the priority areas of business potential.

TECHNOLOGY AND INFORMATION SYSTEMS

Technology and information systems are having the most profound effect upon organizational cultures, trading methods and decision-making processes – yet we are still looking at only the tip of the iceberg. Unimpeded by the constraints of administration-based systems, marketing and sales management is now able to benefit from knowing the facts of a trading situation, which can be pictured uniquely at all levels in the organization. This demands that marketing and sales information needs be treated as prime design criteria rather than being subordinate to administration and support requirements.

Competing successfully demands that customers are provided with what they want and when, where and how they want it. This is now possible through systems based on appropriate market and customer information, rather than product-based account files.

Institutions now stand to gain from the ability to develop and manage their customer bases, an increasingly sophisticated and expert process, in a manner not possible previously. Armed with the power of information, cohesively drawn from various sources, wiser judgements may now be made concerning, for example:

1 corporate business objectives and strategy;
2 specific product volume and market share objectives – set nationally, regionally and for each trading outlet;
3 the appropriate deployment of distribution, sales and communication resources;
4 the siting of branch offices, the development of agencies and the number and deployment of sales personnel;
5 the true nature and success of trading performance.

Only institutions armed with appropriate marketing management information, presented coherently, can make effective marketing decisions. Such information enables local markets to be understood and addressed more effectively. First-class market and customer management is now no longer a dream.

The secret, as ever, lies not only in what information the institution has available but in how it is used. There are four main aspects to this. First, utilizing data held internally will provide an institution with much information about its products and customers. Second, this information needs to be matched with systems for advanced market segmentation and analysis, thereby allowing the prime areas for business development to be identified precisely. Third, syndicated market research data provide a backcloth against which an institution can measure its market penetration and market share. Finally, where such syndicated research is unavailable, primary research studies fulfil an important role in helping to determine a more precise competitive position (see Figure 5.1).

The speed and tenacity of computing power through networks, which allow information to be downloaded within the organization, has facilitated the use of marketing database sources in the most fluid and flexible manner. Moreover, information technology and advanced databases have opened the door to 'relationship marketing', based upon detailed analysis of consumers ways of life and behaviour in order that their wants and needs can be more closely interpreted. Information made available at branch level, at the point of sale, is now vital to facilitate client and customer management on a basis which hitherto was not possible.

The pertinent and appropriate use of information is therefore an imperative and a crucial driving force in the formation of marketing strategy. Institutions are now able to map their trading positions locally (for each branch or distribution outlet, for example), regionally and at corporate level, which establishes a basis for setting appropriate market development objectives and, in turn, the allocation of business resources. This ability has begun to develop what is now commonly referred to as a 'market-driven culture' which has prompted the organization to view itself as a delivery system geared entirely to matching products with markets in the most efficient and profitable manner. In consequence, we are now witnessing changes in organization and the management of activities which more truly reflect the adoption of the marketing concept by financial institutions. For example, customer management throughout the family life-cycle

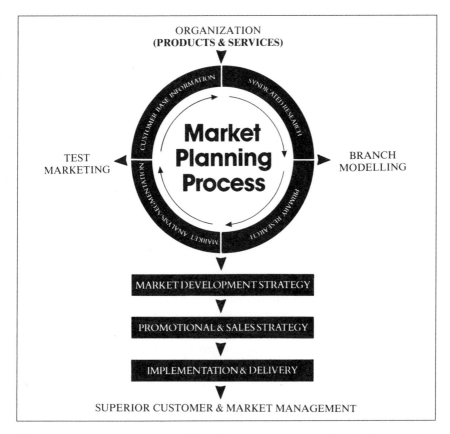

Figure 5.1 The market planning process driving information to produce results (© Profita Ltd)

(see Kotler, 1984, for an explanation of the concept) is no longer a pious aspiration but a more realistic objective. Judgements concerning customer profitability can also be made on a more fundamental basis which extends beyond the immediate acquisition of a new account in direct relation to the cost incurred in such acquisition. Whilst such cost–benefit analysis will always be subject to the closest commercial scrutiny, it need not now be viewed so narrowly that the development of the customer base is impeded because of the institution's inability to assess, even broadly, the potential profitability of a customer's account.

The fruits of the explosion in information technology have forced the realization that information management is prime asset management which necessarily warrants close and constant attention as a high priority. This has prompted institutions to set up an information management function, normally within the marketing organization, to take responsibility for structuring information requirements to provide for the monitoring of key factors and indicators. For example, to facilitate the formation of marketing strategy, information should be defined and analysed within the following five major areas of management control and accountability:

1 product management and development;
2 the management of each channel of distribution;
3 the management of communications;
4 sales and sales management;
5 the management and deployment of all business development resources (giving rise to the concept of a single development budget).

However, it is through the institution's ability to match marketing information to planning and decision-making processes, which enable superior market analysis, customer management and the delivery of products to prime target market sectors, that a sustainable trading advantage can be secured. Therein lies the key to the efficient and effective deployment of marketing resources, in all forms.

MARKETING PLANNING

The business activity that integrates an institution's total marketing effort is marketing planning. This ensures that the institution undertakes a systematic approach to developing products and services to meet and satisfy the market's needs, which will yield positive mutual benefits over time.

Marketing planning involves: assessing the institution's present trading position and how and why it has come about; analysing in which direction it is heading; establishing objectives; defining strategic policies to achieve these objectives; defining what tactical activities need to be carried out, by whom and when; and setting up performance standards to measure and control the institution's progress. Of critical importance, marketing planning ensures that strategic policies are laid down prior to tactics.

However, whilst the need for marketing planning is indisputable, what is now at issue is the basis upon which such planning takes place. Aligned with a review of marketing information requirements, the techniques and methods for marketing planning are therefore being subjected to close scrutiny. The traditional weaknesses associated with the construction of a marketing plan (typically on a central basis within the organization) which is neither adequately communicated to the organization at large nor rarely sees the light of day, are well recognized. The alternative is to make marketing planning a decentralized activity, shared in by personnel within local trading outlets which have close bearing on market development, for example branch offices.

The availability of appropriate information, at all levels within the organization, now enables such participation within a framework which necessarily has to be structured. In this sense, product, distribution, communications and sales-related planning activities are integrated within a process on a basis which allows and provides for a congruence of thought and action which traditional planning approaches deny. A properly constructed planning process establishes a framework within which marketing and sales personnel can perform and through which greater tangible results can be achieved, for the process by its nature ensures greater commitment to defined objectives – adhering to the philosophy, 'let those who make the plans, implement the plans'.

The objective of the planning processes now being developed is to provide a basis for formulating business objectives and strategy, founded upon rigorous market analysis, which enables a more efficient and focused deployment of the various forms of marketing and sales resources. Such processes are a logical evolution from the construction of a sound and responsive information base. They establish the organizational practices to support distribution and customer management in a manner which streamlines operational activities, from which the following benefits derive.

1 Improved profitability, which is brought about by enabling employees, at all levels, to use scarce marketing and sales resources more productively – through a clear understanding of priorities and objectives.

2 Improved branch performance, which derives from actively

involving local sales personnel in market planning, through the process of appraisal and the recognition of their local market's requirements.

3   A broadening of the role of regional and branch office managers, which results from increased responsibility and training in market development.

4   The identification of further opportunities for growth, both for new products and for increasing the sale of existing products into local markets.

5   Improved communications between head office and regional/branch management; this is achieved because all personnel involved in the planning process know their roles in support of specifically defined objectives.

6   Improved allocation of marketing effort, which is achieved through a rationale which aids judgements concerning the deployment of human and financial resources.

7   Improved control of branch performance is possible through an understanding of a branch's trading potential, in relation to the market which it serves.

8   A clearer justification for investment in new branches and support of intermediaries/agents is possible based on valid inter-branch/agency comparisons – drawn from modelling techniques.

The marketing planning processes being implemented by institutions go to the very roots of trading performance and therefore enable superior customer and market management. They assist the task of utilizing resources effectively in support of corporate objectives, local market objectives and customer needs. Furthermore, such processes set the organization free at a local level within a controlled and defined framework and offer a fundamental trading advantage which is not amenable to rapid duplication by competitors.

It is through the implementation of marketing planning, however, that trading takes place and results are achieved.

BRANCH MODELLING

The profitable development of a customer base is a sophisticated and expert marketing activity. Securing market share is therefore increasingly reliant upon acquiring such expertise without which institutions stand to suffer. Traditional initiatives related to the opportune opening of a branch, supported by vigorous sales activity, fall well short of what is now required to acquire and retain market share.

In this respect, marketing planning processes linked to an information base provide the basis for determining the nature and extent of local markets, in relation to competitive standing, from which strategic initiatives derive. This has led to the development and refinement of PROMAP – PROMAP (Profita Mapping is the trademark of Profita Ltd) branch modelling techniques which help to establish, for example, the following.

1   The stage of development of a branch in relation to its market situation (for several branches, this may be extended into an understanding of the branch network life cycle (Kitching, 1982).

    This enables judgements to be made concerning the nature of marketing strategy applicable to each branch (that is, defensive or aggressive) which has very precise implications for product, communications and sales strategy.

2   The viability of the existing distribution network to sustain market share, revenue (or gross receipts, commission and so forth) and profit growth in relation to different volumes of products sold.

3   A basis for determining the appropriate level and allocation of marketing resources (in all forms) in support of the distribution network; branch, intermediary, direct sales and so on.

4   A basis for making comparative judgements about the trading performance of distribution outlets (for example branches) and sales personnel, in relation to the profile of local markets and the business potential opportunity which they provide.

    This helps to establish more realistic and viable marketing and sales objectives, thereby providing a fairer means of assessing human performance.

Branch modelling techniques are therefore of considerable benefit in enabling local trading outlets (in whatever form) to be examined and clustered in trading terms, rather than in the more suspect dimensions of geography or turnover. The techniques also allow much time and effort to be saved by allowing 'What if?' questions to be asked – and answered at relatively low cost. In consequence, institutions are now able to develop a learning curve concerning those factors and attributes which give rise to successful market penetration, in relation to

109

communications and sales activities. Such learning is a precious commodity within the institution as it seeks to avoid waste and maximize the efficient use of marketing resources.

From an operational viewpoint, however, branch modelling provides a basis for establishing and implementing test marketing programmes prior to the implementation of a full marketing strategy. This has a particular bearing on promotional strategy and activity, which are normally associated with high expenditure.

TEST MARKETING

All organizations must face the business reality that, having failed to secure a market share objective, the market rarely goes away. The question therefore arises: 'How should trade with the market be established?' Test marketing initiatives play a central and determining role in answering this question.

Logically, the first stage in this area is customer and market analysis, which involves the interrogation of databases (as referred to earlier) through the use of computer technology. The extruded information base will be of crucial use in evaluating market potential in relation to existing trading patterns. The possession of this intelligence, held both centrally and locally in the organization, is vital for determining strategic promotional and sales initiatives. These can be tested and validated, in relation to local markets and wider geographic trading areas, prior to full implementation, through precisely constructed test markcting programmes.

Information technology has therefore had a considerable impact upon promotional strategy, providing a sounder basis for determining promotional budgets in relation to above- and below-the-line advertising activities, in support of market development initiatives. Institutions also stand to gain considerably from the ability to give their external advertising and promotional agencies clear strategic direction and guidance concerning the development of their markets, from which such agencies can formulate a better creative response. This invariably gives rise to better relationships between institutions and their external agencies, as well as improving the cost-effectiveness of the services which agencies provide.

Test marketing related to a planning process also enables sales activites to be integrated with communications activities such that the marketplace can be approached and managed with sensitivity, continuity and consistency. Field personnel stand to benefit from a precise knowledge of marketing activity which is driven centrally within their organization, to which they can align their local sales activities and endeavours. All too frequently at present, this is not the case, and the intermediary or consumer stands to be confounded by different approaches made by an institution which reflect disorder and sometimes blatant insensitivity. This may damage an institution's reputation, deter trade and certainly give rise to adverse consumer perceptions.

It is therefore understandable that test marketing initiatives, properly co-ordinated at corporate and local level, have enabled the development of sophisticated customer care programmes which give full credence and recognition to the customer's importance to any institution. Such programmes reflect a true customer orientation and are a distinguishing characteristic of excellent organizations; they can, however, be founded only within organizations which have a dedication to first-class customer management based upon a trading culture committed to service.

Test marketing, which has its roots in a well-defined planning process, also enables an institution to continue to learn from the changes which take place in its trading position through any modification to its marketing mix (for example the introduction of a new product) and marketing strategy. Without the knowledge gained from the sophisticated techniques which can now be applied, it is inevitable that marketing resources will be squandered as there is no sound basis for them to be cohesively directed and applied to the development of the market being served.

SUMMARY

The developments outlined in this chapter reflect the moves being made by institutions towards establishing a capability, based upon the selection and retrieval of information linked to a planning process, which enables more effective decision-making within the organization at all levels, in support of business objectives. With the processes for decision-making firmly set in place, progress can be made towards branch modelling and the testing of the market, through the medium of the information base, to the setting of communications and sales strategy. Institutions are therefore establishing the processes and styles of working which are setting the patterns of their businesses for the next century.

In a competitive marketplace it is those institutions which recognize the primacy of the consumer and who can link their organization's operating functions together in support of local markets (either directly or through intermediaries), whose businesses stand to prosper in the fight for profitable market share.

REFERENCES AND FURTHER READING

Drucker, P. (1970), *Managing for Results*, Pan, London, chapter 6.

Gower, L. C. B. (1984), *Review of Investor Protection*, Cmnd 9125, January, HMSO, London.

Kitching, D. W. C. (1982), 'Rationalizing branch banking', *Long Range Planning*, Vol.15, No.1, pp.53–62.

Kotler, P. (1984), *Marketing Management: Analysis, Planning and Control*, 5th edn, Prentice Hall, New Jersey, chapter 4, p.132.

McIver, C. and Naylor, G. (1980), *Marketing Financial Services*, Institute of Bankers, London.

Wilson, A. (1972), *The Marketing of Professional Services*, McGraw-Hill, London.

6

The international dimension

Norman Boakes

Each of the preceding chapters has been concerned with the formulation of marketing strategy. Whether implicitly or explicitly, consideration of the various options will have been influenced by developments taking place across international boundaries. The media, and in particular television, bring the world into our homes and vividly portray the changes which are taking place, both economically and culturally.

This chapter looks at this international dimension and sees how it can be used positively to improve marketing performance.

BACKGROUND

There was a time when UK companies could choose either to market their products internationally or simply manufacture solely for the domestic market. In the latter case, it could be assumed that competition would come almost exclusively from other UK producers. Figure 6.1 shows that this situation has long since passed and there is now virtually no British company, in any industry, which has not been confronted by competition from overseas, whether from Japan, the USA, other European manufacturers, or Third World countries. Life will never be comfortable again.

As with most industrial countries, import penetration has risen consistently in the UK over the past twenty years. From 1971 to 1985 it

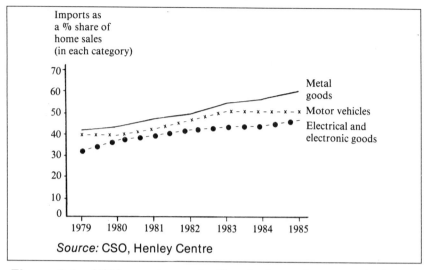

Figure 6.1   UK import penetration (selected categories)

rose from 22.5 to 28.5 per cent of domestic demand. Imports of motor vehicles rose from 41 to 50 per cent, electrical and electronic goods from 31 to 47 per cent and general metal goods from 42 to 57 per cent. As can be seen from Figure 6.1 most of this growth occurred prior to 1983 and the figure for motor vehicles is now falling. However, it should be remembered that overseas competitors have now set up manufacturing plants in the UK so that competition in the domestic market has become even tougher.

For consumers and professional buyers, this exposure to the best the world can produce has had a tonic effect and resulted in a dramatic change in attitudes towards design, quality, service and price. Standards have risen at a speed which would have seemed inconceivable a few years ago, and innovation is now regarded as an essential ingredient for success.

INTERNATIONAL MARKETING

Faced with the fact of international competition in the domestic market, many companies decide to seek new markets overseas with a view to widening their customer base and spreading the risk of an economic downturn in one market. The direct export of products or

114

services from the UK is often the natural starting point and this is described more fully in Chapter 26, 'Reaching overseas markets'.

It is, of course, possible to start, and even continue, exporting solely through UK buying houses but any serious marketer would quickly wish to establish a presence of some kind in the overseas country so as to understand what makes potential customers buy, and then develop a marketing strategy designed to generate a profitable and growing business. Cultural, political, legal, economic and social differences between countries make such an understanding essential.

It should never be assumed that overseas market segments are developing at the same rate as those in the UK. For example, the market for 'healthy foods' which is now buoyant in the UK has lagged behind developments in the USA, Scandinavia, Germany and even France. Similarly, it is very easy for a manufacturer of products with a brand well known in Britain to find himself left in 'yesterday's market'. A classic case would be Australia where the influx of 'new Australians' from continental Europe has resulted in fewer and fewer people being familiar with old-established British brands which were once household names.

In Scandinavia, Danes, Swedes and Norwegians are able to read one another's languages and, with some difficulty, understand one another's spoken word. There has even been an attempt to introduce a common business language – the SAS language, so-called because one of the leading promoters was the airline. The project failed completely because of fierce national independence and, although the countries have a great deal in common, there are a number of sensitivites which need to be considered. For example, the emphasis on 'Made in Sweden' would be less in Norway than in Denmark, and far less than in Finland, another near neighbour.

With the growth of economic groupings such as the European Community, European Free Trade Association (EFTA), Association of South East Asian Nations (ASEAN), Caribbean Community and Common Market (CARICOM), and Council for Mutual Economic Assistance (COMECON), it would at first appear that the trading world is being organized on a supra-national basis. However, such an impression would be misleading, since within each of these organizations, there are significant differences of trading approach and cultural attitudes, even though there may be a common tariff barrier. Within COMECON, for example, the state buying organizations in

Hungary are almost entrepreneurial when compared to those of Romania or Bulgaria. In the European Community, not only does every member state have its own national legislation but, even in a small country such as Belgium, it is necessary to cater for two languages and cultures. However, a Belgian company speaking Flemish is still more likely to buy from a French-speaking supplier in Brussels than a Dutch supplier with which it shares a common language and geographic proximity.

The need to exercise care in the use of colour, words and images has been highlighted many times and yet companies still make mistakes which could so easily have been avoided by some elementary research. There is no such thing as the 'export market': simply a great many countries each comprising a number of different markets and segments which may, or may not, offer opportunities for any particular product or service. Before venturing into any of these, a company must understand clearly what it is hoping to achieve. Is the objective substantial extra volume, or a more gradual growth? Will it be entering an existing market and so need to take a share from competitors, or creating a new market through a programme of consumer or user education? Are the profit objectives in each of these markets identical and does the company have the financial, manpower and material resources to build on success?

Most important, how is profitability to be measured, since this will be the yardstick against which the success of both domestic and overseas operations will be judged. Entry into a new market will require an investment and the size of this investment will depend on the share of the market which it is hoped to obtain within a given period of time and, of course, the strength of existing competition. For most companies, the early stages of overseas marketing are fraught with frustration and the rewards seem small in relation to the amount of effort which is required. A contributory factor is undoubtedly the length of time which elapses before results can be monitored and the necessary action taken.

The companies likely to be successful in international markets are those which have fully understood the reasons for their success in the domestic market, clearly identified their customers and quantified the benefits which they can offer to users and consumers in terms of products and services. They will then have identified the key overseas markets which can generate the greatest return on investment and will

116

have concentrated their resources on each market in turn so as to maximize profitability. Most important, they will have understood and built on their competitive strengths.

By comparison with leading European competitors, many British companies still dilute their resources by trying to operate over too wide a geographical area. Concern for the achievement of long-term strategic objectives should always outweigh short-term tactical gains, and companies must exert discipline so as to avoid being seduced into accepting orders, or following up enquiries, in markets which cannot be effectively and profitably serviced. Far better to pass the responsibility for such incremental business to a third party, such as an export house, which can deal with the administrative hassle and earn a margin on such business.

ORGANIZING FOR INTERNATIONAL MARKETING

Since many overseas competitors will first be encountered in the domestic market, it follows that all concerned with marketing must think internationally, even though they may have responsibility only for the home market. Companies which make an arbitary distinction between home and overseas business, treating overseas marketing as being entirely separate, run the risk that such business will remain small and, particularly in the eyes of production and finance management, have only a nuisance value. The international approach is to regard each market, however small, as having a contribution to make to total volume and profitability and, therefore, subject to the same marketing and financial planning criteria.

When a new product is introduced, or changes made in product formulation or pack design, thought should always be given to the impact of such changes in international markets. It should be mandatory that, before any changes are made, those responsible for overseas markets in which the product is likely to be sold should be consulted. It may be that the demands of the UK market, or other principal overseas markets, make such a change imperative even if the result will be to prevent the product being sold elsewhere. In this situation, the consequences can be clearly thought through and a decision taken. This is very different from some arbitary action, often taken at product manager level without reference to anyone else, which inadvertently results in a significant loss of overseas business because a product no longer complies with market requirements.

For the smaller or medium-sized company, incorporating overseas markets in the marketing plan and providing the necessary support works only when the number of markets is strictly limited. In practical terms, it is virtually impossible to budget for countries which are subject to the vagaries of import licences, quotas, artificially high tariffs and other constraints. Such business is purely speculative and can be estimated only on the basis of previous experience.

For most companies, the first introduction to overseas markets is through direct exports and this may be followed by the appointment of a company employee as a local representative, perhaps responsible for business in more than one market. The next step could be to set up a local marketing company to sell products still produced in the home market.

A number of UK companies have achieved this goal by buying out their overseas distributor with which they may have built up a good relationship over a number of years. Frequently, the opportunity arises when the founder of the business dies, or wishes to retire, without an heir-apparent. Such takeovers, which are usually very amicable, appear to provide an easy solution to the exporter's distribution problem but, quite frequently, they pose another set of problems.

The viability of the distributor has depended on selling a range of products for a number of different principals, with each of whom equally good relationships may have been built up over a number of years. Some of these principals may well have markets or products in which they are in competition with the new owners. They may feel uncomfortable with the new arrangements or, perhaps, have already considered making a change which could now be accelerated.

Most important, the manufacturer will now find itself running a business with which it is completely unfamiliar and it is highly unlikely that anyone from within the organization would have the necessary skills, market knowledge and linguistic ability to take over the chief executive's role. In some cases, it is eventually decided that the business can be managed effectively only if it becomes a local branch handling only that company's products. To achieve profitability following such a decision would usually require a significant investment over a period of time, during which other markets may have to be starved of resources. A better alternative may be to come to joint venture terms with the local company, allowing a period of time for the existing management to build business with increased resources and to train their successors.

Reference is made in Chapter 26 to joint ventures with other UK non-competing companies and local manufacturers seeking product diversification. Taking the UK example first, although the concept of such co-operation, sometimes known as 'piggy-back exporting', has been around for very many years and was actively promoted by the British Overseas Trade Board and others, there is little evidence that it has been successful. Originally, it was thought that larger, experienced exporters would be able to offer assistance to smaller companies but it may be that the smaller companies feared being swallowed up by the giants or the 'chemistry' between the two organizations was simply not right.

Many apparently large companies are really collections of smaller ones, either operating divisions or subsidiaries with quite small budgets. Being part of a larger group may provide financial security but it can also inhibit, rather than develop, entrepreneurial flair. There may well be overseas markets which are closed to some products because of group policy and a considerable amount of executive time may have to be spent in consultation and co-ordination.

There are many examples of smaller companies which have built a strong brand identity in a specialist segment of the market which much bigger organizations regard as being too small to be of interest. A company with strictly limited resources must define its objectives clearly and realistically. An important advantage of small businesses is their flexibility, but equally disadvantageous is their preference for 'seat of the pants' management, and small companies sometimes lack persistence and fail to see a project through to a successful conclusion. Large companies are often more ponderous and take time to get started but, when they do, they usually keep going if only because obtaining a decision to stop may be as difficult as getting one to start!

The next stage of growth for the international company could be arranging manufacture under licence in the overseas market, or setting up an assembly or manufacturing unit, either independently or in conjunction with a local company. Opportunities exist in some markets to obtain significant financial inducements to set up assembly or manufacturing operations and funds may be available at local, regional, national or supra-national level. A thorough examination of all the available funds is necessary before arriving at a decision.

Equally, it is very important to balance the benefits of such financial inducements against practical considerations such as proximity of the production unit to the market, availability of labour and management with appropriate skills, ease of communication with head office, ability to communicate in the local language and political stability.

All joint ventures are a compromise in which each party seeks to maximize its share of the benefit. There must be a common objective and sufficient mutual trust otherwise the project is doomed at the outset. Licensing agreements are complicated and require marketing, financial and legal skills. Ideally, an agreement should be drawn up setting out clearly the basis on which payment will be made and then this agreement can be adapted to meet the specific needs of different markets.

Such an agreement would need to cover:

- what is being licensed
- fees and royalties
- timing of payments due
- audit control
- quality control
- secrecy
- patent and trademark rights and protection
- product development programmes
- supply of ingredients or materials (if relevant)
- performance and market development
- investment
- assignment of agreements or licence
- termination of licence
- disputes and arbitration
- penalties and sanctions for non-compliance or non-performance.

There may well be situations in which, for a variety of reasons, it is impossible to sell products in a selected market. Consideration should then be given to alternative ways of capitalizing on the company's expertise and experience.

Such opportunities may include:

- the sale of technology on a fee basis
- the supply of parts
- a servicing contract
- consultancy services
- personnel selection and training
- operational management contracts
- turnkey projects, perhaps providing design and technology skills within a consortium.

Whatever the organization structure that finally emerges across international markets, it is vital that the company's philosophy and objectives are clearly communicated to all its managers and staff. Similarly, the benefits of cross-fertilization between different cultures should have a positive impact on company thinking and provide a sharper competitive edge.

Within the multinationals, senior managers acquire the patina of the corporate culture and very often develop a business language understood only by their colleagues. This makes communication and decision-making much simpler and bypasses many national prejudices. Companies new to international marketing will find that, even in Europe, the number of hours available for constructive business discussion is limited by holidays, office hours and the availability of executives who spend more and more time in meetings. Add to this the language barrier which still exists, with too few British business executives speaking any language but their own, and one can see the size of the problem which will not be overcome simply by the wider use of fax and telex.

BRANDING AND PRICING

Companies entering international markets must consider what contribution, if any, brand identity will make to the achievement of objectives. Brand building, in any market, is a lengthy and costly undertaking and there will be situations where it is not even an option, either because the brand, or a similar name, is already in use or the image created by that brand is inappropriate to the market segment. An assessment of the importance of branding in the total product offering would have been an essential part of the initial analysis carried out by the company when looking at its UK market position-ing. How far these findings can be transposed on to the new market situation is a matter of careful research and fine judgement.

In a world of ever-increasing travel and international awareness, there is clearly considerable merit in having an international brand but few companies have been able to fulfil this ambition. It may be necessary to use another brand name already owned by the company; create a brand specifically for the market; use the brand of the partner company in a joint venture, or offer products to major customers who would then sell under their own brand. Whichever route is taken will have long-term consequences for the business and may well have a spin-off effect on other markets. It is vital to examine each option carefully, thinking through the consequences of the proposed action and, when a decision has been reached, pursue it single-mindedly.

The method of market entry, branding policy and market position-ing having been determined, it is essential to develop the pricing strategy which should be adopted. Price is only one aspect of the package of benefits which is being presented to the buyer, user or consumer and, as products and services become more sophisticated, so price alone diminishes in importance as a reason for buying. There is, in any case, never one price since few companies sell directly to the ultimate consumer and so their final selling price becomes someone else's landed cost. To this must be added import duties, inland transport costs, wholesale and retail trade margins and marketing support costs, so it is essential to be aware of price in terms of what the ultimate purchaser will have to pay in a particular market.

Studies carried out on behalf of the British Overseas Trade Board suggest that approximately one-third of UK companies do not know this information and are far less flexible in their pricing policies, largely because they are trying to sell into too many markets. A study published as a BOTB Occasional Paper in April 1987, indicated that most UK companies regard exports as at least as profitable, if not more so, than home trade sales. The strength of sterling is occasionally quoted as a reason for lack of competitiveness, but it should be remembered that a number of companies have to import a large proportion of their raw materials which they buy on world markets. There is also the benefit of a good exchange rate when travelling and spending promotional money in overseas markets. Most significantly, the rate of inflation has been falling over the past few years and is now comparable with leading European competitors.

To the economist, price is a mechanism for recovering costs and creating profit or, more precisely, generating a financial contribution towards running the business. For the marketer the problem is to determine what is the 'right price'. Is it the highest figure which can be obtained for a particular item at this point in time and from this specific market? Is it the lowest we can afford to accept and still cover our costs and make some contribution to profits? Or are we really seeking the 'optimum price': that which produces the greatest volume while still providing an adequate excess of revenue over expenditure?

Orders are rarely obtained without effort and an investment in terms of cost, as well as a certain degree of risk, so what are we seeking to achieve and over what period of time? Once these questions can be answered satisfactorily, we are some way forward towards establishing a sensible pricing strategy for core markets. However, it is appreciated that in the real world it is not just what manufacturers and marketers wish to achieve. The whole concept of marketing is based on the necessity of understanding how consumers perceive – and therefore value – the package of benefits being offered.

It is also necessary to take into account those benefits which are being offered by competitors, both exporters from the UK and elsewhere, as well as domestic producers within the market itself. Clearly, the first need is for accurate information: what is being sold, by whom, where and at what price? In particular, what exactly does that price include: are there hidden extras – or hidden benefits – such as credit facilities or free service? Moreover, is the product or service being offered to customers, both trade and consumer, giving them what they really want? They may be asked to pay for benefits which they would prefer to go without, or be willing to pay a higher price for extra value.

As always, it is necessary to balance the benefits which the customer seeks with the financial return required by the company on its investment over a given period of time. This introduction of a time scale is extremely important since most, if not all, companies are interested in building long-term business in a market, rather than making a 'quick buck' by an in-and-out entrepreneurial excursion. There may be nothing wrong with that kind of exercise, provided that it is recognized for what it is: a beneficial injection into the cash flow, not to be confused with international marketing which has to be concerned with the longer-term objectives of the company.

The aim should be to gain a worthwhile share of a particular market segment and to see that share grow at least in line with the market or, if possible, at a faster rate by taking share from competitors. To do this, it is essential to set specific market and product targets for volume, growth and profitability. Where one is selling through distributors or partners, it is also essential to secure agreement from them as to the feasibility of these targets. So far as possible, such partners should be encouraged to contribute to the formulation of objectives so that they share the commitment.

PRODUCT AND PACK DESIGN

The adoption of an international approach will have considerable impact on product and pack design. Simply changing the pack, by using a language in place of English, often appears to be the easiest route into a new market. However, it completely misses the point since the new product has to achieve success within the framework of a completely new situation and a pack designed for the UK, or some other market, may be totally inappropriate.

Every country has its own cultural symbols. These can consist of elements such as choice of packaging materials, choice of typeface, graphic designs, positioning of words and design features on the pack, and an up-market presentation in one country may be a mass-market presentation in another, simply because of greater availability of a particular packaging material. For example, in Germany mass-market confectionery products may be presented in aluminium foil bags which are rarely used in the UK because of their greater cost. The German consumer is prepared to pay for quality of packaging whereas many UK manufacturers are still not convinced that consumers are ready to do so.

Every pack must communicate the benefits which consumers or users will gain from purchasing the product. Packaging must also reflect the consumer's own perception of their place and value in society, and this communication takes place in a form which the purchaser rarely comprehends. It must be transmitted visually in accordance with consumer's own cultural shorthand. The bench-marks against which products are judged can be very different from country to country.

Producing new packaging is costly and time-consuming, even on a fairly minor scale. To this must be added the cost of developing new sales promotional materials, for which the translation should be made in the country where the product is to be sold, by someone who fully understands the way in which the product is proposed to be posit-ioned.

However, such costs are a necessary part of entering a new market and cannot be ignored. Every time a new product is launched and fails, not only is there a financial cost involved but the company's image suffers as well. Damage, sometimes irreparable, is done to the relationship with importers, distributors, partners, consumers and users. Most important, influential buyers will start to regard the company's latest offerings with increasing scepticism.

Some companies are still reluctant to allocate the resources necess-ary to enter an overseas market. The research brief should pay particular attention to all aspects of pack design and product presen-tation since quite small changes could result in considerable benefits when shipping goods by road or sea. Goods are frequently packaged in unnecessarily cumbersome outer cases which occupy additional space and so add a significant margin to freight costs. Failure to mark packs clearly, and in the correct language, may mean goods remaining on the shelf rather than moving quickly through the distribution chain and generating additional sales. The cost of creating a suitable consumer pack for the West German market would probably be no greater than the cost of one prime time spot on a UK TV network.

For many products, the pack represents the last opportunity for the manufacturer to communicate with the user or consumer. All the investment which has been put into securing an order and bringing product and potential buyer together rests on that final decision. Whether the answer is 'Yes' or 'No' can make the difference between success and failure in the market.

There are a very few internationally famous packs which, by dint of weight of advertising over a number of years, have imprinted their identity on the markets of the world. However, few manufacturers today would have the resources to emulate these examples, neither would they be willing to wait for the return on their investment.

Today's international marketers know the importance of identifying their target market, understanding just how buyers and consumers perceive such products, and then tailoring their offering to satisfy this perception.

CONCLUSION

This chapter examined how the international dimension could be used to improve marketing performance. There is no doubt that the exposure of companies in every industry to competition from all over the world has forced management to improve design, quality standards, service and price competitiveness. Companies which failed to do so simply went out of business; those that survived found new opportunities both in the UK and overseas.

The distinction between so-called home and overseas marketing has been recognized in the better company for what it is: an artificial barrier based on a misconception. At the same time, the importance of concentrating resources on clearly defined market segments, not necessarily constrained by national boundaries, has opened up new possibilities.

Finally, we have seen the influence of this thinking on the way in which companies organize themselves and in the branding, packaging and pricing of products and services.

In a world which is rapidly shrinking as the speed of communication accelerates, successful marketing demands an ability to see the whole picture, combined with a meticulous attention to detail. Since it is rare to find these qualities in one individual, the ability to select, motivate and direct a team has become even more important for the marketing professional.

Part II
ORGANIZING FOR EFFECTIVE MARKETING

7

The marketing function and its organization

Michael J. Thomas

Organizations should serve the purposes for which they have been created. This chapter is firmly based upon the assumption that the purpose of any marketing organization is primarily to serve customer needs. At the same time it is recognized that the marketing organization is a vehicle for the company, and in particular for the chief marketing executive, to achieve the goals and objectives of the company.

Marketing executives have two parallel responsibilities. They have to make operating decisions whereby short-term marketing programmes are implemented, and they have to make a vital contribution to the strategic decisions which guide the company into the future and which ensure its long-term survival in the face of social, technological, environmental and, in particular, competitive change. Good marketing organization must accommodate and be responsive to the needs of both operating and strategic decision-making.

Very few companies in the UK are marketing companies. Though many chief marketing executives will happily state that they have embraced the marketing concept, such evidence as we have about marketing organizations in the UK suggests that only a minority of companies are organized to implement it effectively.

Too many chief marketing executives are preoccupied with operating decisions, when they should be concentrating on strategic decisions. Too many marketing executives are concerned with the short term rather than with the long term, with individual customers rather than with market segments, with sales volume rather than with long-term profit. Marketing organizations in the 1990s must be focused on long-term survival, on exploiting long-run opportunities. They must examine how these can be turned into new products and markets, and how strategies can be developed that will ensure long-term growth in markets both at home and overseas.

There is no substitute for market orientation as the ultimate source of profitable growth, and the only way to be market-orientated is to make sure that the organizational structure of the company concentrates on its major markets.

Most companies, even some sophisticated companies, think with some conviction that they are market-orientated, whereas in reality they are product- and production-orientated. There is no guarantee, for example, that a company which uses the product management system (see 'Product management organization', below) will be market-orientated, for, not surprisingly, many product managers can be very product-orientated. In contrast with companies which think they are market-orientated are those which have been forced into new organizational orientation as a result of pressure from very large customers, such as retail grocery chains which require that the companies they buy from use a specialist approach. Such an approach is referred to variously as national account selling, special accounts marketing or trade marketing. Similarly, companies which do business with the government, particularly with the Ministry of Defence, have had to develop specialized marketing approaches in response to the unique buying and contracting procedures of the customer.

The logic of such changes in organization can easily be applied to other markets, both consumer and industrial. A number of companies have made an initial step towards market orientation by differentiating between consumer markets and institutional or commercial markets, developing marketing units to deal with each type of market. Some companies differentiate between distributors and original equipment-manufacturing customers. Some companies differentiate between classes of distributors, organizing their approach to distribution on the basis of the different markets served by different classes of distributors. Ironically, some companies are product-orientated in their approach to the home market, but market-orientated in their approach to overseas markets, an organizational approach forced on them by the special requirements of overseas markets and customers.

There is no one best way in organizational terms to implement the marketing concept, and what follows is not simple prescription. Rather, a series of questions about the marketing organization will be posed and explored: questions that should enable the chief marketing executive of any company to explore the extent to which his marketing organization is marketing-orientated. It should be said that market orientation is first and foremost a state of mind and the chief marketing executive plays the key role in developing strategies, plans and organization to implement the marketing concept.

The chief marketing executive is responsible for guiding his company into market orientation. He is responsible for serving the needs of established markets, for serving new needs in established markets, and for searching out new opportunities in new markets. What type of marketing organization might best serve his needs?

WHAT SHOULD DETERMINE THE NATURE OF YOUR MARKETING ORGANIZATION

The basic principles of organization

Eleven principles of organization are frequently cited (Khandwalla, 1977) as general guidelines for any organization. They are not immutable but provide a sound basis for organizing any management task. They are classified into four basic elements.

1 *Objectives.* The objectives of the enterprise should be clearly stated and understood.
2 *Activities and groupings.* The responsibilities assigned to a position should be confined as far as possible to the performance of a single leading function. Functions should be assigned to organizational units on the basis of homogeneity of objective.
3 *Authority.* There should be clear lines of authority running from the top to the bottom of the organization, and accountability from bottom to top. The responsibility and authority of each position should be clearly defined in writing. Accountability should be coupled with corresponding authority. Authority to take or initiate action should be delegated as close to the scene of action as

possible. The number of levels of authority should be kept to a minimum.

4 *Relationships*. There is a limit to the number of positions that can be effectively supervised by a single individual. Everyone in the organization should report to only one supervisor. The accountability of higher authority for the acts of subordinates is absolute.

The specific properties of an organization

The specific properties of an organization, all of which need to be in harmony with one another, are (Spillard, 1985):

1 people;
2 a mission and set of objectives which together define their tasks;
3 specialization and a separation of skills;
4 a hierarchy of authority as a means through which power is exercised;
5 a control system to secure resources and outcomes;
6 information-flows to enable decisions to be made;
7 procedures for undertaking defined tasks;
8 a system of rewards and punishment to secure compliance;
9 a set of values to bind the whole thing together;
10 a boundary which defines the limits of the organization;
11 linking mechanisms through which to relate to other organizations.

The external environment

Markets
The nature of a company's markets will help to determine the nature of the organization. Where there are relatively few markets, a market-orientated, functional or market management-orientated organization is appropriate. Where the number of market groups is large, and none is very powerful, a product-orientated, product management system is appropriate. A geographically dispersed market, particularly one involving overseas markets, will require some form of geographical organization, though this will be combined with product

or market management. Customer rather than market orientation may be appropriate, particularly when customers are few in number, requiring negotiated sales and/or a high level of after-sales service.

The business environment

The type of business engaged in will influence decisions about appropriate marketing organization. A company producing fast moving consumer goods is not likely to be similar in organization to a firm selling high technology products to a small number of industrial consumers. The role of advertising, for example, will differ greatly between two such environments, and in so far as the marketing organization will to a degree reflect the relative importance of each of the sub-functions of marketing (sales, advertising, new product development, after-sales service and so on) we would expect each marketing organization to differ. Finally, if the rate of change in the markets being served is high, we would expect a marketing organization to be flexible and responsive to change. And, since there are very few mature, unchanging environments around, most organizations must have this flexibility.

Customer requirements

The buying practices of customers become a crucial influence on marketing organization. Where large customers buy through a central purchasing office, when large retail and wholesale chains negotiate 'deals', and where the government is a principal customer, then market orientation is required – the customer is the market.

The internal environment

Management style

Management style influences organizational design and structure, and history cannot be treated as bunk in thinking about the redesign of organizations. Implicit and explicit top management attitudes will to a degree determine the pattern of individual and group action, of centralization and decentralization.

Product policy

As product lines proliferate, simple functional organization must give way to product and market orientation.

People

Organizations are living things, and human attitudes help determine what an organization does. People and not organization charts give life to an organization. One reason why few companies have implemented (in any meaningful way) the marketing concept, is that the same people who held management positions during periods of production or sales orientation have remained in positions of responsibility when the marketing concept has been embraced. The organization charts in many companies have changed, job descriptions have been rewritten, but the same people are in place. Changes in organization must not ignore people, but must be designed to achieve their objectives through effective management of people, sometimes requiring painful shifting or removal of people if the organizational change is to be meaningful.

Organizational choices

The organizational choices available depend to a degree on the impact various contingencies might have on the organization. A fundamental debate over the years has concentrated on the strategy-structure argument. The traditional argument is that the choice of an organization's strategy must determine the nature of the organization, since that organization must be fitted to executing the chosen strategy. This so-called instrumental view of organization derives from the work of Chandler (1962) who showed that many US corporations showed structures that reflected their chosen strategies. In times of change, such as we are currently experiencing, it seems unlikely that each time strategy is changed to cope with the exigencies of dynamic market conditions, structures will have to change in response. Few managements wish to contemplate or cope with ever-changing organizational structure. Thus, ideally an organization needs to be created which can cope with more than one strategy – to respond to changes in focus and direction. 'One cannot say with certainty that structure always follows strategy, or vice versa. What one can look for, however, is a set of contingencies which would help managers in marketing decide in what circumstances one follows the other' (Spillard, 1987; see also Bonoma, 1985).

134

TYPES OF ORGANIZATIONAL STRUCTURE

Functional organization

This is the most basic structure, embracing the activities of sales, advertising and sales promotion, marketing research and product planning. In large organizations, where a divisionalized structure is used, the functional marketing structure may be utilized within each division, as well as at corporate level.

The advantage of this form of organization is its relative simplicity, but its very simplicity makes it suitable for firms which sell relatively few products in relatively few markets. When products and markets grow in complexity and diversity, severe strain is put on the functional organization. A modification of the simple functional organization which does respond to our previously expressed concern for the importance of strategic market planning is shown in Figure 7.1.

Product management organization

The growing complexity of the product lines offered by a company is likely to reduce the effectiveness of the simple functional organization. Then, a product line organization becomes feasible and relevant, and in the large fast moving consumer goods companies the use of a product manager system is of proven relevance. Such a system is by no means to be confined to such companies, however.

In the largest companies, when divisionalization takes place, each division may be organized around a major product or product group. The brand manager structure in one division of Beechams is shown in Figure 7.2. A generalized form of a product or brand management system is shown in Figure 7.3 (Thomas, 1987).

Market management organization

It was stated initially that the purpose of any marketing organization is to serve consumer needs, which is the meaning of the marketing concept. Growing market orientation may require an organizational response as described above, namely greater attention to the product-

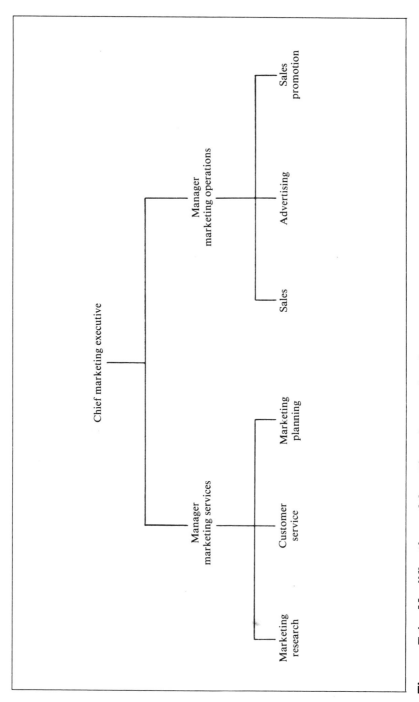

Figure 7.1   Modification of functional organization

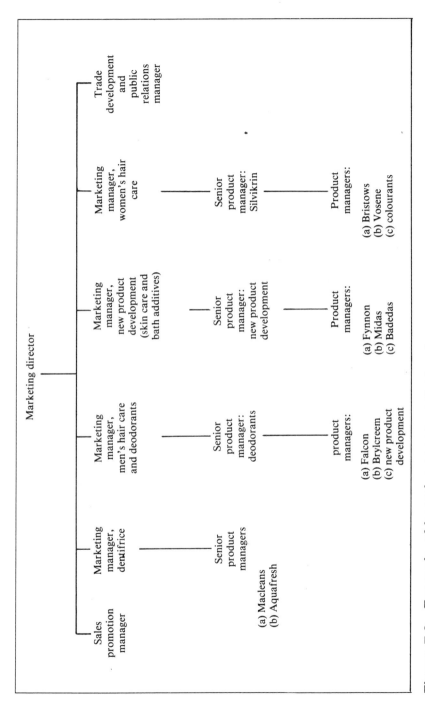

Figure 7.2 Example of brand management structure

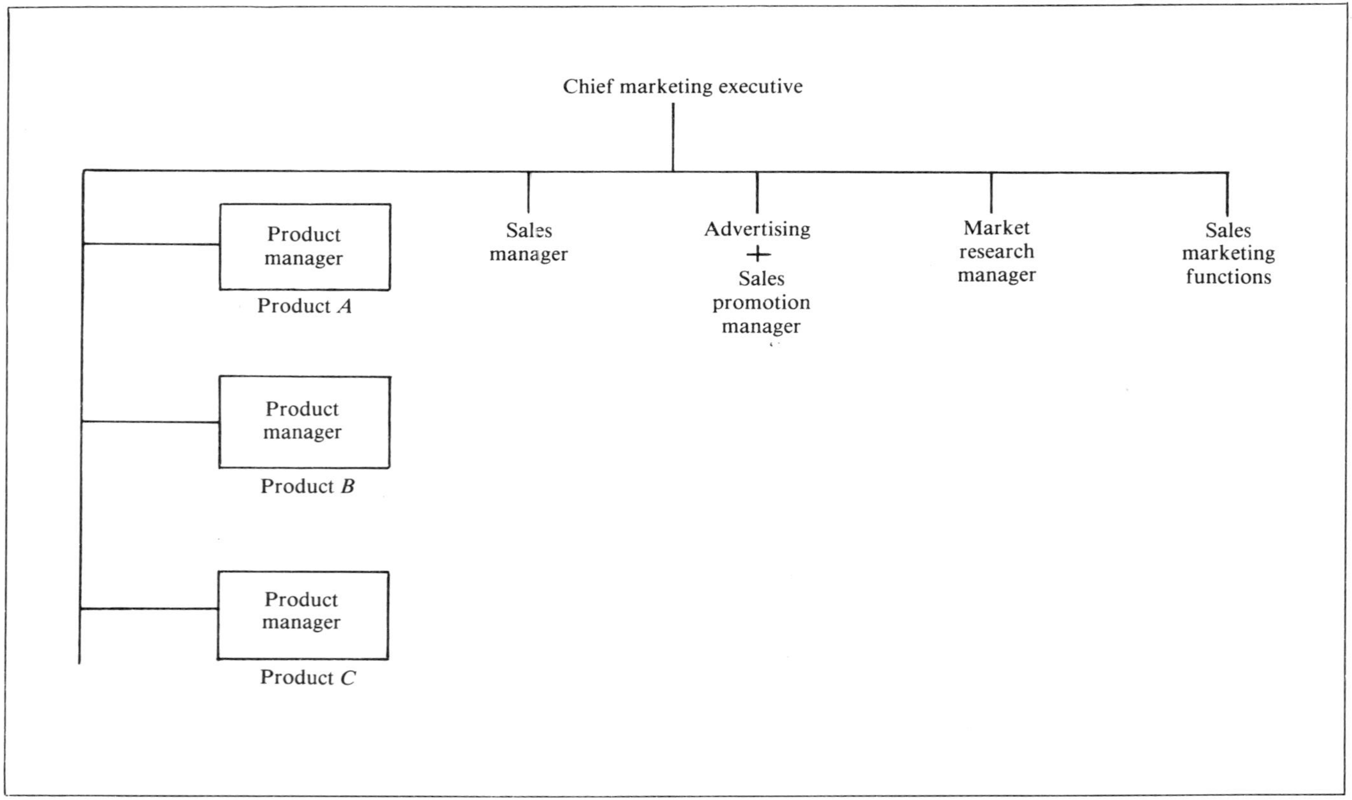

Figure 7.3 General product or brand management system

market fit by use of a product manager system, or a system that concentrates on the needs of particular markets and use industries or channels of distribution. The term 'trade marketing' has been used to describe this organizational approach (particularly in the grocery products trade), though there is little evidence that concentration on key accounts has yet forced any fundamental change in marketing organization – the product manager system can adapt to key account orientation. However, market orientation is vital to implementation of the marketing concept, and the organizational implications of market orientation must be carefully considered. Where markets are sufficiently differentiated from one another, and potentially large enough to warrant special organizational focus, some changes in organization will logically follow.

Geographical organization

Organizational units structured on the basis of geography are relevant primarily to large organizations marketing their products and/or services on an international scale. Geographic organization on this scale usually contains within each geographic entity organizations reflecting functional, product, or market-type organizations.

Customer-orientated organizations

A marketing department based on customer orientation will not differ in essentials from an organization based on markets, but where a few very large customers exist for a company's products, consideration must be given to a customer-orientated organization.

PRODUCT OR MARKET MANAGEMENT?

The most likely dilemma facing chief marketing executives is how to develop their marketing organizations beyond the relatively simple functional structure that serves so many companies. This section summarizes the main advantages and disadvantages of a product or a market management system of marketing organization.

The product manager system enables a multi-product firm to bring a total business management orientation to each product or brand it manufactures. The core responsibility of the product or brand manager is to develop an annual marketing plan geared to the needs of his or her product, and designed to enlarge its market share and profitability. The product/brand manager is the product/brand champion. The product/brand manager in his or her annual planning should be concerned with total marketing opportunity, but his or her strategic thinking will inevitably be limited in scope, since he or she is employed primarily as an operations manager. Product/brand management has limitations in the strategic sense, and characteristically brand managers are interested in their own brands, to the exclusion of much else. New product development fits poorly into the brand management system.

Only where the product defines the market, where the product manager and market manager are synonymous, is the danger of product orientation avoided. Alternatively, in markets where customers are few in number, there is likely to be little danger of product managers being out of touch with significant market developments. But, where a company's products are used by many different types of customers, or in many different ways; where customers' needs are rapidly changing, and new markets are likely to emerge; where technology is available to produce new solutions to customers' problems; and where a company's offering is a mixture of product(s) and service, then a market management orientation must be seriously considered (Thomas, 1988).

SOME QUESTIONS TO ASK ABOUT YOUR MARKETING ORGANIZATION

1   Is current marketing strategy innovative and data-based, clearly expressed and continually re-examined?
2   Does your company have a detailed annual plan, and long-range plans that are continually re-examined and updated?
3   Do contingency plans exist, and how effectively can the company react to changes in the environment?
4   Is the company organized to serve the needs of chosen markets, both at home and abroad, as the means to obtaining long-term growth and profits?

5 Is the company prepared to segment its markets and develop different product offerings for each segment?

6 Does management take a systems view of resource management – is a balance struck between the needs of the marketing mix (sales effort, advertising, product quality, service), the major functions of the company (manufacturing, finance, marketing) and the external environment (customers, distributors, suppliers)?

7 Are the main marketing functions in the company (sales, advertising, product-line management, new product development, after-sales service) managed and controlled in an effectively integrated manner?

8 Does marketing work closely and effectively with research and development management, with manufacturing management, with the purchasing department, with physical distribution and transport management, with accounting and finance, to the end that all departments co-operate in the best interests of the company?

9 Is new product development an effectively organized unit, closely integrated with the strategic planning of the company?

10 How well informed is marketing management about its present and future markets? How recent are market research studies of customers, of buying influences, of changes in distribution channel behaviour, of competitors' performance?

11 How well and how regularly are sales potential and profitability calculated for each market segment, sales territory, product, channel of distribution and order size?

12 Is each area of marketing expenditure regularly analysed for cost-effectiveness?

If the answer is an unequivocal yes to each of these questions, you ought to be managing an effective marketing-orientated company. Any hesitation in answering any of them suggests that the relevant aspects of organization and marketing orientation ought to be closely examined.

REFERENCES AND FURTHER READING

Baker, M. J. (ed) (1987), *The Marketing Book*, Heinemann, London.
Baligh, H. M. and Burton, R. M. (1979), 'Marketing in moderation –

the marketing concept and the organization's structure', *Long Range Planning*, Vol.12, April.

Bonoma, T. V. (1985), *The Marketing Edge: Making Strategies Work*, Free Press, Collier Macmillan, London.

Chandler, A. D. (1962), *Strategy and Structure*, MIT, Cambridge.

Corey, E. R. and Star, S. H. (1971), *Organisation Strategy: A Marketing Approach*, Harvard University Graduate School of Business, Cambridge, Mass.

Khandwalla, P. N. (1977), *The Design of Organisations*, Harcourt Brace, New York.

Spillard, P. (1985), *Organisation and Marketing*, Croom Helm, London.

Spillard, P. (1987), 'Organisation for Marketing', in M. J. Baker (ed), op cit.

Thomas, M. J. (1987), 'Product Development and Management', in M. J. Baker (ed), op cit.

Thomas, M. J., 'Product Management vs Market Management,' in M. J. Thomas and N. E. Waite (eds) (1988), *The Marketing Digest*, Heinemann, London.

See also Bernard Wynne, 'Staff development and training', chapter 10 in this book.

8

Recruitment – qualifications and sources

Martin Duffell

David Ogilvy, (1985) advises young advertising people seeking a marketing training to get jobs as brand managers with a fast moving consumer goods (FMCG) company. It is worth reflecting on why he chooses an FMCG company when there are oil, motor, and electronics companies which are much bigger than the world's largest FMCG business. (The three largest FMCG companies in the world by dollar sales volume are Unilever, Nestlé, and Procter and Gamble, in that order. *Fortune* (1986) lists some seventeen industrial companies in the world as being larger than Unilever.)

Ogilvy may of course be swayed by the fact that the largest single advertisers in both the USA and UK are in FMCG; but a case can also be made that FMCG is the most advanced branch of the science, or art, of marketing. Certainly FMCG marketers have to develop ultra-sensitive techniques and fast reflexes. Motor car manufacturers, for example, would have an FMCG-like relationship with their market only if motorists did not buy cars, but rented them weekly, and every Saturday could choose between keeping their car and sending it back to its makers. The FMCG marketers' consumer is theirs only until the end of the packet, tube or bottle. The need to submit their product to the consumer's choice fifty times a year is what best sharpens marketing operations and the people who work in them. Certainly, marketing managers with FMCG experience are much in demand in other fields, and files on the holders of key jobs in FMCG marketing are essential equipment for any professional headhunter.

I propose to tackle the subject of recruiting and selecting marketing people in the following way. First, in this chapter I examine what marketers actually do, particularly in FMCG, and then proceed to analyse the qualities likely to make them good at it. I then discuss where you will find people with these qualities. In the next chapter I consider how you can attract marketing applicants, and the methods available for selecting the right people for your marketing operation.

THE NATURE OF THE MARKETING TASK

Each year I meet several hundred marketing candidates – young people who want a career in marketing – and I find that many of them have misconceptions about both marketing and management. One is that marketing managers sit in intellectual isolation, with a mass of data, making decisions. Nothing, of course, could be further from the truth. No sane company takes decisions which could cost them millions until all the relevant factors have been weighed and the points of view of all parts of the business have been taken into account. Marvin Bower is quoted as saying that marketing is objectivity (Ogilvy, 1985, p.172), but objectivity is an essence squeezed laboriously from a thousand subjective sources. In marketing, those sources are people, and *you* are always one of the most subjective. Marketers, like many other managers, have as their daily task dealing with a variety of people, and turning conflict into agreement and agreement into action. This *melée* often appears daunting to the more introverted candidate.

The question of introversion and extroversion leads to one of the paradoxes of careers in marketing. The quality on which success depends at senior levels is judgement: the marketing director's judgement can make or break the company. The second most important quality at this level is the ability to motivate subordinates. But at more junior levels persuasive power and persistence lead to success, and these two qualities are more often associated with extroversion. Thus we have the paradox that the best marketing judgement on the board of a company may be that of an introvert – who will have had to behave like an extrovert to get there!

I do indeed know a few marketing directors who are relatively introverted; the answer to the foregoing paradox is that a determined introvert can develop the ability to sell ideas and can even acquire an appetite for complex people problems. For while 'introvert' and 'extrovert' are sometimes useful labels, the qualities we use these words to describe are developed rather than innate.

The task of the junior marketing manager (in FMCG, the brand manager) is at variance with the preconceived ideas of many marketing candidates. The principal decisions brand managers have to make are what ought to happen on their brand, and how to make it happen. The brand manager's vital role in marketing decision-making can be seen from two old conundrums. The first is this. What would happen to a brand if its brand manager's job were abolished? The answer is – nothing. The factory would go on putting the same old formula in the same old pack, the agency would keep screening the same old commercials, and the sales force would keep trying to sell the brand in the same old way and in the same old place. The result would be entropy: a sure recipe for killing a brand slowly in a changing marketplace. From this hypothetical exercise it can be seen that a brand manager is primarily an *agent of change*. Brand managers are judged and rewarded in proportion to their effectiveness as agents of change.

How brand managers bring change about can be seen from the second conundrum. How many people work for a brand manager? The answer is that if they are not very good, no one will, but if they are, everyone in the business will be working for them. Brand managers make things happen by the force of their arguments and their powers of persuasion. Only then do they discover how their ideas fare in the marketplace and develop the judgement to become marketing directors.

Many marketing candidates are surprised to learn that a brand manager's personal staff usually comprises from nought to three brand assistants, and the higher figure only on a very big brand. Such candidates have a faulty model of the power pyramid in a company, which looks like that in Figure 8.1.

The candidate becomes crestfallen when reminded that a medium-sized FMCG company probably has ten brand managers whose brands are usually formulated in the same laboratory, produced in the same factory, and so on. This renders impossible the organization

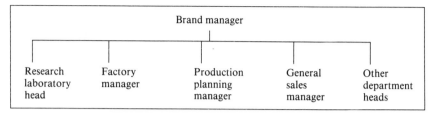

Figure 8.1   A power pyramid

chart in Figure 8.1 where each functional manager would have to report to ten people. The real organization chart is shown in Figure 8.2; it is more like Figure 8.1 turned upside down, and the lines are now broken – indicating not reporting but liaising relationships.

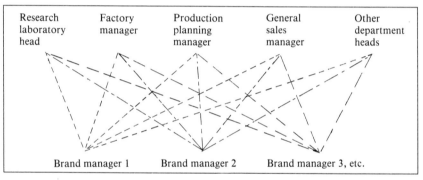

Figure 8.2   An organization chart

In the maze of relationships in Figure 8.2, giving instructions is out of the question. Each brand manager must persuade each functional manager of the priority and importance of the work he or she is doing on that manager's brand. Once our marketing candidate realizes this, he or she will know that success or failure as a brand manager depends on the logical rigour of his or her arguments and persuasive powers.

In fact, the brand management system in an FMCG company is a perfect and rare example of a self-regulating rat race. If a more effective brand manager works on a smaller brand and a less effective one on a bigger brand, the whole company's efforts and priorities become distorted. The board will ask itself why so much resource is being directed towards a small brand. If the answer is that the smaller brand has a more effective brand manager, out of self-preservation the company will have to rebalance its priorities by firing or demoting the bigger-brand manager and promoting the more effective smaller-brand manager. Since market salaries for brand managers vary in 1987 from approximately £12 000 to £30 000 a year there is plenty of scope for promotion and reward in brand management.

I have devoted considerable space to a detailed analysis of the dynamics of an FMCG marketing department because I believe that once the dynamics are understood, the qualities required in marketing recruits become clear. Before I leave the subject of the marketing task, however, I must deal with two important issues: where brand managers go when they are thirty and how marketing and sales careers interrelate in the modern marketplace.

How long can any individual continue being an agent of change, armed only with his or her own persuasive powers and competing to get to the top rung in the brand-management ladder? And where does an individual go once he or she gets there? I believe that the answer to the first question is until the age of thirty, thirty-five at the most. In every career there comes a time when chasing the details of innovation seems better left to younger and fresher minds. At that point, exercising judgement developed from years spent in the front line of innovation, and motivating those younger and fresher minds become more attractive and appropriate challenges.

For this reason most marketing-led FMCG companies staff their marketing departments with 'high flyers'. Marketing departments are usually small in numbers of people, and successful companies find no problems in staffing them entirely with very able and ambitious young people who will either be promoted or leave. Even on the largest and most demanding brands, four years is a long time to be an agent of change. I know one brand manager who stayed on a brand much longer than that. But every three or four years he got a new boss, and this had an amazing rejuvenating and innovating effect. I believe that, on balance, if anyone is to make a lifetime's career of brand management he or she will need frequent changes of brand, market, and possibly country to remain fully stimulated and stretched.

Because Britain, unlike the USA or France, has no fair-trading laws to prevent it, the distributive trade here is growing into a leading marketing force. A small number of very large and powerful retailers control the routes between the largest FMCG manufacturers and their British consumers, and in the last ten years retailers have learned how to flex their muscles. Distributor-owned brands (DOBs) are the main

147

competitors of the market leaders in many FMCG markets in the UK. The British chains are not only large, they are profitable on a scale which makes their US equivalents look second-rate, and their house names are as powerful an influence on the British consumer as even the biggest manufacturers' brands. These chains are usually prepared to stock market leaders in any field, if only to make their own-label product appear aggressively priced, but also-ran brands either hand the bulk of their profits over to the retail chain or quit the battlefield.

The leading distributive chains in the UK have in effect become major FMCG manufacturers and marketers, and their marketing operations are often as sophisticated and high powered as those of even the largest traditional FMCG companies. Their management, at board and negotiating level, is also of the highest calibre and this presents a new and fascinating challenge for British FMCG marketers. If company X develops a new wonder product which all British consumers are likely to want, there is still one further marketing hurdle. Should all the leading chains object to their profit margin on this wonder product and refuse to stock it, the majority of British consumers will never get the opportunity to try it and, however good the product and its advertising may be, it will fail. Moreover, if it does gain stockists in all the major retail outlets, it will probably have eighteen months at the most before DOBs which look very like it and cost 20 per cent less appear on the retailers' shelves. This new situation really stretches the ingenuity of FMCG marketers in Britain. They have to be sharper, more creative, and more efficient than they have ever been before. But this situation throws into high relief the point of contact between the FMCG marketing company and its customer – and now rival – the retail chain. The negotiator who represents the FMCG company at the chain's head office is a key figure, and there are two philosophies concerning who this figure should be.

The philosophy which is losing ground is that the key account negotiator should be a skilful, older sales executive who has known 'old What's-his-name', the buying director of Sadsco's, ever since he or she was filling the shelves at their Tenderham branch. This philosophy is losing ground because, increasingly, the chains' buying directors are very bright, objective people, graduates, perhaps MBAs, who passed through the Tenderham branch so quickly that no one got to know them. And in this arena the canny old sales executive is outclassed. What is more, he or she has no idea of the effect on company profit margins of the small concessions made in negotiation with the new buying director, and so he or she loses every round.

The alternative to the old sales executive as negotiator for the FMCG company is the young marketer, fresh from making a success of running his or her first major brand. Such people can calculate the effect of every concession they make, and can compete with the new buying director as an intellectual equal. There are only two snags. The first is that the retail chains have as much need of bright young marketers today as their suppliers do; so the young account negotiator may go in with a promotional proposition and come out with a job. The second is that the very bright, very ambitious young FMCG marketer may need extra training, not to say special psychological preparation, for this kind of contest, something which was not always on the agenda of brand managers in the past.

Despite these two snags, I have no doubt that the second model is the model of the future. Distributor power is a fact of life for British marketers, at least of FMCG. So young marketing managers should grow up to live with this and should develop the negotiating skills required for managing the new situation; and they will need to plan for this experience as one of the stages of developing a marketing career. This must clearly be taken into account when selecting and recruiting tomorrow's marketing management.

THE QUALITIES REQUIRED IN MARKETERS

From the foregoing analysis there emerges a list of qualities desirable in a recruit to marketing. The first of these is *drive*. This quality lies at the root of persuasive power, and indeed of most human achievement. The young marketer's success will depend on energy and enthusiasm combined with a deep need to influence the environment and *make things better*.

Two other important qualities are competitiveness and self-confidence. For reasons I have explained, marketers must be competitive both internally in the firm and externally in the market. They have to be hungry to succeed and this is likely to show in their record of achievement in life so far. It almost certainly means that they will also be ambitious; to succeed, this ambition must be clothed in social skills and directed into task orientation, but it must be there.

149

It is clearly important for marketing people to be intelligent, to outwit rather than be outwitted, to develop arguments without logical flaws, based on calculations containing no errors. It is easy to say that a marketing recruit should be of the highest possible intelligence. But we must acknowledge that there are many types of intelligence: academic aptitude, practical and 'streetwise' intelligence, the ability to think quickly and deeply. These are all important in marketing with the possible exception of the first. Some employers do set academic minima in recruiting managers, including marketing ones: at least an upper second-class honours degree, or some such qualification. The problem with this approach is that academic performance is not a reliable indicator of IQ. My company has been administering tests of logical reasoning for more than thirty years to candidates for its management traineeships and the low correlation emerges quite clearly. Different undergraduates do very different levels of work and some choose to read subjects which come easily to them while others do the opposite. Moreover, introverts tend to secure better degrees than extroverts and we have already discussed a possible correlation between extroversion and success in marketing.

My own company does not make its job offers to management trainees conditional on degree class, basically because, statistically at least, passing its selection process is more dificult than getting a first. In my own long experience of graduates in business I have observed that a much higher proportion of successful technical managers have firsts than of successful marketers. What is clear, however, is that marketing managers need a high degree of numeracy if they are to persuade their company to spend millions on the basis of their calculations. They also need the ability to absorb and process vast amounts of data logically. The average reading speed among adults is about 300 words a minute. A brand manager with a reading speed of 600 words a minute can examine twice as much data in the same time as an average reader. There are courses which can improve your reading speed, and some guarantee an 80 per cent minimum improvement, but normal adult reading speeds vary from 200 to 800 words a minute and a marketer who can manage the latter has an in-built advantage.

In summary, while academic prowess and intelligence are not the same thing, it must be important to get the brightest marketers you can. They work at the competitive edge of the business and if your company's marketers are brighter than your competitors' then the market, and of course your shareholders, will feel the impact.

The last quality I shall discuss is communication skill or, as it used to be known, the gift of the gab. Marketers spend a large proportion of their time talking: to be effective they have to be good at it. We have noted the brand manager's dependence on persuasive power and while technical managers can afford to be silent guardians of their company's destiny, marketing managers cannot. A company needs the most articulate marketers it can get. Having examined the CVs of many present and future marketing managers I am aware of how many contain in their list of youthful activities 'acting' or, even more frequently, 'debating'. In fact, there is some evidence in my company's thirty-odd years of dusty recruitment files that there is a golden virtue which marketing recruiters should be seeking: the ability to win intellectual arguments with people whose IQ is higher than your own!

Having looked at the most desirable qualities in marketing recruits, I shall now consider where those qualities are to be found.

SOURCES OF MARKETING TALENT

The principal decision to be made by marketing recruiters is whether to buy ready trained marketing people (either by specific job advertising or via headhunters) or whether to recruit and train their own. Both courses involve cost. My experience suggests that brand managers require something like 40 per cent in extra salary to lure them into the unknown from the leading marketing organization that trained them. On the other hand a marketing training such as only a handful of the biggest FMCG companies can give costs many thousands of pounds.

There is one great disadvantage to buying in, and that is the inverse relationship between current career potential and inclination to change employers. Headhunters, in particular, will contact a range of candidates for your marketing vacancy. The candidiate who is about to gain a big promotion in his or her own company, or a glamorous posting overseas, or six months at Harvard Business School, will probably turn down the offer despite the larger salary. The candidate who resents falling behind in the race, or who has been told to pull his or her socks (or whatever) up, will probably accept. Equally, a candidate working for a train-your-own company who is really good is likely to have designs on the job currently held by his or her boss. Joining the company to which the headhunters introduce her may well lead to the problem that the new company will use the same headhunters to obtain his or her next boss. Marketers who switch companies usually learn the wisdom of keeping on good terms with the headhunters who engineered their first move – they will probably need them again.

This consideration has led to the change in practice among large FMCG companies in the UK. In the 1950s and 1960s they relied primarily on buying in marketers from just two companies famous for their training and 'grow-your-own' policies. Today most big FMCG companies recruit new graduates and train them in addition to their buying-in activities. This mixed policy, however, brings problems. Home-grown young marketers get disenchanted by the prospect of being beaten to the promotion they want by a bought-in manager.

I believe on balance that for a company that is big enough, in the UK the best policy is still grow-your-own. Doubtless the UK will follow the US trend towards executives with mobile careers. But US personnel executives, caught in the pantomime of 'golden handcuffs' and 'golden handshakes', are not always happy with the short period for which they can retain the good people they recruit. They envy the employee loyalty of European companies and have admiration, and almost awe, for the very few US corporations which can maintain a grow-your-own policy.

If you decide to buy in your marketing talent there is no shortage of headhunting firms. If you decide to recruit and train your own you have a different problem. Which people would be good at marketing if they were to be recruited and trained? Most marketing recruiters in the UK join the 'milk round', as it is known, and recruit new graduates from British universities and polytechnics. The reason for this is economic. People with the abilities recruiters seek are distributed in fair numbers among the graduating population. Elsewhere, people of the same age and ability are few and far between. So it costs thousands of pounds to screen graduate ranks for suitable talent; it would cost millions to search through the whole population of the same age. I am sure that many bright, forceful and competitive people do not go on to tertiary education. But it seems highly likely that very competitive people with good brains will take up the challenge of academic competition if they can. The way that companies such as my own legislate for exceptions is by setting their qualifications for graduate trainees as 'an honours degree from a British university/ polytechnic or equivalent level of ability'. I will, and have, accepted people as being 'of equivalent ability' – but no company would want to face the cost of considering a quarter of a million applications, and that is why most marketing recruiters stipulate graduates.

I am often asked whether following a particular degree course helps make a better marketer. The answer in technical fields is obvious: chemists are particularly suited to marketing chemicals. But in FMCG there is no proof that having a relevant degree helps. Some 9 per cent of my company's graduate trainees have degrees in business studies or commerce. Although there is evidence that their studies help them in a career in industrial finance, there is nothing to suggest they can be ready earlier for their first brand responsibility if they go into marketing. In fact, it has been argued that since a brand is an abstraction, people who have learned how to handle abstractions – theoretical scientists, philosophers, pure mathematicians and classicists – make better marketers. Certainly there are plenty of examples of graduates in these subjects getting to the top in FMCG marketing.

Companies such as my own in the UK, therefore, recruit graduates of all disciplines, guided by the desire to find the qualities I described in the previous section. There is a drift towards business subjects in British tertiary education (witness the founding of Templeton College, Oxford), but Cambridge still counts business studies as half an A-level because it is not sufficiently intellectually rigorous. There is clearly a long way to go before we begin to train people for specific careers at the infant-school stage.

I am also often asked, 'Do you recruit MBAs?' The answer is, in finance yes; in marketing, at this point in time, no. This, too, will probably change. Diehard practitioners of marketing liken marketing to swimming. If having a Bachelor's degree in aquatic locomotion does not win you a place in the Olympic swimming squad, why should having a Master's? This is perhaps a little unfair, but US experience, once again, is illuminating. In the USA 70 000 people gain MBAs every year, about the same number as that of all new graduates becoming available to recruiters in the UK. American businesses, however, make their target the MBAs of a few 'top-tier' business schools from which some 4000 students get their MBAs – the remainder have problems finding jobs despite having acquired the same theoretical knowledge (Cooper and Dowd, 1987). In other words, the thing that makes the 4000 'top-tier' MBAs desirable employees is the competition to get places in those business schools – only the very brightest make it. In Britain, when the brightest young people all do MBAs, companies like mine will recruit all their management trainees from amongst MBAs. That day may come but it is not here yet.

Minority groups

There are a few points worth making about the source of marketing talent represented by the so-called minorities. No source of talent should be ignored by the objective recruiter. Three of the best young marketers I have worked with in London have been black; all the best (and worst) I worked with in Bombay were black. Currently in Britain there are not many black brand managers but that will surely change.

I have known many first-class women brand managers. However, despite their legal rights, in Britain few women managers who have left to start a family hand their babies over to nannies and continue their careers. Even fewer women marketers return to their careers when their children are grown. In some careers this works, but in FMCG marketing there is a series of drawbacks for you if you are an *emigrée*. In ten years everything has changed, so you have masses to learn before you can begin to be as effective as you were when you left. Meanwhile, things have been happening to those of your old colleagues who were men or childless women. The one you thought much less competent than yourself is now your boss. The one who was almost as good as you is now *his* or *her* boss. Is it surprising that you prefer to start a new career altogether?

It is, nevertheless, a tragedy that so much talent and so many skills are lost to maternity, and I personally believe that companies should make more effort to recall very able women to their marketing departments once their children are grown. The only alternative is to give in to the sexist cynic who averred that if God had meant careers to be combined with childbearing, he (she?) would have made us all women.

A further career problem remains for the woman marketer working for a multinational company who hands her babies over and goes back to work. If she is very good at her job many opportunities for promotion will arise, most of them not in Britain but in any one of seventy other countries. Will her partner pack in his job to go with her, perhaps to a country where he cannot get a work permit? Even if her new job pays three times what his does? Experience suggests that men need emancipating in this respect. Two out of three wives will give up their jobs to go abroad with their husbands, but few if any husbands will reciprocate. Perhaps men will become more emancipated, but it seems more likely that, as divorce rates rise to meet marriage rates, people will accept marriage for the disposable thing it is. Couples split up for poorer reasons than a job in Rio.

There is one other 'minority' worth mentioning with regard to sources of marketing talent. That is polytechnic graduates. Most of the graduates who run companies, especially FMCG companies, in the UK are university graduates. This leads to prejudice in their expectations with regard to candidates from polytechnics, and is as damaging to objectivity as is the Oxford/Redbrick prejudice. Fortunately things are changing. The major FMCG companies recruited 'poly' graduates before the higher Civil Service, but even that bastion has now been breached. The best graduates from polytechnics are as bright as the best from universities even if they are fewer and further between. Polytechnic graduates, many of whom read business studies, are most successful in getting into marketing when they remember that recruiters are more interested in their transferable skills and their capacity to learn than in what they already know. My company offered just over 3 per cent of its management traineeships to polytechnic graduates last year, and I expect that figure to rise.

REFERENCES AND FURTHER READING

Cooper C. and Dowd, K. (1987), 'Mid-life crisis for the MBA', *Management Today*, April, pp.82–86.
Fortune (1986), 4 August, p.165 (international ed).
Ogilvy, D. (1985), *Ogilvy on Advertising*, 2nd ed, Guild Books, London.

9

Selection – media and methods

Martin Duffell

Assuming that you have decided to grow your own young marketers and for good economic reasons have decided to recruit graduates, you will find that there is a great deal of competition for the ablest candidates. As a marketing person you will relish this competition, because it means that there is a graduate market and you can employ your professional skills in marketing your vacancies.

While the market for graduate vacancies is much smaller than for any FMCG product in terms of numbers of consumers, it has nevertheless merited both market research and media expenditure over a number of years.

Graduate recruitment is a mature market. Over 60 000 new graduates become available for employment in the UK each year. Population trends would reduce this by over one-third in the next ten years, but the present government policy is to keep this number almost constant by increasing the proportion of the population going into tertiary education. Over 2000 employers compete fiercely for the best of each year's crop of graduates and the number of recruiters has been rising sharply in the mid-1980s.

The chartered accountancy profession is the market leader by volume, taking up to 10 per cent of all the graduates entering employment. Since most marketers have a low boredom threshold, you will not really be in competition with the accountants. You may, however, find yourself in competition with the City's institutions. The City offers starting salaries which are on average 40 per cent higher than those paid by recruiters and trainers of marketers. The City can afford to pay more because it recruits graduates for narrower jobs; their training costs are lower and the period before productive labour is shorter. The initial salary differential may tempt marketing candidates. But since the City offers jobs which have much less variety and scope for creativity, a small secondary market is developing for marketers, consisting of people who have started a career in banking or finance and have found it hard to keep awake.

GRADUATE RECRUITMENT MEDIA

As with any mature market, regular research information can be purchased and there is a wealth of media available. For a number of years MORI (Market and Opinion Research International) has carried out a regular attitude survey based on a sample of over 1000 final-year students at more than twenty universities. The fieldwork is done in March each year and the results published in June. The names and addresses of all the organizations and publications mentioned in this section appear at the end of the chapter.

Media used in graduate recruitment include press (national, student and specialist recruitment), posters (there are numerous noticeboards in universities and polytechnics), brochures (the biggest single media cost in most recruiters' advertising spend) and video (the newest and fastest growing medium). The most important single graduate recruitment medium I believe to be public relations at universities and polytechnics, particularly with careers advisory services, but also with academic staff and student audiences which can be attracted to presentations, vacation courses, and vacation employment.

If you plan to enter this market you will find two works of reference invaluable. The first is the *Graduate Careers Services Directory* (published by the Central Services Unit (CSU)), and the second is the *Newpoint Guide to the Graduate Careers Services* (published by Newpoint). You can also get expert help from any of a number of advertising agencies which specialize in recruitment consultancy and

157

advertising. Four whose work I know and respect are Trotman and Company and Newpoint (both in the London area), and Hobsons and Publishing Resources (both based in Cambridge).

The graduate recruitment market is as complex as any I have experienced, and consulting the reference books I have mentioned and a good recruitment advertising agency is a necessary preliminary to playing an effective role in it. There are, however, four organizations, four directories of graduate employers, and three national fortnightly publications which must be mentioned in even the briefest survey.

The first organization is AGCAS (the Association of Graduate Careers Advisory Services). This is the national body of professional careers advisers, university and polytechnic staff who provide individual and group counselling on careers to all students, maintain a comprehensive careers library, and offer a variety of other services to job-hunting graduates. AGCAS has its own publishing house based in Manchester, the CSU.

There is a national organization for employers of graduates, AGR (the Association of Graduate Recruiters, formerly known as the Standing Conference of Employers of Graduates), which represents the interests of graduate recruiters. AGCAS and AGR have an agreed code of practice for graduate recruitment and a new recruiter of graduates would be wise to join AGR and obtain a copy of this code.

Two student/business organizations are very active on the campuses in Britain. They are valuable allies, second only to careers advisers, and their officials are energetic students with a strong motivation towards business. AIESEC (l'Association Internationale d'Etudiants en Sciences Economiques et Commerciales) is a well-established international organization which arranges student exchanges for vacation work all over the world. It has branches in more than twenty universities in Britian where students of all disciplines can become members. AIESEC provides a wide range of training experience and business knowledge for its members and has a national committee of full-time officials based in London and an international headquarters in Brussels.

SIS (the Student Industrial Societies), the first of which was founded ten years ago, now have branches in more than fifty universities and polytechnics, arrange presentations for their members, industrial visits and events which will help develop their business knowledge and skills. The SIS have two full-time national campaign organizers, based at the headquarters of the Industrial Society in London. Both AIESEC and SIS can provide recruiters with a ready-made communication route and with student audiences, and both are well worth supporting.

If you intend to recruit any number of graduates for marketing it is worth having details of your vacancies in one or more of the four directories which list graduate recruiters. *ROGET* (the *Register of Graduate Employment and Training*), has the largest circulation. It is published by the CSU and has very full support from the careers advisory services. *GO* (*Graduate Opportunities*) is published by Newpoint, which also publishes *DOG* (the *Directory of Opportunities for Graduates*) which is a set of classified directories for different types of graduate and employment. *GET (Graduate Employment and Training)* is published by Hobsons and competes with *ROGET* and *GO* as a general directory. All these directories are revised and published every year, usually during the long vacations, and they are distributed free to final-year undergraduates throughout Britain.

There are three important fortnightly publications in which graduate recruiters can advertise their vacancies. CSU produces two bulletins, *Current Vacancies* and *Forward Vacancies*, the latter offering jobs to start at the beginning of the next academic year. These are distributed free to students via careers advisory services, as is a fortnightly newspaper, *Graduate Post*, published by Newpoint. There are also opportunities to advertise your presence in the graduate recruitment market in a number of publications which appear annually, such as *The World Outside*, produced by Pagan Publishing, and the yearbooks and other publications of the SIS and AIESEC.

Having mentioned this list of media, I believe that there is no real substitute for visiting the campuses in person and learning from, as well as building good relations with, the careers advisory services.

SELECTION METHODS

Psychologists like Ruth Holdsworth of Saville and Holdsworth classify the data used in selection under a Latin square according to whether input and interpretation are subjective or objective. Figure 9.1 shows the use of a common convention (for example, Mars, 1982, p.29) to label the four boxes.

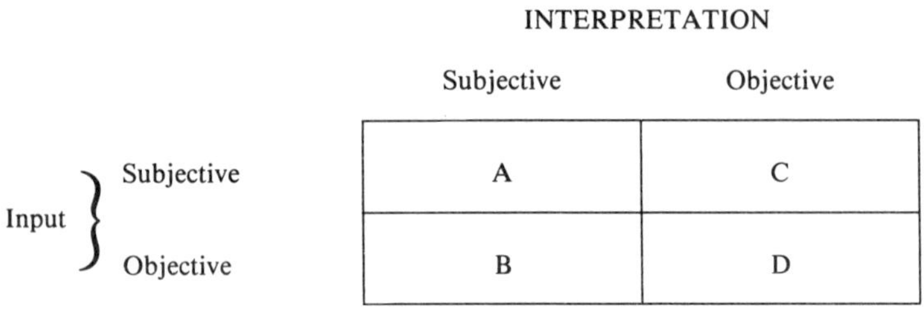
INTERPRETATION
Subjective
Objective
Input
Subjective
Objective
A
C
B
D

Figure 9.1 A Latin square for data classification

Clearly, behavioural scientists will want to maximize the amount of the selection process which falls in box D and minimize the part in box A. Occupational psychologists believe that the two most unreliable ways of selecting people for jobs are references and interviews (see Herriot, 1987, p.79); not surprisingly both fall in box A. Figure 9.2 plots where each of the methods discussed in this chapter falls in the Latin square.

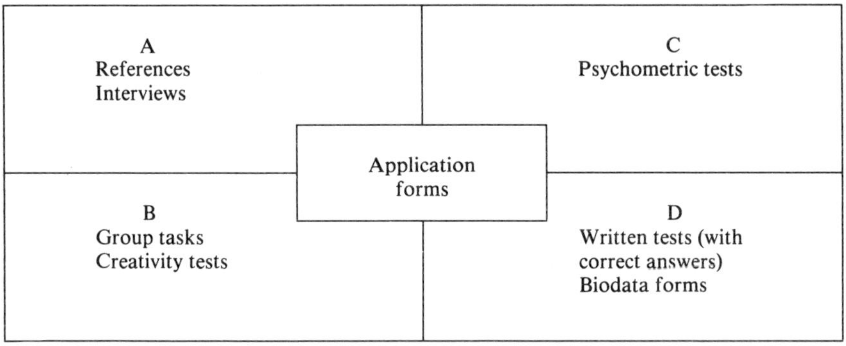
A
References
Interviews
C
Psychometric tests
Application forms
B
Group tasks
Creativity tests
D
Written tests (with correct answers)
Biodata forms

Figure 9.2 Selection methods classified in the Latin square

I have placed application forms in the centre because some parts of them, or some ways of interpreting the information in them, fall into each category.

References

Since references are subjective statements evaluated according to the selector's subjective view of the referee's judgement, they are useless unless your aim is to find the best-connected candidate. References are used as positive criteria only by employers who are too busy or too lazy to find out which candidate would be best at the job. They are also sometimes used to avoid open competition for a post of privilege. You can use them to fill your marketing vacancies but, if you do, you should not expect your recruits to win in any open and competitive market.

Application forms

There is an AGCAS approved standard application form available in all careers services, and many employers accept applications on this form. It helps applicants: some will fill in one, photocopy it a hundred times, and send it to a hundred employers. Some employers worry that this indicates no special interest in *their* job and suggests the candidate lacks confidence in obtaining an offer by applying to only a few carefully selected employers. My own company uses an eight-page 'horror' which puts many applicants off, particularly those who are not very interested in joining us. Some careers advisers run seminars on how to fill in application forms: in so far as this helps candidates not to undersell themselves this is a good thing. On the other hand, help given to a candidate in filling in an application form may not help him or her in the long run. I remember one candidate who was so unlike his application form that I was mystified until he confessed that his father had composed it and his mother had typed it for him. He was not offered the job and would not have been even if he had not confessed. Many application forms look 'coached', but there is one almost blank page in the form my company uses which I do not think anyone has yet found a way of coaching.

In recent years there has been a vogue for using *biodata* application forms which can be computer analysed, so that candidates' factual details can be measured against the data for past successes in the job concerned, or against some defined ideal. The proponents of this system (which is currently used for selecting tax inspectors) argue that it can entirely replace first interviews and thus pay for its high software and running costs. Some years ago my company had a leading consultant in this field examine a large sample of applicants' data which were transferable to such a form. The consultant successfully predicted two out of every three applicants who would suceed in our selection process; this was impressive. But it is interesting to compare the candidates selected by biodata but rejected by our traditional process with those who were selected by our traditional process but not identified by biodata. The striking difference is that those selected by biodata alone are very like the two who were selected by both methods, at least on paper. It suggests that a fair proportion of management trainees produced by our traditional process are 'odd-balls'. I would advise marketing recruiters to keep taking oddballs rather than computer clones. People are a species like any other, subject to a natural selection which is beyond their control. When the environment changes completely, it may be that only one of the oddballs is able to cope. The thought that tax inspectors might go the way of the dinosaur fails to bring tears to my eyes.

Interviews

First interviews for marketing candidates are arranged on campus at most universities in the spring term. The careers advisory services often take over the administration of this 'milk round' and as many as thirty employers may be interviewing on the same day. If you wish to see more than two or three candidates, this is likely to be more economic than paying their fares to your offices.

It can be debated whether personnel managers or marketing managers are better for this purpose. My own view is that if you are interviewing only marketing candidates a marketer is best, but only one who has attended a good interviewing course and gained some experience. Excellent interviewing courses are offered by the Industrial Society, the Institute of Personnel Management, and commercial firms of occupational psychologists such as PA or Saville and Holdsworth. Failing this, a number of good interviewing primers have been written, and one I can recommend is Martin Higham's *The ABC of Interviewing* (1979). It should always be remembered that selection is a two-way process. The candidate you are interviewing is assessing your firm as an employer. For this reason it can be an advantage to make the interviewer the youngest person qualified to do the job. It helps communicate that young people get responsibility in your business. If the interviewer is not competent this youthfulness will backfire – the unsuccessful candidate will tell everyone that the employers who were impressed by him or her in interview sent their managing directors to do it, while you sent the office junior.

Some interviewers put a lot of faith in what they call tough, that is, hostile interviewing tactics. I do not recommend it for marketers, since the hostile interview is the last place where depth of analysis or creativity will have a chance to emerge. All a hostile interview reveals are reflexes in conflict – I can see its use in selecting both spies and marines.

Tests

As we have noted, tests are the most objective method available to selectors but they are useful only if they are appropriate. Basic numeracy tests are unnecessary for people with a good O-Level grade in mathematics, and verbal tests are probably appropriate only for graduates whose course does not require writing essays. It must also be noted that average verbal test scores have been falling sharply ever since television came into the home. A graduate in the top 0.1 per cent of IQs would have been likely to have a vocabulary of 35 000 words (English count) some thirty years ago: today it is likely to be about 25000.

My company employs a test in graduate selection which measures the speed and accuracy of non-verbal, non-numerate reasoning. It is useful to have as an extra piece of information when a candidate's academic record conflicts with the apparent level of intelligence in live performance, or when there are glaring inconsistencies in both. Advertising agencies often use tests of creative writing ability which are obviously appropriate. For jobs where experienced people are being examined an 'in-tray' exercise may be appropriate: candidates can be asked to sort out a heap of correspondence by priority and compose replies. To summarize, tests are good objective data if they are appropriate. One type of test I would not advise in 1987 is spelling. From more than three thousand applications this year, I do not expect the number of application forms without a spelling mistake to reach double figures. Since the advent of television and the demise of Latin in schools even candidates with firsts in English cannot spell.

Psychometric tests appear in one of the boxes in Figure 9.2. Occupational psychologists have done a great deal of work on both

163

sides of the Atlantic on questionnaires which will measure a candidate's personality attributes. Some of the tests produced are very impressive, measuring several dozen attributes on a sensitive scale. It is important, however, to appreciate their drawbacks. The first is that the data are useful only if you are sure where your ideal employee lies on this series of scales. You can, of course, take one of these tests yourself and select only candidates with similar personality profiles to your own. This would bring the cloning problem I have already discussed. It is, moreover, difficult to predict results from personality traits: who would win a war between a man who was more paranoid than he was dogmatic (Stalin) and another who was more dogmatic than he was paranoid (Hitler)?

The second point which must be made about psychometric tests is that they measure a number, albeit a large one, of personality characteristics. But whole people are more than the sum of their parts, and we can never really be sure we have measured the right characteristics.

The third point concerns the classification of psychometric tests into box C (Figure 9.2) – subjective input/objective interpretation. People doing such a test, provided they do not cheat, are giving an accurate picture not of their personality but only of how they see themselves. Thus, for example, these tests measure how logical or persuasive people believe they are rather than whether they *are* logical or persuasive. The input is thus subjective; the interpretation, on the other hand, is an objective tool only when it is used to compare one candidate's self-perception with another's or with an ideal. The ideal may also, of course, be regarded as subjective, thus relegating psychometric tests to box A.

Despite the reservations I have expressed, a large number of businesses have used psychometric testing to select for a wide variety of jobs and are clearly satisfied with the results. Perhaps the blueprint for the ideal young marketer will one day be agreed and, if so, then the scientific tests appropriate to it will rapidly appear.

Group tasks

In the previous chapter I pointed out that young marketers work in a *melée* of people rather than in isolation, and this makes a group selection process very appropriate for marketers. Drive, competitiveness, decisiveness, self-confidence, task orientation, social skills, communication, debating skill, logic, quick thinking, imagination and speed in assimilating data can all be demonstrated in group situations. My own company was among the first to use group tasks, discussions and case studies in the selection of management trainees. Our selection boards, as we call them, were devised many years ago by Harold Bridger, a founder member of the Tavistock Institute of Human Relations, in consultation with the people at the very top of our business. Indeed, today, when many other employers have adopted group assessment, our selection system is distinguished mainly by the unique feature that the chairmen and directors of our main board, as well as those of our numerous subsidiaries, play a regular part in graduate trainee selection. A high proportion of our top management entered the business as graduate trainees and were chosen by the same system. A high proportion of them are also marketers.

In the forty years since their inception, our selection boards have been amended, updated and refined many times. Harold Bridger has passed the baton on to professional colleagues who now form the Oxford Consulting Associates, but the underlying principles of the system are unchanged. The selection day contains four group activities as well as individual tests and interviews for candidates invited, eight at a time, to our London head office. The decision on the candidates' potential for senior management in Unilever is made by an *ad hoc* panel of senior managers usually from four different subsidiary companies. If there are marketing candidates, two of the selectors will be marketers. A senior personnel executive chairs the selectors' discussions, a younger personnel manager manages the candidates' day, and two professional behavioural scientists take part in all the selectors' discussions but have no vote in the decision.

A large number of organizations now use group assessment techniques, which are, I believe, particularly appropriate to choosing marketers. There are also a number of assessment centres run by commercial consultancy firms such as PA and Saville and Holdsworth which offer a selection board service to employers. Armed with the assessment centre results, the employer can interview a short-list and make offers. Many larger companies prefer to organize their own group assessment internally.

One important feature of Unilever selection boards is not always found in other group processes. The behavioural scientists who assist at our selection boards interview candidates individually towards the end of the selection day and offer feedback on any aspect of it the candidate wishes. Some candidates do not want to know what the selectors make of their group performance, style, or personality shown during the day, and the feedback is not forced on them. A majority of candidates, however, want to learn things which they might be able to work on for the benefit of their own personal development. Group activities under observation are often stressful, and candidates usually also appreciate the calming influence of an objective look at their strengths (which are usually many) as well as their weaknesses.

AFTER SELECTION

If you have decided to recruit new graduates to staff your marketing department, and have gone through the lengthy process of selection and hiring them, you are now ready for the crucial task: training. My company has acquired a reputation over many years for training marketers. The underlying principles of a Unilever marketing training are very simple. Such a training includes a series of courses in business and marketing theory which we call our Business Education Programme. It also includes attachments to the sales force, the factories, and every department of the Unilever company concerned. It will also probably include outside attachments, to an advertising agency and a market research company, for example. Most important, a young marketer works in a brand office undertaking increasingly responsible tasks on the brand until he or she is ready to be appointed to manage a brand of his or her own. Such an internal training is not possible for every marketing employer, but there are many other alternatives, as the next chapter will reveal.

REFERENCES AND FURTHER READING

Current Vacancies, CSU, Manchester.
DOG: *Directory of Opportunities for Graduates*, Newpoint, London.

Forward Vacancies, CSU, Manchester.
GET: *Graduate Employment and Training*, CRAC, Cambridge.
GO: *Graduate Opportunities*, Newpoint, London.
Graduate Careers Service Directory, CSU, Manchester.
Graduate Post, Newpoint, London.
Herriot, P. (1987), 'Graduate recruitment – getting it right', *Department of Employment Gazette*, February, pp.78–83.
Higham, M. (1979), *The ABC of Interviewing*, IPM, London.
Mars, Gerald, *Cheats at Work*, Allen & Unwin, London, 1982.
Newpoint Guide to the Graduate Careers Services, Newpoint, London.
ROGET: *Register of Graduate Employment and Training*, CSU, Manchester.
The World Outside, Pagan Publishing, London.

ORGANIZATIONS

AGCAS: Association of Graduate Careers Advisory Services (see CSU).

AGR: Association of Graduate Recruiters (formerly known as SCOEG).

AIESEC Great Britain, Ukin House, Phipp Street, London EC2A 4NR: tel: 01-739 9847.

CSU: Central Services Unit, Crawford House, Precinct Centre, Manchester M13 9EP: tel: 061-273 4233.

CRAC: The Careers Research and Advisory Centre (publish through Hobsons Ltd, see below).

Hobsons Limited, Bateman Street, Cambridge CB2 1LZ: tel: 0223 354551.

IPM: Institute of Personnel Management, IPM House, Camp Road, Wimbledon, London SW19 4UW: tel: 01-946 9100.

MORI: Market and Opinion Researh International Ltd, 32 Old Queen Street, London SW1H 9HP: tel: 01-222 0232.

Newpoint (formerly the New Opportunity Press), Yeoman House, 76 St James's Lane, London N10 3RD: tel: 01-444 7281.

Oxford Consulting Associates Ltd (see also Tavistock Institute of Human Relations, below), 10 Butts Road, Horspath, Oxford OX9 1RH: tel: 08677 3817.

PA Personnel Services, Hyde Park House, 60a Knightsbridge, London SW1X 7LE: tel: 01-235 6060.

Pagan Publishing Ltd, 22 Chancellor House, 17 Hyde Park Gate, London SW7 5DQ: tel: 01-727 3897.

Saville and Holdsworth, The Old Post House, 81 High Street, Esher, Surrey KT10 9QA: tel: 0372 68634.

SCOEG: Standing Conference of Employers of Graduates – now known as AGR (see above).

SIS: Student Industrial Societies, Robert Hyde House, 48 Bryanston Square, London W1H 7LN: tel; 01-262 2401.

Tavistock Institute of Human Relations (see also Oxford Consulting Associates Ltd, above), The Tavistock Centre, Belsize Lane, London NW3 5BA: tel: 01-435 7111.

Trotman and Company Ltd, 12–14 Hill Rise, Richmond, Surrey TW10 6UA: tel: 01-940 5668.

10

Staff development and training

Bernard Wynne

In the eyes of the customer the company *is* the one person who deals with him or her: the telephonist who keeps him or her waiting without an apology; the sales assistant who is not able or prepared to assist; the service engineer who does not arrive on time. As Tom Peters suggests, 'the coffee stains on the table in an aircraft imply that the organization is slack on engine maintenance' (Peters and Austin, 1985). These seemingly very basic functions are those which either enhance or mar the way our company is seen by our customers. No matter how good our total marketing campaign, unless we can deliver effective service at the point of customer contact our products will not continue to find markets.

The one way in which we can ensure that we provide effective service is by ensuring that we have trained our staff.

This chapter focuses attention on the importance of training in marketing; marketing as expressed by the total impact the company makes on its customers and potential customers.

This chapter concentrates on training for three main groups:

1   marketing professionals;
2   salespeople;
3   retail, branch counter, receptionists and service staff.

In addition it looks at three chief approaches we may decide to use in delivering our training:

1   off-the-job courses, internal and external;
2   on-the-job training, coaching, advice and guidance;
3   self-development, personal learning and distance learning techniques.

In addition to this, and especially in relation to the marketing professionals, we will consider the question of education.

In the increasingly competitive environment in which we operate, both in the UK and internationally, effective marketing can help to bring our products to the attention of our customers. It should be remembered that marketing, as Peter Drucker says, is 'so basic that it cannot be considered as a seperate function, it is the whole business as seen from the point of view of its final result, that is from the customer's point of view' (Drucker, 1974). If this is so, and if our marketing is to be really effective, we must be prepared to train the people who deliver our product at the point of contact with the customer.

THE MARKETING PROFESSIONAL

In considering this group, it is useful to start with some consideration of the types of qualities we should be looking for in people working in our marketing departments. Generally speaking, we should be looking for people who are outgoing, who have lively minds and who are socially confident. It also helps if they are able to display a high degree of persuasive skill, good human relations and interpersonal skills.

In addition to these personal skills, a good educational background is essential; a degree, preferably in business studies, which has included a course on marketing is a very useful base upon which to build. It is appreciated that not everybody can start from this position. What must be increasingly true for the future is that the people who run our marketing departments in the leading companies do receive some professional education and training to enable them to function more effectively.

Two recent studies suggest that serious attention should be devoted to the question of marketing education (Walker, 1986).

There are two principal organizations which provide professional education for marketeers in the UK: the Institute of Marketing and

CAM Foundation (Communication, Advertising and Marketing Education Foundation).

The Institute of Marketing

The Institute plays a leading role in marketing education. Its professional qualification, the Diploma in Marketing, is internationally recognized. The qualification is designed to impart a basic knowledge of marketing and to teach students to apply that knowledge and skill to executive decision-making. To acquire these qualifications normally involves a three-year course of part-time study. Many polytechnics, colleges of further education and correspondence colleges offer appropriate courses of study leading to this qualification.

In addition to the basic qualification, it is possible for more mature or senior marketing managers to obtain an internationally recognized qualification via the intensive diploma course. This course consists of a series of residential weekend seminars which prepare participants for the appropriate examinations.

Membership of the Institute of Marketing is in excess of 20 000, and branches and industry groups have a key role in ensuring local backing for those who are interested in increasing their contact with fellow marketing professionals.

The Institute has an effective library and information service. Membership should be seriously considered by any professional marketer working in the UK.

The Communication, Advertising and Marketing Education Foundation

The CAM Foundation is the examinations board for vocational qualifications in the communications industry. CAM provides examinations at diploma level which are designed to enable each student to specialize in subjects which will be of the greatest use in his or her career. Students can sit for the DipCam in advertising, public relations or marketing. Upon successful completion of any one of these qualifications students can go on to take additional subjects which will provide them with the DipCam (Hons) which indicates success across a wider range of subjects.

171

As with the Institute of Marketing, there are several methods of study open to students; evening or part-time day classes at local colleges and intensive weekend courses.

Universities and polytechnics

In addition to the professional institutions described above, many universities, polytechnics and business schools offer a range of courses in marketing which provide an extremely useful introduction to the subject. They also provide the opportunity for people to share experiences and views with inexperienced and experienced marketers. In looking towards the future, it will almost certainly be essential for anyone seeking a career in marketing to have received some formal education in the subject.

Training in marketing skills

All the foregoing refers to marketing education. In addition to the importance of this area of skill development, there is ample opportunity in the field of professional marketing to experience a wide range of training. Training is usually considered to be of a shorter duration than education, and many organizations, including the principal business schools and the Institute of Marketing, offer a range of short courses in particular areas of skill development; a wide range is regularly held at the Institute. They cover introductory level courses into marketing and also provide training for the most senior levels of management. They also provide training in computer-aided marketing, market research, marketing to specific markets and a whole range of other skills.

The Open University, Henley College and Strathclyde University have now produced distance learning packages dealing with marketing.

Familiarity with this range of training and educational opportunities is essential for every marketing executive, both in terms of their own personal development and the continued personal development of their staff. Managers need to identify specific areas of skill development and then seek the appropriate means to meet these training needs.

SALESPEOPLE

The one area which has traditionally been seen as the most important in which to provide training has been that of the sales force. Of all training in relation to marketing, this has perhaps been the one area in which organizations have invested time and resources. This is not to say it has been done universally well or that it has even been done in all organizations. We have all heard examples of inadequately prepared salespeople attempting to sell goods both at home and abroad and being rebuffed at the first stage.

These basic requirements must be addressed by the marketing professional to ensure that the right sort of training is being provided at the right time and for the right people.

In considering the question of sales training, it is perhaps worth restating that selling is an honourable profession. It is a profession which has often been denigrated, perhaps because people have an incorrect picture of the sales executive. The view has been conditioned by the image of the fast-talking type who tries to sell inferior goods, or the rather down-at-the-heel travelling salesman with his suitcase of samples. Neither image portrays an attractive picture of what should be one of the key roles in our organizations.

In looking for people who are likely to be effective salespeople, we need to look for those who are self-motivated, who are frequently able to work on their own without close supervision. Being an effective sales executive requires certain qualities. Although the qualities may vary in degree, in the absence of all of them it is unlikely that the individual will be effective. Such qualities include drive, determination, a high degree of persuasive skill, negotiating skills, being a good listener, being articulate and having good verbal communication ability. Above all, the sales executive must be interested in the contact and must attempt to match the product to the customer's needs. This demands good research into the contact's company; into the contact and into the immediate environment in which he or she works. It also requires effective record keeping. In a more technical sense the sales executive needs to develop a good product knowledge and a good understanding of how the organization he or she represents works, in order to be clear about its decision-making mechanisms and delivery systems.

It has in the past been assumed that many of the skills referred to above cannot be taught and that good salespeople are born rather than trained. This is patently untrue as any behaviour can be learned and modified to fit in with any particular social situation. An important requirement for any trainer responsible for training salespeople is a familiarity with social and behavioural psychology. An interesting chapter on training in social skills is contained in *The Psychology of Interpersonal Behaviour* (Argyle, 1972). All those responsible for sales training should ensure they are familiar with books such as this.

An interesting and up-to-date approach to the sales process and sales training is outlined by Neil Rackham in *Making Major Sales* (Rackham, 1987). People responsible for sales training should become familiar with these ideas as they pose serious questions about many of the sacred cows of selling, respresenting the first significant advance in sales technique for many years.

The main objective of sales training must be to develop the skills referred to above. Essentially, sales training will be most effective if it is carried out both on and off the job. Both these techniques are explained later. All salespeople require to develop skills in off-the-job training situations where they can be in a non-threatening situation and not lose a customer. This training then needs to be followed up with on-the-job practice, guided and counselled by an experienced trainer or sales manager. Attendance at a course alone will not be sufficient for it is important to monitor, review and provide feedback regarding the behaviours displayed in an actual sales situation. This can be achieved only by working closely with a more experienced person.

RETAIL AND COUNTER STAFF

In recent years there has been an awakening to the importance of this group of staff. Traditionally they have been the group with the least status and usually the least training in the organization. Marketing professionals have often been guilty of allowing the importance of this group to be underestimated. Even in recent times they have been described in a marketing textbook as the 'inside order taker' (Foster, 1982). This view demonstrates a complete lack of understanding of the importance of customer service. We should all ask ourselves how many customers meet the marketing manager and how many meet the 'inside order taker'.

Many companies have realized that the role of this group of staff is of paramount importance in the total marketing strategy of any organization.

Any organization which is concerned to ensure that it gets the best from its staff must be prepared to invest training in them. Organizations need to have a training plan which will ensure that all staff follow a set pattern of training and development. This training plan should include both on- and off-the-job training experiences and should be designed to assist employees to achieve clearly identified performance standards at each appropriate stage of their career development.

It is not appropriate to describe performance standards here as they will vary greatly from one organization to another and they are usually most effective when set as close to the job as possible. They should be set by the local manager but should at the same time link in with the general standards required and communicated centrally and have a close relationship with the corporate aims of the organization.

Induction training

The first training for any new members of staff must consist of induction. This should cover all the basic needs of the recruits, namely, where they will be working, who will be their boss, when they will get paid and so on. Local managers who feel that they can ignore these basic requirements are likely to have very confused and therefore ineffective recruits on their hands.

Once this first stage of settling in has been completed, the recruit can then be introduced to the company as a whole, its history and development, its position in the market, the senior management team, how well the organization is doing (last year's results) and most important of all the aims and objectives of the organization. This induction must be carried out early and can be done in a variety of ways: by booklets, but remember that they must be attractive to read and easy to understand; by audio tape; by video film and by interactive videos (each of these terms is described in more detail later). Some companies have a large number of recruits joining at the same time at a central location. Where this is the case it may be preferable to hold a short induction training course in the first few days. In all cases it is essential that induction training is carried out.

175

Skill and product training

The next stage is to put the new recruits to work in meeting and serving the customers. To do this the recruits need to learn all aspects of the product that they will be dealing with. They also need to begin to develop some of the basic skills which will enable them to become quickly effective. This stage of training is designed to develop the ability to help customers to make up their minds. It will concentrate on identifying particular types of customers, creating customer profiles and having some understanding of customer needs. To do this, the employees must understand the product or service which is on offer.

Many organizations believe this training to be so important that they take people away on training courses to ensure that the training is being delivered effectively.

Another useful method of ensuring consistency is to have a formal training period each week. It is not unusual now to find a shop or building society office closed on one particular morning each week for a period of training. Where this is the case, it provides the local manager with an opportunity to ensure that performance standards are regularly being communicated and checked. As with all methods of training, there are difficulties and dangers with it. It is important to ensure that where provision for training is made it is used effectively. Managers need to plan the training in advance and ensure that they stick to that plan and communicate it to their staff. For the organization wishing to introduce this form of training, it is important to ensure that it provides training in training techniques for the people who will be delivering the training.

This section has been dealing mainly with retail and counter staff. There is another group of staff who fall very much into the same category; receptionists, telephonists and service engineers. Many of the same lessons and the same approaches to training need to apply, but they need to be applied thoughtfully as the specific applications to service engineers cannot be the same as training cashiers in a building society. There are special needs and the manager who is responsible for this group of people needs to set special performance standards. The same applies to the telephonist and receptionist. All these groups need to be made to feel a part of the organization as a whole and to be able to see their role in the organization achieving its objectives. They are frequently the main means of customer contact and need to be treated as the ambassadors to our public.

TRAINING TECHNIQUES

There is a range of training techniques which are available to trainers and consideration will be given to these under three subheadings:

1 off-the-job courses;
2 on-the-job training;
3 distance learning and self-development.

Consideration will be given to the meaning of each of these subheadings, and additional information regarding appropriate techniques in relation to each of them will be given under each heading.

How managers or marketing professionals can apply these techniques will depend upon the objectives they set and the skills in which they wish to provide training.

Off-the-job courses

Training courses which take place off the job, which means essentially away from the trainee's workplace, can vary in length from half a day to six weeks. They may be organized internally by the company itself or may involve attendance at a public course run by a college or other professional training organization. There are benefits and disadvantages to both types of course. One of the main benefits of running courses in house, mounted either with the assistance of an external consultant or by in-company trainers, is that you are communicating a consistent message all the time. There is no confusion about this message and you are growing, developing and informing your staff in the way you wish. A disadvantage is that your staff are not being exposed to the usually wide range of people they meet at external courses. Each organization must make up its own mind as to the most beneficial method. Frequently this will depend upon the number of people to be trained. Attendance at external public courses can be expensive, particularly if you have a large number of trainees who require the same type of training.

In considering the training of marketing professionals, it may well be best for them to attend external public courses. It is unlikely that there will regularly be sufficient numbers of people in the marketing department for you to mount specific courses for their skill development. They will also often gain a breadth and depth of knowledge from exposure to other people on public courses that would not be possible in house.

Because many organizations are likely to be dealing with large numbers of retail and counter staff, it will be preferable to arrange their training in house. In-house training provides an opportunity not only to carry out the training you wish to give, but also to build a high degree of company loyalty and commitment. At internal courses and seminars people frequently have an opportunity to identify with the objectives of the company. If this idea of deepening one's commitment and understanding of the company is part of the objectives of this training then the benefits of doing it in house are obvious.

When one considers the training of salespeople, it is necessary to consider also the numbers involved and the methods of training you wish to employ. As with retail and counter staff, there is much to be gained from in-house training. Concentration on one set of products, one set of company objectives and one sales training plan can clearly be of significant benefit. In seeking to ensure that a company communicates a consistent marketing message through all its staff, the benefits of in-house training are substantial. In considering the impact of the marketing message, it is essential that the actual behaviour of the sales force is congruent with the marketing strategy. In many companies this is not the case; training can play an important role in achieving this congruence.

For any organization seeking to run in-house courses, it is essential either to employ trainers or to hire the services of an experienced trainer. It is not sufficient to assume that any departmental manager, even the most effective, can become a trainer overnight. Effective training courses are those which are mounted by professional trainers who have been trained in and have an understanding of what is required both in terms of the trainee's needs and in terms of the range of available techniques.

While appreciating that this approach is not always possible in smaller organizations, a wide range of consultants is available who can easily provide the necessary expertise on a short-term basis for even the smallest organization.

The following is a brief outline of the appropriate techniques which can be used in off-the-job training courses.

Lectures are the most popular method of training, although probably the least effective. The technique involves the trainer standing before a group of trainees and attempting to communicate as effectively as possible the messages he or she wishes to impart. The disadvantage with this method is that it frequently concentrates on the messages the trainer wishes to communicate and pays too little attention to what the trainees are capable of learning. It can usefully be supplemented by a whole range of visual aids, such as a slide projector, a flipchart and an overhead projector. Each of these assists the trainee to understand more easily the message being communicated.

Group discussion is a situation in which the tutor usually breaks the course into smaller groups and asks them to consider a specific subject. Real benefit can be obtained from this method as it assists the trainees to integrate effectively with one another and allows full trainee participation.

Syndicate work and case studies usually refer to a form of group discussion which has to consider a more formidable subject or problem. It will involve a significant amount of time away from the training room and will frequently require trainees to do some group and individual research. If the training course is residential, syndicate work is frequently given as an evening assignment. Case studies often have the additional benefit of providing the trainees with comparative data which can sometimes be extremely useful in developing analytical skills.

Role-playing involves the trainees trying out the behaviours they will be required to use, while away from the real situation. They are frequently used in interview and sales training, it is difficult to envisage sales training courses being effective without some form of role-playing. Trainees always show a degree of scepticism about the benefits of role-playing. Nevertheless, some form of feedback to a trainee is essential and frequently this is best done in a role-playing situation. The act of participation can help the trainee to see the behaviour and attitude displayed in an effective way. The trainer must then relate this to the work situation.

Video recording is used at times to supplement the role-playing exercises as it provides personal feedback. The situation is that the trainees are actually filmed while carrying out their interview or sales presentation and, as well as having the benefit of the feedback from the trainer, they can see themselves in action. Many trainees feel that this situation is somewhat threatening and do not like being exposed in this way. What is essentially true of role-playing in all its aspects is that it provides the trainees with feedback in relation to the behaviours they exhibit. In terms of our specific needs in marketing, to develop effective interpersonal skills for use in market research, sales or customer service, role-playing is an effective technique.

Films and video films are now available from many organizations. Some are extremely good and provide a very useful training aid. It should be remembered that watching a film is essentially a passive exercise, and it is important always to follow up the presentation of a film with some form of discussion so that people can learn to apply the behaviours illustrated in the film in the situation in which the trainer wishes them to be applied.

A training course which lasts for more than one day should endeavour to employ a range of the techniques mentioned above. It is important for trainers to remember that, for most people, attending training courses is an unusual experience. Breaking up the message and using different techniques to introduce it are effective means of ensuring that the trainees' attention is retained and ensuring that the messages are communicated in a memorable manner.

On-the-job training

Learning on the job has a great advantage over all other forms of training. There is, for example, no problem of the transfer of learning from the training situation to the real situation. The relationship between the training and the behaviours required on the job is recognizable and instant. There are unfortunately many significant disadvantages with training on the job although this is largely because managers will not devote the time and energy necessary to ensuring that training by this method is truly effective.

Training on the job will be effective if the trainer is on the spot and frequently sees the trainee in action. The trainer should also be holding regular feedback and coaching sessions. Ideally, the trainer should be an expert performer of the skill and have the sensitivity to be able to interact effectively with the trainee.

Perhaps most training should be carried out in this way. It is clear that most training *is* carried out in this way, although much of it is less than effective, largely because enough time and effort are not devoted to preparing the situation, which involves the trainee, trainer and the manager.

Planning an on-the-job training programme

Having said that most training is carried out via on-the-job instruction and having also indicated that much of it is ineffective, we need to look at how to make it more effective. In the first instance, the manager responsible should identify who is to be trained and in which particular tasks. The manager needs to have a clear idea of the performance standards the trainee is required to achieve at the end of the training programme. These can easily be translated into training objectives and the manager can then communicate these to both trainer and trainee. It is important to realize that training should not be a mystery tour but that trainees should always know in advance what it is they are setting out to achieve. Where possible, training objectives should always be set in behavioural terms. This means that when communicating an objective it should be possible to describe it in terms of the behaviour required. Standards of quality and quantity of work should be agreed between all concerned and monitored throughout the training period.

Training aids
It is essential for the instructor to have a clear understanding of the task to be trained before commencing the training. It is also important

that the instructor takes some time to rehearse the method of communicating the required training. The trainer should look for opportunities to introduce visual aids which will both highlight key points and increase the chances of full comprehension by the trainee. Aids, such as office equipment, marketing literature, product information, dummy files and so on are all readily available in most organizations.

Role-playing is another method which can be employed to improve the quality of training on the job. Informal sessions with the trainer playing a role and requiring the trainee to respond can be a very effective means of communicating, particularly in respect of customer relations training and interaction with other people. This can be done in an office or shop in a quiet period and does not always have to be done away from the job.

Guidelines on instruction

Preparation
Any instruction session is likely to be more successful if the trainer takes steps to ensure that the trainees:

1 are fully at ease;
2 know the objective for the training session;
3 are motivated to feel interested in the job or subject;
4 are able to ask questions and seek clarification at any stage;
5 are not given to understand that the job is either excessively simple or extremely complicated.

Presentation
The trainer should always begin by explaining what is to be done at each stage, and then actually doing it. The key points previously established will be stressd and will provide an opportunity for confirming that the trainee understands each step before progressing to the next.

Practice
If the planning, preparation and presentation have all been effective, the trainee should now be able to carry out the task. The opportunity to try out the new skills or behaviour learned should be given at each stage of the training. Understanding of key points should be verified

as the task is carried out and errors or deviations should be identified and corrected (in an encouraging manner) as they occur.

Most on-the-job training is inadequate because neither managers nor those they make responsible for training are prepared to devote the time necessary for proper preparation, presentation, practice by the trainee and feedback to the trainee. If the above guidelines are followed, on-the-job training will be consistently more effective in achieving the objectives set.

An increasingly popular technique is computer-based training (CBT), or computer-assisted learning. The two terms are essentially interchangeable. This method involves the trainee using a computer terminal which has been programmed with a series of training lessons. The trainee then interacts with the computer, responding to instructions and gradually building up a whole range of learning. A significant advantage of using this method is that trainees can learn at their own pace, make mistakes and go back over old ground as they wish. They have control over the learning period and the trainer has control over the amount of information that is communicated.

CBT is also valuable because it allows the trainee to get on with the training without being constantly overseen by a colleague or trainer. In many businesses this provides a significant advantage.

Interactive video is another method which is becoming increasingly popular. This involves the use of computer and video. It is based upon a laser video-disc player integrated with a microprocessor, thereby augmenting the computer's power with the impact of visual images and sound. The key to successful training of any kind is sustaining interest and maximizing understanding. Interactive video provides this range of approaches in one. This is an exciting development for the future and will be increasingly used by organizations wishing to provide effective training close to the job.

With both interactive video and computer-based training the important element is the program. It is absolutely essential that any trainer contemplating the introduction of either CBT or interactive video consider the software very carefully. Software can either be purchased from a range of organizations or written in house. Whichever route, or even mix of the two routes, the trainer chooses, he or she must ensure that the software is effective and communicates the messages he or she wishes to communicate. Authoring CBT and interactive video is very time-consuming for the trainer; it is therefore most effective when it can be applied to a wide range of trainees. It is essential in authoring to ensure that clear objectives for learning are set, that the trainer has a full understanding of the methods being used and of the task the training is being designed to teach. Much training in marketing skills lends itself ideally to this approach.

Self-development

It is increasingly recognized that people do not spend sufficient time considering their own personal development. Traditionally, we rely on other people to teach us, whether in school or college or at work. Too little effort has been demanded of most people in promoting their own personal development. As Pedler, Burgoyne and Boydell say, 'Most of us, if asked to think how we learned, think of our experiences in situations where attempts have been made to teach us' (Pedler *et al*, 1978). We need to think about when we have solved problems for ourselves, for problem-solving is to a large extent learning. Employees at all levels in any organization should be encouraged to take more responsibility for their own personal development, education and training. Personal development can lead to effective career development and advancement. It will certainly lead to individuals being more effective at the job they are required to do. For anyone aspiring to management, for any marketing professional or for any sales executive who really wishes to become more effective, self-development will be an important element in their plan for personal advancement and career satisfaction.

The means to encourage self-development are now becoming a primary concern in many training departments in leading organizations. Facilities are available where trainees can make use of a range of video, audio and reading materials, all of which are designed to assist personal development. From management's point of view, an exciting aspect of this whole approach to self-development is that people who truly undertake a programme of self-development are highly motivated to succeed, and managers are generally assured that the development will take place outside normal working hours. In implementing schemes of self-development, organizations need to ensure that they do not deny access to formal training procedures to those who are prepared to embark upon such schemes. Those who are prepared to devote the time and effort to self-development should be encouraged by active participation in all the formal approaches to training developed by the organization. Self-development should be seen to be rewarded effectively at all levels.

EVALUATING TRAINING

We need always to consider the importance of assessing and evaluating the training we are giving. There is only one real way of evaluating the effectiveness of training – how successfully the learning acquired from the training has been implemented in the working environment. Generally, training can be most effectively evaluated in three different ways.

1 *Immediate*: This relates to changes in knowledge, skill or behaviour at the end of a training course or particular session of training off the job. To do this we can establish pre- and post-course tests – we can ensure clear-cut training objectives are communicated both to the trainee and the trainer; we can set required performance standards and check whether our training has been successful in achieving those standards. If they are not being achieved, the method of training should be changed.

2 *Intermediate*: It is a fact of life that much of what we learn we tend to forget and therefore we need to assess training in an intermediate way. Over a period of time we need to ensure that the knowledge, skill and behaviour which have been learned are being put to use on the job. Once again, the manager must ensure that he or she is carrying out regular checks to evaluate performance. An important element of this will be the regular appraisal of staff. It is essential that the manager regularly assesses whether or not performance standards which have been learned via training are being attained on the job.

3 *Ultimate* This is the most difficult to measure. It refers to the long-term effectiveness of the individual, the unit and perhaps the organization. To be assured that training is really effective in the long term requires the co-operation and support of top management. Formal appraisal systems need to be effective and used regularly by managers, and also be available to top management

who can assess general performance. This method of evaluation also refers to the 'bottom line'. Training, particularly in relation to quality and service, can mean the difference between make or break for many companies.

It is important therefore for all managers to be aware of the means of evaluating the effectiveness of training. Regular checks should be made at all levels to ensure that money being spent on training is being used well and that the training being given is effective in bringing about the required standards of knowledge, skill and behaviour. While this is true for training in general, it is even more essential in marketing because of the immediacy of the potential impact on customers.

RESPONSIBILITY FOR TRAINING

The manager's role

Many managers believe that the responsibility for training lies with the training manager, or the training department of the organization for which they work. They are completely wrong. The responsibility for training lies with the managers, always the managers. It is the managers' responsibility to ensure that the departments they run are effective. Therefore it is their responsibility to ensure that their staff receive an adequate level of training. To assume that training is the responsibility of somebody else is a complete misconception of its importance. In any business the most important – and, incidentally, the most expensive – resource is the people. All managers worth their salt work very hard to ensure that all the resources they have at their command are working fully effectively. For example, how many managers would accept that the computer within their department could lie idle for many hours without doing something about it. Likewise, with the people they are responsible for, it is the manager's obligation to ensure that they are effective in doing their job; to ensure that they are trained to the required standard.

It is easy for managers to say they do not have the time for training, that there are always competing demands on their time. It is not sufficient for managers to reject their responsibilities; they must ensure that they find or make the time to ensure their staff are adequately trained.

The role of training department

The company may have a training department. A company of any size should certainly have one. The role of this department in providing staff training is to ensure that a framework is available for training to take place within the organization. In many organizations there will be a large number of people requiring similar levels of knowledge and skill and it will probably be more effective if their training is carried out via the training department. A professional training department can provide the means of analysing training needs, of ensuring that there is a consistent level of training throughout the organization and of providing new insights into the most appropriate methods of training. The training department, which should be close to and have a real understanding of the organization's business, can also provide useful insight into future developments, providing managers with the advice and assistance necessary to train their staff effectively.

Training departments can also make recommendations as to the feasibility of internal and external training. Where a training department is staffed by professional trainers, effective use of off-the-job training will always be available. They have the opportunity and responsibility for investigating new methods and techniques for training and for ensuring that employees are trained to the required performance standards. The relationship between the training department and departmental managers is important as training is essentially a service department, there to serve the needs of the departmental managers. It is essential that departmental managers feed back to the training department their requirements and their impressions of the effectiveness of training. Without this regular feedback, training departments can become isolated and unaware of the needs of the organization. Training departments have sometimes been accused of becoming academic ivory towers. This has frequently been due to the training manager not having sufficient support and access to senior management in the organization. Neither in these instances have the senior managers taken sufficient notice of training to ensure that it is closely related to the needs of the business. Training which is not related to the needs of the business is a waste of a significant investment: that which is fully part of the business, especially in the area of marketing and customer service, can make a real contribution to the success of the business.

In a business that is changing and developing in response to new competitive thrusts and market conditions, it is essential that the training manager is involved at an early stage in the strategic decision-making process, to make an effective assessment of the training requirements in relation to planned changes. Training which is always running to keep up with the business is not going to be effective. To be truly useful to an organization training needs to be ahead of the game at all times. Therefore, the involvement of a senior manager with responsibility for training at strategic decision-making levels is essential for the effective company of the future.

Generally speaking, in the UK the investment many organizations make in training has been less than adequate when compared with our principal competitors. This has been true at all levels from the most junior appointment to the most senior management. This must be corrected for the future. Nowhere is this more important than in the marketing function. Marketing represents our major contact with our customers and it is important therefore that the people who deal with our customers are aware of their needs and prepared to respond to them.

Effectiveness in relation to all aspects of training and development can be established only by carrying out constant reappraisals and investigations of the training need and provision. No organization can ever underestimate the importance of effective and continuous training, development and education for all its staff.

REFERENCES AND FURTHER READING

Argyle, M. (1972), *The Psychology of Interpersonal Behaviour*, Penguin, Harmondsworth.

Drucker, P. (1974), *Management Tasks, Responsibilities and Policies*, Heinemann, London.

Foster, D. (1982), *Mastering Marketing*, Macmillan, London.

Pedler, M., Burgoyne, J. and Boydell, T. (1978) *A Managers' Guide to Self Development*, McGraw-Hill, London.

Peters, T. and Austin, N. (1985), *A Passion for Excellence*, Collins, London.

Rackham, N. (1987), *Making Major Sales*, Gower, Aldershot.

Walker, H. (1986), *Marketing*, Pan, London.

ORGANIZATIONS

Institute of Marketing, Moor Hall, Cookham, Maidenhead, Berkshire SL6 9QH. Tel: 06285-24922.

CAM Foundation, Abford House, 15 Wilton Road, London SW1V 1NJ. Tel: 01-828 7506.

11

Sales management

Michael Wilson

THE JOB OF THE SALES MANAGER

The sales manager must first and foremost be a manager. Like other managers in the company he or she is responsible for getting things done, through other people, towards economic objectives. This simple definition has many implications.

'Getting things done' implies that the sales manager must be action-orientated and must be concerned with results rather than means. He or she will be judged by what is ultimately achieved rather than by the processes he or she manages. 'Through other people' suggests that the results will in fact, be achieved by others. The sales manager is not there to do their job for them although this is what far too many sales managers do. It is often easier to handle difficult customers personally than to develop a sales executive to cope with them. 'Towards economic objectives' means that the sales manager must constantly consider the financial implications of his or her actions.

The six basic functions of the sales manager

To fulfil his or her basic duty as a manager of the company, the sales manager must carry out six specific functions:

1   plan objectives and strategies for his or her team;

2 develop an organization structure capable of achieving the objectives;
3 recruit and select staff who can perform the jobs laid down in the organization structure;
4 train them in the further knowledge and skills required to perform the jobs;
5 motivate them to perform their jobs to the best of their abilities;
6 evaluate and control them to ensure the objectives are achieved.

Particular problems of sales management

In performing the six functions the peculiar difficulties of sales management must be recognized. Unlike any other body of staff in the company, the sales force is normally geographically well spread. Thus they cannot be supervised as closely as in other departments. This causes particular problems of motivation, communication and control for the sales manager and feelings of isolation for the sales executive.

Again, unlike other sections of the company the sales force spends the vast majority of its time with people other than company employees, usually, of course, with customers and propsects whose viewpoints are very different from those of the sales executive. This can cause attrition whereby the sales executive's attitudes and skills are worn down by the constant contact with opposing views. For example, it is difficult for a sales executive to maintain that his or her product has a particular advantage when buyer after buyer, month after month (whether correctly or not), says that it is not better than the competing products.

Furthermore, the kind of people who choose this isolated and wearing life are often, paradoxically, those least capable of coping with it. Those who choose selling as a career are normally gregarious individuals, yet the structure of the job ensures that they spend a minimal amount of time with their colleagues.

Need for leadership and training

Sales management must provide strong leadership and training to overcome the particular difficulties of the sales job. The training programme must be powerful enough to inculcate methods of working which will be followed despite the lack of close supervision. Training must also be continuous to counter the attrition of dealing with customers. The leadership shown by the sales manager must be clear and strong enough to support staff who are widely spread and whose nature requires a high level of social contact. Some of the problems can be eased by skilful organization, careful selection and attractive commission systems. However, the basic conditions of the sales job make it imperative that the sales manager places great emphasis on leading and training his or her team.

HOW TO PLAN THE SALES OPERATION

The sales manager will begin by considering the marketing objectives, policies and strategies and control criteria. He or she will probably have a forecast of sales by revenue and volume, a forecast of gross and net profit required, perhaps an expense budget ceiling, a description of the product range available with additions and deletions, price structure, promotional support and so forth.

Forecasting sales

In many companies the sales manager will be involved as a member of the marketing team in the definition of sales forecasts. The process will normally start by forecasting sales for the next period. This is the most critical prediction in the company as it will determine the production schedule, raw material and finished stocks, promotional expenditure and so on. It is best to approach the forecast in two stages. First, what will sales be, assuming all variables in the situation are the same in the future as they have been in the past? Second, which variables will change and what will the impact be? Some of the variables will be internal factors which management decides to change, others will be external factors which are uncontrollable by the company but whose effect must be predicted.

The sales forecast forms the hub of the sales manager's objectives. It will, of course influence and in turn be influenced by the plans he or she formulates. It also represents the heart of each individual sales executive's objective in that the total forecast should equal the summation of the individual sales targets.

Developing the sales plan

Having set the sales forecasts and targets, the manager must now consider how they will be achieved. In formulating objectives, obviously some thought will already have been given to the plan. After the plan is written it might well be necessary to reconsider the goals which have been previously identified.

Basically, the sales manager must ponder five questions.

1 What is to be sold?
2 To whom?
3 At what price?
4 By what methods?
5 At what cost-effectiveness?

In some of these areas, notably the product range and pricing structure, the sales manager may well have limited influence; they are often controlled by the marketing planning department, through a brand or product management structure. In respect of all five facets he or she will certainly have to consider the inputs from other parts of the business: what stocks will be available from production; what money is available from finance; what advertising and sales promotion support is planned and so on.

What is to be sold?

This is the product range definition, and here the sales manager can at least advise his or her marketing planning colleagues on the saleability of the various items in the range as well as new product requirements. From a sales management viewpoint he or she will have to decide whether the full range should be sold to everybody. In some capital equipment markets where the distributor has to make a heavy investment in stock it may not be in the interests of the company to supply dealers whose financial resources may be overreached if they purchased the more costly products. Likewise, companies which have to make after-sales service arrangements may well decide not to sell products to customers who are geographically isolated.

To whom?

The sales manager must next consider the customers and prospects for the company's products.

He or she will first study the existing markets and decide whether business with them is likely to increase, decrease or remain static. This judgement will be based on a study of previous buying records. By analysing customers in terms of their potential and actual purchasing of the various products the sales manager has to offer, the areas to be attacked can be identified. Prospective customers can be analysed in the same way.

By what methods?

Having identified from the product/market analysis the segments to be attacked, the sales manager can now consider the methods most likely to achieve the objectives set.

The main promotional tool is the sales force. The first question to be answered is: What sort of service should the sales force provide in order to influence the buyer? If, for example, the manager of a food firm has identified supermarkets as an area of great potential, this will lead him or her to consider how best to persuade supermarkets to buy more of the firm's products. The best way to approach any problem of selling to a distributive network is to consider what help the dealers need in order to sell the product; in this case, supermarkets will buy more only if they can sell more. One way of selling is to merchandise the product in store, so the sales manager may well organize the field force towards that objective. Obviously such a conclusion will have important implications for the selection, training, organization and control of the field force. The same thinking applies to companies in other industries. For example, a crop protection firm pondering how to increase sales to agricultural merchants will have to consider how the merchant will market the product to farmers. Perhaps the job of the sales force in this case will be to help the merchant develop his own marketing skills.

Even where distribution networks are not involved, the sales manager must still give thought to what service to provide to the buyer. For example, a packaging company must consider whether the buyer needs salesmen who are technical experts in the packaging itself, the packaging process and the machinery required, or the particular

194

packaging problems of individual industries. On the other hand, perhaps the salesman should be more of a design consultant or maybe have a high degree of financial knowledge so that he can discuss the cost-effectiveness of his products. Most important of all in selling packaging, the salesman will need an appreciation of his customers' own marketing problems. Thus the successful industrial salesman selling packaging to, say, a food company will certainly have an awareness of the problems of the food company selling to the retail trade; and, moreover, the retail trade's problems selling to the housewife.

Such an analysis of what kind of sales effort is needed will lead to identification of the sales methods that are appropriate. The complexity of seller/buyer relationships becomes rapidly obvious. It is only by such definition that the sales manager can develop the presentational approach that will enable him to succeed in the face of product/price parity.

Having identified the nature of the sales method he can then consider the scale of effort required. He must calculate how many customers and prospects should be called on how often. The customers are relatively easy to specify because they are known by name to the company. However, it may be uneconomic to have very small customers visited personally, except very seldom. The level of prospecting is more difficult to calculate as in many companies potential customers cannot be identified by name. At least, however, the sales manager can indicate the characteristics of likely prospects. Such a profile can then be used by the sales force to select prospects to be called upon. Alternatively, the sales manager can plan simply to allow a certain percentage of time or calls for the process of looking for new business, giving the salesman the responsibility of using the time or calls wisely.

How often calls should be made is always difficult to assess. Obviously different categories of accounts will require or demand different call frequencies. In some trades where there is an established buying frequency, usually little is gained by calling at a different frequency. For most companies, however, the call frequencies have to be decided by management and the best rule of thumb to follow is to call as infrequently as possible without jeopardising the business. Many companies over-call because they fear that if they are not on the customer's doorstep as often as possible they will lose business. It is worth while to experiment with call frequencies to see if slowing down the frequency does actually affect sales. Even marginal changes can have a dramatic impact on cost. If, for instance, a sales force is calling on average every four weeks and this could be altered to every five weeks, the company could possibly save up to 25 per cent of its sales costs.

The support of the field force will also be covered by the sales manager's study of the methods required to achieve his objectives. It is often the case that various parts of the supplier/buyer relationship can be more economically handled by techniques other than personal visiting by representatives. Telephone selling is one method that is successfully used to handle routine ordering, thus freeing the salesmen's costly time for more creative work. In the consumer goods trades, where point of sale display work is common, many firms have split their field forces into salesmen and merchandisers. In industrial selling, the sales force has often to be supported by technical staff who can advise more expertly on the product and its applications. In the computer market the salesman is usually backed by a team of experts who can advise the customer on systems design, programming and installation.

Furthermore, parts of the sales task may be better handled by other non-personal promotional techniques. For example, it may be more economic to generate prospects for a life assurance company by advertising and direct mail than by cold canvassing by the salesmen. Customer education in using the product may be better handled by producing films than by individual tuition from the salesman.

In other words, the sales manager's task in deciding the nature and scale of the methods necessary to achieve his objectives should not be limited to a simple consideration of how to deploy salesmen. His criteria for selecting techniques must not only be effectiveness and use of his sales force but also cost and use of total company resources. Obviously the majority of the effort will be through the sales force in most companies; this should not lead, however, to ignoring other possibilities.

At what cost – effectiveness?
The planning focus of most companies has been traditionally on growth, particularly profit growth coming naturally from sales volume or at least revenue increases. However the situation facing

Ratios	Comments
1 Sales: sales costs	What is the trend?
2 Sales per sales executive, explained by:	Are there big differences?
3 Number of customers/contacts per sales executive	Are there big differences?
4 Number of calls per day	Relationship to sales?
5 Face-to-face time: total time	Enough time with customers?
6 Orders: calls	Trends in 'strike rate'?
7 Average order value	Differences between sales executives?
8 Field sales costs: total sales costs	Too much 'indirect' cost?
9 Percentage of labour turnover	Is the sales force stable?
10 Most successful sales executive: average sales executive	Difference gives some indication of improvement potential

Figure 11.1   Assessing sales productivity: ten key ratios

many industries is one of stagnant, even declining markets, prices under pressure and most costs rising rapidly. In such circumstances the planning focus has to change from one of simple growth to a search for increased productivity.

Productivity is the measurement of the interrelationship between inputs and outputs, well acknowledged if not totally understood in production processes, but far less well explored in sales because of historic assumptions about year on year sales increases. Improving productivity isnot simply a question of cost reductiom, the dreaded 'head count' exercises for example. Paradoxically such efforts often actually reduce productivity as senior, highly paid sales management have to do the work left behind when junior, lower paid jobs are eliminated.

To analyse and subsequently to increase productivity there must be a clear understanding of what outputs are desired, what inputs are necessary and the nature of the relationship between the two in terms of causation (i.e. what effects result from what causes) and correlation (i.e. how much a change in input will affect the output). Typical desired sales outputs include volume, revenue, product range, mix, market share, gross margin, and net margin. The relative importance and achievability of these will of course vary from company to company and situation to situation. Thus a company which has traditionally sought volume increase may now have to concentrate on margin protection.

Sales inputs are characterized by the type of sales activity used (for example, field force, telesales, van sales), the number of sales personnel (both in the field and in the sales office) and the type of person employed (management:staff ratios, calibre, pay and so on).

There are so many different measures of sales productivity that a sequential approach is needed to concentrate management attention on the key figures and, what is more important, their underlying causes.

A good starting point is to measure the ratio of sales to sales cost. Sales will normally be taken as revenue, but should be analysed by volume, price and mix relative to target. Sales cost will usually include not only field force costs, but also the costs of the sales office, sales management, training etc. This overall measurement can be further analysed as shown in Figure 11.1.

198

Such quantitative assessments of current productivity will usually highlight areas for improvement and at the same time indicate the underlying causes which must be modified if results are to be improved. Furthermore, evaluating sales performance in this way forms a sound basis for the whole planning process.

Major customer planning

Mot companies' sales exhibit strong 80:20 tendencies, that is, a small percentage of large customers taking the bulk of the sales and vice versa. These major customers are so important that they require special planning attention from sales management and, usually, special handling.

In planning this important aspect of the business, the sales manager must first consider the maximum proportion of sales revenue the top customers should account for. One service company, for example, will not allow its top five accounts to represent more than 40 per cent of the sales revenue because above that level it considers itself too vulnerable. An industrial components company decided that no single market should account for more than 15 per cent of its output and that each market segment ideally should consist of no more than five organizations controlling 80 per cent of purchases. Of course, it is not always easy or even possible to control the customer/sales mix in this way, but it is a good start to have a sales policy on this important issue so that if and when major customers are predicted to become too dominant appropriate action can be taken, for example to broaden the customer or market base of the company.

Second, the profitability of business with major customers should be analysed as it is too facile to assume that because they produce most of the sales they must inevitably produce most of the profit. In fact, because large customers demand large discounts, tend to take longer credit, need more stock back-up, expect considerable promotional support and so on, the costs of servicing them are usually dispropor-tionately high. To analyse and control major customer profitability an increasing number of firms produce profit and loss accounts for each top customer. At first, these usually show to the horror of manage-ment that the principal customers produce much less profit than had been believed, and in many cases actually show a net loss. However, only by analysing performance in this detail can a realistic basis be laid for future planning and negotiation.

HOW TO ORGANIZE THE SALES FORCE

Many sales organizations have developed without regular, objective analysis of their purpose or structure. Today they are out of date and unable to fulfil the purposes for which they were originally designed. This is because the traditional hierarchical structure is based upon conditions which no longer hold true in a great number of firms. Such organizations assume that there is a large number of relatively small, geographically separate and independent buying points all with similar requirements, and that these can be serviced by a large number of geographically separated sales executives who can perform similar tasks and who represent the main promotional activity of the company.

Changes in buyer/seller relationships

These suppositions have been made obsolete by a number of fundamental changes in the buyer/seller relationship. First, as has been discussed, the buying power in many industries is no longer evenly distributed. In many markets a few big companies (either distributors or end-users) control the majority of the purchasing. Because of their buying power and importance it is not usually feasible to delegate sufficient responsibility and authority to the sales executive in whose territories they happen to be located. Furthermore, the large customers themselves are increasingly centralizing their purchasing so that branches or subsidiaries which might at one time have been direct customers for sales executives in different territories are no longer allowed to buy.

Second, the development of new marketing techniques has meant that some tasks traditionally performed by the sales force can be more economically or efficiently handled by other methods. The growing use of techniques such as telephone selling, contract ordering, broking, auxiliary or commando sales forces and even franchising is having a significant impact on the nature and scale of the field sales effort required.

It is evident that the sales manager must consider these influences in planning his or her organization. To fit the sales team to the needs of the customers the sales manager must identify:

1 the task of the sales force;
2 how many sales executives are needed;
3 how they should be organized;
4 how they can be managed;
5 how the sales force can be integrated with the rest of the company.

Task of the sales force

It is an oversimplification to say that the job of the sales force is to sell and therefore its members are salespeople. In many industries this is not true within the normal concept of the function – collecting an order. For example, the representative for a pharmaceutical house calling on doctors never takes an order. The grocery sales executive calling on branch stores of a multiple chain may not be able to take an order, as the store manager often does not have the authority to buy. The executive selling plant hire will only occasionally receive an order, when calling on a construction firm which happens to have an urgent need that day.

The sales force structure should also be scrutinized. A geographical split may be most economical in that travel time is minimized. It may not, however, be the most effective. In one glass container company it was seen that the prime service to be provided to the buyer was a technical knowledge of bottling as applied to the customer's particular industry. Thus the sales force was regrouped on an industry basis, changing the organization structure from its traditional geographic basis. Obviously there was some increase in travel costs because each industry group worked nationally but this was more than offset by the increase in sales.

Number of sales executives needed

Many sales managers can give no logical explanation of why the sales force is the size it happens to be. Even when explanations are forthcoming, such as that the sales force is based on population distribution, county boundaries or sales revenue per person, the rationale must still be in question. Such criteria often bear little relationship to the amount of sales effort required. Counties differ greatly in size; population density will seldom correlate directly with sales or potential. Even the assumption that each sales executive should be able to handle a specified amount of sales revenue is very suspect. Generating £100 000 of business in one part of the country can be far harder than it is in another. The amount of sales force effort required to handle 100 customers spending £10 each is likely to be far greater than servicing one account of £1000.

Sales force workload analysis

The aim of building an organization from the bottom up is to give the appropriate level of service to each customer and the appropriate amount of work to each person. The only common factor between sales executives is the number of working hours and this should be the starting point for a workload analysis, which is the only logical way of constructing a sales force. The amount of work per person can then be calculated by assessing the elements of the sales job. If a sophisticated approach is needed, work study and method analysis can be used to establish these elements and the time taken on each. Typically, they include prospecting, travelling, waiting, selling and writing reports. If the number of actual and potential accounts to be visited and the frequency of visiting can be assessed, it is possible to calculate the size of sales force needed (see Figure 11.2).

Territory organization

The organization of each sales executive's workload can now be considered to ensure the territory is covered as effectively as possible. Customers to be called upon have been identified, call frequencies have been set and call rates calculated. Using these three factors the territories can be built up to form appropriate workloads per person. How the workload is handled will have an impact on achievement and cost and, if left to their own devices, many sales executives will work in almost random fashion round the territory, 'territory' in this case

NUMBER OF ACTUAL AND POTENTIAL CUSTOMERS × CALL FREQUENCY
AVERAGE DAILY CALL RATE × NUMBER OF WORKING DAYS PER YEAR

Customer categories and call frequencies
Category A (over £50000 a year)   500 × 12 visits p.a. = 6000
Category B (£25000–£50000 a year)   2000 × 9 visits p.a. = 18000
Category C (£10000–£25000 a year)   5000 × 6 visits p.a. = 30000
Category D (under £10000 a year)   7000 × 2 visits p.a. = 14000
                                                Annual call total   68000

Average daily call rate = 8
Number of working days
    Total days in year   365
    Weekends   104
    Holidays   15
    Sickness   5
    Training   10
    Conferences   5
    Meetings   11   150
Number of working days   215
Call total per sales executive 215 × 8 = 1720

Number of sales executives required $= \dfrac{68000}{1720} = 40$

Figure 11.2   Calculating sales force size

implying a group of customers, not necessarily a discrete geographical area, so the comments are applicable to industry-based territories as well as geographical areas. Some will tend to call more frequently than is necessary on customers near to home and will ignore accounts in distant parts of their areas. Others, particularly industrial sales executives, may give too much attention to customers whom they find technically interesting or from whom they get a pleasant reception rather than allocating their time in accordance with sales potential. The prime aim of territory organization analysis is to maximize selling time by minimizing travel time in particular.

How the sales force should be managed

Having assessed the nature and scale of sales force required, the type and number of managers needed can be decided. Again, following the basic concept of looking at the organization from the bottom up, the first question to be answered is: How many sales executives can the first-line manager manage?

Organizational theorists have long pondered this problem and arrived at different answers by a variety of techniques. Generally, their views range between four and eight to a manager. Because of the variety of different managerial situations, any generalization may well be highly inaccurate and therefore it is more sensible to approach the question by assessing the workload to be handled. There are four principal elements that should be considered.

1 The division of responsibility between line field management and other company staff. For example, how much responsibility and therefore how much time does the field manager need to spend on recruitment, sales promotion, market research and the like? What staff support is available from other departments? How much time must the manager spend in meetings other than with his or her own staff?

2 The nature of the sales task to be supervised. Different sales jobs require different degrees of involvement by the manager. For example, a pioneer sales force is likely to need far more time from the manager than a routine order-taking team.

3 The amount of personal selling undertaken by the manager. Some industries demand a large amount of personal sales time from the manager, operating either alone or as part of a sales team. It is common practice, for instance, in capital equipment selling for the manager to lead a team on important sales projects.

4 The degree to which field training is necessary. This will depend on the type of sales executive and the sales activity as well as on the seniority of the people concerned. A recently recruited speciality sales executive – say, in office equipment – is likely to need far more field training than a senior van sales executive who has long experience of the job. However, because of the attrition process all salespeople undergo, some field training is necessary in virtually every situation.

How the sales force can be integrated within the company

For the sales force to function efficiently it must be viewed as an integral part of the total company effort. To achieve this there must be a clear concept of the role of the sales force in the total communication process with the marketplace. In far too many companies the various promotional tactics are seen as separate units. Thus it happens that the first time the sales force hears about a product modification (which they should be using to sell with) is when a customer comments on it. Even more important is the relationship between the sales force, which is basically an implementational weapon, and the marketing planners. Unless great care is exercised, particularly in companies with product management structures, the sales organization is continuously torn between different brand objectives and plans.

The best way to overcome these difficulties is to involve sales management in the marketing planning process and for the marketing plan to be the basic operating document for everybody in marketing.

HOW TO STAFF THE SALES ORGANIZATION

Sales performance factors

The performance of a sales executive will depend upon three basic factors: innate character traits, training and motivation. The objective of the staffing process is to choose people whose inborn characteristics are suited to the sales job and who can then be developed and motivated. Obviously there are some individuals whose intrinsic personalities are such that little or no training or incentives are required. These are the 'born' salespeople. However, they tend to be few and far between and gravitate towards those industries where their outstanding sales skills are directly rewarded by high commission rates, such as life assurance, office equipment and other forms of speciality selling.

Most sales managers must plan not only to pick staff with the appropriate characteristics but also to train and motivate them. To choose good sales staff, it is necessary to understand some basic concepts of the staffing process and to have a system for handling recruitment and selection.

Basic concepts of staffing

A sales manager needing to recruit somebody new is faced with a predictive problem. How will a person the manager knows little about perform in a job that person knows little about? By some means the manager must match the one with the other, and the failure to achieve congruence causes many of the staff problems in the industry. The manager must therefore appreciate that he or she is not simply looking for a 'good' person, but someone who is appropriate for a particular job: a case of trying to pick horses for courses.

The first stage in the process will be to define carefully the job to be performed. From the organization study that has already been conducted, the general framework of the position will have been delineated. Now it can be specified in the form of a written job description.

From this document the manager can identify the characteristics a successful incumbent would possess, and thus construct a profile.

These two statements contain the criteria against which candidates will be assessed and present incumbents appraised. If new people are required, applications can now be generated by recruitment techniques using one or more sources such as internal staff, newspaper advertising, consultants and so on. To begin to assess applicants, the manager must first gather information about them and, second, have some methods for evaluating and checking these data.

Whenever a prediction must be made of how someone will perform in the future, it is wise to examine in depth what that person has done in the past. Psychological research indicates that in terms of basic behavioural patterns, people do not change very much particularly after the age of maturity. (In fact some psychologists argue that fundamental personality patterns are settled by the age of seven. As most salespeople are well over this age, the precise data does not really matter.) The selection process is therefore concerned with collecting detailed information about the applicant from as far back as possible, verifying that the facts are as stated and then analysing them to identify repetitive behavioural traits.

The techniques which can be used for this collection, verification and analysis process are the application form, psychological tests, reference checking, the structured interview and the placement analysis.

There are eight steps in a systematic staffing procedure:

1 writing the job description;

2   constructing the profile;
3   recruiting candidates;
4   assessing application forms;
5   checking references;
6   psychological testing;
7   structured interviewing;
8   evaluating and placing successful candidates.

HOW TO DEVELOP JOB SKILLS

Planning skill development

The art of selling is the presentation of product benefits in such a way that buyers are persuaded that their needs will be satisfied. To be successful the sales executive must not only be knowledgeable about the product and the customer but also skilful in the presentation of this knowledge. Otherwise, the most knowledgeable people would be the most successful at selling. Increasingly, companies are discovering the lack of correlation between technical knowledge and sales results. For example, for many years it was traditional in the drug industry to employ pharmacists, rather than salespeople, to call on doctors. Both here and in general, an increasing number of companies are finding that staff who are basically salespeople tend to be more successful. Obviously they must be given some technical training but the emphasis is now firmly on the sales aspects of the job.

The training programme must aim to achieve the objectives of giving knowledge and developing skills. The nature and scale of both areas should be specified in advance so that the programme can be directed towards definite goals.

Setting development objectives

This should be approached by identifying the gap between the level of performance expected of the sales force and its current standards. The desired level of achievement can be defined by analysing job requirements of the job specification. For example, if it is noted in the job description that a sales executive will make presentations at trade conferences or be responsible for in store promotions, the

Extracts from typical job descriptions	Knowledge requirement (What do they need to know?)	Skill requirement (What do they need to do?)
In conjunction with his or her area manager, set targets by product group	Customer records Prospect records Market information Sales forecasting technique	Ability to analyse statistics, derive trends and identify opportunities
Must be fully knowledgeable about the products and their applications	Product features and applications in customer circumstances	Ability to relate product features to customer needs Ability to find and interest new customers
Must achieve the targets agreed by obtaining orders from existing customers and prospects	Prospecting techniques Preparation techniques Sales interview techniques	Presentational skills Communication skills Persuasion skills
Must handle all customer queries and complaints	Objection-handling techniques Complaint-handling procedures	Communication skills particularly with irate customers
Must represent the company at trade shows and exhibitions and make presentations when called upon to do so	General company history and background	Public speaking Visual aids
Must monitor and report on competitive activity and state of trade in his or her area	Market research techniques Information sources	Ability to ask fact-finding questions and analyse answers Report-writing
Must ensure the company's products are displayed to best advantage	Merchandising techniques In-store promotions schemes	Display-building Selling merchandising ideas

Figure 11.3   Knowledge and skill requirements analysis

development programme must include training in public speaking and merchandising. Figure 11.3 shows extracts from typical job descriptions and the knowledge and skills required to fulfil the defined tasks. The individual goals of particular parts of the training programme can be derived from this.

Importance of field training

The most important area of sales force development is the continuous field training process. This is normally undertaken by the sales manager concerned. It is difficult to delegate because it is interwoven with other aspects of the management function, such as control and appraisal. Some companies, however, do use a field trainer system. For it to be successful, the division of responsibility and authority between manager and trainer must be carefully defined, otherwise the salespeople will become confused about what guidance to take from whom. Too often, the system is introduced for the wrong reasons – to create a promotion opportunity for senior sales staff or to reward an old company servant who lacks real management potential. If the importance of field training is recognized and seen as an integral part of the sales management function, the need for field trainers seldom arises. Where the volume of field training seems to be beyond the line management capability, the first areas to be examined should be the organization structure and spans of control.

HOW TO MOTIVATE THE SALES FORCE

The motivation of their sales staff is probably the most common topic of conversation whenever sales managers meet. All managers have their own pet theories on how to get the best out of people. The reason why it is such a popular discussion point is because sales staff can be directly supervised only intermittently. It is therefore vital to succes that they are deeply motivated to work on their own. Moreover, the nature of the sales job inevitably involves loneliness and certain customer contacts which can depress the morale of any but the most enthusiastic of sales people.

Because of the geographical separation and the wearing aspects of the job, it is vital for success that sales managers possess or develop the ability to motivate their staff. To do so they need a clear understanding of why people work and what they wish to gain from their work. Only then can they create an environment which will cause their staff to employ their full abilities in their jobs.

Incentives and disincentives

Motivation involves providing incentives which encourage salespeople to give of their best, and removing disincentives which prevent them from devoting their whole energies to their work. Unfortunately, far too often, motivation is equated with incentives only, although it is common to find that the elimination of disincentives – for example injustices, unfair treatment – is the more powerful influence.

It must also be recognized that virtually every incentive brings with it a disincentive, either for the same personal or for his or her colleagues. For example, while a commission system may provide a strong incentive for a sales executive, it may also be a disincentive if he or she feels the payments are unfairly calculated. Likewise, a competition may be a strong motivator for the winners, but it can be demoralizing for the losers, particularly if they believe that because of the construction of the contest they had no real chance of winning.

The task of managers if therefore to consider the needs of their staff both individually and as a group, and to arrange a balance of motivational influences that will encourage them to achieve the company's objectives. In essence, this is best done by ensuring that an individual's own goals in life are consistent with the company's aims. For example, there is little point in recruiting people who are highly motivated by money into a company which offers security as its major satisfaction. Similarly, if the company pays commission as a standard percentage of all turnover achieved, it can hardly complain when the salespeople concentrate on those products which are easiest to sell in volume although they may be the least profitable.

Perhaps the most amusing contradiction is those managers who bemoan the decline of company loyalty as a motivational influence while regularly poaching staff from their competitors.

Although recognizing that everyone has an individual need pattern, there are five main motivational influences the sales manager must fully understand. These are:

1   remuneration;
2   direct incentives;
3   job satisfaction;
4   security;
5   status.

Remuneration

Remuneration and its effect on motivation are a vast and complex subject. Little research has been done, particularly in Britain, into the effects of different forms of payment systems. Nevertheless, certain principles can be identified.

1 That pay, although important, is certainly not the only and may not be the prime motivational influence.
2 That most companies will have to pay at least in part by salary and that salaries should depend upon an assessment of the grade for the job and an appraisal of the employee in order to position him or her within the grade.
3 That where it is possible to pay in part by results, this will have a beneficial effect and lead to the achievement of better sales results; but that certain preconditions must be met to administer commission schemes successfully.
4 That the commission system likely to be most effective is payment on the basis of turnover, probably because it is the easiest to understand.

Direct incentives

This is the term used to cover all the many systems of payment in cash or in kind other than basic remuneration. It includes fringe benefits, merchandise awards, point schemes and competitions. Apart from fringe benefits such schemes do not usually make a significant difference to total earnings and their basic intention is motivational.

Use of direct incentives
Merchandise awards and competitive schemes are best used to focus short-term attention on particular aspects of the business. They are a tactical rather than a strategic motivational weapon. When employed in this way, they can be very effective to concentrate sales force attention on, for example, gaining new accounts, increasing sales of lower volume products, or even submitting call reports on time.

Job satisfaction

In most surveys of salespeople's attitudes job satisfaction is rated as the highest motivating influence. It certainly appears that in an affluent society where at this level, at least, there is little or no unemployment, the major reason a sales executive chooses and remains in a company is because he or she finds the work enjoyable and fulfilling. It is therefore, at least in part, the responsibility of the manager to create a satisfying environment.

As we mentioned earlier, however, everyone has a particular need pattern and, therefore, what constitutes job satisfaction will vary from individual to individual. Some enjoy achieving perfection in the detail of their work, others are motivated by the opportunities of working with a wide cross-section of people. Many different satisfactions can be gained from similar jobs and the manager should emphasize particular aspects for each individual. Likewise, what one finds enjoyable, another dislikes. Again, the incentive/disincentive equation must be handled by management with some care.

Job satisfaction is the most important motivating force for most salespeople. Although each individual has his or her own concept of what is required from his or her career, certain common factors are found. For a position to be satisfying:

1   it must be perceived by the individual as being worthwhile to him or herself, the company and society;
2   there must be clear and challenging goals with regular feedback of results;
3   it must contain a body of knowledge and skills which the individual is given the opportunity to learn;
4   there must be an opportunity for at least some employees to progress either to management or to more important sales tasks;
5   the efforts made by the individual must be recognized and appreciated by his or her superior.

Security

The need for security is a common if seldom admitted motive. The nature of the remuneration system and the relative importance of salary and commission will obviously affect job security and must be considered from this aspect.

However, the less obvious facets of security should not escape the sales manager's attention. First, the degree of security the company wishes to offer must be identified. If the salespeople's jobs are too secure there is a danger that the sales force will stagnate. On the other hand, a high level of insecurity normally leads to high staff turnover and although a great deal of activity might be generated, it is doubtful whether much of it will be purposeful. In companies where insecurity is a constant feature of the environment, morale tends to be low and although there is often an appearance of frenetic action, achievement is usually very limited.

Status

The social status of selling has already been mentioned in the earlier discussions on job satisfaction. By explaining the social worth of the sales function, the manager will also be upgrading its position in society. The manager can also help to improve its status within the company and the market by ensuring that the job titles given carry as much prestige as possible without going to the extremes of 'regional sales director'. The manager should also ensure that the rest of the company realizes the importance of the function so that when a customer telephones and asks for a field sales executive by name, the switchboard operator does not use descriptions such as 'only one of our sales reps' (or, worse still, 'travellers'), when he or she is not in the office. Likewise, when put through to the sales department, the caller should be greeted by someone who says he or she is that sales executive's secretary or assistant. He or she can, of course, adopt a similar role for a number of other salespeople as well.

Identifying motivational influence and planning motivational schemes

Motivation is the business of management. 'Getting things done, through other people, towards economic objectives' implies quite rightly a leadership function.

The sales manager's motivational task starts with setting the job specifications and salary grades of the sales force. In formulating these, he or she will begin to set the framework of motivational satisfactions the company can offer to help achieve its objectives. It is extremely important that conscious thought is given to ensure compatibility between the goals of the firm and those of its employees.

213

Regular objective checking of the level of motivation is thus a wise precaution, particularly in those companies whose sales forces are widespread and have insufficient contact with each other and even with their management. Opinion polls can give a sound basis, particularly in such circumstances, for positive and visible managerial action.

HOW TO CONTROL THE SALES OPERATION

In order to control any activity, there must first be objectives and a plan. Unless it is known what is to be achieved and how, whether it is being achieved cannot be assessed. Conversely, there is little point in setting goals and defining actions unless there is an evaluation procedure.

Management by exception

The problem facing all managers is that they have to achieve results from resources which are scarce. They have only a limited amount of manpower, money and facilities. In particular, they have the most severe constrictions on their own time because although other resources can be expanded where necessary, the number of hours in the day cannot. It is essential, therefore, that their time is used efficiently. One of the prime methods for ensuring this is to devote time only to those parts of the business which are not running according to plan.

The analysis of facets which are not up to standard implies a control system which indicates such variances. This whole process is known as 'management by exception' and can be operated wherever a control mechanism of this kind has been constructed. For example, if the standards set are costs, the result is a standard costing system; if they are budgets, a budgetary control system. To operate such control systems in this way requires that:

1　standards are set;
2　actual information is collected;
3　variances are produced and analysed;
4　corrective action is taken.

214

Setting standards of field performance

To identify appropriate standards for control, managers should ask two questions.

1 What constitutes success?
2 What affects the achievement of success?

Absolute standards

In a sales operation success can usually be defined as the achievement of the sales targets. These serve as the prime standards of control. By themselves, however, they are insufficient. The achievement or otherwise of the annual sales target constitutes an absolute standard. It measures what has happened but it is then usually far too late to redress the balance. Moreover, it does not indicate why the performance has been poor. In a sense it is analogous to the oil pressure warning light on a car. When it glows it indicates that the pressure has fallen below the level necessary for efficient engine operation. It registers this fact after the event has taken place. If the car is being driven at high speed on a motorway, by the time correct action has been taken, damage may well have occurred. Even if that is avoided, the motorist will still not know why his or her oil pressure has decreased.

Diagnostic standards

Diagnostic standards, which help to identify why performance is varying from target are defined by asking the second question: What affects the achievement of success?

In the case of a particular sales executive failing to achieve target, the manager must consider the actions that individual takes which should lead to the goals being met. Surprisingly, there are only four, and these can be identified by the following questions.

1 What kind of people does he or she call on?
2 How many does he or she call on?
3 How often does he or she call?
4 What does he or she do while there?

The construction of standards is the essential first element in the sales force control system. To ensure that appropriate standards have been set, the sales manager should check that they satisfy five criteria.

1 That they are quantitative wherever possible so that variances can be measured.
2 That they cover what the sales force is supposed to achieve.
3 That they measure how the sales force is progressing and help to predict the likely outcome.
4 That they help to diagnose the reasons for sales performance.
5 That they identify likely variances sufficiently early to enable corrective action to be taken.

The secret of effective control is the definition of appropriate quantitative standards. Without them, control is virtually impossible. With them, the manager's task is dramatically simplified and significant amounts of time are saved.

Collection of information

Details of actual performance must be collected so that they can be compared against standards. The better the definition of the standards, the clearer the specification of the information required. Every manager complains about the ever-increasing volume of paper work, facts and figures that has to be handled. One of the main reasons for the explosive growth of available information is that the ability to collect and process data has generally outstripped the skills to use it. In a frantic attempt to gain some form of control management calls for more and more analyses and because of the sheer quantity of available information, believes that it thus has a grip on the situation. Nothing could be further from the truth.

Criteria for information collection

The information collection process should not be started until a clear set of standards is defined. Otherwise, faced with a lack of definition of what should happen, the manager has to search through thousands of facts on what has happened and must somehow arrive at a judgement as to the corrective action needed. The development of electronic data processing has simply worsened the situation because it has improved information capture and processing. Paradoxically, computers are best used as a tool of managerial control when they give the minimum information, not the maximum available data. Once the maximum available data. Once standards have been defined, the computer can be readily used to run a management by exception system pointing out only the variances from plan for management to take corrective action.

Variance production and analysis

Variances are produced by comparing actual results against the pre-set standards. However, this simple method may need to be refined as high variances may result which reflect the forecast error of the standards. For example, although the average daily call rate is set at eight, there is probably no cause for alarm if this varies between six and ten. Because so many of the standards are produced by averaging past performance, it may well be necessary to process the actual results before comparing them against standard.

Taking corrective action

Having identified the true nature of the variance, the sales manager has to decide whether it results from faulty standard setting or inadequate performance. If the former, the standards will have to be modified. If the latter, the performance of the individual will have to be improved, usually by some form of training or instruction. If the individual is to improve, he or she must be given specific targets to achieve within specific time periods otherwise little or no change will result.

If the individual fails to improve and the manager is certain that the standards are correct, and that the appropriate legal procedures have been followed, there is no choice but to transfer him or her from the sales force or, more likely, terminate the employment with the company.

Management responsibility for corrective action

Sales managers must not shirk this fundamental responsibility although it can be extremely distressing to have to dismiss someone who may have been with the company for some years and whom a

217

manager has come to know well. It is almost axiomatic that the worst personnel problems are found in those companies which have tried to pretend that the failures would improve . . . somehow, some time. Sales managers can be absolutely certain that staff difficulties of this nature can only get worse.

Sales managers must realize that there are four aspects to this basic responsibility. First, they are charged by the company to achieve financial objectives. Second, they have a responsibility to themselves to fulfil their tasks as managers. Third, they have a duty to the other members of their teams to ensure their efforts are not dragged down by retaining below-standard performers. Fourth, and most important of all, they have a critical responsibility to the individual to tell him or her as soon as he or she cannot achieve the standards demanded by the company. No one can be happy in a job he or she knows he or she cannot do. The sooner that individual finds a position where his or her talents can be utilized, the better for all concerned. A company is never more culpable than when it retains someone, who is palpably incapable of achieving the desired levels of performance, for so many years that he or she becomes virtually unemployable when eventually asked to leave. Management cowardice or, at best, *laissez-faire* is one of the worst failings companies ever exhibit. Ruthlessness, para-doxically, is often the kindest and fairest attitude that a firm can adopt.

CONCLUSION

The nature of sales management has changed dramatically in the last two or three decades; in many firms even the last few years have seen a complete reorientation of the function. As markets become increas-ingly international, this process of change will not simply continue; it will accelerate as the margins of error become even finer. No longer will finger-in-the-wind management be precise enough to generate profits.

Sales management in particular and marketing management in general must become more professional and more scientific to survive in the future. The great barrier to progress at the moment is the lack of proven theory. To overcome this hurdle, sales managers must be managers must be prepared to hypothesize about better operating methods, not simply perpetuate techniques because they are traditionally accepted. They must experiment with innovative approaches and, most important of all, must attempt to validate their hypotheses by rigorous assessment.

FURTHER READING

Forsyth, P. (1980), *Running an Effective Sales Office*, Gower, Aldershot.

Lidstone, J. B. J. (1986), *Training Salesmen on the Job*, 2nd edn, Gower, Aldershot.

Lidstone, J. B. J. (1978), *Motivating your Sales Force*, Gower, Aldershot.

Lidstone, J. B. J. (1983), *How to Recruit and Select Successful Salesmen*, 2nd edn, Gower, Aldershot.

Melkman, A. V. (1979), *How to Handle Major Customers Profitably*, Gower, Aldershot.

Wilson, M. T. (1983), *Managing a Sales Force*, 2nd edn, Gower, Aldershot.

12

Brand management

Jack Bureau

This chapter looks at the role of brand management as a management discipline.

The discipline is examined under six headings.

1 The need to manage revenue.
2 Revenue sources: brands, product ranges, markets or customers.
3 Key revenue management functions.
4 Planning revenue management: strategy.
5 Planning revenue management: operational planning and control.
6 Brand management, past, present and future.

An analysis of the way business is traditionally undertaken in organizations which do not use brand managers identifies the need for such a role. Such a need is established whether or not the business is brand-based: the case is made as a need to manage revenue. The heterogeneity of revenue sources is identified as the key factor which determines marketing planning boundaries: it is not sensible to attempt to plan two or more distinctly separate marketplace entities. Each requires individual attention from the marketing function. The chapter looks at the planning requirements for such entities, both for the long term (strategy) and the short term (operational). Finally, the chapter examines the objections which have been raised to the brand management function, and forecasts its growth as a discipline in the future.

THE NEED TO MANAGE REVENUE

Revenue may be defined as the money the organization earns in the process of selling its products or services. The heart of all business lies in its capacity to earn revenue – at a profit. The heart of the system known as brand management lies in the concept that revenue earning requires to be managed in just the same way as every other element of the organization. Such a statement may seem to be so obvious as to verge on the fatuous, and yet the practice of truly managing revenue is not at all widespread in Britain. At the birth of every business venture there is – of course – an immediately recognized need for some means of selling the product in order to generate revenue. Thus the selling function, and with it the sales executive, is always seen as the first means of generating revenue. As they are the means of generating the revenue, they are also frequently seen as being responsible for managing it.

Many organizations, having created the sales force, take no further steps to develop their revenue-managing skills, but rely solely on the skills of the sales force to sustain pressure in the marketplace to maintain the flow of orders. For such organizations, the sales force is seen as the only system necessary to manage and obtain revenue.

As the years go by, these organizations come to recognize, of course, that a large number of marketing tools other than the sales force is available to support revenue earning. To produce further pressure in the marketplace the business organization may come to realize that 'marketing' will involve other activities necessary to provide the sales force with the support it needs to ensure the achievement of the forecasted revenue.

Thus, from the simple first step of creating a selling function to generate revenue may grow a large body of specialists and experts who can provide the sales force with a body of help, guidance and expertise in the business of winning orders.

With a fairly complex structure of salespeople, advertising experts, public relations specialists, market researchers, merchandising and promotions operators, the marketing activities of the organization are now a good deal more comprehensive and sophisticated than they were before, when 'marketing' really amounted only to selling. However, even with this level of sophistication, some fundamental problems relating to revenue management still exist.

221

The process of co-ordinating each of these marketing activities – sales, marketing research, advertising, merchandising and sales promotion, public relations and so on – now assumes considerable proportions, and begins to take up more and more of the time of the head of these marketing functions. Under such circumstances, heads of marketing find themselves concentrating on the fire-fighting problems involved in the day-to-day business of administration, at the expense of planning the medium and the long-term future of the products. (Occasionally companies resolve this problem by dividing the functions of selling and 'marketing'. In these organizations you may find a sales director and a marketing director on the company's board, each responsible for just a part of the total marketing function.)

All but one of the marketing tools which contribute to the overall success of the company's products in the marketplace are now professionally managed. The one which is not is, however, the most important in the whole marketing process: the product itself. Unless it is undertaken by the head of the marketing function, no one else will feel the responsibility to undertake the planning of the market position of each product.

Each marketing specialist now has the responsibility of undertaking the detailed planning for his or her specialist activities across the full range of products: no one exists to undertake the full range of planning activities for each of the products individually. If the product requires substantial reassessment because, for example, it has problems in the marketplace; because the way the product is made or presented is in need of re-examination; because the price is wrong; because its general consumer acceptance requires examination, or is found to be declining, then there is no one who is actually paid to resolve such problems. In the marketing department structure under discussion, there is no one who is expected to review each product in terms of its total effectiveness in the marketplace, choreographing total marketing activity in the marketplace, masterminding all the marketing forces the company can bring to bear in order to maximize the success of the product.

It can be said, of course, that such a co-ordinative function already exists in as much as it is the primary function of the marketing director. Such a responsibility might even be considered to reside in

222

the boardroom – even in the person of the chief executive – since full co-ordination of the revenue-earning powers of the organization must be of the utmost importance to the survival of the organization and, thus, be a principal topic for boardroom decisions.

While the logic of this argument is persuasive, the most cursory examination of the amount of work involved in revenue management will make clear that it cannot be managed either by a single person or by a committee.

For most organizations, the work involved in revenue management makes it a full-time job for at least one individual, and frequently for more than one, and the pressing nature of the problems which need to be solved will require their continuous attention. In any case the members of the boardroom should not initially concern themselves with the wealth of small detail inevitable in the planning stages of revenue management.

Once an organization has perceived the logic of these arguments, it will recognize that one of the elements crucial to the continuing success of the organization – the health of its product in the market-place – requires close and continuous planning to maximize the probabilities that the product achieves maximum revenue at the maximum level of profitability.

The overwhelming majority of organizations earn their revenue from a wide spread of products and services, in a wide spread of markets, to widely different segments of the buying population. It really does not make sense for such organizations to work on the principle that revenue management can be effectively achieved by taking decisions about price, product, distribution or promotion across the full range of the organization's products, as if the market-place were homogeneous, and as if decisions taken for one product were necessarily relevant to decisions about any of the others.

Unless the organization produces one offering in the market, and only one, selling to one group of customers, having one set of pricing, promotion, place and product problems, there is a clear and profitable case to support the concept that revenue management must be undertaken at the single product level: even the smallest organization must recognize the segmented nature of its revenue-earning activities and the heterogenous nature of its marketing problems.

Recognition of this logic led the leading American consumer goods corporations to move, in the 1930s, 1940s and 1950s, to the revenue-management, product-by-product approach embodied in the brand management concept, in which each revenue-earning product or service which is identifiably different – as to its marketing problems and opportunities – is recognized as in need of individual revenue-management attention.

It was quickly recognized that such a need could not be fulfilled by giving the task to the people in the disciplines which already existed – salespeople, market researchers, PR or advertising personnel: clearly, they already had their hands full, managing their own specialisms.

The obvious next step was to create a new profession: that of the product manager, the brand manager and the marketing manager. To them were given clearly defined responsibilities, clearly delineated methods of operation and clearly organized reporting and control systems in which to operate.

The definition of their responsibilities turned out to be a good deal simpler than the enactment of the system. In common with most radical changes in the way the organization works, the introduction of this new revenue-management concept, and of the new marketing planners necessary to make it work, created managerial problems. A number of companies introducing the new system reported grave dissatisfaction with its outcomes and gave the system up. A number of such failures received considerable publicity, and a good deal of doubt was subsequently attached to the whole concept of product management. However, with the development of a body of experience associated with the use of this new management technique, managing the organizational problems it creates has become routine: the fundamental problems have been solved.

REVENUE SOURCES

While the principle central to the philosophy of brand management seems logically inescapable – that revenue requires managing and that it must be managed product by product – the ability of organizations to 'lump' their revenue into entities that are meaningful in the marketplace varies considerably. At one end of the continuum lie the consumer goods companies whose market offerings are in clearly unique brands, recognizable as such by producer, distributor and consumer. At the other end of this continuum lie the multitude of companies whose products are not at all clearly distinguishable in this manner, and which are certainly not branded. Producers of raw materials, machinery, maintenance services, insurance policies, security services, suppliers who work exclusively in supplying original equipment manufacturers: the list of items which are less easy to parcel into revenue-manageable portions is endless. It is important, of course, to distinguish here between the problems which arise out of the nature of the market and those which exist because of the (relative) marketing backwardness of the participants.

There was a time when a great many more produts than is the case today were sold as commodities because of a marketing failure among the producers: consumers were in the habit of seeking the generic product rather than any one manufacturer's brand. For example, in the 1920s and 1930s the consumer sought oranges but not Jaffa oranges, raisins and sultanas but not Whitworth's, wallpaper paste was home-made and gave no revenue to the Polycell brand. Many products today continue to sell in the marketplace without any of them – in a marketing sense – 'belonging' to any one producer. There may be a variety of good reasons why this should be the case: more often the reason lies in the marketing backwardness of the producers and distributors operating in these markets. The list of markets which continue to be very largely undifferentiated in this way is surprisingly large: the market for petrol, for household linen (to use an old-fashioned but useful categorization), for a great deal of furniture, for most vegetables, for virtually all meat and fish, and so on. It is not that no 'branding' occurs in these markets, it is rather that such activity appears to be either limited or largely unsuccessful. These markets – and many others – remain determinedly 'commodity' markets and reflect market opportunities that have yet to be seized. It would be a brave man who asserted that such failures are due to any incompetence in applying the revenue-management principles being outlined, but it would be a foolish man who refused to recognize the connection between the practice of revenue management and the establishment of a clear product identity in the marketplace. By its very nature, revenue management abhors a commodity market, as it abhors the economist's construct of perfect competition – and for the same reason: both speak of a supplier's inability to apply some controlling element to the environment in which he or she operates.

And from this it follows that both show a higher propensity for market failure, lower levels of profitability and more uncertainty in employment.

While we may accept that many organizations fail to establish any clear identity for their market offerings because of marketing backwardness, it is now necessary to look at those which have difficulty in so doing for quite different reasons. A number of categories suggest themselves.

1 For the engineering workshop which handles everything on a one-off basis, every element of the revenue it earns is unique, tailor-made, individually costed and may never again be repeated. Marketing control systems of revenue management will not fit easily into such an organization, working in such a way.

2 Many organizations see the market segment or the customer as more dominant than the product. The centre of marketing and manufacturing attention for the maker of automobile parts may well consist of three dozen or so leading motor manufacturers around the world which dominate world demand for made-out parts. What requires to be managed is the revenue not from a product but from each customer.

3 Many organizations will sell the same range of products to different groups of customers, and it is those groups which focus marketing planning attention. For example, the market for household cleaning products (detergents, cleaners, disinfectants, bleaches and so on) lies both in the ordinary household and also in the nation's institutions – hospitals, schools, universities, business premises and factories, office blocks, prisons and so on. The household market and the janitorial market are sufficiently different to warrant separate groups to manage the revenues from each separately.

4 Organizations whose revenue-earning capabilities lie in winning contracts on multimillion pound projects will be unlikely to manage revenue in the same way as the brand manager for a company selling canned soups. Revenue management of this sort is exclusively in the domain of the boardroom and its officers.

Bearing in mind the considerable problems of directly applying the concepts of revenue management by product to these four categories, the decision to be taken is whether it is worth the effort to do so, or whether such efforts will in the end fail in the light of practical difficulties in making the new system work.

A very strong case can be made for seeking always to apply the principles of product management, regardless of the difficulties initially encountered: the system has too many benefits to forgo it. Every business operation needs to identify its market offerings into separate, homogeneous blocks of revenue-earning capability, and structure its marketing department to allow planning managers to manage each separate block of revenue. To this recommendation should be added, however, a useful proviso – it is quite unnecessary for the target of revenue-planning attention to be a product. It may quite satisfactorily and sensibly be a named customer, a group of customers, a segment of the market or any other element which can be identified as being in need of individual planning attention.

Some examples may be useful.

1   A charitable organization like the World Wildlife Fund may very well identify countries – or even continents – as the target for planning attention.
2   A national bank may identify different types of customers as the planning focus. Additionally, it may identify a number of sub-markets among each of its groups of customers: the small business may be planned for separately from the large institutions, the average householder may be planned for separately from the wealthier, investing individual.
3   The jobbing engineering business might identify the different markets from which it does – or could – get its revenue: tool-makers, blacksmiths, sheet-metal fabricators, civil engineering contractors, local government authorities and so on.

KEY REVENUE MANAGEMENT FUNCTIONS

So far, this chapter has attempted to establish:

1   the necessity to plan and manage revenue;
2   The necessity to break down the total revenue into identifiably homogeneous parts: whether such parts are made up of brands, product ranges, customers or markets;
3   That the process of managing the key elements of revenue plan-

ning should be undertaken by specialists who have no other organizational responsibilities.

The recognition of the importance of these three points will lead the organization to create a revenue-management function. Because it will become the hub of marketing activity, this function will clearly be located within the marketing department, together with the selling, market research, promotions management, public relations and other marketing specialisms. The number of revenue managers to be appointed will depend on the complexity of the range of products or services offered in the marketplace, on the one hand, and on the wealth of the organization on the other: good revenue managers are expensive!

The name given to these revenue managers will depend largely on tradition, or on the forces that determine their areas of responsibility in the organization – products, brands, markets and so on. They are generally called product managers, brand managers or marketing managers. If they are at all numerous, they will be grouped, three or four at a time, under group brand/product managers – who in turn report to the head of the marketing function.

The remainder of this chapter refers to this discipline under these many titles, and the reader need not be confused, for their meaning lies in their titles: brand manager, product manager, marketing planner, product planner and revenue manager/planner all describe the same task and the same profession, and only the emphasis is different.

It is now possible to fill out the skeleton so far constructed by examining the functions essential to the revenue-management role.

Analysis

Probably the single most important function of revenue managers is that of analyst. They are hired, above all, to have a better understanding of the products for which they have responsibility than anyone else in the organization. This understanding concerns all aspects of the product as it interacts with the marketplace. Gathering together data about the product, revenue managers will synthesize it all into a coherent interpretation of the product's marketplace behaviour. While market researchers may understand the customer better, works engineers may understand the physical performance characteristics of the product better, the sales force may be better able to sell the product and the purchasing department may be better at buying the product's ingredients, revenue-managers will see all these activities, skills and performances in terms of the need to maximize the criteria of the marketplace: volume of sales, the volume of revenue and the volume of profits accruing to the product, as the result of sales. Whereas other corporate functions are concerned with one stage in the life of all the products – the purchasing stage, the manufacturing stage, the transportation and warehousing stage, for example – revenue managers are concerned with all the stages of the single product, from the forecast of its consumption (as they draw up plans for the future of the product) to its manufacture, delivery, purchase and consumption by the user in the marketplace. Such a role requires that revenue managers see themselves primarily as the product's 'minder'; in constant attendance on the health and effectiveness of the product, prolonging its healthy life on its journey through its life cycle. The primary benefit of such a role to the organization is that it allows the remainder of the organization to concentrate on its specialisms (production engineering, purchasing, bookkeeping and so on) in the knowledge that someone is concerned with marrying up all their skills to the benefit of the product in the marketplace.

Creating solutions

The analysis undertaken by revenue managers will invariably result in the discovery of both problems and opportunities for the product in the marketplace. Probably the single most difficult task revenue managers have is to arrive at a solution for each of the problems, and to arrive at a means of maximizing each of the opportunities. It is in this area in which the 'art' of marketing lies, for to any one set of problems there are probably a thousand satisfactory and effective solutions. The difficulties are not made simpler by the knowledge that the outcome of most solutions is likely to be difficult to measure. Additionally, there is rarely enough money (not to mention courage) to make experimentation possible by testing alternative solutions. Finding a good solution to a marketing problem is the skill which marks out the good from the mediocre marketing practitioner: it is the skill that accounts for the high salaries commanded by top marketing planners.

Formalizing solutions

After a full diagnosis of the product in the marketplace; after establishing the product's strengths and weaknesses there, and determining the proper course of action to take, revenue managers must now find a means of obtaining management's agreement to any changes they are proposing to make to the marketing of the product. For this reason, among others, they will find themselves writing a formal planning document to serve as a basis for presenting their solutions to corporate management.

The reasons for such formality are many.

1 *The role of revenue managers is essentially co-ordinative.* They rely entirely on other departments to enact the plan they have drawn up for the product. They will more easily do so if all the complexities of such co-operation have been formally hammered out and agreed with each of the co-operating departments. Documentation makes more certain that all the Is have been dotted and the Ts crossed.

2 *Revenue-managing documents generally contain elements which are too fundamental to the running of the company for such documentation to be acceptable on an informal back-of-the-envelope basis.* Such crucial elements as unit sales forecasts, profit and loss accounts, pricing structures and media schedules require to be formally as well as very precisely detailed.

3 *Marketing planning is much more an art form than a matter of scientific competence.* If that were not true, there would be no way to account for the widespread failure of new product launches. Because of this high level of uncertainty and risk which normally accompanies most marketing ventures on the one hand and, on the other, the considerable costs associated with marketing activities (selling, promoting, distribution and so on), it is a normal requirement for all major changes recommended by marketing – and most minor ones as well – to require formal, documented review by the corporation's senior managers. Hence the formal documentation.

4 *Great uncertainty in the marketplace requires diagnostic tools to*

give the best chance of reliable post-mortem analysis of failure and success. Whether the marketing activity recommended turns out to be successful or otherwise, planning documentation provides the opportunity to measure changes against forecasts of changes. (This is the reason – it may also be noted – why vaguely worded and fuzzy objectives should be avoided in the compilation of planning documents.) There is also great value in looking back to yesterday's plan against which to check today's: to re-read yesterday's ambitious targets in the light of today's ignominious failure is a salutary remedy against marketing smugness.

Plan approval and authorization

Having pulled together a complete plan for the product in the marketplace, it will now be necessary to persuade the organization to accept the validity of the plan. It is the task which will make the greatest demand on the persuasive and diplomatic powers of the revenue manager.

The personnel to whom the plan requires 'selling' are to be found in the boardroom: the organization's senior management will want to approve the marketing planning activities of the marketing deparment. Crucially, it is this formal approval of revenue managers' plans for their products for the year to come which provides them with the authority they require to enable them to undertake their daily work. For the brand management system to work requires that the revenue managers' undertakings are supported by the clear and overt approval of the boardroom. Such support and such approval may be most simply systematized through the annual approval of plans. Brand managers for their part lay out in detail what they recommend for the product, and corporate management for its part – perhaps after suitable modifications to the plan – provides the approval which then enables brand managers to go to every company department to obtain their co-operation in bringing the agreed product plan to a fruitful conclusion. Brand managers take their product managers' plans to the marketing director and, on receiving approval, emerge with a marketing department plan. The marketing director and each brand manager now take their plan to the board and, if the board agrees with the plan, emerge from the boardroom with a company plan for the product.

The authority which is vested in the boardroom is now the authority vested in the product plan.

Co-ordination and execution

For the fullest co-operation between the marketing planning function and other personnel who are crucial to the plan's successful outcome, the planner will also need fully to persuade the sales force, the manufacturing facility and other functions of the organization of the good sense and value of the solution proposed for the marketing problem.

Much of the day-to-day life of revenue managers is spent in coordinating all the activities necessary to bring the plan to a fruitful outcome.

Monitoring and analysing the results

Once the marketing plan is being executed in the marketplace, revenue managers will want to know whether it is meeting the plan's objectives. The planner will have called for whatever systems and surveys are necessary to enable such measurements to take place, co-ordinating with the marketing information managers to ensure some measuring takes place.

The availability of such measurements brings revenue managers full circle to a new analysis of forces and trends in the marketplace, which in turn may identify new problems and new opportunities which may suggest the need for new solutions and new plants.

PLANNING REVENUE MANAGEMENT: STRATEGY

The circle of activity outlined above describes the circle which is common to all good management. Relating this to the marketplace does not define the activities of the revenue manager. The areas of responsiblity of brand and product managers may be examined under the headings of strategic requirements and operational requirements. By strategic is meant, simply, the longer-term planning horizon. By operational is meant, in contrast, the shorter-term planning horizon. Longer and shorter are, of course, relative terms, and may vary widely from market to market and from organization to organization. To simplify matters, longer term may be considered as always over two years but nearly always less then ten years. Consequently, shorter term will usually refer to one to two years ahead.

By examining what the revenue manager does to plan these time horizons is to understand what the revenue planner does.

The marketing department does not lay down organizational strategy and, therefore, neither do the marketing department's revenue managers. Strategy is the task of the organization's most senior managers – the board. Before it can undertake any serious marketing planning, therefore, the marketing function will call for clear strategic guides from the board. It needs such guidance for particular and important reasons.

1 If he is to manage a product or a service in the marketplace, the planner needs to manage the marketing tools which determine its effectiveness: those elements which Borden referred to as his 'mix ingredients':

- product planning
- pricing
- branding
- channels of distribution
- personal selling
- advertising
- promotions
- packaging
- display
- servicing
- physical handling
- fact finding and analysis

A cursory glance at this list makes clear that important decisions in most of these areas are likely to have long-term effects in the marketplace. In turn that fact makes clear that revenue managers must operate within a set of strategic corporate boundaries which are clear. They need to know where the company is going and where it wants to get to, to ensure that all their recommendations fall within the organization's long-term plans.

2   Sooner or later the organization's strategic objectives will call for growth which cannot be met from its current portfolio of market offerings: it will need to seek new products and/or new markets within which to operate. The organization will turn to the managers of new-product revenue to help create, launch and manage such new business. It will normally fall to the marketing function to provide the manpower to plan and co-ordinate such efforts. Under such circumstances, the marketing function requires clear strategic guidelines:

(a)   as to the scale of new business required, and the time period over which it must be brought into existence;

(b)   as to the constraints which the organization wishes to apply to limit the range of options open to it in its search for new products and markets. For example, the organization may lay down constraints as to the levels of investment maxima and minima in new product ventures or the level of risk; or it may demand that all new ventures should fall within the technological, managerial and marketing capabilities which currently exist in the organization.

3   The function of managing the revenue of a product in the marketplace is intrinsically bound up with the concept of managing the product through its 'life-cycle': the idea that every product is on its way to its demise, and requires, therefore, constantly to be watched and worried over. Thus, the very nature of revenue management is itself long term (and strategic) as is the very nature of the product life-cycle.

4   Many of the most 'creative' solutions to a product or a service in the marketplace results in quite fundamental changes: a significant change in product specification, say, or a complete reorganization of a service facility. If you pay some one to plan the life of the offering in the marketplace, you must occasionally expect a recommendation for radical change. Such changes often require long-term decisions and investments on the part of other functions in the organization: the construction of new buildings, undertaking a major programme of fundamental research in the research and development department, the buying of capital equipment, the complete relocation of sources of production, the development of new distribution networks. All these marketing

recommendations involve the long term for non-marketing functions, and require to be foreseen and forecast in plenty of time: the short-term horizon will not suffice.

PLANNING REVENUE MANAGEMENT: OPERATIONAL PLANNING

Largely through their planning activities in new product marketing, revenue managers will be involved in the development of marketing strategy: that element of corporate strategy which helps the organization to meet its corporate objectives. For the majority of their working lives, however, revenue managers are primarily concerned with the management of the existing revenue from the existing range of products. Such planning is referred to as 'operational planning'.

It should now be clear that the essence of such activity is

to review each product in terms of its total effectiveness in the marketplace, choreographing total marketing activity in the marketplace, masterminding all the marketing forces the company can bring to bear in order to maximize the success of the product.

While the systems each organization uses to achieve those aims vary widely, a number of activities are fundamental.

1 The organization will want to set up a schedule of formal planning which ties in with its budgetary requirements. Thus there will be an annual marketing plan for each major profit earner in the organization. (Some organizations will want such a plan more frequently, calling for a product marketing plan every six months.)
2 The organization will wish to monitor the progress of activity promised in the annual plan, to measure the actual versus the predicted effects of the plan.
3 The organization will want to see recommended changes in marketing tactics when the monitoring systems detect an unfavourable deviation from the annual product objectives.
4 The organization will want to be certain that the revenue managers co-operate closely with other organizational functions in enacting the plans which they have recommended, and will set up systems to guarantee that such co-ordination takes place.

The annual marketing plan

Once a year each principal revenue and profit earning segment of corporate business (that is identifiably different in the marketplace from every other segment), will undergo its annual, agonizing reappraisal. It is, of course, misleading to give the impression that planners spend the rest of the year *not* planning. Quite the contrary: they plan more or less every working day. But most of the time they plan for the very short term, helping to solve very short-term problems, coping with short-term emergencies. But they know that once a year they must commit themselves to a concrete set of recommendations for their products for the next twelve to eighteen months ahead, synthesizing all their activities into a coherent solution to the problems the product faces. Furthermore, they know that such a plan will provide the blueprint for next year's workload.

Plan contents
Every market, and every product or service within the market, is sufficiently different to ensure that no one standard format is perfect for the annual plans of all products. Neither will it be sensible for an organization to insist on an annual product plan for every single product or service it offers in the marketplace, even if it could afford the multitude of marketing planners needed. The essential need is to ensure that annual product planning is undertaken for:

1 all principal revenue and profit earners;
2 all ventures recently launched into the marketplace;
3 all products identified as having serious problems in the marketplace.

Despite differences in markets and their products, there are a number of marketing planning fundamentals which must serve as the core for all annual plans.

Revenue account The end result of the revenue manager's planning efforts and skills are to be found in the financial contributions forecasted for the product. Such a revenue account serves as the ultimate measure of the organization's competence with the product under review. Such an account will:

1 indicate clearly the financial parameters on which the account is

founded: estimated variable product costs per unit; average selling price per unit;

2 show the forecast of units to be sold;

3 clearly itemize marketing expenditure details, both for direct marketing expenditures (advertising and sales promotional expenditure, for example), and indirect marketing expenditures (the cost of the sales force, market research and distribution for example);

4 provide comparisons with previous years' revenue accounts;

5 be percentaged to make such comparisons simpler;

6 clearly show the profitability planned for the product at the gross margin level, the 'contribution after direct marketing expenses' level and at the pre-tax-profit level (always an approximation of the truth, but nevertheless a very useful figure to the motivation of marketing planning).

Sales forecast   While the revenue accounts will have revealed the forecast of total sales, many organizational departments – manufacturing, purchasing and financial, for example – will need a detailed, monthly forecast of unit sales for each product.

Product specifications   The annual plan will make clear any planned changes to be made to the product or service; why such changes are recommended; what their estimated effect will be in the marketplace; how and when they will be implemented; what are the cost and the pricing implications of such changes, and what monitoring devices will be applied to measure the actual outcome of the changes.

Pricing policy   The annual product plan should recommend the pricing policy of the product, together with any recommended changes to that policy; the thinking behind such changes and the effects anticipated as a result. Competitors' prices, pricing structures and apparent pricing strategies may also need to be referred to. Where distributors are in use, distributor margins will need to be examined, compared with those of competitors and policy change recommendations explained and justified.

Promotional policy   Used in the widest sense to include all aspects of sales promotion – personal selling, advertising, public relations, trade and consumer promotions, sponsorship, exhibitions and so on – the promotional policy for a product may involve a great deal of planning activity, accounting for a considerable percentage of the organization's revenue. The promotional effort applied to a product or service is the principal tool the organization uses to ensure that revenue planning is a dynamic response to the marketplace, not simply a passive reaction to events. Creatively and analytically planned, product, price and promotion determine the marketing competence of the organization. Of the three, promotion is the most flexible and the most capable of rapid adaptation to rapidly changing marketing circumstances: it is possible to mount a new promotional plan from scratch in a few weeks. Such flexibility is not possible for product changes, and the options for changes to the price of the product tend to be narrower and should, unlike promotional tools, be used as little as possible. Within the umbrella of the promotional policy lie a number of areas which need to be separately described:

1   advertising policy;
2   trade promotions/sales servicing policy;
3   consumer promotions;
4   public relations.

Selling and distribution policy   The efforts both of the sales force and of those charged with the distribution of the product to the customers will have a significant effect on the competence of the product in the marketplace. To that extent, product planners will be very concerned to re-examine sales policy and distribution policy when they come to write the annual marketing plan for their products. They will have to reconsider, for example, the level of attention given to those products by the sales force – in as much as all the organization's products compete for the sales force's attention – the types of aids they should provide to help the sales force in its efforts to sell the products, and the extent to which the distribution systems employed by the organization are to the best advantage of their products, or require modifications. Marketing planners, the better to know the problems and opportunities affecting their products in these areas, will take particular care to spend time with the specialists running these functions: they will regularly go out on sales calls with the company salespeople, and be sure to keep themselves fully informed about selling and distribution function activities.

Co-ordination systems

It is clear that the role of the brand manager must interact very closely with many of the other organizational functions. Competent brand managers are sensitive to the hazards of interfering with the functional efficiency of other departments. Yet this sensitivity is no substitute for formal systems to ensure that the introduction of a brand management function does not play havoc with existing control and reporting systems. A number of areas are especially vulnerable to the enthusiasm of determined brand managers.

Production planning
Keen brand managers will have a powerful desire to make sure that their products are always available for sale, always delivered on time, always at the forefront of the organization's production schedules. For many markets a forecast of sales, in the short term especially, is likely to be less than reliable, and the person with responsibility for scheduling production efficiently will be constantly pressurized by the brand managers to change production schedules to the advantage of this or that product, to meet unexpected fluctuations in sales. Chaos – and expensive chaos – may result, together with friction and distrust between the marketing and manufacturing departments. Control systems, in the guise of good pre-planning, and routine, regular meetings between the two functions require to be set up.

Technical enquiries
Because they are given responsibility for planning the life of the product in the marketplace, imaginative brand managers will dream up a large number of marketing alternatives which may call for modifications to the product, the product packaging, the production processes and so on. When a number of brand managers each come up with a number of what may be speculative ideas, all of which require investigation by engineers, scientists, cost accountants and other corporate specialists, a great deal of time and company energy can be spent pursuing them. Systems need to be set up which cope with this

239

work flow, and which, ideally, restrict the work to those ideas which have a real chance of being both workable and acceptable to the organization, once the details have been worked out.

Financial

Brand managers must be trained, above all, to view all their activities in terms of profitability and cost-effectiveness. They will be strongly encouraged to speculate – calculator in hand – about the financial outcome of their alternative plans, in order to develop an awareness of the need to allocate limited resources effectively. The wise organization makes sure that the revenue managers have close ties with, and get routine help and advice from, the financial and accounting functions of the company. Some organizations have even developed marketing liaison accountants who devote their time to guiding, helping and double-checking the financial calculations of the marketing planners. Brand managers will need to recommend pricing policy. This, in turn, will require them to have a full understanding of product costs and of the overhead recovery requirements expected of the product. While they are not expected to be involved in capital investment programmes, or cash flow problems, they will need an understanding of both in as much as they are both relevant to marketing decision-taking by the senior management of the organization. Brand managers will also be expected to be guardians of the budget allocated to their products for a variety of marketing expenditures – for example on advertising, public relations, point of sale material and literature and so on.

THE BRAND MANAGER: PAST, PRESENT AND FUTURE

Past and present

This chapter has reviewed the workings of a management system which lies at the marketing heart of many of the world's most successful consumer goods companies, and a system which is beginning to be evident in industrial and service goods companies. The system, and its benefits, are by no means theoretical. As a system, of course, brand management has its problems as well as its advantages.

But the logic that lies behind it is inescapable, and the organizations currently using it would, by and large, strenuously resist its removal.

It may be constructive, however, to examine some of the objections which have been raised to the brand management system.

Responsibility without authority

The commonest criticism in the academic literature concerning brand management as a system is to be found in the statement that the brand manager is a manager with responsibility but without any authority. A number of points need to be made.

1 The areas of the business for which the brand manager is asked to make recommendations are at the heart of the organization's ability to survive, thrive or fail. Changes to product specifications, price and promotional support may very well destroy the product and, ultimately, the company. Even the marketing director is not given delegated authority for most of the responsibilities that belong to the brand manager, hence there is no way such authority would be given to the brand manager, or should be. These responsibilities are the last the board willingly delegates: it only does so because the product planning load could simply not be undertaken at board level. For revenue to be properly managed, someone must be given responsibility for it, *without* being given authority over line management. The alternative is that revenue should not be managed, which is plainly nonsensical; or that each revenue manager is given line authority, which is an even greater nonsense.

2 The revenue manager's lack of formal line authority is more than counterbalanced by the board approval which is given to the annual product plan on which the brand manager bases all his or her work. In a marketing-orientated organization, every other department is aware that the brand manager has the support of the board: it is this which gives the brand manager all the necessary authority.

3 In any case, responsibility without authority applies to every single line manager in the organization. It is only the extent of lack of authority and the level at which it operates that differentiate one manager from another. For example, the board most certainly does not give the manufacturing director unlimited authority over

241

capital investment projects. The board's approval will need to be sought for such expenditures.

The short-term horizon of the brand manager

It is said that brand managers, sensing the necessity to make their mark on the new range of products they have inherited, will attempt to make unnecessary changes to the product and seek to maximize short-term success in the marketplace at the expense of the medium and long-term health of the products. To this criticism is added the fact that brand managers are notoriously 'on the move', constantly seeking to go faster and higher up the promotional ladder, and that such ambitions inevitably result in a short-term focus. Of course this is true. It is equally true that the group brand manager and the marketing director must ensure that such short-term views do not prevail at the expense of success in the market. In any case, it takes no great insight for ambitious brand managers to recognize that they will seriously damage their reputation – and, hence, promotional prospects – by seeking short-term benefits to their personal advantage but to the disadvantage of the company.

Brand managers wastefully compete against each other

It is the nature of brand managers – and one of their virtues – that they quickly become fervent champions of the products for which they have been given responsibility. As such they will make every effort to get the rest of the organization to pay maximum attention to their products, and are quite indifferent to the rest of the organization's range. The effect is that of a group of managers avidly competing for the organization's limited resources, inevitably resulting in waste. Once more, this would be true were it not for the controlling forces applied to brand managers by more senior members of the marketing department. Marketing directors hardly encourage such tactics. And it is the function of other managers in the organization – the general sales manager and the production manager, for example – to balance the needs of one product with those of the others.

The future

It is likely that the brand management system will grow in acceptability and usage in the business community. It will, of course, need to adapt to changes, as it will need to adapt to being used in the new types of organizations to which it will be introduced. The greatest threat to its development lies in those companies which are organizationally and emotionally not yet ready to accept the system: many cases, if not most, of the failure of brand management as a system – and marketing practice in general – can be traced either to a poor understanding of what is involved, a failure to develop the systems necessary to underpin the new discipline or a fundamental failure to give full support to the practitioners and their systems when they are introduced. The introduction of brand management as a new system into a business may, of course, prove to be a traumatic experience to existing systems and, above all, to the power structure of the existing managers. For this reason it can be argued that the standard procedures and goals in the recruitment of today's brand managers ought perhaps to be re-examined and reassessed. Currently the brand management structure, where it is employed, has – on its lowest rung – bright young graduates taken straight from the universities and polytechnics and hired to act as assistant brand managers, where they 'learn the business'. After a period of eighteen months to two years, they will graduate to handling the smaller of the company's products; two to three years after that they may achieve the stardom of a set of important, high profit earning brands.

There are problems in such a system.

1   A good deal of the goodwill towards the marketing department is routinely frittered away because, from the point of view of the usually older senior managers in all the other departments, too many important decision areas in marketing are left in the hands of twenty-three and twenty-four year-olds who are still learning the basic rudiments of business operations (few things are more calculated to irritate the old hand than the young marketer!)

2   To overcome this problem, the marketing function routinely protects its young brand managers and assistants with a bevy of experts, who are hired partly to take decisions (which might be better taken by the brand manager), partly to provide advice (which an older brand manager would need less). Policy here differs widely between different companies, but very young brand managers, inexperienced in the ways of business generally,

243

are the norm in many organizations.

Some companies are beginning to take another route. They are refusing to take graduates directly into the revenue-management function. Instead they are recruiting brand managers directly from young middle managers – twenty-seven to twenty-eight years old – who have already had five or six years' experience with the company, who know other company managers, already have a wide experience of another discipline (sales, market research, accountancy or some other managerial discipline) under their belt and who have proved their managerial competence in these disciplines to the satisfaction of the company. The fact that even the junior brand manager is responsible for a set of brands (and their associated profit contributions), which are of importance to the company, and whose corporate health is more truly in the brand manager's hands than in that of any other company manager, suggests that the product's 'minder' should never be less than an able and experienced company executive. It might be an improvement in company recruitment policies if the post of assistant brand manager became a position at which to arrive, instead of being a post at which to start a business career.

Problems with introducing the revenue manager system

It would be unrealistic to conclude this chapter without a brief examination of some of the hazards in brand/revenue management, which are particularly acute when the system is first introduced to an organization which has not previously used it.

Problems of transition
The advent of the brand manager inserts a new layer of management into the system. It has the effect of changing the lines of communication between managers and between departments; of providing a quite new focus of responsibility; of diluting existing power bases. For the brand manager system to work requires that all the company's senior and middle managers both understand and appreciate the value of the new system. The probability that such appreciation will be felt by all the managers of an organization is remote. The system will suffer buffets and storms in the first few years of its operation.

Problems of diplomacy

Most of the working life of the brand manager is spent in persuading other managers to provide what is necessary to achieve the objectives agreed in the product plans. Not all brand managers manage this task with tact and the persuasiveness of logic. Many find that the short route to success lies in aggression and general abrasiveness. In few other functions are the selection and recruitment criteria more important than those used in the selection of brand managers.

Problems of delegation

It is an inevitable corollary of the function of the brand management that there must be responsibility without delegated authority: the case for this has already been elaborated. As a result, the role of the brand manager may very well prove disheartening if care is not taken to handle such a problem intelligently. One of the most successful means of solving the problem is to make sure that, up to the highest levels, brand managers are always expected to present whatever case they have planned for the marketing of their products. So long as they have to fight for themselves, they will come to recognize that authority for marketing activity is largely dependent on their skills both as a planner and a presenter. If they are not allowed to carry out the plans they have recommended, it will be because they have failed to persuade the board of the soundness of their recommendations. Obversely, when the board agrees with those recommendations, they will know that it is their policies which are determining the marketing success of the products for which they have responsibility.

Problems of interference

Unless fairly carefully controlled, brand managers become a ubiquitous presence in all the departments of the organization, seen to be 'sticking their noses in where they have no business'. The need here is for a planner who is sensitive to the territorial defensiveness of line managers, as well as for sound, formal control systems which prevent undue interference by brand managers in the running of non-marketing functions in the organization (already discussed above). The classic means of overcoming resentment by other managers towards such 'interference' is to train brand managers to take an active interest in the functions of those other departments under the guidance of those charged to manage them. In a manufacturing organization, for example, the brand managers should know the factory process, the people and the problems on the factory floor in order to sustain good communications and information about 'their' products where they are being made. When this is achieved, the effect may very well improve tolerance of each discipline towards the others, in the light of a real understanding of each other's operational and managerial problems.

CONCLUSION

For many business organizations, revenue management is already seen to be as useful and as necessary as any other business discipline used to improve organizational efficiency and effectiveness in the marketplace.

In this chapter the case has been strongly made that revenue requires planning, controlling and managing. The chapter has examined the means of achieving such control.

Ultimately the logic of brand management lies in its capacity to generate more profits, to secure greater certainty of secure employment and to generate a sense of greater competence and professionalism in the organization which uses such management disciplines.

FURTHER READING

Bureau, J. R. (1981), *Brand Management: Analysis, Planning and Control*, Macmillan, London.

Davidson, J. H. (1987), *Offensive Marketing*, 2nd edn, Gower, Aldershot.

Jones, J. P. (1986), *What's in a Name? Advertising and the Concept of Brands*, Gower, Aldershot.

Ward, J. (1984), *Profitable Product Management*, Heinemann, London.

Winkler, J. (1972), *Winkler on Marketing Planning*, Cassell, London.

13

Financial controls in marketing

J. E. Smith

ATTRACTING AND USING FUNDS

Whatever the business, manufacturing or distributing, consumer products or technical products, funds are required to allow launching in the first instance, and then to permit continuity of operations. These funds have to be used effectively if the business is to survive, and so be in a position to generate or attract more funds. Looking at a business from a financial control viewpoint means first of all examining the separate aspects of fund raising and fund using.

Attracting funds to a business is not an easy matter. Capital is never in plentiful supply; it has always to be prised out of a reluctant money market and inevitably costs something to obtain. The sources of capital are many and they can be classified from a duration point of view as short term, medium term and permanent. Short-term capital is that which is attracted from the banks as overdrafts on current accounts or from creditors, that is, suppliers prepared to supply materials and services on credit. Such capital is in theory immediately repayable and normally used in the business as working capital. Medium-term capital is debt capital, money borrowed from banks, financial institutions and the public, where the capital is required in the business for a longer period of time, often to purchase assets like land, buildings, plant and equipment. Permanent capital is, in the case of the limited liability company, the share capital provided by the owners which is normally kept in the business and added to by the profits made by the business and retained in it. The responsibility for finding funds for the business is often called a 'treasury' responsibility.

On the other hand, the funds are not normally sought unless someone on the operations side of the business has uses for such funds. The spending of the capital in a business is of two types.

1 Capital expenditure – spending large amounts of the funds at particular points in time on fixed asset items such as land, buildings, plant equipment, office fixtures, fittings and so on. Quite often, such spending is significant in that it alters the direction of a company's activities for years ahead.

2 Revenue expenditure – day-to-day spending on the bought-out materials and services of the trade and upon wages, salaries and the other costs associated with making products or providing services for sales.

In practice, it is usual for many managers in the business to have responsibility for the use of funds.

OPERATING STATEMENTS

One of the important financial statements, the balance sheet, depicts this aspect of raising and using funds. Examination of the balance sheet will tell one just how much capital is available in a business, where it is being used and has come from. Most important, it will indicate how much of the capital is invested in fixed assets and how much is being used as working capital. The other financial statement, the profit and loss account, looks at the business from an income point of view. It shows the sales turnover or gross income, the operating costs being deducted from this, leaving the net profit. The balance sheet and profit and loss account are statutory documents of stewardship accounting for limited liability companies, that is, they must be submitted with an annual return to the Registrar of Companies. They are intended to give an annual account of the directors' stewardship of the shareholders' funds.

ANALYSIS OF BUSINESS PERFORMANCE

To analyse the objectives of a business is a complex matter, since so many of these objectives prove to be unquantifiable, but there is usually common agreement on the fact that some of them are financial in character. The most important financial objectives are:

1 making an adequate profit return on the resources emloyed in the business and in particular on the capital employed;
2 proper balancing of cash flows in and out so that the business never runs short of funds and never has funds lying idle.

It is necessary to measure regularly the achievement of the business in these terms and this is usually done in terms of certain accounting ratios. A periodical critical examination of results by the use of ratios can be a very useful management discipline. The right starting point is an internal comparison with the previous years' results, giving a breakdown of the return on capital employed into its basic constituents, that is, the profit margin on sales and the sales turnover of capital employed (see Figure 13.1).

Even this simple ratio analysis over a number of years will normally reveal some substantial variations as well as some consistent trends. For the marketer, such measurements have implications. It can be readily seen that:

$$\text{Percentage return on capital} = \text{Percentage profit margin} \times \text{Sales turnover of capital}$$

with all that this implies in terms of pricing policy, either low prices to encourage volume or high prices to give a good profit margin ratio. This form of ratio analysis can be extended to relate the profit made to the fixed assets, the working capital, and the sales to the same expressions of the capital employed. Then, bearing in mind that the difference between sales turnover and profit is in operating costs, these costs can be analysed by type or function and related either to the sales turnover or to the total of operating costs. It is sound management practice, for example, to know what percentage marketing, selling and distribution costs bear to the grand total, and to keep this under regular observation. Often lines of enquiry are prompted by ratio analysis which can lead to the spotting of corrective action. Two areas of great significance in day-to-day operations of a business are

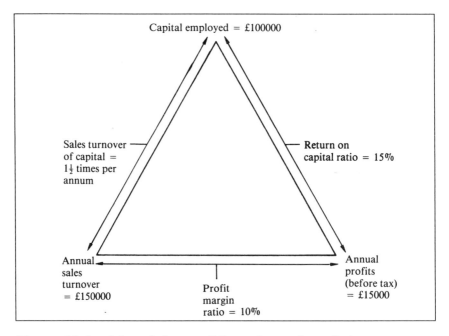

Figure 13.1 A breakdown of the return of capital

stockholding or inventory levels and the amount of money owed by customers. It is as well to check the relationship of both these figures to a suitable measurement of output, inventory levels to both production and sales and debtors to sales. This often reveals undesirable trends which have not been planned, and ought to be of interest to the marketer.

The need might become apparent to discover whether other firms in the same or other industries showed different ratios and trends. This implies the possibility of the company joining in some form of inter-firm comparison which is carried out by some trade associations or rather more specifically by the Centre for Inter-Firm Comparisons Ltd. The use of such comparisons and ratios is no substitute for management but it can be a very considerable aid to management.

PLANNING THE USE OF FUNDS

Capital expenditure

Capital expenditure on fixed asset items is normally so significant as to demand special planning. Procedures are necessary to attempt to stimulate the innovation which is very often the forerunner to capital expenditure, and then to ensure proper authorization of the spending after it has been systematically evaluated. Later, control of the spending is required and finally a post-audit of the progress of the project in financial terms.

The word 'project' has been used because a company's capital expenditure budget normally comprises many such projects with different characteristics. A look at an annual capital expenditure budget would reveal some projects merely designed to maintain existing business, for example, machine replacement; some which indicate extensive expansion, for example, new products for new markets, while others would be made necessary by government legislation. Other items of capital expenditure might be directed specifically at cost saving or productivity improvement, but others might be entirely different, the acquisition of other businesses or other forms of outside investment. Clearly, capital expenditure can affect the amount of capital employed in a business and the effectiveness of it can affect the return made on that capital.

There are various methods of evaluating proposed capital investments, the simplest being the pay-back period method, in which the estimated annual cash flows (or cost savings) which arise from the project are related to the initial cash outlay to finance the project, so that it becomes clear how many years will be required to replace the capital fund. The internal rate of return method requires one to estimate the profits which will be made during the life of the project, convert these to an average annual profit, which is then related to the capital employed, to give an average rate of return. A more sophisticated yet realistic approach is afforded by the use of discounted cash flow techniques which reflect the time value of money in the appraisal.

It is important that the appraisal of capital expenditure should be carried out systematically, and that a financial analysis is made. This means estimating the capital expenditure and the cash flows that will arise from that capital expenditure. In many projects this will mean forecasting sales and estimating the cost of those sales. This is work to be done partly by the sales organization and needs to be treated seriously. If the capital expenditure is significant, the whole future of the business coud depend upon the accuracy of the assessment of the market and the share of that market which the business can capture.

251

Working capital

Taking British industry in general, some 40 per cent of the funds employed in it are in use as working capital, that is, capital basically employed in the form of stock (raw materials, work in progress and finished goods), debtors and cash. The view taken by accountants is that the last two items are liquid – in cash or readily convertible into cash – whereas the stock items have to be sold (in the case of raw materials and work-in-progress, the products still have to be made). It is not overstating the case to say that many quite profitable businesses have been wound up because of a failure to plan and control the liquid resources.

What are required are policies of stockholding, credit control and cash holding, and clearly these are relevant to, and therefore need to be set in conjunction with, the marketing manager. There the problem is not only what can be afforded from the point of view of liquid resources, but what must be aimed at in the way of stocks carried and credit terms to encourage trade and, therefore, profitability. The setting of the policies required in this area is a combined management task, and clearly this is another area in which the marketing manager has a role to play in the effective use of funds.

FINANCIAL PLANNING THROUGH BUDGETARY CONTROL

A technique often used in financial planning is that of budgetary control. This implies expressing the plans of the business inquantitative and monetary terms and then exercising control, that is, measuring actual performance, costs and cash flows against the budget, and taking corrective action where necessary.

There are two main stages in budgetary control.

1 Deciding upon the budget period, which must be appropriate to the nature of the trade and the time of production, and then forecasting and planning activities for that period. High, yet attainable, standards of performance will be the basis of the budget.
2 Taking action and evaluating performance in the light of the plans and standards developed in the first stage.

Budgetary control is aimed at the planning and control of the performance of the business, costs and cash flows. The budgets required can be reviewed under three main headings, operating budgets, financial budgets and the capital expenditure budget. The two main questions which arise when preparing the operating budgets are:

1 What will be sold, in what volume and at what prices?
2 What, therefore, will need to be produced, and what should the costs of production, administration, marketing, selling and distribution be?

The sales budget deals with the first question and is often the starting point and lynchpin of budgetary control procedures. This is the area in which the marketing manager will be expected to be thoroughly involved, and so he or she should be. The effective use of resources in the business cannot be planned without a meaningful sales budget, taking into account not only current market, customer and product aspects but also any limiting factors within the business such as control space, labour skills or bottlenecks in particular plant or equipment. Care needs to be taken in the preparation of this budget because the estimating of cash flows in and out of the business depends upon it. All operating costs in the business have to be budgeted by managers in charge of their respective budget centres, and these have to be translated into cash outflows, whereas the sales budget figure are converted into cash inflows. The accountant is essentially the person responsible for the flow of funds in the business, and has responsibility for making arrangements for the availability of funds at the appropriate times. The accountant inevitably becomes heavily involved in the plans and aspirations of other managers.

The discipline of expressing plans in quantitative and monetary form represents an invaluable exercise because managers are forced to face the future. The budgeting system can act as a co-ordinating device and as a means of communication. Managers become more aware of their specific roles in the business and, most important, standards of performance and cost have to be developed. The feedback of control information comparing actual performance and costs with the budgets motivates managers, reminds them of their responsibilities and prompts corrective action. If there is a danger in the use of budgetary control, it is that it is a short-period technique concentrated upon providing assistance in the control of day-to-day operations within the framework of an annual budget. Concentration on the annual budget could lead to neglect of the necessary longer-term planning. The marketing function would be largely responsible for ensuring that this did not happen.

Out of the system of budgetary control should come useful information for the marketing function, for example, comparisons of actual sales achievement compared with budgets, all figures being analysed as appropriate to representatives, areas, customers, product groups and products. There should also be available details of all actual costs in the marketing area compared with budgets. To the extent to which some selling and distribution costs are likely to vary more or less directly with sales, there should be a 'flexible budget' for these costs, in other words, a budget based upon standard costs which can be adjusted up or down in accordance with the sales achievement.

PROFIT CENTRES

The marketing organization may not be seen by the management accountants as a budget centre. The latter implies that the marketing manager is a budget holder responsible for the performance and costs of a part of the business against an agreed budget. This budget approach is not the only one which is used to try to instil profit orientation in managers throughout the business. A very popular approach in these times when the overall business objective seems to be an adequate return on investment is the investment centre or profit centre approach. The latter phrase will be used to imply both.

The idea of profit centre accounting is that a particular section of the business, function or department is regarded as a separate business from a profit and loss account point of view. In other words, in each trading period the complete business profit and loss account is broken down into these departments, in respect of each of which is known the sales turnover, operating costs, net profit and, in some cases, the capital employed. It is then possible to calculate the return on investment made by each of the profit centres. It is felt that a suitable measure of profit performance is needed wherever management responsiblity is divided among subsidiaries, divisions and departments for such purposes as guiding the operating managers in their day-to-day control and decision-making and helping top management to appraise their work.

Theoretically, the profit centre is a good idea, but it creates problems. First, it is not universally applicable. It is not really possible to talk about the sales income of a department which has output measurable in quantities but not in value. This is particularly true of service departments, for example, the maintenance department in a manufacturing business. Some businesses have tried to overcome this problem by setting up a system of transfer prices, that is, artificial selling prices for the transfer of products or services from one department to another. Several organizations treat the production department and the selling function as two separate profit centres, transferring production from the former to the latter at transfer prices. At the best, such prices can be only arbitrary, and the level at which to set them is likely to be a subject for discussion for a long time into the future. In practice, the danger in the profit centre approach is that there will be an over-concentration on the achievement of the wrong objectives. What is required in the end is not the profitability of individual profit centres but of the business as a whole.

COSTING AS AN AID

Management accounting is different from stewardship accounting. Whereas in the latter the emphasis is on year-end financial statements prepared for the business as a whole in accordance with the Companies Acts and accounting standards, the work of management accounting is directed towards measuring activities within the business and providing financial and cost information which will assist management in its day-to-day work of planning and control as well as in its decision-making. Much of the work of management accounting is costing, and the objectives of costing are as follows.

1 A knowledge of what costs are incurred, which are significant, and in what locations of the business they are incurred is a pointer to cost control and a stimulant to cost reduction.
2 Cost data, particularly departmental cost rates, are required to enable cost estimating for price fixing to be accurate. The cost estimating function also requires feedback information to assess the accuracy of its work.

3   Product cost information is required both for checking upon the adequacy of existing selling prices and also to facilitate the calculation of the relative profitability of product.
4   The planning of future operations and the setting of budgets cannot be done without information on costs in the various functions of the business and the behaviour of such costs. Feedback of actual cost information against the budgets is also needed.
5   There are many decisions which management has to make which involve financial and cost considerations, and the cost information needs to be available.

The two primary functions in the business, production and marketing, are in need of help from the costing function.

COST ANALYSIS AND THE TECHNIQUES OF COSTING

At the outset, costing is essentially a matter of analysis. Costs have to be analysed:

1   into materials, labour and overhead costs and into the particular items within each;
2   by locations within the business;
3   by product groups, products, contracts or jobs according to the production methods of the business;
4   by those costs which vary more or less directly with the output of the business and those which remain more or less fixed.

Where one is using cost information which recognizes the different proportions of variable and fixed costs, one is using a particular costing technique called marginal costing. Where cost information which is not bringing out this point of cost variability is employed, a technique called the absorption cost or total cost approach is being used.

If the business is to be profitable, the total costs of running it must be recovered (or absorbed) in the long run, but this does not mean that total cost information is the relevant information for every decision, neither does it mean that every product can or should have a selling price which is greater than its normal total cost.

To look at it from a marginal cost point of view, one divides the

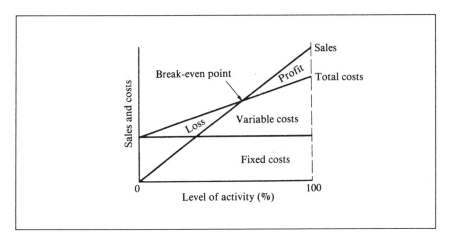

Figure 13.2   Break-even chart

costs between marginal or variable (with output) and fixed (irrespective of output). To do this means observing the behaviour of costs over
a long period. It will probably be found that direct material costs,
direct labour costs and certain overheads such as power, tools and
consumable materials vary directly with output, whereas
depreciation, rent and rates, salaries and the like remain relatively
constant. The marginal costs are much more directly the costs of
products, whereas the fixed costs tend to be period costs or policy
costs.

BREAK-EVEN ANALYSIS

When the above breakdown of costs is known, a break-even chart can
be prepared (see Figure 13.2).

   This is a useful tool for costing. Plotting the levels of fixed and
variable costs against sales income discloses the break-even point, the
point at which neither profit nor loss is made. Above the break-even
point are profits, below are losses. The break even chart shown in
Figure 13.2 is an over-simplication because the lines of cost and sales
are not in practice straight lines. At the very best it provides a rough
guide to the profits and losses likely at different levels of activity; it is
only a rough guide because it assumes a certain product mix, and this
is a dangerous assumption. Consider the same chart drawn in a

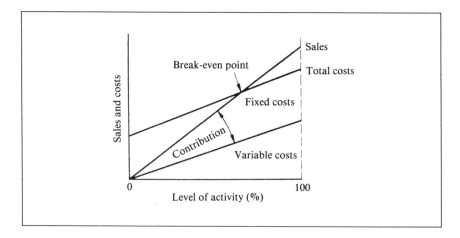

Figure 13.3 Break-even chart

different way (Figure 13.3). Exactly the same basic figures are used upon which the alternative chart is drawn, but in this case the block of fixed costs has been imposed on top of the variable costs. The advantage which one obtains from this chart is that an additional measurement called 'contribution' can be gleaned from it. This is the margin left after deducting the variable costs from the sales value, and is the 'contribution to fixed costs'. When the fixed costs have been fully absorbed or recovered, then contribution becomes profit.

This is the reality of the business situation. Some of the costs of running the business are not directly related to production or the provision of services: they are the fixed or constant period costs. Profit arises only when the total contributions from the production activity exceed these constant costs, so that to maximize profit in the short term contribution has to be maximized, and this is not the same as maximizing turnover.

PRODUCT COSTING AND PRICING

Marketing managers must have a knowledge of what products cost to make, sell and distribute either as an aid to the fixing of selling prices for those products or in order to calculate the relative profitability of different products. This is basic marketing information. Once again,

Table 13.1 Three products made from material in short supply

	Direct material cost	Direct labour cost	Variable overhead cost	Marginal cost	Sales price	Contri-bution	Contribution as percentage of material cost
Product A (£)	100	50	100	250	300	50	50
Product B (£)	80	50	100	230	290	60	75
Product C (£)	60	50	120	240	300	60	100

the approach to calculating product costs can be on a total or marginal cost basis.

The total cost of a product is the sum of materials, labour and overhead costs of that product. It is not usually too difficult to calculate the direct materials and direct labour costs of products: the problem is normally with the indirect materials, indirect labour and expense items which comprise the overhead costs. A common practice is to collect these overhead costs according to function or department in the business and then calculate cost rates by which they can be absorbed into the costs of products. This involves the apportionment of many items of cost, notably the fixed costs, on what are at best arbitrary bases. It also means that cost rates calculated for individual departments are based upon the costs for a period related to the departmental activity for that period, so that inevitably the 'total cost' of a product holds good only at a certain level of output and contains arbitrary apportionments of certain costs. In this respect, it is no more than a rough guide as a basis for price fixing.

The marginal cost of a product is much easier to compute, comprising only the directly attributable variable costs. In this way apportionments are avoided. The marginal cost of a product normally comprises the prime costs of direct materials and direct labour plus variable overheads. If the product marginal cost is deducted from the product selling price, the contribution the product makes is apparent, and a good way of ranking products is to relate their individual contributions to whatever is the limiting resource factor in the business. Table 13.1 ranks three products made from the same direct material which is in short supply.

It will be clear from this example that product C is the best contribution earner in relation to the limiting factor. This is an oversimplified example but will serve to make the point that assessments of product profitability need to be made if a business is to be and remain profitable, and they need to be made accurately and on the basis of cost information which is relevant.

This is vital information for the marketing function which must be pursuing policies aimed at maintaining and improving profitability. A knowledge of which products to be pushing is necessary. The other point is that in the long term, prices of products should be reflecting the required contribution from the limited resource.

RELEVANT COST DATA FOR DECISION-MAKING

It is also important that reliable cost information is available for other decisions such as make-or-buy, the desirability or otherwise of overtime or second-shift working, which particular production methods to use, and so on. Such cost information will need to take into account the different characteristics of cost and particularly that of variability.

THE MARKETING CONTRIBUTION TO THE EFFECTIVE USE OF FUNDS

It has already been explained that funds are used either to buy fixed assets or to provide working capital. It will be obvious that such spending needs to be planned and controlled, and the marketing function must join in the management exercise to ensure effectiveness of such spending. In practice, the business will almost certainly use budgetary control procedures, so that a sales budget and a sales cost budget will be focal points of financial planning. Upon the accuracy of the sales budget will depend the estimates of resources required and the precision in allocating financial resources. No doubt the marketing manager will have capital expenditure proposals to put which will need to be evaluated. Certainly he or she will have some say in the matters of inventory levels and credit terms allowed to customers.

The marketing manager must be aware of the effect of volume on costs and profits, and have some knowledge of break-even points at different levels of activity. He or she must have reliable information on the relative profitability of different activities, product groups and products. Only in this way can his or her contribution be effective.

FURTHER READING

Drury, J. C. (1985), *Cost and Management Accounting*, Van Nostrand Reinhold, Wokingham.
Ray, G. and Smith, J. E. (1982), *Hardy Developments Ltd. Text and Cases in Management Accounting*, Gower, Aldershot.
Westwick, C. A. (1987), *How to use Management Ratios*, 2nd edn, Gower, Aldershot.

Part III
DEVELOPING THE PRODUCT

14

Understanding customer behaviour

Gordon Foxall

CUSTOMER-ORIENTED MARKETING

Only the simplest socio-economic systems avoid marketing. Any society whose economy extends beyond subsistence or simple barter must make arrangements for orderly material exchange, that is, for the systematic creation and implementation of the marketing mix. This requires that decisions be taken with respect to the kinds of product and service that will be produced, the ways in which the availability of goods for sale will be communicated, their distribution, and their pricing.

But, while all exchange economies require, by definition, that such marketing decisions be taken, societies differ widely in the styles with which they discharge the corresponding functions. Fundamentally, they vary according to who takes these decisions. In the majority of cases, marketing decisions have been taken by or on behalf of producers, that is, by manufacturers, distributors or governments, while customers' choice has been severely restricted by their lack of discretionary income and the absence of effective competition among suppliers. These circumstances have ensured that the managerial style with which basic marketing functions have been discharged is over-whelmingly *producer*-oriented in its outlook, aspirations and results.

Those economies – typically industrialized and affluent – in which the style of marketing management is predominantly *customer*-orientated differ primarily because, to a considerable extent, economic power lies with buyers and users. By virtue of their capacity to choose among competing firms, competing industries and competing nations, buyers influence ultimately the product, promotion, place and price decisions which determine the marketing mix.

Simply as this distinction has been put (for further discussion, see Foxall, 1984a), its implication is that marketing success depends upon the creation and use of marketing mixes that are more sensitive to and more considerate of the actions of buyers than are those of one's competitors. Sometimes the effective matching of corporate resources to customers' revealed requirements appears to result from no more than a managerial hunch or spontaneous insight. But appeals to 'entrepreneurial insight' do little to help managers make decisions. Detailed examination of the factors which make for successful new product development – in consumer durables and non-durables, and industrial goods – indicates that those companies which consistently produce winners have managers who understand customers' needs and behaviour, who work with the users of their products to develop more satisfactory innovations, rather than relying on guesswork or intuition (for example Foxall, 1984f).

Marketing management, especially the functions of marketing planning and the gathering and use of marketing intelligence, is inescapably based on some idea or other of how (and perhaps why) customers behave as they do. In the interests of effective marketing, it is necessary that those responsible for such ideas add appreciation of the subtleties and complexities of buyer behaviour to their entrepreneurial insights. The very success of behavioural science in marketing makes this emphasis important. Over the last two decades in particular, ideas about the psychological motivation of consumer choice have become increasingly current with the result that many unsophisticated and uninformed conclusions are frequently drawn with respect to the nature of consumers' decision processes. A person who has just purchased an inappropriate, expensive consumer durable, such as a video recorder, is unlikely to respond by going through an extensive decision process in which he or she calmly examines all the available alternative models and goes on to purchase one of them – but this is precisely what a recent, managerially oriented book on marketing suggests! Similarly, there is all too often a tendency to ascribe industrial buying decisions to either unalloyed ratiocination or emotional irrationality. A little knowledge can be misleading and even dangerous. This chapter, therefore, discusses, albeit briefly, the main ways of looking at consumer and industrial buying behaviour from the viewpoint of behavioural theory and research; it does so on the assumption that each perspective can be relevant to a particular set of circumstances but that none is universally valid.

THE CONSUMER BUYING PROCESS

Buying is a process, not a single act. It is a sequence of pre- and post-purchase activities which surround and influence purchase decisions. All the stages of buying are of interest to the marketing manager who seeks to influence pre-purchase awareness of needs or wants, any ensuing search for and evaluation of information about products and brands that might satisfy them, the topography of buying (what? where? how many? how often? and so forth), and the consequences of consumption, all of which may shape patterns of purchase and repurchase. Marketing strategies have been sought from understanding of the social and psychological factors which affect consumers' decisions at each stage of this sequence on the assumption that patterns of choice can be strengthened or modified by acting upon the social identification or mental state of the buyer. The behavioural sciences have been strongly invoked in this task: social psychology supplying concepts and measures of attention, perception, motivation, personality, attitudes, intentions and so on, whilst sociology and anthropology have provided concepts of status, social class, group influence and culture. Each of these influences has inspired *ad hoc* studies of consumer choice using, say, brand attitudes in an attempt to account for brand selection. A more sophisticated approach has attempted to organize the disparate behavioural science concepts – taking account of their interactions with one another, as well as their separate influences – into systematic models of human behaviour rather than a checklist of potential determinants of choice.

The most widely-established models of this kind (for example Howard and Sheth, 1969) depict the consumer as a processor of information who is involved in:

1 receiving via the senses data from the environment (say an advertisement for a new brand of a fast-moving product), and perceiving and interpreting them according to experience, opinions,

goals, personality structure and social conditioning;
2 searching for additional information to clarify the want/need so aroused, and evaluating the alternative competing brands available to satisfy it; and
3 developing the beliefs, attitudes and purchase intentions which in turn determine brand choice.

The consumer is thus portrayed as an active collaborator with the marketing system, engaged in establishing relevant cognitions (beliefs) and rationally modifying them on the basis of novel information, subsequently responding affectively (with like or dislike) to each alternative, and finally acquiring the conative (motivational) intention to buy the favoured brand (that which most closely fits the consumer's goals and aspirations) which precedes choice in the marketplace.

The sequence of events and accompanying mental processes and states assumed by such models is an elaboration of the cognition–affect–conation hierarchy proposed by the mechanistic models of advertising response of more than a quarter of a century ago. The resulting stimulus–organism–response (S–[O]–R) psychology of the comprehensive models is shown in simplified form in Figure 14.1.

Comprehensive modelling has played a useful, though limited, role in attempting to organize and integrate a mass of possibly explicative concepts, measures and research findings into a meaningful sequence which promotes understanding, prediction and, perhaps, control of consumer behaviour. In as much as testable hypotheses have been derived from the models, knowledge has increased; even when research has suggested that the models should be radically revised or alternative explanations sought, such modelling has played some part in stimulating systematic investigation in place of *ad hoc* enquiry. However, during the 1970s and 1980s, this approach to explanation has been strongly criticized both on scientific grounds and as a practical device for the prediction of such managerially useful aspects of consumer choice as brand and store choice.

The comprehensive models have depicted the individual consumer as too rationalistic an information processor, failed to make allowance for explanations which do not demand that the consumer is inevitably a highly involved and committed problem-solver, and otherwise made assumptions which have not been confirmed by observation, at least not sufficiently strongly to be of much use in marketing (Foxall, 1980). Empirical evidence for the models has always been scant, but most damaging is the revelation that except where conditions are highly conducive to a particular purchase, there is little relationship between those main determinants of attitude and intention to purchase suggested by the models and the buying decision itself (Foxall, 1983, 1984b).

Particularly in the non-laboratory contexts which are directly relevant to marketing, brand attitudes and brand purchase intentions may mean little as predictors of buyer behaviour. Situations which intervene between the expression of a purchase intention (say, as part of a market research investigation concerned with new brand development) and the opportunity to buy the new brand (when it eventually appears on the market) are responsible for low attitude–behaviour correspondence; this effect is, moreover, to be expected, given the limitations of the psychological theory and the research instruments employed. The implication is that analysis of the external environment within which consumer behaviour occurs, and of patterns of similar, prior behaviour, will lead to a more complete understanding of consumer choice (Foxall, 1984c, 1984d), and some comprehensive modellers have already moved in this direction.

LOW INVOLVEMENT, LOW COMMITMENT

For others, however, the central causal chain remains information – attitude–intention–behaviour, and there is no reason to abandon the information processing approach in its entirety simply because it is not unequivocally the key to understanding consumer choice in every circumstance.

Admittedly, there is support for sequences of consumer behaviour other than the familiar cognitive–affective–conative hierarchy which underpins many textbook accounts and much market research activity. In particular, there is the suggestion that, whilst minimal cognitive learning often precedes purchase, behaviour (purchase) is the next stage in the hierarchy, and affective or attitudinal effects follow rather than precede buying and consuming. But the experimental work which played a large part in establishing the predominance of

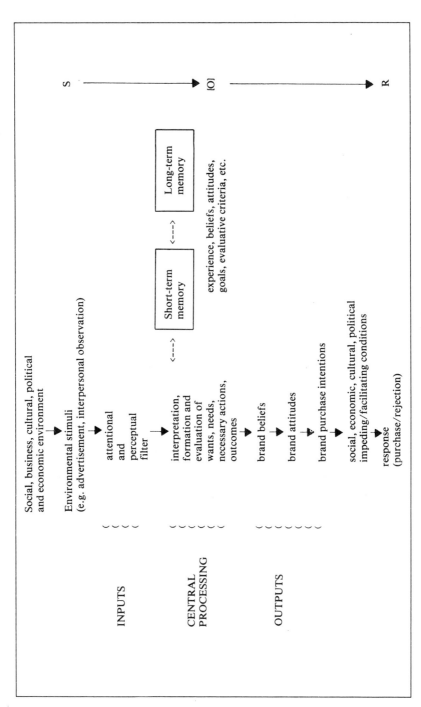

Figure 14.1   The consumer as an information processing system

this 'low-involvement hierarchy' also led to the conclusion that cognitive information processing, while occurring far less frequently, is the viable alternative (Ray, 1973). The sophisticated view which is slowly emerging among consumer researchers is that understanding should concentrate on the circumstances to which each sequence is appropriate rather than on trying to establish one or other as the sole explanatory mechanism.

This reasonable approach is adopted here, though it is important to emphasize the pervasive nature of low involvement/low commitment consumer behaviour: as the following discussion indicates, much of what is known from direct observation about consumer behaviour is consistent with this.

First and foremost, the evidence indicates that the frequently encountered uncommitted consumer uses information in a far more *ad hoc*, less structured way than the comprehensive models claim. In the key area of consumers' comprehension and use of additional nutritional information on food packaging, empirical research demonstrates that most buyers neither understood the extra data nor employed them in making purchasee choices. Although the consumers claimed to like more rather than less information and to feel more satisfied when it was provided, they did not as a result use it extensively or make more rational decisions (see Driver and Foxall, 1984). (This is not to argue against the provision of such information or the further education of buyers: but it hardly provides evidence of information-hungry buyers whose decision mechanisms are geared to the economically rational processing of information.

Even when relatively expensive, infrequently purchased consumer durables are bought, there is considerable evidence that buyers severely limit their pre-purchase searches for information. Customers in such circumstances often visit only one retail outlet and consider only one brand, using price and the reputation of suppliers as short-cut indicators of quality, and relying extensively on in-store sources of information such as sales staff, avoiding such 'neutral' sources of information and evaluation as *Which*? or Consumer Reports (Foxall, 1975; Robertson, 1976; Olshavsky and Granbois, 1979; Driver and Foxall, 1984).

This does not imply an irrational consumer but is consistent with the nature of human attentive and perceptual processes: only a small fraction of the information aimed at consumers penetrates their perceptual defences; still less is attended to, interpreted, yielded to, or allowed to exert influence over behaviour. Indeed, how else could the consumer cope with the massive volume of such information available from advertising and other sources?

Consumers, after all, shop and consume partly for fun; these leisure or semi-leisure actions have high emotional content and spring from a variety of non-work, non-intellectual motivations (Foxall, 1984e).

If extensive, formal information gathering, the first phase of comprehensive decision-making, is absent from much consumer behaviour, the whole process falls into doubt. Indeed, the elaborate sequence favoured by the early models is strikingly difficult to detect over a considerable range of consumer purchasing. The evidence supports the view that brand choice is usually not the outcome of any detectable decision process at all, not simply because the decision process becomes compressed with repeat buying, but because in many instances there is no such process at all 'even on the first purchase' (Olshavsky and Granbois, 1979, p. 99).

Again, this is hardly surprising: the opportunity costs of extensive problem-solving preclude an information-processing approach to selection within most product classes where, typically, the differences between competing brands are minimal or of little or no consequence to buyers: where, in other words, the consumer is relatively uninvolved, uncommitted and indifferent to the available substitutes. The notion of the consumer whose behaviour exhibits a narrowly defined rationality based on discriminations born of extensive information processing is difficult to sustain as a general model in face of evidence that in so many cases brand-level choices are determined by the social and physical environments in which buying occurs, notably the arrangement of supermarket and other store interiors which give rise to so-called impulse or unplanned purchasing on a large scale.

The concept of the information-processing consumer who is invariably an active problem-solver and decision-maker rests upon an exaggerated evaluation of the power of external stimuli to control behaviour, especially marketer-dominated information sources. Television advertising, widely cast as the strongest of these stimuli, far from involving its audience and creating determinative attitudes to brand purchase, effects – at most and after enormous repetition – small changes in viewers' perceptions. The viewer, far more concerned with the programmes, makes few if any connections between the advertising and his or her life, and even the minimal learning of brand names which may follow massive doses of repeated advertising is preconscious. It is the in-store opportunity to purchase the advertised brand that activates whatever perceptual learning has taken place, stimulates point of-sale remembering and, possibly, leads on to brand trial (Krugman, 1965).

Any affective response towards an advertised brand expressed at the pre-purchase stage must be extremely weak and speculative, perhaps reflecting feelings towards the advertisement itself rather than the advertised item. Attitudes, likes and dislikes based on evaluation can form only after purchase when the item's performance can be judged from direct experience. Even then, brand attitudes remain so weak (absolutely and by comparison with opinions about more involving social and political issues) that some investigators have asked whether recorded brand attitudes constitute anything more than measurement artefacts (Lastovicka and Bonfield, 1982).

Direct observation of sequences of consumer purchases over time bears this out. Since most product classes are composed of many brands, each similar to the others in terms of physical attributes and formulation, it is not surprising that the vast majority of buyers do not discriminate among them by preferring one brand above all others and showing 100 per cent loyalty to it in their purchasing. A small proportion of buyers of a product is completely loyal in this way, selecting the same brand on every occasion, but most are not. Most consumers purchase different brands on different occasions, selecting from a relatively small subset of available brands which are close, tried and tested substitutes. Thus, not every brand in the product class has an equal chance of being purchased – customers are not random buyers – and, while a typical consumer may purchase among the brands in his or her 'repertoire' in some systematic way (say, choosing brands A, B and C in a series of shopping trips in the order A B C A B C A B C ...), he or she is more likely to exhibit a fairly haphazard selection of repertoire brands over time. Strict brand switching, in the sense that a brand is totally abandoned as another is irrevocably substituted, is rare indeed (Ehrenberg and Goodhardt, 1988). Similar patterns of consumer behaviour over time also characterize store choice (Keng and Ehrenberg, 1984).

273

Awareness, trial, repeat

The identification of the uncommitted consumer, apparently indifferent at the brand level (however important and involving the *product* may be), and the careful monitoring of his or her choices over long series of shopping trips, has led to the development of a much simpler model of consumer behaviour based on the sequence awareness–trial–repeat buying (ATR) (Ehrenberg, 1974; Ehrenberg and Goodhardt, 1988). This depicts repeat buying (all-important to most consumer goods suppliers) not as the outcome of elaborate cognitive learning on the part of the individual buyer, but as a function of brand trial, the experience of buying and, more important, use of the selected brand. It is during this trial stage (which may involve several acts of purchase and consumption) that the consumer is able to make the evaluation on which the development of brand attitudes and future purchase intentions relies. Repeat buying rests upon the reinforcement of whatever positive benefits such use confers on the customer, his or her personal evaluations of its value in use, rather than on the mental conditioning inculcated by powerful marketing stimuli (which advertising is often assumed to present) and the strong, determinative mental states supposedly derived from them.

Trial itself is a function of awareness: consumers seldom purchase brands of either durables or non-durables of which they have not previously heard from acquaintances or advertising. Advertising *is* important, therefore, especially in the case of new brands, in achieving awareness of brand names. But its role is principally to arouse curiosity, at best an extremely weak positive evaluation which will lead to trial of the item.

The ATR model of purchasing and consumption, a dynamic representation of the sequence of consumer choices, does not deny the importance of the marketing mix – the advertising which creates awareness before trial and reminds the customer of any rewarding outcomes, thus reducing dissonance and encouraging repeat buying; distribution which provides brand availability for trial; pricing, the facilitating/impeding mechanism – but neither does it attribute to it the power to shape continuing brand choice before the buyer has even purchased the brand for the first time. ATR emphasizes the part played by evaluative trial, a facet of consumer behaviour which entails appraisal of the tried brand (especially in comparison with previously

274

adopted brands within the same product class) in determining the composition of the buyer's repertoire of brands and pattern of long-term purchasing.

Further, the ATR approach, together with the painstaking empirical research upon which it rests, helps clarify the nature of consumers' commitment and rationality. At the product class level, the buyer is likely to be highly involved and committed to purchase: the very frequency of purchase and the assiduous manner in which buyers try out and evaluate the available product class members in order to construct a repertoire of suitable alternatives support this. But the similarity of these alternatives, at least in terms of their physical composition, promotes relative indifference such that the individual buyer is uncommitted as a rule to any particular brand. As long as at least one repertoire brand is available, the consumer is likely to make a purchase, though most opt for variety when it is offered in the course of several purchase occasions.

This implies not a random, indifferent consumer but a sensible, informed and experienced buyer who knows what he or she wants and which brands supply it. This buyer's sensibility is not narrowly economic, however: a few extra pence to pay for an acceptable non-durable item, a few extra pounds for a durable, will not necessarily deter purchase. But the consumer is technically aware and experienced as a result of the frequency of purchase opportunities and the large amount of trial experience gained. The consumer is knowledgeable, within the requirements that make the product purchase desirable or necessary, and hence able to be a reasoning and alert purchaser if not a rational information processor.

CONSUMER BEHAVIOUR IN NEW AND MATURE MARKETS

The conclusion that both high- and low-commitment consumer behaviour exist, though the latter predominates, alone offers limited practical insight. At the least, it is necessary to know when each is likely to occur in order that appropriate marketing responses can be decided. One approach to understanding the contributions of these distinct concepts of consumer choice is to trace buyer behaviour over the life-cycle of a typical product market – at first, discontinuous in that it is founded upon a genuinely novel product whose adoption considerably modifies buyers' consumption patterns, but which, as it progresses, is characterized by the emergence of a number of continuous (that is, incrementally different) product versions, which have little if any disruptive influence on the consumption behaviour of buyers who are, by this time, familiar with the established product class.

Howard and Moore (1982) describe the behaviour of customers who are confronted by a discontinuous innovation (the first brand in an entirely new product class, for example video recorders or home computers in their initial manifestations) as 'extended problem-solving'. In the absence of similar brands, prospective buyers compare the innovation with products as similar to the new item as exist (say, tape recorders or hand-held calculators). This comparatively lengthy procedure occurs during the introduction and into the growth stages of the product life-cycle and allows the buyer to judge the discontinuous brand on the basis of perceptions of its additional benefits. Those who buy at this stage are relatively insensitive to price, typical consumer innovators who are inner-directed, affluent compared with later adopters, and venturesome (Foxall, 1984e).

During the growth stage of the cycle, consumers who have become familiar with the characteristics of the product find it easier to compare the various brands which emerge. Now that potential buyers appreciate the features of the product, more manufacturers have an incentive to enter the market, offering slightly different versions, knowing that customers can make straightforward judgements of the incremental innovations, and their repertoire decisions accordingly. Price becomes an increasingly salient variable in the purchase behaviour of the later adopters who now enter the market.

Once a dominant product design emerges for the industry (Abernathy and Utterback, 1978), the result of technological refinement and the alignment of production and marketing with clear knowledge of customers' requirements and purchase propensities, brands become increasingly standardized. Market segmentation based on customers' differing willingness to pay for brands of varying quality or performance emerge and, within each segment, competing brands satisfy the specific wants of buyers whose 'limited problem-solving' entails a sophisticated and informed process of choice.

The mature phase of the life-cycle sees the emergence of fewer new brands, but those which are launched conform closely in their formulation/construction to the design dominating the particular segment whose requirements they match. Customers are by now capable of comparing and evaluating a new version by reference to the attributes of a wide range of alternatives which make up the product class. Their purchases are accurately described as 'routine response behaviours', and the most important purchase criteria are price, availability, and the requirement that new brands reach the standard set by incumbent versions (Howard and Moore, 1982, p. 129).

This life-cycle approach embraces the highly involved consumer who, when highly discontinuous brands first appear, attempts to make informed decisions through careful evaluation of the costs and benefits likely to ensue from adoption; the somewhat sophisticated buyer whose purchase of one of the competing similar brands which later appear is preceded by minimal decision-making; and the apparently uncommitted consumer, involved at the product level to obtain certain well-defined benefits but less committed in advance of purchase to particular competing brands which supply them in a standardized manner.

INDUSTRIAL BUYER BEHAVIOUR

Industrial markets involve the economic transfer of products and services between business or other organizations. They include markets for such goods as primary produce, capital equipment, raw materials, and intermediate products such as components. They also include catalytic inputs which facilitate production without entering into products or the processes by which they are made: routine office supplies, for example, and corporate banking and insurance services. The nature of industrial buyer behaviour is somewhat different from that encountered in final consumer markets – notably because of the derived nature of demand for non-consumer goods – but the differences can easily be exaggerated.

Both consumer and industrial buying can be specialized and novel, taking on the appearance of a highly rationalized activity; both can be routinely repetitive, apparently entailing no decision process at all. Each can be socially influenced and result in group rather than individual choices. The main difference derives from the fact that

277

industrial buying is a professional activity, undertaken on behalf of formal organizations. While purchasing by final consumers is normally a prelude only to consumption, industrial buying usually represents an early stage in a process of investment, from which economic returns, perhaps at a prespecified rate or level, are sought. It is, therefore, an activity which forms part of the strategic management of the company and it is undertaken (indirectly if not directly) in competition with the strategic buying activities of other businesses.

As a result, industrial buying often attracts larger risks, both corporate and personal, and is marked by greater complexity and uncertainty than consumer buying. But not invariably: business organizations usually have far greater resources to withstand risk and uncertainty, and can bear the consequences of some purchasing mistakes that would break households. Similar considerations of selective perception, individual personalities and motivations, cognitive limitations, social status and group dynamics give rise to only boundedly rational decision-making in both spheres.

As was the case in the development of consumer buying models, determinants of purchasing which extend beyond the simplifying micro-economic assumption of economic rationality have tended to come to the fore in modelling industrial buying. Many examples – from that of the purchasing agents who were rewarded for achieving maximum discounts rather than minimum prices (Bonoma, 1982) to the emotional and political factors which influence fleet car buying – attest to the constraints on economic logic which characterize much organizational buying.

Indeed, the progress of industrial buying models closely parallels that of consumer behaviour models, from the 'task' models which confined decision-makers' motivations to the maximization of economic and technical utilities, to the 'non task' models which emphasized social, psychological, emotional and other non-economic influences, and on to the decision process and composite models which have tried to encapsulate the complexity of buyer behaviour by endeavouring to integrate economic, technical and behavioural considerations. Figure 14.2 summarizes the analytical and conceptual framework within which these models have been derived.

The central component is a decision sequence which implies a high level of economic and technical efficiency on the part of the purchasing organization. Aware of a problem, the decision-maker searches

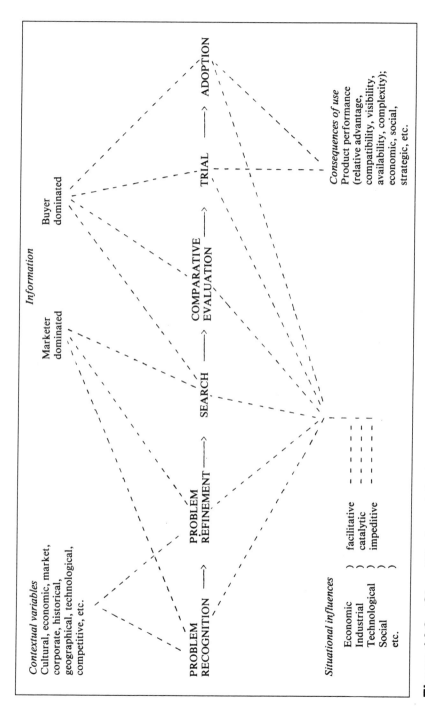

Figure 14.2 Simplified model of industrial buying

279

extensively for likely solutions, carries out thorough comparative evaluations of these, and ultimately selects that which promises the optimal returns. Empirical investigation and measurement have shown that a large proportion of purchase decision-making cannot be attributed to economic and technical logic alone: organizational and behavioural factors exert a significant influence on the shape of purchase outcomes (Baker, 1975; Parkinson and Baker, 1986). Most formal models have, therefore, attempted to indicate the nature of the antecedent and concurrent influences on industrial purchasing situations and the ways in which the consequences of previous purchases impinge upon new buying decisions.

This is not the place to review these models individually. It is instructive, however, to take account of the advance in understanding provided by the Buygrid analysis of Robinson *et al* (1967) which describes the situational influences which help shape buying behaviour and decisions.

The Buygrid distinguishes three buying situations: the new task, the modified re-buy, and the straight re-buy (which have much in common respectively with extended problem-solving, limited problem-solving, and routinized response behaviour).

New task buying occurs when the purchaser's uncertainty is greatest: because the problem in question has not previously arisen, decision-makers must draw upon whatever general experience they have; but, because their specific experience is nil, they rely heavily upon information from marketer-dominated sources to compare and evaluate as many feasible solutions as possible. These situations do not occur often, the decision processes they involve are thorough and careful (since not only the firm but the buyer's career may be at risk) and, frequently, the decision outcome plays a decisive part in determining future choices of supplier and make. A typical new task situation would occur when a novel make of capital equipment is introduced into a new product market at the beginning of the life-cycle of an innovative technology, for example the development of advanced manufacturing techniques. In this situation, the buying decision requires a number of formal and informal stages; all the buyphases depicted in the Buygrid (Figure 14.3) are probable.

Straight re-buys are the opposite of this: recurring purchases which can be dealt with by routine procedures. Previous suppliers are most likely to be considered at this stage and it is most probable that the present in-seller (the existing supplier) will receive the new order. Most industrial/organizational buying decisions fall into this category; there is no need for the buying organization to go through all the buyphases to reorder satisfactory products and the sequence of buyphases shown in the Buygrid is thus severely telescoped.

The out-seller (that is, not an existing supplier) is clearly at a disadvantage. His or her strategy is usually, therefore, to persuade the buyer that some element of the purchase situation has changed: he or she may offer a significant price advantage, new technology, a more extensive system or other inducement. Buyers faced with such new information normally attempt to obtain the benefits from the in-seller before considering a switch: although most stay with the in-seller, the out-seller has introduced some change in their routine buying behaviour. The point is usually to alter the buyer's decision criteria in some way.

If the out-seller is successful in persuading the buyer that some important facets of his or her purchasing situation have altered, the task situation becomes a modified re-buy and the buyer is likely to reconsider a number of the buyphases depicted in the Buygrid, possibly phases 2 to 8.

THE SOCIAL CONTEXT

Both consumer and industrial buying are socially influenced but the latter differs in that it is generally undertaken within a formal organizational structure in which responsibility for buying has been consciously apportioned. At its simplest industrial buying requires no more than a purchasing agent acting knowledgeably, perhaps on behalf of others: such straight re-buys can be safely delegated to professional buyers. At its most complex, as in the case of new task buying, it may require the multiple interactions of many executives of differing status and functional responsibility. The term 'buying centre' is used to denote the various individuals within the organization who participate in a buying decision. Its composition varies from transaction to transaction and its members are often difficult to identify in complex buying situations, for instance for a new data processing system.

Such new task buying typically involves managers of differing

		Buyclasses		
Buyphases		New	Modified	Straight
1 Anticipation or recognition of a problem (need) and a general solution				
2 Determination of characteristics and quantity of needed item				
3 Description of characteristics and quantity of needed item				
4 Search for and qualification of potential sources				
5 Acquisition and analysis of proposals				
6 Evaluation of proposals and selection of suppliers(s)				
7 Selection of an order routine				
8 Performance feedback and evaluation				

Source: Patrick J. Robinson, Charles W. Faris and Yoram Wind, *Industrial Buying and Creative Marketing* (Boston: Allyn & Bacon, 1967), p. 14. Reproduced with permission.

Figure 14.3   The Buygrid

status, both in terms of the executive levels and the functional areas represented. In addition, the roles and interactions found in such infrequent purchasing are complex: *gatekeepers* may facilitate or impede the flow of information, and will certainly edit it, before it reaches *deciders*; *influencers* attempt to ensure that specific features are available in the required product or that a particular supplier is favoured; *users* may be responsible for initiating the entire purchase-decision sequence, with or without taking any further interest or part in the ensuing operations, though if they do they are likely to play an important role in determining the specifications of the chosen product. The actual *buyers* in new task contexts, those who negotiate and place an order, are likely to be senior managers who are not purchasing specialists.

Establishing the precise composition of the buying centre is no simple task; researchers' ideas of who participated in a specific decision vary according to the methodology they employ (Moriarty, 1983). However, it is interesting to note Johnston and Bonoma's (1981a) report that, on average, four functional departments, three strata of managers, and seven individuals were required to make a typical capital equipment purchase in the sample of firms they investigated; in the case of service acquisitions, four departments, two levels of management, and five individual managers participated.

Straight re-buys, by contrast, involve much simpler social relationships. Responsibility can, as has been noted, be safely delegated to the specialist buyer who may need to consult no one else in the organization. However, even in such circumstances, the buyer is subject to the attempts of some out-sellers to modify the topography of the buying situation, possibly by circumventing the buyer's authority by appealing to a senior manager.

This is a useful reminder that industrial buying is a political process and sellers' failure to consider the distribution of power within the purchasing organization has not infrequently resulted in failure to sell. The control of information and communication is central to the nature of industrial buying; the capacity to exert control over the gatekeeping role of purchasing managers is especially valuable (Johnston and Bonoma, 1981b). For important decisions, buying power does not necessarily reside with those who carry formal authority in the organization; neither is influence over the buying-decision process confined to any particular functional area. Bonoma (1982) notes, however, that those who wield power in the buying centre can be identified through careful observation of managers' verbal and non-verbal communications behaviour.

However, those managers who have ultimate authority to make purchases (especially in complicated new task buying) are frequently the most anonymous and least visible members of the buying centre: knowing that they alone can ratify decisions, they are often content to leave negotiations to juniors who must defer to them for the final say-so.

INDUSTRIAL MARKET SEGMENTATION

Recognition of the similarities between consumer and industrial buying, especially in mass markets, has led to an increasing use of research concepts and techniques originally developed for, and for years confined to, the former sphere in the analysis of organizational buyer behaviour (Foxall *et al*, 1987). While it has been customary to segment industrial markets according to non-behavioural factors such as product, company size, geographical location and supplier, there has been steadily mounting interest in more sophisticated approaches which take purchase and consumption behaviour into consideration (for example Wind and Cardozo, 1974).

A particularly interesting development is the segmentation of industrial markets according to the benefits sought by buyers, a technique applied originally for consumer goods (Haley, 1968) and recently exemplified by Moriarty (1983) in a study of buyer behaviour in the non-intelligent data terminal market. This market contains over forty competing suppliers but is dominated by IBM which accounts for about two-thirds of sales. Segmentation has traditionally been based on the division of buyers into IBM and non-IBM purchasers. On the basis of an extensive survey of non-intelligent data terminal buyers, 40 per cent of which had bought IBMs, Moriarty compares such supplier-orientated segmentation with that which emerges from consideration of the benefits sought. It is instructive, in view of changing conceptualizations of industrial buyer behaviour, to follow his comparison.

His research indicates that IBM machines appeal disproportionately to large firms (employing more than 1000) and firms in the distribution and financial sectors. IBM deciders emerge as low-risk purchasers, keen to please their superior managers by making a visibly 'safe' purchase, selecting a terminal which is supported by a full range of software and complementary equipment, and which is compatible with their firms' existing mainframe computers. IBM selectors have more experience than non-IBM deciders in purchasing terminals; their companies also buy significantly more terminals which may give rise to this. IBM-buyers' purchases are generally funded by their data processing departments. Participants in the buying decision report greater need (than their opposite numbers in non-IBM buying organizations) to feel confident about what they are buying and perceive the decision as risky, but their conservatism in buying belies a high degree of self-ascribed innovativeness.

Non-IBM machines appeal disproportionately to small companies (with up to 250 employees) and companies in manfacturing. Non-IBM buyers apparently used a more formal purchase decision procedure, considering more sellers at the initial and final stages; they also attach more importance to formal information sources, significantly more than IBM-buyers to such external sources as trade advertisements, literature and trade shows (Moriarty, 1983, pp. 99–109).

Cutting across these supplier-based categories is another basis for segmentation: the different benefits sought by relatively homogeneous groups of buyers of data teminals. Moriarty identifies two main benefit segments in this market. Both rate service and reliability as extremely important and, in addtion: segment 1 seeks price flexibility, that is, a willingness on the part of the supplier to negotiate, high sales competence and ease of operation; segment 2 is concerned primarily with the quality of software available, the breadth and compatibility of the manufacturer's product line, the visibility of the chosen machine to top management and the stability and reputation of the manufacturer. This second segment is relatively insensitive to price.

Consideration of these two segments gives a rather different impression of segment structure from that suggested by a supplier-related classification. Segment 1 firms are more likely to be located in distribution and manufacturing, segment 2 in business services. Segment 1 firms are of small and medium scale (having up to 1000 employees), segment 2 large (over 1000), though the former are more likely to have larger operating units (employing over 1000). The decision participants in segment 1 firms are most probably middle managers from the sales, production, and administrative functions and general managers, while those in segment 2 are more likely to be finance and data processing specialists but senior or first-line managers. The former perceive greater risk in the decision, believing themselves to be under greater time pressure; the latter have greater need for confidence in the product and value prior experience of a supplier.

Finally, 31 per cent of segment 1 firms and 51 per cent of segment 2 firms had purchased IBM machines (Moriarty 1983, pp. 110–120).

MARKETS AS NETWORKS

Every frame of reference has its uses and its limitations and it is worth concluding by noting the criticisms of the framework assumed in this chapter (and in the majority of marketing publications) advanced by those academics who portray industrial markets in terms of networks

285

of organizations which share long term, stable relationships (Hammarkvist *et al*, 1983).

The typical 'marketing-mix-based' approach to markets assumes the viewpoint of the supplier and concentrates on a single time period; but the networks approach (Mattsson, 1984) emphasizes their interactions over time. It is based on the understanding of the market environment as a vast network of related firms. Rather than separate the values exchanged in the marketplace into the four major marketing mix elements controlled by a marketing manager, the networks paradigm is concerned with the totality of resources and activities of seller and buyer and the resulting interdependencies. The dominant framework for understanding marketing assumes that information is usually gathered through market research, that is, separate investigations remote from normal commercial interactions, but the networks approach stresses that marketing intelligence is received and interpreted during the market exchange process, that is, as part of everyday commercial relationships. While the former approach delineates the firm clearly according to its legal and constitutional boundaries, the latter is based on an open systems viewpoint in which the firm's boundaries are behaviourally determined and, therefore, cannot be fixed. While the firm is portrayed in the 'marketing-mix approach' as a self-contained entity engaged in persuading or otherwise influencing the consumers and competitors, the interaction approach emphasizes the co-operation and trust that exists between firms, their joint mechanisms for handling conflict (Mattsson, 1984; see also Turnbull and Cunningham, 1981).

This emerging framework, which has been applied predominantly to industrial markets but has scope for application in consumer markets too, probably applies mainly to buying situations involving straight and modified re-buys rather than those involving considerable discontinuity. But it places a valuable emphasis upon the frequent long-term relationships encountered by market participants and provides a useful antidote to the too constrained view of the market which is the received wisdom.

REFERENCES AND FURTHER READING

Abernathy, W. J. and Utterback, J. M. (1978), 'Patterns of industrial innovation', *Technology Review*, Vol.80, pp.41–47.

Baker, M. J. (1975), *Marketing New Industrial Products*, Macmillan, London.

Bonoma, T. V. (1982), 'Major sales: who really does the buying?', *Harvard Business Review*, Vol.60, No.3, pp.111–119.

Driver, J. C. and Foxall, G. R. (1984), *Advertising Policy and Practice*, Holt, Rinehart and Winston, London; St Martin's Press, New York.

Ehrenberg, A. S. C. (1974), 'Repetitive advertising and the consumer', *Journal of Advertising Research*, Vol.14, No.1, pp.25–34.

Ehrenberg, A. S. C. and Goodhardt, G. J. (with G. R. Foxall) (1988), *Understanding Buyer Behaviour*, Wiley, New York.

Foxall, G. R. (1975), 'Social factors in consumer choice', *Journal of Consumer Research*, Vol.2, No. 1, pp.60–64.

Foxall, G. R. (1980), 'Marketing models of buyer behaviour: a critical review', *European Research*. Vol.8, No.5, pp.195–206.

Foxall, G. R., (1983) *Consumer Choice*, Macmillan, London; St Martin's Press, New York.

Foxall, G. R. (1984a) 'Marketing's Domain', *European Journal of Marketing*, Vol.18, No.1, pp.25–40.

Foxall, G. R., (1984b) 'Evidence for attitudinal–behavioural consistency: implications for consumer research paradigms', *Journal of Economic Psychology*, Vol.5, No.1, pp.71–92.

Foxall, G. R. (1984c), 'Consumers' intentions and behaviour', *Journal of the Market Research Society*, Vol.26, No.3, pp.231–241.

Foxall, G. R.(1984d) 'Developing new products: attitudes, intentions and behaviour revisited', *Marketing Intelligence and Planning*, Vol.2, No.1, pp.23–32.

Foxall, G. R. (1984e), 'Meanings of marketing and leisure: issues for research and development', *European Journal of Marketing*, Vol.18, No.2, pp.23–32.

Foxall, G. R. (1984f), *Corporate Innovation: Marketing and Strategy*, Croom Helm, London; St Martin's Press, New York.

Foxall, G. R., Gutmann, J. N. and Moore, R. M. (1987), 'Mass marketing and the role of consumer-style research in non-consumer markets', *1987 Conference Papers*, Market Research Society, London, pp.167–184.

Haley, R. I. (1968) 'Benefit segmentation: a decision oriented tool', *Journal of Marketing*, Vol.32, pp.30–35.

Hammarkvist, K.-O., Hakansson, H, and Mattsson, L.-G. (1983), 'Markets as networks', in: M. Christopher *et al* (eds), *Back to Basics: Marketing and the 4P's*, Cranfield School of Management.

Howard, J. A. and Moore, W. L. (1982), 'Changes in consumer behaviour over the product life cycle', in M. L. Tushman and W. L. Moore (eds), *Readings in the Management of Innovation*, Pitman, London, pp.122–130.

Howard, J. A. and Sheth, J. N. (1969), *The Theory of Buyer Behaviour*, Wiley, New York.

Johnston, W. J. and Bonoma, T. V. (1981a), 'Purchase process for capital equipment and services', *Industrial Marketing Management*, Vol.10, pp.253–259.

Johnston, W. J. and Bonoma, T. V. (1981b) 'The buying centre: structure and interaction patterns', *Journal of Marketing*, Vol.45, pp. 143–156.

Keng, K. A. and Ehrenberg, A. S. C. (1984), 'Patterns of store choice', *Journal of Marketing Research*, Vol. XXI, pp. 399–409.

Krugman, H. E. (1965), 'The impact of television advertising: learning without involvement', *Public Opinion Quarterly*, Vol.29, No.4, pp.349–356.

Lastovicka, J. L. and Bonfield, E. H. (1982), 'Do consumers have brand attitudes?', *Journal of Economic Psychology*, Vol.2, No.1, pp.57–75.

Mattsson, L.-G.(1984), 'An application of a network approach to marketing: defending and changing market positions', in N. Dholakia and J. Arndt (eds), *Changing the Course of Marketing: Alternative Paradigms for Widening Marketing Theory*, JAI Press, Greenwich.

Moriarty, R. T. (1983), *Industrial Buying Behavior*, D. C. Heath, Lexington.

Olshavsky, R. W. and Granbois, D. H. (1979), 'Consumer decision-making – fact or fiction?', *Journal of Consumer Research*, Vol.6, No.2, pp. 93–100.

Parkinson, S. T. and Baker, M. J. (1986), *Organisational Buying Behaviour*, Macmillan, London.

Ray, M. L. (1973), 'Marketing communication and the hierarchy-of effects', in P. Clarke (ed), *New Models for Mass Communication Research*, Sage, Beverly Hills, pp. 147–176.

Robertson, T. S., (1976) 'Low commitment consumer behavior', *Journal of Advertising Research*, Vol.16, No.2, pp.19–24.

Robinson, P. J., Faris, C. W. and Wind, Y. (1967), *Industrial Buying and Creative Marketing*, Allyn & Bacon, Boston.

Turnbull, P. and Cunningham, M. T. (eds) (1981), *International Marketing and Purchasing*, Macmillan, London.

Wind, Y. and Cardozo, R. N. (1974), 'Industrial market segmentation', *Industrial Marketing Management*, Vol.3, pp.369–377.

15

Marketing research

Bill Blyth

Marketing research is dynamic. Market research is passive. Marketing research is the collection and synthesis of primary or secondary data and their transformation into *information* that is relevant, timely and accurate for the task.

DEFINING THE INFORMATION REQUIREMENTS

The principles of defining information needs are completely independent of the product being offered or conceived, be it a consumer product, a business-to-business service or heavy capital plant. Unless users of research have a clear and concise definition of the information they require, they will carry out unsatisfactory – and at worst misleading – research.

Once the information requirement is defined, together with a number of straightforward criteria, the most apposite research should be apparent to a skilled market researcher. When carrying out market research, use skilled professional advice, and involve the researcher in defining the information need – the research brief. Research is not a science; however, it follows certain logical principles which have developed over time and which rarely fail to produce an answer *if* the proper criteria are observed.

STRUCTURING THE INFORMATION NEED

In any management environment, data are continually being made available in a myriad of forms. In identifying a research need one asks two questions:

1   What do I know?
2   What do I need to know in addition?

To identify what one knows it is useful to have a simple way of structuring available and potential data. For any market there are a finite number of questions research can answer about actual or potential purchasers.

1   Who are you?
2   What do you buy?
3   How much do you buy?
4   What do you pay?
5   Where did you buy it?
6   When did you buy it?
7   What else could you have bought?
8   Why?

From this data set one then infers the answers to:

9   What will you buy next?
10   What if ... (for example) price/advertising/ distribution/packaging/product specification are changed?

The ultimate market research study would contain answers for questions 1–8 all obtained simultaneously from individual entities purchasing or potentially purchasing in a market. In practice this is never obtained, although it must be acknowledged that developments related to EPOS technology and other microcomputer advances, are making this partly possible in some consumer markets in the USA.

The reasons why it is not possible are the other criteria by which the information need is defined:

• time
• depth

- accuracy
- obtainability
- cost.

Time

Research takes time. Even if the data already exist they have to be found and accessed in a relevant way. Good marketing management starts from a clear understanding of what it knows or what it can access. Then, if the information need can be quickly defined, the research has to carried out. Typically, the more accurate the research, the longer it takes and the greater the cost. One needs to trade off these variables, particularly for tactical applications. The need for punctual and accurate information can often be met by subscribing to one of the available subscription databases, but at a cost.

Depth

Irrespective of whether the unit of information is an individual, a household, a commercial establishment or an organization, there is a limit to the amount of information that can be collected, be it by personal interview, by telephone, or self-completion either in writing or now, in some instances, via a keyboard. Here the trade-off is between depth and breadth. The deepest information comes from 'qualitative' research, interviewing consumers either individually or in small groups. Here the questioning is unstructured, with a trained executive interviewer guiding the questioning. Such research can go deep into underlying attitudes and motivations. However, it is extremely expensive and rarely conducted on a scale of more than fifty individual interviews or six group discussions with six to eight individuals in each. Consequently, the findings are not quantifiable in the sense of having statistical accuracy.

In the UK the opposite end of the spectrum is the Target Group Index which interviews some 25000 people about almost everything they could possibly buy, watch, read, or do. However, the depth of questioning is relatively low and relies on recall of behaviour. The latter will give you a quick guide to the percentage of the population who ever buy a product, the former an in-depth analysis of 'Why?'

Table 15.1 Accuracy of sample sizes

Sample size	True population (within ± %) 19/20 of the time	9/10 of the time
250	9.0%	7.5%
500	7.0%	5.5%
1000	4.5%	4.0%
2000	3.0%	2.5%

Accuracy

In so far as market research has a scientific basis, it lies in statistics. The application of statistical theory provides the ability to draw a representative sample of a population, and further the ability to calculate the probability that the answers given by that sample lie within certain limits of the true population value.

Table 15.1 gives simplistically the accuracy of various sample sizes.

To halve the error, one has to quadruple the sample size. Unfortunately costs are linear but accuracy is not. Furthermore, there are many sources of error other than that related to sample size:

- the sample selection
- the wording of the questions
- the order of the questions
- the interviewers
- the analysis of the data

All these factors potentially increase the error. Good research will reduce these errors, and will measure them. It cannot eliminate them. In a strict sense errors of this type are random.

The second factor affecting accuracy is bias. Bias is factors inherent in the research design which consistently lead to mis-estimation. Sometimes they can be built knowingly into the research, at others they occur in an uncontrolled manner. An almost universal and planned bias in much consumer research is that institutional residents are excluded, for example imprisoned criminals, members of the armed forces, students in halls of residence. An uncontrolled bias might be brought about by the difficulty of interviewing in high deprivation areas. This probably results in under-representing the young, unskilled unemployed. For most purposes this does not matter

Table 15.2 Approximate ad hoc research costs

Type of research	Cost (£)
Depth interview	180–300 +
Group discussion	600–1000 +
Hall test (200 × 20-minute interviews – housewives)	2500–3500
Personal interview (1000 × 20-minute interviews – adullts	9000–12000
Telephone (1000 × 10-minute interviews – adults)	6000 – 8000
Omnibus survey (1000 × 10 questions – adults)	2000–2500

in either instance, but for some it might. Accuracy requirements and key areas in which to avoid bias must be identified in advance and then traded off against other elements.

Obtainability

By this is meant:

1 Do people know the answers?
2 Are they prepared to give them to you?
3 Do they have the time?

If the answer to any of these is no, there is little point in pursuing the research without amendment. Research typically relies on the good-will of the respondents and little or no fee is generally paid. Abusing that spirit of co-operation produces bad research not only for oneself, but over time alienates respondents.

Cost

By international standards research in the UK is still cheap. Very large amounts of data are available 'off the shelf' (see Chapter 1). Typically subscriptions for commercial research range from the £10000s to in excess of £100000. Most research is still *ad hoc*, that is, tailor-made. For this type of research the market is very competitive, prices quoted varying depending on quality, overhead structure and the state of the order book. The prices quoted in Table 15.2 are intended to be a rough guide.

For minority groups, cost will be higher.

TYPES OF RESEARCH

The best information for any market must be:

1   What are my sales?
2   How big is the market?

The success of retail audit market research data in the 1950s was arguably founded on the fact that they told manufacturers what their own sales were, and in the 1960s what their competitors' were. In every gross oversimplification there is a grain of truth. Even today in the era of expensive and complex marketing management information systems one is continually surprised by the number of companies which do not possess basic data about their own business. Examples are the inability to distinguish domestic and export sales; in financial services to distinguish accounts and customers; the lack of any customer classification data; the confusion of sell-in and consumer offtake.

The lack of hard data about one's own business precludes most of the benefit of external data.

The size of the market can generally be simply and roughly estimated by *desk research*. Desk research is the use of published secondary data. For almost any market government statistics are available which enable the calculation of market size in terms of volume or value. Published data represent just the tip of the iceberg. Relevant departments are generally willing to co-operate to produce relevant data. For most consumer markets the Family Expenditure Survey gives the ability to calculate market sizes, for others production statistics together with import and export statistics will suffice. The CSO publishes a guide to what is available – *CSO Guide to Official Statistics* – and it is an invaluable tool for all marketing departments. Government data also serve to fill in the basic margins of much other data – detailed population data, employment data and many other little-known but valuable series. Great care is taken in their construction and so far as possible their accuracy should be assumed to be as good as possible. Accordingly, they also serve as an additional cross-check on other ancillary sources.

Beyond government data there are a rapidly growing number of database providers who sell data from a variety of sources. For first-time users an approach to one of them may be the most cost efficient route, rather than trying to pursue their own desk research. A list of some prominent suppliers appears at the end of the chapter.

With the growth in information technology this trend can only continue to grow. Much ingenuity is being addressed to repackaging existing data or cross-referencing it, for example linking census data to postcoded address lists, and the applications go beyond market research to a number of other related services such as direct mail.

If one's sales or potential sales are low in relation to the total market the need for formal market research will also be small, unless one is seeking difficult-to-identify sub-groups of a market. Potential customers will be contacted via point of sale or address lists; substantial sales increases will still be relatively small to the total market and thus regular monitoring of the total market unnecessary; advertising will be low and often local or specialized, perhaps requiring testing for comprehension, but with directly observable effects.

Above this level there will be the need for research, and potentially research against every chapter heading of this book. Over time researchers have developed techniques suitable for providing relevant information for aiding management of different aspects of marketing. The actual techniques will vary by type of business depending on how the data in the overall data model need to be obtained. Readers are referred to the reference material given at the end of the chapter if they require further information on this subject.

For any specific information need there will be more than one way in which the information can be obtained. There are no perfect solutions. The requirement of the marketing manager is to define *all* the parameters of the information need as clearly and in as much detail as possible, and then to test the proposed research against those parameters. For those totally new to research, without an internal department to provide expertise and experience, the employment of a consultant to guide planning at the early stages would be sensible.

COMMISSIONING MARKET RESEARCH

There are over 300 companies providing market research as their main business service in the UK. In addition, large numbers of other consultancies claim to provide expertise in this area. The professional bodies of the industry – the Market Research Society and the Industrial Market research Association – have a code of conduct covering all aspects of research which their members must observe. It is advised that research is commissioned from companies where at least the senior executives are members of one of these associations. The Market Research Society publishes an annual list of organizations carrying out research in the UK together with details of company size and specialization. It also publishes a list of similar companies operating in other countries and a list of consultants. It is possible to commission a UK-based agency to co-ordinate research in several countries simultaneously and some companies specialize in this, either through overseas subsidiaries or associated companies.

Word-of-mouth recommendation is a good start for those new to buying research. Research companies rely on repeat business. Users need to find the right blend of technical skills, organization and people that gives them the best service.

However, at the end of the day good research requires a good brief, and the researcher becoming involved in understanding the client's business and their needs. To achieve this both sides need to make a contribution.

FURTHER READING

Bradley, U. (1987), *Applied Marketing and Social Research*, 2nd edn, Wiley, Chichester.

Crimp, M, (1986), *The Marketing Research Process*, 2nd edn, Prentice-Hall, New Jersey.

Dillman, D. (1978), *Mail and Telephone Studies*, Wiley, Chichester.

Foxall, G. R., (1983) *Consumer Choice*, Macmillan, London.

Mort, D. and Siddall, L. (1986), *Sources of Unofficial UK Statistics*, Gower, Aldershot.

Moser, C. A. and Kalton, G. (1978), *Survey Methods in Social Investigation*, Heinemann, London.

Worcester, R. M. and Downham, J. (1986), *Consumer Market Research Handbook*, 3rd edn, Elsevier North-Holland, Amsterdam.

USEFUL ADDRESSES

Information providers

Datasolve Ltd 99 Staines Road West Sunbury-on-Thames Middlesex TW16 7AH

Euromonitor Publications Ltd 87–88 Turnmill Street London EC1M 5QU

Finsbury Data Services Ltd 68–73 Carter Lane London EC4V 5EA

Harvest Information Services Ltd The Mall 359 Upper Street London N1 0PD

Maid Systems Ltd Maid House 26 Baker Street London W1M 1DF

Mintel Publications 7 Arundel Street London WC2R 3DR

Institutions

Association of Marketing Survey Organizations (AMSO) Ince House 60 Kenilworth Road Leamingtom Spa Warwickshire CV32 6JY Tel: 0926 36425

Industrial Marketing Research Association (IMRA) 11 Bird street Lichfield Staffordshire WS13 6PW Tel: 0543 263448

The Market Research Society 175 Oxford Street London W1R 1TA Tel: 01-439 2585

16
Product planning

Simon Majaro

The marketing concept is no longer new. It has been in existence for almost forty years and has been absorbed into the strategic and operational culture of many companies. Nevertheless, it is disappointing to observe what a superficial hold the underlying philosophy of marketing has attained in many organizations. So many years after Theodore Levitt (1960) wrote his classic *Marketing Myopia* we still find many companies talking about their products in production or technology terms rather than customer benefit terms. Too many companies consider marketing as an organizational function whereas the true converts to the marketing creed treat it as an organizational ethos, a 'way of life'.

Peter Drucker summarized this simple notion many years ago by saying 'Until the customer has derived final utility, there is really no "product "; there are only "raw materials".' In other words, the production people must be involved; the department must be aware of the customer and his or her needs and so too must the personnel and finance functions. The paramount objective is to ensure that the customer derives final utility and satisfaction; without them there is no 'product'.

If this statement is true, one is entitled to ask a very fundamental question: 'What is the product?' This question represents a very subtle shibboleth. The reader may recall the biblical story of Gileadites who could identify their enemies by asking them to say 'Shibboleth'. Whoever responded by saying 'Sibboleth' was an enemy and was slain. The inability to pronounce the test word correctly betrayed the person's nationality. Ask a person: 'What is your "product"?' and the answer will help you to judge the level of understanding and commitment that the interlocutor has towards the 'marketing concept'.

THE VARIOUS FACES OF THE 'PRODUCT'

A product has many faces. What the manufacturing person sees can be very different from what the marketing person should be seeing. Let us take an example. A company manufactures ball bearings and roller bearings in a vast assortment of sizes, alloys and configurations. The production manager will respond to the question: 'What is your product?' by simply saying 'ball bearings and roller bearings'.

The marketing manager should be punished if he gives the same reply. To him the product or products are 'anti-friction' devices. They are aids to the reduction of friction in a number of machines or instruments, such as motor cars and machine tools. The true marketer knows in detail the various sectors of the Standard Industrial Classification and will be able to enumerate the needs for anti-friction devices of each of the sectors listed. Where there is no friction there is no need for the product, or to be more precise there is no product in Peter Drucker's terms. This example is quite simple. Let us look at more complicated cases.

A pharmaceuticals company manufactures a number of drugs. By the nature of the industry and its level of technology the drugs represent complex chemical compounds. The production people and the research and development people are very tempted to define the product in units of the 'wonder drug' that the firm produces. The enlightened marketing person will describe the product in terms of the illness which the drug combats or the discomfort which it alleviates. The production-orientated man will boast about the units of the antibiotics which the firm manufactured in a given period; the truly marketing-orientated person will talk about the number of pneumonia sufferers who were cured by 'our product' and, when attempting to measure the firm's market share, will do so in relation to his or her perception of the market, namely the number of pneumonia cases that occur in the course of the year.

Normally the more intricate the product and the more sophisticated the technology the greater the chasm between the perceptions of the product among the various functions of the enterprise. Obviously the research and development person who has been instrumental in the development of a highly innovative analgesic would prefer to talk about the complex chemical molecule of the product, rather than its headache alleviation characteristics. They are of course both right, but the research and development person talks about the physical properties of the product; the marketer talks about what the product does for the consumer. In marketing terms the latter utility is the one that really matters. Unless you have a headache you are not in the marketplace and the product has no relevance to you. If you do have a headache you become passionately interested in the product, not because it contains the x or y wonder ingredients but simply because it will alleviate your condition.

A manufacturer of diesel engines will tend to talk about the number of units, the size of the units and the number of cylinders produced in the course of the year. 'What is your product?' will inevitably be answered with 'Diesel engines of 50 h.p. or 75 h.p. etc. configuration'! The marketer should say: 'We manufacture energy producing units of a particular design as an auxiliary facility in process plants, or ships or hospitals and at a cost per unit of electricity of x pence etc.' The marketing person must respond to the question as if he or she were the buyer of the product.

The message should be fairly clear. The marketer who has absorbed the marketing concept as a way of life will always seek to identify the product in terms of what it does for the customer and the cost/benefit it is capable of generating for the consuming environment, whether it is an industrial environment or a domestic one.

THE 'PRODUCT' – A NEW DIMENSION

Much has been written about the product life-cycle and what happens to sales and profitability during its course. The concept is a useful one but one of its pitfalls is the fact that we often forget to identify the product in terms that are really meaningful to the marketing process. The product may be progressing well towards 'growth' in the context of its technology or manufacturing processes, yet it may have reached its 'saturation' point in terms of its market or segment penetration. The two levels of performance are not necessarily congruent. Let us take an example.

A manufacturer of running shoes supplies the fraternity of professional and quasi-professional joggers with specially designed shoes that provide arch support when running or sprinting. The sales follow a classical pattern which indicates that a 'product life-cycle' is in operation. As a result of the ravages of competition and the fact that the product has reached the saturation point in the cycle, pressure on margins is heavy and erosion of profitability is taking place. Nonetheless, rather unexpectedly the life-cycle takes a twist upwards and sales are starting to boom again. The obvious implication is that the laws of gravity have been defied and that the theory of the product life-cycle should be relegated to academic manuscripts only.

What has really happened is that the 'marketing ecology' has changed. A new market has sprung up for the firm's product: the amateur joggers, people of all ages who have read about the health value of jogging and decided to join the throng of early morning enthusiasts. In truth what has happened is that a new market has developed and to all intents and purposes the product has acquired a new face and should be treated as a new product. On this basis one would have one product for the professional runner and one for the enthusiastic jogger. The physical product may be the same but the marketing product will be different and each will deserve its separate analysis *vis-à-vis* the life cycle evaluation.

In the light of this it is instructive to re-examine the earlier example from the pharmaceuticals industry. Imagine that Stanton Chemicals manufactures an antibiotic product, Stantalyn, which is used effectively in the treatment of a wide range of infections. If the product is looked at as a technological package its life-cycle could be traced on the basis of its total sales and profitability. On the other hand, we can rightly assume that each infection type represents a separate market with the result that one can plot the life-cycle performance in relation to each sickness. Thus, without getting too involved in the technicalities of a complex industry, one can have a product life-cycle in respect of each identifiable 'indication': infections of the throat, ear, lungs, bile duct and so on. Each 'indication' will have its own product (with or without different brand names) and each one of these products will have its own life-cycle.

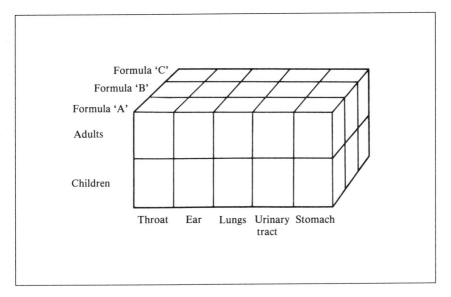

Figure 16.1 Product/market/segment vectors

The situation can be further embellished by saying that the drug used by children in relation to one kind of illness is a different product from the one used by adults. Thus we finish by getting a three-dimensional matrix of product/market/segment *vectors*.

It is quite possible that the product will need to undergo a slight differentiation process, such as the production of a sweetened syrup for children, to facilitate absorption or swallowing, but essentially the product characteristics in technical terms are probably unchanged. Thus this illustration would suggest that we have many products as shown in Figure 16.1, and not just one. If this is so, we can now look at the new dimension of the product life cycle by plotting the cycle of each 'vector' in turn, as illustrated in Figure 16.2.

This concept opens a new perspective for the marketer in as much as the product life-cycle gains a meaningful and more practical dimension. The product becomes the instrument of satisfaction for each market segment and it is the progression of the product in relation to each sub-market that is being monitored. The marketer who learns how to monitor the product in this way will also acquire the skill of applying the most appropriate marketing tools for each stage of the 'vector' life cycle.

'Vector' in mathematics means a quantity having direction as well

303

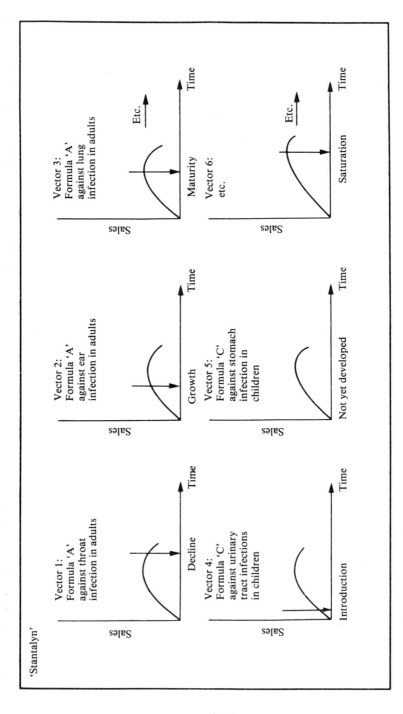

Figure 16.2 Vector life-cycles

as magnitude, denoted by a line drawn from its original to its final position. To the marketer 'vector' means the market segment which is 'satisfied' by a specific product. The segment in question may be capable of 'satisfaction' by a number of products offered by the firm. Each 'product/segment' unit of activity is a vector. In other words, what is being suggested is that instead of talking about the progress of a product or a brand along the life-cycle one should plot the behaviour of the vector life-cycle, namely the 'utility rendered to a specific market segment'. Thus diesel engine manufacturer who has designed a small power generating plant that can supply energy for a factory and also propel a vessel has two distinct 'vectors': the supply of energy to a plant; and the supply of propulsion to ships. The physical and technical product may well be the same but in marketing terms two separate vectors exist and their development will probably take totally separate patterns towards growth and success.

Top management often expects the identical performance from all its products. In many instances this is neither possible nor justifiable. Different vectors have to cope with totally different marketing environments and to expect the same level of results from such environments just because the physical product is the same is illogical. The level of competition, the cost/benefit requirements and the distribution problems can tilt the balance in favour of one product/ segment and make the other look unattractive. Marketing people understand this much better than accountants or production people. The latter feel that a machine is a machine and the level of profit it provides to the selling company is the same irrespective of who uses it and what it is being used for.

MARKET SEGMENTATION REVIEWED

The theory of market segmentation has taught us that very often a company does better by devoting its efforts and creativity to developing a marketing programme specifically designed to appeal to a segment of the market rather than to the market as a whole. The theory goes on to say that having studied the firm's strengths and weaknesses in some depth the marketer decides to seek to satisfy a selected part of the market rather than attempt to be all things to all people. However, when approaching the market with a segmentation policy it is necessary to recognize that it is essential to gain a significant portion of the submarket whilst a small market share of the whole would have sufficed.

Segmentation policies often fail for the simple reason that having decided to segment the market and concentrate one's effort in that area, one has acquired too small a share of the segment in question. It is therefore vitally important that the person who decides to concentrate on a segment should seek to dominate or obtain a significant part of that segment. The would-be segmenter should carry out thorough market measurement studies to establish beyond all reasonable doubt that the selected segment justifies the firm's attention. After all, having opted for a part of the market instead of its totality one takes the risk of 'placing all one's eggs in one basket' and before taking such a decision one must be satisfied that the strategy selected is right.

Market segmentation offers considerable scope for creativity. It is an area in which the innovative marketer can identify opportunities which competitors have missed or have decided to ignore. Thus, when one looks at the more successful car manufacturers in the world such as BMW, one soon recognizes that the real reason for their success was the fact that they had identified a very attractive, albeit small unexploited market segment. However, in selecting one's target segment for marketing development one must ensure that three fundamental conditions are adhered to: the segment must be measureable; it must be sufficiently substantial to justify the effort to be invested in it; it must be accessible in the sense that the institutional systems that facilitate the marketing process (for example channels of distribution, media availability) exist.

These three conditions are of course interrelated and perfectly logical. Yet it is sad to watch how often fairly experienced marketers fall into the trap of selecting segments which do not meet one or more of these conditions, and consequently fail. A further pitfall lies in attempts to 'cheat old age' of a declining product by simply differentiating it *vis-à-vis* a specific segment which happens to be on the decline as well.

In our modern and very competitive environment it is not enough to assume that a segmentation policy is *per se* a formula for success. One must refine the concept beyond what we have attempted to do in the past. Before indulging in product planning we must break down the market into consumer-oriented and cost/benefit-oriented sub-markets or 'vectors'. Obviously there is nothing to stop the marketer from standardizing a product for a cluster of 'vectors', but it must be by design and not by accident. This is not dissimilar to the kind of problem one encounters in international marketing where the effective marketer seeks to identify the needs of each country but then attempts to standardize the product for as many countries as lend themselves to such standardization.

For example, suppose a large transport company has decided to specialize in the field of carrying very heavy cargoes (over 150 tonnes per cargo). This is in itself a segmentation policy in as much as the company has opted out of the very competitive field of transporting ordinary cargoes. One hopes that before embarking on this strategy, which demands a very heavy 'infrastructure', the company has gone through the process of measuring the size of the market for heavy cargoes and found it to be substantial in marketing terms. Furthermore, the company should have extablished that the segment in question is accessible.

The strategy may prove to be successful but if the company wishes to pursue the logic of this argument a step further it must undertake a vector analysis. That would help to ensure that the marketing effort is more directly geared towards the real marketing opportunities and that the product is totally congruent to the needs of each vector.

How should the company go about it? It should analyse step by step in quantified terms who needs to carry very heavy cargoes. The Standard Industrial Classification offers a useful division of the industrial scene. Thus the mining/quarrying and the chemical and shipbuilding industries are all relevant vectors, and each one probably needs a different product. Moreover, some of these many vectors will offer better marketing opportunities than others.

If one could plot all these opportunities on a 'dart-board' type chart (see Figure 16.3) the best will fit into the 'bull's eye' centre; the next on the adjacent circle and so on. Once the implications of this philosophy are grasped by the creative marketer, he or she will have acquired an excellent tool for planning. First, the product will be more directly designed to meet the best vector's needs. Second, the promotional mix can be geared towards the most attractive target audience. Third, the sales force can be directed towards the 'bull's eye' buying environment. It is a totally different story from sending a sales force in search of people who need to transport very heavy cargoes.

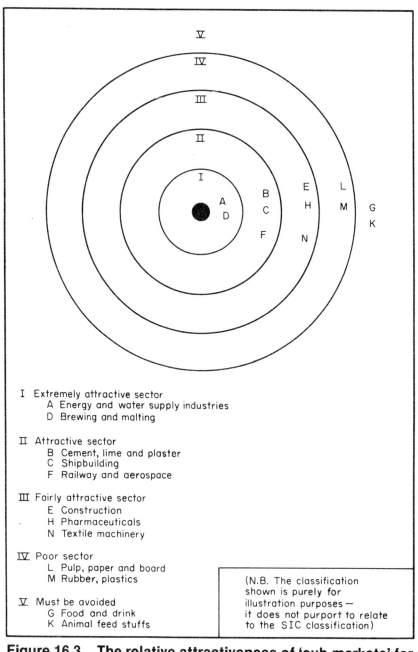

I Extremely attractive sector
    A Energy and water supply industries
    D Brewing and malting

II Attractive sector
    B Cement, lime and plaster
    C Shipbuilding
    F Railway and aerospace

III Fairly attractive sector
    E Construction
    H Pharmaceuticals
    N Textile machinery

IV Poor sector
    L Pulp, paper and board
    M Rubber, plastics

V Must be avoided
    G Food and drink
    K Animal feed stuffs

(N.B. The classification shown is purely for illustration purposes — it does not purport to relate to the SIC classification)

Figure 16.3 The relative attractiveness of 'sub-markets' for a 'heavy-cargoes' transporter

ORGANIZATIONAL IMPLICATIONS

It is worth exploring the organizational implications of what has been suggested. Many companies have so-called product managers or brand managers. Quite a few of these firms must reflect upon the real role of these managers and its appropriateness to a truly marketing-orientated business. In many situations these managers are the hidden manifestation of a bias towards the product as seen by production people rather than the one seen by marketing people. What, for instance, is the marketing relevance of a flooring product manager in a firm that manufactures and supplies flooring for domestic, industrial and institutional markets? Surely what such a company needs is a domestic flooring *market* manager, an industrial flooring *market* manager and an institutional flooring *market* manager.

The word 'market' is emphasized because the product as such does not exist until such time as the market/segment/vector in question exists. It is the needs of the market which the manager has to satisfy and not the needs of the product. In seeking to meet the needs of the market the marketer has to develop a total marketing mix and not only a product. By calling him or her a product manager we simply fog the issue and detract from the importance of the job.

It is not suggested that the role of product managers has disappeared. In many firms such managers are most appropriate and their role is an important one. At the same time it is recommended that before opting for a structure that encompasses the product management concept top management must explore the alternatives and consider the relative merit of each in relation to the marketing aims of the firm. In fact in certain circumstances one can envisage solutions which embrace both product management and market management in a matrix combination (Majaro, 1986).

The whole essence of the matrix approach to organization development is based on the theory that two vital, albeit slightly overlapping structures can coexist. One of the structures is traditional, hierarchical and results-orientated. The other structure is co-ordinative, integrative and in many instances seeks to impart a truly marketing-orientated dimension to a system which by its very nature is less capable of being dynamically so. Referring back to the earlier example of Stanton Chemicals, one can envisage a matrix type organization like the one shown in Figure 16.4.

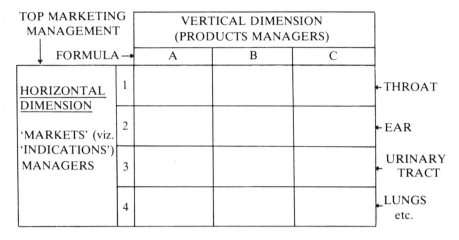

Figure 16.4   Matrix organization for Stanton Chemicals

A structure like this may well prove to be the best way of combining the more traditional way of managing the product with the much more progressive, albeit more complex, marketing-orientated approach.

Finally, a simple checklist for the more enlightened reader:

1 Do not attempt to structure your organization until you have established clearly what your products are.
2 Before defining what your products are, attempt to identify the size and accessibility of the various market vectors that your company is best equipped to satisfy. The 20 per cent of the vectors that offer 80 per cent of the results for your firm will direct you towards the most sensible and effective structure.
3 Maintain enough flexibility in your structure to enable you to cope with the dynamism of the marketplace. The matrix approach to organizational structuring can offer such a flexibility in many situations.
4 Never forget that the most successful marketing takes place when the company knows exactly who it is trying to satisfy.

REFERENCES AND FURTHER READING

Heller, R. (1984) *The Supermanagers* E. P. Dutton (Truman Talley Books), New York.

Levitt, T. (1960),'Marketing myopia', in E. C. Bursk and J. F. Chapman (eds), *Modern Marketing Strategy*, Harvard University Press, Cambridge, pp.24–28; also *Harvard Business Review*, Vol. 38, July–August, pp. 45–56.

Levitt, T. (1965), 'Exploit the product life cycle', *Harvard Business Review*, Vol. 43, November–December, pp. 81–94.

Levitt, T. (1983) *The Marketing Imagination*, Macmillan (The Free Press), New York.

Majaro, S. (1986), *International Marketing – A Strategic Approach to World Markets*, fourth impression, Allen & Unwin, London, chapter 11.

O'Shaughnessy, J. (1984) *Competitive Marketing – A Strategic Approach*, Allen & Unwin, Boston.

Porter, M. E. (1980), *Competitive Strategy* , Macmillan (The Free Press) New York.

17

Product design

Patrick Bruce

The objective of this chapter is to establish the need within organizations to adopt a considered approach to design in the development of new products and the redesign of existing ones.

Product design is seen here in the context of classical marketing thinking and is identified as a critical tool in matching the firm's resources to market opportunities. The skills of the designer are discussed, and the characteristics of a design hierarchy described. It is argued that it should have the close attention of senior management, and should be directly and independently represented at this level.

It is suggested that subordinating design to the management of other business disciplines will inhibit the use of design as a competitive weapon in the marketplace. As design affects almost every area of organization from production through to finance and distribution, it is identified as a necessary aid to the management of change both inside and outside the firm.

To gain maximum benefit from a product design facility, either in house or consultancy-based, the explicit consideration of resources required and provision for their sound management are necessary. Some of the issues surrounding the choice between in-house and consultancy-based design are explored and the benefits examined.

Finally, the need to approach product design in a structured way is supported by a method developed through thirty years of consultancy work by a design practice in the unique position of servicing both members of its own holding company and a substantial external client base. The method breaks the design process down into distinct stages, using client involvement to help eliminate perceived and actual risk. Each phase is examined showing the importance of adequate research before the process starts, and the need to use the integrative skills of the designer to seek the solutions across company divisions, not simply within them.

THE SCOPE OF THIS CHAPTER

There is no shortage of literature on the subject of design, and arguably an over-abundance of attempts to define it through the written word. It is clear that, however it is defined, design as a business tool affects a bewildering array of issues from the corporate image or identity of a company; through the tangible aspects of its product range; the means of communication used to reach end-users, financial institutions and employees; the appearance and performance of its means of distribution, including vehicles, warehousing and final outlets; and so on. To keep this section to manageable proportions, product design will be considered here as it applies to tangible goods aimed at consumer and commercial end-user markets.

Despite this closely defined area, product design will have had some impact earlier in the development cycle, for example in shaping the components and sub-assemblies that make up the finished product.

Many of the issues relating to goods design will also apply to the intangibles of service industries, to fashion products and to food products. The reason for keeping to design of end-users products is that it allows for a clearer discussion on how design fits into the business environment and how the process works.

PRODUCT DESIGN AND MARKETING

When considering the subject of product design the key question is why it matters at all. The marketing literature is a fruitful source of arguments justifying new product development, or the redevelopment of existing product. Product life-cycle theory indicates a finite time span during which a product can be expected to be profitable, and gives a clear description of the need for initial expenditure to support the development of the product market.

It also highlights the need to support the development of new product with the proceeds of successful products currently on the market to ensure that continuity of income and profit is maintained. The work of the Boston Consulting Group further underlines product life stages, and their cash-generating or cash-absorbing implications.

Judging the finite life of products is, of course, the key to the successful use of such models. It is the one issue which is, perhaps, simplest to understand but most difficult to measure before the event. Plotting sales will allow some measure of life-cycle progress at a given point, and will allow a commercial view on whether the redesign of an existing product should be undertaken, or when a new replacement product needs to be introduced.

However, the underlying assumption is that the generic product form is still appropriate in the marketplace. One might question whether a typewriter manufacturer should be redesigning or developing new typewriter products on the basis of a life-cycle plot, or whether the generic form itself is under threat from low-cost word processors. Clearly a much wider view of what is happening in the marketplace is required, including serious evaluation of substitute products arriving from an industry sector outside traditional industry competition.

The typewriter example shows life-cycles curtailed by technological change. There are also circumstances where national and cultural differences impose limits on potential market growth. All the direct and indirect influences should be evaluated before product development takes place to ensure the differences are accommodated, and the market size implications clearly understood.

One variable not often made explicit is the influence of fashion on product design and development. Taste has always influenced the end-user, and with the advent of global marketing and exposure to ever wider varieties of cultural and visual choice, this has become an issue of critical importance in many areas of industry and commerce. Lifestyle marketing in consumer goods has sought to address this factor, clearly targeting defined segments.

It would be dangerous to assume that taste has no effect on products targeted at commercial purchasers. The office furniture industry has had to adopt domestic influences in the appearance of their products in terms of colour, texture, fabric usage and style, as well as the ever-changing functional requirements imposed by office electronic equipment. Manufacturers of heavy goods vehicles have readily accepted many elements of design from saloon car manufacturers who, in turn, are bowing to the demands of corporate image and domestic influence.

What this means is that without a thorough audit of company resources and the wants and needs of the market, and working towards matching resources and opportunity, no amount of product development and design will ensure success in the marketplace.

DESIGN AND THE CORPORATE MANAGEMENT STRUCTURE

Professor Bruce Archer (1974) in his book *Design Awareness and Planned Creativity in Industry* described the need for design and its management in the context of the total business entity. He suggested that design should be considered a business tool, and that its use and proper management could be shown to affect the whole business operation. The question of what constituted good design was posed by asking who it should be good for. Good design would consider many corporate issues: the generation of profit over the product life; the satisfaction of consumer needs; the ability of the company to produce, market, and distribute the product; and the contribution of the product in visual and functional terms to the environment.

He argued that while good design did not, by definition, create any visual offence, neither did it set out to be fine art. Its purpose must be to optimize and accommodate the often conflicting requirements of the business enterprise.

The influence design has on so many aspects of corporate and end-user life is underlined by Mark Oakley (1984), author of *Managing Product Design*. He argues that as a business discipline product design should be independently represented at senior level within the management structure. If it becomes subordinate to any other traditional business discipline it cannot achieve optimal solutions to satisfy the multitude of conflicting interests in the business.

Christopher Lorenz (1986), in his book *The Design Dimension* identifies a number of international companies which have established

315

that design is no longer to be considered 'a low level creature of marketing'. He quotes Professor Philip Kotler's view that the only way for corporations to ensure market success is to design better products. Among the companies Lorenz identifies as having elevated design to 'fully fledged membership of the corporate hierarchy' are Olivetti, John Deere, Ford, Olympus, Sony, and Philips. They have recognized the value of design as a competitive weapon and integrated it into their corporate structure.

Lorenz's list of a designer's skills and attributes includes imagination, creativity, the ability to demonstrate three-dimensional relationships, communication skills in words and sketches, and the ability to synthesize multi-disciplinary factors into a coherent whole.

It is because of this combination of skills, and the ability to comprehend and work across traditional business disciplines, that Peter Gorb of the London Business School believes that designers have high potential in the role of general management. Gorb refers to the conservative nature of organizations which correctly seek to preserve the assets of their shareholders and their employees, and who will therefore resist change. However, the increasing globalization of markets and shorter product life-cycles have meant that companies must cope more and more with the issue of change, both internally and externally.

The development and implementation of new products are for many companies disruptive activities and underline the perception of designers as change agents. Oakley points to the incidence of organizations which have resisted such change to the point where their very survival has been at stake. He points out that many firms pay lip service to the need for design while laying down internally inconsistent policies which prevent product innovation. He quotes twelve reasons established by J. R. Bright in a 1964 publication explaining why companies and their employees resist change. Among these are the protection of status or habit, the protection of the capital base of the company, and preserving the equilibrium of the business atmosphere and society.

While most commentators believe that change is a necessary fact of business life in order to protect the survival of the business entity, one does not have to look far to see the conflict caused within organizations which seek to introduce changes to working habits, manufacturing techniques and product ranges. In the examples quoted by Lorenz earlier it is clear that the need to change has been grasped, and the integrative synthesizing nature of the designer's skills have been adopted at senior level.

Oakley (1984) shows examples where design, having been made subordinate to another discipline, failed to produce optimum results. Seen as an agent of change design becomes an overt threat, and the firm loses the opportunity to use available skills constructively as a competitive weapon.

The case made here, then, is that to provide the greatest potential to an organization in managing its way into the future, the design function should not be considered a subdivision of some other business discipline. As an integrative discipline it should receive the attention of top management. It is an area of key importance in the whole range of the company's activities. It straddles all the traditional business functions within an organization, and acts as the interpretative interface between the organization and its markets. Without it the company will not generate new products. Put in the wrong hierarchical relationship it will not ensure that opportunities in the marketplace are matched to internal resources, present and future.

THE ORGANIZATION OF PRODUCT DESIGN

This subject is dealt with succinctly by Oakley (1984) and it is not intended to deal with it in great detail here. Oakley points out some of the essential differences in hierarchical relationships between design departments in relation to other traditional business divisions. The design hierarchy tends to be flat, with decisions being taken on a team basis, not top down. Expertise is distributed throughout the organization, and authority is assumed by the knowledge holder, not necessarily the hierarchical head. All members of the team will contribute to decision-making, with tasks and roles being frequently redefined to suit the prevailing needs of the situation. This organic style of management structure is contrasted with the mechanistic style which is formal, hierarchical and bureaucratic. Most situations will demand a mix of the two styles located along a continuum from one extreme to the other. This would roughly equate to the need for design expertise along a continuum from pure engineering design to pure appearance design. Figure 17.1 shows this in diagrammatic form.

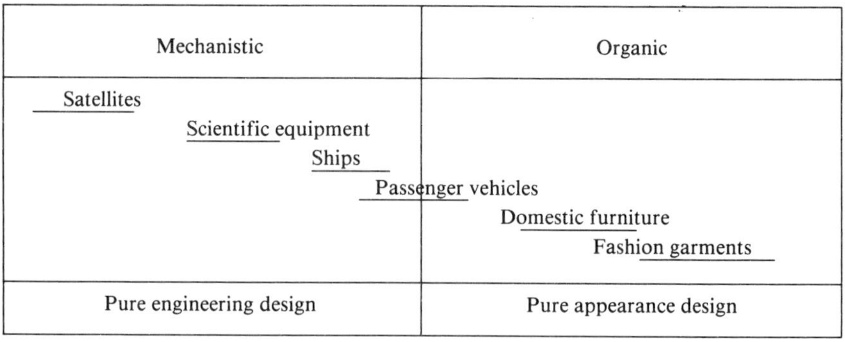

Mechanistic	Organic

Satellites
  Scientific equipment
    Ships
      Passenger vehicles
	Domestic furniture
	       Fashion garments

Pure engineering design	Pure appearance design

Figure 17.1 Organic and mechanistic management structures

Clearly the organization must decide on its own management needs and style depending on the match of internal resources with external opportunity. What is of critical importance is the decision to use an internal resource or an external consultancy to meet its design needs. There are strong arguments in favour of both approaches. Those organizations which establish in-house teams make a substantial commitment to the direct use of management time, the ongoing associated staff and space costs, equipment allocation, and so on. This commitment forces explicit recognition of the issues surrounding design.

The decision to use an external consultancy, however, is often not considered as explicitly. Because it is felt to be a low-risk option allowing a quick exit if something goes wrong, there tends to be less commitment to the design function. However, to maximize the match of resource to opportunity demands commitment to make the process work. Designers, while having a broad range of skills and attributes, do not possess a magic wand. They need to work within defined parameters which can be established only by the careful investigation and evaluation of the matching process, and this can be done only with the explicit input of the commissioning company. This means an appointment at senior level to establish and control the necessary budgets, co-ordinate the information from all departments within the firm, establish time scales and monitor the design programme against agreed criteria.

Decisions on how the external consultant is to be used must be made explicit. Is it necessary to concentrate on purely conceptual ideas? This may be the case where the company has become so production-orientated that it assumes internal constraints. Is the company too small to support the necessary staff on a full-time basis? Can the consultancy offer a range of skills unavailable in-house? Will an external consultant produce consistently better results 'because his life depends on it'? With a consultancy an unsuccessful scheme can be dispassionately aborted, where in-house there may be pressures preventing such a course of action. Whether the design resource is internal or external, management must make explicit the resources required and responsibility levels in the management structure. Both methods of organizing for design must be considered in the light of their contribution to the organization's future. Competitive success is born of commitment to the key issues in all senior management disciplines including the design function.

THE DESIGN METHOD

What follows is a description of a design process which has grown from the need to manage design for both in-house and external clients by a design consultancy which is part of a large holding group. As a group member the design consultancy offers a comprehensive service to each group company on a long-term basis. The service includes the design of the client's communications (both corporate and trading), the retail environment (architectural, interior and merchandising), the selection and design of the product as well as related packaging and graphics, and its fashion goods requirements. The result of this consistent commitment to design can be seen in the group's extraordinary expansion through organic growth and acquisition and merger, and its consistent level of profit despite the needs of a business in an expansionary phase of its life. The design skills on which this business rests were established over thirty years ago when the consultancy was the only element of the group in existence. The aspect of non-group consultancy was developed and expanded at the same time as the group business grew, reaching the point where it now offers a fully developed range of design skills to both group and non-group clients. As a result of this experience it has been able to develop a design method made up of several clearly identifiable stages, each complete in itself. This method is used to ensure that the design programme is kept on track, that it starts with the right information, that it suits the particular requirements of the individual company and that wherever possible risk is eliminated.

Risk limitation

Perceived risk is of central importance to the client using a design consultancy. Like all service businesses, the service cannot be stored, and the nature of the whole process is intangible. For all the success stories of similar clients with similar problems, there is always the doubt of possible failure. V. A. Zeithaml (1981) comments on the high level of perceived risk in services marketing. The article describes a continuum ranging from high search qualities (those attributes which can be established with certainty before purchase) through high experience qualities (those which cannot be determined before purchase but which can be evaluated afterwards) and high credence qualities (those which cannot be evaluated even after purchase). Risk increases from easy evaluation in the former case to difficult evaluation in the latter. Zeithaml places professional services in the difficult to evaluate (high credence qualities) sector where perceived risk in purchases is high. It is suggested that methods of risk reduction are critical in service businesses.

This is a most important factor to the consultancy, and leads to the involvement of the client as closely as is practicable in the whole process. Risk reduction should start before the client contacts the consultancy, with the definition of the problem and evaluation of resources and opportunities as the first step. Once the client has established the basic criteria he or she is in a position to discuss the formulation of the brief and to evaluate the correct consultancy to undertake the work.

The brief

The brief is all-important. It establishes the boundaries of the problem, the methods and extent of the work to be done, and the time scales and budgets within which results are expected. It is in the context of the brief that a sound estimate of time expenditure and therefore cost can be evaluated, and critical decision points can be established. Substantial input from the client is required at this stage and understanding of the problem is reflected back from the designer. Clear understanding of the problem, the manufacturing constraints, the market objectives and the timing, eliminates the first element of perceived risk.

Orientation

This stage is the development of an appropriate 'visual language' to be used to guide the designer's hand. Orientation is a useful method of visually interpreting qualitative market data which describe several different 'segment opportunities' in terms of appearance and consumer lifestyle. The client can see his or her research in pictures. It is important because it imposes agreed constraints on the problem in terms of appearance and materials. In terms of ranges of appropriate products available off the shelf it identifies product gaps very early in the programme. This eliminates an endless search for ill-defined ideas and starts to manage the process in a disciplined way. It also seeks the direct involvement of the client at an early key decision point, ensuring that the programme does not put the company beyond its ability to cope with the change inherent in product development and design. It is also reassurance that the designer has fundamentally understood the brief.

Sketch design

Following agreement on which visual language should be adopted to suit the now explicit characteristics of the end-user, the next stage is the generation of design concepts. These must meet the objectives of both the identified customer base and the organizational resources available. Commonly known as 'sketch concepts', the ideas are generated in volume with detail limited to critical areas. The ideas must conform to the criteria agreed in the previous stages and give the client the widest variety of choice and stimulus. Despite the focusing effect of earlier work, the designer will still produce a bewildering array of conceptual work conforming to the criteria laid down.

Depending on the nature of the programme there may be several decision points during this stage, forcing client and designer continually to target or refocus the design effort, evaluating and refining earlier ideas and directions.

Often the client will be starting preliminary costings now to ensure that those ideas widely off target can be eliminated. So further risk is removed through the creative collaboration of both client and designer. At the end of this phase there will be no unexpected shocks or utterly impossible propositions, although through the collaboration the client's view of the end product may well change substantially as alternatives are generated and evaluated.

The working relationship between designer and client enables the decision-making process to be approached in a dispassionate manner when selecting the concepts to be taken to the next phase. The origin of the ideas becomes submerged and the decisions are made jointly, avoiding conflict and maximizing the likelihood of a productive end result.

Design development

Following agreement on the appropriate concept the next element in the programme is the detailed development of the design. This stage deals with the refinement of all the external, user-orientated aspects of the product. Given the designer's knowledge of the manufacturing system the product idea is developed both in general form and in detail. This stage reconciles the needs of the manufacturing process and the end-user. It is an integrative stage, developing the best match of resources to opportunity and incorporating cost constraints, profit requirements and so on. It is at this stage that the client's technical personnel have a greater input into the process, advising on technical feasibility and cost, while the designer works to ensure that the original concept is not lost to purely technical expedience. A product which satisfies the perfect operational manufacturing criteria but which will not sell is valueless.

As an aid to evaluation it is often useful and necessary to produce a sketch model. This is a three-dimensional representation of the product which allows assumptions about size and proportion of the drawn form to be checked thoroughly. It is extremely cost-effective in that it prevents too much detailed development taking place in the wrong area or according to the wrong dimensional criteria. The combination of sketch model and detailed visuals allows a proper assessment of the product's physical and visual characteristics, having taken into account all the critical manufacturing and financial criteria. Once again the emphasis is on eliminating perceived risk. The committed input of technical personnel now starts to limit actual risk in manufacturing as well.

Measured drawings and model-making

The final design stages involve the production of fully measured drawings and the building of a finished model or prototype. Here again, the input of the manufacturing company is crucial in controlling costs of design and product manufacture. While the designer is capable of producing toleranced piece-part drawings, this usually proves unnecessarily expensive, and where possible the task should be undertaken by the manufacturer. The production of general arrangement drawings, showing all key control dimensions of the fully assembled product, is in most cases adequate and relatively inexpensive. The choice between model-making and prototyping will depend on the manufacturing method. Where there is a substantial tooling commitment, modelling the product in its finished form is the only method to adopt. This will allow the highly finished model to be used in final market testing and appraisal before committing to tooling and other associated launch costs.

Implementation

Following the final costings of piece parts, sub-assemblies, final assembly and the amortization of tooling, the final stage is to commit to production and implement the new product. Once again, it is essential that there is commitment from the designer to protect the marketable idea from excessive manufacturing constraints which might dilute it and make it unsaleable. The support and appraisal during the implementation phase by both the designer and manufacturing staff are extremely important in ensuring the maximization of the product's value in the marketplace. The design industry is littered with examples of time and effort wasted due to the lack of resources for this phase. The successful product sells, performing well against all criteria laid down. The product lacking implementation resource can only fail.

Packaging

One might think that at the successful conclusion of the implementation phase the role of design is over. This is not the case. Very few products can be transported or displayed or even sold without some form of packaging and branding, ticketing, guarantees, instructions and so on.

These aspects must also be considered explicitly in terms of costs and benefits. A good product with poor shelf presence ceases to attract the end-user in the competitive environment. At an early stage therefore it is necessary to establish what routes of distribution are to be used, and the criteria for the packaging and two-dimensional design work. Is the packaging to be protective, or is it decorative? What competitive products exist, and what is their market presence? What information about the product must be displayed, and how? The opportunity to use these elements to add value, to influence the purchase decision, and reinforce the choice of the end-user should not be missed.

However, it is often ill-conceived, and not considered part of the whole bundle of benefits made available to the customer. It is an area where the integrative skills of the designer can maximize the marketing opportunity by ensuring a product solution which meets the user's needs and aspirations, and is internally consistent in every aspect.

CONCLUSION

This chapter has attempted to confront some of the issues surrounding the role of product design within the company. It has examined the interface between design and marketing, arguing that it allows a visual assessment of marketing criteria, and that its proper management will often cause necessary shifts in marketing thinking.

It has shown that the design process affects all areas of corporate life. To achieve maximum benefit from the integrative skills of the designer, the place of design in the management hierarchy must be at senior level. If the discipline is to be subordinated to any other business function, this will impose severe limitations on the design function, preventing it from seeking product solutions which adequately match company needs and resources with market opportunity.

Whether the company chooses to use an internal team or an external consultancy, the need for management and other resources must be made clear. No amount of product design expertise will guarantee success if commitment in terms of time, money and information is not made at senior level.

Finally, a well-tried design method was discussed. This breaks the design process down into distinct and manageable phases, encouraging client input at all key decision points, thereby reducing perceived and actual risk.

The design process touches every aspect of corporate existence, from production to finance, marketing, distribution and so on. If it is to work effectively across all business disciplines, the approach to design must consciously deal with the issues of its place in the company hierarchy, its resourcing, management and design method.

An increasingly global market and shortening product life-cycles put great pressure on companies to change. A key element in the management of change is the use of the creative and integrative skills of the designer, to ensure that competitive new products reach the market in a form which clearly matches the ability of the company to produce them at a profit with the desire of the consumer to buy them.

REFERENCES AND FURTHER READING

Archer, L. B. (1974), *Design Awareness and Planned Creativity in Industry*, the Design Council, London.
Lorenz, C. (1986), *The Design Dimension: Product Strategy and the Challenge of Global Marketing*, Blackwell, Oxford.
Oakley, M. (1984), *Managing Product Design*, Weidenfeld and Nicolson, London.

Zeithaml, V. A. (1981), 'How Consumer Evaluation Processes Differ Between Goods and Services', in *Marketing of Services*, (1981), American Marketing Association, Chicago.

18

Packaging as a marketing tool

Bill Stewart

Packaging is becoming increasingly recognized by marketing professionals as one of the most powerful tools available to them. The days when pack design could be relegated to a purely functional role are long gone. In this chapter we shall consider why packaging justifies marketing attention, the tasks packaging must perform and the potential for maximizing this performance.

THE IMPORTANCE OF PACKAGING AS A MARKETING TOOL

Packaging in one form or another has been a part of human civilization for a long time. Historically, its use was restricted to being the medium for collating produce. We may assume that archaeological artefacts such as pots and jars were indeed items of packaging designed to hold powders and liquids. No doubt less durable materials were used but did not stand the test of time – early biodegradable packaging! While the containment role of packaging, therefore, has long been recognized, it is only in recent times that the promotional aspects have begun to be fully appreciated. Until some twenty-five years ago, there were no specialist packaging designers in the UK although they were already playing a part in marketing activities within the USA. In Britain, there were graphic designers, transit packaging engineers and packaging suppliers who also offered design services restricted to their particular packaging medium.

As the level of marketing sophistication grew, so the need for true specialists increased and, taking a lead from the pattern established in the USA, in-house packaging engineering facilities and packaging consultancies were established to service the needs of the marketing function. Even then, few organizations could offer a total service, combining graphic and technical disciplines. Today, with packaging accounting for around 3 per cent of UK gross national product, its importance is firmly established. Design, in general, has now been accepted as a means of increasing sales, albeit rather late in the day for much of British industry. Nevertheless, the increasingly high calibre of marketing personnel recognizes that imaginative packaging design, if used correctly, forms an integral part of marketing strategy.

There is little doubt that the most important influence on packaging today has been the rise of self-service outlets. Often the pack is the only sales aid available at point of purchase. Informed assistants are generally not available to explain the product's attributes – the pack itself must do this and, if the product is to be successful, do it better than the competition. The retail grocery sector currently operates on around a 96 per cent self-service basis.

It would be wrong to suggest that packaging is the only tool to assist the marketing function in these areas but it must be considered one of the dominant factors.

Although the retail grocery area accounts for a huge slice of the consumer spend, there are other areas of self-service where packaging plays an equally important part. Out-of-town superstores, the so-called 'sheds', sell a wide variety of prepacked goods, with car spares and DIY materials being of prime importance. Here, where goods often require complex and technical selection, the pack must work even harder.

So far, we have mentioned the retail trade. Wholesale operations too have been affected by the trend to self-service. Cash-and-carry outlets are a further example of the selection of goods being influenced by pack design. After all, in some respects the wholesale pack must perform the same functions as its retail derivative, even though in collations of prime units.

WHAT PACKAGING MUST DO

All packs must meet several criteria although the degree of emphasis on individual aspects will vary according to the product nature and markets envisaged. All aspects should nevertheless be considered. Failure to do so is likely to result in packaging problems which ultimately reflect on the product itself and could create lack of faith in that product and possibly the brand itself.

Containment

The first function of packaging is to contain the product. This may seem to be stating the obvious. Think, however, of those instances where, as consumers, our experience shows that even this function has not been given the attention it deserves. Bottles that leak and bags that burst are all too frequent occurrences and will negate other hard-won marketing advantages. It may also be necessary to build in tamper-evident features to proctect the consumer and, ultimately, the manufacturer from the effects of prying fingers. Theft from prepacked goods, 'shrinkage' as the trade would term it, is yet another unsavoury feature of modern retailing. Many multiples are critical of pack styles which permit goods to be removed while the pack appears unhandled. There are instances where buyers for leading multiples will refuse to stock the product line unless this problem has been satisfactorily resolved. If this problem is not tackled at an early stage of product/pack development, there is a real danger that the manufacturer may already be committed to an unacceptable pack style – an expensive mistake.

While effective containment is essential, the method of opening the pack needs consideration also. Consumer research shows a marked aversion to packs which are difficult to open. Biscuits are the most often cited in this respect. The standard response from the packaging industry has been that the consumer has a choice – soggy biscuits or a pack that may be slightly inconvenient to open. Furthermore, the industry has been rather too ready to suggest that the problem is due to the consumer's lack of training. After all, argues the industry a tin of beans needs a tin opener and the consumer accepts this without question; in the same way, some packs require the use of common household equipment to open them. The implication is that the answer is to 'educate' consumers. While this may have been the case when the consumer was faced with little choice, this attitude will not win sales where multiple choice is now often the norm. We ignore the consumer at our peril.

329

Insufficient attention to the consumer's needs is not only arrogant but short-sighted in today's competitive climate.

Protection

As with containment, protection is a basic technical requirement which at first sight, does not seem to warrant further discussion. Consider, however, what the pack must protect against if it is to present the product in pristine condition to the ultimate consumer. First, it is important that the likely hazards are identified throughout the distribution chain. These can be broadly divided into two categories, transit and climatic hazards.

Transit hazards are those physical hazards encountered during the product's journey from manufacture, through storage and distribution to the point of sale and, ultimately, to the end consumer. Inevitably, multiple handling will be involved during this cycle, the extent and severity of which will depend upon the nature of the journeys, methods of handling, and weight and size of the product. Collations of unit packs are also a factor in determining the level of handling likely to be encountered. Transit damage results from impact brought about by dropping, crushing through excessive stacking and vibration during transport.

Climatic damage is likely to result from damp, excessive heat or cold, or indeed any combination of these. Remember that, even if the product withstands such climatic variations, the pack may not. A weakened pack may lead to transit damage in these circumstances.

Legal compliance

Packaging must of course comply with the law in all respects. The requirements will vary considerably depending upon the nature of the product, the countries of sale and type of transport used. With greater attention being paid to safety, legal requirements are becoming increasingly more complex. Greater consumer awareness, governmental actions and the trend to more international trade have all played a part in this. While, in the past, some manufacturers may not have adopted quite such a responsible attitude as they should have done, the move towards strict liability has encouraged greater legal compliance. Disasters directly attributable to packaging are, in these circumstances, likely to attract prison sentences in addition to possibly huge financial penalties. In the extreme, leaking chemicals which are a contributory cause of, say, an aircraft crash, could have serious repercussions for even the largest of companies. Aircraft are not cheap! It is not appropriate here to detail the many legal requirements which require consideration; this is itself becoming a specialist area of the packaging operation. Suffice it to say that legal clearance should be obtained as a matter of course.

Environmental considerations should form part of all marketing programmes, even where not a legal requirement. The environmental lobby in Britain is small but growing. If, for no other reason, the product is perceived as offending the environmentalists, sales may quite possibly suffer. In any case, as responsible people, we should consider the implications of our actions in this respect.

Identification

Packaging must identify the contents. For some military and industrial types, this alone may be sufficient. It is, however, equally important to the soldier and the trader in the field that, when they open the pack, the goods inside match the description of the outside markings. While this holds true for retail products, it is plainly not enough in itself and other, promotional requirements may be of additional importance.

Promotion

Promotion in this context means the pack acting as a positive selling agent, promoting the product. It does not mean special offers. The first task of packaging is to stand out visually. It must achieve this in the prevailing lighting conditions at point of sale and must be distinctive when compared to the products in close proximity. These are likely to be competitive products but may also be other classes of goods. The principal tools available here are shape, colour and texture. Individual circumstances will dictate which of these will be most effective. It is worth noting that shape is often the most useful feature and yet is often the most neglected. Some products are instantly recognizable by shape alone – triangular Swiss chocolate can mean only one brand.

Cost

The criteria outlined above must be achieved in a cost-effective manner. It is important that total cost be considered, not simply the cost of the pack itself. This should include labour in assembly, storage and transport as well as material cost, if a true picture is to be obtained.

WHAT PACKAGING CAN DO

By use of good design, both graphic and technical, the opportunities provided by packaging can be exploited to the full. The product, however, must live up to the expectations conveyed by the pack. If the anticipated promise suggested by the packaging remains unfulfilled, the product will ultimately fail.

A good design is one which meets the objectives laid down in the marketing brief. It can be judged by these criteria and, if the brief is correct, by the sales generated. Other judgements are subjective and of relatively little value. The aim should not be to win an award or to be clever for its own sake, but simply to be on target with marketing requirements. The designer, nevertheless, should exercise his or her ability by challenging the brief, moving outside it to explore fresh areas and then narrowing down to the terms of the brief once more. In this way, both designer and client can be sure that all design directions have been adequately explored. Those directions which, clearly, are outside the brief can be rejected. Often, however, such exploratory work will provide the difference between an ordinary and outstanding pack design.

Imagery

Packaging is a superb medium to use for imparting the required imagery by use of shape, surface graphics, colour and texture. It is vital that marketing management is clear about the image it wishes the pack, and hence the product, to project. Problems tend to occur where compound imagery is required, the pack consequently needing to work much harder to convey more than one message. The result often has the effect of diluting each individual imagery requirement and introducing blandness to the design. This may be acceptable if that is what is required or it is unavoidable for other reasons but not if one quality alone is to be dominant. It is a marketing responsibility to identify such imagery and to communicate it clearly to the designer.

When the image by which the product is to be perceived has been identified, the designer's role will be to achieve it within the parameters of the brief. Most design studies are a compromise between conflicting requirements. Practical considerations must inevitably assume greater importance as the study progresses. There is little point in meeting imagery targets when the cost of production, for example, is well above the budget set or indeed impractical in any other way.

It is important to recognize that shape is significant in aligning the pack with its required imagery, an area often neglected in favour of surface graphic treatments alone. If, for example, the product is a luxury shower gel aimed specifically at the female market, then the pack may need to be soft in image terms. Clearly, features such as hard edges may be inappropriate. This often poses a problem for the designer who may, for several reasons, be limited in the choice of packaging media. There simply might not be sufficient latitude to select materials or processes which allow the use of soft curves, although it should be stressed that every opportunity should be taken to try to incorporate a medium which does reflect the imagery requirements. In this instance, the only available options may be to use texture or surface graphics to achieve the desired effect.

It would be misleading to conclude from the above that graphics represent a fall-back position when shape options are exhausted. The optimum design solutions are achieved when physical pack design and graphics are developed in tandem, each augmenting the other. Indeed, the twin disciplines of technical and graphic design can never truly be separated. Technical designers know the limitations of the processes and materials with which they are working while, unfettered by such constraints, graphic designers can visualize the desired end effect. Between them, imaginative and practical solutions emerge with physical shape and graphics in harmony.

Every opportunity should be taken to build consumer benefits into the packaging. This is one way of differentiating your pack from the competition and providing a further reason for purchase. Be warned, however, such benefits must actually work in a practical sense. Consumers quickly learn to avoid packs which do not function as well as expected. Ideally, any consumer benefit should be readily perceived without recourse to printed explanations. If, for example, it is thought that a liquid product which is poured in use requires a handle to ease dispensing, the container should be designed so that 'pourability' is visually communicated at a glance. In this instance a vestigial handle is simply not enough. The total design should indicate how the product works.

HOW TO USE PACKAGING AS A MARKETING TOOL

We have seen, in outline, the criteria packaging must meet, and have looked at some areas where packaging is uniquely positioned to assist the marketing strategy. In this section, we can now begin to consider how the full potential of packaging as a marketing tool can be harnessed. There are no short cuts. Only by following a disciplined series of events, can you be sure that all opportunities and potential pitfalls have been given full consideration.

Conduct of the study

The study should be structured to follow a series of logical steps, the first of which consists of gathering further information.

No two design studies are the same. Each will vary according to the product type and the market to be entered. The activities described below must be regarded as the ideal pattern, one indeed typical of many studies.

Developing the brief

To direct packaging design work with the greatest possible accuracy, it is necessary first to build the fullest possible brief. Checklists 1 to 7 below show the type of information which is needed, and will help build such a brief. Not all the points listed will be relevant to every study but they should all be considered. Checklist 1 covers the general information on the market and the product's position in that market, which will be applicable to any study. Checklists 2 to 6 deal separately with the facts required for a technical design on the one hand and graphic design on the other. Finally, checklist 7 covers administrative information.

The information demanded by the checklists is typical of that needed by packaging design agencies, but is equally applicable for briefing other groups servicing marketing requirements such as, for example, advertising agencies.

Some marketing groups will provide much of the data within a written brief; others will depend upon the agency extracting them through a question and answer session. Whichever method is adopted, it is important to ensure that all the points are given full consideration.

Checklist 1   General information
This checklist covers the points to be checked with regard to the product and the market.

1   The market

- Total size – volume and value – trends – brand fragmentation and shares
- Regionality
- Seasonality
- Wholesale distribution breakdown
- Consumer profile
  - Age
  - Sex
  - Socio-economic groups
  - Special characteristics

2   The product

- History
- Brand share
- Description and usage
- Frequency of purchase
- Sizes
- Prices
- Advantages and disadvantages against competition
- Brand loyalty
- Regionality
- Seasonality
- Wholesale distribution breakdown
  - By outlet type

- By counter versus self-service
- Direct
- Prospect profile (existing/future)
  - Age
  - Sex
  - Socio-economic groups
  - Special characteristics
- Copy strategy
- Planned advertising and promotion

Checklist 2   Technical design requirements
The following points refer to the requirements of the consumer and the product.

1 Design objectives

(Here list specific design objectives.)

2 Consumer requirements

- Ideal quantities, sizes, weights
- Size/value for money impression
- Importance of
  - Style
  - Shape
  - Colour
  - Texture
  - Visibility
- Requirement of consumers to inspect and handle prior to sale
- Ease of take-home/delivery
- Need for storage
- In-use life required
- Opening/closing requirements
- Childproof/tamper-evident
- Usage
- Dispensing/extraction
- Measuring
- After use
- Protection of the consumer against hazard from the product
- Environmental and ecological considerations
  - Disposability

- Returnability
- Recyclable materials
- Over-packaging

3 Product requirements

- Compatability of materials and product
- Product life/deterioration characteristics
- Shelf life
- Product size/weight/volume
- Protection against
  - Liquid/moisture
  - Microbiological contamination
  - Gases/odour
  - Temperature extremes/thermal shock
  - Infestation
  - Light: UV/artificial
  - Mechanical damage
    - Crushing
    - Dropping
    - Squeezing
    - Puncture
    - Additional transit hazards

Checklist 3   Further technical design requirements
The following points refer to production and legal requirements.

1 Production requirements

- Need for use of existing plant
- Machinery, lines and manpower available
- Opportunity for introduction of new processes and machinery
- In-plant facilities for
  - Material manufacture
  - Package/component manufacture
  - Printing/decoration
- Tied or favoured suppliers
- Suppliers who definitely should not be approached
- Contract packaging
- Cost breakdowns of existing packaging
- Forecast sales quantities

- Forecast purchasing quantities
- Pack cost budget
- Processes
  - Sterilization
  - Pre-weighing/metering
  - Filling
  - Closing/sealing
  - Checkweighing/headspace
  - Labelling/printing/decoration
  - Overprinting
  - Inspection/quality control
  - Collation
  - Outer packaging
- Storage
  - Methods
  - Time requirements
  - Stacking weight/height restrictions
  - Pallet size/type
  - Despatch methods
- Opportunities for standardization and cost reduction

2 Legal requirements

- UK
- EEC
- National country of sale
- Transportation (local and international)
- Weights and measures

Checklist 4 Further technical design requirements
The following points refer to the distribution and merchandising aspects of the technical design brief.

1 Distribution requirements

- Method of distribution – Mail order
  - Wholesaler
  - Retailer
  - Direct
- Estimated length of time stored at
  - Warehouse
  - Wholesaler (including cash and carry)

- Retailer
- Consumer
- Method of
  - Transportation
  - Loading
  - Warehousing
  - Wholesale storage (including cash and carry)
  - Retail storage
- Importance of divisibility at all stages
- Transportation weight requirements
- Requirement of standardization for range
- Anti-pilfering/tamper-evident requirements

2 Merchandising requirements

- Size with own/other display fixtures
- Use of planograms
- Hanging slot configuration
- Carded products
  - Radius/square corners
  - Price mark area
  - Product orientation
  - Product visibility
  - Need for tactile product examination

Checklist 5   Pack graphic design
Areas to be considered for graphic design projects.

1 Design objectives

- New design
- Redesign/updating
  - Design continuity/analysis of existing elements
  - Range integration/extension

2 Consumer requirements

- Size impression
- Appropriateness of pack for product
- Importance of pack appearance in use
- Preferred/associated colours
- Usage instructions

3 Retail display requirements

- Shelf sizes
- Estimated display life
- Position of display
  - Shelf
  - Counter
  - Dispenser
  - Check-out
  - Window
- Position in relation to purchaser
  - Eye level
  - Above/below
- Display by brand/product group
- Panels most often seen
  - Facings (front, back, top, sides, bottom)
- Lighting levels at point of display
- Proximity
  - Competitive products
  - Other product lines

4 Wholesale display requirements (including cash and carry)

- Need for coding/labelling on outer case
- Degree of branding necessary
- Need for subdivisible sales units

5 Production requirements

- Number of colours/varnish
- Size of print area
- Method of reproduction
- Materials
- Quantity
- Run size
- Artwork requirements
- Cost limitations

Checklist 6   Special graphic requirements
Additional considerations which apply specifically to graphic design studies.

1 Special requirements

340

- Anticipated future copy changes
- Foreign/multilingual copy
- Price flashes
- Promotional flashes
- Bar codes
- Need to tie in with advertising/point of sale

2   Legal requirements

- Cautionary information to be included
- Legislation to be observed
  - Correct style and size of copy
  - Content weight/volume declaration
  - Ingredients copy, order and size
  - Maker/supplier's name and address
  - Special claims
  - Warning symbols
  - Use of EEC symbols

3   Restraints
- Materials
- Processes
- Inks
- Pack style/form

Checklist 7   Administrative requirements
Administrative information which should be considered at an early stage of the project and at interim points throughout.

1   Time requirements for development and completion
2   Availability of existing research
3   Packaging research and testing planned for the project
4   Need for additional shipping case or associated point of sale studies.

Acknowledgement
The author acknowledges permission from Siebert/Head Ltd to reproduce, in modified form, the 'Checklist for a packaging brief', from which checklists 1 to 7 are abstracted.

Intake of additional information

Designers, however imaginative, are working to a brief and the results of their work will be measurable by their success in meeting the design objectives. To understand fully what these objectives are, the designers' first task is to familiarize themselves with the market, the environment in which the product will be sold. While a casual stroll around a supermarket, for example, might yield some information, it really is insufficient. One of the most successful methods is to organize a structured store survey. This should be conducted in a number of outlets, representative of the product's distribution. The list of outlets to be visited needs careful selection in conjunction with the marketing department. Allowance should be made for regional bias or variation, outlet sizes and degree of sophistication, location (out of town, high street and so on) and any other factors of importance to the product's sales pattern. International studies require such detailed consideration for each country of sale.

A store survey looks for opportunities and limitations at point of sale. To assist in identifying these, measurements are required. Lighting levels at point of sale are of prime importance. If the product is often displayed in poor lighting conditions, any design will have to take this factor into account if the pack is to stand out. Stores are unlikely to alter their lighting arrangements simply to assist you to sell your product. If, therefore, your product is going to be relegated to a poorly lit area of the store, dark pack colours may be a poor choice. Lighting can be measured by using a camera set on one-thirtieth of a second, using a film speed of 200 ASA. The aperture required to allow photography at this setting can be recorded. Using these settings, experience shows that lighting levels of f4 and below are progressively poor, while those above f4 indicate good lighting.

It may also be important to know what facings are being displayed. For example in the case of a breakfast food cereal packed in a rectangular carton, the survey may indicate that more ends than fronts are displayed on the shelf. While the designer may concentrate on decorating the large main panel, he or she ignores the ends at his or her peril. These should at least be branded and not, as is often the case, show bar codes only. We are not in the business of selling bar codes!

The third measurable factor in the store survey is to chart goods which are in proximity to our product, or its likely position should it be a new product. This involves charting those products which are above, below and to each side of our product in each of the locations being researched. In this way we can learn what packs our product needs to stand out

342

against. In some instances, this might mean direct competitors but can often be products from our own company or totally different product lines. We may wish to make use of the association of surrounding products in a positive sense by deliberately designing in a link between our product and, say, the brand leader – a 'me-too' product – or concentrate on brand name being shared with another product in the range. Alternatively, we may wish to distance our product from all those around it, deliberately making it different in pack form and decoration. The choices are presented when the facts are available.

The store survey can be disciplined by the use of a simple form, an example of which is shown in Figure 18.1. In practice, the use of photography and, in particular, colour slides, assists enormously with the analysis of store survey data. It is surprising how much more detail can be appreciated viewing slides in the relative calm of the office, rather than when caught up in the hustle and bustle of a busy supermarket.

Photography also enables a complete design team to participate and become familiar with the product's environment. It would be difficult to take a complete team of designers around each location; apart from the logistical problems, store managers are likely to object. Commercially too, there are obvious advantages to this approach. Film is cheap, executive time is expensive.

Interviews with buyers are increasingly becoming a feature of many studies. This is true at both retail and wholesale level. With a large proportion of business in the hands of five or six companies, particularly in the retail grocery trade, it is nonsensical to commit to a repackaging programme without consulting the appropriate buyers at an early stage. Contrary to many marketing managers' fears, buyers are generally most helpful and willing to express their expert knowledge. Perhaps it is a refreshing change to be given the opportunity to comment on the pack forms they admire, what their stores wish to see in packaging terms for now and the future and what packaging they definitely would not wish to see – rather than be subjected to a sales pitch. Also important, buyers can advise on merchandising requirements and arrange for planograms to be made available.

Factory visits are essential to enable the practical parameters to be established. While much of this should have been included in the brief, it is nevertheless important to see the operation at first hand, Again, photography is a useful aid. The complete process from goods inward to the despatch bay needs to be studied. Of particular interest would be the

STORE SURVEY
CANNED READY MEALS

LIGHTING LEVEL

1/30th sec: 200 ASA					

BRAND	FACINGS	BRAND	FACINGS
			-

PROXIMITY TEST

BRAND

GENERAL OBSERVATIONS

OUTLET NAME ....

OUTLET ADDRESS ....

CLASSIFICATION
Grocers
Multiple/Co-op/Independent Symbol/Independent
Self-Service/Counter Service

Figure 18.1 Simple store survey record form

condition and storage of incoming packaging, those areas of the production operation related to packaging, handling and storage of packed stock and the type of transport being used for delivery. Depending upon circumstances, central distribution warehouses and wholesale warehouses may require a separate visit. The opportunity should be taken at each stage to obtain information from those initmately involved with the product. This might typically include production, quality assurance, warehousing and distribution management. Opportunities for packaging improvement and any packing line problems can be identified.

The advertising agency responsible for the brand will invariably have a viewpoint and this should be obtained. It may not always coincide with the marketing point of view and is often slanted in a different plane, offering a fresh insight into the area of packaging.

We have assumed that the original brief was a full one. Most studies, however, will require a further briefing session to complete some of the blanks that are bound to arise once the project is in progress. It is worthwhile introducing additional input from sales management, which is, after all, at the forefront of the business. Sales and account managers know their markets and, in addition, may have to sell any pack changes to their sales team. They will have a view and it should be listened to.

By now, we are in possession of a vast store of information, some fact and much opinion. It would be wrong to suggest that all those we have consulted and whose opinions we have elicited must be correct in their pronouncements. There will have been some contradictions and all will have spoken from their own standpoint, some possibly influenced by company politics. Certainly few will have been without any opinion; as with religion, politics and education, everyone has an opinion about packaging! Almost certainly there will be a consensus of opinion on many leading issues, and design parameters can now be set with potential opportunities and problems clearly identified.

The design

The design phase can now begin. It is for the design director to judge whether to reveal all or part of the information to his or her team during the initial project work. Too early and the numerous constraints may impair creativity; too late and time may have been wasted pursuing unworkable solutions.

It makes sense to identify first the technical design solutions, the pack forms and constructions having most potential. This, however, should not be done in isolation. A graphic overview is needed to establish the graphic potential of each technical design candidate. This early conceptual work is often considered as a first stage of a project, probably leading to a large number of possible design solutions. As packaging is three dimensional, so most conceptual designs should be worked up to three-dimensional mock-up packs. The range of candidates is reviewed and recommendations made. There is rarely one solution to a problem so, at this point, there may be more than one candidate recommended for further development. Usually, the full scope of work is presented to the client and the rationale explained in selection and elimination of individual designs. In this way, the client can follow the design team's thinking, and narrow the alternatives in the same way as the designers.

Stage two of the design process will see further development of those technical directions agreed as having potential from stage one. Extensive graphic experiments will begin, at this point probably concentrating on the important face panels only but not forgetting the results of the earlier store survey which will have shown which panels are most likely to be displayed. If a total range of products is to be packed, a representative selection will probably be tackled to enable broad guidelines to be established which can later be implemented across the total range. At the conclusion of this stage, the work is reviewed and presented, again in total and leading to firm recommendations. Should market research be required, it is generally at this point in the study that it is introduced. This will often mean that highly finished models are needed.

Stage three sees refinement taking place, often fine tuning following the results of the market research. Technically, specifications are finalized and detailed costings obtained. Graphically, there may be a need to extend the range at this point, perhaps to incorporate foreign language variants.

Finally, as stage four in our idealized study, artwork would be prepared to the printer's requirements. It is sensible to organize a handover meeting with the finished art department, printers and client present. Proofs will be approved in due course. Where required, quality control manuals would be issued and, if necessary, guidelines laid down for corporate graphics use.

By tackling the problems in a logical sequence, as outlined in this chapter, the packaging project can be fitted into a critical path analysis plan, ensuring that no deadlines are missed and no areas overlooked.

19

Pricing as a marketing tool

Rory Morgan

In a competitive enterprise system, price flexibility is an essential enabling mechanism that stimulates the creation of desired goods, and removes gluts caused by over-production. In every price-controlled system, two views exist: that of the *producer*, and that of the *consumer*. From the earliest societies that used money rather than barter as a basis for the exchange of goods, setting the correct price level – the level that balances the interests of both parties – has exercised the greatest minds. The satirist Juvenal, speaking in classical times, noted that 'here in Rome, all things can be had', but added the wry consumerist aside, 'at a price'.

Nevertheless, before the development of modern economic theory, price setting by the producer relied almost entirely on practical experience, 'gut feel' and the immediate feedback of market outcomes. While many would argue that this still remains the basis of many marketing price decisions, there is no doubt that the usefulness of the economic tradition, first expounded by Adam Smith and David Ricardo nearly two centuries ago, has been to stimulate the investigation of markets for *systematic* relationships between the price of goods and the subsequent demand for them (or vice versa).

THE THEORY

A fundamental notion in classical economics is that of the *demand*

347

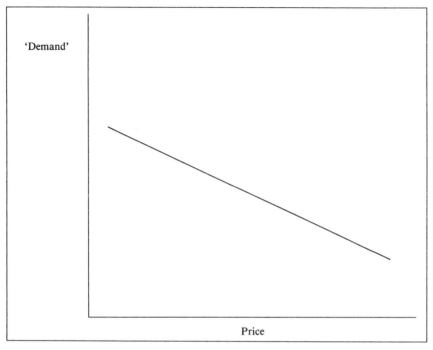

Figure 19.1   Linear demand curve

function. In its simplest form, the argument is that in a given market, and for a given price, there is a level of quantity demanded. This level of demand can be expressed as sales volume, brand share and so on; but ultimately represents the degree to which the 'consumer' is prepared to accede to the prices imposed by the 'producer'. A possible graphical representation of this relationship is shown in Figure 19.1 which shows a linear function. Since every line has its mathematical equation, the equation that expresses the relationship between price and demand is known as the *demand equation*, and the resulting graph the *demand curve*.

There are a few points to note about this curve.

First, as can be seen the slope of the curve is downwards, or *negative*, implying that demand decreases as prices rise (or conversely, that demand increases as prices fall). Most markets comply with this, although it is worth pointing out that some do not: for example, products with great 'snob' appeal, or luxury markets in general often reverse the slope so that demand rises as prices rise.

348

Clearly, there must be a point on the price axis where this relationship no longer holds; generally at the extremes of very low and very high price. Nevertheless, the rule may well apply within the price bounds normally encountered in the market. (This reversal is also true for markets with negative slopes to the demand curve – if a huge price were charged, it may instil in consumers' minds the notion that there must be something special about the product, and hence increase its value.) An important point about demand curves is that they refer to local phenomena of pricing, and should not be extrapolated too far.

The slope of the demand curve is of great interest, therefore, since it indicates the magnitude of response to price changes. This rate of response is termed the *elasticity of demand*. If the curve were perfectly horizontal, there would be no change in demand for notionally a very large change in price, and the demand in the market would be described as being perfectly *inelastic*. In contrast, a vertical (or near vertical) curve suggests dramatic changes in demand for very little change in price, that is, demand is *elastic*.

However, in real life many markets do not possess linear demand curves, and the relationship between price and resulting demand in less regular. This is particularly true when the demand for particular products is considered. For example, Figure 19.2 shows the typical 'S'-shaped curve found in many branded markets. As can be seen, at the extremes of low and high price, the demand is considerably more inelastic, but quite elastic in between.

This is explained as follows: in many competitive markets, a very low price will not attract all the possible buyers to the product, since there will be some who are not aware of it, or do not have it available, or who are strongly attached to other products. Further decreases in price therefore attract diminishing numbers of customers – hence the curve at the low price end will tend to the horizontal. At the other extreme of high price, the loyal buyers of the product will be more resistant to switching as high prices are encountered – hence the curve in this region will again tend to the horizontal. The region in between represents the switching in and out of more price-sensitive consumers, and the curve in the mid-price region will therefore show greater elasticity of demand.

In these curvilinear situations, there is no single measure of a product's price elasticity, since the slope of the curve depends upon the point at which price is measured. It is usual therefore to agree a band either side of a particular price, and define the *price elasticity* of that

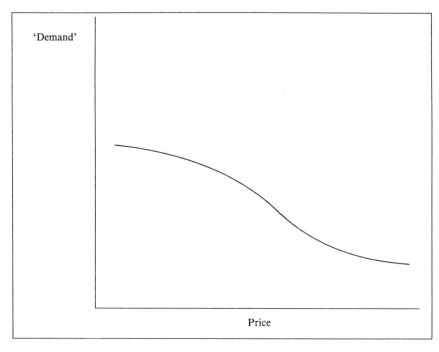

Figure 19.2   Curvilinear demand curve

price as the percentage change in demand resulting from a percentage change in price. Since slopes are commonly downwards, elasticities are generally negative in value. For example, if a 1 per cent increase in price results in a 4 per cent drop in demand, the elasticity would be -4.

The significance of this figure can be best seen in revenue terms. If the elasticity is -1, sales will rise or fall by the same percentage as prices change, and total revenue will therefore be unaffected. However, an elasticity greater than -1 implies that revenues will rise if prices rise; and conversely fall for cases where the elasticity is less than -1.

It should be clear that knowledge of the shape of the demand function is essential for price setting. For example, in Figure 19.3, a product priced at point A1 is in a quite different situation from one priced at point B1. The demand curve at price A1 represents a 'plateau' situation where an increase in price to A2 would incur only a small drop in demand. However, a product priced on the 'cliff' at B1 would suffer a

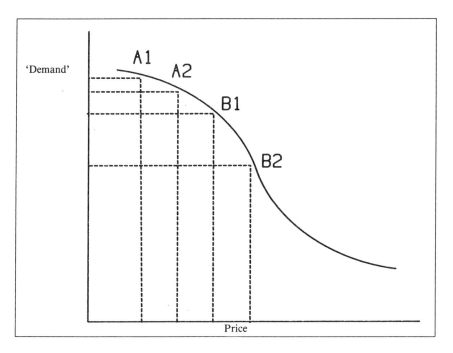

Figure 19.3   Evaluating price changes

considerably greater loss in demand if it increased its price to B2, even though the price increase were the same in both cases.

Note also that in some markets, *thresholds* exist, often involving the 'next rounded value', such as £1, or even 10p intervals for some low-priced products. These thresholds exhibit themselves as local discontinuities in the demand curve, or 'steps'.

THE PROBLEM FOR THE PRODUCER

While it is true that some markets are exempt some concern for correct price setting (for example, highly competitive markets at one extreme, and highly oligopolized markets at the other), most marketing concerns have some latitude in setting prices, and therefore must face continual pricing decisions. This is as true for non-manufacturing organizations (such as those providing services) as for manufacturers. While in many cases the need is the simple one of maximizing sales (and/or profits), it is clear that this must be done in the context of the particular constraints facing the marketing organization, together with its strategic objectives.

While this chapter concentrates on method rather than objective, it is worthwhile noting that the objectives of price setting can vary considerably.

'Internal' objectives

For example, the need may be to *reduce* price to gain product trial among customers (penetration); or, in stark contrast, to *raise* price where the increase in line profits more than offsets the likely loss in sales volume.

Moreover, price alteration strategies may be undertaken in differing contexts. Thus, the marketing goal may reflect needs as different as that of promoting a new product recently launched, or of treating an ageing brand or product as a 'cash cow' to fund other parallel developments.

Equally, pricing policy may reflect the need to meet internal organizational targets such as a satisfactory rate of return on the investment made. What is almost certain is that different pricing policies will be required for products at different points in their life-cycles.

'Competitor' objectives

In addition to 'internal' constraints, pricing decisions frequently reflect the constraints facing the competitors, in a fixed market within which a number of marketing organizations operate.

Perhaps the simplest objective of a pricing strategy here would involve the need to maintain, grow, or control the decline of a particular product's or brand's share of the market, whether this be expressed in volume (for example thousands of cases, or tonnage), or monetary value (for example 'sterling' share).

In competitive situations, price setting is frequently complicated by differing production overhead costs encountered by different organizations, leading to differing profit levels for similar products. Here the decision-making frequently incorporates some notion of the capacity of a competitor to respond to a price change initiated by one organization. This is one of a number of scenarios which can lead to long and protracted pricing wars: the threat of rapid retaliatory price cutting acting as a barrier to the entry of new competitors, or as a means of waging a lengthy war of attrition against a less favoured competitor.

In general, competitive markets provide some of the greatest problems for price setting, since theoretical demand analysis conducted at the consumer level often does not provide for an estimate of competitor reactions. Frequently, the 'room for manoeuvre' on pricing is less than expected, since the market may well have formed a dynamic equilibrium that will tolerate only small price movements before 'self-correcting' price reactions are triggered among competitors.

Consumer objectives

In some cases, pricing strategy may react to the knowledge that sensitivity to price can vary considerably between consumers: that is, there are those consumers who are very *price conscious*, and who would be very likely to switch products in the event of a price change; and those who are particularly attached – or loyal – to a particular product or service, and who would tolerate quite large changes in price before contemplating switching. Clearly, not everyone can be described in such black and white terms, and this distinction represents the two extremes of a dimension upon which most consumers can be positioned.

Nevertheless, knowledge of the composition of the consumer marketplace expressed in these terms in invaluable for some pricing policies, since it allows the producer to target a product or service to particular segments, possibly in the light of current production or distribution constraints. For example, a 'skimming' policy would price a new product high to gain a premium from likely loyal buyers, even at the expense of failing to attract price-conscious buyers who would require a lower price before buying. Later in the product life-cycle, perhaps when production capacity has been built up, greater distribution achieved, and competitors have entered the market, the price can be reduced both to appeal to a wider group, and to present greater difficulties to competition.

Strategies such as these, however, obviously require a good knowledge of the segmentation of the market in these terms, and the sizes of relevant groups. While this can be acquired by the trial-and-error method, specific research techniques have been developed to quantify this issue.

'Trade' objectives

While the consumer is the ultimate arbiter of success or failure of a pricing strategy, the growing trend of the concentration of the retail trade (in the fast moving grocery sector as well as the durables sector) in most developed countries means that the modern producer has, in practice, an intermediate customer, and by *force majeure* has relinquished to the retailer a good deal of control over end pricing. This has a number of consequences.

In some cases the retailer in effect sets the end price, and has taken over the role of the producer. Many of the arguments made above therefore now apply to the retailer and it remains for the manufacturer to negotiate (possibly via volume discounting) satisfactory distributor margins. Of course, since the interest of the retailer is ultimately concerned with the *volume* of sales (at a given margin), the manufacturer is faced with presenting convincing arguments (for example from market research, previous track record, support media expenditure and so on) that satisfactory sales volume will in fact be achieved. Given that failure to meet retailer objectives in these situations can lead to delisting, and that an unprecedented proportion of sales in some markets is now concentrated in the hands of a progressively smaller number of retailers, one outcome is that responsibility for trade negotiations is becoming increasingly centralized, and less the function of a sales force.

In other cases, the manufacturer can heavily influence the end price, or even dictate it. Alternatively, the retailer is allowed the flexibility to alter the end price by offering the consumer discounts. In either case, the manufacturer has determined the price to the trade, but needs to ensure that sufficient margin exists to provide a reasonable incentive to the distributor. This can lead to pricing policies which have more to do with maintaining trade margins, than presenting the end consumer with consistent prices (the motor car industry is an example).

THE PROBLEM FOR THE CONSUMER

It takes two parties to make a contract, and if the producer has one viewpoint, the other side of the price-setting coin is the final purchaser. Underlying the 'demand' stimulated by a particular pricing strategy lie the large number of individual consumers who have chosen to accept the price, or who have chosen not to. Moreover, the average elasticity of demand in a market may or may not be a good representation of the many individual consumers who will have widely varying degrees of price sensitivity.

In this context, price plays a psychological role to the consumer. There are a number of aspects to this, and as we shall see later, these have a considerable impact on the research methodologies designed to assist price setting (Morgan, 1987a).

Price as information

To the producer, changes in price represent deliberate responses to marketing pressures, and priced products are therefore, in legal terms, unemotional 'propositions to treat'. To the consumer, however, prices often represent more than cold economic utility. Work originally carried out by Stoetzel in 1954 suggested that price possesses a psychological *information content* to would-be purchasers, as do pricing movements (Stoetzel, 1954). For example, a price reduction may well reflect general price trends in the market, but may signal to the customer a variety of other messages: the item may be faulty; or about to be superseded; or the price will fall further; or that the quality has been reduced. Similarly, a price rise could suggest scarcity (and hence desirability) or higher quality (Oxenfeldt, 1961).

Judging price

Extensive research carried out in the 1960s and 1970s into the psychological processes consumers undergo when evaluating price established an important principle: most consumers in most markets do not make absolute judgements about brands or products in isolation. Instead, *relative* judgements are made about products within a person's repertoire. Moreover, this comparative basis for assessment typically extends beyond an evaluation of performance or image characteristics, into the area of price judgement. For most purchasers, it is the relative price considerations when compared with alternatives that convey the most information, and which therefore by extension contribute to purchasing decision-making.

To some extent, this issue of the relativity of price perception is exacerbated in markets where prices vary considerably by distribution channel. For example, in some fast moving consumer goods markets, the price of the same product can vary by as much as 100–200 per cent between cut-price multiples and corner shops. To a consumer, a fixed reaction to a specific price would be less than useful in situations where the product might be purchased from a number of outlets.

Familiarity with price

Possibly as an extension of the above, consumers may be unfamiliar with prices, and unaware of the price of alternatives not immediately on display at the point of sale. A recent research project in the USA, which involved intercepting shoppers emerging from supermarkets and asking in detail how much they thought they had paid for items they were carrying in their shopping basket, found an astonishing lack of recall of prices paid. Of course, this does not imply that prices are unimportant, since the displayed prices on the shelves may well prompt discrimination on the part of the buyer, rather that the decisions are often made locally and prices not stored in long-term memory for future reference and comparison.

It is clear from a number of recent studies, however, that in many low cost/outlay grocery markets the *involvement* of the consumer with the decision task itself can be very low indeed in developed countries. While this could reflect the boring and repetitive nature of buying in these fields, an alternative (or supplementary) view might be that the quality differentials within many product fields have grown smaller, so that the consequences of making a 'wrong decision' are much less. The development of retailer own labels, with assurances on quality (and therefore value for money), may well have contributed to this.

In some cases, especially in the purchasing of consumer durables, research has shown that the purchasing decision can extend a considerable period before the actual purchase. This *information-gathering* period will of course include the collection of information on price, as well as product performance criteria. In the six months prior to the typical purchase of a motor car, the average consumer will progress from a situation of very vague pricing awareness to detailed 'on the road' costs, including a knowledge of possible trade-in deals and dealer discounts.

Repertoires

A common finding from consumer panel data in repeat purchasing markets is that the proportion of product buyers who are 'solus' (that is, have bought the same product – and no other – a defined number of times) is very small, and typically less than 8 per cent. In most markets involving repeat purchasing, it is clear that consumers maintain 'repertoires' of products, between which they are prepared to switch periodically. This does not mean that all products within an individual's repertoire have equal likelihood of purchase; in fact they can each be thought of as having their own probability of purchase greater than zero and less then one (except in the case of single brand repertoires, where the probability for that brand is therefore one). A number of factors may contribute to this switching.

The most obvious example in the area of household purchasing arises when a *single consumer* (for example a housewife) is making purchasing decisions to satisfy the tastes and needs of others in the same household. The degree of independent decision-making allowed by these other members may be wide (as in most foodstuffs) or more restricted (for example alcoholic beverages). The decision made by the actual purchaser may not therefore be totally autonomous.

In some markets (for example confectionery, breakfast cereals or snacks) there can be a distinct search for novelty or variety, which can overcome a price barrier by prompting an 'impulse' purchase.

In other markets, a number of products can be purchased with a view to use on a number of *occasions*. Examples here can range from personal toiletries to alcoholic beverages: the important point is that a single consumer is acting in effect as a number of different consumers, depending on the occasion. Again, this can have an important implication on price setting, since the same person can be extremely price sensitive for some occasions, everyday perfumes for example, and much more price tolerant in others, for example fragrances for special occasions.

The perception of price

Finally, but by no means exhaustively, there is the issue of how the consumer actually evaluates the effect of the 'magnitude' of a price. For example, in the case of multiple purchasing where more than one unit is bought at the same time, does the buyer think (and hence make decisions) in terms of the unit price, or of the total outlay? Or indeed, in terms of pack price, or price per 100 grams?

At this point, the role of the psychologist takes over from that of the economist, and the concern is more to do with the understanding of *individual* choice processes than of their aggregated effects.

This can be a relevant issue when products are sold 'unbundled', that is, where the purchaser must put together a number of individually priced components to satisfy his or her needs. In consequence, should the marketing organization concentrate in its price-setting policy on the price sensitivity of the individual components, or on the 'gestalt' of the total price? A good knowledge of the 'optical' price premium attached to discretionary product components by customers can lead to a pricing policy that is more in line with consumer expectations, than a production-based 'cost plus' system. Moreover, premiums gained in one area can support losses made in others. For example, most car manufacturers charge more for larger engine options, even though the cost difference is rarely justified by the extra production costs – simply because there exists a consumer expectation that this should be the case. Different paint finishes, however, are often given parity costing even though production costs may vary significantly.

RESEARCHING DEMAND RELATIONSHIPS

In the event, the marketing organization will need some systematic research to determine the nature of price relationships in the market. In view of the considerations noted above, it is not surprising that most research methods in some way attempt to derive the demand curve for a product, or for a market.

In broad terms, there are two different ways of doing this.

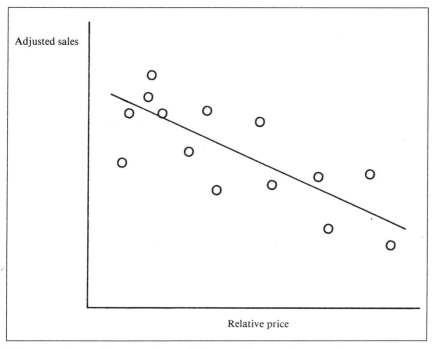

Figure 19.4   Scatterplot of demand at various relative prices

Econometrics

The most obvious way of establishing price–demand relationships is to examine past sales data, and note the way in which patterns – or correspondences – exist between pricing movements and sales. Thus, for example, one might plot the average selling prices of a product in a number of successive sales periods against cases sold. In fact, because of random effects, the relationship would be unlikely to be perfect, and some means would be needed to make a 'best estimate' of the relationship between the two variables.

It is possible to use mathematical curve-fitting techniques to derive a 'best fit' for data of this sort. For example, the method of linear *regression* would calculate a line through the data points that was 'best', in so far as the sum of squares of distances of each point to the line was at a minimum. This is shown in Figure 19.4. This line, represented by an equation, could be used to assess the elasticity of demand in the market, and also to predict the outcome of possible pricing movements.

In reality, this statistical approach, known as *econometric analysis*, is considerably more complex than this simple example suggests.

To start with, as noted earlier, most demand relationships are non-linear and possibly discontinuous, so that considerably more sophisticated mathematical models (such as Box–Jenkins, or ARIMA approaches) must be fitted to past data. Just a few of the problem areas encountered in this area are discussed below.

Data points

Most econometric techniques require a large number of data points before reliable models can be constructed from them. As a general rule of thumb, at least twenty measurements are required as a minimum, or around two years' monthly (or four-weekly) sales periods. This naturally poses problems in new markets, so that this approach is difficult to use for the price setting of innovatory new products prior to launch.

However, the large number of data points required brings its own problems. Markets change over time – and great care must be taken to avoid merging data from periods where different circumstances applied: for example, different competition, or tax rates.

Variables

So far, just one variable has been suggested that could have an effect on sales – that of price. In reality, of course, there are a large number of 'independent' variables which can affect a 'dependent' issue such as sales: for example, advertising activity (both for the product, and for competitors), promotional campaigns, trade incentives, facings, out-of-stocks, changes in retail distribution levels and so on, to name just a few. Complex econometric models may well incorporate a large number of factors, all designed to 'explain' apparent changes in demand, or sales, and often at a regional level, or by grocery multiple.

Some of these factors are not continuous; that is, they are of very short duration. For example, a short but intense burst of TV advertising is designed to have an effect long after the campaign finishes. This may need to be modelled also, as will any variables that are 'lagged', or whose effects linger on after they have themselves ceased. In some cases, it is possible to specify the degree of lagging to the model, which will then optimize the 'fit' with the data. In other cases, the modelling procedure will itself suggest the pattern of lagging in the data.

Variable definition

In addition to specifying the number of variables in the model, great care must be taken to define these in the most appropriate manner. For example, 'price' may be expressed as absolute average retail selling price (RSP), or RSP relative to other products.

The measurement of sales effect may come from ex-factory sales, an industry deliveries audit, consumer panel data, or retail audit; and each of these has its own advantages and disadvantages. Moreover, the expression of the level of sales may be simply in terms of absolute volume, or adjusted for variations in distribution, as in 'rate of sale'.

In some markets, care should be taken to discriminate price–demand relationships between different variants or pack sizes of the same brand. This is especially true when sales fluctuate, or exhibit seasonality, since in peak periods there is a natural tendency for larger pack sizes to be bought.

Patterns or trends

A particularly confounding feature of some markets (at least where econometrics is concerned) is that there may be distinct trends, stemming either from the growth of the market as a whole, or its decline. If prices have changed systematically through this period of change, false premises can be deduced from the apparent relationship, and need to be corrected for.

The most frequently occurring periodic trend is shown by seasonality of demand, where the cycle is often annual. In some cases this can be anticipated as an effect of known magnitude (for example sales of lawn mowers), while in others the amplitude of the effect can vary (ice cream sales and weather are an example).

Competitive reaction

Where the econometric model is used to predict the outcome of possible price changes, care must be taken to take full account of the potential reactions by competitors, since the model will often not have taken these into account if they have not featured in the past periods on which the model was based.

In general, econometric models can be a useful tool in the marketing armoury, for calibrating markets and as a basis for prediction. Nevertheless, they suffer from a fundamental philosophical shortcoming. By placing great emphasis on the apparent correlation of variables, they may stimulate misleading conclusions about the nature of the relationships between them. In short, 'just because A occurs with B, does not mean that A causes B'. Very little can be said about why A or B happen anyway.

Another cause for caution arises from the inescapable nature of the data themselves, which are of course exclusively derived from past events. In many cases, and in many stable and mature markets, this 'historicality' of the data is perfectly acceptable for short-term tactical planning. But in others, rising on the tides of fashion or requiring long-term strategic planning, a reliance on the pattern of past events to predict the future may be at best irrelevant, and at worst dangerous.

Ad hoc methods

If the origins of econometrics arose from the methods of classical economic theory, those of the *ad hoc* approaches derived from consumer psychology. In these methods, the aim is not to look at past aggregate sales data, but to adopt an experimental approach by recruiting a sample of consumers, and asking them to undertake a specific task that will uncover their reaction (and hence, by inference, the reactions of the universe of consumers as a whole) to particular pricing options.

There are a number of distinct advantages to these approaches. First, they avoid the 'historicality trap' of using past data (noted earlier), and can be adapted to new markets where no data exist. Second, they are particularly suitable for new product development concepts or prototypes which have yet to be launched. Third, because they involve the recruitment of specific samples of consumers (which can be defined in particular ways), they allow the market to concentrate on target consumers that have been defined elsewhere. Finally, they are the only way to identify the extent to which individual consumers in a market vary in terms of price sensitivity, and therefore provide a means of performing market segmentation.

In recent years, this area has witnessed a considerable growth in the number of methods available, all of which have their advantages and disadvantages in particular situations. Nevertheless, they fall into dis-

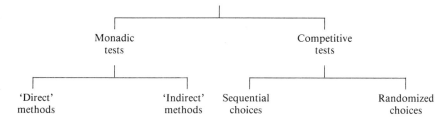

Figure 19.5 Classification of *ad hoc* methods

tinct 'schools' of thought, as shown in Figure 19.5 (Frappa and Marbeau, 1982).

Monadic approaches

In monadic methods, respondents who are recruited to take part are exposed to a *single* concept or product, and asked to deliver an opinion about their inclination to purchase at one or several prices.

The simplest (and oldest) system involves asking just that: 'Would you buy the product at price X?' and obtaining a 'Yes' or 'No' answer. In fact, this 'direct' approach is rarely used, since consumers are often reluctant to commit themselves in such a strong fashion during a market research interview; and if the stimulus is an unknown product or service, there may need to be a period of familiarization before a purchase decision is made.

Therefore, a more usual approach is to use a 'buying intention' scale, which allows the respondent to make a more graded reply. Such a scale might be as follows:

I would definitely buy	5
I might buy	4
I am not sure	3
I probably would not buy	2
I definitely would not buy	1

The number of responses from the study given to each category would be summed, and a mean score calculated by using the category weights shown (in this case, 5 to 1). Although the mean score generally has no intrinsic meaning in itself, experienced researchers can compare the scores achieved with those from previous studies, and judge how well the product has performed in stimulating purchasing intentions among consumers.

Although scaling approaches clearly require back data (or 'norms') for comparison, they have been shown to be well correlated with actual purchasing (Riddle and Wilkinson, 1979).

A more 'indirect' approach dealing with the presentation of a single product stimulus was developed by Gabor and Granger (1965). In this, respondents are presented with a series of prices in random order, and for each price asked whether they would buy or not. If they respond in the negative, they are asked whether this is because it was too cheap (that is, dubious quality), or too expensive. From these data, cumulative response curves can be charted for the proportion of likely buyers at any price (that is, those who thought the product was neither 'too cheap' nor 'too expensive'), thus generating a quasi-demand curve to which pricing-setting principles can be applied.

Van Westerndorp (1976) proposed a similar approach in his 'price sensitivity meter', which attempts to increase the precision of the response by collecting it on a five-point scale, although the methodology is essentially similar.

While these monadic techniques have been extensively documented – and are particularly appropriate for ill-defined markets (where the nature of the competition is difficult to specify) or genuine 'innovation products' – they can be criticized for not taking into account some of the findings mentioned earlier about the way in which consumers evaluate price. In particular, monadic approaches make no allowance for *relative* judgements which consumers might make between alternatives at different prices, or indeed that a given 'price' might itself *vary* in distribution. What might be an 'expensive' price for a hypermarket shopper might after all be a 'cheap' price in a village store.

The first point was addressed by Gabor and Granger in their 'randomized shop situation' method (Gabor *et al*, 1970). In this, respondents are shown a number of prespecified scenarios of products at particular prices. A typical scenario would consist of more than one brand, which would therefore allow the respondent to make relative judgements. Faced with a scenario, respondents can either select a single product as the one most likely to be purchased under those conditions, or specify the proportions of each they might buy over time (for example in repertoire situations) (Morgan and Godfrey, 1985).

While this approach is clearly more appropriate for well-defined markets, the researcher must spend some time in advance designing the specification of the scenarios to be presented.

Perhaps the most advanced methodology currently available for use in well-defined markets using competitive scenarios is the 'brand/price trade-off' (BPTO) method, developed by my company in the late 1970s (Morgan, 1987b). In this system, respondents are faced with a scenario of competing brands, which can be tailored for each individual's repertoire, or availability at his or her usual source of purchase. The elicitation method proceeds by starting all items at given prices, and successively asking the respondent to examine the priced items and state the one he or she would be most likely to purchase. The 'chosen' item is then increased to a higher price, and the question asked again. The interview stops when either the respondent refuses to purchase any of the brands at the prices they have reached, or when the range of prices under review is exhausted.

A practical advantage of this method is that scenarios do not need to be specified in advance, and the only prespecification required is the actual range of prices to investigate. However, there are a number of other advantages to the approach.

Typically, the data collected from each respondent in a BPTO exercise are subjected to 'conjoint analysis' to derive weights representing the relative desirability of the product items to that respondent, as well as the relative sensitivity to price levels. This allows a computer model to be built that is capable of 'simulating' respondent 'choices' for any combination of brand and price. This analysis is conducted at an individual level (technically known as 'micro-modelling') before aggregation, and so in theory offers the most sensitive way of handling individual differences in brand appeal and price tolerance. Moreover, since the analysis is conducted at the individual level, the individual predictions can be weighted for heaviness of consumption to provide *volume* share estimates, in addition to *usage* shares.

The advantage to the market is that the resulting computer models can be used in a totally flexible way to predict market outcomes, often via an interactive session at his or her personal computer. For example, a single simulation could be conducted to examine the effect of a single brand's price change, or changes to a number of brands, or even the effect of a competitor reaction. This is shown in Table 19.1 where the five percentage point gain in brand share experienced by Brand B has been achieved at the expense of a two percent loss in share for Brands A and D, and a one percent loss for Brand C.

Alternatively, a series of simulations can be conducted in which the

**Table 19.1   BPTO simulation of a price increase for brand B
(brand shares)**

	Current market %	Simulation %
Brand A	22	20 (-2%)
Brand B	13	18 ($+5\%$)
Brand C	42	41 (-1%)
Brand D	23	21 (-2%)

price of a target brand is systematically changed, with the remaining
brands kept constant at their 'market' prices. A graphical plot of brand
share movements resulting from this will reproduce the 'demand curve'
for the target brand, as well as the gains/loss from competitors. From
the example in Figure 19.6, it can be seen that the result of price increases
for brand B reproduces the expected 'S' demand shape, and also shows
that brand A is much less likely to benefit (that is, to compete) than
brand C.

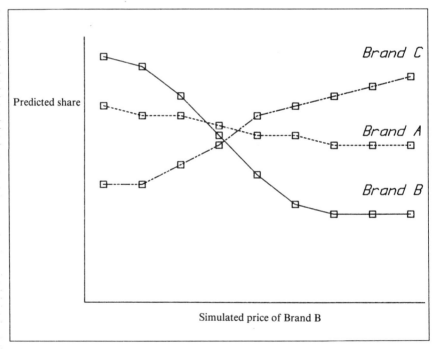

Figure 19.6   BPTO simulated brand shares

In general, BPTO modelling represents the 'state of the art' in *ad hoc* methods, where competitive product displays can be employed.

CONCLUSION

This chapter presents a general review of pricing problems in marketing. Of necessity much has been omitted, both in terms of general theory as well as details of case practice. Nevertheless, the References and further reading section below should provide the interested reader with further sources.

As in most branches of marketing, the most useful asset remains common sense. While the old adage; 'There ain't no brand loyalty that two cents off can't overcome' may not hold in all circumstances, it still remains a good rule of thumb until proven otherwise.

REFERENCES AND FURTHER READING

Frappa, J. P. and Marbeau, Y. (1982), *Pricing New Products at Better Value for Money*, ESOMAR Congress, Vienna.

Gabor, A. and Granger, C. (1965), 'The pricing of new products,' *Scientific Business*, No.3,August,pp.141–150.

Gabor, A., Granger, C. and Sowter, A. (1970), 'Real and hypothetical shop situations in market research', *Journal of Marketing Research*, Vol.VII,August,pp.355–359.

Morgan, R. P. (1987a), 'Ad hoc pricing research – some key issues', *Journal of the Market Research Society*, Vol.29,No.2,pp.109–121.

Morgan, R. (1987b), *Brand/Price Trade-Off – Where We Stand Now*, EMAC/ESOMAR Symposium on Micro and Macro Modelling, Munich.

Morgan, R. and Godfrey, S. (1985), *The Role of Pricing Research In New Product Development*, Market Research Society Conference, Brighton.

Oxenfeldt, A. R. (1961), *Pricing for Marketing Executives*, Wadsworth Publishing Company, San Francisco, p.28.

Riddle, M. and Wilkinson, J. (1979), *New Product Development in an Evolving Market*, ESOMAR Seminar, Dubrovnik.

Stoetzel, J. (1954), 'Le prix comme limite', in P. L. Reynaud (ed) *La Psychologie Economique*, Paris,pp.184–188.

Van Westendorp, P. (1976), *Price Sensitivity Meter: A New Approach to Study Perception of Prices*, ESOMAR Congress, Venice, pp.139–167.

20

Developing and launching a new consumer product

Pamela Robertson

Possibly one of the hardest tasks in the development programme is determining the scale of the opportunity or opportunities needed, but it is very important to define this at the outset as it has implications for the likely scale of investment required. Thus a company which has had a recent history of strong growth products, which are still very vigorous, may not need very significant new products to achieve its growth objectives, as the momentum of existing products will play a large part in meeting them. A company whose brands are mature, however, may need a significant programme of new product development (NPD).

The board of a company will have defined its growth targets; usually for a three- to five-year period. The scale of the NPD task can be identified by assessing what contribution existing products will make in terms of the desired growth and, thus, the gap remaining to be filled by new products. In considering the potential of existing products, there is a need for a high degree of realism, as sales of most products can be increased, but the level of investment required to achieve increased sales may not be justified in terms of the profit return.

A number of questions must therefore be asked about existing products before deciding on where resources should be allocated.

1 How much more is the market likely to grow for current products?
2 How much larger share of the market can the brand realistically

achieve?

3 How much money will need to be invested to achieve this share?

4 How much needs to be done on the current business just to defend the current position – what could happen if the brand is not defended?

5 What sort of profit can be expected?

6 Is this a good return on investment?

If a market is static or declining it is unlikely that much growth in sales can be achieved from the market itself. Again, if it is an established market any significant shift in brand share is likely to be expensive. It may be that significant sums will need to be spent just to defend the current position.

If such an investigation into an existing product's potential suggests that a significant additional investment is not likely to produce a good return, then the investment level should be such that the product's position and profitability are maintained or even grow slightly, but the main resources should be put into new products.

After assessing the gap between the contribution of existing products and the financial objective, the targets for NPD will have been identified. If the gap is very large the level of resource required, both financial and human, is likely to be of a high order, and it is important to ensure that this is recognized. Significant development activity cannot be carried out on 'shoestring' budgets and this needs to be made clear at the outset.

DEVELOPMENT STRATEGY AND OBJECTIVES

Successful new product development relies heavily on an appropriate development strategy. A company which is currently very good at making baked beans, is unlikely to achieve a high degree of success with a new product in the cosmetics market, because the inherent skills of the company are not in fashion and imagery, which are essential to success in the cosmetics market. Tailoring the development programme to the company's strengths and areas of competitive advantage, is more likely to lead the company into markets and products appropriate to its skills.

Defining where the company's competitive advantage lies is not easy and requires a very objective assessment. The factors which need to be examined include:

1 *brands* – their strength and degree of elasticity;
2 *distribution* – flexibility and capabilities, current utilization;
3 *sales* – key areas of strength in terms of retail channels, current utilization;
4 *technical* – areas of expertise and those areas where the expertise could be utilized;
5 *consumer image* – innovative, traditional, fashion-orientated, reliable and so on;
6 *finance* – funds for investment, return on investment criteria, payback and cash flow considerations;
7 *management* – basic ethos, flexible, dynamic, cautious and so forth;
8 *marketing* – strong, aggressive, proactive, reactive, attitudes to levels of marketing investment and so on;
9 *research and development* – fast, slow, in high-tech development or quality control and the like.

It is important to look at all these aspects of the business in relation to competition – for example, a company might view its distribution base as being good in relation to other aspects of its business but, when viewed in relation to its competition, it may not be as good as the competition's.

Each aspect also needs to be looked at in relation to the markets the company serves, as market forces may be such that what was considered a strength a few years ago might now be a limitation.

A good example of this would be a company selling products to the hardware trade. Five to ten years ago the small independent retailer would have been very important and a company with good distribution in this sector would have had a real strength. With the development of the DIY superstores, the independent hardware trade now accounts for only a minor share of sales and six or seven major DIY multiple retailers account for over 60 per cent of hardware product sales. A supplier which has not achieved good distribution in these key multiples has a severe limitation in terms of sales and distribution profile.

The development strategy should encompass the principal strengths of a company in relation to the market. Thus, a company might determine its development strategy as being a company which produces innovative, heavily branded, patentable, high frequency of purchase products or which is 'lowest cost producer of own-label products' and so on.

By combining the objectives, the strategy and key criteria, it should be possible to develop a new product policy for the company which will provide the direction for the programme. This policy should cover:

1 definition of business area in which the company is/will be operating;
2 development time scale;
3 attitudes to acquisitions versus internal development;
4 maximum capital available for:
   (a) acquisition;
   (b) internal development projects;
5 minimum size of acquisition
6 minimum turnover for a new product;
7 requirements for return on capital;
8 attitudes to investment/payback policy; and
9 other relevant criteria such as use of brands, production facilities, sales and distribution facilities, the type of competitive environment considered appropriate for the company.

SEARCH FOR MARKET OPPORTUNITIES

Perhaps the most difficult problem a company faces is how to allocate priorities and where management time and other resources should be channelled. Some companies study every possible opportunity in depth without cutting down to a short-list of the most suitable ones, so they produce nothing except paperwork. In other companies an idea catches on and it cannot be stopped however badly it performs in research, often because there is nothing else to take its place.

To ensure that the development programme is targeted at the most appropriate markets for the company, the use of a simple screen devised on the basis of the company's objectives, strengths and criteria can help pinpoint quickly and easily those market areas which should receive some priority.

Such a system is no magic formula for success, but it has many advantages.

1 It allows evaluation of a large number of opportunities, yet enables the company to concentrate quickly on the best ones.

Table 20.1   Example of a market screen

	Maximum score	Baby foods	Canned meat	Fruit juice	Greetings cards	Toys
Factors						
Market size	15	4	14	7	15	15
Past growth	10	1	2	9	6	5
Profitability	20	8	2	13	18	19
Competition	20	6	8	15	16	16
Chance of originality	20	5	7	9	14	17
Seasonality	5	5	3	3	1	1
Fir for:						
Company production	25	2	5	5	0	0
Sales force	20	8	14	14	7	7
R & D	10	7	7	7	2	2
Branding	15	2	8	9	1	2
Distribution	10	6	8	8	5	5
Internal total	*80*	*25*	*42*	*43*	*15*	*16*
Total score	170	54	78	99	85	89

2   It is a disciplined approach which takes some of the subjectivity out of such decisions.

3   All the opportunities can be compared on the same basis.

4   It is possible to understand in what ways one opportunity is better than another.

Table 20.1 shows a typical, though simplified, example of a market screen.

Such a system pinpoints the problems and opportunities in each case; thus the example shows baby foods to be a very poor market, canned meat to suffer from both lack of profit and poor sales trends, while fruit juice has the best score for a food company because it is a reasonable market and it is suitable for internal resources. Greetings cards and toys are far more exciting markets, but do not fit in well with internal resources; acquisition or a joint venture would solve this, if either were within the scope of the development policy.

To save time in the screening process, which usually involves the collation of a great deal of market data, it is useful to isolate perhaps two or three key criteria which provide a first screen, to reduce the number of markets or product categories for more detailed evaluation in the main screen. These key criteria might be anything from 'fit with existing brand', to 'utilizes production facilities'. The importance of this exercise is to identify those criteria which are fundamental to the development programme, and ncthing should be assessed in the detailed screening exercise which does not meet those criteria.

MARKET EVALUATION

Once the screening process has been completed, the development team has a short-list of priority areas for further consideration. The markets highlighted now need to be considered in some depth in order to understand their structure and dynamics, factors which will influence change in these markets thus opening up new opportunities. Knowing the current market size is therefore relevant, but being able to understand what is likely to make the market or segments within it grow will offer greater insight to the new product developer.

The obvious aspects to investigate include market size and trends, main market sectors and trends, product types and ranges, prices, trade margins, companies in the market, distribution profile, trade and consumer attitudes, consumer profile, usage, profitability, opportunities and threats.

For the development process it is also essential to investigate such factors as:

1 lifestyle trends and likely impact on the market;
2 strengths and weaknesses of companies involved in the market;
3 changes in distribution structure;
4 the impact of own label;
5 product failures in the past ten to fifteen years, an analysis of the reasons for failure and the lessons to be learnt;
6 recent successes and the reasons for success;
7 developments in other countries, particularly North America, Europe, Japan and Australasia and the relevance to the UK market;
8 price sensitivity and the potential for added value;
9 different ways of segmenting the markets. For example, in recent years many companies have looked at markets in terms of health opportunities, leisure and so on.

This type of data should be available from a combination of desk research and selective trade interviews. Using executives experienced in such interviews can yield a wealth of highly valuable information and can be the most important factor in evaluating the market.

IDENTIFYING A DISTINCTIVE ROUTE

The market evaluation may highlight a specific opportunity, but this is rare. It is more likely to help identify possible routes such as added value, or niche product for one sector, or health or similar. If an opportunity is clearly identified purely through the evaluation of the market, one should be wary, since if the idea is so obvious, many other companies may also have identified the gap and as with such large markets as cracottes, snack pots and instant custard, a large number of products entered the market at the same time. This will inevitably lead to price cutting, and several product failures as the market evolves.

Finding distinctive and appealing ideas is not easy. It is also important that the idea should be simple; if it is not, it will be difficult for the consumer to understand and appreciate the benefits.

There is no magic formula to provide a distinctive and appealing idea and usually a number of different methods are employed in the search for a product idea which will have the required level of appeal.

Some of the following approaches have been found useful.

1 *Search for ideas or products in overseas markets:* if a product is performing well in, say, North America, Japan, Australasia or Europe, it is quite possible that the product will have at least some measure of appeal in the UK, even if modifications are necessary.
2 *Search for market gaps:* search for opportunities through simple grid analysis, market segmentation, gap analysis based on existing market data.
3 *Research and development production ideas:* it is important to involve the technical personnel wherever possible; research and development often has relevant ideas and it can be useful to unearth its old suggestions/projects which have never been progressed for various reasons; what can be produced on under-utilized plant may be another starting point.
4 *Synectics:* lateral thinking, in conjunction with the more 'logical' approaches, often leads to the more original ideas.
5 *Lateral brainstorming:* there has been some development of an approach combining the best aspects of lateral thinking with traditional brainstorming. Such sessions can often be quicker and so more cost-effective than formal synectics.
6 *Consumer creative groups:* these are not easy to conduct, largely

because most consumers are not familiar with idea-generating techniques and can be somewhat reserved at the prospect of apparently being somewhat outrageous. However, when employed successfully using lateral and synectics techniques with consumers, such groups can be very rewarding.

7 *Product evaluation:* a very analytical assessment of products and their performance in relation to requirements and usage can provide an insight to possible areas of opportunity.

8 *Packaging developments:* in recent years consideration of the packaging as a vehicle for innovation has become quite important, and developments in packaging such as the tetra brik have lead to significant market development, such as fruit juice. Therefore keeping abreast of new developments by packaging companies, and evaluating pack development in other markets, such as wine boxes being adopted for use as paint containers, can provide new opportunities.

9 *Merchandising and service:* in some of the less developed and competitive markets opportunities may be found simply in the way in which the products are sold. A recent example of this is Polycell and home security, where few of the products sold were new, but Polycell took advantage of the lack of sophistication in packaging, provision of information and the poor product merchandising by providing bright, attractive stands with a fairly comprehensive range of home security products. More importantly Polycell used 'user friendly' language rather than the technical language used on most other home security packaging which was designed for use by the tradesman rather than by the DIYer. Consumers could see exactly what the packet contained, where the product could be used and how to install it, and the tools they would need. This gave the DIYer the confidence to tackle a task which many had decided previously was too complex.

DEVELOPMENT OF THE CONCEPT

A good idea alone is not enough. Even for startlingly good ideas, consumers need to understand the benefits fully:

- why they should use
- when they should use

- how they should use
- who it would appeal to
- what it offers that existing products do not

The actual words used are important: inappropriate terminology can easily evoke a negative reaction, as can inappropriate visuals, product description and brand name. Therefore early stages of consumer research not only act as a filtering process in terms of good ideas, ideas with some appeal but requiring further development and basically poor ideas, but provide guidance on consumer communication.

Initial concepts vary in format and much will depend on the type of product being developed. The medium for communication for a very functional product is likely to be a concept board with clear statements of benefit; if, however, it is a product area with a high degree of imagery, the medium may well be packaging plus concept. Where imagery or emotion plays a significant role the concept may well be communicated through what appears to be advertising, but in reality is not because advertising is designed to be persuasive, whereas concept positionings are developed to assess the genuine appeal of the idea or product.

Concept and product development and evaluation

The amount of evaluation required for a new product will depend very largely on the level of risk and opportunity. If the opportunity is relatively small, there is probably little point in spending vast amounts of money developing and refining the product, packaging, and advertising. However, as a minimum there should be both qualitative and quantitative evaluation of the concept, product, packaging, advertising and pricing.

Developing samples of the product for consumer and retailer testing can sometimes be difficult. In practice these procedures are not difficult in most food and drink markets; the initial product development can be done in a rudimentary way and kitchen samples can be used for such research; in toiletries the product examples can be obtained usually without too much trouble. In household chemical products – polishes, laundry products, DIY, gardening – the problems can be more difficult, but 'fudging' the products on the basis of what is already on the market is often possible.

In durables, on the other hand, where the design element is critical, this is a real problem, because the cost and time needed to develop a prototype make it difficult to have several different ones developed at the same time. Nevertheless, use of photographs or initial drawings is rarely satisfactory and it is important to have at least one prototype which can be shown to target consumers; thus car clinics have been extremely popular for all new car development.

Stage by stage planning and evaluation

Once there is a definite new product concept with initial consumer interest in it, it is likely to be developed by means of a staged process which must vary considerably according to the type of product concerned and the risk and opportunity at each stage. Some of the stages are likely to be simultaneous, others sequential; some can take under a day, others years. A typical programme is shown in Figure 20.1 but it must be regarded as an example only.

Ideally there should be a senior project leader within the company, with the personality and the authority to 'pull the project through' an organization which is likely to be unconsciously against him or her. Such a person must represent the very difficult combination of realism and enthusiasm, so that he or she can kill the project if at any time it does not meet criteria, and inspire everyone else's enthusiasm if it does. In the latter case he or she must have top management backing to ensure full co-operation from technical development, sales management, financial, production, distribution and management itself, so that the new product has the correct priority. For example, at Heinz the marketing of soup is, in a way, child's play compared with the launch of, say, creamed rice, and it is significant that Heinz made headway with new products in the early 1970s only when Tony O'Reilly appointed his most senior manager to be in charge of new rather than existing products.

TRADE RESEARCH

One aspect of the development programme which has become increasingly important is trade research. In most consumer goods markets there has been a concentration of retail distribution, so that for many new products it is critical to gain acceptance by a small number of important

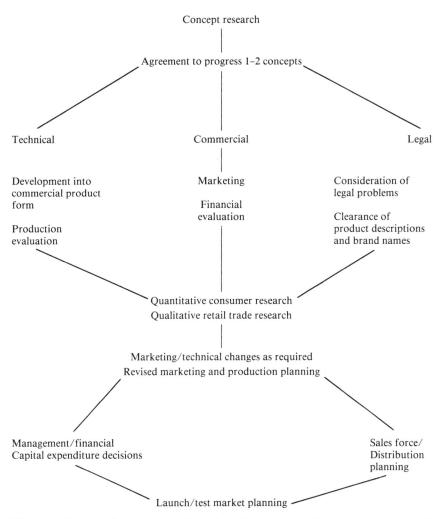

Concept research

Agreement to progress 1–2 concepts

Technical

Commercial

Legal

Development into
commercial product
form

Production
evaluation

Marketing

Financial
evaluation

Consideration of
legal problems

Clearance of
product descriptions
and brand names

Quantitative consumer research
Qualitative retail trade research

Marketing/technical changes as required
Revised marketing and production planning

Management/financial
Capital expenditure decisions

Sales force/
Distribution
planning

Launch/test market planning

Figure 20.1   Stages in the development of a new product concept

multiple retailers. This is particularly true of food, drink, toiletries, cosmetics, DIY, electrical and many other markets. A handful of major multiple buyers often controls the destiny of a new product.

Although some retail outlets are becoming larger, few outlets have room for more products; new products have to displace existing products and, much as most manufacturers like to believe that the delisted product will be a competitor's – and, indeed, recommend that it

379

should – as often as not the retailer will want to remove from the shelf another product from the manufacturer's own range.

Ensuring a listing for a new product must be a top priority for manufacturers, and trade research is therefore an integral part of the total development programme. However, trade research need not and should not be confined to assessing the appeal of a product and the trade's requirements for it in terms of service. Trade research can be used from the start of the development programme to ensure that the product ultimately developed has every possible chance of success. Trade research is used to find out about potential markets and potential competitors' and buyers' views on new products.

Once short-listed ideas have been developed into concepts and have come through at least one stage of consumer research successfully, it is often useful to carry out a preliminary, and necessarily relatively superficial, evaluation of the concept with the trade; superficial in that the concept may well change or develop as it is progressed, and there is also a danger in alerting the trade too early by giving too much away. But the concepts can be evaluated in outline and this helps to pinpoint any likely problems.

At this stage it is important to gain an in-depth understanding of trade requirements concerning such aspects as trade margins, bonusing, promotional policy, merchandising policy and service needs, representational requirements, distribution systems, administration systems and so on. It is useful to determine when buyers hold their reviews of new products and how far ahead of launch. This is critical information for any product, but particularly one which has seasonal sales where the timing of its launch is critical to its success.

This information is not only essential to ensure that the right service is offered to the trade, and the trade marketing strategy is appropriate and appealing, but the information can also form part of the basis for the financial evaluation.

Several months before the planned launch, and with sufficient time to make any necessary modifications, a total product proposition test should be carried out. This should cover products, (prototypes are sometimes suitable), packaging, merchandising material, promotional programmes, trade support programmes, margins and bonusing.

This research prior to launch usually helps to smooth the sell-in and there is a much greater chance of success for the new product since good distribution is much more likely. This is because the trade will have been involved in the development and therefore commitment to manufacturer and product is that much greater.

TEST MARKETING

Because of the risks likely to be involved in launching a new product it usually pays to test it first in a limited area. Mini-van research, as developed by Unilever, can at times be a substitute means of bridging the gap between product research and national marketing. Alternatively a simulated test market can be used such as BASES or ASSESSOR.

However, the main benefits of a proper area test in realistic conditions are twofold.

1   It teaches the company how to handle the new product, as it provides a pilot plant situation. This is particularly important if the new product is outside the company's previous expertise.
2   Test marketing provides a basis for future sales and profit forecasts, though these must be treated with care, because no one area is typical and the market varies from one year to the next. Test market performance must obviously be more reliable for future forecasts than estimates based on artificial research alone. This is particularly true if the test is long enough to allow for a settled pattern of repeat buying to take place.

Test markets are rarely possible in the case of durables, but there are times when it is possible to import a limited number of products or to obtain sufficient from another source for an area or for one large customer. It is always worth considering such methods of cutting the risk.

THE LAUNCH

Finally, at the end of all this work, comes the national launch. In practice not enough attention is paid to it; it is also quite wrong to consider it as the final step in the project – it is still only the beginning. A few points should be made.

1   The national launch needs to be planned a long time in advance. Some companies will not accept any launch, even in a limited area, unless all the details are agreed at least six months beforehand.

2   The sales force must be given a very full product and marketing briefing.
3   The trade must be given a full presentation of the thinking behind the product, the main research and test market results and the future aims.
4   Forecasts need to be made of consumer and trade penetration each month or every two months, and monitoring procedures should be set up accordingly.
5   High priority should be given to the launched product throughout the company.
6   Ideally the executive who has been behind all the planning should also be the person responsible for the launch; this is vital to ensure the required level of commitment as well as for the sake of continuity.
7   Despite all the work done to date, there are likely to be at least some problems. If the product has indeed passed all the hurdles satisfactorily there must be no panic at the first problems; some of the biggest new product successes found it hard going at first. The launched product needs careful nurturing over the first few years to ensure that it has a good chance of joining the list of significant successes.

REASONS FOR NEW PRODUCT FAILURE

It has been mentioned earlier that any new product should have a champion, preferably at a senior level.

Anyone involved with NPD will acknowledge that the failure rate for new products is high, although just how high has never been accurately measured. Usually when a product fails it is not just one aspect of the product or launch programme which has led to failure, but a combination, some aspects being more important than others.

There are seven main areas where problems arise which are either a root cause of failure or are contributory to a company not meeting its objectives for a new product launch. These are:

1   inappropriate development strategy;
2   the people factor;
3   too little investment;

4   lack of understanding of the consumer;
5   lack of understanding of the trade;
6   no real distinction in the product;
7   timing.

Inappropriate development strategy

Every company has its own strengths and limitations, and in most cases an aspect of its business will provide the company with a competitive edge. If incorrectly identified, a company's development strategy may lead it into areas where it is ill-equipped to develop successful new products.

The people factor

It is often the case that NPD is left in the hands of relatively junior and/ or inexperienced people who, however good, do not have the experience to ensure that all aspects of the development are properly carried out or are appropriate to the scale of the development. Another people factor is that the development team is under-resourced, and the NPD team is often trying to run current brands, with their pressing day-to-day problems, whilst developing new products, or just one or two people without the necessary breadth of skills are left to develop the new product on their own. NPD requires creativity, knowledge of markets, trade, consumers, competitors, packaging, promotion and so forth, and while such knowledge/experience might be vested in one or two individuals, an expert team is likely to do the job better.

Investment

Even in the largest companies, the NPD department and its activities are often funded with only small budgets. To obtain significant new products a company must be prepared to invest large sums of money in finding and developing an idea or product and then making sure that all the elements are to optimize success. The greater the objectives the greater the investments, and with insufficient investment the quality of the product launched is often damaged to an extent that what little investment has been made is wasted because the product is a failure.

'Misreading' the consumer

It is often said, correctly, that the way the question is asked will determine the response. Understanding the end consumers and what will appeal to them is fundamental to successful NPD. Without the expertise to know what to ask and when to ask it, and to understand the response, failure is inevitable.

Understanding and acknowledging the importance of the trade

As with consumers, the requirements of the retail trade need to be clearly understood. What is it that will make them take a new product and displace an existing product?

Distinctiveness

It is generally accepted that for a new product to succeed it must be distinctive and appealing to its target market.

Developing distinctive and appealing ideas is not easy, and a high degree of creativity is required to come up with an idea no one else thought of, but with wide appeal.

Quite frequently products are developed which lack genuine distinctiveness, because companies have not been sufficiently objective in their assessment of the differences between their new product and existing competition.

Timing

Timing is a very difficult area – a good idea can be ahead of its time and the market therefore is not ready for it, or it can be too late. While the product is being developed competition may also be active, and when launched several others may already be on the market. This does not inevitably mean failure, but it will if the product reaching the market last is very like those already available.

Another problem of timing is more avoidable – the actual length of the programme. Companies often demand very fast programmes with the almost inevitable result that not everything is done properly, or the programme is allowed to drag on losing momentum and, often, sight of the original objectives.

The last timing problem is that the product is not ready in time for the retail buyer's range review and so perhaps six months or a year are lost, by which time the competitive situation has become more intense.

These pitfalls can be avoided – largely by commitment, experience and expertise; knowing what level of investment is required to meet objectives, being committed to NPD to the extent that financial and human resources are available to the appropriate level required, having the right expertise to ensure a distinctive and appealing product for both trade and consumer.

FURTHER READING

Kraushar, P. (1977), *New Products & Diversification,* Business Books, London.

Kraushar, P. (1985), *Practical Business Development, What Works What Does Not,* Holt, Rinehart and Winston, London.

Kraushar, P. (ed) (1986), *New Product Development,* ESOMAR Monograph Series, Vol. 1.

Peters, T. and Waterman, R. Jr (1982), *In Search of Excellence,* Harper & Row, London.

Porter, M. (1980), *Competitive Strategy,* Free Press, London.

Porter, M. (1985), *Competitive Advantage,* Free Press, London.

Ramsay, W. (1984), *Seventeen Basic Precepts for New Product Development,* Paper to Oxford Management Centre, April.

21

Developing and launching a new industrial product

Michael J. Baker

For many years it has been argued that there are more similarities than differences between industrial and consumer marketing so that it is divisive and often counter-productive for practitioners in either field to ignore practice and experience in the other. Nonetheless, in the particular, it is clear that there are important differences in degree which merit separate consideration and treatment. In the preceding chapters a number of authors have dealt with many of the key concepts related to new product development and the same ground will not be covered again – the primary objective here is to focus attention on some of the more distinctive features associated with the marketing of new industrial products.

Clearly, within the scope of a book of this nature, it is possible to provide only a brief overview of some of the main factors and the reader is strongly recommended to consult some (or all) of the books listed in 'References and further reading' at the end of the chapter in order to gain an appreciation of the complexity and richness of this field of marketing activity.

The chapter is organized in the following manner. First the importance of new product development to the firm's survival and growth as the principle plank in its competitive strategy. Next, the reasons why users and markets resist innovation with the result that many new products are deemed to be failures. Arising from this analysis, some guidelines are proposed for identifying early buyers so that the firm can develop the most effective launch strategy to ensure rapid penetration and the development of the market for its new product.

THE IMPORTANCE OF NEW PRODUCT DEVELOPMENT

While it is true that demand does exceed supply in certain markets, this is largely confined to new markets for new products. In more traditional and familiar markets, such as those for steel, ship-building, car tyres and even cars themselves, potential capacity far exceeds effective demand with the result that firms compete with each other for the customer's favour. Classical economics would have us believe that this competition would focus on price, but the reality is that manufacturers choose to recognize that demand is not homogeneous and so seek to differentiate their product to match more closely the needs of specific subgroups or market segments. Clearly if manufacturers are successful in distinguishing their products in a meaningful way, then they provide prospective users with a basis for preferring them over other competing alternatives and so create a temporary monopoly which allows them a measure of control over their marketing strategy.

The desirability of exercising some control over a market rather than being controlled by it – being a price maker rather than a price taker – is self-evident. The wisdom of doing so is equally compelling, for a number of surveys have shown conclusively that while price ranks third or fourth in the selection criteria of most industrial purchasing agents, product characteristics or 'fitness for purpose' ranks first.

For these reasons product differentiation has become the basis for competition between suppliers competing for a share in a market and this explains the importance attached to product development by most companies today. It also helps to explain why new product development (or innovation) has become increasingly sophisticated and much riskier than it used to be. This is because, with so many more companies investing heavily, minor features are quickly copied or made obsolete by more radical changes. In the same way, the accelerating rate of change has had a similar effect on major innovations so that the average life of products is becoming shorter and shorter (compare, for example, valves, transistors and microprocessors as basic inputs to computing devices). Thus many companies are faced with the apparent paradox that if they do not innovate they will be left behind, while conversely if they do the probability of failure is very high and this could ruin the company too. As Philip Kotler has put it:

> Under modern conditions of competition, it is becoming increasingly risky not to innovate . . . At the same time, it is extremely expensive and risky to innovate. The main reasons are: (1) most product ideas which go into product development never reach the market; (2) many of the products that reach the market are not successful; and (3) successful products tend to have a shorter life than new products once had.

With regard to the first point it is clear that discarding products during development must impose some cost. However, a great deal of advice is available on this phase of development, and it is believed that companies have become much better at weeding out weak ideas earlier in the development cycle and so are able to minimize losses from this source. Similarly, a shorter life might be preferable to a long one if one can generate similar volumes of sales, because the discounted value of present sales is greater than future ones and early capitalization of an investment gives the company greater opportunity for flexible action. This point will be developed later.

Much the most important cause for concern is the fact that many products are not successful at all. In these cases not only has a company incurred all the development costs but it has also incurred the marketing costs of launching the new product, not to mention the possible loss of goodwill on the part of the users who discover the product is unsuccessful and likely to be withdrawn from the market.

THE NATURE AND CAUSES OF PRODUCT FAILURE

While claims concerning the incidence of new product failure are commonplace, few such claims are based on hard evidence. Those which are usually conflict with one another, due to the absence of any agreement about precisely what is to be measured, so that trying to quantify the proportion or value of failures is largely a matter of speculation. However, managers are agreed that the number and cost of failures are high and are anxious for advice as to how they can reduce this risk. To do so it will be helpful to propose a simple definition of failure and then see if at least the main causes of it can be identified.

A simple definition of failure is that this is deemed to have occurred when the innovator so decides. While this may not appear to be very helpful, it should help to clear the ground by making it explicit that success and failure are comparative states and there is no yardstick or criterion for deciding when one ends and the other begins. To argue otherwise would be to claim that all companies subscribe to the same managerial objective – for example, a return of x per cent on capital employed – and clearly they do not. It follows that your failure might be someone else's success and attempting to define the states precisely is a sterile exercise.

This is certainly not true of establishing the perceived causes of failure because by so doing it should be possible to develop guidelines and tests for identifying and avoiding these in future. Unfortunately, relatively few companies appear to be willing to document their failures and there is a marked dearth of case history material on the subject. In 1964 the National Industrial Conference Board in the U.S.A. conducted a survey as a result of which it offered the following list of factors underlying failure in rank order or importance:

1 inadequate market analysis;
2 product defects;
3 higher costs than anticipated;
4 poor timing;
5 competitive reaction;
6 insufficient marketing effort;
7 inadequate sales force; and
8 inadequate distribution

Over 50 per cent of all respondents cited the first three reasons.

A more recent study was carried out by Roger Calantone and Robert Cooper of McGill University in which they asked managers in 150 industrial companies in Quebec to categorize the nature of the causes leading to market failure: 'those products where sales had failed far short of expectations'. Table 21.1 summarizes the responses to this survey and reveals strong support for the findings of the 1964 study.

Table 21.1 Specific causes for poor sales performance (N = 89)

Specific cause	Percentage of product failures	
	Main cause	Contributing cause
Competitors were more firmly entrenched in the market than expected	36.4	13.6
The number of potential users was overestimated	20.5	30.7
The price was set higher than customers would pay	18.2	33.3
The product had design, technical or manufacturing deficiencies/difficulties	20.5	25.0
Selling, distribution or promotional efforts were misdirected	15.9	23.9
The product was the same as competing products . . . a 'me-too' product	14.8	25.0
Did not understand customer's requirements: product did not meet their needs or specifications	13.6	26.1
Selling, distribution or promotional efforts were inadequate	9.1	31.8
A similar competitive product was introduced	10.2	22.7
Were unable to develop or produce product exactly as desired	11.4	19.3
Competitors lowered prices or took over defensive actions	12.5	13.6
Timing was too late	8.0	13.6
No market need existed for this type of product	5.7	18.2
Timing was premature	6.8	13.6
Government action/legislation hindered the sale of the product	2.3	3.4

These causes of new product failure have been summarized as six 'failure scenarios' as shown in Table 21.2.

By contrast, in 1982 Booz, Allen and Hamilton updated their 1960s survey and came up with seven factors contributing to new product success, namely:

1 product fit with market needs;
2 product fit with internal functional strengths;
3 technological superiority of the product;
4 top management support;
5 use of the new product process (normative theory);
6 favourable competitive environment;
7 structure of new product organization.

In between these studies Andrew Robertson and his colleagues at the Science Policy Research Unit at Sussex University conducted an analysis

Table 21.2   Failure scenarios

Reasons for new product failures

Product characteristic	% of failures
The better mousetrap no one wanted (innovative, unique products rejected by the market)	28
The me-too meeting a competitive brick wall (similar to products on the market already meeting customers needs)	24
Competitive one-upmanship (me-too products hurt by the concurrent introduction of similar competitive products)	13
Environmental ignorance (products not well suited to customer needs)	7
The technical dog product (technically new products not performing)	15
The price crunch (products well suited to customer needs but priced too highly)	13

of a series of thirty-four new product failures and concluded that their main cause was a lack of market orientation.

While the evidence may not be as extensive as one might wish the conclusion appears inescapable – failure is the consequence of managerial ignorance or, worse still, managerial neglect. Ignorance because there is a very extensive managerial literature, based on well-documented practice, which emphasizes the importance of thorough market analysis as an essential prerequisite of any new product development; neglect because it is management's responsibility to keep itself informed of the best current practice and, if one is well informed, it is difficult to conceive how one could excuse commercial failure in a variety of ways which fundamentally all come down to the same thing – inadequate market analysis.

Several other chapters in this book provide advice on aspects of market analysis and measurement all of which is applicable to industrial marketing. Accordingly, it will be assumed that the reader is informed and responsible and will put to good use the advice contained in these chapters. Unfortunately, while this will greatly enhance the probability of success it cannot guarantee the eradication of 'failure' for one or other of two basic reasons.

First, failure is defined in terms of not achieving a target sale volume within some prescribed period of time, usually determined on the basis of the time necessary to earn a satisfactory rate of return on the capital employed. The difficulty in applying such a criterion is that the great

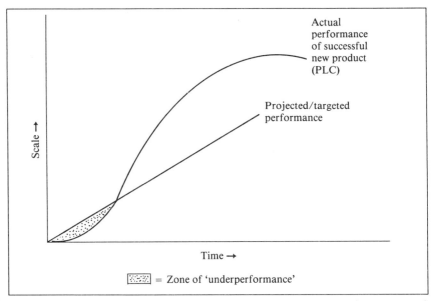

Figure 21.1   Product life-cycle and projection of expected sales

majority of managers tend to use a straight linear extrapolation when projecting future sales despite the fact that all the available evidence on the sales performance of successful new products points convincingly to some form of exponential growth. The theoretical expression of such a phenomenon is the well-known product life-cycle concept which postulates that all products pass through a life-cycle characterized by slow initial development. This is followed in turn by a period of rapid growth and a period of maturity or stability, whereafter sales will begin to decline unless management takes positive steps to extend or even rejuvenate the mature phase. Such a product life-cycle is reproduced in Figure 21.1 together with a straightforward linear projection of expected sales. From figure 21.1 it is abundantly clear that in the initial phases the new product will consistently underperform against the target – indeed the gap between the two will increase. Depending upon the time scale involved it seems quite likely that many managements will withdraw a product from the market because of its apparently deteriorating performance (the gap between 'projected' and 'actual') without ever knowing whether it would 'take off', in which case actual sales would later greatly exceed those projected.

Of course this is the major criticism levelled against the PLC concept – it can tell you only what the sales performance of a *successful* new product will look like – it cannot tell you if any given product experiencing difficulty in penetrating a market would be successful if you persevered with it.

The second reason why existing advice on market analysis and new product development will never result in a 100 per cent record of success is that there is another important factor which has been omitted from conventional analysis and which accounts for a significant proportion of failures. This factor has been described in a number of ways, the most familiar of which is 'resistance to change'. But, however we describe it, it is an expression of managerial attitude towards new products and it helps to explain why such products make slow initial progress when first introduced to a market.

It is vital that managers responsible for launching new products should understand why prospective customers may be slow to appreciate or accept the benefits claimed for such innovations. Clearly, if one possessed such information it might be possible to devise strategies to overcome these difficulties. Basically, the problem seems to be that while most managers feel that they can pre-identify the most receptive market for an innovation the evidence is that by and large they are not very good at it. With the benefit of hindsight it is not difficult to see why company 'A' could not seem to make up its mind about the benefits of adoption while company 'B' accepted it almost immediately. The question is can we identify any patterns in the reactions of companies to new product propositions which would enable us to pick out the 'B' companies in advance? The next section summarizes some of the factors which should be taken into account.

MANAGERIAL ATTITUDE AND 'RESISTANCE TO CHANGE'

It has been suggested that a leading problem with economic theory is that many laymen mistake its models for reality. Much the same problem seems to beset our attitude to industrial purchasing decisions for, while it is argued that consumers (too often disparagingly dubbed 'silly housewives') may act irrationally, it is unquestioningly accepted that companies follow the precepts of economic rationality and make decisions which maximize a price/quantity relationship in the manner prescribed by economic theory.

My own view is that *all* buyers use objective criteria in determining which purchase will give them the most satisfaction, that is, they behave 'rationally'. Unfortunately, such a process frequently fails to enable a prospective buyer to come to a decision for the simple reason that after exhausting all the available objective criteria he or she is still left with two or more apparently equivalent alternatives and has to make a choice between them. As a theoretician we can assume away this problem by stating that if two or more products are objectively the same then they *are* the same and it does not matter which we choose. In the real world it is not like that at all – Daz is different from Omo, Rover is different from Mercedes, Goodyear is different from Dunlop, JCB is different from Caterpillar and so on. In the absence of any means of distinguishing between close substitute products life would become intolerable for we would live in a state of constant uncertainty. Thus the reason products are perceived as different is because we believe them to be so (usually with more than a little help from their manufacturers) and it is this belief or attitude which determines how we make purchase decisions.

But subjective factors do not influence only final purchase decisions when we are required to make a choice between what otherwise might be considered objectively identical products, they also influence our perception of the objective factors themselves. Thus it is not a question of what the seller claims are the attributes of a product or the benefits which will flow from its adoption that is important but the prospective buyers' interpretation of these claims, and there are numerous reasons why their views may differ. For example, James Bright (1964) cites twelve major sources of opposition to innovation and it is significant that only two of these, 3 and 6, make any pretence to economic objectivity:

1   to protect social status or prerogative;
2   to protect an existing way of life;
3   to prevent devaluation of capital invested in an existing facility, or in a supporting facility or service;
4   to prevent a reduction of livelihood because the innovation would devalue the knowledge or skill presently required;
5   to prevent the elimination of a job or a profession;
6   to avoid expenditures such as the cost of replacing existing equip-

ment, or of renovating and modifying existing systems to accommodate or to compete with the innovation;

7 because the innovation opposes social customs, fashions, tastes, and the habits of everyday life;

8 because the innovation conflicts with existing laws;

9 because of rigidity inherent in large or bureaucratic organizations;

10 because of personality, habit, fear, equilibrium between individuals or institutions, status, and similar social and psychological considerations;

11 because of a tendency of organized groups to force conformity;

12 because of reluctance of an individual or a group to disturb the equilibrium of society or the business atmosphere.

There is now a considerable body of evidence which confirms beyond doubt that industrial buyers are just as subject to the processes of selective perception and distortion as are individuals making purchases for their own needs, and it follows that industrial sellers should follow the example of their consumer counterparts in seeking to develop a better understanding of the factors which shape and influence the buyers' attitudes and behaviour. The final section of this chapter attempts to isolate certain guidelines which may prove helpful in this task.

IDENTIFYING THE INDUSTRIAL 'EARLY BUYER'

From the foregoing discussion it should be clear that:

1 commercial failure is usually the result of delay in building up an acceptable sales volume;

2 the sales of a new product grow exponentially so that after an initial slow start successful products 'take off' and sales grow very rapidly indeed;

3 There is an inherent resistance to change and it is this which delays early sales;

4 while one may define a new product's economic and technological characteristics in objective terms these characteristics are viewed subjectively by prospective purchasers.

If we accept these conclusions it seems reasonable to hypothesize that the first person to buy must perceive the innovation more favourably than those who defer a decision or else reject the new product. It follows that if this is so there must be a significant advantage in being able to pre-identify potential early buyers for it will then be possible to target one's initial sales efforts at them. As noted above most sellers would argue that they already try to do this, but if their preselection is based upon their perception of who is likely to benefit most from purchase then it is unsurprising if this differs from the potential user's view.

For example, many innovators concentrate their sales efforts upon market leaders or those with the greatest potential demand for the new product on the basis that they have the most to gain. They also have the most to lose and it is this alternative interpretation which invariably predisposes the bigger company to proceed cautiously. This is not to say that they will not be among the first to buy, because given their scale of operations large users can often afford to buy an innovation solely to test it without any final commitment to it either way. Conversely, small companies may need only one unit of the innovation if it is a piece of capital equipment, or may have to standardize upon it if it is a raw material or component with the result that they are wholly committed and have to make the innovation work. Other things being equal, then, smaller companies have a greater commitment to any innovation they adopt and so will make strenuous efforts to make it successful.

Smaller companies are also likely to respond more quickly for the simple reason that decision-making is more concentrated than in large companies and does not have to proceed through a hierarchy of committees. Further, in the smaller company it is usually simpler to discover who the key personnel are – the 'gatekeepers' who allow in or exclude information on new products, and the opinion leaders who gain job satisfaction through influencing their colleagues' views on specific matters such as the technical merits of a new piece of machinery. The benefit of being able to identify key individuals is obvious because we can then get to know them as such and achieve a much better knowledge of what conditions their perception.

Extensive research has shown that the firms most likely to respond quickly to new products are those which are experiencing some difficulties or problems of their own. For example, Jim Utterback of the Massachusetts Institute of Technology found in a study of five industries in Europe and Japan that 'successful projects were seen to be related to a fairly or highly urgent problem faced by a firm', and this conclusion is confirmed by numerous others. In broader terms, innovations are likely to appear more attractive to unsuccessful than to more successful companies. The conventional wisdom tends to favour the more successful, if for no other reason than that they will be able to pay, and this increases the probability of delay in market penetration.

A third factor of considerable help in pre-identifying the receptive companies is determination of the policy on depreciation and replacement. Most innovations are substitutes for something else and it is clear that a need to replace may give rise to the urgency discussed in the preceding paragraph. Certainly, if organizations are actively reviewing replacement possibilities there would seem to be a greater likelihood of their being willing to evaluate a new product than would be the case if they are entirely satisfied with their present supplier or installation. Most organizations have explicit depreciation and replacement policies, and time taken to determine these and the stage in the cycle at which individual companies are placed could repay handsome dividends in identifying the most receptive market segment.

A study of replacement policies may also uncover opportunities for joint product development, an approach which work by Eric von Hippel has shown to have a very high success rate. Most companies are flattered that their suppliers should take an interest in their likely future needs and are often willing to participate in joint product development, thus making it quite clear what benefits users are seeking and also providing facilities for field testing and trials. In addition, one of the most persuasive arguments to encourage the purchase of a new product is to be able to point to its successful use by someone else (another risk-reduction strategy).

Collectively all the foregoing factors emphasize the need to know your customers and to put yourself in their shoes when considering the perceived merits of an innovation.

Most new products are introduced by existing companies into existing markets and this is obviously much less difficult than is the case when developing an entirely new market. In the latter instance the same advice still applies, but much of the information will be more difficult to come by and may have to be inferred from other indicators. In such circumstances considerable benefits can be obtained by regarding the market development phase as a capital investment project (like research and development) and offering inducements to early buyers which help reduce the high perceived risk of being first. For example, it is possible to limit the financial risk by leasing or sale-or-return clauses, and running-in problems can be reduced by providing technical assistance and a generous policy on losses due to start-up difficulties. Alternatively, it is possible to join forces with a supplier/distributor with a proven track record in the market and benefit from its marketing skills.

WHO IS RESPONSIBLE FOR NPD?

Until now the emphasis in this chapter has been upon the launch phase with little or no reference to the internal process of NPD. In part this is because earlier chapters have looked at issues of product planning and product design. However, reference has also been deferred to reinforce the point that launching new products is a decidedly risky business from which it follows that those with responsibility for the activity bear a particular burden to guarantee that every possible effort has been made to ensure that the proposed product will meet the needs of a clearly defined target audience.

While these issues have been discussed in general terms earlier it might be helpful here to report some of the findings from an ongoing research project at Strathclyde University into the association between marketing and competitive success. Thus far the project has pursued two main thrusts. The first, 'Profit by design', is sponsored by the Design Council and has concentrated on the specific contribution of design – both aesthetic and technical – as an element in the marketing mix. The second – 'Project MACS', funded by the ESRC and Institute of Marketing – has adopted a much broader approach and set out to evaluate the findings of populist and anecdotal accounts of the correlates of competitive success (see, for instance, *In Search of Excellence*, *The Winning Streak*, and the like) in a rigorous and closely controlled survey.

Given that attention to design factors and their importance in determining success have become management motherhoods it would clearly have been naïve to approach the question of the precise role and contribution of design in a direct way. Accordingly, Profit by design adopted an indirect approach and purported to be an exploration of the process of new product development. Thus by bundling in design with a whole host of other considerations it was felt that specific reference to design would both be spontaneous and reflect its comparative standing *vis-à-vis* other relevant factors.

In that the full report of the study is much longer than this chapter it clearly is not possible to do justice to it here but one particular finding is felt to be particularly apposite and this relates to the involvement of different persons and functions within the process of NPD from conceptualization to launch. A diagram speaks a thousand words, and Figure 21.2 summarizes the findings.

From Figure 21.2 it is clear that marketing has an important role to play at all stages of development, that both engineering and aesthetic design are key elements and that top management involvement is significant at key stages in the process. However, the importance of the findings is even greater than appears at first sight for the data were split according to the actual *performance* of the respondent companies into successful and less successful categories. It emerged that a company's ability to be successful is determined by the range of people it employs and the involvement of these people in key decision-making areas such as new product development. The evidence suggests that the greater the functional representation and the greater the integration of functions the greater is that company's ability to develop commercially successful products. Companies in the study learned from experience that new product development is a repetitive, synthetic activity which can be continually refined and quickened to increase new product leverage over competition. This ability to shorten and refine the process of NPD is particularly important in dynamic markets where technological advances are frequent and result in new products being outdated prematurely.

SUMMARY

In the scope of such a short chapter we can only scratch the surface of an enormous subject. Hopefully the discussion will encourage reading of the specialist books, some of which are listed below, as well as underline the relevance of the other chapters in this book. Marketing is a highly complex activity in which the practitioner must combine a multiplicity of factors to meet a dynamic and continually changing situation. Nowhere

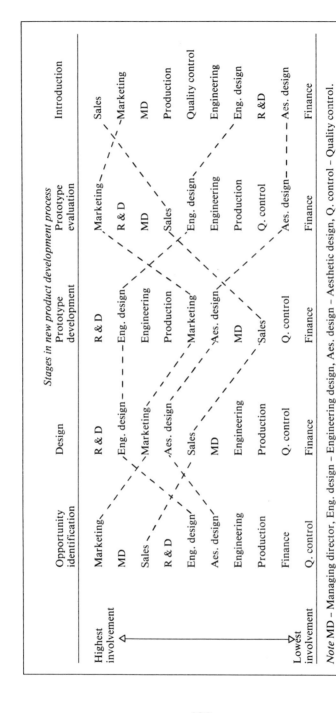

Figure 21.2   Personnel involvement in the design and development of new products

Note MD – Managing director, Eng. design – Engineering design, Aes. design – Aesthetic design, Q. control – Quality control.

is this more true than in the case of new product development, yet it is an activity which we cannot afford to avoid if we wish to remain competitive. It follows that any guidance on how to improve our success rate is to be welcomed and it is hoped that this chapter has provided some insight into the more important factors.

FURTHER READING

Baker, M. J. (1975), *Marketing New Industrial Products,* Macmillan, London.

Baker, M. J. and McTavish, R. (1976), *Product Policy and Management,* Macmillan, London.

Baker, M. J. (ed) (1979), *Industrial Innovation,* Macmillan, London.

Baker, M. J. (1983), *Market Development,* Penguin, Harmondsworth.

Booz, Allen & Hamilton Inc. (1982), *New Product Management for the 1980s,* New York.

Bright J. R. (1964), *Development and Technological Innovation,* Richard D. Irwin, Homewood, Illinois.

Cooper, R. G. and Calantone, R. J., A discriminant model for identifying new scenarios of industrial new product failure', *Academy of Marketing Science,* 1979, 7(3), Summer.

Hart, N. A. (ed.) (1984), *The Marketing of Industrial Products,* 2nd edn., McGraw-Hill, Maidenhead.

Hisrich, R. D. and Peters, M. P. (1978), *Marketing a New Product,* Benjamin/Cummings Publishing, Menlo Park, California.

Kotler, P. (1972), *Marketing Management,* 2nd ed, Prentice-Hall Inc., Englewood Cliffs, N.J., p. 465.

Parkinson, S. T. and Baker, M. J. (1986), *Organizational Buying Behaviour,* Macmillan, London.

Pessemier, E. (1966), *New Product Decisions: An Analytical Approach,* McGraw-Hill, New York.

Stone, M. (1976), *Product Planning,* Macmillan, London.

Twiss, B. (1974), *Managing Technological Innovation,* Longman, London.

Utterback, J. M. (1979), 'Product and Process innovation in a changing competitive environment', in M. J. Baker (ed) *Industrial Innovation,* Macmillan, London.

Von Hippel, E., 'The dominant role of users in the scientific instrument innovation process,' *Research Policy,* 5 (3), 1976.

Von Hippel, E., 'Users as innovators', *Technology Review,* 80 (3), January, 1978.

22

Developing and launching a new service

Don Cowell

The British economy is now a service economy. That is, in terms of output and in terms of employment, services have become the largest sector of the economy. Corresponding with this service revolution, marketing scholars have begun to study the subject of services marketing much more intently, systematically and rigorously.

The development and launching of new products have been an important topic for marketing academics and marketing professionals for a number of years. There is a significant volume of published literature on the subject which reflects both the extensive research which has been undertaken and the importance of the topic to practitioners. A number of potentially valuable insights, frameworks and experiences are available in this new product literature and are applicable to developing and launching a new service. However, it is increasingly recognized that there are a number of issues which are distinctive to services. For this reason the topic of new service development has been identified as an area of great importance. For example, in 1983, the American Marketing Association sponsored a symposium on developing new services, and 'new services development' has been designated as the top priority area by the Marketing Science Institute in the USA. It is very likely that our knowledge of new service development and launching will increase over the next few years. The purpose of this chapter is to examine the factors that should be considered when preparing for the launch of a new service.

REASONS FOR DEVELOPING NEW SERVICES

There are a number of reasons why service organizations develop new services, including the following.

1 *Obsolescence:* service organizations cannot continue to rely on their existing range of services for their success. Sooner or later they become obsolete. They mature and then decline in their product life-cycle. Change is a way of life for the innovative service organization.
2 *Competition:* new services are required to maintain present sales success and customer loyalty as well as to capitalize on changing marketplace needs in competitive markets.
3 *Spare capacity:* new services may be introduced to use up spare capacity, for example vacant theatre seats or low levels of usage at off-peak times on transportation systems.
4 *Seasonal effects:* many service organizations (tourism, for example) may have seasonal patterns of demand. New services may be introduced to even out these fluctuations.
5 *Risk reduction:* new services may be introduced to balance an existing sales portfolio where heavy dependence is placed on just a few services offered within a range.
6 *Opportunities*: new opportunities may emerge through a competitor withdrawing from a market or market research revealing unmet customer needs.

Whatever the reasons for introducing new services they are usually obtained in two ways. First, they may be obtained externally through acquisition or through licensing (for example, as in international marketing). Second, they may be developed internally through the process of new service development. Both strategies are risky and can result in failure; this chapter is concerned with the latter.

SERVICE/MARKET STRATEGIES

An important influence upon a service organization's new service development and launch procedures and processes will be its service/

market strategy. This relates to decisions regarding target markets to be served and services to be offered to those target markets. The strategic options for service organizations are similar to those available for organizations marketing products. They are:

1 attempting to sell more existing services to existing clients;
2 attempting to sell existing services to new clients;
3 attempting to sell new services to existing clients;
4 attempting to sell new services in new markets.

The word 'new' can have a number of meanings attached to it in service contexts. One categorization of product innovations lends itself to service settings and identifies six groups ranging from major innovations to style changes (Heany 1983).

1 *Major innovations:* are new services for markets still largely undefined. They include both new types of services (the first carphone systems are an example) as well as new service delivery systems, for example distance education schemes.
2 *Start-up businesses:* are new services for a market already served by services meeting the same generic needs. Examples include private health-care services; building society cheque-book accounts; and a new kind of retail business such as Tie Rack.
3 *New services:* for the currently served market are an attempt to offer existing customers of the business a new service not available before but which may be offered by a competitor. Examples include building societies extending into fields like insurance and brokerage services.
4 *Service line extensions* are additions to the existing service range and line. They include restaurants adding new menu items or airlines enhancing their services by adding a new route.
5 *Service improvements* involve a change in certain features for services already on offer to an existing market. They include speedier execution of an existing service through automation, an airline increasing leg room on seats or a bank extending opening hours.
6 *Style changes:* represent a highly visible series of changes. They include new livery and design schemes for a transport company, refurbished interiors in a chain of opticians or new uniforms for hotel and restaurant staff.

Opportunities in the marketplace are the impetus for new service

405

development and launch policies. However new the service may be, a systematic process for new developments has its virtues.

NEW SERVICE DEVELOPMENT

It has been found that an ordered and systematic process for developing and introducing new products may help reduce the risk of product failure. Although procedures vary considerably, some procedures may be highly elaborate and formal, others informal and much less specific. Where such systems exist they tend to include a series of steps or phases between the decision to look for new ideas and their ultimate commercialization in the marketplace. While the terminology of new product development and the range and order of steps included in the process vary, the underlying notions behind their use do not. These are, first, to create as many good ideas as possible and, second, to reduce the number of ideas by careful screening and analysis to ensure that only those with the best chances of success get into the marketplace. One such sequence of steps is:

- idea generation
- idea screening
- concept development and testing
- business analysis
- development
- testing
- commercialization

Not all these steps may be necesssary for all services. Much will depend upon factors such as the characteristics of the particular target market, the nature of the new service, competitive pressures, the time and resources which can be devoted to the process and the degree of innovation involved.

Idea generation

Ideas may be generated in many ways. They can arise inside and outside the organization; they can result from formal search procedures, for example marketing research, as well as informally; they may involve the organization in creating the means of delivering the new service product or in obtaining rights to the service product, as with a franchise.

The creative process of developing new ideas has long intrigued marketers although the process itself still defies detailed understanding. This has led in some cases to the adoption of techniques like 'synectics', brainstorming and lateral thinking to help improve the creative dimension of new service development.

Idea screening

This stage is concerned with checking out which ideas will justify the time, expense and managerial commitment of further research and study. Two features are usually associated with the screening phase.

1 The establishment or use of previously agreed evaluative criteria to enable the comparison of ideas generated (for example, ideas compatible with the organization's objectives and resources).
2 The weighing, ranking and rating of the ideas against the criteria used.

Screening systems range from the highly sophisticated, involving the collection and computer analysis of a mass of data, to simple checklists of a few factors considered to be vital. But it is important to stress that no single set of criteria is appropriate for all organizations – they must develop and adapt their own set of criteria to their particular circumstances.

Concept development and testing

Ideas surviving the screening process must then be translated into service concepts. In the service context this means concept development and concept testing.

1 *Concept development:* is concerned with translating the service idea (where the possible service is defined in functional and objective terms) into a service concept, the specific subjective consumer meaning the organization tries to build into the product idea. Thus, in attempting to sell the idea of regular saving to young, unmarried people, a building society might market the idea on the basis that

participants would be saving towards house purchase and might later receive preferential mortgage treatment.

2   *Concept testing:* is applicable in a services context as well as in goods contexts. Concept testing consists of taking the concepts developed by idea generation and idea screening, and securing reactions to them from groups of target customers.

An associated stage of the development of the service idea is that of service positioning. Service positioning is a concept increasingly widely referred to though it remains imprecisely defined, loosely used and difficult to measure. Essentially it is the visual presentation of the image of an organization's service in relation either to competitive services or to other services in its own mix. The principle underlying this method of presentation is that it enables service attributes to be compared with competitive offerings and with the customer's perceptions of services relative to his or her needs.

Some services, for example tour operators, are best positioned directly against competition. Other companies have developed effective strategies by deliberately not confronting competition directly. For example, Avis admitted it was number two in the car rental market in the USA and advertised that it must try harder. On the other hand economy motels in the USA such as Motel 6 Inc, Scottish Inns, Days Inns and Econo-Travel, have stressed low-cost lodging, eliminated swimming pools and restaurants and used pay television in positioning themselves against rivals with more elaborate services.

Business analysis

This stage is concerned with translating the proposed idea into a firm business proposal. It involves undertaking a detailed analysis of the attractiveness of the idea in business terms and its likely chances of success or failure. A substantial analysis will consider in detail aspects like the manpower required to implement the new service idea, the additional physical resources required, the likely estimates of sales, costs and profits over time, the contribution of the new service to the range on offer, likely customer reaction to the innovation and the likely response of competitors. Obviously it is not possible to generate accurate forecasts and estimates and it is customary to build some degree of tolerance into the analysis to allow for the uncertainties and ambiguities involved.

This stage may typically involve some initial technical and market research and initial timings and costing for a new service launch.

Development

This stage requires the translation of the idea into an actual service for the market. Typically this means that there will be an increase in investment in the project. Staff may have to be recruited or trained, facilities constructed, communications systems may need to be established. The tangible elements of the service will be designed and tested. Unlike goods the development stage of new service development involves attention to both the tangible elements of the service and the service delivery system.

Testing

It may not always be possible to test new services. Airlines may introduce a new class of service on a selected number of routes or a bank may make a new service available initially on a regional basis; but some new services do not have such an opportunity. They must be available and operate to designed levels of quality and performance from their introduction. The American Express Bank, after conducting detailed research which indicated that opening a London branch would be successful, had ultimately to take the plunge and go ahead by establishing a branch with a range of services (Flack, 1978).

Commercialization

This stage represents the organization's commitment to a full-scale launch of the new service. The scale of operation may be relatively modest, such as adding an additional service to an airline's routes, or large scale involving the national launch of fast-service footwear repair outlets operating on a concession basis. In undertaking the launch some basic decisions must be make:

1   when to introduce the new service;

2 where to launch the new service, whether locally, regionally, nationally or internationally;

3 to whom to launch the new service – usually determined by earlier exploration in the new service development process;

4 how to launch the new service – for example, unit trusts may offer a fixed-price unit on initial investments during a certain period.

With highly novel and innovative services, organizations may be guided by the extensive literature and experience on innovation and diffusion. However, like many areas of marketing, most documented experience in this area had concentrated on tangibles rather than intangibles, and innovation in the service sector require further empirical study.

SERVICE RANGE

Few service organizations offer only one service; they usually offer a mix of services for use or purchase. The particular range will be developed in response to internal needs or external influences. For example, high street banks now offer between two and three hundred different kinds of services for personal customers, partly as a response to business development but partly also as a result of competitive pressures and customer demand. A typical service range has both width and depth. Width refers to the number of different service lines offered, depth refers to the assortment of items within each service line. A service line is a group of service items sharing similar characteristics in terms of customers, sales methods or price. Figure 22.1 illustrates the concepts of service range, width, depth and service line, using simple customer categories, for a local authority leisure centre.

In designing a service range careful attention should be given to the following.

1 What the optimum range of services should be. Most service organizations rely on market research evidence and trial and error in making this decision.

2 The positioning of the range of services provided against competitors' offerings.

3 The length and width of the range and how the services within it complement one another.

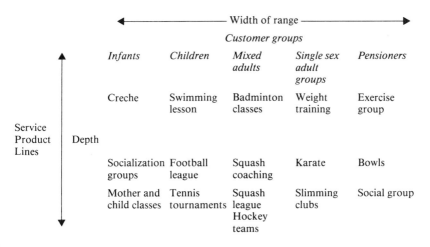

Figure 22.1 Illustrative service product range

4 The profitability of the range where profit is a key concern, as it will be with most commercial services.

The new service development process outlined above is similar to that for new products. There are, however, a number of distinctive features of services which in turn create special considerations for service marketers. The remainder of this chapter deals with these matters.

DISTINCTIVE FEATURES OF SERVICES

Intangibility

Services are essentially intangible. It is often not possible to taste, feel, see, hear or smell services before they are purchased. Opinions and attitudes may be sought beforehand, a repeat purchase may rely upon previous experience, the customer may be given something tangible to represent the service, but ultimately the purchase of a service is the purchase of something intangible.

Refinements of the notion of intangibility have been suggested by Wilson (1972), Bateson (1977), Rathmell (1966) and others. These largely suggest that the goods–service continuum can be represented as a tangible–intangible dominant continuum. Illustrated in the work of Shostack (1977), and reproduced as Figure 22.2, the continuum idea

411

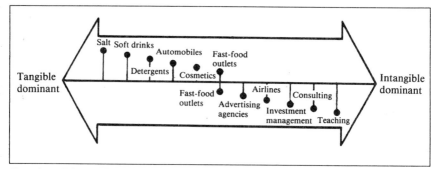

Reprinted from Shostack, G. L., 'Breaking Free from Product Marketing', *Journal of Marketing,* Vol. 41, No. 2, April 1977, American Marketing Association, p. 77.

Figure 22.2   A goods–service continuum

emphasizes that most 'products' are combinations of elements or attributes which are linked. There are few 'pure' products and 'pure' services.

Shostack suggests that marketing 'entities' are combinations of discrete elements, tangible and intangible. Her molecular model provides a way of visualizing and managing a total market entity. It can show the elements making up a product, the interrelationships between them and the dominance of goods or services, tangibles or intangibles in an offer. Figure 22.3 is a simplified example to demonstrate her notion of a product entity.

In Figure 22.3 airlines and motor cars are divided according to some of their main attributes. The two products have different nuclei and they also differ in dominance. Airlines are more intangible dominant – there is no ownership of a tangible good. Airline travel cannot be physically possessed, only experienced. The inherent benefit is a service. On the other hand, a car is more tangible dominant. A car can be physically possessed, though the benefit it yields is a service too.

Inseparability

Services often cannot be separated from the person of the seller. A corollary of this is that creating or performing the service may occur at the same time as full or partial consumption of it. Goods are purchased, sold and consumed whereas services are sold and then produced and

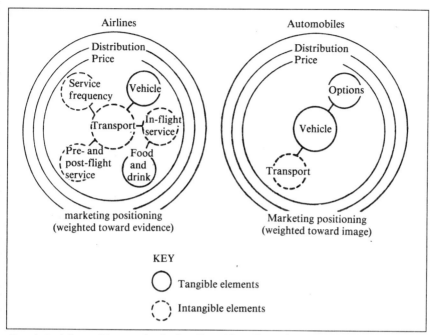

Airlines   Automobiles

marketing positioning
(weighted toward evidence)

Marketing positioning
(weighted toward image)

KEY

◯ Tangible elements

⌒ Intangible elements

Reprinted from Shostack, G. L., 'Breaking Free from Product Marketing',
Journal of Marketing, Vol. 41, No. 2, April 1977, American Marketing Association, p. 76.

Figure 22.3   The molecular model

consumed. The inseparability of the creation and the performance of certain kinds of services applies particularly to some personal services, for example dental or medical treatment, professional services.

Heterogeneity

It is often difficult to achieve standardization in the output of certain services. The standard of a service in terms of its conformity to what may be prescribed by the seller may depend on who provides the service or when it is provided. So even though standard systems may be used to handle a flight reservation, book a car in for service or quote for life insurance, each 'unit' of service may differ from other 'units'. Franchise operations attempt to ensure standards of conformity but ultimately with services it is difficult to ensure the same level of quality of output as it may be with goods. From the customer's viewpoint, too, it is often difficult to judge quality in advance of purchase.

Perishability

Services are perishable and cannot be stored. Spare seats on a package tour or an empty hotel room represent capacity lost for ever if they are not 'consumed' when they are available at any point in time. In addition, considerable fluctuating demand patterns may apply to some services which aggravate this perishability feature further. Important marketing decisions in service organizations relate to the service levels they will provide and how they will respond in times of low and excessive usage, for example through differential pricing, or special promotions.

Ownership

Lack of ownership is a basic difference between a service and a good. With a service a customer may only have access to or use of a facility (a hotel room, for example). Payment is usually for the use of, access to or hire of items.

With the sale of goods, barring restrictions imposed by, say, a hire-purchase scheme, the buyer has full use of the product.

A summary of these characteristics of services is shown in Table 22.1. Also shown are some implications of these characteristics and suggested means of overcoming the problems posed.

There is, however, still difference of opinion as to whether some of these characteristics do help to discriminate between goods and services. For example, Wyckham *et al.* (1975) provide cogent arguments why intangibility, heterogeneity and perishability at least are not of themselves sufficiently discriminating. They believe there are too many exceptions to their use for services alone and believe that what is required is not a simple product/service scheme differentiating on the basis of the characteristics of the offer itself but a more complex taxonomy of offerings which differentiates on the basis of product/service characteristics and market characteristics. That said, these features of services do seem to have an influence upon creating special considerations for service marketers concerned with developing and launching new services.

414

Table 22.1 Some constraints on the management of services and ways of overcoming them

Characteristics of service	Some implications	Some means of overcoming characteristics
Intangibility	Sampling difficult. Places strain on promotional element of marketing mix. No patents possible. Difficult to judge price and quality in advance.	Focus on benefits. Increase tangibility of service (e.g. physical representations of it). Use brand names. Use personalities to personalize service. Develop reputation.
Inseparability	Requires presence of producer. Direct sale. Limited scale of operations.	Learn to work in larger groups. Work faster. Train more competent service providers.
Heterogeneity	Standard depends upon who and when provided. Difficult to assure quality.	Careful personnel selection and training. Ensure standards are monitored. Pre-package service. Mechanize and industrialize for quality control. Emphasize bespoke features.
Perishability	Cannot be stored. Problems with demand fluctuation.	Better match between supply and demand (e.g. price reductions off peak).
Ownership	Customer has access to but not ownership of activity or facility.	Stress advantages of non-ownership (e.g. easier payment systems).

SPECIAL CONSIDERATIONS FOR SERVICE MARKETERS

Most special considerations for service marketers stem from the differences between services and products.

Problems deriving from the characteristics of services

Some differences between marketing research for new services and for new products stem from the characteristics of services themselves, some of which together with their suggested effects on the use of marketing

415

Table 22.2   Service characteristics and their effects on marketing research

Characteristic	Effects upon marketing research
Intangibility	• Where a dominantly intangible service, home use tests not appropriate • Often appropriate to move directly from concept testing to test marketing in new product development • 'Researchability' problem for dominantly intangible services
Patenting difficult	• Reduces incentives for large R & D investment • More focus on 'me-too' services • Tendency towards service improvement rather than innovation • Ease of competitive entry influences viability of new service concepts
Standardization difficult	• Difficult to develop accurate concept descriptions • Problems in concept testing
Direct relationship between service performer and client	• Judgements of service influenced by who performs the service and the client's involvement in performance
No clear lines of demarcation between a service and the place in which it is delivered, the process and the people	• Concept testing difficult because of need to assess impact of performer and physical evidence on service itself.

research, particularly for new service development research designs, are shown in Table 22.2.

Problems in researching new services

Many of the difficulties shown in Table 22.2 apply to marketing research for new services. The general problems of researching services with their often elusive, ephemeral and intangible qualities are aggravated when new services are being researched. The uncertainty and ambiguity of the service, the difficulty the customer may have in articulating what benefits are sought from a service innovation, and finalizing the elements the service should consist of, provide a 'researchability' problem for the market researcher. One scheme represents a service as a constellation of tangible and intangible attributes. A particular problem in new service development is to identify, weight and rank the separate elements that make up a service offer. These are difficult judgements for researchers to obtain from customers for existing services. They become even more difficult with new services.

The very nature of services means that researchers and users must be prepared to use 'soft', qualitative data particularly in conceptualizing a service. Because services possess the characteristics of perishability and intangibility their value is more often judged in terms of benefits rather than features. This can mean that to determine what a service entity is to a market, a marketer must conduct more initial marketing research than in product marketing. Also, a tight service specification may be difficult to produce. These problems of measurement have led to the development of new techniques in marketing research. They have also led to attempts to clarify the concept testing process for services. One suggested framework for concept testing a service which outlines the steps involved is shown in Figure 22.4.

In this framework concept testing goes through a number of steps. The service idea begins with analysis of consumer needs. Ideas are then generated to meet these needs; these ideas are subjected to a preliminary analysis during which the competitive environment is considered; ideas are examined internally and subjective judgements are made about the market; and a preliminary external reaction from potential customers and suppliers is obtained. The 'positioning' of the service in the market is then considered and field studies are undertaken to present the concept specifically to a carefully selected sample of potential customers. Finally, the concept is evaluated. Customer understanding of the concept, customer buying and usage intentions, and customer benefits are sought in particular. Unfavourable results may mean revising the concept; favourable results may mean test marketing (where applicable) or direct introduction of the service (where possible). The purposes of this framework are thus to find out whether a potential customer:

- understands the idea of the proposed service
- reacts favourably to it
- feels it offers benefits to meet unmet needs

Concept testing processes for services have been a relatively neglected area of marketing management. However, the growing interest in service marketing and the importance of clearer definitions of services, suggest this will be a significant area of development over the next few years.

Compared with products, some differences experienced with services

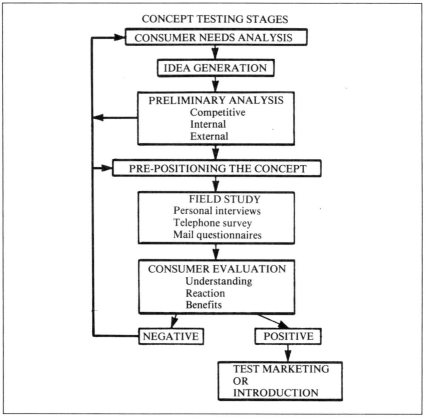

CONCEPT TESTING STAGES

CONSUMER NEEDS ANALYSIS

IDEA GENERATION

PRELIMINARY ANALYSIS
Competitive
Internal
External

PRE-POSITIONING THE CONCEPT

FIELD STUDY
Personal interviews
Telephone survey
Mail questionnaires

CONSUMER EVALUATION
Understanding
Reaction
Benefits

NEGATIVE   POSITIVE

TEST MARKETING
OR
INTRODUCTION

Reprinted from Murphy, P. E. and Robinson, R. K., 'Concept Testing for Services' in Donnelly, J. H. and George, W. R., *Marketing of Services,* American Marketing Association, Chicago, 1981, p. 218.

Figure 22.4 Framework for concept testing

offer advantages to the marketing researcher. First, the researcher has the opportunity to evaluate services before, after the sale and during the sale (that is, during the performance of the service). Unlike a product, which is produced and then consumed, some services are consumed as they are being produced. The provider can thus obtain feedback while the service is being produced and make appropriate adjustments where these are required by customers. One study has shown that participating in a marketing research investigation on site does not actually interfere with enjoyment of a service. However, the consumer's evaluation of being a respondent is sensitive to the costs and rewards of participation and the service organization needs to maintain the respondent's good-will.

Second, direct customer involvement with many services allows the user to specify the type of service required direct to the seller or performer:

> Most companies selling services start out with an enormous market information advantage over the consumer product company; the service company knows a lot about its customers. With the increasingly effective use of internal data processing and computer applications, most service companies can effectively provide their customer characteristics entirely with internal data. (Hardin, 1970)

Third, the relatively more recent use of marketing research by service organizations has given them certain advantages. They are able to use proven techniques developed in other contexts. They can benefit by avoiding earlier mistakes and misapplications of marketing research techniques in product fields.

Problems associated with new service features

The buyer's choice of a new service may be influenced by features associated with it. These features may be seen by the consumer as a fundamental part of the 'core' service or as 'peripheral' to it. In tangible product marketing the brand, the colour, the design or the package may be important contributory factors to the consumer's purchase decision. Generally such elements are less conspicuous features in service marketing but they may nevertheless be integral components of some forms of service planning. The relevance of some of these features is described below.

Service branding
Branding is difficult because of the problems of maintaining consistency of quality in service settings, and it would seem not to be used in services marketing as much as it should. This is surprising for, given the intangible nature of services and the difficulty of distinguishing one service from another, branding provides a significant method for achieving some degree of service differentiation.

419

Service patents

The intangibility of services means that there are no patents. It is thus difficult to prevent competitors from copying service innovations, even though trade names can be protected. This means that innovations may have short life-cycles since they are easy to copy. Banks and airlines are examples of where the absence of patent protection has brought large-scale copying of practices, for example the classes of air travel available. The absence of patent protection is one of the characteristics which present unique problems to service organizations and their clients. The British Invisible Export Council has pointed out that with regard to certain traded services, the expertise they require makes them difficult to copy quickly.

Service warranty

The provision of a service is formally undertaken within a framework imposed by the law of contract. This framework of legally enforceable obligations is a complex combination of those undertakings which were agreed expressly by the parties precontractually and those which are imposed from outside. Terms are implied into contracts by statutes. For example, the Supply of Goods and Services Act, 1982, implies into contracts for the supply of services terms which stipulate that the service will be supplied with reasonable care and skill, within a reasonable time and at a reasonable cost (unless time and cost are expressly fixed). Indeed, other statutes (such as the Unfair Contract Terms Act 1977) severely restrict the potential for limitation or exclusion of such obligations as these. Moreover, terms can be implied into such contracts as these because they are trade usages or customs or because they have become normal between the parties over a previous course of dealings.

However, in discussions about the nature and content of what is provided in the supply of a service the marketer may overlook the essential importance and the value to increased market share of the supply of more than that which must be supplied to avoid the threat of action for breach of contract. For example, if at an airport the passengers are delayed by circumstances beyond the control of the service provider, the supply of facilities which are over and above the legally enforceable obligations will inevitably improve the profile of the service product. Thus if the passengers are set to be delayed for hours on end, the personal attention of the service provider to the maximum practicable comfort and convenience of each of his customers becomes a marketing tool in itself. The customer is aware that more is being supplied than, in his perception, is being paid for.

After-sales service

After-sales service is usually associated with the sale of tangibles. However, it is also relevant to services markets. For example, an airline may assist passengers to arrange hire cars and book hotels as part of its service; an insurance company may advise clients on changes they should make to their policies as their personal circumstances change; a stockbroker may assist a client to readjust a portfolio of shares; a dentist may provide a check-up some time after providing dental treatment.

After-sales service can be an important element of the service marketing mix. Its availability can help to secure a sale in the first place; it can maintain and develop customer loyalty and goodwill; it can provide a means of obtaining feedback about service performance; it can provide a means for obtaining suggestions for new and improved services.

Problems associated with the design of the service process

A significant influence upon a customer's perception of service quality is how well the process of service delivery functions. The way in which service systems operate is crucial to customer satisfaction. Those which operate effectively and efficiently can give marketing management considerable marketing leverage and promotional advantage. It is clear that a smooth-running service operation offers competitive advantages particularly where differentiation between services is minimal. But effective and efficient systems do not operate by chance, they operate by design. Developing and launching a new service is as much concerned with the design of service delivery processes and procedures as with the design of the services themselves. Often the service product is the service process. Many service operations, particularly those operating multi-site operations, need to codify operations procedures to ensure some consistency in service performance. Some service operations have extensive procedures manuals to try to ensure some uniformity of operation.

The area of service design and service delivery is traditionally viewed as the responsibility of the operations manager, but in service organizations co-operation between marketing and operations is vital. In service systems the implications of operational performance and malpractice are too visible to be solely operational concerns. The customer is so often involved as a participant in the service delivery system that operational concerns about service delivery effectiveness and efficiency are marketing concerns too. Particular problems associated with the design of the service process therefore stem from the much closer relationship needed between operations managers and marketing managers. The design of service processes from a marketing perspective has received scant attention by many service organizations, but is increasingly recognized as an area in which a new service can be differentiated from competitors' offerings.

Problems associated with the use of people in new services

Service personnel are important in most organizations. They are particularly important in those situations where, in the absence of clues from tangible products, the customer forms an impression of a new service from the behaviour and attitudes of staff involved in the service delivery system. The design and launch of a new service therefore demand attention to the service product, the service process and service personnel involved. How a new service is performed will ultimately influence the image of a service organization. As with the new service process, the design of the new service employee – customer relationship should not be left to chance. Attention must be given to the people aspects of the service. Many service organizations which launch new services now recognize the importance of careful selection and training of service personnel, standardization of patterns of behaviour towards customers, ensuring consistency of appearance and conducting quality control studies through service personnel audits. The significance of the relationship between employee and customer has begun to receive the attention of academic researchers in marketing as the role of the service 'encounter' and the role of employees in new services development has begun to be fully recognized (George and Marshall, 1984).

CONCLUSIONS

Service marketers can benefit considerably from existing knowledge of the new product development and launch process derived from studies of new consumer products and new industrial products. However, this chapter suggests that some distinctive aspects of services may create special issues for service marketers. Since services themselves vary considerably in terms of their nature, form, processes and delivery, generalizations about new service delivery and launch should be treated with caution.

REFERENCES AND FURTHER READING

Bateson, J. (1977), 'Do we need service marketing?', *Marketing Consumer Services: New Insights*, Report 75-115, Marketing Science Institute, Boston.

Flack, M. (1978), 'Research for financial and investment marketing decisions', *Journal of the Market Research Society*, Vol. 20. No.1, January, pp.14–29.

George, W. R. and Marshall, C. E. (eds) (1984), *Developing New Services*, Proceedings Series, American Marketing Association, Chicago.

Hardin, D. K. (1970), 'Marketing research for service industries', in V. Buell (ed), *Handbook of Modern Marketing*, McGraw-Hill, New York.

Heany, D. F. (1983) 'Degrees of product innovation', *Journal of Business Strategy*, Vol. 3, Spring, pp.3–14.

Rathmell, J. M. (1966), 'What is meant by services?', *Journal of Marketing*, Vol.30, No.4, pp.32–36.

Shostack, G. L. (1977), 'Breaking free from product marketing', *Journal of Marketing*, Vol.41, No.2, pp.73–80.

Wilson, A. (1972), *The Marketing of Professional Services*, McGraw-Hill, London.

Wyckham, R. G., Fitzroy, P. T. and Mandry, S. D., (1975), 'Marketing of services', *European Journal of Marketing*, Vol.9, No.1, pp.59–67.

Part IV
DISTRIBUTING THE PRODUCT

23

Distribution channel management

Jack Wheatley

The process of distribution is not merely concerned with physically getting goods from manufacturer to eventual customer. Distribution strategy covers the following activities: the choice of available channels, whether or not to confine distribution to one channel or several; whether to go direct to the customer or deal through intermediaries; how much expenditure to allocate for distribution and whether to take a complete or partial financial interest in the available channels.

What might seem the best or only channels available at the start of a marketing campaign may prove to be inadequate or too restrictive for subsequent development of sales, so manufacturers who opt to distribute entirely through wholesalers may regret their lack of contact with retail outlets when they need extra sales or when they realize that the wholesaler is also promoting a competitor's output, perhaps to the exclusion of their products.

The choice of distribution channels therefore requires careful thought and full consideration of the available alternatives.

PLANNING FOR DISTRIBUTION

In arriving at a final decision on which channel or combination of channels should be used many points must be taken into account. The choice depends not only on costs in relation to funds available, but also on the location of the consumer, the places where he or she is most likely to see the product and the extent to which it is desirable and/or necessary to maintain direct contact with the consumer. It also depends on the bulkiness of the product, anticipated average order value, credit risks involved in the alternative methods available and the risks entailed in placing all distribution in the hands of an outside and independent agent or wholesaler.

With a new product and particularly if the market is a new one to the manufacturer it still takes great courage to try to bypass traditional channels. The patterns of distribution and demand are now changing, however, as the ranges of choice open to consumers widen.

Not so long ago, nobody would have considered garages as an outlet for confectionery and soft drinks, newsagents for pop records, chemists for wines and spirits or food supermarkets for clothing and furniture, but all these changes have taken place to the advantage of the retailing outlets and the manufacturers.

Distribution itself cannot be considered in isolation from other aspects of the marketing plan because it is usually up to manufacturers to promote their products to the eventual consumer and to stimulate demand that will materialize into a decision to buy at the chosen point of distribution.

New methods of large-scale distribution such as hypermarkets and cash and carries are attractive in that they facilitate bulk distribution to a limited number of outlets but, in opting for this method as a sole means of distribution, manufacturers are vulnerable in the sense that changes in the buying policies of one or two of the outlets can have a significantly adverse impact on sales volume. The ultimate decision on which distributive channels to use must depend on the costs involved and the estimated net profit contribution available within the various alternatives.

What might seem the best short-term solutions are not necessarily in the long-term interests of the manufacturer and therefore extreme care must be taken before placing all distribution in the hands of an outside body be it a wholesaler, agent or merchant.

The ideal is to have full control over all aspects of distribution, but this may well involve the manufacturer in direct selling costs that the product could not carry in the light of the anticipated sales forecast.

THE WHOLESALER

Wholesalers have traditionally been one of the oldest links in the distribution chain, but while still popular, this method is losing some of its appeal with manufacturers beginning to develop their own images to their consumers. Even so, wholesalers still offer the cheapest form of distribution as they take responsibility for storing in bulk and delivering in small quantities to the consumer. This relieves manufacturers of the greater part of delivery costs for they are concerned only with making the more economical bulk deliveries to the wholesaler's warehouses. The wholesaler takes all the small credit risks and absorbs direct selling costs, but will very rarely avoid selling a competitive product.

Because of the nature of their business, wholesalers carry wide brand ranges and their sales staff become initially 'order takers' with no specific selling emphasis on any particular brand. They tend, therefore, to reflect consumer demand rather than create it.

Although wholesalers can handle all distribution it is advisable for manufacturers to employ at least a small sales force to call on and persuade ultimate outlets to place orders for their products from the designated local wholesaler. Orders can be taken and passed to the wholesaler as a gesture of good faith but also as a positive encouragement to stock a manufacturer's product.

Some companies have set up their own wholesaling operations. The speedy, prompt, delivery (SPD) organization set up by Unilever is an example, and in this case the wholesaling/distribution company stores and distributes for other organizations on a proper commercial basis. In the main, it is better to regard wholesaling as a specialist function and to set up an in-company operation only if it can be done properly and expertly. Few organizations have the required range to do that.

A combination of direct distribution and wholesaling is preferable as the sales contacts the wholesalers have built up over the years are very useful, but if wholesaling is used it is important to remember that the eventual consumer will need to be exposed to product promotion from the manufacturer. Wholesalers cannot be expected to create the demand for they have too many competing interests.

To avoid conflict with a wholesaler's selling policy manufacturers can give a different brand name to their products sold through the wholesaler. This technique is used successfully with such products as stationery, clothing and certain foodstuffs.

THE RETAIL TRADES

The structure of the retail trades had altered considerably since Napoleon referred to Britain as 'a nation of shopkeepers'. Many smaller shops have been forced out of business but many that have changed their style of management to compete with the larger, and often impersonal multiples and supermarkets, have survived. Often location has proved to be the prime factor.

Independent retailers

Independent retailers provide an efficient local service at higher prices than the larger chains and multiples and they often provide extended credit and/or free delivery for their customers. As outlets, they tend to sell the products for which there is an established demand, but are often very responsive to good sales promotion of new products and can be more easily persuaded to try new lines than wholesalers.

Voluntary groups

To combat the threat posed by multiple chains and supermarkets, independent retailers have banded together into voluntary groups which started as central buying groups but have now developed into highly efficient retail outlets following common policies extending to product ranges, stock control, accounting, store layout and store promotions. Other groups have been formed by large wholesalers to guarantee outlets for the lines they sell and this, in turn, has led wholesalers to develop their own label brands for distribution via the retailers in their group.

Multiple stores

The advantage of using this channel of distribution is that the buying points can be covered by a very small sales force as most items are bought centrally from head offices. Store managers work to central promotional and stocking policies and, providing manufacturers can persuade the central buyer to stock their products, they are assured that the necessary efforts will be made at store level. Because of the need to achieve fast turnover on what are often narrow margins, multiple stores will not persist with slow-moving lines and so manufacturers need to back up the stores with adequate promotion to consumers. Multiples have developed from being the outlets set up by food manufacturers who wished to extend vertically into retailing, but some have taken the opposite path backwards into manufacturing; this is what has stimulated the growth of 'own label' brands.

Alternatively, some multiples have arranged own-label production by outside manufacturers. This is useful to independent producers as a channel of distribution but they must be assured of long-term contracts if they use this channel as a sole outlet for distribution.

Retail chains

Again, store managers follow centrally laid-down policies but there is usually more flexibility allowed according to local conditions. Stores often trade under different names, but the manufacturer is usually offered multiple outlet distribution and, consequently, a wider coverage.

Local chain store managers are usually very responsive to store promotions backed up by press and television advertising. The combination of a television spot naming a particular retail chain as a stockist of a product and a display of that product with a card saying 'As seen on television' is very successful.

Department stores

Department stores carry a wide variety of merchandise under one roof with specific departments under their own separate buying and selling management. Each department is organized to sell particular product ranges.

The standard of personal service is often very high. Some of the larger

431

stores have almost become institutions to the criterion of good service and are respected as such all over the world. Buyers are usually highly skilled professionals who anticipate fashion trends and buy accordingly. Manufacturers using this channel can obtain extremely useful market research information by maintaining contact with store buyers. This channel is also used by companies setting up their own boutiques or 'shops within shops', a method particularly suitable for such products as jewellery, cosmetics and clothing. Exporters would find this a useful means of getting established in a new overseas market. Travel agencies are another example.

Co-operative societies

These are becoming combinations of multiples, department stores and supermarkets with the apparent aim of selling their own manufactured products. This is the complete evolutionary cycle, for the first co-operative societies in the middle of the last century were manufacturers setting up as manufacturers and retailers.

Private brands, however, still account for a significant proportion of total turnover and the use of this channel offers the possibilities of large-scale distribution from a limited number of outlets.

Supermarkets

These are a natural development of multiples and self-service outlets and now account for a significant proportion of total retail trade. Product ranges have extended from food into a wide variety of non-food items operating under very tight control and measuring a percentage of sales.

Because of their vast buying power, supermarkets are able to extract hard bargains from manufacturers and lay down very strict conditions as to delivery times, quantities, packaging, and so on. Manufacturers are offered economic distribution in that delivery points are far fewer than for independent retailers; buying, however, is in the hands of an equally small number of head offices. Manufacturers who opt for supermarkets as their only outlets are subject to sudden changes of buying policy.

Supermarkets are becoming increasingly concerned with multiple product ranges to such an extent that specialist supermarkets dealing solely in product ranges such as carpets, radio and television are appearing to attract the customers who are becoming somewhat disenchanted with the lack of choice in the non-food departments of supermarkets.

Hypermarkets

Regarded as the ultimate in retailing, this type of outlet is now well established in the UK. The principle is to provide 'one-stop shopping' for a wide variety of products in an out-of-town location where space is available at lower rents than in town centres. These outlets are very attractive to manufacturers as access and egress are usually easier because of geographical location.

Cash and carry

These outlets have been developed by wholesalers and voluntary groups whereby retailers select the goods they are going to sell from the wide range displayed and collect, pay and transport them back to the shops. This method tends to be used by the smaller retailers, for example restaurants, canteens and newsagents. The cash and carry outlets usually maintain regular promotional mailing to their retail customers and run special offer campaigns, but otherwise provide a minimum of service.

As a channel of distribution manufacturers can make good use of cash and carry outlets to deal with the problems of small deliveries provided they can create a demand by promotion to the eventual outlet and consumer. However, as cash and carries are retailers' supermarkets, good packaging and presentation can be very helpful in persuading retailers to pick products off the shelves and to try selling them in their own stores.

Discount stores

A comparatively recent innovation to the retail scene is the discount store which provides cut-price products with the minimum customer service. This channel is particularly useful for sales of consumer durables and toiletries. Chemists' lines are being increasingly distributed in this manner. Discount trading became increasingly evident following the banning of resale price maintenance.

Mobile retailers

To strengthen the personal service there has been a growth in the number of retailers taking their products direct to the home. Grocers, greengrocers, bakers and butchers are using this method and yet dairies, which by tradition have made deliveries of milk direct to the consumer, are trying to cut down on the number of deliveries to reduce costs. Prices charged do not reflect the service provided. Dairies are adding soft drinks and confectionery to the range carried by their milk floats in order to increase sales per journey.

Ready-cooked foods like fish and chips, hamburgers, meat pies and chickens are now sold from mobiles as well as the normal tea, coffee and light refreshments.

Van selling

Van selling is used by manufacturers of perishable foods, particularly bread and meat products, and allows complete control of the distribution operation. Cost per order can be high, particularly in large items where so much time can be lost in finding a suitable parking place or waiting in traffic jams, but total distribution costs can be lower than would be incurred with a separate delivery fleet and a sales force.

Door-to-door selling

A very expensive method of distribution, and apart from a few highly successful exceptions, door-to-door selling is not widely practised. Government legislation was formulated to prevent the worst excesses of this type of selling whereby people were persuaded by unscrupulous sales staff to buy products that would not work or that they did not need or could not afford. It is often used in combination with a national or local advertising campaign. The regular wider promotion gives an air of respectability to the sales staff who follow up and call from door to door.

Considerable success has been achieved by companies selling cosmetics, but to be effective the use of this channel for such products requires a very large sales force as the average unit of sale is very low in value. Double glazing, central heating and encyclopaedias are more applicable to this type of distribution as the average unit of sale tends to be much higher than with the smaller products.

Garages

Apart from selling petrol and oil, garages are now retailing wide ranges of motor accessories and food lines. The appeal is largely geared to impulse buying because consumers do not normally go to garages just to buy the ancillary items. As channels of distribution, however, garages are becoming increasingly important.

THE COMMODITY MARKET

Perishables are usually distributed through the commodity markets in the UK, but many of them have become so heavily congested that producers are tending to fix up long-term contracts with outlets and deliver direct. Such contracts can be beneficial to the producer in so far as selling prices are stabilized, but they must be fixed in the light of a very accurate assessment of future supply and demand which the commodity markets reflect on a daily basis. Other commodities such as rubber, copper, tin, tea and gold are still bought and sold through the traditional markets in London.

Franchising

This is a method of distribution used mainly to further the sales of an idea or a process rather than a product itself. Successful exploitation of this method had been achieved with a wide variety of products including fried chickens, hamburgers, instant printing, drain cleaning, tyre and

435

exhaust fitting, ice-cream, steaks and Chinese food. Financial assistance is provided to the franchisee to set up his or her business, with the manufacturer taking a share of the resulting profits and providing training in business management. Common standards and common forms of presentation are very important and are enshrined in agreements between the franchisor and franchisee.

Party plan selling

Under this method a manufacturer appoints agents – usually women – who hold sponsored parties in their homes and invite their friends to see the products. Orders are taken and more agents are recruited and so the operation develops. This channel is useful for selling kitchen and other domestic ware, clothing, jewellery and cosmetics, but is difficult to use in conjunction with distribution through traditional retail outlets for these do not take kindly to this type of sponsored competition from their suppliers.

Mail order

This has become a popular channel for a very wide range of products and services. Large department stores and mail order houses are investing large sums in postage, printing and distribution of catalogues direct to the public. At the other end of the scale, rare books, classical records and even collections of specially minted coins and medals are promoted and distributed via direct mail to a specialist public. The big attraction of this method is the direct promotion to the consumer to the complete exclusion of any intermediaries. But perhaps the most spectacular growth in recent years has been direct selling through couponed advertisements in newspapers and magazines – through the Sunday supplements in particular. The method has also spread to television.

Direct selling costs are negligible, but advertising costs are extremely high; however, companies successful in this field continue to use this channel and are clearly satisfied with the returns obtained. Some distributors have extended their operation by setting up their own stores selling nothing but the products advertised by their direct mailing, thus relieving them of small distribution costs. This combination of previously separate channels is typical of what often happens as a marketing operation develops.

AGENTS, BROKERS AND MERCHANTS

The advantage of all these channels is the personal contact and knowledge they have of a particular market. Agencies are established on an exclusive and semi-exclusive basis and can be very helpful to the supplier entering a completely new market or to those which want to employ their own sales force. The agent should act as a member of the manufacturer's sales team as distinct from the wholesaler who is more concerned with the burden of physical distribution.

Clearly, granting a sole agency is a step not to be taken lightly for, if the wrong agent is appointed, considerable harm can be done to the principle's image and development plans before such an agent can be replaced.

Brokers act as intermediaries working on very fine profit margins but, as with agents, they often have very useful contacts. A danger with brokers is that they can depress the market price by selling at cut rates sufficient for them to earn a minimal margin, particularly on volume sales.

Merchants generally operate as a mixture of agents and whole-salers and usually have a good standing in the marketplace. Care must be taken in passing them sole selling rights because they tend to carry a wide range of lines and are sometimes unable to put significant emphasis behind any one product.

EXPORTING

Selection of the proper channels of distribution for overseas markets is even more important than in the UK markets where the lines of communication are shorter and mistakes can be more speedily rectified. It is essential that proper account be taken of local customs and practices, attitudes and patterns of demand. For entry into an overseas market the best method of distribution is probably through an export agent. Selection of the agent is clearly very important and the Chamber of Commerce, the Department of Trade and Industry and trade associations can all offer good advice on where to find agents.

Direct representation in large department stores is another success-fully used method of distribution because, as in the UK, leading stores are barometers of current demand and can usually place sizeable orders offering economies of scale to distributors.

With some countries, particularly those of the Eastern bloc, the distribution has to be through large buying offices in the UK and often there is no direct contact between manufacturer and ultimate consumer.

INDUSTRIAL DISTRIBUTION

Techniques of good marketing are being applied increasingly in the industrial field. As far as channels of distribution are concerned the choice is almost as wide as that available for consumer goods.

Industrial products tend to be of a more technical nature so consideration must be given to after-sales service irrespective of the chosen channel of distribution. Very often manufacturers will deal with their customers via an agent on all matters of sale and supply, but will deal direct on servicing and maintenance.

Package deals involving products from within a large group of companies can be offered to one common outlet; similarly, a manufacturer may well find many captive outlets within his or her own group. This opportunity is often missed or just not pursued.

Licensing is a method often used in the engineering industry, for example with motor cars and aeroengines. Under these arrangements, the licensee undertakes to produce and sell goods to the licensor's specification in consideration of a share of the resultant profits. This method enables a manufacturer to expand revenue without a corresponding increase in investment.

Heavy engineering industries make use of consortia to distribute their products. This applies to such projects as offshore drilling equipment, building and civil engineering contracts, power station supplies, ship-building and the like.

CONCLUSION

Inevitably, the final decision on which channels to use must be a compromise, but it is the purpose of this chapter to provide an outline of the range of possibilities, and even if it has done no more than stimulate more detailed and rational thinking on this vital aspect of marketing it will have served its purpose.

24

Trade marketing

Jerry Parker

Trade marketing is a fashionable phrase for what is an important part of modern marketing and selling. But what do people understand by trade marketing? What do they mean by the term? Does everyone have the same definition? Do retailers, consumer product companies and industrial goods manufacturers see eye to eye about what is involved in trade marketing? To answer these and a whole string of other relevant questions my company conducted detailed research. We interviewed a substantial cross-section of both industrial and consumer goods manufacturers and their marketing and sales departments. We also spoke to a number of leading retailers (both buyers and marketing personnel).

Nearly 70 per cent of the industrial companies we spoke to stated that trade marketing had no particular relevance to their market (even though a surprisingly large number used distributor companies to supply their goods and services to end-users).

Almost half the marketing people in consumer goods companies defined trade marketing as marketing, producing and selling to the trade.

These responses interested us. In fact they rather disappointed us because my own definition involves marketing, promotion and selling through the trade to the consumer or end-user.

THE RETAILER

Nearly 70 per cent of the retailers we interviewed mentioned only two or

440

three manufacturers as star suppliers, in terms of the usefulness and relevance of the plans they proposed. 'Most suppliers do not thoroughly understand how modern retailers operate'. This was especially interesting to me since my definition of trade marketing includes 'understanding the channels of distribution, and their own marketing ambitions – thoroughly enough to implement effectively branded goods plans and promotions *through* these channels and on to the consumer'.

The criticisms from retailers continued. Three-quarters observed that most suppliers do not fully appreciated the factors and techniques they use to make listing decisions and determine the allocation of shelf space. Nine out of ten said there is still a wide variation in standards across a broad spectrum of supplier companies.

Companies should perhaps conduct some inexpensive independent research to check what their major customers think of their trade marketing operations, compared with those of other suppliers – even though the results of such research might be rather embarrassing for a company which markets successful brands.

Parallel to this observation, 60 per cent of retailers observed that strong brand portfolios masked weaknesses in individual negotiators. The problem could be laid at the marketing department door, because more than half the retailers interviewed believe that many good account managers are 'let down' by their own marketing departments. They are expected to present national initiatives for the product, which fail to recognize the needs of the retailer and the important subsector of the public at large which chooses to shop in the leading multiple's stores. However, far from being inherently hostile to suppliers' marketing departments, 40 per cent of retailers noted in their negotiations with suppliers that the best performing account managers have marketing as well as sales experience.

Many retailers are concentrating on the role of marketing within their own organizations. Two out of three of all those interviewed claimed already to have a well-developed separate marketing department. Nearly all of these expect their own marketing people to work alongside buyers and provide support on request. Most expect their marketing specialists to play a more active role in assessing activities proposed by suppliers on new and existing brands. Suppliers must therefore expect their propositions to be met with an increasingly considered response.

At a strategic as opposed to tactical level, what we are seeing is an increasingly determined attempt by leading retailers to brand their stores. More and more manufacturers of branded products are required to regard retailers not just as distributors but rather as brand manufacturers to whose requirements their own brand activities need to be accommodated.

The 'star performers' mentioned by the retailers in the interviews are companies which recognize that trade marketing is more than just a working knowledge of their trade sector customers and developing trade and tailor-made promotions for them. The successful industrial companies recognize that trade marketing is not solely the province of FMCG and have developed and adapted the approach of the consumer goods companies to suit their own needs and the needs of their chosen channels of distribution.

THE APPROACH TO TRADE MARKETING

Trade marketing is the linch pin between the sales strategy and the marketing strategy, the former being concerned with appeal to the trade customer, the latter with appeal to the consumer.

It is important to note that of all the multiple factors of the marketing platform designed to appeal to consumers, they are reached directly, independently of the intervention of the trade by one single factor – media advertising. All the other ingeniously planned features are totally dependent on the distributive trade performing the functions assumed of it, if they are ever going to influence the consumer or end-user.

Product performance, appearance, pricing, promotion and support must have consumer appeal. They must also be suited to the customer needs of each trade sector and each major account to gain their support. While media advertising is aimed principally at influencing the ultimate consumer, it must not be overlooked that it has a highly important indirect effect – influencing and impressing the distributive trade. A campaign must not only be effective in persuading consumers, it must also convince distributors that it will be effective.

It should be clear from the product marketing strategies who the intended product users are and how the range of individual product or products and services should be defined: the number of potential and actual users and any geographical bias in these numbers. The objective must be to develop the trade marketing culture within the company and create the opportunity for joint planning by sales and marketing. The strategy for marketing through the distributive trade is to define how resources in manpower, staff, supply services and financial reward to chosen trade sectors will be used to move products through to the consumer at the right level. So how should you start to develop the approach to trade marketing?

IMPORTANT ELEMENTS IN TRADE MARKETING

Sales objectives

Are the sales objectives clearly defined?

The sales objectives must clearly define the volume and margin requirements for a particular trading period. They must take into account historical, current and future distribution trends and set individual brand priorities for both mature, developing or declining brands. Further refinement is then necessary to determine individual product objectives by distribution channel and large trade customers or groupings of trade customers. Those objectives must then be translated and developed into realistic and achievable sales targets.

The achievement of these targets through a planned programme of standard amd promotional initiatives should also be underpinned by contingency planning to ensure a swift response to market, volume and profit fluctuations.

Trade sector knowledge

What do you need to know to develop an effective sales strategy?

If you are an established company you will have a clear understanding of what the distribution options are. It is important continuously to update your knowledge of the types and classes of trade which act as distributors for your product group. There are usually many levels within a distributive system and you need detailed knowledge of their functions and relationships; the appropriate numbers for each grouping and their geographic spread. Both sales and marketing need to appreciate the long-term potential of these groups and the prospects for growth that they offer.

In most markets there has been a concentration of trade power particularly in the retail sector. These major accounts are represented in their negotiations with suppliers by sophisticated, marketing-orientated buyers, with better information technology at their disposal. It is therefore imperative that suppliers develop a comprehensive under-standing of the way their large customers operate. This goes beyond the usual information on distribution depots, numbers of outlets, branch lists, important field personnel, head office management structures. You need to know more than simply the promotional programmes they operate and what financial support they expect if they feature your products, as well as their profit margin expectations for particular product groups, their stockholding policy, the type of servicing they require and how active they are in selling, displaying, promoting and canvassing for suppliers' products.

More important, the supplier also needs to know how they use the wide range of information at their disposal. What does the current technology provide for them and how is the information used to evaluate product performance, particularly yours? What other criteria do they measure and evaluate? What advantages will future technologi-cal development give them? How should your company plan to respond and adapt?

It means knowing what standard research they buy, what research they commission and why. How do they measure success? How do they measure competing brands and their own competitors on the high street or within the industry? What plans do they have for own label? And so on and so on. Suppliers' national account negotiators should know the limits of the buyer's flexibility. The buyer's own performance is eva-luated and measured by his or her management against prescribed result areas, and every buyer has targets and margin objectives to achieve.

Only with this type of comprehensive approach to trade knowledge can you develop product or service initiatives which relate to the real needs of the different trade customers and trade sectors.

Activity planning

How much planning does the overall sales strategy need?

It is at this stage that joint planning between marketing management and sales management first arises, although close communication and co-operation should exist at all times.

It is essential that joint planning for the products and the trade should be conducted simultaneously and co-operatively by both groups of managements – not pre-empted by one group and then agreed by the other. If the two planning exercises are carried out independently it is inevitable that one will dominate the other (and the other will be subject to a reconciliation which defeats the purpose). This is why many companies have set up trade marketing departments to act as the pivot between sales and marketing, co-ordinating and developing the planning process in an impartial manner.

Full-year marketing plans are produced for each product by most marketing departments. Suprisingly many do not produce to the same detail full-year sales and marketing plans for the major trade customers. Company targets must be phased across the trading time frame. An annual calendar of promotional and support activity planned in detail for consumers, trade sectors and individual major trade customers is the next stage. It must so arrange these initiatives to promote maximum trade acceptance, consumer impact and sell through, without promoting conflict within the trade or duplication of effort for little real increase in volume.

Trade lead times will determine the forward planning and production requirements for both presentation and agreement deadlines. In-store or 'buying in' periods will determine production dates for both special products and promotional and support material.

The calendar of promotional activity should also take media schedules into account to ensure the support programme develops and increases volume and profit in line with the trading objectives.

In some leading FMCG companies individual product managers have each been allocated one major customer. Their objective is to champion and represent the marketing needs of the customer for all the brands within the range with their marketing colleagues. They co-ordinate and co-operate with their counterparts in sales to produce a joint sales and marketing plan for that individual customer. I believe this recognizes that trade marketing skills are a day-to-day requirement in brand management, particularly as many companies develop pan-European initiatives on production, design, packaging and advertising, co-ordinated at the international level for implementation in local markets.

Sales force organization and control

Is the sales force organized efficiently and cost-effectively to meet its targets?

The effectiveness of the sales organization should be, and usually is, continuously reviewed by sales management. Within a trade marketing framework it is crucial that resources are tactically employed to implement trade marketing strategy effectively.

Professional sales managers will systemize the measurement and control of their staff. They will know current sales costs per year/day/hour for each category of selling staff. In dealing with the trade they must also identify differences in its selling function and ensure they are adequately provided for. They should also question the extent to which other trade support activities are justified by marginal costings. Specialization within the chosen channels of distribution must be set against the sales staff's specialization by function. What should it be and what could it be? The answers may indicate scope for outside sales support staff as a more effective response to trade needs particularly at individual outlet level.

It is cheaper and easier to provide incentive for up to a hundred sales people than for the thousands of consumers who buy the product or services. Carefully constructed incentive programmes offer maximum tactical flexibility within a trade marketing strategy enabling you to meet highly specific trade objectives. Motivation and reward programmes need to address the traditional virtues of extra effort and selling more. They must also have a trade dimension to channel effort into achieving customer objectives as well as total sales and margin targets.

Modern sales forces must also place more emphasis upon the customer planning process and it is therefore important that management information and support systems provide comprehensive detail. Factual assessments can then be made on the organizational efficiency of the sales force, and the development of both human and marketing support resources to the mutual benefit of both the trade customer and the company.

Pricing and discount control/account profitability

How do you achieve the right balance between controlled shelf prices, satisfactory trade margins and your own volume and margin targets?

It is important to establish controllable discount schemes, which must apply equitably across the range of trade customers. Many companies operate schemes which create anomalies – overpaying some, underpaying others, encouraging undercutting – instead of providing incentives for greater sales by motivating the trade to support your products and rewarding their efforts.

A controllable discount scheme must also create the opportunity for the supplier to manage the ongoing shelf price and cut-price special offers in co-operation with the trade. What do you know about the margins actually realized on company products by each category of distribution? What margin will the trade expect if the shelf price is to be reduced for a period? What are the ranges of shelf prices you would like to see established in each trade sector and for each level of customer type? Are these differentials realistic? Should your discount programme reflect these margin aspirations to give you more control? What additional rewards should you offer to the larger customers in line with the extra volume potential they provide? Can these rewards be structured to ensure they are not included in their margin calculations and yet still provide the incentive the customer is looking for?

For the larger accounts you should also conduct account profitability studies. They will highlight not only the true costs and operating profit but also those elements in the mix of total support that need adjusting. This exercise can also be developed into a standard module (using simple equations and ratios) for completion by the major account handlers.

Some UK companies have established such systems. They categorize or apply specific expenditure under fourteen headings for the products listed or stocked by the major customers. The simple format used by these companies is shown in Figure 24.1. It is supported by a number of appendices which detail ratios, percentages and equations to be applied to the current sales statistics. Explanations provided with the format include:

1 *Overheads transferred in* – multiply unit sales figures by the overhead transferred in figures provided in the appendix.
2 *NAM costs* – national accounts managers' costs equal £38,000 a year divided by the numbers of accounts and apply the time factor equation.
3 *Direct cost variances* – variant of actual costs of goods set percentages for the year of 1 per cent; calculate 1 per cent of full revenue sales and add to the direct marketing contribution; favourable.

This exercise is completed annually by each member of the national account team.

Account name ....

Account profitability study

Dec–Nov

	Total value	GSV %
Full revenue sales		
Standard direct cost		
Overheads transferred in		
Standard profit contribution		
Discounts		
Advertising		
Sales promotion monies		
Overriders		
Direct marketing contribution		
Field costs		
NAM costs		
Merchandiser's costs		
Debtor's interest		
Other overhead expense		
DCVs		
Operation profit contribution		

Figure 24.1 Account profitability study form

Such an approach, however simple or complex, not only provides the additional controls on pricing and discount levels but also ensures that managers of accounts develop the range of business skills and objectivity to manage their customers better.

Trade and tailor-made promotions

Can you improve your volume and margins by promoting more effectively?

Each stage of the approach to trade marketing is interdependent.

Effective sell-out promotions can be developed only by applying the detailed trade sector knowledge and margin information to the wide range of promotional options available. Any promotion needs consumer and retailer appeal; without retailer appeal the consumer never gets to see it. But a retailer who accepts the promotion will also require reassurance that it will sell through. The joint planning process by sales and marketing should ensure that promotional strategies are developed to achieve the volume and margin objectives for the promotional period. The promotional initiatives combine the important elements of customer appeal with a range of customer benefits which will impress and influence the retailer's decision to support the promotional programme.

Major account organization and control

Do you have the right organization and control for the business with your major customers?

Within the organization of the sales team there is the need to create this specialist approach. The calibre of the people nominated to handle the major customer is critical. In most markets relatively few customers account for a large proportion of the company's sales and demand a similar proportion of the discount and promotional support budgets. I have already highlighted the increasing sophistication of their buying and marketing departments. Negotiators who represent your company must be able to negotiate competently at this level, earning respect for business acumen. Their proposals must be built around the key customer benefits of improving, increasing, saving, solving, reducing, to develop real two-way communication and understanding.

These managers require specialist development and training. They must be capable (jointly with marketing) of creating the major account sales and marketing strategies, and planning the detailed, volume, margin, listing and promotional customer activity. These plans must reflect the forward negotiating and agreement requirements, and create the necessary in-house lead times for the production (at both the presentation and implementation stage) of all the important components in the programme.

Shelf management

How do you ensure that shelf facings and displays do justice to your brands?

Again, I must stress how important it is to know the customer's criteria for listing and display. Who is responsible for shelf layout programmes? What formulas, techniques, research, do they use? Who do they consult? How often are programmes produced, and when and how frequently are they reviewed? What input can the supplier make formally and informally? What services, support can you provide?

Once these criteria have been established, programmes and initiatives must be developed to influence shelf positions. Leading retailers often feel they know more about merchandising and display technique than any supplier. Our research with retailers showed their confidence in this area to be well founded. It seemed to 50 per cent of those questioned that suppliers react only 'when their products are moved to the bottom shelf'.

A long-term merchandising strategy must be developed which is not based upon pure self-interest and minimal research. The way forward is first to develop the same skills as the customers and then develop *joint solutions* with them.

Own label management

How do you handle the own-label competition in your markets?

Do you manufacture own label or not? Is it a threat (in terms of market share percentage)? Is it growing? Who makes it/supplies it to the retailer? Clarify your company attitude to own-label manufacture. To which retailers is own label most important? For those retailers – do you know their promotional policy and timings? Do you know their display policy? In each account (or as a general principle) what is the most effective pricing? Do you know the ideal pricing differentials for own-label and branded goods? Do you really understand the promotional (timings and type) and display (site and facings) policies?

Do you consider gaining knowledge and developing strategies against own label like other brands. If not, why not?

Can you use other non-competing own-label products to promote your products with certain retailers?

These are some of the questions you need to ask. Recognize the status of own label. Be clever, not scathing about it. Treat it with respect and then fight it if you perceive it as a threat to your brands.

From a strategic point of view, becoming an own-label supplier/

manufacturer can help you compete in a dual way with the number one brand. It offers opportunities to control retail prices, gain knowledge of pricing and promotions for own label and competitors, and to be pre-emptive with your own strategy. Most important by supplying both own-label and branded goods the number two company could become the effective number one supplier.

Training and development/recruitment

Is your team skilful enough consistently to achieve the targets and objectives you set?

Once you have developed the information and organization base, you must question if you have the right calibre of people to implement your trade marketing strategy. Will they respond to training and development and can they increase their level of planning and selling skills? If not, you will have some important recruitment decisions to make. Before you develop your training programmes you must identify the separate needs of development and backbone personnel. Development personnel are those who demonstrate potential for increased responsibility and can aspire to more senior positions within the management structure. For them, individual training/development programmes should not only increase current skills but also substantiate and qualify potential against a range of more senior positions.

Backbone personnel are those who have reached their level of competence and are unlikely to move further up the ladder. They are still valuable and successful in their current positions and need training to ensure their skills keep pace with the needs of the marketplace. They need development to improve their business perspective and maintain their motivation to perform consistently year in and year out.

The same approach obviously applies to management development. The individual training and development programmes will identify the potential managers of the future and the range of positions to which they could aspire. Succession planning will ensure that there is a pool of candidates who have been better prepared to make the next move.

Utilizing field sales support/merchandising

Is there a role for alternative forms of sales support?

Although this is part of sales force organization and control, it is worth separating out the alternative forms of sales support because they should be pre-tested and evaluated before decisions are made on structural changes. The objective is quite simply to ensure that you maximise the opportunities. First, you must evaluate the alternative forms of sales support available. Will they merchandise and display, freeing up sales force time? Can they also carry out a stock and order function? Will they be directly employed by you and, if so, full time or part time? How will they be managed? Should you use an outside force? What are the benefits and limitations? Again, is this full time or tactically on a 'blitz' basis? How will your measure/evaluate performance? Can test results by replicated nationally? What will be the reaction of the trade, will they see it as a benefit? How will it be funded? What will be the reaction of your current sales force? How should the benefits be communicated? Are redundancies or cut-backs necessary or is this an additional cost?

You must ensure that you develop the right merchandising combination in response to the real needs of your marketplace and not just as a cheaper (and possibly inferior) alternative.

Using telesales

Can telephone selling help me?

The same criteria apply to telesales as to alternative forms of sales support. You must identify the scope from telesales, then decide its long and short-term value. The telesales effort would need to be co-ordinated into the mainstream activity and could potentially deliver cost savings with no reduction in effectiveness. Pre-testing is again a critical requirement and initial and ongoing training programmes would have to be developed and in place if you decided to test and then go live with this activity.

CONCLUSION

Successful trade marketing involves strategy, knowledge, good organization and planning.

It should also be a 'culture' within a company rather than being treated as a topic for a sub-committee or a department. It is a way of thinking which questions every aspect of the operation and its ability to respond to the needs of both the consumer and the customer. I have briefly outlined an approach to trade marketing that poses many of the questions in a range of important areas. Trade marketing is a thought process which enables you to go on extending the list of questions to whatever length is appropriate for your brands and trade customers. Many of the key aspects of trade marketing are applicable to industrial goods suppliers and they must tailor their approach to suit their own needs. While trade marketing should be a more established theory in consumer goods companies, they still have far to go. The highlights from our own research prove the point.

25

Physical distribution and logistics management

Martin Christopher

Distribution, and the wider business philosophy of logistics, have always been a central feature of all economic activity. Yet paradoxically it is only in recent years that they have come to receive serious attention from either the business or academic worlds. One very obvious reason for this neglect is that, while the *functions* that comprise the logistics task are individually recognized, the *concept* of logistics as an integrative activity in business has developed only within the last twenty years.

What is logistics? It can be variously defined, but expressed at its simplest it is (see Bowersox, 1978):

> The process of strategically managing the movement and storage of materials, parts, and finished inventory from suppliers, through the firm and on to customers.

Logistics is thus concerned with the management of the physical flow which begins with sources of supply and ends at the point of consumption. It is clearly therefore much wider in its reach than simply a concern with the movement of finished goods – a commonly held view of physical distribution. In the logistics scheme of things we are just as much concerned with plant and depot location, inventory levels, materials management and information systems as we are with transport.

One of the features of the logistics concept – which is its greatest attraction while simultaneously being the greatest obstacle to its widespread adoption in industry so far – is that it places the emphasis on integrating activities that traditionally have been located in different functions of the business. Thus in many companies responsibility for, say, inventory on the one hand and transport on the other may be vested in the production function and the distribution functions respectively, and decisions on one will often be made without regard for the other. The logistics viewpoint, however, forces the decision-taker to recognize the connections between the component elements of the materials flow system – indeed it encourages comprehensive systems thinking rather than functional tunnel vision.

It is interesting to trace the evolution of thought in the logistics activity and then to assess its importance for business today.

As early as 1915, writing from Harvard Business School, Arch Shaw took a view of the logistics activity which was radically far-sighted. He said (Shaw, 1915):

The relations between the activities of demand creation and physical supply . . . illustrate the existence of the two principles of interdependence and balance. Failure to co-ordinate any one of these activities with its group fellows and also with those in the other group, or undue emphasis or outlay put upon any one of these activities, is certain to upset the equilibrium of forces which means efficient distribution.

. . . The physical distribution of the goods is a problem distinct from the creation of demand . . . Not a few worthy failures in distribution campaigns have been due to such a lack of co-ordination between demand creation and physical supply . . . Instead of being a subsequent problem, this question of supply must be met and answered before the work of distribution begins.

This view of logistics as a bridge between demand creation and physical supply is as valid today as it was when first expressed seventy years ago. However, no matter how fundamental this idea was, very little attention seems to have been paid to it and, indeed, in 1962 one of the gurus of management, Peter Drucker, writing in *Fortune* magazine, said (Drucker, 1962):

Physical distribution is today's frontier in business. It is one area

455

where managerial results of great magnitude can be achieved. And it is still largely unexplored territory.

There are signs, however, that management consciousness of the importance of logistics is growing and the last ten years have seen a considerable upsurge in interest in this area.

A number of factors have contributed to this growth in interest in logistics management. One is that as companies seek out areas for productivity improvement they are forced to confront the substantial corporate costs represented by distribution. Production and marketing have both been subjected to scrutiny by academic commentators and the more efficiency-conscious companies. Now it is the turn of the materials flow system that binds production and marketing to receive similar examination.

Giving increased urgency to this examination is the growth in the costs of movement and storage. Energy crises have had a direct impact upon transport costs and soaring interest rates have made the costs of holding stocks a sizeable expense. Beyond this the vast proliferation in the size of most companies' product ranges has meant that the total stockholding investment of these companies has increased dramatically. When one considers that ten years ago a typical frozen food company offered a range of only 200 items whereas now it has a total range of over 500, it can be appreciated how important a factor in the corporate balance sheet inventory has become.

Changes in the channels of distribution have themselves forced many manufacturers and distributors to take a fresh look at their distribution systems. Grocery retailing in the UK is a prominent example of how power in the marketing channel has dramatically changed hands. Twenty-five years ago there were 150,000 retail grocery outlets; today there are only 60,000. Clearly the size of these outlets in physical and turnover terms has increased considerably and so too has the centralization of retail buying power. For example, Tesco and Sainsbury together account for over 25 per cent of the UK sales of groceries. The impact this has had on manufacturers, and in particular on their distribution systems, has been far-reaching.

Similar changes in channel relationships have occurred in many other industries too.

The combination of all these factors has brought the distribution problem into sharp focus. In particular, awareness is growing both of

456

the impact of logistics upon corporate profitability and, underlying this, its impact upon the national economy.

THE CONCEPT OF LOGISTICS MANAGEMENT

As we have already noted, the logistics concept is based on a total systems view of the materials and goods flow activity from the source of supply through to the final point of consumption. It recognizes the interrelationships between the multitude of functions involved in this movement from source to user and in so doing forces management to think in terms of managing the total system rather than just one part of it.

The specific functional areas encompassed by logistics might be termed the 'logistics mix' and could be summarized as follows.

- Inventory, for example:
  - service level decisions
  - materials requirements planning
- Information, for example:
  - order processing
  - demand forecasting
- Warehousing and handling, for example:
  - depot location
  - unitization and packaging
- Transport, for example:
  - mode decisions
  - scheduling

The logistics management task is concerned with the integration and co-ordination of these activities in such a way that end markets are served in the most cost-effective manner.

The whole purpose of the logistics activity is to provide 'availability'. Everyone will be familiar with the cliché: 'The right product in the right place at the right time.' If one adds 'at the least cost', that is precisely the objective of logistics management.

Another way of defining the objective of logistics management could be in terms of 'customer service', which is in effect an elaboration on the notion of 'availability'. The idea of customer service encompasses all the points of contact between the customer and the supplier in terms of physical fulfilment of orders. Customer service is the output of the logistics system and it results from the combined effects of the activity centres within the 'logistics mix'. All these activities are important in establishing a desired level of customer service performance. They are also interdependent; if one activity fails, the system fails, creating poor performance and destabilizing workloads in other areas, resulting in the end in poor cost-effectiveness for the system as a whole. A failure in sales forecasting, then, may influence materials requirements planning which then results in low product availability of finished goods inventory. This in turn may result in either lost sales or an increased number of back orders which may in turn delay order processing and hence extend the order cycle time. This may result in the need to expedite shipments which increases the cost of service to the customer (Christopher *et al*, 1979).

Obviously, providing improved customer service will normally incur additional costs for the company. The higher the level of service offered the higher will be the costs. In fact it can be shown that once the level of service increases beyond the 70–80 per cent mark, the associated costs increase far more than proportionately ('service level' being defined for our purposes as the percentage of orders which can be met from stock within a given period.

The implications of this cost function for the distributing company are worth some attention. In the first place, many companies, far from having any explicit service policy, are unaware of the level of service at which they are operating. Even if the company does have a declared service policy it is often the case that service levels have been arbitrarily set. Offering a 97 per cent level of service instead of a 95 per cent level may have only a slight effect on customer demand, yet it will have a considerable effect on distribution costs – for normally distributed demand this 2 per cent increase in the level of service would lead to a 14 per cent increase in safety stock.

Clearly, therefore, it is essential that management recognizes the cost implications of a service strategy. Indeed, by offering logistics service the company is absorbing a cost that would otherwise have to be borne by the customer. For example, if the supplying company delivers twice instead of once a week, it is relieving the customer of a certain responsibility for holding stock – the more frequent the deliveries, the less stock the customer needs to hold. Similarly, if the customer knows that when placing an order with that supplier, the supplier will rarely be out of stock on that item and can deliver it speedily, then again the customer's stockholding can be lower. Because it costs money to hold stock – currently about 25 per cent of its value a year – by offering such a service the supplier is absorbing this customer cost.

WHAT ARE THE COSTS OF DISTRIBUTION?

There has been a tendency in the past for companies to consider only the costs of transport and, perhaps, warehouses, as their distribution costs. Recently, however, more companies have adopted the 'total distribution cost' concept. This concept recognizes that many more costs are incurred through the provision of availability than just transport and warehouse costs. For example, decisions about service level, as we have seen, affect the amount of inventory that needs to be held in the system; thus the cost of holding inventory must be included as a distribution cost. Likewise, order processing costs are influenced by the distribution activity, so they too must be included; indeed, there is a case for including invoicing costs. The costs of materials handling and protective packaging also form part of the total distribution cost, as should the costs of managing and administering the distribution system.

We could express the total distribution cost concept in the form of an equation:

$$TDC = TC + FC + CC + IC + HC + PC + MC$$

Where

TDC	=	Total distribution costs
TC	=	Transport costs
FC	=	Facilities costs (depots, warehouses and the like)
CC	=	Communications costs (order processing, invoicing and so on)
IC	=	Inventory cost
HC	=	Materials handling costs
PC	=	Protective packing costs
MC	=	Distribution management costs

Various surveys have been made of the relative costs of distribution in industry and their findings seem to suggest that these costs represent about 15 per cent of sales turnover for a typical company. Averages can of course be misleading and, depending on the nature of the business, the figures can be very much higher or lower. Table 25.1 shows one company's analysis of its total distribution costs.

Table 25.1 A leading food company's total distribution costs

Cost	% of total sales	
Transport inwards		
Materials to factories		1.00
Transport outwards		
Palletization	0.02	
Factories to depots	1.71	
Depots to customer	2.09	3.82
Warehouses, depots		
Clerical wages	0.16	
Warehouse labour	1.29	
Other costs	1.19	2.64
Order processing		
Rental of terminals	0.11	
Operating terminals	0.07	
Computer	0.03	
Sales accounting	0.68	0.89
Protective packaging		2.00
Management		
Management costs	0.17	
Stock auditing	0.02	
Stock planning	0.01	
Training	0.01	0.21
Stock losses		0.26
Interest on capital		
Stocks	0.24	
Building, vehicles, plant	0.46	0.70
Total		11.52

While this company has placed some costs under slightly different headings from those used in the TDC equation above, they amount to the same thing in total.

One of the benefits of being able to identify the specific sources of total distribution costs is that it becomes easier to identify potential 'trade-offs'. A trade-off occurs where an increased cost in one area is more than matched by a cost reduction in another area, leading to an improved situation overall. Thus, a distribution system with ten regional depots has high warehouse and stockholding costs compared with a system of only five depots, but the savings on trunk haulage and the reduction of stock-outs may more than compensate for the extra costs involved in the ten-depot system. In this case, an increase in warehouse and stock carrying costs has been traded off against a reduction in total system costs.

Generally, the effects of trade-offs are assessed in two ways: first from the point of view of their impact on total system costs, and second from their impact on sales revenue. It is possible to trade off costs in such a way that total costs increase, yet because of the better service now being offered, sales revenue increases. If the difference between revenue and costs is greater than before, the trade off may be regarded as leading to an improvement in cost-effectiveness.

In addition to the possibility of trading off costs between the various elements in the distribution system, for example between depot costs and stockholding costs, there is the possibility of identifying trade-offs within an individual element. Thus, stock levels of finished goods in the logistics system may be reduced at the expense of the level of service offered, but the reduction in sales revenue resulting is more than compensated for by the reduction in stockholding costs – or vice versa in different circumstances.

TOTAL SYSTEMS MANAGEMENT

For the benefits of such trade-offs to be fully achieved managers must begin to think in terms of total systems rather than in terms of narrow functional areas. A great deal has been written and talked about systems, systems approaches, systems thinking and systems management. While as a generalization it would probably be correct to define anything that converts an input into an output as a 'system', the concept of a logistics system is rather more complex. As we have seen, the logistics system is concerned with the movement and storage of products from their raw state, through various stages of sub-assembly, manufacture, packaging, transportation and delivery to the final customer. Depending upon how widely one wishes to define the 'system' it can be seen that logistics considerations are involved throughout the marketing and exchange channel from the sources of supply to the points of final consumption. To add to the complexity it is unlikely that the same corporate entity will be involved, or will have control, over the entire system. Furthermore, within the company itself many functional areas, or sub-systems, will exist which may have conflicting goals or objectives.

This latter feature is of particular concern to logistics systems management. Table 25.2 shows some of the conflicts that can occur between functions of the firm (that is, sub-systems) when goals are determined by

461

functions without regard for the impact of their actions upon the total system. This very common feature of corporate structures is called 'sub-optimization' by operations researchers – in other words, a failure to recognize that, unless carefully managed, the whole can sometimes be less than the sum of its parts. The ultimate rationale of the logistics concept is that it reduces sub-optimization within the company through a greater integration and co-ordination of connected activities.

Figure 25.1 represents the materials and information flows which must be managed to provide cost-effective customer service.

Many companies fail to recognize that the materials flow through the firm and the related flow of information (that is, orders, forecasts, stock reports and so on) should logically be seen as an integrated system. Typically, responsibility for the various functions involved in those flows is fragmented. At best there will be a partial attempt at integration through the development of a materials management function to manage goods inwards and the procurement of materials, and a parallel distribution management function responsible for the delivery of finished goods. The logistics concept suggests that greater efficiency and effectiveness can be achieved through an even wider, total systems view.

Some companies are in fact moving towards the adoption of such an approach to logistics management. Indeed, it has been suggested that there is a process of 'evolution' by which the company might progress on its way to the adoption of a logistics orientation. Looked at broadly there are three stages.

The first of these stages might be described as a *transport management* orientation. In this very basic situation the organization will not have recognized the function of transport except as a means of moving the product from the factory or warehouse to the customer's premises. It will be viewed as a purely mechanical task which does not need senior management attention. Often it will be managed by personnel with little status in the organization and no attempt will have been made to integrate the transport activity with other demand-fulfilling tasks such as warehousing, order processing and inventory control. The emphasis will be on cost minimization, the transport function being evaluated in terms of cost per mile or cost per case shipped or some such similar measure. Many companies have still not moved beyond this stage.

The second stage could be termed the *physical distribution management* or PDM orientation. This stage reflects a significant transition for the company because it requires a recognition that distribution is more

Table 25.2 Situations which can give rise to inter-departmental conflicts

Sub-systems goal	Purchasing	Production	Finance	Marketing	Logistics
Bulk purchases of materials	Advantage/ larger discounts		Disadvantage: working capital tied up		Disadvantage: warehousing costs increased
Long production runs		Advantage: low costs	Disadvantage: working capital tied up	Disadvantage: narrow product range	Disadvantage: warehousing costs increased
Broad product range	Disadvantage: discounts small on low volume	Disadvantage: short, high-cost runs	Disadvantage: finished goods stocks high	Advantage: more sales through wider customer appeal	Disadvantage: higher costs through more administration and warehousing space
Tighter credit control			Advantage: greater use of working capital	Disadvantage: possible loss of sales	
Four-day delivery (from seven days)			Disadvantage: higher operating costs	Advantage: more sales because of better service	Disadvantage: system costs increased in order to meet service requirements
Unit loads			Advantage: lower operating costs	Disadvantage: loss of sales to small customers	Advantage: system costs can be lowered by eliminating uneconomic calls

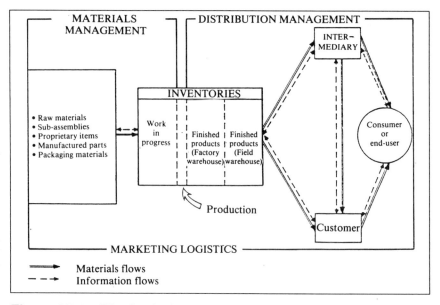

Figure 25.1   The logistics systems concept

than simply moving goods from A to B but instead is a vital link in the customer satisfaction process. Now the emphasis is on customer service and the use of distribution as a means of gaining leverage in the marketplace. A greater status is accorded the distribution manager and the function may even be represented at board level in its own right. Now the functions of warehousing, order processing and finished goods inventory control will probably be incorporated in the total distribution activity and the performance criteria will be as much about delivery as about costs. This second stage is perhaps the most common in British industry today.

Finally comes the third stage: the *logistics management* orientation. The logistics orientation, as we have seen, recognizes that to improve the performance of the system, as measured by the cost-effective provision of customer service, all the interrelated activities in moving materials and goods from source to user must be managed as a whole.

Clearly the logistics concept as we have defined it involves a radical transformation of the way a company faces up to the needs of the marketplace in terms of its entire operations management.

What is implicit in this new approach is the recognition of the need to balance the requirements of customer service against the internal

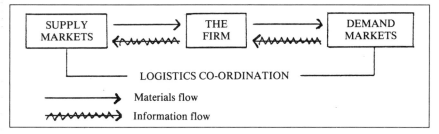

Figure 25.2   Logistics links supply with demand

management of its resources. Figure 25.2 highlights the integrative nature of the logistics task in bridging the operations gap between source of supply and final demand.

This conceptual framework is analogous to the concepts of materials management and distribution management presented in Figure 25.1. The suggestion here is that logistics is a *planning framework* rather than a business function. In other words, the management task inherent in logistics is *not* so much concerned with the *management* of materials flows but rather with providing the mechanism for establishing objectives and strategies within which the day-to-day activities of materials management and distribution management can take place.

LOGISTICS' ROLE IN CORPORATE STRATEGY

It is often forgotten that there is an important role for logistics in the development of corporate strategy. Instead a narrow cost-reduction view is taken and as a result many opportunities for improved market performance are missed.

Increasingly, however, more sophisticated organizations are recognizing that logistics has a wider role to play within the business. Decisions taken now on distribution networks, management of materials flow, information systems and so on can be crucial in determining the ability of the company to respond to changed market circumstances or new business opportunities.

A good example of how logistics can have impact at the highest level is provided by SKF, the Swedish bearings manufacturer. Several years ago SKF was facing severe competition in its European markets from Japanese suppliers which were able to supply standard bearings at a price not much higher than SKF's production cost. Analysis of the situation highlighted the fact that while SKF was producing over 50,000 variants the Japanese were concentrating on a very limited range of fast-moving lines. Moreover, SKF had plants in Sweden, Germany, the UK, France and Italy, each of which was generally providing the full range of variants. It became clear that SKF was unable to gain the benefits of scale at the production level because the typical batch run length was so small. The Japanese on the other hand were mass producing a much smaller number of items and consequently were much lower down the 'experience curve' which was reflected in their lower costs.

SKF's response was essentially logistical. It first reviewed the product range with the object of substantially reducing the number of items manufactured. Beyond this, however, it decided to concentrate the production of certain categories of bearings at individual manufacturing locations. Thus the French factory would make bearings which would be produced only there, Italy had its own unique line and similarly at each of the other manufacturing locations.

The end result was a classic trade-off in logistics costs. On the one hand, the costs of transport involved in distributing finished produce from the plant in, say, Sweden, to a customer in the UK were substantially higher than hitherto when that customer had been supplied from the UK. On the other hand, the production cost savings more than offset this extra cost.

To make it all work SKF installed a sophisticated information and planning system which enabled a centralized control of production and the allocation of inventory to local stocking points. This system, which it called the Global Forecasting and Supply System (GFSS), is essentially a logistics management system.

While SKF has faced severe trading conditions in recent years due to recession in its principal markets, it is probably true to say that its position would be much worse were it not for the adoption of this radical approach to logistics management.

In a quite different context one of North America's largest wholesale distributors, Foremost-McKesson, revised its logistics strategy to rescue a fast-deteriorating profit situation. The company was faced with a classic 'middleman squeeze' with more and more manufacturers delivering direct to the retailer. The company's response was to seek additional ways in which it could 'add value' to the basic distribution process (*Business Week*, 1981). Amongst Foremost's responses to the situation it faced were:

1 taking waste products as well as finished goods from chemical manufacturers, and recycling the wastes through its own plants – its first entry into chemical waste management;
2 creating a massive merchandising service by providing teams to set up displays of manufacturers' goods within stores;
3 acting as middleman between drug stores and insurance offices by processing medical consumer claims;
4 using the information from its computer to help manufacturers manage inventories, collect and analyse market data, and even plan sales and new product development;
5 leasing electronic ordering equipment to retailers, offering shelf management plans, and even providing price labels.

These and other actions have transformed the company's profitability – a transformation which has been achieved by the recognition that logistics is essentially a strategic orientation.

One further example underlines the positive impact on the market-place that a well-thought-through logistics strategy can achieve. The Whirlpool Corporation is a leading US manufacturer of domestic appliances such as washing machines, spin dryers and so on. To give some idea of its size, the company estimates that every day of the year approximately 25,000 customers buy one or more appliances which have been manufactured by Whirlpool. A significant percentage of these appliances are purchased from 900 Sears retail stores and 1700 Sears catalogue outlets. A further significant proportion of Whirlpool's annual sales volume is purchased from 13,500 franchised Whirlpool brand retail and builder outlets which are supplied from forty-five wholesale distributors. As might be imagined, the logistics of supplying these various channels of distribution from eight manufacturing facilities located in six different states are extremely complex. For example, the company estimates that its daily shipments throughout the system are equivalent to a freight train seven miles long!

The company recognized some years ago that in a competitive marketplace product availability and customer choice were highly important. Yet given the size of Whirlpool's product range the cost of holding high levels of inventory throughout the channel would be prohibitive.

To solve this problem the company has installed a 'real time' inventory control and order processing system. If a customer walks into a Sears retail store on, say, Monday and selects a model he or she wishes to buy it can be in the customer's home by Thursday. The way it works is that on Monday evening all the orders for Whirlpool products from that store are transmitted to the nearest Sears regional distribution centre (RDC). On Tuesday morning the Sears RDC combines all orders from its assigned retail stores and transmits their total needs directly into Whirlpool's computer which automatically processes the order, reserves inventory and transmits a shipping document to the appropriate Whirlpool distribution centre by Tuesday afternoon. That same afternoon or evening a trailer is loaded for delivery overnight to the Sears RDC early Wednesday morning from where it is broken into local delivery routes for delivery to the customer's home the following day.

The effect of this is to minimize the total inventory in the system. Apart from the items held in the retail store, which are for display purposes only, the only place inventory is held is in the nineteen Whirlpool distribution centres. Not only is inventory reduced through this consolidation but also vehicle space utilization is maximized by shipping complete trailer loads to Sears' warehouses. A further sophistication that has recently been introduced is to offer a greater range of colours for appliances but not actually to hold all these colours in stock. Instead, orders are consolidated by colour and unpainted appliances (which are held in stock) are then sprayed the appropriate colour. This postponement of the commitment to colour allows a further substantial reduction in total stockholding.

The end result of these logistical decisions has been to enhance the customer service offering both in terms of speedy availability and choice and to improve Whirlpool's market position.

These examples demonstrate that companies are increasingly recognizing the importance of distribution and logistics and its impact on their marketplace performance. It seems that the 'dark continent' that Peter Drucker wrote about twenty-five years ago (Drucker, 1962) is about to be explored.

REFERENCES AND FURTHER READING

Bowersox, D. (1978), *Logistics Management*, Macmillan, London. (The definition in the text is an amended version of Bowersox's.)

468

Christopher, M. (1985), *The Strategy of Distribution Management*, Gower, Aldershot. (Chapter 25 is based upon material in this book.)

Christopher, M., Schary, P. and Skjott-Larsen, T. (1979), *Customer Service and Distribution Strategy*, Associated Business Press, London.

Drucker, P. (1962), 'The economy's dark continent', *Fortune*, Vol.72, April.

Shaw, A. W. (1915), *Some Problems in Market Distribution*, Harvard University Press.

26

Reaching overseas markets

Norman Boakes

Harold Macmillan will be remembered by many as the man who said 'exporting is fun'. In fact, although these words were contained in a copy of his speech released to the press, he never actually used them. Exporting is hard work, frustrating and not to be entered into lightly. However, carried out professionally, it can be very profitable and should improve the long-term prospects for a company by providing more customers than can be found in the home market. Occasionally it can also be fun!

The purpose of this chapter is to summarize the most important considerations and suggest where further help and advice can be obtained. It is written with the newcomer to exporting in mind but the experienced exporter may find it helpful to be provided with a concise overview.

Table 26.1 gives some exporters' views on the profitability of exporting. Nearly two-thirds of 'active' exporters believed that export business was as profitable or more profitable than home sales. Many companies consider that exports contribute to overall profitability even where unit profit is lower.

THE DECISION TO EXPORT

The decision to enter a new market cannot be taken lightly. A company successfully selling its products through retail outlets, would

Table 26.1 Exporting versus domestic sales (profitability)

	All exporters %	Active exporters %	Passive exporters %
Exporting is:			
More profitable	20.6	24.5	21.4
Same/cannot distinguish	41.0	39.6	35.1
Less profitable	38.4	35.8	43.5

Source: DTI Occasional Paper, *Into Active Exporting,* April 1987.

be unlikely to start selling the same range to the catering trade without considering whether packaging and pricing policies were correct, what extra demands the new business would impose on production capacity and whether the existing sales force could cover the new outlets.

It would soon become apparent that the structure of the catering trade was very different from the grocery business in that there is a wide disparity between industrial, institutional, hotel and traditional outlets. Similar problems would be experienced by a company supplying accessories to the automotive aftermarket which chose to enter the original equipment business and sell directly to major manufacturers.

Yet one sees companies attempting to sell their products overseas, and even appointing exclusive agents or distributors, simply as the result of an enquiry received or a chance contact, perhaps in the airport lounge while on vaction! Even today, there is a certain excitement and glamour attached to exporting which results in decisions being taken in haste and commitments entered into which may well inhibit profitability in the market concerned for many years to come. Figure 26.1 shows the greatest difficulties in exporting as seen by exporters.

Concern over the financial aspects of exporting was expressed by more than one-third of those responding to a DTI-sponsored survey. Handling export paperwork was also considered a deterrent and this problem is being tackled vigorously by SITPRO, the Simplification of International Trade Procedures Board.

No company would expect to win business in its home market without properly understanding its customers' needs and then setting out to meet those needs more effectively than its competitors. Commitment from top management is essential for success. There

471

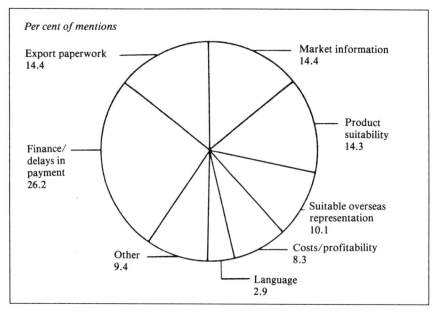

Per cent of mentions

Export paperwork 14.4

Market information 14.4

Product suitability 14.3

Finance/ delays in payment 26.2

Suitable overseas representation 10.1

Other 9.4

Costs/profitability 8.3

Language 2.9

Source: DTI Occasional Paper, *Into Active Exporting,* April 1987.

Figure 26.1 The greatest difficulties in exporting

must be a realistic appreciation of the level of investment required and the length of time which will elapse before results are achieved.

The benefits to be derived from exporting should include:

1 increased profitability in the longer term;
2 better utilization of production capacity;
3 a wider customer base;
4 increased security by spreading risk over a variety of markets;
5 sharper marketing skills through exposure to competition in international markets.

Table 26.2 shows the reasons given by exporters for starting to export. Exporters, particularly the 'active' ones, are more influenced by opportunities abroad than by declining home markets. Nearly half the 'passive' exporters were motivated by an unsolicited order or enquiry.

RESEARCHING OVERSEAS MARKETS

For the company new to export, the first question must be 'Where do

472

Table 26.2   Why exporters start

	% all exporters	% active exporters	% passive exporters
Saw market potential	38	45	30
Unsolicited enquiry/order	32	22	43
Long-term policy	9	12	6
Spare production capacity	7	4	10
Technological/product advantage	6	6	5
Declining home sales	4	5	2

Note: 'active' exporters are those with 15 per cent plus exports in one of the past three years; 'passive' those with 1–15 per cent.

Source: DTI Occasional Paper, *Into Active Exporting,* April 1987.

we start?' Even companies which have been exporting for some years should carry out a regular appraisal of the markets in which they are currently working, as well as those which may offer even more attractive possibilities. Very few exporters would claim that they have entered every one of their markets as the result of careful research and logical reasoning. More often, it is chance events which create opportunities.

For most new exporters, drawing up a short-list of overseas markets is largely a matter of common sense. They are likely to avoid countries which are politically unstable, or where there is considerable risk that one will not be paid. There are also markets with a high level of discrimination against imports which may manifest itself in embargoes, quotas, tariffs, technical approval and health certificates and excessive labelling requirements. Positive attributes would include the frequency and regularity of shipping links, remembering that distance increases cost in every aspect of exporting. The ability to conduct business in the language of the country will also be a significant advantage.

Companies providing products or services which are highly specialized may find it necessary to generate sales in a number of markets simultaneously, since no one market would be large enough to sustain the necessary investment. This may also be true if a company is at the leading edge of technology, with innovative products which quickly become outdated.

With these exceptions, it is always better to short-list two or three

473

markets where the product is likely to find acceptance and then select one market in which to concentrate effort and resources.

In arriving at the short-list, ask the following questions:

1 Which industries currently use your product?
2 In which countries are these industries to be found?
3 Which countries have significant imports of this product?
4 To what international standards does your product conform?
5 Which countries accept these standards?
6 What restrictions are placed on imports?
7 Is the business environment likely to remain stable?
8 Are there adequate shipping facilities?
9 Do social or business customs differ greatly from the UK?
10 Which language is used for business?

Having made an initial selection, compare one market with another. This can be done, initially, by desk research. At a later stage, it will be necessary to undertake field research in which each market is visited so as to check out the facts and examine the current situation at first hand.

When comparing short-listed markets, ask the following questions:

1 What is the size of the market for this product category?
2 What proportion is supplied by local production, what from imports?
3 Has the market increased in volume or value over the past five years?
4 What changes are occurring in user industry/buyer behaviour?
5 Are there plans for new investment in these industries?
6 Who are the main suppliers of competitive products?
7 Is proposed legislation likely to affect either demand or the structure of the industry?
8 What factors might limit future demand?

When looking at the requirements of the market, consider the following factors:

1 What position will the product occupy in the market and is there a gap or must one be created?
2 How does the product compare with those in the market in terms of quality and price?
3 Is it likely to be acceptable to potential customers?

4   What standards and regulations apply to this product, and does your product meet these requirements?

5   Is it necessary to have the product approved and, if so, how long will this take and what will it cost?

6   What will be the cost of new product design, packaging and sales literature?

7   How will potential customers be identified?

8   What channels of distribution are used by competitors?

9   Are these the best for this product ... and what are the alternatives?

10   What level of marketing support will be required?

11   What are the normal terms of business?

When carrying out research, the starting point for any new exporter in the UK should be the Department of Trade and Industry, which can offer a wide range of services. The Export Marketing Research Scheme, for example, would provide a grant of up to 50 per cent towards the cost of a research project up to a maximum of £20,000 at the time of writing. Information about the scheme can be obtained from any DTI regional office or directly from:

Department of Trade and Industry
Export Marketing Research Section
Room 148
1 Victoria Street
London SW1H 0ET
Telephone: 01-215 5277

Research is not a substitute for decision. The results may be inconclusive and the company concerned will have to decide whether or not to take the risk. Almost certainly, research will have been unable to quantify precisely what share of a market it will be possible to achieve, since it is impossible to predict the level of response from existing competitors or from new competitors who may decide to enter the market.

One mistake which many companies make is to underestimate the total cost necessary to enter a new market. Research expenditure is only the first small step. The real costs start when products and packaging have to be changed to meet customer requirements, and samples and sales aids provided to the selected distributor who then looks to the exporter for continuous marketing and service support.

475

The important points to remember when selecting an export market are:

1 Don't spend time examining too many markets, concentrate on a few.
2 Select a market which has sufficient potential.
3 Remember, a small market may still have a significant niche and less competition.
4 Select a market where your product has some competitive advantage, for example design, performance, quality or price – but do not rely exclusively on price.
5 Visit the market yourself before commissioning a detailed field study. Talking to leading buyers or visiting an exhibition can help you to identify key questions.
6 Use the services of BOTB, banks, chambers of commerce, trade associations and any other contacts you may have.

ENTERING THE MARKET

When the research has been completed and the market offering the greatest immediate potential identified, it will now be essential to secure commitment from top management and allocate production capacity, based on the anticipated level of demand, with a built-in safety margin so as to be able to support success. It is also essential that, at the outset, a marketing plan is drawn up and a budget made available: not just for the first year but for the first three years.

A large part of the research will have been concerned with identifying how best to enter the market by looking at the available channels of distribution. Only when this decision has been made, will it be possible to assess the financial viability of the project and carry out pricing calculations.

For each market it will be necessary to set specific objectives. Since every company has finite resources, it must define these objectives clearly and realistically. A written marketing plan encourages systematic thinking and provides the means by which performance can be evaluated. Initially, the plan may be quite short, but it should be revised and expanded to contain both short-term and long-term projections. It should certainly include sales forecasts for each product and market segment, together with the costs necessary to achieve these sales and the required contribution to profit.

Entering a market is usually achieved in one of four ways:

- Selling direct to users
- Appointing a commission agent
- Appointing a distributor
- Working with a non-competitive manufacturer

Selling direct to users or, in the consumer goods business, to leading retail organizations, requires a good knowledge of the market and the ability to communicate in the local language. It is also expensive in terms of travel and executive time.

However, some large companies do prefer to purchase direct from the manufacturer but they must be sufficiently competent to handle the import documentation and the exporter must have the capability and resources to sell direct. This involves identifying the people who make purchasing decisions; selling the product; arranging distribution; labelling and packing the goods according to instructions and complying with the buyers' requirements. Companies which purchase direct are usually very demanding about service and delivery dates.

Two other possibilities are selling through mail order companies or selling by direct mail.

Consumer purchasing through mail order catalogues is a growing business and there are many hundreds of specialized catalogues produced by stores and mail order companies. Buyers generally wish to enter into negotiations at least twelve months before the catalogue is published and exporters must be able to supply on time and in the quantities required.

For an exporter to sell by direct mail requires sufficient funds to cover a heavy investment in the production and circulation of the catalogue and in advertising. It is usually essential for the exporting company to build up its own mailing list and this will take some time.

Appointing a commission agent is often essential if one is selling capital equipment, particularly where it forms part of a major contract. The commission agent is a 'Mr Fixit' who can guide the exporter through a labyrinth of local regulations and customs, identifying specifiers, buyers and users. For most consumer products, commission agents are a less satisfactory solution than distributors

477

since they have no title to the goods and cannot provide the sales and merchandising service which is usually needed by the exporter.

The commission agent represents the exporter in the overseas market and takes orders on its behalf. The exporter ships the goods and invoices the customer direct. When the customer pays for the goods, the exporter pays the agent a commission on the sale. This is normally included in the price quoted to the customer.

Distributors, who will accept full responsibility for the marketing of products through the various levels of the trade to the ultimate customer, are preferred by many exporters. The distributor imports the goods on its own behalf, warehouses them and sells to a third party. Unfortunately, in most industries, efficient distributors are in short supply and already handling a wide range of products which may include those of competitors.

Working with a non-competitive manufacturer can be a satisfactory alternative. This can either be a manufacturer in the overseas market for whom the exporter's products would be complementary or, alternatively, a UK company selling into the same market. An overseas manufacturer may insist on marketing the product under its own brand which then significantly reduces the opportunity for the UK exporter to change distributor. Logically, it may lead to a local manufacturing agreement under licence with the overseas partner paying a royalty to the exporter.

Arrangements between two UK companies can run into difficulties because the priorities of each company in one particular market are unlikely to be identical. There can also be a difference of opinion concerning the allocation of resources and costs, and whether or not objectives have been achieved.

Within the UK, there are two other kinds of organization which can be of value to handle the total exports of small companies or to complement the exports of the medium-sized and larger company. These are confirming or export houses and export agents. The confirming house buys on its own account and supplies overseas markets. Many work on behalf of specific countries or selected buyers and may have access to bank or other lines of credit. A number of overseas companies do, of course, have their own UK buying offices.

The export agent can be an individual, or a small company, probably specializing in selected markets and working on behalf of a number of non-competing principals. Most work on commission,

478

leaving their principal responsible for collecting payment but others will take full responsibility for buying, selling, shipment and payment.

Whether working through agents, distributors or manufacturers, it is of paramount importance to have an unambiguous agreement which details the rights and responsibilities of both parties. Agreement must also be reached as to which legal code is to be applied in the case of a dispute. It must be recognized that the appointment of a local marketing representative, in whatever form, does not take away from the exporter the responsibility for managing the business.

To summarize:

1 identify the appropriate market segment for the product;
2 ensure that the distribution channel used matches this segment;
3 set specific objectives for each product and market segment;
4 allocate adequate resources;
5 prepare a marketing plan;
6 do not abdicate responsibility.

SELECTING AND WORKING WITH DISTRIBUTORS

The survey mentioned above showed that 22 per cent of 'active' exporters regarded finding the right agent or distributor as the most important key to success in exporting. Nearly 50 per cent of the companies responding to the questionnaire chose this method of distribution. Table 26.3 shows the views of the exporters who took part in the survey.

Finding the right partner, in the right market, is clearly regarded as the key to success, closely followed by commitment and confidence.

The names of suitable importers should have been identified at the research stage and comprehensive information obtained in respect of each one. Essential questions include:

1 correct title and company address;
2 details of offices, branches, subsidiaries and warehouses;
3 ownership of the company and date of establishment;
4 paid-up capital and reserves;
5 three years' accounts and financial data;
6 companies and products represented, with length of representation;

479

Table 26.3   Keys to success in exporting

	% all exporters	% active exporters	% passive exporters
Finding right agent or distributors	18	22	15
Choosing right market(s)	15	15	15
Commitment, confidence and persistance	13	15	12
Cost competitiveness	9	7	12
Understanding customers and competitors	6	10	11
Getting sound outside advice	7	5	6
Modifying products/packaging	7	6	5

Source: DTI Occasional Paper, *Into Active Exporting,* April 1987.

7   trade and bank references;
8   distribution capabilities including regional distribution facilities;
9   availability for servicing or any other special facilities required for your product;
10   company organization chart and staffing levels;
11   sales and marketing organization structure in detail;
12   sales performance history and, if possible, market share data for existing products.

It is necessary to establish that the potential distributor is financially sound, professionally competent and able to build new business for your product without jeopardizing its existing business. It is important to identify the kind of outlets which are regularly serviced and the geographical area which is covered. Does the distributor build business for its existing principals or simply grow by taking on new lines? Has it an effective management and marketing organization? The export manager must personally visit the distributor and meet as many people as possible within the organization to arrive at an informed judgement.

When seeking a distributor, the exporter should also talk to potential customers in the market who buy from a number of distributors so as to compare their performance and reputation. Clearly, in preliminary discussions with buyers and distributors, it is helpful if the identity of the principal can remain confidential so as to avoid alerting the competition and also to prevent bias in the answers given. Where a principal wishes to change a distributor, this is absolutely essential and, in both cases, confidentiality can be achieved by using an independent consultant who knows the market and the industry.

It must be remembered that the distributor will also be assessing the competence and commitment of the principal. Many distributors are able to choose the companies for which they will work and it is essential that both parties feel that the 'chemistry' is right.

A provisional agreement should be entered into with the chosen distributor which allows a trial period of, say, twelve months during which both parties can satisfy themselves that the relationship is one on which a successful business can be built. At the outset, it is important to build a partnership in which both principal and distributor can work together to achieve a common objective.

The distributor will wish to visit the principal's offices and factory, familiarize himself or herself with the product range and get to know the management team. The principal and distributor will then work together to produce and implement the marketing plan, and the distributor agreement will refer specifically to the part which each has to play and their respective financial contributions.

Before the distributor or agency agreement is signed, it is essential to check which local laws may be applicable. There can be protection to agents, after termination of a contract, in respect of future commissions and an importer who has invested at the request of a principal may also be able to recover some of these costs.

The agreement should cover:

- geographical territory or specific customer coverage
- brand or product exclusivity
- marketing responsibilities
- marketing information and reporting procedures
- method of payment
- rights of principal and distributor/agent
- pricing, promotion and costing
- performance criteria
- trademark and patent protection
- training of personnel
- duration of agreement
- procedure for handling disputes, including legal code to be invoked
- termination

Every agreement should specify those areas where failure to comply, by either party, would invalidate the contract. Examples could be where the distributor fails to pay on time in three consecutive periods or, alternatively, the principal fails to deliver.

Once the relationship has become established, there is a temptation for the exporter to leave more and more of the decisions to the distributor and concentrate attention on other markets. One of the main complaints of overseas buyers and distributors is that British companies fail to visit a market sufficiently often, or at an adequately senior level. The experience of successful exporting countries such as Germany, Switzerland and Sweden shows that it is far better to concentrate effort on a few markets, rather than spreading resources too thinly. The export executive responsible for the market must visit regularly and spend sufficient time working with sales staff and meeting important buyers. He or she must tread a very careful line between maintaining friendly relations and becoming over familiar. The executive's responsibility is to manage his or her company's business through the distributor's organization.

A relationship must be built based on mutual trust and respect between the principal and distributor. It is important that the export executive is given the authority to take decisions in the knowledge that they will be implemented. He or she will also need to spend time gaining the confidence of those within the company who contribute to export performance, whether in marketing, production, finance or distribution.

To summarize:

1 agents or distributors should be selling to the right kind of outlets and have good contacts;
2 their products should be compatible and not in direct competition;
3 where necessary, there should be technical competence, an understanding of the process in which the product is used and the ability to provide service;
4 the agent or distributor must be able to offer effective coverage within the exclusive territory;
5 the agency agreement must be checked out by a lawyer and should allow a trial period before commitment;
6 every potential distributor must be visited before an agreement is reached;
7 check the company's financial standing;

8   the distributor is an extension of your sales force and requires management and motivation;
9   maintain a businesslike relationship and avoid accepting hospitality which cannot be returned.

DELIVERY AND PAYMENT

The customer will be satisfied only when the order has been delivered. Many exporters still quote ex works or FOB (delivered on board ship) when the customer often expects delivery to the door, especially in Europe. It is important to find out what the customer prefers; how the competition quotes, and then match it. Some buyers in Europe will send their own vehicle to collect from several suppliers and so prefer ex works terms.

Delivery includes transport and customs clearance and means bearing the associated risks and costs. A freight forwarder can arrange all of this, but remember to include the charges quoted by the forwarder, including the fee, in your quotation to the customer.

A good fowarder should:

1   have a good knowledge of your markets and all the necessary transport, documentation, customs and banking requirements;
2   be well represented in the market;
3   be familiar with the requirements of your products, especially if they include dangerous goods or need specialized handling;
4   have the time and interest to help and advise you;
5   be financially sound, with good liability cover and, preferably, be a member of the Institute of Freight Forwarders which lays down strict professional standards.

The main delivery options are: road, especially for Europe; sea or combined sea/overland transport for longer distances; air freight; post, especially air parcel post; and express or courier services. The decision as to which to select is based on speed, cost, and customer and product requirements.

Many exporters continue to quote in sterling but it is important to ascertain what customers prefer, what the competition quotes, and then match it. Advice can be obtained from the bank which can also offer cover against fluctuations in exchange rates. Matching both

Table 26.4   Letter of credit documents rejected on first presentation

Date	Scope	Sets presented	Sets rejected on first presentation	Failure rate (%)
1981	Four banks	3261	1778	54.52
1983	Midland	1215	595	48.97
1986	Midland	1143	587	51.36
1986	Five banks	10096	5276	52.26

delivery terms and currency can add to the competitive edge of a good product at the right price. Ten thousand presentations were surveyed in November 1986 by Barclays, Hambros, Lloyds, Midland and National Westminster Banks. On first presentation, 52.26 per cent were rejected. Results of this and earlier surveys are shown in Table 26.4.

Export documentation is no longer difficult to understand thanks to the work of SITPRO. However, it is more complicated than home trade invoicing and an order can be held up because of a simple error, omission or missing document. Training courses are readily available for export staff and information can be obtained from SITPRO and also from local chambers of commerce.

Delays in payment are costly and bad debts even more so. Advice should always be sought from the bank's international specialist rather than simply dealing with a local branch. Seventy per cent of UK exports are sold on open account, 20 per cent under bankers' letters of credit and 10 per cent in other secured ways.

It is important to match competition and, in Europe and North America, most exports are sold on open credit terms. Thirty days is common but, realistically, this means two months from date of invoice until the arrival of payment. Remember that 60 days' credit will probably cost 3 or 4 per cent of the invoice value in interest.

Insurance against default by a customer can be provided by the Export Credits Guarantee Department and also by a number of private companies. Again, the bank can advise. A very useful checklist entitled 'How to control floating money' has been produced by SITPRO and can be obtained from that organization at the following address:

Simplification of International Trade Procedures Board
Almack House
26/28 King Street
London SW1Y 6QW

In export marketing, efficient documentation is vital and can make the difference between profit and loss. Here is a summary of points to watch.

1 *Setting up*
   • Find a good freight forwarder
   • Talk to your chamber of commerce
   • Talk to an international specialist from your bank
   • Talk to SITPRO
   • Check if you can take further advantage of other export services such as those of BOTB
2 *At the market research stage*
   • Check competitors' delivery terms
   • Check competitors' currency of sale (probably buyer's currency)
   • Check competitors' terms of payment (30, 60, 180 days, letter of credit, and so on)
   • Check normal methods of transport and obtain quotations
   • Check if subject to special controls or financial arrangements, such as for processed foodstuffs or textiles
3 *At the quotation stage*
   • Consult your freight forwarder and bank as necessary
   • Quote delivery terms and include these costs in the price
   • Quote in suitable currency
   • Specify a suitable method of payment
   • Quote the terms and methods of payment clearly
4 *When the order is received*
   • Check that the terms are as quoted and all delivery, paperwork, and payment requirements can be met
   • Arrange cover against foreign currency fluctuations and default
5 *When the order is ready – or preferably beforehand*
   • Contact the forwarder to arrange transport and insurance
   • Allow time to complete and process the documents, especially for special certificates or methods of payment where other organizations are involved

- Use the most appropriate SITPRO documentation method
6 *At regular intervals until payment is in your bank account*
    - Check progress of payment and other commercial factors such as the customer's total indebtedness to you
    - Check cumulative costs of interest, both from date of invoice and back to the date of receipt of order
7 *When payment has been received*
    - Check whether the intended margin has been realized after deducting all costs and overheads
    - Review the success of the transaction and what points to improve on next time

If all these points are carefully monitored, it is likely that you will, given hard work and some luck, build a profitable export business.

27

Direct response

Jack Zimmermann

Direct response advertising, or direct marketing as it is frequently called, is poised to become the most important part of the marketing mix. It is on the brink of stardom. Not because it has 'come of age' or has espoused 'professionalism', or for any of the other pseudo reasons so commonly quoted by practitioners of various sectors of marketing, but because market forces are right. (See also Chapter 36, 'Direct mail', which examines in detail this important subject of direct response advertising.)

The rising cost of advertising in the mass media to reach a decreasing audience and the knowledge that the target sector is a mere fraction of the declining total, coupled with advances in technology which few would have believed possible ten years ago, have made direct response the slumbering giant of the promotional industry.

But, soon everyone will realize its potential and the discipline will not only enter the mainstream of the marketing pool, it will swamp its erstwhile detractors in advertising and promotion. And the next five years will bring an increasingly attractive climate in which direct response can thrive. For the segmentation and proliferation of media will act in its favour, creating wholly new opportunities. The strengths of the medium are the tight targeting and precise monitoring it allows. Its weakness is that tight targeting has been the opposite of mass marketing. How can you tight target to four million people?

By using a combination of lists, socio-demographic targeting and a careful selection of the proliferating media it will be possible to select the most likely prospects without missing so many that the exercise becomes self-defeating. And it can be done so cost-effectively that it makes other forms of promotion look profligate.

THE EARLY YEARS

There was a time when it seemed that direct response advertising had exhausted its potential. In the 1920s, 1930s and early postwar period direct mail, mail order and direct response, aimed mainly at the C2D market, were thriving. Black and bloody advertisements in the national press were very successful. High circulations and low-cost advertising rates made it relatively easy to make a profit.

Most of the items were sold on price. The direct response advertisers had cut out the retailer, removed the necessity for expensive showrooms and needed to employ very few staff, so they could afford to sell goods cheaply.

There was also a shortage of disposable income which made price cutting even more desirable, and research showed that people liked receiving parcels through the post; it made them feel remembered and important.

Most items on offer were family goods; boots, shoes and, in the early days, patent medicines and pick-me-ups – the sort of goods which today would not be allowed to be advertised.

Direct response continued to thrive after the war, when there were huge supplies of army surplus goods and acute shortages of just about everything. Many a fortune was made in those days selling anything from army boots to army surplus chairs. One advertisement, in a national Sunday newspaper sold 16 000 pairs of boots.

It took about three years to clear the bulk of the stocks. Most of the advertisements appeared in the national and associated media, but *Exchange and Mart* was playing its part in building many of the postwar direct response giants. But as the supply of consumer goods improved and the advertising rates increased in relation to circulation, these small ads in the national press became less and less viable.

For many years there had been two or three pages of small ads in the national and, after the surplus boom, there was always great reader interest in the type of items promoted – lift-up shoes, trusses, copper bracelets to cure rheumatism – and every conceivable angle seemed to be explored. Readers were still attracted by low prices, however, and the margins were no longer there. The three pages shrank to three columns, and the specialist agencies, which might each have handled twenty such clients, turning out advertisements by the dozen and making a lucrative income, hit hard times. But as the C2D 'gold-mine' dried up, the ABC1 'diamond-mine' was being discovered.

THE 1970s

In the 1960s the first Sunday colour supplements were launched and their ingenious salespeople set about convincing advertisers of all kinds that up-market colour would bring undreamed-of sales.

People like Bob Scott, founder of Scotcade, and advertisers like MFI, were the trail blazers. (MFI is now the biggest retail advertiser in the UK spending more than £20 million a year to promote its 130 huge stores, but in those days it was just emerging from a total reliance on direct response advertising by opening the first of its retail outlets.) They saw the sense in showing their products in colour and targeting a little further up-market to the people who earned more money. Their pragmatism paid off.

Without the Sunday magazines the 1970s direct response boom would never have happened and many of the giants such as Scotcade and Kaleidoscope, which became household names, would never have made their first million.

Some of those who set out to master this market were rewarded with massive success. Some once-famous names may no longer be in the marketplace but their successors are still there, successful, organizations such as the John Harvey Collection and Harlington House.

There were some spectacular failures too. But it must be remembered that most of the companies which prospered were very small initially. Some lacked the vision or experience to change their operations as their sales grew. They failed to expand, or did not have sufficient warehouse space to house the turnover they could now expect and so started to disappoint loyal customers. More often, they could not properly handle the buying for their expanding businesses. And, with direct response, the buyer is usually more important than the marketer because the product is the most important ingredient in the mix.

THE PRODUCT

Direct response marketing has always offered people something which is either not freely available or is not available elsewhere at the price on offer. To succeed, the direct response marketer must be able to source such goods and acquire them in sufficient quantity and quality to fulfil demand and keep the buyer satisfied. And the next offer must always be waiting in the wings. Scotcade gained its first success with non-stick saucepans from Taiwan – a good product aimed at the right sort of customer. But it's a tough business and very difficult to keep producing unusual items. Once the products become too familiar, buyers rapidly lose interest.

The best items are light, robust, durable and capable of being presented well in print – black boxes pose problems. It helps with targeting if the product is also attractive to a definable type of consumer. In fact, the golden rule of marketing must be followed: the product, audience, pricing, timing and proposition all need to be right. Pure creativity does not work in isolation, it must be used to harmonize with characteristics of known customer groups or to fit the desired prospect's profile.

The best products are usually items which people know but which are offered in, say, a wider range of colours than usual or at a particularly attractive price. Brand new concepts will sometimes fail because people cannot understand them, or do not believe they will work.

Direct response companies cannot afford to educate the public – it would take too much space. But interesting, as opposed to complicated, items will usually work because you can tell a good story about them. The product's benefit to the buyer is of supreme importance. Once this benefit has been identified, simplicity is often the keynote of success. All that needs to be done is to show how the product meets the need, as clearly as possible.

TECHNIQUES

There are also techniques which the 'old hands' of the direct response world use to increase response rate. These are some of them.

1   Where a product has perceived monetary value, a discount can

work wonders. This does not have to be 'money off', it could be 'buy within the next three weeks before the price increases' or 'only 2000 available at this price'.

2   Researchers say that peak goodwill exists at the time the customer receives his or her first order and feels pleased with the purchase. At this moment it is possible to employ the 'bounce back' technique by including in the fulfilment package such things as information on another product, news of a special discount on related products or details of old offers.

3   Time limits can prove very persuasive, especially when linked with a token reward. (Since people who do not reply to an advertisement or mail shot within seven days are very unlikely ever to do so, it is worth offering them an incentive.)

4   Valued customers can be offered free gifts as incentives – either to buy more or to introduce a friend.

5   First impressions do count, so the creativity and style of the advertisement should ideally be linked to the graphics and colour of the packaging or envelope and its contents. When the initial contact with the customer is being made by letter or leaflet delivered to the door, an unusual envelope size or colour can make it more tempting or memorable.

6   Since the postage/delivery price will be the same irrespective of its contents (and this will usually be the biggest cost involved) it is worth considering increasing the quality of the contents of the leaflet/letter. Would beter paper or more colour make a difference for very little extra cost per item?

7   Where a letter forms part of the promotional package it should be conversational, have short paragraphs, and underlining and capitals should be used to add prominence to the main propositions. A second colour can help, and postscripts can be effective.

8   Even the most profitable formula can be improved, so try 'liberating' the product – 'FREE' is a wonderful word.

9   The response mechanism, which might be a coupon, telephone number or sticker, should probably be planned and designed first. Avoid giving customers too many choices – it can confuse them.

10   All media should be considered, television, radio and even posters can all be used to lift response in certain cases. Bonusprint was the first advertiser to link a nationwide door-to-door

distribution of photo-processing envelopes with a national TV advertising campaign telling people to look out for the envelopes and use them. It was an expensive and daring move, but it paid off handsomely.

11 There is nothing wrong with long copy. It often works by increasing commitment. But lower creative standards should never be accepted simply because it is a direct response promotion. And if someone else's good idea is working – borrow it. It might work even better for you.

12 Loose inserts can be far more cost-effective than on-page advertisements, and more noticeable and colourful. This format will also impose fewer creative constraints and can be used in several different ways, for example as showroom literature, in a door-to-door drop, and for testing. Most publishers will agree to part-circulation inserts, and in media testing cost per thousand is normally the most important factor.

13 Testing is vital. Test, test and test again. Test the product, the media, the copy, the layout, everything you can – and keep testing. But test only one element at a time, unless a comparison is being made between a completely new advertisement and the control advertisement (the one that secured most response last time).

14 The list is the crux of the business, even where regular advertising is taking place. Purging (getting rid of duplications, people who have 'gone away' or died) is vital, as is file segmentation to provide targets for the next offer. The minimum segmentation should be: product bought, credit scoring, order value, buying channel, geographical location, customer's value and buying method (cash or credit). The list can also be segmented demographically.

15 There are several ways of judging results. The best five are probably percentage conversion of enquiry, cost per enquiry, cost per order, sales per order and percentage conversion of enquiry to order.

These points are known to any experienced direct response marketer. But what separates professionals from gifted amateurs is that they know that things are likely to go wrong – which is why it is sensible to test as many variables as possible.

TESTING

The product is obviously the most vital factor. It follows, therefore, that its potential saleability must be the first thing to test.

The offer is also important. Should credit terms be made available? What about a free trial? Should there be a reward for speedy response? Then there are the media. Will mailings be better than door-to-door deliveries? Will advertising space or loose inserts be more effective?

The format of the advertisement or mailing can make a big difference. Unless all the sensible alternatives are examined, the product has not really been tested.

Even when everything has been researched and the client is delighted with the results, the control should be perpetually analysed and tuned. The new advertisement which secures a response 50 per cent higher than the control advertisement is not a figment of a fevered imagination, it happens all the time.

The product, offer, media and creative work can all be tested before a campaign goes national.

MEDIA

Before the tests can start it is necessary to make decisions about the target market and which media are likely to work best.

Any company which does not have a list of existing customers, and most of those that do, will need to rely on advertising. For consumer products, the Sunday supplements or the credit card magazines (Access, Barclaycard, Trustcard) are probably best.

It is possible to test in, say, the *Observer*, by using half a page, which costs about £6 000 and offers a circulation of about 600 000. The run can be split if necessary. If the advertisement worked in the *Observer*, you could then place it in other national colour supplements knowing that the product was satisfactory. Test the range of media to discover which works best. If the initial advertisement did not work, there would be no point in trying it in, say, the *Sunday Telegraph* without either changing the creative concept or the pricing.

Women's magazines tend not to be as successful as the colour supplements – unless you are selling fashion, and even then for most of them the price range would need to be modest: £30 to £40 would be too much. Goods sold under the name of the magazine itself, for example the IPC Women's Magazine Group direct response company, will attract a far greater response than offers of similar goods at a similar price from an unknown company.

The same is true of brand name packages in the financial services area. People in Britain are still a little afraid of mail order, unlike customers in America for whom it is an accepted part of life. Although the various customer guarantees and the safeguards offered by publishing companies tend to make it relatively safe in the UK, nevertheless most respondents prefer the security of a 'big name' company.

Whether the offer appears through their door, in the mail or in the pages of a magazine or newspaper, the 'household' name will always do better than the unknown contender. This is why banks and insurance companies have been so successful in 'piggy-back selling', that is, approaching their current account customers and policyholders with offers of, for example, mortgages or pension schemes.

Until this year very little research had been dome into attitudes to and the effectiveness of door-to-door distribution. However, in 1987, Circular Distributors, the longest-established and largest of the UK distribution companies, commissioned research company Millward Brown to carry out a survey into the medium.

The sample comprised 400 households in towns throughout Britain, which had been part of a CD Share Plan – that is, the delivery of several different leaflets at the same time – plus a further 200 where distribution was 100 per cent guaranteed. Respondents in 85 per cent of the CD sample homes and 89 per cent of the control sample remembered receiving at least one of the items delivered. Millward Brown comments: 'The general level of distribution achieved by Circular Distributors was very high, only marginally below the realistic maximum. And much of the distribution took place during a period of extreme weather conditions, when communication was often difficult.'

Fifty-seven per cent of recipients, when questioned about their reading habits, said they 'usually look through and read things that interest them' and 39 per cent agreed that they welcomed receiving leaflets through the door.

Door-to-door distribution has been one of the leading growth media of the decade, yet is still looked upon by many potential clients

494

with scepticism and fear. Rumours of dumping (throwing away bundles of undelivered leaflets) and fears that recipients dispose of items unread have stopped many potential clients from using the medium. Perhaps the research will help change such attitudes.

It is a medium much used by photo-printing companies, double and secondary glazing firms, mail order catalogues in search of new agents and, more recently, personal finance companies – CIS has long done its direct response marketing via the medium.

The emergence of more sophisticated targeting techniques (CACI's Acorn has been widely used in the medium for about eight or nine years while Pinpoint has been used extensively for the last three) has made door-to-door distribution even more cost-effective as a direct response vehicle.

Those media which prove to be effective should be used at regular intervals and should continue to generate a response for a relatively long time – until the law of diminishing returns sets in. With the Sunday colour supplements the best level of repeat tends to be about five weeks. Since there are several supplements this enables direct response companies to place at least one advertisement in a different colour magazine every week. The larger companies will run five or six offers simultaneously, so that they have a different offer in every magazine every week on a regular cycle.

It is vital to have the next offer ready in anticipation of replies tailing off on an existing one.

Almost all advertisers use their respondents as the basis of lists of targets to whom they can sell further products, often via direct mail shots. They can also sell, swap or merge these lists with companies which have similar types of customers. However, some companies still do not compile lists. Bonusprint, for example, claims that lists are irrelevant for its purposes since people will use the service only when they have a film to be developed. Instead, Bonusprint sends two new envelopes along with the prints. Some photo-developing companies also enclose free films or leaflets promoting other goods or services.

THE MERGER OF MARKETING DISCIPLINES

Bonusprint is the exception rather than the rule. Direct mail's personal approach has been used successfully in generating a response from people who do not seem to be influenced by other forms of advertising. Many charities rely on it for the bulk of their donations, and some of the biggest retail stores, such as Harrods and Debenhams, use their list of customer account holders to market goods as well as for sales promotions and loyalty-building exercises.

In the motor industry, the names and addresses of new car buyers have been used to support dealer-based direct mail campaigns, sell accessories, introduce new products and market services. They are also sometimes used to quote a trade-in figure on the existing car when it becomes a couple of years old and even to encourage the owner to upgrade to a larger model as the family grows.

Within realms such as these the boundaries between advertising, direct response, direct mail and sales promotion become blurred. This is why the experienced direct marketer will be unafraid to recommend a client to go one step beyond direct response if the possible outcome will benefit some part of the client's business.

A client who has separate above- and below-the-line agencies, and possibly even separate PR, design and sales promotion companies too, may fail to benefit from this merging and mingling of the different disciplines. However, the concept of what Stan Rapp, chairman of Rapp and Collins (the world's third largest direct response agency, which has billings of more than 150 million dollars) calls MaxiMarketing, in his book of the same name, offers perhaps the most cost-effective way forward for today's advertisers. Rapp says:

> Many US marketers act as if they do not really want the customer in the first place.
>
> Many fulfilment packages seem like an afterthought. Last year we answered every automotive ad that offered additional information. Most of the time we received a showroom catalogue and a printed form letter that did not even have our name on it. This happens because the department that does the ad does not send out the information. This is a weakness with advertising everywhere in the world.
>
> Sometimes, the follow-up takes many weeks or longer to arrive, which is a sure way to kill a sale.

Rapp adds that studies have proved a precise correlation between prompt follow-up and sales.

On the merging of the various disciplines, Rapp says:

You have to do awareness advertising, or the competition will bury you. You have to do sales promotion. But to get an edge you have to use databases, and the company that uses them most extensively and effectively will win the market share fight of the 1990s.
Whereas, today, the primary advertising battle is on television, tomorrow the primary battle will be between databases.

An example of how the separate promotional techniques are beginning to merge is the link between premiums and direct response marketing – which used to be the exclusive domain of book clubs, mail order companies and publishers, like Readers Digest. Now premiums are being used in many areas of direct response. Insurance companies, investment brokers, credit card companies and banks are using them in mail and door-to-door shots to speed replies. A 'speed premium' can increase the total response level by 10 to 15 per cent.

'Member get member' techniques can be enhanced by the offer of a reward; since an average of 30 per cent of new prospects are discovered in this way, it is often more cost-effective than advertising.

Time-Life supported a new series of DIY books on home repair and home improvement with the offer of a free belt-style tool pouch to consumers who agreed to try the books for ten days. Anyone who subscribed to the series within seven days also received a free tool kit.

The financial institutions have also been quick to see the value of gifts. Most of the credit/charge cards have offered the standard credit-card calculator as an incentive in door-to-door or mail shots to enlist new customers. The financial sector is, in fact, one of the main users of all forms of direct response advertising at present. It has taken over from the retail sector as the biggest press advertiser. Organizations such as Sun Life, Abbey National and most of the other big insurance companies, building societies and loan companies are running advertisements in which coupons feature prominently. This is not surprising, since many people are keen to learn more about such subjects but do not want to be pestered by salespeople, either face to face or on the telephone. Direct mail and response offer a private and convenient option.

Computer and software companies, charities and retailers are other big users. Often the promotions to the sort of consumer interested in these areas can be termed 'lifestyle marketing'. This means that the sellers have taken the trouble to find and list the sort of people/families which will be interested in the sort of products they have to offer, on a long-term basis. They then carefully create propositions which will fit the consumers' needs in the years to come.

This is most easily illustrated in the children's goods marketplace. The marketer can be virtually certain that children will need more and different toys/clothes/sports equipment as they grow, so he or she follows up the first order (which will probably come as the result of a direct response advertisement) with regular mailings about other products. The sporting and leisure goods companies operate similarly.

Direct response techniques are also being used more widely in business-to business selling, but the marketplace and the media have not yet been quite right for massive expansion. However, the advance of technology and targeting techniques will eventually make this another huge growth area.

All this might make it appear that everyone's letterbox must be permanently stuffed with fulfilment packages and that the press is bristling with coupons yet it is a fact that most households receive fewer than one unsolicited mail package a week, and the average annual spend per household on direct response goods is still only around £15. The growth potential is still incredibly large.

In 1986, 71 per cent of the MEAL and Times top 100 companies used one or more of the direct response marketing disciplines, but research into exactly what they did is scanty. Direct mail figures are fairly comprehensive (the British Direct Marketing Association says that spending increased from £324 million in 1984 to £445 million in 1985, a rise of 37.3 per cent) but they tell only half the story. In America, direct response marketing is reckoned to account for 65 per cent of total marketing budgets.

Some of the biggest UK advertising agencies seem to believe that direct response marketing has a bright future. Since Young and Rubicam pioneered the multinational interest in direct marketing back in the early 1970s, when worldwide boss Ed Ney bought Wundermans, agencies have been acquiring direct marketing arms.

Ogilvy and Mather launched O and M Direct in 1977 and expanded it in 1985 with the purchase of Trenear-Harvey Bird and Watson. In the same year Davidson Pearce, McCann-Erickson, Leo Burnett and Grey all bought into the sector, and in the previous three years D'Arcy

MacManus Masius, Ted Bates, Doyle Dane Bernbach, Benton and Bowles and Foote Cone and Belding had all done so.

Agency clients are proving the validity of these moves as media costs rise while the computer byte (upon which so much of direct marketing's success depends) becomes cheaper. Most clients have their own computers and these are providing information about customers and prospects which they have never before had or been in the situation to exploit. Direct response marketing is offering them the ability to use these databases and to relate spending to results in a way never before envisaged.

As an extension of this they are able to run 'loyalty management' schemes which enable them to keep in touch with their customers, not only to sell them more but also to reduce the risk of successful predatory raids by competitors.

Although computers have made all this possible, they have not really created any new marketing techniques. They have merely added power and accuracy to the old ones.

TARGETING

One area which has seen massive improvement is targeting in the UK. Almost all targeting disciplines are based on a combination of the post code and the census.

The Post office divides Britain into 120 postal areas, subdivided into 2700 districts and 8900 sectors. A single sector contains 2500 households and is described by the first four characters of a postcode, for example NW1 5. CACI and Pinpoint use map-tracing techniques and computer power to convert these sectors into co-ordinates and store them in the memory. They then store data gleaned from 130 000 enumeration districts in the National Census (with some twelve to twenty enumeration points per sector) and combine the two sets of data, so that the geographic distribution of consumer characteristics can be easily seen and studied.

The targeted sets of consumers can be chosen and the information is coded in such a way that the desired addresses can be laser printed.

These techniques do much to explain the massive growth of direct mail and the current boom in door-to-door distribution. These systems do work, although why people should want to buy the same goods just because they live in similar houses in identical streets does seem to be an incredible coincidence. It is probably easier to understand why someone who can, say, afford to go on a Kuoni holiday could be presumed to have a large disposable income. This is where lists become relevant.

LISTS

Lists have been around for forty years, and some companies have been progressively building them for all that time. The computer revolution hit this marketplace about twelve years ago – until then it was a laborious process to collect names and addresses and almost impossible to keep lists clean.

The saying goes: 'The only list worth having is your own'. And your own customer base will certainly work the best, but it will need to have new blood added at regular intervals if it is to continue to produce results. This can be injected by advertising for new customers, or list buying.

Buying is becoming commonplace but it can be a precarious move because many lists have been overworked or are not quite correctly targeted. It is easy to get into the realms of junk mail in households which are fed up of being inundated with offers of the same type of product. Also, someone receiving several offers a week cannot possibly afford to buy them all – or might have sent for another offer and been disappointed with it.

Quite simply, it is easy to put the right propositions to the wrong people. Then there is the problem of the non-respondent. When should he or she be deleted from the list? Spalding, the bulb catalogue company, used to send catalogues to previous customers in the spring, autumn and spring and then delete anyone who had not reordered.

Women are by far the greatest 'responders', both for themselves and their families. Direct response advertisement and catalogues appeal particularly to people who see their time as valuable, not to be squandered. Working women fall very much into this category.

Many years ago people who lived in the country used to be the main mail order buyers, because they found it difficult to get to the shops. The car has changed all that. Now it is the 'townies', for whom traffic congestion, unhelpful shop assistants and lack of parking space make shopping in large towns a nightmare. They often turn to advertisements and catalogues for their goods.

CATALOGUES

In the postwar period, catalogue companies were the backbone of the direct response industry. They advertised in women's magazines and the national press, favouring the strong use of colour and emphasizing fashion – in those days half their sales came from that area.

At one time they were in a position to satisfy the UK's household needs – and they did not need to sell on cheap prices since they offered credit. They could sell products for £1 a week – for ever. People just kept adding to their order as they paid off part of the debt – a kettle this week, a dress next. They sold branded goods to a receptive audience.

Difficulties arose when agents stopped selling goods outside their immediate family. A catalogue the size of two telephones directories, printed on top quality paper and brimming over with full colour, was seen by an average of three and a half people. The massive on-cost this represented was daunting. But the catalogue industry is professional and clever and it had the bonus of being able to keep agents for many years once it had recruited them.

Databases were formed to indentify the buying habits of current and potential customers and new, smaller catalogues produced to suit their exact needs. These are more profitable since a smaller catalogue does not involve such large overheads and is sent to people more likely to buy from it.

THE FUTURE

As one door began to close others were technologically opened, and this will happen again and again with direct response. It will be used more and more, and seldom in isolation, since its strength is its position within the promotional and advertising mix. It will increasingly provide the basis for narrower casting to target audiences, rather then the broader appeal of television and the press.

As the various emergent communication technologies become commonplace, making viewdata, cable and satellite television and electronic mail everyday shopping tools, the shopping basket will be replaced by the computer 'mouse' and bracing advertisements will be superseded by those with response mechanisms.

28

Agents

Bernard Katz

A distribution channel, in marketing terms, is a pathway from the supplier of a product or service to the buyer. An agent is one form of distribution channel; a distributor is another. There are a number of different channels. A supplier makes use of one or more distribution channels as appropriate to the business.

THE DIFFERENCE BETWEEN AN AGENT AND A DISTRIBUTOR

The roles of agent and distributor are frequently thought to be the same. But although the terms are loosely interchanged, each has a specific function.

An agent is a person or company who sells goods and services on behalf of a principal. Goods are delivered by the principal directly to the customer – agents do not usually carry stocks. Payment is made by the customer directly to the principal. Remuneration is obtained by way of commission achieved on sales made to customers.

A distributor buys for his or her own account from a supplier and holds stocks. The distributor then sells on to the end-user. The manufacturer or supplier does not necessarily know the identity of the final purchaser. The distributor is responsible for securing payment for deliveries sold to his or her own customers.

Figure 28.1 illustrates how agents and distributors service a market. The operation of agent and distributor is the same in the home market and the export market; overseas, factors of language and business practice intrude. For example, in the Middle East agents and distributors carry stocks. Both are called agents.

In selling through agents and distributors, each method has advantages and disadvantages.

Advantages of selling through agents

1 The principal has direct contact with each customer. If the services of the agent are discontinued, the relationship with established customers can be maintained.
2 A full selling price is chargeable to all customers. Agent and principal must agree on whether commission is payable on the ex-works factory price , on the delivered site price or, overseas, on the FOB or CIF or any other export contract price. If it is payable on the CIF price, commission is being paid on the insurance and freight charges. Commission rates vary with the industry. On fashion goods the commission rate may be 10 per cent. In the steel industry it is 2 per cent or less.
3 Selling costs are minimal. There are the initial setting-up costs of attracting and screening applicants; the costs of interviewing prospective agents, with travel and hotel costs if the selection is made overseas. When appointed, an agent must be provided with samples of the product, either free or at a substantial discount. There are also printing costs for literature, visiting cards or special instructions. Overseas, printing is in the local language. Theoretically, after the set up-costs, agents begin working at their own expense and orders start to flow in.
4 Selling through agents requires little initial investment. That is why it is seen as an easy pathway to new business by companies wanting to grow. But all too often agents are appointed and the principal then waits and waits for orders that never come. The principal/agent relationship is rather like a marriage: as such both parties must work to achieve success. The principal's sales manager must visit the agent

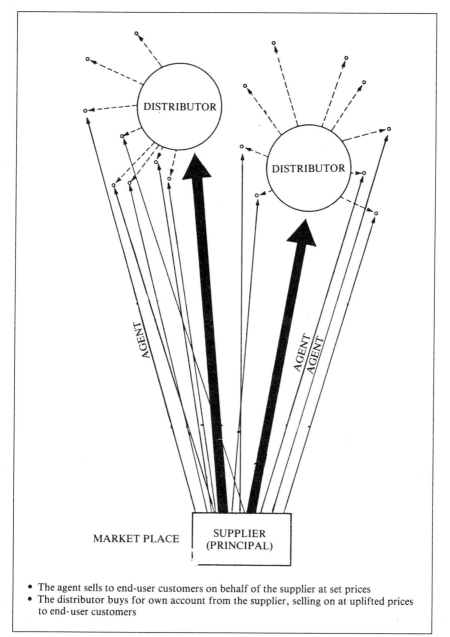

Figure 28.1   How agents and distributors service a retail outlet market

regularly to provide support and motivation. Every such visit can be merchandised by the agent setting up customer appointments.

5 There are opportunities for securing ongoing feedback from the marketplace. This requirement should be built into every agency agreement. An agent must report on progress regularly at weekly intervals. Overseas, particularly, agents are well placed to provide news of impending changes in legislation, demand, fashion trends and new product usage. The agent with his or her ear to the ground is often the first to encounter competitive action and strategies. This important market intelligence must be relayed to the principal.

Disadvantages of selling through agents

1 The unit order size is small rather then large.
2 Credit control management is necessary for a large rather than small number of customers.
3 Packaging and delivery costs are necessary for many small consignments.
4 The principal has no control over the sales effort exerted by the agent for the product.

Advantages of selling through distributors

1 Orders are large rather than small.
2 There are savings in packaging, delivery charges and insurance by making container-sized deliveries.
3 The opportunities for bad debts are reduced by having a small rather than large number of buyers.
4 Established distributors are often prepared to make prompt payment for their purchases to benefit from the maximum cash discounts.
5 When sales are contingent on pre or after-sales service, distributors are in a position to provide such service. They also have the organization to maintain spare parts stock.

Disadvantages of selling through distributors

1 When bad debts do occur they can be substantial due to the volume of business transacted by distributors.

2   Distributors demand a large discount off list prices because of the size of the orders placed. Margins vary with industries, but distributors require a high return, to compensate for their risks, investment and input. Overseas, distributors clear the goods through customs at the port or airport of entry, unpack and store them, and process them for sale to customers.

THE OBLIGATIONS OF THE PRINCIPAL TO THE AGENT

From the agent's point of view there are good and bad agencies. The agent lives by selling – from the sales, commissions are earned. Possession of an agency does not automatically guarantee that the agent earns money. An agent will require the following.

1   *A good product to sell.* Products that are new to a market and demand much groundwork before being accepted by customers, are unattractive to agents. The time required to gain consumer acceptance might more profitably be spent selling readily saleable products from other principals.

2   *Reliable early deliveries.* Commission is not usually earned until the goods have been delivered. If the delivery time is extended the agent must wait for the commission.

3   *Favourable commission terms.* Commission rates are frequently stable within an industry. The payment of larger than usual commission rates diminishes profitability for the principal. A higher than usual commission sometimes is offered to an agent for an introductory period, to launch a product new to a market. This is designed to compensate for the additional effort required. Careful consideration must be given to the demotivation factor, if a commission rate is to be reduced after an agreed period to that considered appropriate for normal sales.

   The time at which commission payments are to be made requires thought. Agents would like payment immediately the principal receives the orders. This system is open to abuse by sending fictitious orders to claim commission, which orders are subsequently cancelled. One option is for payments to be made when the principal receives payment; another – when regular business is sent by the agent – is monthly payments on a set day, subject to appropriate safeguards.

One situation where a higher than normal commission rate is payable is in a *del credere* agency. Here, the agent agrees to take financial responsibility for customers' orders, in the event of their default. Due to this commitment the agent will make the effort to ensure that there are no bad debts. *Del credere* agencies are not common. Usually they are created in export markets where credit and financial control by the principal is difficult.

4 *Favourable credit terms for customers.* The more attractive the deal for the customer, the easier it is for the agent to build up sales.

5 *Advertising and promotional support.* In distant areas of the home market, and overseas, the agent is often better placed than the principal to advise on promotional input appropriate to the territory – outside, that is, of judgements made by specialist advertising agencies. Most agents ask for and expect the principal to bear the cost of advertising and promotion. Full support or a negotiated compromise is a matter of judgement for the principal.

6 *Training in product knowledge and product usage.* Without doubt, a sound knowledge of the product is a precursor to effective selling. Whenever appropriate, the agent is invited to the factory for indoctrination and training. Any activity that reinforces a relationship between agent and principal is to be encouraged.

7 *Competitive prices.* Non-price competition is a marketing activity: it is quality, it is reliability, it is innovation – and it is something every manufacturer should explore and achieve. From the agent's point of view this is a complication. In general terms, agents believe that if the price is competitive, that is, low, they can sell. If it is high, it is difficult or impossible to sell.

THE RESPONSIBILITIES OF THE AGENT TOWARDS THE PRINCIPAL

The agent/principal relationship is two-way. Both principal and agent have expectations. When they are fulfilled the relationship is mutually rewarding. This does not always happen. Agents sometimes seek relationships in order to prevent a principal from competing against the products of another of the agent's principals. The agent is expected to fulfil certain obligations.

1 *Attract customers.* The agent's task is to find new customers with

whom to do business. The agent must be a self-starter, continually motivated to find new business from existing and new customers.

2 *Have a thorough product knowledge.* Incomplete knowledge inhibits sales. It also diminishes the credibility of the principal's image and products in the marketplace.

3 *Know all the regulations.* In the home market this means the implications of the Trades Descriptions Act; the current VAT regulations. Overseas, the agent must keep the principal informed of changes in tariff regulations, exchange control, health, safety and local legal requirements.

4 *Acquire and maintain a thorough knowledge of the market.* The agent should identify all the different segments into which the goods can be introduced.

5 *Report regularly.* Market intelligence is the life blood of a marketing plan. The agent must report regularly. A weekly report on the agent's activities helps the principal plan production and identify promotional help that could be made available. The report has two essential ingredients: what the agent has been able to achieve; and the constraints, in the form of external market forces, impeding progress.

For many agents paperwork is unpalatable. Their strengths lie in their selling skills. Filling in reports is felt to be unproductive and the task is delayed or ignored. Figure 28.2 illustrates an agent report form. A structured form eases the task for an agent and should always be provided.

6 *Maintain regular contact with customers.* An understanding of customers' needs and problems, reliability and regular contact are the ingredients of good business.

7 *Deal with complaints.* This aspect of the agent's work is often resented. It is not felt to be productive. The same resentment is felt towards filling in report forms. The time spent does not directly generate new business, but it is an integral part of the agency function. Overseas, delays at the docks and airports, and difficulties in customs clearance are problems local agents are better placed to deal with than their principals. In the home market, the agent who has taken the customer's order usually has a closer relationship with the customer than the principal, and is in a better position to understand, pacify and resolve the customer's complaint.

8 *Identify appropriate training requirements.* The agent's perception

Agent _____

Territory _____

Week No.	Date	Customer contract		Business Taken	ACTION
		Old	New		
1					
			Total £		
2					

Figure 28.2 Agent's weekly report form

of training needs reinforces the principal's marketing approach to meet customer needs precisely. Product usage training is particularly important.

9 *Stockholding*. Strictly speaking, an agent is not called upon to carry stocks. In certain trade sectors agents do, particularly in the Middle East. Title to the goods does not pass to the agent, but remains with the principal. The agent provides storage and handling facilities on an expenses basis, and earns commission in the usual way, from sales. Commissions are increased to reflect the additional obligations.

A variation of this situation, usually in export trade, is when business is increased through *consignment trading*. The principal decides, in consultation with the agent, that there is the potential business additional to the orders already placed. So goods are sent by the manufacturer and stored in a bonded warehouse until called forward against fresh orders taken by the agent. The principal then authorizes their release, and they are delivered to the customers. Bonded warehouses are used because only storage and transport charges are incurred; customs duty and import taxes are not payable until the goods are despatched from the warehouse.

SELECTING AN AGENT

The problems of selecting an agent able to generate good business are considerable, particularly in small or specialist markets. Agents with a good track record are already committed. There is usually no shortage of would-be agents, but how does one identify which inexperienced agent will be able to overcome the problems of customer resistance and disinterest? Figure 28.3 provides a checklist of points to be considered. Other items can be added which are pertinent to specific industry and market requirements.

Would-be agents are invariably optimistic. They are certain that good business will ensue. They are also determined to wrest a sole agency agreement from the new principal – for as large a territory as can be secured. Exclusive rights are a powerful marketing tool, when business goes well. Such rights should not be granted lightly. Performance-related safeguards can be introduced.

Territory demarcation is an important issue. It relates both geographi-

	YES	NO
Are there live contacts in the market place?	☐	☐
Is there a sound knowledge of the market?	☐	☐
Is there evidence of a good business reputation?	☐	☐
Is the agent financially sound?	☐	☐
Has the agent provided details of other agencies held?	☐	☐
Does a cross-check with the agent's other principals confirm that the information given is complete?	☐	☐
Is there evidence of the agent's competence technically?	☐	☐
Is there evidence that the agent can sell?	☐	☐
Is there evidence that the agent can cover the projected territory effectively?	☐	☐
Is the agent able to justify his or her projection of future business if the agency is granted?	☐	☐
Overseas, does the agent have adequate language capability?	☐	☐

If the answer is *yes* – OK. If *no*, probe to discover the extent of shortcomings.

Figure 28.3 Criteria for agent selection

cally to a market and to specified products or services supplied. How and when commission is paid on business obtained from a territory must be precisely defined, or circumstances may rise where two agents claim commission on the same transaction, each believing the claim valid.

To give an example, agent Smith sends in an order from a multiple retail outlet customer, whose head office is in his territory. Some of the goods are for a retail outlet in the territory of the adjacent agent, Jones. Jones claims commission on all goods delivered within her territory. Smith claims commission on all goods delivered against his original order.

LOCATING A NEW AGENT

There are various channels for finding an agent. Each may be employed concurrently, to generate a pool of names from which selection is made. The channels are described below.

Personal contact

Suitable candidates may be found from the spectrum of contacts acquaintances built up in the course of business. Experience of the trade develops a repertoire of knowledge and skills helpful in resolving agent selection needs.

Recommendations

There is a difference between recommendation and personal contact. Existing customers are asked to recommend an agent likely to be interested in handling the principal's goods.

The customer is often willing to do this when he or she is satisfied with the service provided by an agent already calling for another firm. A local agent keen to meet a customer's specific needs offers attractive commercial benefits when the principal's factory or warehouse is remote from the customer.

Advertisements

Advertisements inviting contact from agents are placed in the national or local press, and in the trade press. A useful directory is *British Rates and Data* (BRAD), obtainable from:

British Rates and Data
McLean Hunter House
Chalk Lane
Cockfosters Road
Barnet
Herts
EN4 0BU
Telephone: 01–441 6644

It provides details of every trade publication listed by title and by product or service. Help overseas for the names and addresses of suitable publications is available from:

Department of Trade and Industry
1 Victoria Street
London SW1H 0ET
Telephone: 01-215 7877

If an advertisement is translated into a local language overseas, it is essential that the text is colloquially and grammatically correct. This criterion applies to all translation. An appropriate check is to use three stages:

1   translate from English into the local language;
2   translate from the text back into English, by a third party;
3   compare English translation with the original text.

Chambers of commerce

Agents who are members of a chamber of commerce use the services of the chamber to further their activities. Contact with chambers may therefore produce names and contacts wishing to be considered. As a general rule chambers supply lists of names and addresses to anyone who asks, if it will promote the business of the members of that chamber. There is less co-operation if the objective is only to promote the business of the person or company making the enquiry. It is sometimes expedient, particularly overseas, to take out membership of a chamber of commerce – provided that research shows the potential for business in the particular market is good.

Department of Trade and Industry representative service

When seeking overseas agents the department is able to provide help. For a fee it provides a short list of businesses in the marketplace. They will all have been screened, and are specifically interested in working with the exporter's product or service.

IDENTIFYING THE TRAINING NEEDS OF NEW AGENTS

At the selection interview it is important to identify the competence and selling skills of the agent. This can be evaluated by probing methodically into the different activity areas.

Figure 28.4 illustrates a training audit grid. The interviewer marks the response at each level on a scale of 1 (weak) to 7 (strong). The mark is a subjective judgement based on the agent's responses to the prompt questions listed below, which follow the format of the grid.

Prospecting

By telephone
- Do you use the telephone to sell?
- Do you use the telephone to make appointments?
- Do you use the telephone to advise if you are late for an appointment?
- How do you eliminate calls having little chance of success?
- Do you use a script for the telephone calls?
- What do you do when the customer says 'No'?
- When the call is not succeeding how do you pave the way for future contact?
- Do you maintain careful records of all prospecting calls?

By letter
- Do you have the resources to prospect by letter?
- Do you have an effective format for a prospecting letter?
- Do you confirm business appointments by letter?
- Is your correspondence with customers businesslike and efficient?

By cold canvass
- How frequently do you make cold calls?
- Is block canvassing likely to generate good business?

Distributing the Product

Agent_____Market_____Date_____Controller_____

	Weak 1	2	3	4	5	6	Strong 7
PROSPECTING SKILL							
by phone							
letter							
cold canvas							
SALES REPRESENTATION SKILL							
Visual aids							
Qualifying customer needs							
Passing benefit messages							
Overcoming customer objections							
Closing Increasing order size							
NEGOTIATING SKILL							
Preparation							
Tactics							
Ability to create variables							
Bargaining skills							
GETTING REPEAT BUSINESS							
Post-delivery visit							
Regular visit							
By telephone							
By referrals							
PLANNING							
Call cycle							
Personal time management							
Report writing							

Use the training audit prompt questions to probe agent's performance and abilities. Evaluate on a scale from 1 to 7. Enter mark by ticking appropriate column.

Figure 28.4 Training audit grid

- What target number of cold calls per customer visit is practical?

- Have you evolved an effective introductory gambit for the cold call?
- Do you maintain records of all cold calls made?

The sales presentation

Visual aids/samples
- What visual aids/samples do you normally use?
- How can visual aids reinforce your sales presentation?
- At what stage of the presentation should samples/visual aids be introduced?

Qualifying customer needs
- What questions identify customer interest?
- What questions pinpoint customer needs?

Product benefit messages
- What contribution do benefit messages make to winning sales?
- What techniques are useful in passing benefit messages?

Overcoming customer objections
- How do you overcome a customer's 'No'?
- What do you do when a customer says 'I'll think about it?'
- How do you identify whether a customer's objection is the real objection?
- What important rule or rules apply when countering a customer's objections?

Closing
- How many closing techniques do you know?
- How many closes do you use?
- How often do you use the trial close?
- What do you do when the customer says 'No'?

Increasing the customer's order size
- When should one attempt to increase the order size?
- How is the order size increased?
- How frequently should pressure be applied to the customer to give bigger orders?

Negotiating skills

Preparation
- What is the difference between negotiating and selling?
- How does one prepare for negotiations?
- What do you understand by the three negotiating positions:
  - must achieve or deadlock
  - intend to achieve
  - would like to achieve?

Ability to create variables
- What is the value of the variable in negotiation?
- What can be termed variable in respect of the products we are discussing?

Tactics
- What different tactics are effective in negotiation?
- How can you create time to think in a negotiation when the other side takes you by surprise?

Bargaining skills
- What questions should be asked before granting a concession?
- What do you consider to be the most important rules of bargaining?
- What is the effect of the other side linking all its issues toegther?

Getting repeat business

Post-delivery visit
- What are the objectives of calling on a customer after a delivery is made?
- What is an appropriate pattern for a post-delivery visit?

Regular visit
- How frequently should regular visits be made to customers?
- Is it feasible to sell the idea of a telephone call instead of a visit, to save the customer time?
- What is the approach you adopt on a regular call to a customer?

- What innovations are likely to increase the volume of business obtained?

Telephone call
- Is it possible to take repeat business by telephone?
- Should the telephone be used to make an appointment before calling for repeat business?
- Has a script been developed to secure repeat business by telephone?

Referrals
- Have you ever asked customers to recommend other buyers?
- When is the best time to ask for a referral?
- Have you ever asked a buyer to introduce you to another buyer?
- What form of incentive should motivate a buyer to recommend another buyer?

Planning

Call cycle
- Taking into account your other commitments, how frequently would our customers be called on?
- How frequently would potential customers be called on?
- What proportion of business is likely to come from what proportion of customers – that is, would, say 80 per cent of orders come from 20 per cent of the customers?
- How frequently do you call on the most important customers?
- How much time do you consider is necessary to build up a satisfactory customer base?

Personal time management
- Do you achieve everything that you set out to do?
- Do you plan your day?
- Would you like help in improving the management of personal time?

Report writing
- When do you write up your notes on performance?
- What records do you keep?
- What is the most common cause of interruption to your report-

writing programme?

• What is your understanding of the reason why we insist on receiving regular reports from you?

PROTECTION FOR THE PRINCIPAL AND THE AGENT

When business is good there seems little need for protection. Agent and principal can work together without any formal agreement: orders are sent; deliveries are made to customers; commissions are paid.

Sometimes the relationship is soured by problems arising from disputes. For example, an agent passes an order to the principal for specialist equipment for urgent delivery by a particular date. The order is accepted. Due to incomplete delivery instructions, the subsequent delivery is misrouted, the equipment arrives late, and delivery is not accepted by the customer. The agent claims commission on the order value, which the principal is reluctant to pay, considering that the non-acceptance is the agent's fault for providing incomplete delivery instructions. There is also the loss to the principal in having to dispose of the rejected equipment.

One method of resolving disputes before they occur is to enter into a binding agreement constructed to deal with all matters of dispute likely to arise. When a problem arises, the agreement provides the solution. The absence of a formal contract safeguards neither agent not principal. Performance can be evidence that a contractual relationship was the intention of the parties, whether or not an actual document is signed.

Whether an agreement is intended to cover all likely areas of dispute or simply the most important, there are a number of essential considerations. The following aspects should be discussed by both parties and incorporated in a principal/agent agreement.

1 *A statement of the parties to the agreement.*
2 *The purpose of the agreement.* One party agrees to appoint the other as agent. The other agrees to act as agent, subject to the terms and conditions stated.
3 *The territory.* Geographically the territory may be a country, a county or region, a town or, say, all land north of a given river. The description must allow precise understanding of the territory limits. The boundaries may also be political, for example the EEC, so long as the understanding is clear.

520

4 *The product range.* Sometimes a manufacturer employs more than one agent in the same territory, selling different items produced by the organization. The products are usually differentiated by value added, for example a textile manufacturer sells piece goods and made-up garments from those piece goods into the same territory.

5 *The principal's discretion to accept orders.* The agent's duty is to obtain orders but not to enter into binding contracts for the principal. The principal confirms all orders placed. This is a safeguard against orders being placed which cannot be executed for reasons of inadequate production capacity, time limitation or exhausted stocks.

6 *Commission.* The basis on which commission is paid is clearly stated – when, how frequently, subjected to what exclusions, and whether on orders received directly or indirectly.

7 *House accounts.* There are often existing clients within a territory before the agent is appointed. When very strong personal relationships exist between the principal and a client, such clients are nominated as falling outside the agent's sphere of activity. No commission is payable for goods delivered to these clients, notwithstanding arrangements for commission payable on all direct and indirect business.

   A new agent appointed to an existing territory expects to inherit live accounts. House accounts are likely to be few in number.

8 *Consignment goods.* The terms are given under which consignment deliveries are made, how they are to be insured, and how to be disposed of on termination of the agreement.

9 *Term of agreement.* The period for which the agreement is binding must be stated, together with the period of notice of termination to be given by either party. Termination is to be notified formally in writing.

10 *Duties of the principal.* The main duties of the principal are: to pay the agent's commission due; to pay expenses, where agreed, and provide an indemnity if loss is suffered.

   The principal's right to deal with other agents or to make sales to the territory other than through the agent is to be clearly defined.

The final document reflecting the needs and objectives of both parties should be ratified by appropriate legal advisers.

APPENDIX

Form of agency agreement
This document sets out the terms of the agency agreement prepared and sold by the Manufacturers' Agents' Association of Great Britain and Ireland (Incorporated), of 13A West Street, Reigate, Surrey RH2 9BL.

[copyright of the Manufacturers' Agents' Association]

THIS AGENCY AGREEMENT   made the

day of   198

BETWEEN   of

(hereinafter called the Principals) of the one part

and   of

(hereinafter called the Agent) of the other part WHEREBY IT IS AGREED AS FOLLOWS:

1   The principals hereby appoint the Agent as their sole agent in
    area for the sale of all goods manufactured or dealt with by them
    for a period of [say five years] and thereafter until the appointment
    shall be determined by six/twelve [delete as necessary] calendar
    months' notice in writing which may be given by either party after
    the said period expiring on the   198 [end of such five years or
    as the case may be] on the 1st day of any month.

2   The agent shall exercise all reasonable care and skill in the perfor-
    mance of his duties and shall act faithfully on behalf of the
    Principals.
        The Principals will do all things reasonably necessary to enable
    the agent to earn his due commission and will supply him with such
    information as he may reasonably require.

3   The agent will forward to the Principals all enquiries he may receive
    and shall not (without express authority) enter into any contract on
    behalf of the Principals nor bind or attempt to bind them in any
    way, nor shall the Agent (without express authority) receive any
    cheques or money on behalf of the Principals.

4   (a) The principals will provide the Agent with all necessary samples
    patterns demonstration models catalogues price lists and sales
    literature generally to enable him to conduct the agency, and the
    Agent shall not be liable for any loss or damage to any such samples
    or other of the aforesaid items if not caused or contributed to by the
    negligence or default of the Agent.
    (b) The Principals shall pay all carriage, freight, customs and excise
    duties, insurance and all other payments reasonably neccessary in
    respect of the said samples and other items, including the cost of
    delivery to the Agent in the first place and their return to the
    Principals or as the Principals may order on the termination of the
    agency.
    (c) The agent shall have a lien on any such samples or other items in
    his possession in respect of any moneys outstanding from the
    Principals by way of commission or expenses or any other sums due
    to him from the Principals.

5   The Principals shall forward all goods which they agree to sell to
    customers in the said area direct to such customers together with
    invoices and other documents in respect of any such sale but they
    will at the time of sending the customers any such invoices or other
    documents send to the Agent a duplicate or copy thereof and they
    will also send a copy or duplicate of every order when received to
    the Agent.

6   (a) The remuneration of the Agent shall be by way of commission and shall be at the rate of [rate of commission to be filled in] per cent upon the invoice price of all goods sold to the customers in the said area whether from orders received by the Principals through the Agent or from customers direct.

(b) After termination of the agency the Agent shall be entitled to commission at the same rate on all orders accepted from such customers up to the date of such termination.

(c) The commission shall in all cases be at the said rate on the normal invoice price and no deductions may be made from the commission by the Principals in respect of any rebates or other concessions granted by them to the customers (other then the usual trade discounts).

7   The Principals shall pay to the Agent such expenses as are reasonably incurred on behalf of the Principals (or as may be otherwise agreed upon between the parties). The Principals shall also pay the cost of all advertising and publicity but no such expense shall be incurred by the Agent without the consent of the Principals.

8   The Principals shall on the [date to be filled in] day of each calendar month send to the Agent an account showing the particulars of all sales during the preceding calendar month to customers within the said area together with a statement of the commission due to the Agent and a remittance for the amount of the commission shall accompany the said statement. After termination of the agency the Agent shall be entitled to commission on all orders as set out in clause 6 hereof and the Principals shall continue to deliver commission accounts accompanied by remittances as above mentioned until all such orders have been executed.

9   (a) The Agent may upon presentation of any account in respect of commission by the Principals request an extract from the accounts and other books of the Principals relating to such commission, and the Principals shall deliver to the Agent an extract from all such relevant books.

(b) Where the Principals fail to deliver such an extract or where the accuracy of such extract is disputed by the Agent, the Agent shall be entitled either personally or by his solicitor or by a qualified chartered accountant acting on his behalf to inspect the relevant books and accounts of the Principals.

10 The Agent shall not be entitled to commission on the amount of any invoice if such amount shall be wholly or partly lost by reason of the insolvency of the customers, and in the event of any commission having already been paid in respect of such amount the same shall be refunded by the Agent to the Principals.

11 (a) In the event of the agency lawfully being terminated by the Principals for any reason other than wilful misconduct on the part of the Agent, the Agent shall be entitled to an amount to be paid to him by the Principals by way of compensation for loss of goodwill suffered by the Agent.

(b) Such compensation shall be an amount equal to the average annual sum earned by the Agent in respect of commission under the agency during the five years immediately preceding the said termination.

(c) In the event of the agency having subsisted for a shorter period than five years, the amount of the compensation shall be the average annual sum of the entire period of the agency.

(d) Where the Agent has completed more than five years' service as Agent to the Principals the amount to be paid in compensation shall be increased by 2.5 per cent in respect of each completed additional year of service.

(e) Such compensation is payable three months after the termination of the agency.

12 Compensation as is contained in clause 11 above shall also be payable where the Principals sell lease hire mortgage or otherwise dispose of their business or where for any reason the Principals cease to carry on business or become bankrupt or (in the case of a company) become insolvent or go into liquidation.

13 In the event of the agent retiring after the age of sixty-five, or on his death, compensation shall also be payable to him or his personal representative or representatives as the case may be as contained in clause 11.

14 This agreement shall be construed in all respects in accordance with English law and for this purpose the Principals hereby submit themselves to the jurisdiction of the English courts [*this clause is required for principals outside England and Wales*].

525

As witness the hands of the parties the day and year first above written

Signed ....
in the presence of:

Signature of witness
Address
Occupation
Signed ....
in the presence of:

Signature of witness
Address
Occupation

FURTHER READING

Katz, B. (1987), *Managing Export Marketing,* Gower, Aldershot.

29

Wholesaling

John A. Dawson and Ian Watson

'Wholesaling' is a somewhat nebulous concept. One possible definition would be that it is a stage in the distribution channel where an independent agency provides the facility for buyers to purchase a variety of product lines for non-personal consumption. It must, however, be noted that a number of other types of organization meet several of these criteria and yet are not strictly in the wholesaling business.

Agencies such as third party specialist transport and distribution firms, dealers and brokers are all middlemen in the exchange process, but they differ from wholesalers in two vital ways. The wholesaler takes title to the goods while these other agencies are employed by suppliers to distribute and do not normally take title. Second, wholesalers are responsible for the buying decisions in respect of the goods they handle, which differentiates them from the distributors and agents who do not take buying decisions.

WHOLESALING IN THE PRODUCT CHANNEL

Before examining the function of the wholesaler it is useful to establish its position in the distribution chain. Figures 29.1 and 29.2 illustrate its position as an intermediary between the source of products and their end use. Product sources may include primary producers, manufacturers, importers and other wholesalers. End use, as indicated in the definition, is not strictly confined to retail outlets. For worked raw materials such as

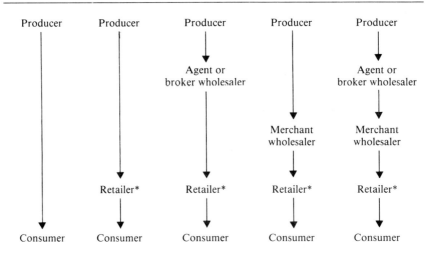

*This may include delivery to the retailer's regional distribution centre (RDC) or to the stores themselves.

Revised from T. E. Barry, *Marketing: An Integrated Approach,* CBS International Editions

Figure 29.1 Principal channels of distribution for consumer products

steel and timber, and finished products such as components, the end-user is the next stage in the production or marketing process; for finished products such as photocopiers the end-user can be any business operation.

Throughout commercial history there has always been the need for the middleman as part of the exchange process. Before the industrial revolution this function was carried out by individuals dealing in specialist markets. The industrial revolution brought a change from cottage-industry production to mass production. A feature of mass production was that more was produced than was actually demanded immediately. Inventory was established. Consequently, some sort of regulatory control and bulk buyer was required to satisfy both the needs of the producer and those of the end-user. Not only was the retail trade inexperienced in handling demand from a mass consumption society but the producer was equally inexperienced in catering for this society. The

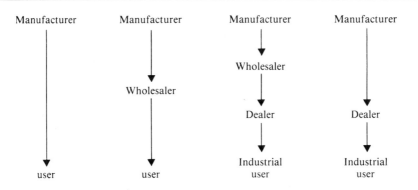

Note: Agent can be inserted after manufacturer in any channel above, when the manufacturer uses some form of agent to do his selling.

Adapted from V. P. Buell, *Marketing Management – A Strategic Planning Approach.*

Figure 29.2   Principal channels of distribution for industrial goods

wholesaler therefore had to satisfy new conditions of supply and demand. This established the wholesaler's place in the channel.

FUNCTIONS OF WHOLESALING

The range of activities and services the modern wholesaler offers includes:

1   The facility of breaking bulk orders to manageable quantities, for example from pallet to case load. In some cases this may include repacking.
2   The carrying, including storage (sometimes specialist), of a wide range of products from diverse sources.
3   Credit facilities to customers for the purchase of products or loans for the advancement of the customer's business.
4   Service support and management expertise to selected business areas, for example merchandising, stock control, security.
5   Knowledge of local markets to foreign-based companies wishing to

529

Table 29.1 Criteria for deciding which wholesaler to use: manufacturer's view

---

1 Evaluation of sales efforts of wholesaler:
  (a) Extent and activity of sales force of wholesaler.
  (b) Does sales force sell, or does it just take orders?
  (c) Extent to which manufacturer must supplement wholesaler's sales efforts with own promotion, sales, and/or retail personnel.
  (d) Number of lines handled by wholesaler. Does the firm handle too many lines to give sufficient attention to manufacturer's line?

2 Evaluation of relationship of wholesaler to channel of distribution for the product:
  (a) Type of wholesaler that can give widest distribution and assurance of sufficient retail outlets for line.
  (b) When particular types of retail outlets are desired, can the wholesaler handle them?
  (c) Quality and continuity of relationships maintained between wholesaler and retailer.
  (d) Degree to which wholesaler co-operates in promotion, pricing, financing, and other marketing activities.
  (e) Willingness of wholesaler to maintain continuous relationships with manufacturer.

Source: Department of Marketing, University of Pennsylvania, Wharton School of Finance and Commerce.

export to the market in which the wholesaler operates, for example toys from Hong Kong.

6 The storage of products where there is an excess of supply over demand, for example agricultural surplus products.

7 Distribution over a wide geographical area.

Wholesalers are familiar with local markets. Because they are close to customers they can make the initial selling moves by identifying prospective customers and exploring their particular needs. The value of wholesalers lies also in their facility to hold local stocks to supply small orders. Suppliers generally have difficulty with these small orders and wholesalers provide an effective means of entry into a very fragmented market. The wholesaler also acts as a channel of information back from the customer, who may be more willing to supply information to a wholesaler's representative than to a supplier directly.

Table 29.1 shows a list of possible criteria to be used by a manufacturer in evaluating the wholesale channel and a particular wholesaler. The essence of the choice of wholesaler is the level of service the wholesaler provides to both supplier and customer. The retailer, in making the same decision, uses slightly different criteria. From a retailer's viewpoint, the benefits of using a wholesaler include:

Table 29.2 Criteria for deciding which wholesaler to use: retailer's view

1 Lines
   (a) Does the wholesaler supply all or most of the lines needed by the retailer?
   (b) Does wholesaler supply all or most of the brands required by the retailer for each of his or her lines?
   (c) Does the wholesaler stock an assortment of varieties, styles, sizes, and colours sufficient to meet the retailer's needs?

2 Services
   (a) Can the wholesaler assure a continuous and regular supply of merchandise without excessive out-of-stocks or back-orders?
   (b) Extent of aid given to the retailer by the wholesaler (for example, promotion, pricing, inventory maintenance and so on)?
   (c) Extension of credit by the wholesaler?
   (d) Delivery by the wholesaler?
   (e) Does the wholesaler send salespeople on too frequent and time-consuming calls?
   (f) Is help given by salespeople?
   (g) Does the wholesaler's costs structure permit selling price to the retailer such as to allow the retailer sufficient margins?

Source: Department of Marketing, University of Pennsylvania, Wharton School of Finance and Commerce.

1 provision of selling aids, including merchandising support;
2 provision of expert advice on activities such as shop layout, building design and so on;
3 obtaining access to a wide range of products from several manufacturers;
4 provision of credit;
5 provision in some cases of sale-or-return trade conditions.

Thus, from the retailer's viewpoint the choice of wholesaler depends on different criteria from those from the manufacturer's viewpoint. Table 29.2 lists the possible criteria from a retailer's viewpoint. Again, the key element is service.

THE UK WHOLESALE INDUSTRY

The wholesale industry plays a key role in linking suppliers and consumers and makes a significant contribution to the economy of the UK. The turnover for the industry in 1985 was £170 billion, which

Table 29.3   Wholesale distribution 1985

	No of businesses	Total turnover (£ excl. VAT)
Total wholesaling and dealing	109779	170551
Wholesaling of food and drink	16491	28984
Wholesaling of petroleum products	961	31308
Wholesaling of clothing, furs, textiles and footwear	9714	6847
Wholesaling of other goods	51409	53656
Coal and oil merchants	3939	3102
Builders' merchants	4286	5445
Corn, seed and agricultural merchants, dealers in livestock	3137	8641
Dealing in industrial materials	4791	20164
Dealing in scrap and other waste materials	4330	2767
Dealing in industrial and agricultural machinery	7715	7736
Operational leasing	3006	1901

Adapted from *British Business* (1987). Distribution and Services Trade Inquiry, 17 July, p. 32.

compares with a total retail turnover of £88 billion for that year. Value added for the industry in 1984 amounted to 6 per cent of gross domestic product.

Table 29.3 shows the breakdown of the wholesaling industry into specific categories. The table reveals that the wholesaling of consumer goods accounts for approximately 52.5 per cent of the industry turnover, with 27.3 per cent made up by industrial dealing and 20.2 per cent by petrol, coal and oil wholesaling.

There has been a steady increase in the number of businesses in wholesaling, an increase in volume of trade and a relative decrease in stockholding in recent years, as is shown in Table 29.4. The reasons for the increase in number of wholesaling firms are far from clear. Many of the firms in wholesaling, particularly in non-foods, are small, and entry barriers are relatively low. It is nonetheless surprising that as wholesalers account for a lesser share of retailing purchase so their numbers increase. One possible explanation may be an increase in wholesalers supplying various small firms in the personal, financial and household services and in the number of wholesalers dealing in office consumption products.

In March 1987 the wholesaling and dealing trades in the UK employed approximately 870 000 people; this compares with 2 049 000 currently

Table 29.4 Total wholesaling and dealing

Year	No of businesses	Total turnover (£ million)	Stocks (£ million)		Stock turn (total turnover ÷ end of year stock)
			Beginning of year	End of year	
1980	91403	105842	9654	10258	10.32
1981	95968	114618	9977	10781	10.63
1982	100660	123825	10585	11099	11.16
1983	104426	139256	10938	11985	11.62
1984	108112	158167	11984	12842	12.32
1985	109779	170551	12957	13292	12.83

Adaption from *British Business* (1987). Distribution and Services Trade Inquiry, 17 July p. 32.

employed within the retail trades. Wholesaling is dominated by full-time workers, 90 per cent of employees being full time. The total number employed in the wholesaling and dealing industry has remained relatively constant.

There is considerable variation in the extent to which wholesalers handle goods reaching retailers. Nonetheless consumer goods wholesaling still accounts for over 50 per cent of current wholesaling and dealing turnover. Estimates of the extent of wholesale penetration are shown in Table 29.5. For the most part these proportions are decreasing, with some products – particularly food – showing quite rapid decreases in recent years. The level of wholesaling activity within a specific product sector depends upon a wide range of factors.

1 *Size of product demand.* If the product has a large market there is likely to be some level of wholesaling activity. A large market does not necessarily mean a high percentage of wholesale penetration but it usually means a substantial sales volume in the wholesale sector.
2 *Retail fragmentation.* If the retail trade within a sector is very fragmented with relatively low penetration by multiple retailers, there are likely to be wholesalers breaking bulk. If both manufacturing and retailing are fragmented, wholesaling will flourish.
3 *Perishable products.* These have always relied on wholesalers because of their proximity to and knowledge of the source and its markets in relation to storage and distribution.
4 *Complexity.* The complexity of dealing with imports has allowed wholesalers to specialize within these fields, as they have built up the

Table 29.5 Estimated penetration of wholesale trade into commodity retail sales 1982

Commodity sold by retailers	% supplied by wholesale trade
Fresh meat, fish, fruit and vegetables	90
Alcoholic drinks	45
Other food and drink	40
Chemists and sundries	70
Jewellery, clocks and watches	15
Clothing	25
Footwear	20
Radio, TV and electrical goods	40
Photographic goods	30-40
Toys and games	50
Furniture and floor coverings	50
Hardware, china and glassware	50
Chocolate sugar confectionery	45
Tobacco	40
Stationery and books	40
Newspapers, magazines and periodicals	95

Adapted from Euromonitor (1982), *Wholesaling.*

contacts. In some cases even the larger retailers deal with wholesalers for imported goods.

5 *Legal requirements.* There are certain products still subject to price control by the manufacturer: books, magazines, newspapers and prescribed medicines. The lack of price advantage in favour of large multiples in these fields has allowed wholesalers to thrive.

6 *Cross-over.* The ability of wholesalers also to supply industrial customers has helped them protect their consumer business.

Food and drink wholesaling

The wholesaling of food and drink is a large component of the UK's wholesaling industry. Total turnover is now approaching £30 billion a year. Over the last twenty years the sector has become increasingly competitive as multiple grocery companies have expanded and moved to reduce their dealing with wholesalers. Opportunities for wholesalers have decreased but there remain about 40 000 independent retailers who provide a core market for wholesalers. Food wholesaling to retailers in the UK is divided into two distinct types of operation: cash and carry and

Table 29.6   UK grocery wholesale sales 1981–85 (£ million)

	Cash and carry	Wholesale delivered	Total	% annual change	% volume change (inflation adjusted)
1981	3166	1823	4989	—	—
1982	3356	1836	5192	4	−2
1983	3670	2020	5690	10	7
1984	3950	2130	6080	7	1
1985	4320	2290	6610	9	4

Note: Figures include grocery product sales to all sectors including catering.

Adapted from Retail Business (1986), *Food Wholesaling*, September, p. 32.

delivered trade. These together account for a 1985 turnover of £6.6 billion: £4.3 billion through the cash and carry sector and £2.3 billion through the delivery trade (Table 29.6). The remaining £20 billion of wholesale sales in food and drink are accounted for by purchasing by manufacturers, processors and leading contracts in the service catering sector.

Cash and carry

Originating in the USA during the 1950s, cash and carry warehouses arrived in Britain in the early 1960s. They began partly because of the need for delivered wholesalers to seek new uses for their redundant depots. Initially cash and carry operations were very small in both size of depot and product range offered.

The cash and carry warehouse copies a store-type format in which customers purchase their requirements in much the same way as a consumer uses a supermarket. The principal advantage they offer is that they are usually between 5 and 10 per cent cheaper than a full delivered service. The 1960s were a period of rapid growth for cash and carry methods from both traditional wholesalers and new specialist cash and carry companies. Cash and carry growth reached a peak in 1969 with a total of 632 depots. Since then there has been a gradual decline through rationalization and competition in depot numbers. The number of cash and carry depots in 1985 was 594. The average depot size has increased from 12 000 square feet in 1969 to 37 000 square feet in 1985.

Three types of cash and carry wholesaling operations have evolved

535

Table 29.7 Leading cash and carry operators 1985

	Sales (£ million)	Number of depots
Companies		
Nurdin and Peacock plc	728	33
Linfood (Dee)	477	86
Makro	375	10
Booker (cash and carry business)	212	112
Batleys plc	175	7
M6 Cash and Carry	62	7
Watson and Philip	60	8
Groups		
PIA	2000+	NA
Landmark (Spar Landmark)	900	77
ICCG	410	43
Keencost	350	51
NIWA	300	50
Target	160	21

Notes: Sales figures include all products including non-grocery items.
In 1988, Linfood were bought by Booker.

Source: Mintel (Summer 1986), *Food Wholesaling*, p. 136.

(Table 29.7). These are the cash and carry chains which provide no delivered service and which are not part of any buying group, for example Nurdin and Peacock, Makro, Linford and Batleys. These four companies currently account for approximately 40 per cent of the UK cash and carry market in groceries.

Second, there are independent companies which belong to cash and carry buying groups. These are organizations which by group purchasing obtain the best possible purchase terms and overriders, can have a national marketing company which involves promotion and advertising which co-ordinates own-label operations. The largest is PIA (Producers Importers Alliance) which basically operates as a bulk-buying function with none of the marketing support offered, but it does offer a range of own labels. PIA is associated with groups such as ICCG, Keencost and Target, which offer full marketing support. Although not having widespread publicity PIA has grown quickly and with its sales to sectors other than retail has a total sales volume of over £2000 million. Third, there are the traditional wholesalers which opened cash and carry outlets while retaining their delivered business. These outlets are usually linked in buying groups that operate parallel to their wholesale voluntary group involvement. Thus the Landmark buying organization has close links with Spar wholesalers.

Delivered trade

The main development in delivered trade wholesaling has been the emergence of the voluntary group. In 1954 voluntary group retailing began in the UK. The impetus for subsequent growth was provided by the relaxation of building laws (Fulop, 1962) and the collapse of resale price maintenance in the late 1950s and early 1960s. Both these developments fuelled multiple retailer expansion in the grocery trades and increased the pressure on small retailers and wholesalers alike. In an effort to protect their market share wholesalers combined with retailers to form voluntary buying groups. In 1954 there were fifty shops in voluntary buying groups. By the early 1970s this figure peaked at about 30 000 and it has since reduced to around 14 000 in 1984.

For the retailer the cost of joining a voluntary chain is usually a weekly membership fee and a contract binding the retailer to purchase an agreed percentage of products from the linked wholesaler. For a small retailer the main advantages of belonging to a voluntary buying group are the benefits of a national image in relation to advertising, promotions and own labels, access to a wide range of consultancy services linked with retail operations, and a defined trading area with no other member of the same symbol group encroaching. This has become an interesting issue as some wholesalers supply rival symbol groups within the same geographical area.

The main disadvantages are twofold: first, the retailer's loss of independence as the wholesaler in part dictates the operation; second, the cost of belonging to the group, which includes not only the membership charge, but being obliged to purchase a set requirement from that wholesaler and the missed opportunities for purchasing the products possibly more cheaply elsewhere.

The wholesaler gains two advantages from sponsoring a voluntary buying group – a consistent order from a stable number of retailers and the ability to help raise retailing standards amongst members to increase turnover for both retailer and wholesaler.

537

ARE WHOLESALERS ADAPTING TO CHANGE?

The market for wholesaler services in the consumer goods sector is declining. For the most part the figures in Table 29.5 may be expected to decrease in coming years. To assess the responses of wholesalers it is first necessary to examine the causes of the change. Key areas of concern to the wholesaler are changing consumer lifestyles, a shift in power from the manufacturer to the retailer and the effects of new technology.

In a society in which there are increasing numbers of women in the workforce, increasing leisure time for the employed and changing family roles and structures, different shopping habits have emerged. Large retailers have been able to identify and respond to these important changes in consumer behaviour. This is partly because they are constantly in contact with the consumers throughout the UK and become aware of changes as they occur. As a result large retailers have been able to formulate well-defined marketing strategies. This, when linked with the price advantage of buying direct from the manufacturer, has resulted in the multiple retailers taking market share from independents, on whom the wholesaler is largely dependent.

Ever since retailers grew large enough to bypass the wholesaler through direct purchase from the manufacturer, the wholesaler has lost its power within the channel. The strengthening of buying power by the large retailers associated with their growth of own label, has reinforced the market power of the retailer within the total channel. The wholesaler therefore has become less important to the manufacturer but remains for the manufacturer an important entry point into the independent retailer market.

Advances in warehouse technology have enabled retailers to operate efficiently their own warehousing function, taking control of a greater volume and wider range of products. Additionally, manufacturers are able to operate more flexible production lines which are more responsive to changes in demand, and so there is a diminished need for the wholesaler's stockholding service.

Within the food trades the introduction of new processing technology has allowed retailers to increase the shelf life of fresh and frozen foods. Large grocery multiples now offer nationally some products that previously were distributed only on a regional basis. Additionally retailers have been able to integrate these short-life products within a uniform distribution system without having to invest in costly transport equipment.

In response to these shifts in the operating environment the wholesaler may explore various strategies for continued growth and survival. The first set of possible strategies requires the wholesaler to become more directly involved with retail operations. In this group two distinct strategies are open to the wholesaler.

1 The creation of a voluntary group of retailers linked together with specific contractual obligations, for example Spar, Stern Osmat Group. This has the advantage of ensuring that standards set by the wholesaler are achieved by the group of retailers through continual contact. In return the retailer receives the benefits of belonging to a national organization and sharing in its resources.
2 Alternatively wholesalers may run and operate their own chain of stores giving more profit and control but with added effort and outlay of resources. One example is the McCarthys chain of company-owned chemists.

One big drawback of these strategies is that they can cause a conflict of interests within the same organization.

A third strategy which extends wholesaler operations towards the final consumer is the opening of wholesaling depots to the public. There are important implications to be understood and overcome before wholesalers can contemplate this course of action.

1 They must be in a position to benefit from good market potential in both growth and size.
2 They will be entering a market where they will have to compete with established names.
3 A good location is necessary in relation to the markets and the competition.
4 Legal requirements must be complied with, in opening the depot to the general public.
5 The wholesaler must be aware of consumer perceptions regarding shopping environments and products sold in them.
6 The announcement that the depot is to be opened to the public may alienate trade customers.

A company that successfully overcame these barriers is Magnet and

Southern, which crossed the divide from building suppliers to DIY retailers. At the time of its diversification the retail DIY market was beginning to emerge. The competition was minimal and the opportunity was there for a company to take advantage of the growth potential. Consumer perception of DIY products and uses coincided with the builders' merchants environment.

These three strategies all aim to extend wholesaler influences within the vertical channel. There are also strategies associated with diversification of activities and of products.

The fourth strategic alternative results from the opportunity to diversify into third party warehousing and distribution. This is available to some wholesalers who have evolved into specialist distribution agencies for large multiple retailers. This is possible because of their specialist knowledge of the product market and their facilities and experience in the distribution of products. A number of the leading multiple food retailers subcontract the distribution of their perishables to third parties (for example, Tesco and Argyll to Glass Glover) and it is possible for established wholesalers to diversify into this area.

Fifth, product diversification can be developed as a strategy. Most wholesalers are continually adapting and changing their product mix in an attempt to target more profitable segments of business. The catering industry has grown rapidly to become an important customer to the food wholesaler, resulting in large catering sections within cash and carry outlets and the emergence of cash and carry's and delivered wholesalers specializing exclusively in the catering market, for example Booker Catering supplies and Linfood's Chefs Larder. With the growth of large ethnic communities, wholesalers are also extending product range into the ethnic food markets such as Chinese and Asian.

A sixth strategic alternative is the extension of services. The provision of a range of services is the core of wholesaler operations and a strategic option is to focus on these core activities. This approach includes extension of credit services, advice and support for customers (often involving advice on new technology), support services to suppliers, and faster and more efficient provision of traditional product services. Wholesalers have traditionally offered credit as a way of maintaining customer loyalty. Other wholesalers have chosen to expand other aspects of their service offering. An example is the privileged buying schemes by delivered wholesalers operating in the food and drink sector. They are used as a way of increasing the amount of business with the

Table 29.8 Watson and Philip trading profile

	1984	1985	1986
Total sales (£ million)	93.4	114.8	150.0
Profits before tax (£ million)	1.61	1.12	1.66

	1984		1985		1986	
	Sales mix %	Trading margin %	Sales mix %	Trading margin %	Sales mix %	Trading margin %
Cash and carry	44.3	0.38	52.6	0.83	61.9	1.18
Catering	20.3	2.30	15.8	1.99	11.6	1.96
Delivered grocery	21.3	1.29	18.7	1.30	17.9	1.33
Retail	4.2	1.46	4.0	1.60	4.2	1.76
Imports	9.4	0.49	8.9	0.96	8.3	1.01

voluntary group retailer and in return the retailer receives special discounts with his or her purchase.

These six strategic options are not the only ones available nor need they be used exclusively. To survive, and certainly to grow, the whole-saler of the 1990s will need to take a more strategic view of the business and this may involve implementing more than one of these basic strategies.

The firm of Watson and Philip illustrates a number of key features discussed in this chapter. The company operates cash and carry, catering services, delivered grocery and retail operations. The balance amongst these has changed in recent years as is shown in Table 29.8. Cash and carry has become an increasingly important activity in the company due to its acquisition of several companies in order to expand into new market areas and also because of investment in new depots and extensions of older ones. There are significant economies of scale both at depot and company level in cash and carry operation; thus Watson and Philip has sought to increase volumes (sales £78.6 million in 1983, £149.65 million in 1986) and the size of cash and carry depot (in 1987 a new depot of 100 000 square feet in Derby, and extension of Kilmarnock depot by 13 500 square feet). Cash and carry remains the core activity of the group and diversification is taking place, for example through the acquisition in 1987 of Ian Yates Ltd, the specialist confectionery and tobacco cash and carry. The strategy adopted in this case is a concentration on some business to obtain the cost economies of scale but within this to explore modest diversification in specialist areas and also to increase the services offered to customers. The results of earlier strategies involving vertical integration and diversification into catering can be seen still in company structure which has moved from its origins as a food importer.

Wholesaling remains a significant industry in the UK economy servicing the industrial and consumer sector of the economy. The industry is complex. Sectoral activities extend from the wholesaling of steel to supplying the local Spar 'Eight Till Late' shop. As a consequence strategic and operational management needs are extremely varied, from operating heavy lifting and handling equipment to planning packaged grocery shelf layouts. While the physical handling of goods remains a common characteristic of all wholesale activities, the factor which differentiates competitive firms from each other is service. Much of what wholesalers offer to suppliers and customers can be considered as service. The service offering of wholesalers provides them with competitive advantage. That a service is offered which is useful and valuable to customers and suppliers has ensured the continued existence of the wholesale sector.

The future of wholesaling rests with the way wholesalers respond to the changes in their operating environments. Environmental change requires the wholesalers continually to reposition themselves by moving from declining to growing markets. In this way they can renew differential advantage by measures such as moving into new vertical relationships, diversifying, adapting new technologies and providing new mixes of services. Firms which fail to take the opportunities presented by the need to reposition themselves as a result of environmental change lose contact with both suppliers and customers, and these firms will inevitably give way to those with better communications and a more market-orientated approach. Marketing orientation is the key to wholesaling success in the future even more than in the past. The successful wholesalers of the 1990s, irrespective of their sector of operation, will be those which have the development strategies able to take advantage of the changing environment in which the firm operates. Only by continually changing their management and operations can wholesalers continue to be effective and efficient.

REFERENCES AND FURTHER READING

Barry, T. E. (1986), *Marketing An Integrated Approach*, CBS International Editions, New York, p. 449.

British Business (1987), Distribution and Services Trade Inquiry, 17 July, p. 32.

Buell, V. P. (1984), *Marketing Management – A Strategic Planning Approach*, McGraw-Hill, New York, p. 337.

Euromonitor (1982), *Wholesaling*.

Fulop, C. (1962), *Buying by Voluntary Chains*, Allen & Unwin, London, p. 67.

Institute of Grocery Distribution (1987), *Grocery Wholesaling*, IGD, Watford.

Mintel (1986), *Food Wholesaling*, Summer. p. 136.

Retail Business (1986), *Food Wholesaling*, p. 32.

30

Retailing

Eric Morgan

For several years after the war, marketing people liked to think that retailers did not matter, seeing them as an almost mechanical channel of distribution whose only purpose was to allow the wise and seductive manufacturer to make contact with happy and persuaded consumers. Provided that goods were pushed into retail distribution, the marketer's skills would pull them through into consumption. Some retailers contributed to this image of the effortless middleman, but the picture was really created by the expansive economic conditions in which almost any goods sold readily. It coincided with a period of greatly increased marketing awareness and training, and the recruitment of self-confident young men and women who were encouraged to be aggressive.

SIGNIFICANCE OF THE RETAILER

Times have changed. We have forgotten what expansion was like; most of our markets are actually declining in volume, although inflation in selling prices gives a spurious impression of growth. Competition is much more severe among manufacturers and among retailers – and some of the retailers have become part-time manufacturers, too. Consumers are far better educated about products and spend their money with more discrimination; they expect, and get, great freedom of choice. High inflation, together with shortages of cash and credit, forced retailers to be more discriminating about their purchases; inventory control has become a principal concern of their business.

Many retailers are now running bigger businesses than they used to do and the professional manager can count as well as anyone else. All this has forced the significance of the retailers back upon us. It could be objected that they are still effortless middlemen, now the victim of circumstances instead of their beneficiary, but this would be condescending and inaccurate. We can see that many retailers are very good indeed at understanding their customers, providing what they need and helping them to enjoy it. This calls for a new response from the marketer.

ECONOMIC FLUCTUATIONS

Selling-in, once again, really matters – and very often it is not easy. Economic restrictions alone ensure that retailers will wish to buy smaller quantities and to restrict their inventory to lines which really sell through quickly. One of the most dramatic examples was seen in Venezuela, in the winter of 1979/80; after nearly three years of rigid price controls, restrictions were suddenly removed and prices shot up by 30 per cent. Retailers quickly ran out of money. The cost of borrowing was increased and credit was controlled, so they could not borrow money. Manufacturers also found it difficult to borrow. So purchasing was forced to slow down or stop altogether, as retailers liquidated their stocks. Best-selling lines went out of stock first, but the retailers did not reorder because they now had a chance to get rid of slow-moving items and turn them into cash. Eventually retailers could start to buy again and, if they were sensible, they concentrated on best selling lines and allowed the slower ones simply to go out of distribution.

The Venezuelan example was extreme, but something like it has gone on in many other countries, including Britain. The outcome is probably healthy, so long as consumers themselves do not run out of purchasing power. Retailers need to sell their old stock at the new higher prices. This is not profiteering; it is the only way to collect the money they need to purchase new stock. But if the state of the market is competitive and depressed, they may not be able to raise prices as much as they should.

This happened to retail jewellers in early 1980, when the price of gold had more than doubled. For many weeks retailers continued to sell their

545

stock at the old prices because they simply could not sell it at all if they put their prices up to the new replacement price of gold. As this did not make sense either, the business virtually came to a halt. Some jewellers simply stopped buying, locked up their stocks and waited for the madness to subside. Fortunately for the jewellers, they had other things to sell, but the specialist manufacturer of gold articles was in serious difficulties.

PITFALLS OF EXCESSIVE DISTRIBUTION

The manufacturer must sell-in, that is obvious enough, but the selection of customers is not so easy. Let us dispose of the idea that you do better if you sell to more and more retailers – you do not. The reason is clear. Markets are not indefinitely expandable. Once consumers can find the goods readily, and these goods are pleasantly offered with adequate ranges of choice, it is unreasonable to expect that consumer purchasing will increase further just because more retailers compete with each other for the market. Why should it? At some point distribution must reach its optimum.

This optimum might call for 200 000 outlets for baked beans or detergent, but it might be only twenty outlets for Rolls-Royce. If you go beyond this optimum number, you simply reduce the amount sold by each retailer, so giving him or her a poorer income on your goods. The retailer will be disenchanted with you; stock will become stale. Excitement fails: consumers are turned off. The magic disappears. Several retailers then stop selling these over-exposed goods – probably sending their unsold stocks back to the manufacturer or, at least, refusing to pay for them until they are sold out. Such an exercise does nobody any good. Distribution can, of course, be inadequate but, once it has been built up to a satisfactory extent, any further extension is counter-productive.

Selling excessive quantities to retailers is similarly self-defeating. It does not guarantee that they will make special efforts to sell your brands to eliminate the burden of high stocks. It might do this in some cases, but it is just as likely to result in a number of other, disagreeable situations. Some of your stock will go stale. Some will sit in the stock room and remind the retailer not to buy any more from you. Meanwhile they represent the trouble you are causing them and so they become bad payers. You convince them that your brand does not sell well – they will return it to you, if they can get away with it. Alternatively, they may try to move the stock by means of drastic price cuts or other bargain offers. This may be harmful to the image and prestige of your brand and it will certainly be irritating to competing retailers who bought your brand from you in good faith, at normal prices. Such results are clearly undesirable. 'Adversary' positions like this should be avoided; they do not succeed, and they represent an awful way to live. It is much better to make your interest coincide with the interests of your retail customers; then both can prosper and enjoy it.

A NEW PERSPECTIVE ON SALES

Do let us understand what 'prosper' means. It has to do with money in the absolute. People do not live on percentages; retailers make money because they buy, sell at a profit, buy again, sell again at a profit and so on. They cannot buy more than they can afford, but the faster they resell their stock, the faster they can repurchase and make another round of profits. The more they do this, the more money they make. They invest the money in stock and they need their stock to turn over as frequently as possible.

'Turnover' is interestingly ambiguous in English English; the Americans use it much better and do not make it synonymous with 'sales'. They use it to mean the number of times that stock turns over in a given period. The sales of a brand in a department store might be $100 000 per year, with a turnover of 6; this means that every two months, on average, the store sells its total stock of $16 700 worth of the brand. If everything could be controlled perfectly, the store would never hold stocks of the brand in excess of the $16 700 and just as it sold the last item, at the end of the two-month period, it would take in a new delivery.

The Americans have another useful term – 'open to buy'. This means the investment which the store is willing to make in the inventory of a given manufacturer. Clearly, it is in the manufacturer's interest to manage this 'open to buy', so that it is invested in brands that sell well, because the manufacturer will then make new sales to top up the inventory, back to the 'open to buy' figure. By contrast, if the manufacturer made a sale which used up all the 'open to buy' but did so with products which did not sell through to the consumer, no further sale to the retailer would be possible because there would be no 'open to buy' available. This concept is obviously different from the alternative of a monthly allocation of purchasing funds. 'Open to buy' is a superior concept because it relates the retailer's new purchases to the sales made by him or her; it ensures that the company which has done well can have a good chance of continuing to do well. It is just another example of 'To them that hath shall be given' – a principle which is much in evidence in retailing.

'Open to buy' has an interesting dampening effect on price changes. Sales managers normally can do the simplest arithmetic when they forecast the effects of a price increase; once they have decided whether or not to assume any reduction in the unit volume of sales, they just apply the new price to the agreed volume, and the value of the sales is found. (If there is no change in unit volume – and in times of inflation, we have seen price increases have much less effect on volume than they used to have – the amount of the price increase simply 'falls to the bottom line', which is to say that it represents precisely the resultant increase in profits.) However, under an 'open to buy' system, the total amount of money available for the inventory of the manufacturer's products is fixed until the date when the store next reviews it, probably in several months' time. Therefore, as manufacturers sell in new stock, they can sell in only fewer units at a higher price, than had been sold out at the old price. This is an automatic volume restriction which has nothing to do with any reluctance on the part of consumers to buy at the new price.

All these ideas, and the tougher times that have brought them about, are quite good for us. They force us to think about what is really happening to sales and how money is really being made to work. It is self-defeating, as we have seen, for salespeople to pump more and more stock into more and more retail outlets. It is similarly pointless for retailers to demand higher and higher profit margins and special discounts. Manufacturers cannot afford them. They have to live, too, and are subject to the same economic difficulties as the retail customer.

It behoves us, rather, to concentrate on moving the goods through to consumption. Let us build a franchise of interested retailers and loyal consumers. The whole cycle makes sense when consumers come back to repurchase: the retailer resells to them; the retailer repurchases and the manufacturer resells to the retailer; the manufacturer remanufactures and repurchases materials. This enables the manufacturer to be more economic, and so prosper and offer a better deal to customers. This pleases retailer and consumer alike and everyone benefits. The most dramatic example of this mechanism has been provided by electronic calculators, which now cost one-tenth of their price a few years ago and are now owned by almost everyone in the population. It looks as though microwave ovens are starting to move in the same direction.

INSIDE THE SHOP

In view of this need for fast and efficient turnover, it is not surprising that so much emphasis is put on activity inside the shop. This is not to say that all the activity is well thought through or is beneficial – there is nonsense among in-store activities, just as there is among TV advertisements. There are always very many ways of doing any good job badly. But display work has been studied for decades and is known to be extremely helpful. It is not particularly profound but is nonetheless true that shoppers are more likely to buy brand X if they can see it, if it looks nice, if the presentation is relevant to them and if they believe that they are offered value for money. So, merchandising demands that we know where to put brand X: into the right shop; into the right place in that shop; and on the gondola where your competitors are (ideally at the right height for easy vision and handling, in good light, where most of the people pass by, and so on). We cannot all put all our brands into just this ideal spot, but we must try. After all, some of our competitors are not paying attention and are not even attempting to compete for this space, while others are too weak to insist. 'To them that hath shall be given' applies in this respect too. The manufacturer with the most 'muscle' is the one whose products are the most important to the retailer; the one who is apt to demand special co-operation and privileges in the store, and be likely to get them. Some people object that this merely makes the big bigger and that it restricts competition, but you can hardly blame the retailer for wanting to help the manufacturer whose goods produce the most profit. It is a fact of life and one which means that you should be concerned to be strong in those outlets which carry your goods; it is better to be important to your retailer than to be in widespread distribution with minimized sales per outlet.

INCENTIVES TO THE RETAILER

So there is competition among manufacturers for the support and good will of the retailer. Your scheme to promote your brand to the consumer may need, itself, to be promoted if it is to get into distribution at all. The old way was to give a cash bonus to the retailer. Later this switched to a bonus in goods. Then came personal incentives for the people who actually sold the goods to the public. Then came more business-orientated incentives, such as extended credit or consignment payment terms. Finally, perhaps, we see that the professional retail manager is offered answers to his or her particular problems.

The manager does not want too much stock to occupy too much space but does want rapid turnover (in the American sense). He or she is likely to feel co-operative towards promotions which sell substantial quantities during a limited period of time. This helps to solve his or her problems. It also enables more promotions to be fitted into the space available in the store and in his or her calendar, and this makes him or her more competitive versus other retailers.

Other chapters in this book deal with planning what the promotional activity itself should be. There is a wide choice to suit different economic and competitive circumstances. Some promotions are just what they seem; a cut-price offer, for example, is the simplest attempt to persuade consumers to buy this brand rather than another (or to buy larger quantities of it or to buy it sooner than one otherwise would). Other promotions appear to have one purpose but actually have another. The offer of a very expensive, mail-in premium, for instance may really be a dramatic vehicle for impressive display in the shop, while masquerading as a consumer offer. Some promotional offers have forgotten what they are for (such as the 'gift with purchase' when the gift is irrelevant to the purchased product and possibly even irrelevant to the purchaser). But no matter what the promotion, the retailer's co-operation is needed, and we all must realize that this is not automatically obtained. We must be able to think in the retailers' terms, to be concerned about their problems and to find solutions to them if we hope to procure their participation and help in the promotion of our brands.

There are some other motivators which almost amount to 'licences to trade'. The most obvious – and the most abused – is co-operative advertising. The idea is that manufacturers and retailers share the cost of advertising the brand and also advertising the store where the brand may be found. Often the message in the advertisement is simply that brand X is on special offer at the specified store, and retailer and manufacturer naturally share the cost of the advertising between them. In practice, this can well prove to be an expensive disappointment. For instance, the manufacturer's 50 per cent contribution can be calculated on the worst rate (the single insertion price) of the newspaper or other medium concerned, whereas the retailer gets large quantity discounts from the medium, based on his or her total advertising. Some retailers put more than one brand in the advertisement and if unwary manufacturers each pay 50 per cent the retailer is almost printing money. Obviously, a little caution can prevent these abuses.

Now we come to the advertisement itself. All too often the advertisements are placed in local newspapers whose printing is terrible and whose editorial ambience is unsuitable to your brand. The message in the advertisement is usually the wrong one; the retailer wants to push the bargain offer, the cut price or whatever, rather than the quality of the brand and information about its features and uses. It is very dangerous to give your advertising money to retailers if they will not spend it properly (perhaps because they do not really understand advertising or because they take a very short-term view of the motivation of consumers). At least, the marketer must try to control the editorial content of the co-operative advertisement, by providing layouts, matrices, radio tapes and so on, and by insisting that they be used. Be prepared to spend enough time and to exercise controls so that your co-operative advertising expenditure has a chance of being effective, not just as a licence to trade, but as a sensible motivation of the consumer.

Other 'licences to trade' exist. In continental Europe, a firm favourite is the 'year-end bonus'. This is a payment to the retailer whose purchases of a manufacturer's products have achieved a pre-agreed annual total. Each year the target is negotiated, invariably demanding growth on the actual purchases in the previous year. Care needs to be taken in setting these targets, particularly because price increases alone can seem to produce growth, yet they cannot justify what is, in effect, an increase in retail percentage margin. Some marketers find that the year-end bonus can be put to good effect, particularly to encourage a retailer to increase his or her purchases towards the end of the year when there might be a danger of falling below the target. (This is a two-edged sword; retailers who have already reached your target by early December may well stop buying your product to concentrate on a competitor's, whose total is still below target.)

'Natural rabatt' (for example, supplying thirteen units of a product but invoicing only twelve) is a 'licence to trade' much used in Germany. It has nothing to recommend it because it cannot be used in any positive way. It is merely a means by which the retailer gets an increased profit margin. By contrast, the cash discount is coming to the fore again, pushed by the shortage of cash and the high cost of borrowing. A discount for prompt payment may well be worth the manufacturer's while, provided that he or she can prevent powerful retailers from taking the discount without actually remembering to pay promptly at all!

RETAIL CHAINS

In all the foregoing discussion there is not very much difference between independent retailers as a class and retail chains as a class; we find all levels of intellect and all levels of probity. There is, of course, a difference of muscle. The big chain is more important to the manufacturer than the individual small independent. That is why many independents now bind together to form voluntary chains. These are frequently known as 'symbol' groups, because they usually adopt a name and a symbol with which to identify themselves. Some have brands of their own and the symbol features as their private label. Some groups are composed of totally independent co-operating retailers, while others have made some financial investment in their central organization but, essentially, they are the independent entrepreneur's answer to the large chain.

A group facilitates economic buying; this may be the negotiation of some overriding discount which will apply to the independent purchasing by individual members, or it may depend upon the existence of a central buying office which actually purchases on behalf of members. Some central offices commit members to promotional programmes, while others execute advertising campaigns for the benefit of the whole voluntary chain. Almost every variation of organization exists from one country to another and from one retail segment to another. Much of the pioneering work was done in the grocery field in Holland while Britain and Canada were active early in pharmacy.

552

A rather specialized form of the same principle is practised by the franchise chains (of which Kentucky Fried Chicken is probably the best example). Franchised dealers usually own their own shop and are personally responsible for its business results but, in return for fees, are almost completely 'managed' by the central organization, which controls shop layout, product specification, pricing and promotion and which conducts a central advertising campaign. Franchising is growing, and actually includes perfumeries in Australia and car mechanics in Britain.

It can be supposed that the strong central control in a major retail chain, must give greater negotiating strength, provide better facilities and make more economic use of resources. This is probably true, so long as central bureaucracy can be kept under control. But it can also be argued that there is a much stronger motivation for the owner–manager to give service and to build a clientele, compared with the shop assistant who is bored and watches the clock until closing time. This, in turn, is countered by the training programmes of such companies as Marks & Spencer and by the joint ownership arrangement of John Lewis.

Chains are succeeding in unexpected quarters; in Germany, for instance, the Douglas chain consists of extremely sophisticated and exclusive perfumeries. This is providing honourable but very tough competition for the stylish independent retailer. Chains of discount stores produce less honourable competition, with their unauthorized and roundabout purchasing and their promotion of 'parallel imports'. These outlets do not build anything permanent or useful but merely spoil the consumer franchise which others have painstakingly built.

Chains not only offer private-label goods (as in the leading supermarket chains) but some manufacture for themselves (consider the major own brands of medicines and cosmetics which are skilfully marketed by Boots). Others sell little or nothing but their own brands Marks & Spencer, for example). The manufacturer's relationship here is simply that of a contract manufacturer who makes to the retailer's specification but does not supply any brands from the manufacturer's own stable. Such very powerful retail companies obviously have a double relationship with the manufacturer; they can be his or her biggest customer and biggest competitor at the same time. One might think that such situations could be abused, although monopoly laws and fair trading codes exist in many other countries to prevent this. In reality, the ethical standards of these chains are very high and their trade practices are proper and constructive.

The retailer who turns manufacturer does need to rethink some of the basic economies. The straight retailer has to supply capital for land, buildings, fittings and fixtures but, after that, largely operates on suppliers' money; goods can be received and sold on to consumers before the manufacturer has to be paid. The manufacturer, however, has to finance the stock, and this can easily represent working capital which is much greater than the investment in fixed assets. Retailers' own brand business, therefore, may give them extra sales and a strong promotional image but it is questionable whether it offers them a very attractive return on the capital employed. In stringent economic times, we may well find that retailers will do rather less of this sort of manufacture, because they will find it is extravagant in its demands on capital (and because the profit in absolute money, per article sold, is a good deal smaller than they could get from selling higher priced branded lines).

There is no point in the marketer's complaining about competition from retailers, because it is a fact of life. It can even be helpful to the manufacturer by making a market lively and expansive. When it is unhelpful, the marketer's duty is to try to persuade retailers to change their ways, but this should be a businesslike process. Above all, do not go to war with retailers, but find ways of making their interests lie in the same direction as your own. Not only is this more profitable but is a much more agreeable way to earn your living.

FURTHER READING

Brown, A. J. Chapter 9, 'The Distributive Trades,' and Chapter 10, 'Channel management', in Baker, M. J. et al. (1983), *Marketing Theory and Practice*, 2nd ed, Macmillan, London.

Buttle, F., 'Retail space allocation', *Int. J. Physical Distribution and Materials Management*, 1984, Vol. 14, No. 4.

Davies, R. I. and Rogers, D. S. (1984), *Store Location and Store Assessment Research*, John Wiley, Chichester.

Gattorna, J. (1985), *Insights in Strategic Retail Management*, MCB University Press. Bradford.

Knee, D. and Walters, D. (1985), *Strategies in Retailing*, Philip Allan, Deddington, Oxford.

McCall, J. B. and Warrington, M. B. (1984), *Marketing by Agreement*, Wiley, Chichester.

31

Franchising

Danielle Baillieu

Franchising as a method of operating a business was invented by Isaac Singer of Singer Sewing Machines in 1858. It came to the UK in the 1960s having been practically dormant in the USA for over a hundred years. Franchising is still in its infancy in the UK, although over the last several years there has been substantial growth.

According to a report carried out by Power Research Associates (of 17, Wigmore Street, London W1) there are currently some 530 businesses which claim to be involved in franchising, 440 of which are actively in business and 348 of these are involved in business format franchising.

The actual units in operation at the present time have been calculated to be 19 800 with total sales in the region of £2.2 billion and employing some 149 000 individuals.

Since 1984 the total number of business format franchisors has practically doubled. The Power report predicts growth to 42 000 franchised outlets by 1989 with a turnover of £5.25 billion, and 53 250 outlets by 1991 with a turnover of £6.1 billion, allowing for closures at 18 per cent of the total.

In fact, the growth may prove to be even more substantial. Franchise awareness is increasing amongst both potential franchisors and potential franchisees, especially through exhibitions and seminars throughout the country.

FRANCHISING AS A LEGAL CONCEPT

Franchising is not easily defined. The term is sometimes applied loosely and even inaccurately to distribution and licensing arrangements, for example petrol distribution and manufacturing licensing. Sometimes one comes across the terms 'first generation' and 'second generation' franchising. These tend to be used by the US Department of Commerce. The first-generation franchises are the petrol service stations and soft-drink bottler types where there is a franchised dealer concentrating on one company's product line. This chapter is primarily concerned with the second-generation franchise – that is, business format franchising.

In business format franchising the franchising company (franchisor) grants a licence to its franchisees for a predetermined financial return (usually an initial franchise fee with or without future royalty payments). The franchisee is then entitled to a complete business package which the franchisor makes available to the franchisee. This consists of:

1 expertise and market research;
2 financial planning based on their expert experience gained from pilot operations;
3 training;
4 an operating manual with ongoing support;
5 the use of the corporate name.

In theory this package should enable the franchisees to operate their own business to exactly the same standards and 'format' as all the other units in the franchised chain.

It is widely agreed that a franchising arrangement has the following characteristics.

1 A franchise is a contractual relationship under which the franchisor grants a licence to the franchisee to carry on business under a name owned or associated with the franchisor.
2 The franchisor controls the way in which the franchisee carries on the business.
3 The franchisor provides the franchisee with support.
4 The franchisee provides and risks his or her own capital.
5 In many cases a franchisee is given some territory within which to operate and this will be stated in the franchise contract.

The franchise relationship has both advantages and disadvantages. Everyone must be aware of these and should weigh them up carefully.

ADVANTAGES AND DISADVANTAGES OF THE FRANCHISE RELATIONSHIP

Advantages to the franchisor

Many people, whether they are established corporations or successful entrepreneurs, want to franchise because:

1 they can expand more quickly;
2 they are not using their own capital – it is the franchisee's money that is at risk.
3 they benefit from the economies of scale of bulk buying;
4 as they can build a chain of units quickly they are in a better position to negotiate keen purchasing contracts than an individual;
5 management of franchisees is easier because they tend to be highly motivated (it is their capital at risk, after all!) and are prepared to work anti-social hours to achieve success.

Advantages to the franchisee

1 The biggest advantage to franchisees is that they can set up a business at a lower risk than with traditional methods; the franchise business will have been tried, tested and proved successful by use of pilot operations. According to the Power Report, between 1984 and 1986 there were 14 per cent withdrawals in business format franchising. Withdrawals are not necessarily failures – they could be the franchised business changing hands. The report states that over 10 per cent of units at any one time will not be trading under the same franchisee a year later.
2 The franchisee benefits from the market research and support the franchisor provides.
3 Franchisees will be given assistance in setting up the business: everything from funding a site, fitting it out and then continuing day-to-day assistance.

4 Franchisees will benefit from bulk buying.
5 They also benefit from advertising as a group.
6 One of the biggest advantages to the franchisee is the use of the franchisor's 'name' or 'brand'.
7 The franchisee will also get preferential treatment from banks. In many cases banks will lend up to 75 per cent of the investment – something they would rarely do for people setting up a business on their own.

DISADVANTAGES TO THE FRANCHISOR

1 Failure of a particular franchisee may reflect badly on the franchise operation as a whole.
2 Exercising control over franchisees may be a problem and a watertight system is necessary. Nevertheless, a situation of continual default by a franchisee may prove difficult for the franchisor to handle because franchisees are not employees but people who have invested their own money. In such a situation the franchisor may ultimately be faced with only one option – to terminate the contract or buy-in the franchise.
3 Once franchisees are established in the business they may resent the payment of royalties, feeling their success is due to their own efforts and not the franchisor's assistance. The franchisor should therefore always maintain a high profile within the franchise relationship.

DISADVANTAGES TO THE FRANCHISEE

1 Franchisees are not their own boss and will have to operate the business in accordance with the franchisor's wishes.
2 There will be little scope for the franchisee to exercise initiative even when it may seem to benefit the business.
3 The franchisee may feel that the payment of all or part of the royalty fee is not justified as the franchisor is not providing adequate support.
4 The royalty fee is usually based on sales turnover. Therefore the franchisor will wish to increase this – and this may jeopardize the

profitability of the business. The franchisee must ensure that a balance is maintained.

5   A franchisee may be restricted in the disposal of the business and will most certainly have to obtain the franchisor's approval.
6   A franchisee may also experience difficulty in renewing the agreement (most of which run for five to ten years).
7   A franchisee may have to participate in advertising and promotional activities which may be of little or no benefit to his or her particular unit.

Anybody contemplating franchising as a method of doing business must understand that for the franchisor to succeed the franchisee must succeed first. It has been known for potential franchisors to comment that franchising is just a way to expand quickly without risk. Needless to say they generally do not succeed. Franchising must be regarded as a symbiotic relationship at all times.

FRANCHISING IN THE UK

Franchisors can be classified into three groups.

1   Established companies which realize the potential of franchising in the UK market and are stepping forward by using franchising to expand their existing business.
2   New companies which develop a business format franchise by opening pilot operations and, when these are proved successful, offer franchises to members of the public.
3   Foreign companies from countries more developed in franchising wish to franchise in the UK because they rightly feel that the UK market is underdeveloped and wish to diversify into the franchise market, which has a substantial growth potential.

Few franchise operations in the UK have reached market saturation. Those which have are trying to diversify into developing other franchises. For example, the Youngs Group, which has Pronuptia and Youngs Formal Wear franchises, developed La Mama (maternity wear) – a chain which subsequently collapsed. Prontaprint plc (instant printing) developed Poppies (domestic and industrial cleaning), which is no longer being run by it.

Most experts in the field agree that franchisors are better off specializing in their own particular field rather than trying to diversify.

In 1985 sales by franchise businesses in the USA totalled about $530 billion (Department of Commerce). In 1984 one-third of all US retail sales were made by franchises. If the UK follows the trend in the USA it is clear that a market with enormous potential is opening up and waiting to be exploited sensibly. The present state of the economy in the UK is ripe for franchise development because there are many people losing jobs and receiving sufficient redundancy payments to start a franchise. This is assisted by the leading banks recognizing franchising and lending up to 75 per cent of the franchise investment.

The Power Report estimates that 93 000 new jobs have been created by franchising (not including franchisees). The greatest expansion seems to be in leisure products and services, mobile food and drink and business property maintenance. The lowest growth is in clothing and fashion, transport of parcels and goods, and fast-food retailing.

Franchising is an excellent method of doing business for both franchisor and franchisee. Where failure does occur it unfortunately sets the franchise industry back by shrouding the franchise concept with suspicion, and all too often the franchisees are blamed. In fact, failure usually occurs because of inherent defects in the franchise format set up by the franchisor. These flaws are not discovered or are ignored during operation of the pilot schemes and are passed on to the public. The potential franchisor must realize from the outset that it is no easy task to set up a franchise operation which will prove successful and profitable for both franchisor and franchisee.

Setting up a franchise

Franchising involves a large investment in time and money. Potential franchisors should familiarize themselves with the franchise concept. They should appreciate that franchising is a unique method of doing business and that they will require new skills and expert advice. They will be changing the emphasis of their business, from drawing income from operating it directly to deriving that income from setting up other people in business.

The key to success in franchising is careful planning and sufficient market research.

Can the business be franchised?

The potential franchisor should ensure that the business is franchisable. For this to be possible the business should be unique in some way, that is, it should offer a special product or service, it should be difficult to imitiate and it should be fairly easy to teach the method of operation to franchisees.

Market research

It is necessary to determine the strength of the product/service in the consumer marketplace and to ensure that there is a developing market for that particular product/service. It cannot be stressed enough how important market research is. Franchises have failed because the market research carried out has been embarrassingly inadequate. It will be of no avail to try to force-feed the public to accept something there is no market for. On the other hand, if there is a gap in the market we have only to look at outstanding examples of success such as the Body Shop, Tie Rack and Sock Shop to see the rewards that can be achieved.

Pilot operations

By its very nature, franchising offers potential franchisees a tried and tested business concept. At least one, preferably three, pilot operations should be set up to ensure that the concept works. These should be located in completely different areas to ensure that the concept is indeed successful and not just dependent on a unique or typical location. By setting up the pilots the franchisor will be building up goodwill and reputation – which are essential ingredients of the franchise package. The pilot operations test out aspects of the business – the operating manual, the contract, the business plan and whether the business can make a profit. At this stage, the franchisor is experimenting to see what works: the business structure or layout may receive modification in the light of experience. Once the system is perfected the franchisor can start franchising. The franchisor should retain some of the pilot operations (even when taking on franchisees) as company-owned shops. This will ensure that the franchisor stays ahead of new developments and continually experiments with new ideas to the benefit of the whole format. There is no better way to demonstrate to franchisees that they should make a particular change than to show them how well it works in a company shop.

Planning the company organization

Some franchises fail because they have an inferior management structure. They have inadequate and inexperienced staff who are incapable of providing franchisees with sufficient support to operate successfully. In such cases failure is inevitable. The franchisor should indentify key personnel and their CVs should be made available to franchisees. To begin with it is better to use in-house staff who the franchisor can trust, backed up by expert advice. In time additional personnel will need to be recruited and trained. Staff must be given adequate training to enable them to help franchisees in starting the opertation, and later to act as 'trouble shooters'. Franchisees will need continual support and this should be provided to a high standard – after all, this is why the franchisee makes royalty payments. If adequate support is not given it is certain that franchisees will begin to resent the payment of royalty fees and problems will begin.

THE FRANCHISE PACKAGE

Once the franchisor has shown that the pilot operations are successful the experience gained can be used to develop the franchise package.

Site selection for retail operations

Market research and the pilot operations will reveal which type of site is best for the business. The franchisor will need to assist the potential franchisee in selecting the best site. Some businesses will need a primary site while others will function just as well in a secondary location. The potential franchisee will also need advice on optimum trading hours and trading space. Enough time must be spent in finding the correct site. All too many franchisees fail because of inferior locations.

Fixtures and fittings

The fixtures and fittings should be tailor-made to suit the franchise. The franchisor should always bear in mind the cost. If it is too high the franchise package will not be attractive to franchisees. The design should be attractive and practical.

Franchise selection

A franchisor should be extremely careful in the choice of franchisees. In the early stages it can be tempting to sign up an individual too quickly simply because the franchisor wishes to expand quickly and obtain a return on the money invested to date. It is wise to make a list of all the qualities a fanchisee should have and to stick to it. Under no circumstances should franchisors deviate from their requirements. It is always better to wait for the right person. Special deals with initial franchisees as a means of luring them to the franchise package are not recommended and should be avoided. Where this has been done problems have arisen because such franchisees always expect special treatment as they feel they are special cases. In addition, it causes ill-feeling among other franchisees who are not recipients of the special deal.

Presentation material and marketing the franchise package

'Hard sell' should be avoided at all times. Successful franchises tend to sell themselves. The franchisor should concentrate on demonstrating success. This can be achieved by success in the pilot operations followed by successful franchisees. Some franchisors employ public relations consultants. They are expensive and probably better avoided in the early stages. Initial marketing can be extremely effective even when carried out in house. Editorials in newspapers are a superb form of advertising, followed by advertisements and editorials in business magazines and franchise magazines such as '*Franchise world*'. Franchise exhibitions and seminars offer an excellent opportunity for franchisors to market their franchises.

Details of the franchise package should be incorporated in a brochure. This should be attractive and easy to read. The brochure is the shop window of your franchise package. The information in it should be factual and a true representation of the business opportunity you are offering, and any financial projections included in the package should be conservative and realistic. Some franchisors have videos that potential franchisees can view (usually for a period of a week). This is a good idea but not recommended in the early stages where the franchisor may be working to a tight budget.

Franchise fees

Fees are usually based on sales turnover. A certain percentage, say 10 per cent, will be payable by the franchisee to the franchisor. The franchise fee provides the franchisor each week with a source of income which should cover expenses and leave a profit. If the franchise is a good and viable system and is run efficiently by management, each new franchisee will increase the franchisor's income. Some existing franchisees may well wish to take on additional units, again adding to the franchisor's source of income.

Mark-ups

Where a unique product is being sold in the franchise the franchisee will normally be required to undertake to purchase that product exclusively from the franchisor. In such cases it is normal for the franchisor to make a mark-up. The mark-up should be reasonable and the franchisee should be told what it is. A franchisee should never be exploited. If the mark-up is too high the franchisee will find it difficult to sell the product and turnover will fall, leading to a reduction in royalty fees for the franchisor.

A careful balance between franchise fees and mark-ups needs to be calculated to ensure that both franchisor and franchisee can make a profit.

The initial franchise fee

A fee will be payable by the franchisee to the franchisor on signing the contract or opening the business. It is a front-end fee for the initial support and advice the franchisor must provide. When payable, such fees provide the franchisor with gross income. A franchisor should be fair and realistic in the amount of this fee: a vey high fee is suspect as it could indicate that the franchisor is there just to relieve a potential franchisee of capital and is not committed to providing satisfactory ongoing support.

The average front-end fee is between 5 and 10 per cent of the total cost of the franchise package.

Other sources of income for the franchisor

The franchisor can quite legitimately derive an income from franchisees for such things as sale of equipment, leasing premises, leasing equipment and financing arrangements.

Allocating territory

How much territory to allocate to each franchisee will depend very much on the nature of the business. A franchisor must carry out market research to find what the optimum territory allocation is. It is very easy to make mistakes in the beginning and allocate too much territory to a franchisee and then have to buy it back. On the other hand, if units are placed too close together franchisees sales will suffer and obviously this will be detrimental to the franchisor. Franchisees will feel vulnerable without an exclusive territory yet a franchisor could be extremely vulnerable if one is granted especially in a situation where a franchisee is not exploiting the market to the full. One solution is for an exclusive territory to be granted with a proviso that is could be changed at any time if the franchisor thought it would be beneficial and necessary in promoting further business.

Training and communication

The franchisor must have a good management team and a franchise manager who can communicate well with franchisees and deal with all problems that arise. Remember that franchisees are not employees: they have invested money in a business and they will expect (and rightly!) that when problems arise they will be dealt with immediately and efficiently by the franchisor. Good communication must start from day one. It can be followed up by a weekly or fortnightly newsletter.

Initial training

Training will have to be provided to a high standard by experienced staff. The franchisor imparts his or her expertise to the franchisee, showing the franchisee how the business can be run successfully using the tried and tested formula. Depending on the business the training can last from one to four weeks. There are bound to be teething problems, and franchisees should be given the additional support of a full-time franchise manager for their first week. This will boost their confidence and trust in the business and the franchisor. Training will need to be practical (for example at a company shop) and theoretical (at company headquarters).

Continuing training

The franchisee must be kept abreast of new developments in the business. The franchisor will need to make the franchisee aware of new products and ideas.

The operating manual

The training given to franchisees revolves around the operating manual. This is exactly what it purports to be – a manual which demonstrates to franchisees how to operate the business. The manual must be given to franchisees before they commence training and should be retained by them. The manual will contain the know-how of the business and as such will normally be protected by copyright. It must be comprehensive and detailed.

Preparation of the operating manual

An outline of what the manual must contain can be obtained from a solicitor or consultant, who can also be used for further advice. There is no point in asking a solicitor or consultant actually to write the manual – it would be prohibitively expensive and they would not know your business as well as you do. The manual must be written by someone who knows the business thoroughly. It will take that person usually at least three months to write, and even then it may have to be amended in the light of experience gained from the pilot operations.

A typical operating manual will contain the following information.

1 Introduction and philosophy of the business.
2 Details of the way in which the business is to operate together with details of the equipment that must be used and the servicing agents to be used.
3 Methodology of operating the business:
   (a) franchise fees – calculation of, accounting and specimen forms;
   (b) accountancy – calculation of VAT, PAYE, weekly returns, forms to be used;
   (c) insurance – recommended cover, guidance;
   (d) advertising – guidance and recommendations;
   (e) trading times;
   (f) staff:
   • how many to employ – full time/part time, general guidance
   • training in staff disciplinary procedures
   • uniforms
   • statutory regulations, for example dismissing staff and employment protection laws
   • job descriptions and contracts of employment
   (g) use of all standard forms and procedures;
   (h) stock:
   • pricing and purchasing policies
   • quality control
   • stock mix recommended
   (i) trade name/mark – goodwill;
   (j) personnel guidance – a list of everyone working for the franchisor and who to contact for a particular problem;
   (k) premises – design, layout, list of telephone numbers of service centres, housekeeping.

These matters will be covered in most manuals. Obviously manuals will differ according to the business. For example, a fast-food franchise will contain full details of preparation of food and portion quantities while a retail outlet will detail stock requirements, merchandising and window displays.

The franchise contract

There are many variations on the franchise contract. A franchisor must obtain the advice of a lawyer specializing in franchising. The same contract will be signed with each franchisee, and to maintain uniformity should be non-negotiable but at the same time fair and just to the franchisee. Unfair contracts do exist but succeed only in creating resentment and problems in the long run. For a franchise business to suceed both franchisor and franchisee should have a 'good deal'.

The contract must be flawless. It should be tested on the pilot operations and amended if necessary.

A typical contract will comprise the following.

1 A statement of the parties to the contract, their registered offices and the date.
2 The grant of the franchise and commencement period.
3 The renewal option.
4 Territory clause.
5 The business premises.
6 The operating manual.
7 Advertising.
8 Training.
9 Stock, supplies and equipment.
10 Trading hours.
11 Price policies
12 Royalty payments.
13 Sale/assignment by franchisee and franchisor.
14 Termination.
15 Secrecy clause.
16 Inspection clause.

17 Indemnity clause.
18 Restraint of trade.
19 Choice of law.
20 Arbitration.
21 Death/incapacity.

Obviously contracts will differ according to the type of business, and other clauses may be included, for example a 'franchise association' clause allowing franchisees to set up an association. The contract is the legally binding document. Franchisors should ensure that staff stick to statements in the contract and do *not* make promises over and above what is dealt with. There are cases where franchisor staff have made misleading oral representations to induce franchisees to enter into the contract. This usually ends in litigation and must be avoided. Honesty is undoubtedly the best policy in franchising.

Financial considerations

The development costs of setting up a franchise will be in the range of £100 000 to more than £300 000. For this reason the banks will be cautious and the franchisor will have to prove a number of things.

First, that the pilot operations are successful and, second, that the business is franchisable and could provide a franchisee with a return on investment in two to three years.

The cost of setting up a pilot operation will vary. It will usually cost more than a franchise unit simply because it is an entirely new venture. A franchisor should bear in mind that the investment level by franshisee should be kept at a realistic level.

Professional fess, consultants and solicitors will cost at least £25 000.

The training and operations manual will cost at least £15 000 to prepare and print.

The corporate identity logos and production of a prospectus will cost a further £10 000 at least.

Advertising for initial franchisees will cost about £5000.

Staff will need to be trained in aspects of franchising and recruitment. A consultant may need to be employed to assist in all aspects of setting up a franchise.

Consultancy cost

The larger consultancy firms will charge £700 or more a day. On top of this there will be travelling and subsistence expenses. On the other hand a franchisor could employ an indivdual experienced in franchising to act as a consultant on a part-time basis at a fee rate of £100 a day. His or her charge will be lower because it is part-time employment and he or she will not have overheads to cover. The consultant's role should be to liaise with the franchisor and his or her other advisors on all aspects of the franchise.

Some consultants prefer to quote a stage or project fee cost.

Any terms should be agreed in writing. The franchisor should select a consultant with whom he or she gets on well because they will be spending a lot of time together making crucial decisions.

Franchisors will need to provide their bank with a detailed business plan for both the pilot operation and the franchise development programme, showing clearly how they intend to obtain an income, that is, details of the service fee and mark-ups.

CONCLUSION

This chapter has attempted to show the considerable scope franchising can offer to any business person or company wishing to expand. It has also indicated the time and cost involved in setting up a franchise network, which must not be underestimated.

The UK is highly suited to franchising both home-grown franchises and franchises from abroad (especially from English-speaking countries such as the USA). Some authorities expect the European franchise market eventually to surpass the USA. If this does happen the UK will have a large share of the European market. It is clear that reputable franchising is here to stay, and to grow, providing franchisors and franchisees with a new and successful dimension for conducting business.

Part V
THE PRACTICE OF MARKETING

32

Market segmentation

David Tonks

There will be few occasions when the practice of market segmentation is irrelevant. It will apply to mature products and to new products, to industrial products as well as to consumer goods and services, and it will be relevant to both non-profit and profit-making concerns. It is a theme that will run through the organization from defining the business mission and undertaking the marketing audit down to the fine detail of assembling and implementing an appropriate marketing mix. It is *the* strategic concept and technique which act as a pivot for the marketing concept and for the practice of marketing.

With the customer as the focus for a marketing-orientated operation, that focus would be blurred without recognizing the different kinds of customers in terms of who they are, their buying behaviour and their relative importance. For the purpose of this chapter, market segmentation is taken to mean the subdivision of a total market into useful component parts. This begs the question of what 'useful' means. With the business mission given and the specific objectives of the corporate and marketing plans also known, the concern is with target marketing that can be implemented, that is *actionable*.

Some organizations may still see themselves as providing one thing for all people; for a small number, this may still be more or less the case. However, most marketing organizations are faced with choices in terms of which of many possible markets and sub-markets they can decide to target. Consumer markets in particular have become much more varied during the course of this century. The general rise in disposable incomes, higher standards of education and more complex and subtle systems have all helped to generate more complex arrays of wants and needs. On the supply side the extent of competition is also varied but, as a general rule, markets have become more competitive so that an organization seeking to ensure long-term success and survival must recognize the existence of a number of market segments and choose from among them so as to maintain a competitive edge.

Organizations such as Levi Strauss, Coca-Cola, Amstrad, Sainsbury, Next, Benetton, and Saga have demonstrated effective target marketing. The Levi 501 launch in 1986 was a classic example of segmentation in practice. The general history of Coca-Cola also provides good examples such as 'Tab' for the diet market but other examples, such as the more recent introduction of 'Classic Coke' in the USA are not entirely convincing. It is also interesting to conjecture what moves certain public utilities will be making when they are exposed to the harder reality of a competitive market.

TARGET MARKETING AND THE ALTERNATIVE APPROACHES

Kotler (1984) draws the conventional distinction between mass marketing, product-differentiated marketing and target marketing. Mass marketing, typified by Henry Ford and his Model T – 'Any colour as long as it's black' – now survives only in a few commodity-type markets. Product-differentiated marketing can have the apperance of target marketing but it is very different. With this approach, a number of product variations are offered to appeal to more or less the whole market. Conversely, with target marketing, the approach is led by the customer so that the organization identifies the individual market segments within the total market, assesses their worth and only then provides a marketing package designed accordingly.

IMPLEMENTING TARGET MARKETING

A central issue is therefore to decide how to segment the markets of interest and then how to position the organization amongst those segments – how to target markets. Selectivity of this kind can lead to

Table 32.1 Implementing a policy of target marketing

Identification
Which specific variables should be used?
Which descriptor variables should be used?

Assessment
What are the important criteria for evaluating the segments?
Which of the segments are actionable?
Which of the resulting segments are the most desirable?

Differentiation
Position the product for the target segments(s).
Assemble a marketing mix for the target segment(s).

Answering the questions in the table, particularly those concerning identification and assessment, is the concern of this chapter. The emphasis is on consumer markets.

improved customer satisfaction and to greater profitability. *Identification, assessment* and then *differentiation* are the essential stages in target marketing. The first two are more concerned with analysis, to determine the intrinsic worth and the desirability of the segments. The third is largely the decision-making stage when differentiation at the product/ market level and a suitable marketing mix will have to be determined. Table 32.1, adapted from Kotler (1984), provides a simple summary of these three important steps in developing a policy of target marketing.

IDENTIFICATION OF MARKET SEGMENTS

Frank, Massy and Wind (1972) suggested a particularly useful overview of the alternative variables that can be used for segmenting markets. They are allocated into one of four categories. Here, those variables which are direct and which concern particular buying behaviour will be called 'specifics'. The term 'descriptors' is used for those variables which are indirect, which define the customers but which are not related directly to acts of purchase, acquisition or consumption. As for the method of measurement, there are degrees of 'objectivity' associated with the variables chosen.

For example, one way of segmenting a consumer market is by TV region. This may or may not link with buying behaviour and some specific variable; it is therefore a descriptor. It is also objective in the sense that location of the customer can be measured accurately. Alternatively, attitude towards a given brand is a specific variable because it

Table 32.2   Alternative variables for market segmentation

	Descriptor	Specific
Objective	e.g. Age, region	e.g. Brand usage rate, buying situation
Inferred	e.g Lifestyle, personality	e.g. Brand attitudes, brand preferences

does relate to a particular act or potential act of purchase. It is also 'inferred' as opposed to 'objective', because of the difficulties associated with obtaining a precise measure of attitudes. Table 32.2, adapted from Frank, Massy and Wind (1972), gives examples of descriptor and specific variables, objective, and inferred.

Clearly, the specific variables are of ultimate interest to the marketing manager in that the need is to identify how individuals and groups of individuals differ in terms of their buying behaviour. Descriptors alone are of limited value although it is frequently assumed that buying behaviour is associated with such descriptions of customers. Quite often, the relationship is known and quantified. This is referred to later, but for the time being it can be seen that if you are interested in, say, heavy users of a brand, and they are known to be in a particular age group and tend to live in a certain area, they are much easier to access with these descriptor profiles.

Some confusion can result when this distinction between descriptor and specific variables is not made clear. The former attach convenient labels to the latter, types of cutomers who buy in certain ways or for certain reasons.

Which specific variables should be used?

The following would be included among the objective, or more objective, specific variables.

1 *Product usage/purchase rates*
   • Are they non-users, medium users, heavy users?
   • Are they solus users in that they buy only one brand?
   • Are the purchasers of interest as well as the users?
2 *User/buyer status*

- Are they current users, former users, non-users, potential users, regular users, first-time users?
- Again, in some cases, it may be the buyers who are of interest rather than the users.

3 *Loyalty status*
- What degree of brand loyalty do they display?
- Is it strong, medium, weak?

4 *Marketing factor sensitivity*
- How do they respond to the various marketing influences?
- Are they susceptible to price or to advertising?

5 *Purchase situation and occasion*
- Is it an impulse or considered purchase?
- Is the context social or business?
- What is the setting for the purchase?

6 *Media habits*
- Which media are they exposed to?

Using these variables, a target audience might be selected, comprising heavy users with marked brand loyalty who are price-sensitive.

The more inferred variables might include the following.

1 *Needs*   What do they need, or say they need, from the product?

2 *Benefits sought*   What particular benefits do they expect from the product?

3 *Attitudes and perceptions*   What attitudes do they have towards the product? How is it perceived?

4 *Product preferences*   What do they prefer and how do they choose between brands?

Using these variables, a target audience for, say, denim jeans might be those who require the status afforded by a high-profile brand image. By mixing the two types of variable, objective and inferred, a target market might be defined as non-users with low brand loyalty who require a durable, functional pair of jeans and who read particular specialist magazines. Various permutations are possible. Wind (1978) gives some examples of combinations which might be appropriate. He suggests that for a general understanding of the market, important considerations will be benefits sought, purchase and usage patterns, needs and brand loyalty.

Which descriptor variables should be used?

Descriptor variables, the labels which are attached to important target markets, have received much attention in recent years. It must be remembered that the specific variables are of primary importance. The relationship between the two is often left implicit so that the target market might be defined as housewives in the Granada TV region although the main, underlying concern is to reach, say, potential heavy users – it being known or assumed that they are potential heavy users. Again, there is a mix of objective and inferred measures. Those falling into the 'objective' category are by far the more widespread and often speak for themselves.

Geographical region

The use of geographical region to identify market segments is very common in marketing. TV regions have the particular advantage of allowing relatively easy and perhaps cheap access to the desired target audience. More important, some buying behaviour does correlate strongly with region.

Demographics

Demographics as a sub-group contains the usual variables of age, sex, social grade, family size, family life-cycle, income, occupation, education, religion, race and nationality. All these variables have at least three advantages in common with geographical area. First, they are relatively easy to measure compared with some other variable types; second, they are easy to understand and, third, they are well established. The issue is the extent to which they can discriminate buying behaviour in a way which is useful to the organization doing the target marketing. For example, in seeking to distinguish between users and non-users of a product, a demographic such as age will be of little value if the age profiles of users and non-users are identical. We return to this aspect later.

The use of social grade as a descriptor merits special mention. In the UK social grade (also known as socio-economic group) is very often encountered as a way of classifying consumer markets. Thus, a target audience may be defined as C1/C2 teenagers. The classification, based on the occupation of the head of household, is given in Table 32.3.

There has been much debate about the value of social grade as a

Table 32.3   Social grade in the UK

Group	Status	Occupation	% adults
A	Upper middle class	Higher managerial, professional or administrative	3
B	Middle class	Intermediate managerial, professional or administrative	13
C1	Lower middle class	Supervisory or clerical and junior managerial administrative or professional	22
C2	Skilled working class	Skilled manual workers	32
D	Working class	Semi and unskilled manual workers	21
E	Subsistence	State pensioners or widows (no other earner), casual or lowest grade workers	8
			100

Source: Adapted from JICNARS national readership surveys.

method of segmenting consumer markets. Leach (1987) pointed out that the method conceals more than it reveals and also that the implicitly assumed correlation between social grade and income is often incorrect, giving the example of a coal miner (class D) and a vicar (class A or B). The groups themselves are very large with the result that the popular combination of C1/C2 contains 54 per cent of the adult population. It should also be borne in mind that, while social grade is probably as good and bad a rough and ready descriptor as it always has been, marketing people are simply becoming bored with it, particularly with the arrival of more interesting and potentially more useful methods of segmenting markets.

Geo-demographics

Notable amongst more recent methods and worthy of some special attention are those descriptor variables which have the generic term 'geo-demographics'. These methods have emerged over the last ten years. Dissatisfaction with more conventional methods, effective marketing and the availability of cheaper computing power have all contributed to their growing popularity although some remain sceptical. They are all descriptors of the UK population based on a mix of demographic and household composition variables, with the resulting consumer types or segments linked to geographical area.

The best known of these geo-demographic systems is ACORN (A classification of residential neighbourhoods). Neighbourhoods are

579

Table 32.4   The ACORN groups

ACORN groups		1981 population	%
A	Agricultural areas	1811485	3.4
B	Modern family housing, higher incomes	8667137	16.2
C	Older housing of intermediate status	9420477	17.6
D	Poor quality older terraced housing	2320846	4.3
E	Better-off council estates	6976570	13.0
F	Less well-off council estates	5032657	9.4
G	Poorest council estates	4048658	7.6
H	Multiracial areas	2086026	3.9
I	High status non-family areas	2248207	4.2
J	Affluent suburban housing	8514878	15.9
K	Better-off retirement areas	2041338	3.8
U	Unclassified	388632	0.7

Source: CACI

identified and grouped according to the similarity of profiles created by applying cluster analysis to a set of descriptor variables obtained from census data. Cluster analysis is a technique which creates, in this case, groups of people who are similar across a range of such variables. Although the approach originated in attempts to measure social deprivation, the relevance to market segmentation was soon recognized in that the groups that result – the market segments – may well discriminate buying behaviour. ACORN uses forty census variables to create thirty-eight types which are often compressed into the eleven basic groups shown in Table 32.4.

People belonging to group A are described in summary as:

This type of area contains the 3 per cent of the population living in communities which depend directly on farming for their livelihood. Generally, these areas are too far from large towns to prove attractive to commuters. Poor local job opportunities result in generally low household incomes and few chances for women to work. Housing conditions in many cases are also poor with a large proportion of tenants in tied cottages lacking basic amenities. Low wages and the absence of retail competition result in somewhat unsophisticated consumer preferences and leisure is spent less through commercial outlets than in social activities and rural pursuits.

Similar systems to ACORN include PIN (Pinpoint identified neighbourhoods) from Pinpoint, Mosaic and Super Profiles, which uses sixty-five census variables to create 150 clusters. The other systems tend to differ in terms of the services offered rather than in the underlying logic that leads to the market segments. None has gone uncriticized.

A notable advantage of geo-demographic systems such as these is that the resulting market segments can be linked to postcodes thus allowing more efficient access to appropriate market segments within or across a specified geographical area or areas. They are also connected to other databases such as TGI (Target group index) and NRS (National readership survey), allowing portraits of key segments to be identified. For example, comparing 1986 with 1982, people living in 'less well-off council estates' take 28 per cent more package holidays, open 16 per cent more current accounts and own twice as many stocks, shares and unit trusts', according to CACI.

CACI, which introduced ACORN, now offers extended services through Marketfile GB, which integrates a number of marketing databases including ACORN. With this type of knowledge, such systems are very powerful for particular applications of target marketing such as mail order and store location.

No doubt the forces which have led to the emergence of these geo-demographic descriptors will continue and further 'clones' will emerge. They will probably concentrate on particular product, brand or market types and this could well be an exciting and useful development – as could the development of such systems for foreign markets. The USA, Germany and France all have geo-demographic classifications of consumer markets based on census data and the like.

Personality and lifestyle

This is the final category of descriptor variables and contains two main approaches, both of which result in inferred measures of the segments.

Many attempts have been made in the past to link personality with buying behaviour. For example, the extent of 'innovativeness' might well be connected with brand choices. Success has usually been limited and this has very often been attributed to the methods used. The future may hold more promise for this approach, but in the meantime it has been overshadowed by the relative popularity of an associated segment descriptor – lifestyle or as it is sometimes known, psychographics. With lifestyle segmentation, people are classified according to three main dimensions – activities, interests and opinions. Typical of this method is

581

Table 32.5   Male lifestyle segments – McCann Erickson

Segment		% adult males
Avant guardians	Concerned with changes and well-being of others, rather than possessions. Well educated, prone to self-righteousness.	13.5
Pontificators	Strongly held, traditional opinions. Very British, and concerned about keeping others on the right path.	15.0
Chameleons	Want to be contemporary to win approval. Act like barometers of social change, but copiers, not leaders.	11.5
Self-admirers	At the young end of the spectrum. Intolerant of others and strongly motivated by success and concerned about self-image.	15.0
Self-exploiters	The 'doers' and 'self-starters', competitive but always under pressure and often pessimistic. Possessions are important.	13.0
Token triers	Always willing to try new things to 'improve their luck', but apparently on a permanent try-and-fail cycle. Includes an above average proportion of unemployed.	10.0
Sleepwalkers	Contented under-achievers. Don't care about most things, and actively opt out. Traditional macho views.	13.0
Passive endurers	Weighted towards the elderly, they are often economically and socially disenfranchised. Expect little of life, and give little.	9.0

Source: Marketing/McCann-Erickson

that used by McCann-Erickson (shown in Table 32.5) but there are many others such as that from Taylor Nelson.

Combinations of specific and descriptor variables are more likely to provide segments which discriminate buying behaviour in some useful way. Thus, the segment of interest might be loyal brand users with high usage rates who are known to be males, aged twenty-five to thirty-five living in the South East, belonging to ACORN group J and who read the quality press. This type of information may come from primary research into a market or it might be available from the likes of TGI. Table 32.6 gives an example of the combinations made available by TGI, which analyses, amongst other things, market segments for products and brands in terms of both specific and descriptor variables. In this example, which concerns all male users of after-shave lotion, there are 4.5 million users in total. There is a basic specific variable for segmentation – users rather than non-users – and the users are then classified according to a variety of descriptor variables. The market segment

Table 32.6 Target group index data

	A	B % down	C % across	D Index
	'000			
All men	4478	100.0	21.9	100
15–19	567	12.7	25.2	115
20–24	691	15.4	33.7	154
25–34	1220	27.2	31.4	144
35–44	789	17.6	24.4	112
45–54	569	12.7	18.6	85
55–64	412	9.2	14.4	66
65 and over	230	5.1	7.3	34
AB	658	14.7	18.6	85
C1	920	20.5	21.1	97
C2	1868	41.7	26.2	120
D	918	20.5	21.0	96
E	114	2.6	10.5	48
ABC1	1578	35.2	20.0	91
C2D	2786	62.2	24.2	111
ABC1 15–34	781	17.4	25.4	116
35–54	532	11.9	20.4	93
55 or over	265	5.9	11.9	55
C2DE 15–34	1697	37.9	33.2	152
35–54	826	18.4	22.4	102
55 or over	377	8.4	10.0	46

Source: Adapted from TGI, BMRB

defined as 'C2/D/E 15–34', a combination of social grade and age, shows 1.7 million males in the category, 38 per cent of all users. Of the males with this descriptor profile, 33 per cent are users of after-shave. This leads to the 'index' figure which shows that usage rate in this category is 52 per cent higher than that for all males. Clearly, these decriptor variables of age and social grade do identify different sub-groups amongst all male users of after-shave lotion. Such information, used intelligently, is essential for effective target marketing. In applying the concept of market segmentation problems are frequently caused by a surfeit as well as an absence of data.

Choosing from among these many variables for segmenting a consumer market can be a problem. Of ultimate concern is the extent to which the variables and the segments which result are of some use, but in the case of a new approach this may well be speculative. Some forays

583

into segmentation of the market will be based on the premise that segments do exist and can be identified with particular specific and descriptor variables.

Principal questions will include the track record of any one variable in identifying useful target segments for similar products, the extent to which the approach is understood and accepted and the complexity and cost of obtaining worthwhile data.

All this applies equally to industrial markets. End-use as a specific variable and geographic location as a descriptor are very popular. Additional specific variables include buying situation (straight re-buy, modified re-buy and new purchase) and other characteristics such as the nature of the buying centre and the buying criteria employed. Other descriptor variables concentrate on the broader characteristics of the organization such as size, and SIC group. In general, the principles of market segmentation and target marketing apply equally to consumer and to industrial markets.

ASSESSMENT OF MARKET SEGMENTS

What are the important criteria for evaluating the segments?

There are certain standard requirements of market segments but chief amongst these is the extent to which the segmentation variable chosen and the segments which result do in fact discriminate between the buying behaviour of consumers in a useful way. Are the segments 'unique'? This must be the acid test for any approach. If the approach taken cannot stand up to the 'So what?' question at this level, there is little point in proceeding.

It is no doubt tempting to take a simple, cheap and accepted approach which gives potentially actionable segments – and then reflect on the power of that approach to discriminate. In the absence of existing and available information on markets and market segments, this temptation could be irresistible and the results may be disappointing.

Some descriptors offer no explicit logic, no identifiable link between the descriptor and the specific variable of interest. Thus, geo-demographics based on census data might be seen as a surrogate measure of lifestyle which, in turn, will determine or be associated with some buying behaviour. The actual connections are rarely made clear and it is often necessary to be content with association rather than causation. The inevitable response to all this is that if the method works, if it *does* discriminate – 'Why worry?'

In addition to the main requirement of effective discrimination, the criteria suggested by Kotler (1984) can be used.

Measurability

It may well be that a prescise audience can be identified as a desirable target market but if data are difficult or costly to obtain, the extent to which that knowledge can be used will be very restricted. If, for example, a product is to be launched towards high income 'self-exploiters' aged twenty-five to thirty-five who live in the Yorkshire TV region and who belong to Super Profile Lifestyle B, data on this market segment may be hard to come by, or at least expensive. Without appropriate data on, say, the size of such a target market, marketing planning becomes very judgmental.

Accessibility

One of the main reasons for redefining a key target segment such as heavy users by superimposing descriptor variables is to facilitate choice of an appropriate method and style of communication and to determine the best way to deliver the product. Some descriptor variables hold up very well against this criterion. The geo-demographic descriptors have the marked advantage that their databases are linked to postcodes, rendering the target audience easily accessible. No doubt the marketing information revolution which is taking place will further encourage the precision possible with these methods. Conversely, other descriptors present problems. If the target audience is defined or redefined using some of the lifestyle variables, reaching it with an effective communications mix may be extremely difficult or expensive.

Substantially

While it may be possible to identify a target market which displays 'unique' and suitable buying behaviour and is measurable and accessible, the worth of that segment and the justification for assembling a marketing package for it will be a function of the segment size. It may simply be too small to warrant any special marketing effort. Markets can be over-segmented or they might be too small in the first place to

585

justify any attempt at segmentation. In addition, the stability of the target segments(s) over time will be important. This applies strongly to segment size and to the 'benefits sought' within it. In markets for consumer goods and services, product life-cycles, or more accurately market life-cycles, can be erratic and brief.

Which of the segments are actionable and desirable?

The criteria – 'uniqueness', measurability, accessibility and substantiality – will determine the actionability of the identified target segment. Going beyond the target segment itself, the organization's capacity to serve that segment and the activities of the competition will determine its overall desirability. Issues such as business mission, SWOT analysis (strengths, weaknesses, opportunities and threats) and in particular, the competitive position, are dealt with elsewhere in this book. The outcome will be differentiation – positioning the product(s) along the identified dimensions, determined by the requirements of the target segment(s) and the offerings or likely offerings of the competition. The marketing mix of product characteristics, price, communications and distribution will be assembled to create this positioning, to satisfy the needs and wants of the target segment(s) and to establish a competitive advantage.

SUMMARY

When market segmentation and target marketing are appropriate, and this is usually the case, *identification* is first necessary. The market segments will be identified and defined with an appropriate combination of specific and descriptor variables. Then, *assessment* will require the resulting segments to be evaluated according to their intrinsic actionability. Discriminatory power, measurability, accessibility and substantiality will be the main criteria. The goals and the capacities of the organization and the configuration of the competition will determine which target segments are desirable. This is followed by *differentiation* to position the product in accordance with the needs and wants of the target segment(s) and to secure the competitive edge.

REFERENCES AND FURTHER READING

Frank, R. E., Massy, W. F. and Wind, Y. (1972), *Market Segmentation*, Prentice-Hall, London.

Kotler, P. (1984), *Marketing Management: Analysis, Planning and Control*, Prentice-Hall, London.

Leach, C. (1987), 'How conventional demographics distort marketing realities', *Classifying People – Are Lifestyles Threatening Demographics?*, Campaign/Admap Seminars, April.

Wind, Y. (1978), 'Issues and advances in segmentation research', *Journal of Marketing Research*, Vol.15, August, pp. 317–37.

33

Advertising

Charles Channon

Advertising is typically one element in the persuasive presentation of a product or service to its buying or using public. For many of those involved in it, whether as advertisers, agencies or consumers, it is *the* communication element in the marketing mix. What we really mean by this is that it is the most obvious and separately identifiable.

ADVERTISING AND THE MARKETING MIX

In fact, the whole of the marketing mix contains potential or actual communications and all of them, when they are found, are designed to be persuasive to purchase and consumption. A cleaning product may contain coloured particles to highlight certain claimed ingredients and their benefits; a small electrical good may have design elements which highlight its suitability for youth or that it is fashionable; in most instances a pack does far more than simply 'protect' what's inside – it will 'brand' the contents at the very least, and sometimes a great deal more.

Even distribution can 'say' something about a brand. So can price: whether our price is higher or lower than the competition is, potentially, a communication to our market about things other than price. As a relative price it can produce, say, lower margins and higher volume or higher margins and lower volume and either route may mean more or less total profit. But as a communication it can say something about our quality, our market segment, our end use, and so on. In this respect it must be consistent with our strategy as expressed through the rest of the marketing mix, including, of course, promotion, of which advertising is a part.

In this sense the whole of marketing strategy, directly or indirectly, is a communication with the marketplace. It must be so because in most developed marketplaces the buyer, the customer, the consumer is usually free to choose – to buy or not to buy, to buy our product or service or someone else's. To make that choice, consumers need 'information' – information which they have in some way processed and responded to at the rational and/or emotional level, consciously or unconsciously. The response may be as vague as a heightened sense of familiarity or as definite as a feeling of total satisfaction with previous trial or the belief that the product contains added fibre or is selling for 20p off at Tesco's. Of course, as we have seen, this information which is being used and responded to does not just come from advertising. In the last analysis, the response is to the whole of the marketing mix. So, advertising is not unique as a tool of marketing; rather it is like the other communication aspects of marketing, only more so. Its sole function is to evoke a response through communication in paid-for space – usually from the consumer, often (indirectly) from the trade as well, and sometimes from other audiences.

What it communicates may be a claim about value for money or a product performance benefit. It could equally be just a reminder or it could be an association or an image in which words as such, let alone claims, have little significant role to play. Whatever it is will be (or should be) determined by the nature of the product field and the consumer needs within it and by the part that advertising can play in the context of the rest of the marketing mix.

We should never think of advertising as isolated from the rest of marketing. It plays just one part in helping to solve a marketing problem or exploit a marketing opportunity, and to be effective the part it plays must be right. If the marketing problem is distribution, advertising may be able to contribute only a little to its solution; if the problem is price, advertising as such may contribute even less. And if the problem is the product itself, advertising may even be counter-productive. Advertising which generated widespread trial of an unsatisfactory product, could well render a later 'new improved' version unsaleable. On the other hand, if the problem is awareness advertising can be very powerful, and

589

even more powerful (because the effect lasts longer) if the problem is positioning, that is, if potential consumers have not grasped where your brand fits in to their needs or lives in a way that is different from the competition.

Where advertising fits, it will work to *simplify* consumer choice in your favour, provided that *the advertisements themselves also form a fit between the brand and the consumer in the real world*. Implicit in this statement of the obvious are some important fundamentals about the nature of advertisements and of the advertising process.

First, advertisements relate products or services to people. To do this effectively, they must be appropriate to the former and relevant to the latter *in a way that helps to express and sustain competitive advantage*. This, if you like, is the generalized or generic version of the strategy to which any advertisement is written (whether consciously or unconsciously). The specifics of the brand, the specifics of consumer needs in the product field, and the specifics of competitive advantage will determine the strategy to which a particular advertisement or campaign is written. Yet, however specific the strategy, *it will not write the advertisements* (though there are still some advertisers and some product fields where it can appear to come very close to doing so). For every given strategy there will be, in principle, an *in*definite number of possible creative solutions.

This gap, as it were, between strategy and execution is not unique to advertising. Nevertheless, it is particularly evident in advertising and helps to explain the high profile of the creative function within it. What matters is the response. Strategy will define the response we want but it is a creative execution – an advertisement – which must elicit it. In some cases the content of the strategy and the literal content of the advertising message will be almost identical; in others this will not be so, due to the nature of the required responses and the way such responses are achieved – emotions, imagery, involvement, and values must be re-created, not just stated.

Target consumers and their needs, however, are only one side of the connection an advertisement makes. The other side is the product or service, which we often speak of as the *brand*.

ADVERTISING AND BRANDING

At the most basic level it is obvious that the one thing an advertisement must do is to identify what it is selling. However, a well-branded advertisement is no more than the final link in a whole process of *differentiation* from the competition, which good marketing will attempt to achieve in the marketplace wherever it can. It is a process to which advertising is peculiarly well suited to contribute and, indeed, it is this power in advertising which has historically accounted for its prominence in the marketing of fast moving consumer goods.

We talked earlier of advertisements relating products to their target consumers in a way that helps to express and sustain competitive advantage. Looked at more closely, this statement can be seen to be almost a redefinition in communication terms of the ultimate operational objective of the whole of marketing. Although the concept of profit is not explicit in this definition, we would do well to remember that it is there by implication as the *business* objective for which all good marketing is simply the strategy: *profit defines the purpose for and constraint under which competitive advantage is created and sustained.*

Competitive advantage can take many forms but, whatever it is, the consumer needs to know about it and needs to know that it belongs to us. It could be a price advantage; it could be a performance benefit like 'washes whiter', 'gets stains out', 'kills 99 per cent of all known germs', or 'kind to hands'. Or it could be a generalized promise of reliability and value which adds up to 'the name you can trust'. It could concern *authenticity* – 'the real thing' – or be a form of social gratification like an enhancement of the role in which the product is used or of the end use (or end-user) to which (or to whom) it is addressed. It could be that our brand is easier to identify with, or has a more distinctive identity or more attractive personality – or just more fun. Being a better advertiser can sometimes constitute our competitive advantage. But whatever it is will be relevant at some level to consumer choice and the link between it and our product will be forged by branding.

Branding links a reputation to a name and creates an *owned difference in the marketplace* which is relevant to consumer needs. It provides a focus for interest, credibility and loyalty and, of course, it can be used to identify and reinforce any form of stimulus to sales. It is a powerful aid to the simplification of choice and to the creation of a *protected* franchise among your target consumers.

Branding works by counteracting the erosion of advantage which is the natural tendency of any competitive product field. It creates a sort of patent in the mind or, if you prefer, helps to build what accountants call

591

'goodwill', which, properly supported, has a good chance of surviving attempts by our competition to match or equal us on our own ground. Successful branding can be very valuable: it becomes our differentiated asset in the marketplace and may be worth more to us than any other assets the company has.

In this sense a brand is a unique identity, a whole which is greater than the sum of its parts. You *can* build a brand *without* advertising, but many products need advertising to help them do this because the experience of the product in use will not by itself be enough to establish its unique identity without the projection, the associations and the amplification which advertising can provide.

ADVERTISING AND ADDED VALUES

Most consumers will admit that there are many products which mean something more to their users than simply what they deliver in terms of pure performance. This is most obvious in personal purchase product fields like, say, lager or fragrances, where what we buy is also a statement about ourselves. Yet most household purchases which are not retailers' 'own brands' make some statement, even if only the residual reassurance and guarantee that the product in question will deliver up to expectation. Even 'own-branding' will have a meaning in this context either because it means something anyway (Sainsbury's wines, for example) or, negatively, because we have decided that this is a product field where price alone ought to be decisive.

All these 'meanings', except the last, constitute in some sense an *added* value. For reasons that will now be obvious, added values help differentiation in the marketplace, are a natural product of the creation of a brand and are usually very suited to projection and reinforcement in advertising, although, as with everything else, there are other ways of doing it.

We need to be clear that added values are not a marketing invention but are fundamental to our social nature as human beings. As anthropology has shown, we use goods to define our values, reinforce them, and express them to other people. In this perspective, if, as has been said, money is information in circulation, then *goods are information delivered and received*. Gifts, such as a box of chocolates, are obviously like this but so are houses, furnishings, cars, holidays, clothes, what we serve at a meal and even savings and insurance. All these things serve a functional or rational purpose, but to us as human beings in society they often mean more than the purpose they serve – more to ourselves or to our families and friends or to the world at large. This does not mean that consumption behaviour is necessarily *irrational* but rather that 'rationality' must not be confined to a limited functional and economic meaning.

VALUES, ECONOMIC VALUE, AND EVALUATION

The importance and legitimacy of values and meanings in consumption behaviour have some practical implications for the relationship between marketing and advertising on the one hand and the science of economics on the other. In the end, economics can deal with *values* (that is, all the various consumer needs and satisfactions which marketing and advertising must address in the marketplace) only in terms of their *economic* value, expressed in the form of such relationships as the price elasticity of demand (what percentage change in demand will result from a 1 per cent change in price) and so on. This type of analysis can be very useful *retrospectively* in evaluating what marketing has achieved but necessarily gives very little guidance on how you might set about achieving it in the real world in the first place.

The assessment of what has been achieved can still be very valuable, however, and it can be particularly valuable for an *optional and controllable* marketing cost like advertising. It is not easy to achieve because the marketing mix is not just a mix as far as sales and profit are concerned but a *blend*. It requires us to *isolate* an effect due to advertising over and above the effect of the rest of the mix (to which, of course, advertising may also have contributed – if, for example, there is an *underlying* long-term upward trend in sales). It must not only isolate an advertising effect from the rest of the mix which *we* have created but also isolate it from all those other influences on purchasing which we do not control, such as competitors' activities, and a variety of economic, social, technological and even political pressures.

It *can* be done, as the IPA Advertising Effectiveness Awards have shown, and done more rigorously than simple-minded arguments like 'advertising went up and then sales went up' which used to be the staple and inadequate basis of such demonstrations. It is easier to do if planned for in advance and the case histories of the published books of the Awards provide extremely useful models of how to do it. The analyses they deploy, of course, are not solely those familiar from economics textbooks, indeed rather the reverse, but they do go a long way towards demonstrating how in practice advertising helps to convert values into economic value, and economic value into profit.

The bottom-line accountability of advertising will become more important as markets become more competitive and as the *business* objectives of marketing activity come into sharper and sharper focus through the stock market and its analysts. But this is only one aspect of a changing competitive environment for advertising which has tended to shift the aims of advertising activity away from the long-term brand-building effects, which can be inferred but not separately quantified (at least on a consensus basis), to strictly short-term effects where, in certain circumstances, other means of promotion may appear to be equally or more efficient.

ADVERTISING AND THE COMPETITIVE ENVIRONMENT

Two of the most important changes of this kind, apart from the ever-increasing pressure on financial performance as such, have been the growth of retailer power and the shortening life-cycle of many markets.

Historically, brand advertising developed as a weapon of the manufacturer against the retailer and wholesaler. In 1964 the abolition of resale price maintenance in the UK began a process whereby retailers of packaged goods could begin to wrest some of this power back into their own hands. They could, as it were, stimulate demand (by cutting the price of brands at the expense of the manufacturer's margin rather than their own), concentrate demand (by creating larger and larger outlets whose volume would give them economies of scale), and differentiate demand (by creating 'own brands' and, latterly, by making the stores themselves into an added value 'brand' which could compete on basis other than price alone).

The effect of this in the UK over time – in the USA the relationship and its consequences have been rather different – has been a tendency to reduce the resources available for supporting manufacturer brands in ways other than cutting the price (or some equivalent incentive to stock) to the retailer. It has also created a double jeopardy for brands which are not brand leaders; the retailer can 'afford' not to stock them but they cannot afford not to be stocked. Other things being equal, it is clear that in a situation where three or four retail chains control half the sales of a brand which itself holds less than 0.1 per cent of those retailers' sales, marketing must shift its emphasis to *pushing* the product through (that is, getting product into stock) and, to that extent, less into *pulling* product through (that is, differentiating demand among consumers.)

There are other reasons too why classic packaged goods advertising has begun to be less dominant in total advertising activity than it used to be. For one thing, there has been a growth in service markets generally and in financial services markets particularly. In many of these markets there is a tendency for the advertising task to polarize between highly generalized 'corporate' support and highly specific support and promotion for often short-lived products. Another factor is the quickening pace of the life-cycle of a number of advertised products. This applies both to the financial services products which we have already mentioned and to other product fields like consumer electronics. Shorter product life-cycles mean that there is less time to recover the initial investment. With manufactured goods there is also less likelihood that the economies of scale potentially open to those first into the market could offset the steep decline in the general manufacturing costs of the technology which so often characterizes technological markets. In these situations there may well be less to allocate to advertising but, equally important, what is allocated must 'move a lot of boxes' before price- and distribution-led competition absorbs most of marketing's resources.

There is also a broader thrust at work in many *high* frequency of purchase markets whose implications are harder to predict. This thrust comes from the information revolution particularly as it has affected data capture and data analysis. With (or even, on occasion, without) bar coding of goods, it is now possible to retrieve information about sales as they occur at the till and analyse these so as to control stock, facings, reordering and pricing, and, of course, to provide an up-to-the-minute information base for the buyer at head office doing a deal with the manufacturer. One effect of this is greatly to reduce the scope for traditional manufacturer influence on *in-store* marketing, but as these activities have traditionally competed with media advertising for a share of the marketing cake the result may be to increase the importance of advertising in the mix.

A stage further on (quite a bit further on) in the use of electronic point of sale (EPOS) data would be the ability *to cross-analyse sales by purchasers by media exposure* as the ultimate form of instant single-source data. Ad-lab data of this kind obviously have huge potential though it should be noted that generating them is one thing and using them effectively is quite another – most information systems in marketing and advertising have been significantly underused. Be this as it may, it seems reasonable to suppose that it would increase and sophisticate the dialogue on media policy between client and agency, provided that the client could have access to these largely retailer-generated data. This is not to say that it would always tend to increase total media spend.

With or without the ad-lab development, EPOS is part of the evolution of the retail sector towards higher margin strategies and away from price competition (in which the lever to profit is sheer volume). In principle, this should make manufacturers' added value brands (and the advertising that builds and maintains them) more attractive to the retailer. Equally, however, it highlights the fact that switched sales between brands, which change brand shares but not margin or total volume in the product field, are of no particular interest as far as the retailer is concerned. Switching sales, gaining share, are what advertising does best; it can also help to expand the market, if there is room for growth. In future manufacturers' marketing objectives may need to be at least as much margin led as they are share led. Added value competition at a price premium is more difficult than at price parity and represents a challenge both to new product development and advertising. It could also imply fewer winners unless there is a more effective segmentation of the market.

On balance, this particular development looks as if it will tend to maintain the importance of brand-building advertising, but it may also make it even more competitive for the agencies concerned as the *real* index of performance becomes sterling 'margin share'.

Increasingly, distributed computer power will also greatly expand the potential for applying statistical modelling to markets – and not only to packaged goods markets. This will, as noted earlier, sharpen the element of accountability in the client agency relationship, but it is a long haul, requiring good data and a long time series over which the data have been collected. It also has one disadvantage, not unknown elsewhere in advertising, which is that the data are very difficult to communicate *with all their proper qualifications* to those who have to act on them. The 'boffins' should not be asked to bear the responsibility for this problem on their own – marketing and advertising management must advance half way to meet them.

MARKETING AND THE ADVERTISING PROCESS

With one significant exception the whole thrust of this review so far has been to emphasize the necessarily close relationship between the ways marketing and advertising work. Yet whatever the focus, short or long term, just moving unit sales or building a consumer franchise, this symmetry between the tasks and objectives of marketing and advertising is very easy to lose sight of in the real world of the client–agency relationship and the agency's way of working.

One factor here is that clients can be concerned about the confidentiality of key financial performance data, so the agency may not know, for example, the client's margin, other costs and so on. While understandable this is also limiting, not only on the agency's ability to offer general advice but also on the extent to which the agency can really understand the total contect of its work as when, for example, it recommends an advertising budget.

Two other necessary factors that arise in the translation from a marketing problem to an advertising objective however are just as important. One of them is the 'gap' we have already mentioned that exists between the advertising strategy and the actual advertising recommendation. Most, if not quite all, advertisements have to be based on an advertising *idea*, which is *not* the same as the advertising strategy. It will be based on the strategy of course, and designed to achieve the consumer responses which the strategy says will help the sell, but it is not created *by* the strategy: it is created *to* the strategy. The ideas that the agency's creative department devise may or may not contain words or claims that reflect the strategy in a literal and direct way.

Creative ideas and their treatment in advertisements constitute the 'language' of advertising. That language has its own conventions, resources and skills. It can draw heavily on the style and typical content of the medium in which it appears (for example, when television advertising uses a 'sit-com' idea as the basis of a campaign). It has its own conventions, too, which arise out of all those approaches, devices, and techniques which are the natural armoury of simplifying communications and persuasive communications – like product demonstration,

597

product endorsement, analogy, imagery, humour and wit. Not every advertisement, of course, uses these resources to the same extent – an 'earpiece' advertisement (those you sometimes see either side of the name of the newspaper on its front page) may simply repeat the brand's 'logo' – this will depend on the job the advertisement is trying to do. But every advertisement, even the simplest, will be trying to have an impact on its audience and leave an 'impression' (consciously or unconsciously) about the product. How effective an advertisement is at doing this job will depend in part on how many target consumers it reaches (its coverage) and how often it reaches them (its 'frequency') but it will also depend on how well it uses the resources of the language of advertising which we have been discussing.

Advertising as a *craft* – the craft of the creation and production of advertisements – is, therefore, unlike many other marketing tasks in its specific skills and in its product. Both are decisive for the character of an agency, for the work satisfaction of all those employed in it (not just the 'creatives' themselves), and for its success in winning and keeping business. So, although in the multi-disciplinary world of the agency there are many relevant skills and resources which to a greater or lesser extent overlap those in the client's marketing department, there are other *defining* elements in it which make it different and mark out its operational goals as in many ways peculiarly its own.

Good advertising is one such goal, and good media planning and buying another. Indeed, media planning and buying, though it receives in its own right less attention from the general public, is the other distinguishing activity of an agency and the other service which its clients are buying, apart from advertisements themselves. They may buy these services from separate sources rather than from one full-service advertising agency but, whether they buy their media from the same source or separately from a media independent (as 'media only' agencies tend to be known), media planning and buying is a craft in its own right with its own special skills and resources. The world of media with its audience research data, its comparisons of cost-per-thousand (the cost of reaching 1000 of a given audience or circulation), its analysis of reach and frequency, its schedules (the media chosen for a campaign together with the timing – and size or length – of the ads to appear in it), and its optimizations (maximizing what can be obtained for a given campaign cost against specified criteria of coverage and frequency) is also a very different world from that of marketing and, it should be said, from that of creating and producing the advertisements themselves.

We have spoken of these distinctive outputs of an agency as its operational goals to distinguish them as activities from the marketing ends which they both serve. It would be more accurate to speak of them as the distinctive *operational activities* of the advertising business which in their turn have their own distinctive operational goals. If this sounds like more word play on a sort of Russian dolls basis (when each doll opens to reveal another doll which opens to reveal another doll ... and so on) that is because in any multi-disciplinary and multi-stage business *one person's strategy is always likely to be another's objective.*

For example, a company's business objective may be growth in profits and its strategy to milk existing brands in saturated markets while expanding brand share for its brands in growth sectors. In the light of this the marketing director and his or her brand people may have an objective of increasing share while maintaining margins in their growth markets and a strategy of achieving this by increasing distribution and advertising support. The agency may, therefore, have the objective of stimulating trial among non-users of the brand and a strategy of doing this by increasing awareness and emphasizing its suitability for certain end uses to which product quality is particularly relevant. The agency's creative department will have the objective of increasing awareness and improving perceptions of quality along with the salience of certain end uses, and the creative recommendation will in effect constitute its strategy for achieving this. The final 'strategy' in this chain of objectives and strategies is the advertisement or the campaign. In the agency part of the chain, the objectives and their strategies are framed in terms of what advertising can achieve *per se* (for example increase awareness, modify attitudes, stimulate trial – not gain share, increase volume) so that, in this respect, the disciplines of thought which guide the advertising process are distinctive of that process just as much as the craft skills and activities which constitute its end-product to the client.

This contrast between marketing's and advertising's common pursuit of differentiation in the marketplace, on the one hand, and their distinctive differences in craft skills, operational goals and disciplines of thought on the other, is nothing special or unusual. Similar contrasts will be found wherever there is specialization within a common endeavour.

One other aspect worth noting, however, is how the search for differentiation in the creative product of advertising leads to a great deal of stress on the new and the original. This is *not* to say that original and creative thought are not found in the rest of the marketing mix – they are and they should be – but the importance of originality in the creative idea and the skills which make that originality work in terms of television, press, radio, posters or cinema, bring into sharp focus a necessary connection between the craft of advertisements and the arts, entertainment and editorial skills of the media in which advertisements appear.

Emphasizing this aspect of the business must be done with care. It can all too often seem like a covert plea for self-indulgence by the agency and an excuse for weakening the need for relevance. That it should neither be like this nor have this effect goes without saying. Equally, however, it is not to be despised simply because it can be abused. It can make an extremely valuable contribution to the sales effectiveness of advertising in the marketplace, as is shown by the number of cases in the IPA Advertising Effectiveness Awards where the advertisements concerned win creative awards as well.

THE ADVERTISING CYCLE AND THE AGENCY ACCOUNT TEAM

Advertising is a cyclical process of which advertisements and media schedules are the recurrent product. The cycle starts with what might be called a planning baseline; this leads to the development of a strategy, which leads to the development of a creative brief and a budget, which leads to creative and media recommendations, which lead to running the advertisements, which in turn lead to monitoring our apparent progress in the market place, which will, sooner or later, become the new planning baseline, with the cycle starting all over again.

As described, the process sounds simple enough. In practice it can be a complex process, which is feedback-intensive, prone to error, and as dependent on sound judgement as on good data. Of course, advertising accounts can differ enormously in their complexity and in the scope and nature of the feedback which is provided, while agencies themselves differ in how they are organized to apportion the various responsibilities to which the process gives rise. For this reason it may be most useful to distinguish the responsibilities as such prior to any consideration of who fulfils them.

600

In fairly simplistic terms the responsibilities can be listed as follows.

1 *Agency responsibilities to the clients*
   - to advise them generally in their own best interest
   - to provide creative and media recommendations which are relevant and appropriate to the client's business and marketing objectives and strategy
   - to effect this at an appropriate level of quality, professionalism, timeliness, and cost-effectiveness
2 *Agency responsibilities to the brand and to the consumer*
   - to relate the brand to the target consumer through the advertising so as to help the sell
   - in such a way as to be true to the heritage, character and performance of the brand *and* relevant to the current needs and satisfaction of the target consumers
   - to do this as far as possible so as to protect *future* sales of the brand
3 *Agency responsibilities to itself*
   - to keep the business and handle it profitably
   - to ensure so far as possible that the client not only receives the best advice but is persuaded by it.
   - not only to produce but to run work which merits the respect of its peer group agencies in the business
   - to attract and retain good talent and, as far as possible, to provide the scope and incentive for its development at every level in the agency

At first sight such a list may seem somewhat surprising in its structure and emphasis. It is not, of course, a list of legal responsibilities, so it says nothing about the fact that an agency is a principal and not an agent when it acts on behalf of its clients. It does not tell one whether the agency's remuneration will be commission-based or, as is increasingly the case, fee-based. It gives little indication of the terms of business to be agreed with the client. Furthermore, it appears to draw a surprising distinction between the interests of the client and those of the brand and an invidious distinction between both of these and the agency's own interest.

In reality, of course, all these interests overlap: they are complementary rather than contradictory, but is is important to remember that they are not identical. They *can* clash when things get out of kilter. The advertising management task which is shared between a good agency and a good client is to ensure that all these critical responsibilities remain in their proper complementary relationship to one another.

For example, it is not in the client's long-term interest that good agency service should remain unprofitable to that agency, any more than it is in the long-term interests of consumers that a good brand should not make any money for its manufacturer. Again, clients with a portfolio of brands may well be tempted to improve the bottom line by a short-term policy of under-supporting one brand or purely price promoting it in a way that undermines its long-term franchise, securing sales today at the expense of sales tomorrow. If the agency doesn't 'stand up' for the brand in this situation, who will?

Similarly, it is the brand's relationship to the consumer's needs and perceptions, not to those of the production manager or sales manager, that matters. Production may want to stress features or ingredients (or even, according to agency folklore, the factory) rather than consumer benefits or uses or social gratifications; sales may want to emphasize the logo, the value for money, and a slogan they think will appeal to the trade.

Again, agencies cannot best serve their clients through glorious failure. Good work which doesn't run is a loss to the client and a blow to the agency. True, not all 'good work' (in the agency's eyes) is necessarily sales-effective and not all 'dull work' is sales-*in*effective, but in a situation of trust such a dichotomy should be resolvable by research feedback and judgement. It can always be argued that if dull work can sell *n* boxes then good work *of the right kind* should be able to sell *n +* boxes.

Not all agencies and not all clients could be induced to underwrite all the responsibilities stated here. Some on both sides set their face against creative awards, for example, as a permanent temptation to self-indulgence and irrelevance. Others, by contrast, believe the real temptation to be in the other direction: work that is nominally relevant in that you can match all the points in it against the strategy, but which never in fact comes to life and never engages the consumer such that its relevance becomes meaningful and effective. There is obviously a question here of balance and fitness for purpose, and a different balance may have to be struck in different situations.

All these responsibilities involve issues and different areas of expertise which have to be handled within the resources of the account team, drawing where necessary on internal agency resources or from outside.

Leadership and the primary interface with the client will lie with the account director, media and creative responsibilities with the appropriate members of the team. In respect of those responsibilities which we have described as being to the brand and to the consumer, practice is more variable: they can be handled by the account director working with either an agency researcher or outside research suppliers when research is called for. Increasingly, and particularly in larger agencies in the UK, they will be separately identifiable as the proper sphere of the 'account planner' in the team.

The account planner in this situation will be responsible for generating the advertising strategy in the first place, and for any research-based creative development of the creative ideas produced to that strategy. The account planner will, therefore, be responsible for selecting and interpreting the research evidence both at these stages and at the final stage of evaluation in the marketplace, which leads to the next planning baseline and the next round of the advertising planning cycle. In this sense, as *the representative of the consumer's needs and perceptions* the account planner gives a separate and independent voice to the marketing principle as adapted to the agency's own specific product and way of working.

Throughout the advertising cycle, feedback in the form of research or other data has potentially a large and important role to play. The kind of research that is deployed will have much to do with the particular stage in the cycle that has been reached – at the beginning it may tend to the exploratory, the 'open-ended' and the qualitative, at the end to the structured, focused and quantified. It will also have much to do with the respective philosophies of the agency and the client and with the way they have respectively understood the marketing and advertising task. In a nutshell, *how you think the marketing works will influence how you think the advertising works which in turn will influence how you think the research works*. This symmetry is perfectly proper and many of the arguments about research technique and methodology simply conceal a lack of congruence between the way the client and the agency understand the fundamental task. Here, as elsewhere, it would often be more fruitful to bring the assumptions out into the open and see why they differ rather than argue, often fruitlessly, about the methodological consequences that simply follow from them.

In the end there are as many models for marketing and advertising as there are types of differential advantage. Certainty is rarely attained and even more rarely held on to, because solutions wear out and problems change. In any case, the 'how' and 'why' questions, which are so important to consumer choice, do not give *actionably certain* answers whether or not we *count* the answers to them across a representative sample or simply listen to them in group discussions. So advertising decision, however well or extensively informed, is always, in the end, based on judgement, which is why respect and trust between all the parties to it, including the client, are the foundation on which everything else is based.

THE CONTROL AND REGULATION OF ADVERTISING

Advertising in the UK is carried on within a regulatory framework which acts to curb abuse and to make advertising responsive to the public consensus as well as to the letter of the law.

It has not always been so. Ninteenth-century patent medicine advertising in the UK, as elsewhere, was singularly free of any regard for the truth, however laxly defined. The gradual application of legal controls and a rising standard of education in the marketplace as a whole were two important pressures in raising standards. The present regulatory system can be regarded as the product of the culmination of these two pressures in the development of consumerism in the 1960s, accelerated by a new consciousness of the potential power of advertising which followed the introduction and spread in coverage of commercial television from 1955 onwards.

As a result the UK now has a mixed system of statutory control and self-regulation. The civil law deals also with such matters as copyright, trademark infringement, passing off and defamation. Broadcast advertising (that is, TV and radio commercials) is subject to a system of statutory control. The Code of Advertising Standards and Practice for these two media is the statutory responsibility of the Independent Broadcasting Authority (IBA) and its day-to-day implementation in clearance procedures is the responsibility of the Independent Television Companies Association (ITCA) and the Association of Independent Radio Contractors (AIRC) respectively. The code is specifically designed to avoid confusion between advertisements and programme material. Changes in the code and its application are the responsibility of the Advertising Advisory Committee which is an independent and broadly representative body appointed by the IBA.

Print advertising is governed on a non-statutory self-regulatory basis, administered by the Advertising Standards Authority (ASA) and funded by a levy on all display advertising. It is this body which deals with complaints from the public. The intra-industry complaints and issues are dealt with by the Code of Advertising Practice Committee, which represents all the main parties to the advertising business and is responsible for the British Code of Advertising Practice (BCAP) and the British Code of Sales Promotion Practice (BCSPP). These codes are not legally enforceable but bad publicity is a powerful corrective, backed up by the willingness of media to refuse space to the rule-breakers. On the whole, the system works well, not least because the spirit of the code is regarded as being as important as the letter and because specific provision is made for difficult areas like taste and decency. It is in the interests of marketing and advertising as well as consumers that it should continue to work well. As a result of the Misleading Advertising Regulations 1987 self-regulation has received some statutory back-up in the form of a reserve power by which the Director General of Fair Trading can have legal recourse in those few cases where the ASA cannot act quickly enough or cannot secure compliance.

Nothing is ever perfect, of course, and some controversy still surrounds the effect of the regulation of various financial markets in the city, which affects increasingly important areas of advertising activity like flotation. In general, however, the system keeps advertising 'clean'. If it were not so, advertising would be less effective and, it should be said, less attractive.

FURTHER READING

Broadbent, S. (ed) (1987), *Twenty Advertising Case Histories*, Holt, Rinehart & Winston, London.

Broadbent, S. and Jacobs, B. (1984), *Spending Advertising Money*, 4th edn, Business Books, London.

Channon, C. (ed) (1985), *Advertising Works 3*, Holt, Rinehart & Winston, London.

Channon, C. (ed) (1987), *Advertising Works 4*, Cassell, London.

605

Douglas, M. and Isherwood, B. (1980), *The World of Goods: Towards an Anthropology of Consumption*, Penguin, Harmondsworth.

Douglas, T. (1984), *The Complete Guide to Advertising*, Macmillan, London.

Jones, J. P. (1986), *What's in a Name? Advertising and the Concept of Brands*, Gower, Aldershot.

King, S. (1970), *What is a brand?*, J. Walter Thompson, London.

White, R. (1988), *Advertising: What it is and how to do it* Revised edn, McGraw-Hill, London.

Wolfe, A. (1986), 'The effects of scanning on the manufacturer/retailer relationship', *ADMAP*, Vol. 22, No. 10, October, pp. 56–59, 70.

34

Sales promotion

Alan Toop

Arguably, sales promotion is the most important marketing tool in use today; firstly, because promotional activities, especially price-cutting, have a direct and considerable effect on the fortunes (literally) of most mass-manufacturing and mass-retailing companies; second-ly, because monies spent on sales promotion, as far as they can be estimated, are greater than the expenditure on any other marketing function.

So starts Chris Petersen's book, *Sales Promotion in Action* (1979). And he continues by defining sales promotion as:

- a featured offer
- of tangible advantages not inherent in the product or service pro-moted
- for the achievement of marketing objectives.

'A featured offer' is one that is not just a normal and unremarked and taken-for-granted aspect of trade in the product or service being promoted. 'Of tangible advantages not inherent in the product or service' means that the offer must be of tangible, physically quantifiable nature, not just an appeal to the emotions or intellect, as is often the case with classic media advertising. And the offer needs to be of something which is not *essential* to what is being promoted to make it fit for its purpose. For example, the offer of fuel injection as a superior alternative to carburettors, at no extra charge, might form a sales promotional offer for a car; a free engine would not.

'The achievement of marketing objectives' can mean a whole variety of possible objectives, as is illustrated by the following list of examples of sales promotions.

1 '2p off', which has as its objective the selling of more product to the consumer.
2 'Half-price this week only!' is aimed at selling a lot more, very quickly.
3 'We won't invoice you for ninety days' is intended to persuade the trade to take delivery now when you have delivery capability to spare, even though the consumer buying season does not start for another two months or more.
4 'A free case to you the wholesaler, for every ten cases you sell to your retail customers' aims to motivate someone else to sell more.
5 'Your first month's stock free!' may persuade a retailer to stock your product.
6 'You could win this gold bar if you're displaying our Gold Seal when Miss Goldilocks visits your store' may persuade retailers to erect displays.
7 'Try this sample, then take this 10p coupon to your nearest ... ' prompts trial of a new product.
8 '30p a case discount, enabling you to offer it to your customers at only 22p a packet' should encourage retailers to feature this low price in their own principal advertising campaign.
9 'Free colour licence when you rent this TV' overcomes the barrier formed by the cost of the licence fee when renting colour television.
10 'Send six proofs of purchase to obtain this tea towel free' has as its objective to retain repeat purchase loyalty over six purchases.
11 'Save for your old age as you smoke Filter X' is intended to retain repeat purchase loyalty forever.
12 '£25 off these language tuition tapes when you book your holiday with us' communicates the fact that we specialize in holidays for the intellectually curious.

Is sales promotion really so very different from advertising, then, if its objectives can include communicating the character of holidays? The answer must be yes, even though the differences are not necessarily those implied in the old distinction between 'theme' advertising and 'scheme' promotions; the classic dividing of support activities 'above' or 'below the line'; the distinction between long-term, strategic, media advertising and short-term tactical sales promotion.

One difference has already been noted. This is the more tangible, physical, character of many sales promotions, appealing through the tactile qualities of three-dimensional physical objects as much as through the senses of sight or sound which are more the province of television commercials or press advertisements.

Indeed sales promotion has media of its own which have just this dimension of physical immediacy:

1   door-to-door distribution of, for example, a sample of a new product and a coupon worth 10p when taken to the shop and redeemed against a full-size first purchase of the new product;
2   promotional teams of in-store demonstrators, or display checkers (as in example 6 above), or promotion announcers, or sample or coupon distributors in store;
3   the promoted product's pack, in which promotional premiums can be packed.

Of course sales promotion does also make use on occasion of classic media such as press advertisements to help communicate an offer.

Much sales promotion activity is short term, concerned with the here and now. It is designed to produce a quick and numerically measurable result: more sales to the trade; or more customers buying this month than last; or more agents handling the service than ever before; or 1500 grocers displaying pre-packed display units.

But sales promotion is not *necessarily* short term. There are many case histories to prove the contrary. The annual Miss Pears Competition is still going strong, having been originated in its present form in 1957, and dating back to 1932 in an earlier version. Similarly, the British co-operative movement started offering dividends as a loyalty bonus, a classic sales promotional technique, in 1844 (rather longer than most current advertising campaigns have been running!). Of course, not everybody notices the dividend was a sales promotion until co-op societies started offering instant dividends in the form of co-op dividend stamps, in the 1960s.

Similarly, much sales promotional work is concerned with offering incentives: 'Buy this and I'll give you that', or 'do this and I'll make it worth your while'. Co-op dividend stamps illustrate this approach but

609

incentive is a very inadequate description of many other sales promotions. The annual Miss Pears Competitions, for example, generate a number of entries which though high compared with many other competitions are low compared with the total number of purchases of Pears soap made during the year. The competitions are therefore offering a direct incentive to buy to only a rather small minority of all the users to whom Pears needs to sell to reach its sales targets. The rationale of this promotion, the reason why Pears has persevered with it over the years, must clearly lie elsewhere. We can safely conclude it is because the competition communicates a message about the brand, associating it with skin of girlish freshness.

ADVERTISING OR PROMOTION?

So when does one use advertising, and when sales promotion, to achieve given marketing objectives? As in so many areas of marketing, there are few hard and fast rules. It is essentially a case of 'horses for courses', of one technique being more likely to succeed than another in a given set of circumstances.

Budgets are important in this context, the amount of money available to finance sales promotion and/or advertising. Your advertising agency will tell you that it is not worth spending below a certain minimum level in the various classic media, and that below this level your brand or service's 'voice' will be drowned in the hubbub of other advertisers shouting their wares. And this minimum level is likely to increase in line with your immediate competitor's spending.

Among British manufacturers of packaged goods more and more advertisers have been dropping down to and below this minimum level of media budget over the past twenty years. This is not least because such manufacturers have channelled more and more money into sales promotion, including price cutting, under pressure from the ever more powerful retail trade on which they rely for the final distribution of their goods to the end consumer.

Sales promotion is such a great rag-bag of methods and media, of techniques and tactics, of possibilities and opportunities, that more often than not some sort of cost-effective promotional scheme can be created on budgets significantly lower than those required to sustain a classic advertising campaign. Indeed, as I wrote (Toop, 1978):

The very lack of clearly defined boundaries to sales promotion activity represents its constant potential for original solutions to marketing problems. The very lack of well-established traditions in sales promotions encourages innovation, encourages radical answers to fresh challenges as they arise.

In no other part of the whole spectrum of marketing activities is there more call for imagination and inventiveness; for lateral as well as logical thinking; for understanding of what will not just gain attention but will also maintain an audience's interest. In no other marketing activity is there greater scope for creativity; and in no other can creativity produce commercial dividends so cheaply.

Budgets are not of course the whole story. Some marketing tasks have become almost the preserve of sales promotion, since sales promotion techniques have proven so effective in accomplishing them. For example, sampling new products, where the letterbox distribution of small-size samples and/or high-value coupons can produce a wide-scale trial by consumers quicker and probably in greater depth than waiting for media advertising to persuade them to go in search of the product in the shops. Again, a series of in-store demonstrations of the new product will create a level of consumer purchases that will convince the retail chain that the new product is worth stocking and being assigned shelf space.

The competitive situation cannot be ignored either. Some markets have become so heavily promoted that an unpromoted product or service has become well nigh unsaleable. And it is not just competition with outsiders that counts: some large food manufacturers, for example, often formed from a series of takeovers or mergers in recent years, ask their sales forces to handle so many different products that to get the sales force to redirect the necessary attention to any one of these products requires the product to carry a new promotion. This may or may not be an appropriate way to get the company's employees to do what it wants, but that is often the way it is.

WHO IS RESPONSIBLE?

This brings us to the who and how of sales promotion. Who should be responsible for sales promotion in a promoting company, and how should they organize the creation and implementation of sales promotion? The topic is important. As suggested at the beginning of this

611

chapter, expenditure on sales promotion now probably exceeds that on almost any other marketing function. In many companies in which the division of total support budgets between advertising and sales promotion twenty years ago was typically advertising 60 per cent, sales promotion 40 per cent, these proportions are today reversed. The first observation about who docs what in salcs promotion is that fcw companies as yet involve their senior management in sales promotion as fully as their huge and growing spending on sales promotion would seem to justify.

Most commonly sales promotional activity is regarded as a marketing department responsibility, in which the initiator of any single promotion is most likely to be a senior brand manager. The marketing manager, to whom this senior brand manager reports, may or may not be closely involved in approving the proposed promotion. It is quite likely to depend on his or her personal taste, rather than on any clearly defined responsibility written into a job specification. The marketing director is unlikely to be involved, except in the most general terms of approving annual promotion budgets and broad promotional strategies. He or she is much more likely to be closeted in meetings with the company's advertising agencies, deciding on the next television commercial, even though the money to be spent on it may be modest in relation to the sales promotional fortune being spent by his or her subordinates. 'Below the line' can mean out of sight.

The management structure of some companies is even worse adapted to the realities and needs of sales promotion in another respect: that is, by far the fastest growing part of sales promotion spending over the past decade has been on trade bonusing, trade discounting, 'special allowances' and on price-cutting activities of all sorts. A large part of this expenditure is channelled through the hands of sales managers, who in practice take decisions as to how precisely it is used.

These sales managers have a variety of titles, including 'national accounts manager', but they all have in common the fact that they report to the sales director; they are not part of the marketing department, and they are not often responsible for profit. Much of the price-cutting budget is therefore used to gain sales, and the cost of these sales, and their profitability or otherwise, are only rarely the responsibility of the sales personnel spending the money. Not surprisingly, therefore, the promotional cost of these sales – in a situation where competitors respond to a discount of 20p a case' with '22p a case' and to '2p off' with '3p off' – rises steadily. Thus the sums of money available for other forms of brand support, notably advertising, are steadily eroded.

Thus, the growth of retailer power, about which we have all heard so much in recent years, has in part resulted from the weakness of manufacturers' management structures: their slowness to adapt to the realities of promotional spending.

Be that as it may, the promotions need creating and need implementing. Price promotions, almost more than any others, need a touch of imagination, a spark of creativity, an element of the new, the different, the surprising, to transform them from pedestrian, take-it-or-leave-it offers into offers that cannot be missed and probably will not be refused. So how does that senior brand manager (or whoever it is that is responsible) set about the task?

ORGANIZATION OF PROMOTIONS

First, at the risk of stating the obvious, he or she needs to know something about sales promotion. Such is the comparative youth of sales promotion in its modern form, and on its contemporary scale, that knowledge and experience of sales promotion and expertise in its use are still less widely diffused than is the case with other marketing functions such as the media advertising, market research or new product development.

If there is any doubt about the responsible person's understanding of sales promotion, it should be improved. He or she should buy a book or two on the subject (see the reading list at the end of this chapter); attend a training course on sales promotion (there is a small but growing number); study the code of practice issued by the Institute of Sales Promotion; read any available reports on the results of previous sales promotions carried out by the company; persuade one of the better sales promotional consultancies (more of them in a moment) to arrange a two-day visit to observe sales promotions being created and implemented.

Much depends on the human resources the company does or does not have. Some, for example, handle all sales promotional work in house. Such companies typically have a sales promotion manager running a department which may well include a premiums buyer, a print buyer and an executive controlling the handling and clearing operations of internal departments responsible for redeeming coupons channelled back from the distributive trade; fulfilling applications from the public for mail-in offers of premiums and cash refunds; and judging entries for prize promotions such as competitions and draws. How the starting ideas or concepts for such promotions are originated in these in-house operations is less clear (though none the worse for that), and certainly some such companies have careful methods and techniques for evaluating and developing at least those concepts, perhaps the more orthodox, which lend themselves to, for example, consumer panel pre-testing.

SALES PROMOTION CONSULTANCIES

At the far end of the spectrum other promoting companies buy-in or contract-out their promotional work. At its simplest, this consists of appointing a sales promotion consultancy (one that can demonstrate its facilities for implementing as well as creating promotions) to look after the total sales promotion operation. They do so in much the same way as a full service advertising agency creates the advertisements, commissions film production companies or finished artwork studios to produce them, selects the media, negotiates price with the media, books the media, and commissions the research required to check these decisions, at both before and after stages. In sales promotion terms this full service includes:

1 creating the ideas for the promotions;
2 producing designs and writing copy for all forms of communication of the promotions in sales promotional media, such as pack, point-of-sale display, in-store leaflets, sales presenters and so on;
3 commissioning finished artwork for these sales promotional media;
4 briefing, seeking competitive quotations for and then commissioning the manufacture of any premiums required by the promotions;
5 briefing, seeking competitive quotations for and then commissioning all print material required by the promotions;
6 briefing, seeking competitive quotations for and then commissioning companies specializing in these fields to handle postal applications or entries from the public, to redeem coupons returned from

the trade, to distribute promotional material door-to-door, to send promotional teams into stores to demonstrate, to distribute coupons or samples, or to erect or check displays;
7   commissioning whatever research may be appropriate to check the correctness of decisions both, before and after the running of promotions.

As with advertising agencies, the key contribution is the creative function. Well-managed implementation is vital, but should be taken for granted in any first class sales promotion consultancy. But good administration alone will not justify the substantial fees such consultancies earn; good ideas will. They will provide the means of cutting through the ever-increasing promotional clutter that disfigures so many markets today.

Between the exclusively in-house and entirely bought-in extremes there are many gradations and variations. Most promoting companies cluster round the mid-point of this spectrum of possibilities: probably employing consultants to create the concepts either on *ad hoc*/one-off of projects or (more and more commonly nowadays) on a retained basis; possibly buying print through the company's print buyer when his or her quotations are more attractive than the consultancy's; perhaps leaving the consultancy to buy any premiums that need creating, but contracting direct with premium manufacturers when the premiums are available off the shelf, and so on. Thus a division of responsibilities and functions is arrived at which best suits the needs and resources and, indeed, the management philosophy of the promoting company.

The first-time user of sales promotion can apply to the secretary general of the Institute of Sales Promotion, Arena House, 66–68 Pentonville Road, Islington, London N1 9HS, Tel: (01) 837-5340, to obtain further details of the growing number of sales promotional consultancies, as well as details of companies offering specialist services in fields such as coupon clearing, postal application handling, prize promotion judging, in-store demonstrations and merchandising.

Any company using or proposing to use any outside services such as these can be sure that Britain is as developed and sophisticated in terms of skills in all these sales promotional functions as any other country with which this author is familiar, including the USA. Indeed, it is measurably in advance of many other countries, including most in Western Europe.

REFERENCES AND FURTHER READING

The Institute of Sales Promotion recommends the following short reading list, and offers the comments which are made. A very comprehensive reading list is also available from the Institute.

Petersen, C. (1979), *Sales Promotion in Action*, Associated Business Press, London. A basic textbook covering the strategy and tactics of sales promotion.

Piper, J. (ed) (1980), *Managing Sales Promotion*, Gower, Aldershot. A comprehensive review of sales promotion in the UK, with contributions from many leading practitioners.

Toop, A. (1966), *Choosing the Right Sales Promotion*, Crosby Lockwood & Son, London (paperback (1978), The Sales Machine, London). A pioneering book on the subject, now revised and updated.

Toop, A. (1978), *Only £3.95?! – The Creative Element in Sales Promotion*, The Sales Machine, London. Creative solutions to sales promotion briefs, illustrated (colour) with numerous case histories.

35

Public relations

Frank Jefkins

Public relations can make a considerable contribution to marketing strategy, and is not limited to product publicity and what is sometimes regarded by marketing people as 'free advertising'. Moreover, since public relations concerns the total communications of a company it can make many indirect contributions to successful marketing. These range from employee relations to financial and political relations. Nor is PR limited to the corporate identity and the corporate image, two very different things which impinge on marketing.

A large volume of PR is conducted by non-commercial organizations which are not or are seldom involved in marketing or advertising.

And unlike advertising, where most practitioners are employed by advertising agencies, the majority of PR personnel work in-house and not in PR consultancies. Nevertheless, the consultancy world has grown immensely in the past three or four years.

These general statements are made to stress the breadth and nature of PR. It reaches into every facet of every kind of organization, commercial and non-commercial, private or public sector. This is because PR exists whether one likes it or not, or whatever one cares to call it, and whether one has specific people handling it. Any organization has to communicate with numerous groups of people and individuals. The purpose of that communication is to make itself understood. That will mean effecting changes in attitude if it is not understood or, worse still, misunderstood.

It is difficult to market successfully if a company is misunderstood –

or not even known – to the countless people who influence successful marketing. They are not just distributors and ultimate customers. They could be employees, possible recruits, politicians, civil servants, bankers, investors, stockbrokers, all kinds of opinion leaders as well as those more directly in the market place. They could be people with whom the marketing department normally has no dealings. Public relations extends far beyond the confines of marketing.

POSITIONING OF PR

This begs the question where should PR be positioned in a company? Sometimes it depends on who thought of it first, who decided there was a need for an organized PR unit. Much of PR is located in the marketing department, but this can be a handicap. Ideally, PR should report to top management (and in large companies PR is handled by a director) so that it can service the whole organization *including marketing*. The independence of the PR department will enhance its ability to operate broad scale.

No criticism of marketing is implied by this. To position the PR manager independently of marketing can actually strengthen his or her services to marketing. It is rather a case that PR is not a part of marketing but marketing *can* be a part of PR!

One of the reasons for undervaluing and misplacing PR is that it costs relatively little compared with promotional activities such as advertising. A main reason for this inexpensiveness (but cost-effectiveness) is that the primary PR cost is time or manpower. There may be expensive items like video or print, but PR costs are mainly those of human skill and manhours in a labour-intensive activity. This may be increased by the use of modern techniques such as desk-top editing, electronic mail, databases and other electronic aids to communication.

How can PR aid specific aspects of the marketing strategy? Let us start with the corporate identity.

CORPORATE IDENTITY

The creation of a corporate identity is the responsibility of PR, because it embraces every physical aspect of an organization, although an outside specialist may be commissioned to devise the scheme.

Corporate identity should not be confused with corporate image, to which the former may contribute. The first is how the company is seen physically – its visible uniformity – but the second is how it is perceived mentally, and this depends on knowledge and experience which will differ between individuals. While both employee and shareholder may be aware of, say, BT's yellow livery and distinctive logo, they could have very different mental images of the company. A corporate image can be volatile, and it may depend on how a company is seen to behave. BT's many categories of customer will each have their particular images, very much according to how they are deserved!

This is therefore a good point at which to dismiss one of the myths of PR often found in marketing circles – that PR is about creating favourable images – or favourable anything! PR is about facts not fiction. A favourable image cannot be created any more than a tarnished image can be polished. Life is full of good and bad: PR has to win understanding of both – why Intercity trains are fast and comfortable and why they are late, break down or have accidents.

But to return to the corporate identity scheme. Whether a new scheme is devised or an old one is changed it is a huge job. A distinctive logo is necessary but it must not be so clever it obscures the identity it is supposed to represent. A distinctive colour scheme is also necessary, and the colours of the rainbow have many shades to choose from. A typeface is required which, again, will enhance appearances, but lends itself to both elegant display and legible text. Specially designed clothing and accessories such as dresses, blouses, shirts, ties, scarves, headgear, overalls and badges may be required. Premises and transportation will have to be decorated. Logo, colours and typography will have to be applied to business stationery, annual reports, share certificates, calling cards and so on as well as to advertising, packaging and sales promotion materials. These needs stretch right across the organization.

All this uniformity gives strength to the organization, not merely providing identification. Promotionally, it is a company's warpaint, but also it represents the company's pride, its signature, its character, its separate and distinct being. And that communicates within and without the organization to everyone. It extends far beyond marketing, although marketing is one of its greatest beneficiaries, and it is something which marketing can exploit at every opportunity.

The public relations department has to ensure that the corporate identity scheme is carried out properly by all who are responsible for making purchases throughout the organization at home or abroad. For this purpose, an instruction manual has to be produced and distributed. This can take many forms such as a bound book, a spiral-bound manual, a wall-chart or a video, and it may have to be produced in a variety of languages and maybe with national variations. Sometimes, different colours may have to be used because of the special colour, the languages or preferences of certain societies, e.g. the Chinese or Muslims.

ADVERTISING

There are two aspects of the PR input regarding advertising. While PR exists whether we like it or not, advertising is optional. There are growth companies like Rentokil which have become leaders in their field, expanded internationally, and maintained a very healthy stock market quotation, which have spent little on advertising but exploited virtually every PR technique over the past thirty years. This was largely due to the faith put in PR by Bob Westphal who retired as chairman in 1987. But perhaps the classic example of a PR-oriented management and meagre advertising spend is Marks and Spencer.

This is not to deny the power and necessity of advertising, and its contribution to the success of many other companies. Nevertheless, there is a PR aspect which seriously concerns marketing and that is the extent to which a company's advertising enhances its reputation and both dealer and customer goodwill – or is it embarrassing?

An example of embarrassing advertising is 'knocking copy' in which certain companies indulge, the worst for many years being in the motor car industry. There have been other examples from the energy and computer industries and in 1987 even from a trade association, the Association of the British Pharmaceutical Industry (ABPI), which 'knocked' meat pies, beer, and eggs and bacon as being unhealthy, much to the annoyance of the food and brewing industries. There is supposed to be a self-regulating British Code of Advertising Practice (BCAP), yet over-zealous advertising agents (or over-demanding clients) regularly produce unethical advertisements which are reported to the Advertising Standards Authority by members of the public. Every month the ASA publishes its freely available *Cases Report*, in which all investigated complaints are reported. To be named in an ASA *Cases Report* (whether or not the complaint is upheld) is very bad PR.

There is, therefore, a serious need for marketing people responsible for advertising to be familiar with the BCAP, to see its advertising is beyond reproach, and perhaps to invite comment from the PR manager or consultant on advertisements at an early copy, visual, script or story-board stage. The famous names which appear in the ASA *Cases Report* every month indicate a very sloppy marketing attitude to the PR effect of advertising.

NAMING AND BRANDING

Naming and branding are essential pieces of communication, where PR and marketing should work together. Yet we can find the strangest and most confusing or forgettable names in the newer sunrise industries. Most computer company names sound as if they are in pharmaceuticals. Others have silly, inapt and confusing names like Apple, Apricot, and Acorn which are as bad as those for Nissan motor cars.

Naming, whether of a company, a product or a product range, is a vital form of both marketing and general business communication. Names should be distinctive, memorable and easy to pronounce and spell. Some of the best are short like Oxo or Omo, or simple initials like IBM or KLM, or pleasant acronyms like Fiat or Toshiba. True, it is not easy to create a new name, but how often is it conceived as the most elementary and yet valuable element in the marketing mix? What's in a name? Everything! It is basic PR.

Ford seem to be among the experts in this field. They start with a very simple household name, and then enhances their products with a galaxy of splendid names like Prefect, Consul, Granada, Capri, Fiesta, Orion, Sierra and so on. How much nicer to drive a car with one of those names than something with a forgettable name like Montego.

PACKAGING

Today it is possible to pack products, especially small unit FMCGs, in an amazing choice of containers and materials. It is possible to sell a product because of its container and in spite of the additional cost – the handy but expensive aerosol, for example. People are lazy and money-wasting – or call it convenience-minded and willing to pay for the benefit. They would rather have something measured or prepared rather than have to measure or prepare it themselves, hence the popularity of sachets or ready-made meals. All this relates to modern distribution methods such as the supermarket.

It is interesting that in Britain, Lean Cuisine was launched with a PR campaign whereas in the USA it had depended on an advertising campaign. While the emphasis was on the quality of the meals, it was also an example of how convenience foods lend themselves and their form of packaging to PR.

The added value of many modern packaging devices is a PR marketing plus because it is bound up with goodwill and customer satisfaction. Anticipating and satisfying customer demand is a matter of marketing and PR semantics. Goodwill may be regarded as an intangible asset but where packaging is concerned it results in very tangible sales and profits.

One feature of good packaging – which can include labelling and on-pack or in-pack instructions – is that when it is easy for a consumer to enjoy the benefits of a product or service that consumer is likely to buy again. Packaging is not therefore a matter of economics – is it cheaper to pack in a tube or a blister pack, is it cheaper to use plastic or foil – but will this or that packaging not only sell the product off the supermarket shelf but will it induce repeat purchasing? That is better economics, more practical marketing, and exceedingly good PR.

PRICING

Is the price not only economically right but right from the point of view of the customer? For example, the press carries a great deal of motor car insurance advertising (including direct response), yet the premiums are seldom as low as one can obtain through the AA brokerage service for members. Some of these prices are obviously not right and depend on gullible customers who are unaware of the market price.

To what extent does marketing adopt pricing policies which in the end prove to be good PR? Will people feel they have got value for money and paid a fair price, or will they resent being over charged? Will they prefer to pay more because in the end it proves to be cheaper, as when one buys a more expensive but more reliable motor car which is never off the road?

In Britain we live in less of a waste economy than the Americans who prefer to buy cheap motor cars that guzzle gasoline than more expensive sophisticated cars that last longer and consume less fuel. It is not surprising that *The Price is Right* should appeal to a large British TV audience: right pricing is a psychological truth in British marketing, as we see with Sainsbury's slogan 'Good Food Costs Less'. In a price-conscious society, price is a PR consideration bound up in goodwill, satisfaction, confidence and reputation.

While the marketing man may juggle with his pricing policies of skimming, psychological, economic, bargain, market and so on the bottom line is what sort of image does a company earn by its pricing strategy? Once upon a time it was how could we keep the price down: today there is sometimes a fear that a low price rubbishes the product. It is in fact easier to raise a price than to reduce it, for one suggests superiority and the other inferiority.

DEALER RELATIONS

Not everything is bought off the shelf, and only certain items are impulse purchases. Many products still depend on the advice, knowledge and enthusiasm of the man or woman behind the counter. Just how much does he or she know and understand about the product? Does the sales assistant just take the easy option and sell the smallest or cheapest size to make sure of a sale, or does he take the trouble to find out what is most likely to satisfy the customer's need? Does the supplying company depend only on trade terms, trade advertising or even sales promotion, or does it establish a relationship with dealers?

Dealer relations is often neglected by marketers who rely on the baker's dozen technique or think TV advertising will do everything. It won't. Marketing history is full of disasters because the shop assistant was too ignorant to sell the goods. The assistant who retorts 'Well, that's what they say in the advertising' isn't going to sell anything. But there are still companies which let their advertising agents spend their millions and think the buck begins on ITV.

A PR campaign can be developed around dealer relations alone. It can incorporate works (or other product visits); a dealer house journal; retail staff training courses; invitations to visit stands at exhibitions; dealer conferences (including previews of commercials at TV stations);

dealer videos and slide presentations, window or store dressing contests; and trade press relations to keep dealers informed through their trade journals.

MARKET EDUCATION

Otherwise known as pre-selling, this is a major PR activity which has been used by many successful companies as diverse as holiday and transportation firms, insurance companies, electronics and computer manufacturers and pharmaceutical companies. It is less applicable to FMCGs, but has been used by more sophisticated producers as in the case of Lean Cuisine.

With more technical or newer products market education consists of PR methods to prepare the market for an eventual launch which may be in from six to eighteen months' time.

It may depend on the innovator or dispersion theory whereby one influential person or customer is encouraged to make an experimental purchase. This initial purchase, by demonstration or recommendation, encourages others to copy and become adopters. Gradually, the idea spreads until finally the most conservative laggards become purchasers. One of the earliest examples was McCormick with his mechanical farm equipment in America's mid-west, while modern examples have ranged over pest control, fruit pickers, computerized trains, direct-input type-setting and hospital equipment.

Sometimes market education requires a familiarization process, so that when the product is eventually available on the market the particular consumer public is aware of it and ready to buy. This may entail all sorts of PR activity such as reports, pictures and features in both print and broadcast media. This happened over three or four years with the Metro motor car, and its eventual appearance on the market was welcomed. But it failed to happen with the Sinclair tricycle, which was expected to be an 'electric car' and turned out to be something that could be ridiculed on *Spitting Image*.

THE AFTER MARKET

If customers are assured of after-sales service and spare parts facilities, if manuals and instructions are clear, if guarantees are worthwhile or better still comprise of simple promises, if customer interest is maintained, another important aspect of PR is achieved. Confidence and goodwill may encourage the initial purchase, produce recommendations, and result in habit buying or eventual replacement of the same make.

Why is it that so many companies are careless or complacent about the after-market, being concerned only with the immediate sale?

Yet this is the most important PR aspect of marketing. It does not require the advice of PR management, only the PR-mindedness of marketing management. That is perhaps the real secret of PR. It is not always an outside technique performed by a PR functionary. In most of our successful companies PR is implicit in management, executive and supervisory philosophy throughout the organization. Yes, it may be best if PR techniques are integrated in an independent PR department answerable to top management, but a great deal of PR is simply communication to achieve understanding and that is the responsibility of everyone, especially marketing personnel.

PR TECHNIQUES

Apart from PR's broader relationship with the marketing mix, there are those PR activities which are distinct from advertising but which have marketing implications.

A major area of PR is internal management–employee relations, which have developed rapidly in recent years, partly because of the democratization of industrial relations, partly because smaller work forces are more intimate, and partly because electronics have made internal communications so much easier. More harmonious staff relations mean better productivity, better quality products, and better delivery, which are all aids to more successful marketing.

Media relations, a basic PR technique, operates at all levels and conveys information to the community or neighbours, employees, suppliers, distributors, the money market, consumers and users, and opinion leaders. The marketing effort is aided by the company, its people and its products or services being constantly in the news.

To reach more specialist publics, the PR department also creates its own media such as external house journals, documentary films and videos, educational print, private exhibitions, audio-visuals and visual aids. It also organizes events for the media and for special groups, and these may include works visits, talks and video shows, seminars and conferences.

Another PR activity (but one which may also have advertising and marketing appeals) is sponsorship, which can aid the corporate image, create goodwill and, through repetitive media coverage, increase awareness of a company or its products or services. With some advertising media (TV for example) becoming non-cost-effective beyond a certain point, many companies have preferred to invest in sponsorship. There are specialist consultancies that bring together those seeking to be sponsored and those wishing to sponsor, and which will organize the entire undertaking.

On the whole, PR is about overcoming the negative situations of hostility, prejudice, apathy and ignorance by informing, educating and creating knowledge, and thereby establishing and maintaining understanding, goodwill and reputation. Much of this calls for solving communication problems, effecting change, and giving advice to all sectors of management. Ideally, PR starts with the chief executive. It is significant that during recession and the development of new high-tech industries, the most successful companies have been those where PR has been recognized at board level, either because of enlightened management or because the PRO has had board director status.

OUTSIDE PR SERVICES

Reference has been made so far to the in-house PR unit, either as part of the marketing department or, more realistically, as an independent department servicing the whole organization including marketing. But what of the PR consultancy? It should not be called an 'agency', a term confused with the advertising agency which is strictly speaking the agent of the media from which it traditionally earned commission. PR consultancies are nobody's agents and earn no commissions. They give advice to clients and are paid fees based on manhours. It is also a misnomer to refer to retainers, unless they are paid (like retainers to lawyers) for exclusivity but no service (which must be paid for additionally).

Unlike advertising agencies which are appointed when the volume of advertising makes this viable and better creativity and media buying skills are required, PR consultancies tend to be appointed either when a company undertakes too little PR to justify a PRO, or because it is so busily engaged in PR that it needs to augment the PR department with extra or specialist services.

In Britain today there are many specialist PR consultanices, a major specialism being financial PR, while another concerns parliamentary liaison. Others handle exhibition PR, or the production of house journals, while still more specialize in certain fields such as high technology, food, fashion, travel or entertainment. The *Hollis Press and PR Annual* lists some 1200 consultancies, and a similarly large list appears in *Advertisers Annual*. The larger ones belong to the Public Relations Consultants Association which lists its members in the *Public Relations Year Book* which it publishes jointly with the *Financial Times*. Lists of clients also appear in these annuals.

Individual public relations practitioners may be elected to membership of the Institute of Public Relations, and membership of this professional body indicates that the individual has a minimum of five years' comprehensive experience and upholds the IPR's Code of Professional Conduct. The recognized vocational qualification is the CAM Diploma in Public relations (DipCAM or MCAM indicating membership of the graduate body) awarded after a three-year examination conducted by the CAM Education Foundation. There is also the Group Diploma in Public Relations awarded by examination by the Examinations Board of the London Chamber of Commerce.

36

Direct mail

Nicholas O'Shaughnessy

Direct mail is something we are instantly familiar with, part of the clutter of daily living. It is part of the much larger category of direct response advertising (Livingstone, 1982), and therefore cousin to all the colour supplement advertisements, televised record sales, catalogues and such like. Yet mention of it seldom evokes affection in the consumer. We seek to explore why in this chapter, and to substantiate our claim that when properly done it ceases to have 'the character of an afterthought', and can become the essence of the marketing campaign.

THE CASE FOR DIRECT MAIL: TARGETING

Segmentation, the ability to target and tailor, is the critical consideration in the measurement of any marketing medium. On this, direct mail scores very highly indeed: for its distinctive merit is the potential to target market segments with greater precision than any other method apart from the sales visit itself. Direct mailing segments can be refined to an infinite degree, as long as we can obtain further information about target prospects.

Direct mail is so effective because, being personalized, it flatters people's own importance: they appear to have been chosen by invisible judges to join an élite group – perhaps they do not realize how mechanical the whole business is, and think that great effort has been invested in discovering and writing to them: 'Direct mail succeeds because unlike other media it can deliver a specialized message to distinctive groups, made personal through the agency of new technology and therefore engendering unqiue loyalties' (O'Shaughnessy and Peele, 1985). Because direct mail has the special ability to be made personal it can create a strong adherence, with the impression given that the needs of some particular group are being especially targeted. It can be tuned to specific elements in the market – those wanting a more lively appeal perhaps, or those whose loyalty needs reinforcing, or people contemplating purchase for the first time.

In contrast to direct mail, television as a medium has serious deficiencies. Its costs have continued to soar above the level of inflation. There is the difficulty in targeting, since most programmes are delivered to a broad audience, so that television advertising is best suited to consumer non-durables. But the future in marketing lies in precision targeting, where direct mail excels. A general market appeal, communicated through more public media, may be bland because of the heterogeneous nature of the target audience; mail will allow us to be more lucid and vigorous with specific groups, heightening the message and tone of the original appeal. Seldom can television attain the personal, intimate voice of direct mail. But the two can work together: television makes us feel familiar with a product or personality, and direct mail is a logical extension of this association. They can create a sense of relationship in the consumer. The illusion of personality is cast over an automated process.

THE CASE FOR DIRECT MAIL: OTHER BENEFITS

Direct mail is rich in creative possibilities. The letter can ostensibly come from a corporate potentate or a celebrity. The tone can range from bargain basement to élitist, and all kinds of imaginative ingenuity are possible – pop-ups, three dimensions, stamps, coins. All such alternatives can be pre-tested. Gifts, collectables, photos, peel-offs, numbers, seals, samples, tokens, brochures and so on – all can be experimented with. And the intangible incentives it can offer are numberless – clubs and memberships, price offers, guarantees, to name a few (Nash, 1986).

Direct mail can be speedily produced, unlike a conventional advertising campaign. Thus it can respond to fluctuations in taste, new assaults by rivals, the threat from new substitutes and the like. It is a potential public relations tool which can counter negative publicity: it does not demand the contracts, deadlines and long-range planning of other media. It is very well suited to fluid commercial operations such as share issues and financial products: anything in fact where a sudden shift is an important part of the commercial environment.

This speed and flexibility of direct mail explain its use in American political campaigning. For certain product categories and situations it could be critical – for a firm that wished to bemuse a competitor with an updated model, or introduce a new product, it would be a way of announcing the news speedily and dramatically to the target markets.

Another merit of direct mail is that its effectiveness can be accurately evaluated. The mail can be pre-tested, and we determine from a sample the impact of the final mailing. Different types of copy, package and offer are tested for their response rates. Thus an alert direct mailer can continually improve, and learn the most persuasive types of appeal to make: the assessment and refinement of other forms of advertising and promotion are necessarily much vaguer. The consequence of this is that the labour of finding details and fashioning appeals would be handsomely repaid. Currently the targeting potential created by the information revolution goes unexploited.

Direct mail confers many other benefits on its sponsors.

1 It enables us to publish a lengthy, reasoned appeal, and in some selling contexts this could be a merit. It can lend the appearance of logical argument, of a rationally constructed case, even though the covert appeal is nearly always to emotion.

2 Direct mail has curiosity appeal – our wish to unpack it and discover what is actually there. Indeed, there is a virtual guarantee that this sort of advertising is noticed, because it intrudes on our attention in a way that newspapers, magazines and even television cannot wholly match.

3 Direct mail can create a latent want, with the consumer subsequently stirred to purchase action by some other more immediate market or situation stimulus.

4 While direct mail marketers incur the cost of list hire, printing and posting, they avoid many of the costs associated with wholesale/ retail distribution.

5 Direct mail offers great potential for comparative and even negative and alarmist advertising, although it would be tactless to

630

advocate this. Personalized, negative mail appeals garnered high levels of support for many American politicians and pressure groups: the same tactics would probably work in some commercial situations (Crawford, 1981).

6 The use of several different media can be reinforcing and create variety, using perhaps the same motifs and personalities to lend a consistent identity.

7 The mail can also compensate for weaknesses, allowing for a firmer revival than might be obtained by investing more money in more costly mediums: for example, when a few extra television advertisements may have scant effect. Again, though, it is a mistake to see these elements as conflicting: responses to a television advertisement can in themselves build a mailing list.

8 It has been claimed that direct mail increases the efficiency of the sales force by 50 per cent when the two are used in conjunction (Gosden, 1985).

9 Technology in the area is constantly improving: the effects – increased speed and lower price – make direct mail more attractive and within the budget of smaller businesses. A personal computer can easily deal with 10 000 letters.

10 Business-to-business direct mail is also growing in popularity, partly as a consequence of the increasing cost of the sales call (Gosden, 1985).

Historically direct mail has not been fully understood and therefore imperfectly exploited; often in the past it has been employed by firms which could not afford conventional distribution channels. It is bound to perform better as a habitual pattern of ordering things by mail or telephone solidifies. Indeed, younger people may adjust more easily: the more the behavioural trend moves in that direction, the better the prospects. Consumer acceptance of direct mail is growing, partly as a consequence of the increasing professionalism and sophistication of the mail itself (Gosden, 1985). It is widely believed that suspicions of a mail 'glut' are unjustified, that in fact people like it (Gosden, 1985). 'Junk' mail is only perceived as such if it looks tawdry.

SOCIAL DIRECT MAIL

Direct mail is also useful for non-commercial institutions as a highly effective technology for fund raising. Charities – as indeed commercial organizations – are finding that, having performed an initial act of commitment, people feel predisposed to do so again. This makes direct mail a powerful tool for public pressure purposes, for it is an adept lobbying instrument as a consequence of its ability to foment emotional adherence. For example, Alaskan legislators were influenced over balanced budgets by constituents encouraged by a direct mail campaign (Snyder, 1982).

It represents a device for discovering and exploiting potential supporters, and its potential in this area has yet to be fully recognized: 'it is effective because it introduces the concept of membership – people are made to feel part of a group, the essence of which is shared information' (O'Shaughnessy and Peele, 1985).

In America direct mail fund raising was the rightist response to the agitation politics of the left: conservatives were attracted by its ability to mobilize public pressure without the need for public demonstrations. It helped to defeat twelve liberal senators between 1976 and 1980. Mailers satisfied the American right's need for a ringing articulation of their values that cut through the compromise, evasion and restraint of ordinary politics, and in so doing they seemed for a time to be undermining the party system. The Republican party, however, began to draw strength itself from direct mail, expanding its donor base from 34 000 in the early 1970s to 2.7 million in 1983; contributions amounted to $8 million in 1975 and $92 million by the end of 1982, and 80 per cent of this sum was the result of direct mail solicitation (Harris, 1982).

From political mail, in particular, consumer marketing has much to learn. The mail is the demagogue's own medium, and through its agency 'new right' entrepreneurs have raised fortunes. Rightist consultant Richard Viguerie, for instance, has the names and addresses of 30 million conservative Americans on tape in a guarded vault.

America's political consultants employ the large amounts of available census data; and the so-called ethnicity tapes. They accumulate large lists of names. They are expert in the art of composing a letter, the subtle artifice in a superficially unsubtle product. The quality of political direct mail is often higher than the commercial, because the consultants have learnt to exploit the potential of precisely targeted direct mail to stir emotion. There is no endeavour to build up a reasoned, factual case. Arguments always present a picture which even true believers know to be overdrawn. By contrast, the targeting of commercial direct mail is often more vague: its sponsors make less effort to segment their audience and hence their mailings are more general, therefore less effective. Nor do they exploit emotion beyond material desire: there is no passion in what they do. And clearly, with many products, passion is irrelevant: few, for example, would feel genuinely infatuated with a food mixer. But other products do potentially involve deep emotion – the connection between insurance and fear for example.

THE CASE AGAINST DIRECT MAIL

Direct mail yields its best dividends over the long term. Testing and building lists are laborious operations: the logic of this is that mail gives its optimum performance when it becomes a permanent institution rather than an occasional experiment – to be effective it must be made an established marketing ancillary. Other limitations include the expense of prospecting (Gosden, 1985).

Direct mail suffers from many of the drawbacks conventionally associated with advertising. There is the danger of exhausting one particular kind of creative approach or thesis, and therefore a need for vigilance. Then there is the often quoted danger of over-solicitation. In America the average household now receives fifteen items of commercial direct mail every week, and there is an obvious risk when people recruit from the same list. On this subject we have argued (O'Shaughnessy and Peele, 1985):

> Some claim that direct mail has an optimum level of impact after which its effect declines. This might be true if every direct mail shot were similar, but it is arguable that the medium can be given infinitely varied content that might push back a saturation point, if within limits it exists at all.

The mail has curiosity appeal and ministers to a sense of being wanted.

Direct mail is misunderstood, especially in the UK. Mailings resemble each other too closely, they may appear cheap, they target the same lists too often and too imprecisely: it is therefore not surprising that people complain, and that the genre is discredited. Fault lies not with the concept but the tactical execution. Superior direct mailings will not arouse antagonism in people: they will be accepted and even welcomed as a mature way of seeking business among adult citizens.

Table 36.1 Art and artefacts: overview of list markets (Harper, 1986)

List category	No. of lists	Universe (000)
Cell 1		
Art, antiques, collectables	31	2995
Cultural books and magazines	31	5232
Cultural arts	7	485
Subtotal	69	8712
Cell 2		
Upscale gifts and decorating items	24	2088
Photography	5	969
Regional publications	20	2732
Subtotal	49	5789
Cell 3		
Luxury foods, home entertainment	16	3316
Affluent, upscale lifestyle	8	843
Miscellaneous (credit cards)	5	1732
Subtotal	29	5891
Total	147	20 392*

*Reduced by 25 per cent due to duplication factor.

THE MECHANICS OF DIRECT MAIL

Mailers must clarify their target audiences via operational criteria which state the exclusive characteristics of those in the segment. The essence of direct mail is the discovery of reliable names: the house list is the key strategic armament. This is a composite of names obtained by past prospecting and other names already in the firm's possession, and replies from lists supplied by research and commercial purchase. The quality of such lists will dictate the success or failure of direct mail operations. They must be cleared of habitual non-respondents, absentees and so on (Nash, 1986): they must be laden with detail so the list can be divided into sub-segments.

Lists are therefore critical. They can be derived from membership and subscription lists, banks, retailers, newspaper clipping bureaux, public records, professional registers and magazine readers. They can also be brought from professional list brokers. In America the Standard Rate and Data Service Guide to Consumer Mailing lists (Skokie, Illinois) provides 1000 pages of detail about every consumer list on offer (Nash, 1986). Lists can be bartered and exchanged between firms. There are of course business lists as well as consumer (here the rate of change is high – in America 20 per cent). Technology is supple enough to disaggregate names into every conceivable kind of list: in America there are even 'ethnicity tapes' that pinpoint the national origins of names.

By way of example, Table 36.1 shows the number of lists and list members available in certain product categories in the USA.

Lists are also generated by 'geo-demographics'. The availability of local data makes it possible to label small areas according to class, social and other demographic and economic factors. We can evolve a fixed number of labels applicable throughout the country and use this as a method of targeting: the ACORN system does this in the UK. In America the richness of census detail makes it possible to use this method with some refinement – for instance, the thirty audience cell and subcell demographics (Gosden, 1985) which the census provides about each community include the following.

1 Percentage of households with income of $25 000 a year and over.
2 Percentage of owner-occupied households.
3 Percentage of households with children under three years old.
4 Ratio of children of five years old and under to household.
5 Percentage of black households.
6 Percentage of households that are one-unit structures (based on Metromail count).
7 Percentage of households that are ten or more unit structures (based on Metromail count).

Periodic mailings, rather than the isolated mail shot, may cement loyalties aroused, for the initial commitment becomes a decision precedent so that we may feel like buying again.

In direct mail, errors are often made with the letter. The evidence suggests that the more it resembles a real letter the more persuasive it is. I am not qualified to comment on the psychological intricacies of this: it simply works. Poor direct mail is a pastiche of a real letter: quality work looks exactly like a personal letter from a professional individual. The letter will be based on empirical investigation, but as in any form of copywriting its power will also be a function of intuitive insight.

The letter should motivate to action, the sole criterion of its effectiveness. Consequently the appeal is often squarely to emotion. Details of print and layout are significant; it may even look like a handwritten letter, perhaps a rather artificial device. It is particularly important to seek to overcome the inertia and inconvenience of reply: the reply must be prepaid and easy to complete; telephone payment via credit card should be available.

The envelopes should be smart; depending on the target market they may be attractive and eye-catching. Letters are often long, though there is no set orthodoxy here: but usually their language is fairly simple, with reader attention retained by subheadings, brief, snappy words and the use of colourful images. There is ample room for vivid graphics. Business mail, of course, would be somewhat different in tone as it performs a different function – at the very least, it reaches the same audience in another mood and capacity.

Good copy is the way to successful direct mail. This demands skill to attain a seemingly effortless effect: the art that conceals art. In practice much direct mail exudes a false euphoria: it is a genre that has not really caught the popular imagination – people perceive it as mediocre. It exhibits none of the artifice of, say, a television advertisement: it remains marketing's poor cousin. Does the banality really represent direct mail executives' opinion of the status of their market?

Much direct mail remains an obtuse instrument because it is imitative in vein: success can be achieved, as in all forms of advertising, by simply going against the convention and surprising public expectations.

CONCLUSIONS

Writing in an earlier edition of this book, Bill Livingstone (1982) summarized the future prospects for direct mail:

> The increasing number of working wives means that 'shopping' as a skill has declined in status: convenience is more important now – and buying by mail is very convenient. Mail order business now totals well over £2000 million a year, and is taking an increasing share of total retail trade. The percentage of non-food retail trade carried out through mail order has increased from 7.1 per cent in 1971 to close to 9 per cent today. Another indicator of increasing direct mail activity is the number of business reply/freepost items handled by the Post Office: up from 96.9 million in 1971 to an estimated 305 million by 1980. Information systems such as Prestel Viewdata will make

'homeshopping' even easier, especially if linked with interactive home computer terminals.

The potential of direct mail is enhanced by several contemporary trends. The information revolution has entailed more obtainable information about increasing numbers of people. This means that the central conditions under which direct mail is sustainable will be there; enabling the fine tuning of copy to segment.

Direct mail's effectiveness is magnified by the social trend to home centredness and convenience; shopping, business, political and social activities are increasingly located in the home rather than in the external community – hence Alvin Toffler's 'electronic cottage'. One day shopping itself will be possible on direct response television, with electronic catalogues; printed direct mail will one day become anachronistic. However, direct mailers now benefit from this trend to a society of muffled introverts. Yet the medium remains only moderately exploited because it is moderately understood – conventional wisdom in the area has not developed the same sophistication as in other marketing media. It has the characteristic of an afterthought.

Elsewhere I have argued (in the context of politics, but the same applies to commerce) that direct mail reflects two trends – from mass media to tailored and targeted media, and from direct action to the armchair approach, and that having grasped that the element of personalization is central to the success of direct mail, technology will seek ways of taking this further. Companies will speak with an increasingly private voice: even the television medium will become targeted as channels and outlets expand. But at the moment 'it is infrequently trusted with a pivotal function and this junior role may make it a relatively unfruitful use of resources' (O'Shaughnessy and Peele, 1985). Finally, there follows a direct mail checklist.

1   Test mail different types of copy first. Much of the profit comes on subsequent mailings, not on the first, cold mailing.
2   Direct mail can be used in conjunction with other media, for example radio, telephone, personal visits.
3   The identity of the person who purports to send the letter is important, and ideally has some special relevance to the person who receives it.
4   The letter must be intimate and personal.
5   It must completely resemble a 'real' letter.

6 Direct mail is a subtle and much misunderstood medium. How the copy is written is critical to its success; copy can be much more hard-hitting than when aimed at the general, unsegmented public.
7 The danger in direct mail lies in mass, undifferentiated solicitation. The key ingredients of good mail are:
 • emotive copy
 • smart, highly personalized letters
 • ease of reply
 • good lists.

REFERENCES AND FURTHER READING

Clark, E. (1981), 'The lists business', *Marketing (UK)*, December, p. 25.
Crawford, A. (1980), *Thunder on the Right*, Pantheon Books, New York.
Dale, A. *Direct Mail List Building*, the Post Office, London.
Fairlie, R. (1978), *Direct Mail Testing and Measurement*, the Post Office, London.
Gosden, F. F. (1985), *Direct Marketing Success*, Wiley, New York.
Harris, P. C. (1982), 'Politics by mail: a new platform', *Wharton Magazine*, Fall, pp. 16, 18, 19.
Harper, R. (1986), *Mailing List Strategies*, McGraw-Hill, New York.
Holtz, H. (1986), *The Direct Marketer's Workbook*, Wiley, New York.
Livingstone, B. (1982), 'Direct marketing', in *Marketing Handbook*, ed. Michael Rines, 2nd edn. Gower, Aldershot.
Nash, E. L. (1986), *Direct Marketing*, McGraw Hill, New York.
O'Shaughnessy, N. J. and Peele, G. (1985), 'Money, mail and markets', *Electoral Studies*, Vol. 4, No. 2, August.
Sabato, L. (1981), *The Rise of Political Consultants*, Basic Books, New York.
Snyder, J. P. (1982), 'Playing politics by mail', *Sales and Marketing Management*, 5 July, pp. 44–6.

37

Speciality selling

Stuart Thomson

Speciality selling refers to the work of those who sell to industry and commerce by calling upon existing clients, customers and prospects. Depending on the type of product or service they sell, speciality salespeople will also visit national and local government authorities and, in certain instances, private individuals in their own homes.

Speciality salespeople sell capital equipment, products, materials and services. They are expected to have specialized knowledge of what they sell and to be capable of offering prospective purchasers compelling reasons for buying. They are responsible for initiating sales, and usually conduct their negotiations at the premises of those to whom they are selling.

THE QUALITIES DEMANDED OF SPECIALTY SALESPEOPLE

The personal attributes desirable in a would-be speciality sales executive at the start of his or her career are extensive. An employer is hoping to find recruits for the sales force who are honest, sincere, conscientious, cheerful, polite, reliable, enthusiastic, industrious, loyal, co-operative, imaginative, intelligent, well informed, courteous, determined, resourceful, articulate and ambitious. They should also have a pleasant personality, possess initiative, be well turned out, have sound judgement, be efficient self-organizers, be blessed with a positive attitude of mind and have the strength of character to contend with the inevitable disappointments and onsets of physical and mental fatigue, with courage and stamina.

When all these desirable personal qualities exist in an applicant who has never previously been a sales executive, but is intent on becoming one, the prospective employer is entitled to celebrate his good fortune.

After being selected, a new recruit to selling must acquire, through training, experience, thought and study, an impressive amount of knowledge, selling skill and appropriate work habits. These include product knowledge. Without adequate product knowledge salespeople cannot sell competently. The more they know about their product or service – what it is, what it does do and what it could do – the better equipped they are to fulfil their selling responsibilities. Product knowledge, though, does not of itself make a sales executive. He or she must be able to put that knowledge to effective use and this cannot be done unless he or she has, or develops, the ability to influence people. The orders which speciality salespeople secure could not have been achieved without being able to influence people to buy.

Speciality salespeople are expected to have up-to-date information about the industry or trade to which they sell. They need to be familiar with the market in which they work. Newly recruited people should be able to discuss and, if possible, solve the problems of a customer or prospect which relate, directly or indirectly, to the product or service being sold. They are expected to possess a sound knowledge of business finance, and to learn as much as they can, depending on circumstances and availability of time, about the organization and operation of the companies they call on.

Salespeople should have a detailed knowledge of the company for which they work, including its past history and recent development. They must be aware of the many company activities which will affect their personal work.

It is clear from what has been said so far that a speciality sales executive needs to be intelligent and of good character. However, there are other areas to be considered relating to selling activities and they illustrate the extent of the demands which are made on resources of character and spirit.

Two people working for the same company may have an equivalent degree of product knowledge. The potential of their territories could be similar. Both appear to work industriously. It might be difficult to detect a difference in their personal courtesy. Does this mean, though, that their sales figures would be similar? Sales directors, sales managers and experienced salespeople realize that this is unlikely. One of the two will almost certainly produce more business for the company. He or she will be the one who has reached a higher level of selling skill, has stronger motivation and is more determined to obtain orders.

Successful selling is directly related to personal attitudes, perception, beliefs, strength of character and an understanding of what to say, how to say it and when to say what needs to be said. Of two salespeople with the required amount of product knowledge, both knowing exactly how their sales presentations should be made, the one who is more accomplished in his or her use of words, more attentive in listening to what is said to him or her, more perceptive as to how to deal with a sales situation, will be more productive.

Being an accomplished user of words in personal selling does not mean being a brilliant conversationalist or employing unusual words in the hope that they will sound impressive. Words are the tools used to obtain orders. Capable salespeople deploy words with care and controlled economy. They are adept at asking polite, well-phrased questions at the appropriate time and they listen intently to the answers they receive. They are not engaged in a monologue but in a two-way discussion in which listening to what is said to them is important. They must provide information to a potential customer because without it the prospect is unlikely to buy. But they also need information from the prospect in order to direct their sales story advantageously. Listening attentively to, and thinking about, what has been said, is vital.

It is not easy to call for the first time on a prospective purchaser, a stranger, and as a result of what the sales executive says and what he shows, to influence that stranger to buy or, at least actively to consider purchasing in the future. When meeting a prospect for the first time the executive does not know, in advance, the prospect's temperament or personality. He or she cannot know whether the prospect is worried about some business or domestic problem, is feeling unwell or how much time the prospect has available. Notwithstanding all this, the sales executive knows that it is his or her responsibility to succeed, as far as possible, in attracting and holding the prospects attention; interesting and continuing to interest him or her in the sales story about the product or service that is being sold; and then developing that interest into a desire to buy and thus obtain the positive action which will convert the prospect into a customer. No sales executive can achieve this result at every sales interview. To be able to secure orders sufficiently frequently, and therefore make the selling effort profitable in relation to costs, indicates selling skill and the exercise of determination.

A great deal is heard, in the world of speciality selling, about the need to think positively. Accentuate the positive, eliminate the negative, the saying goes! While this is sound advice it does not alter the fact that salespeople are often on the receiving end of other people's negative decisions.

Unless able to accept 'turn-downs' philosophically, a sales executive's future will be bleak. The job is certain to provide a large number of such disappointments. Mature, productive salespeople are conditioned to this. Beginners are apt to become disconsolate after many turn-downs. They take them as indications of personal rejection. They fail to realize that their sales stories have lacked appeal; that the propect may not have been appropriate; or that an appropriate prospect can have genuine reasons for deciding not to buy at that particular time. Far too many young speciality salespeople retire hurt from selling in their first year because they had expected selling to be far easier than it is.

People conversant with the work of speciality sales executives understand the significance of high morale, physical endurance, determination and selling skill in obtaining orders. They know, as well, that other accomplishments are necessary for sustained success. They also appreciate that unless the sales executive can manage his or her use of time, is systematic in his or her approach and is prepared to do the necessary paperwork, he or she will not be in a position to apply selling skills effectively. Every company has had the experience of employing people with outstanding ability to sell but who are personally disorganized and for this reason are outsold by less gifted colleagues who 'plan their work and work their plan'.

Report writing

In most types of speciality selling salespeople are expected to compile reports on their calls. Most people dislike writing reports but unless they complete their reports they are failing to do their work efficiently. The sales office needs information: without it it cannot fulfil the tasks required of it. Not only do salespeople need a copy of their own reports for reference but they should keep a statistical record of their own results.

To lessen the burden of report writing, and to speed the receipt of reports at head office, much progress has been made in recent years in the use of various types of electronic communication between sales staff and their headquarters. These modern methods of transmitting information do not, however, eliminate the need to keep accurate records for planning purposes.

THE BENEFITS OF SELLING

Having surveyed the broad spectrum of what speciality salespeople have to do, the qualities they are expected to display, and what might seem to be the disadvantages of a career in selling – the uncertainties, travelling, mental and physical fatigue, the constant need to meet and beat the sales efforts of competitive companies, the loneliness, and the pressure – let us now consider the very real attractions and benefits which are obtainable from the work. Provided an individual reaches a standard of ability which ensures that sales figures are maintained at no less than the minimum acceptable level of profitability, his or her working life offers advantages which are seldom found in other forms of employment.

A sales executive has a large measure of personal independence. With the exception of those who sell drinks, groceries and other consumer products to retailers and who, for the most part, must keep to a prescribed pattern of regular calls on retail outlets, speciality salespeople create their own pattern of dealing with their work. Except when carrying out a specific instruction from their companies, it is they who decide whom they should contact and how much time to allocate to each customer, client and prospect, depending on the circumstances of each interview.

There will be opportunity after opportunity to exercise personal initiative, with the comforting knowledge that the sales executive is entitled to exercise this initiative.

To a great extent speciality salespeople are free from daily supervision. There is no 'boss' standing over them checking every move they make and every word they utter. They can enjoy many of the benefits of self-employment and at the same time the comparative security that working for an employer provides.

643

Then there is the variety. No two working days are the same. Because the sales executive travels from one place to another, and is meeting many different people, there is much less boredom than in many other occupations.

Speciality selling as a career is exciting, adventurous and challenging. There is always the possibility that tomorrow will be a day of particular achievement and, if it is not, there will be other tomorrows. Competition sets the adrenalin in motion. There is the stimulation of being engaged in a competitive activity. Not only is the sales executive competing for orders against rival sales forces but he or she is competing also, as far as results are concerned, against colleagues – and against himself or herself in the attempt, which should always be made, to beat his or her previous best.

Most salespeople are well paid. Systems of remuneration vary from company to company. In well-established concerns there will be a salary and in many instances commission on sales and/or a bonus. Salespeople, other than those whose work is closely confined to inner city areas, will probably be supplied with a company car. Financially ambitious and capable salespeople feel that 'the sky's the limit' as far as earnings are concerned, if not with their present company then with another, or as a result of going into business on their own account. Even many who are less materially ambitious earn more than they expected to do before deciding to enter selling.

The demands of different products

The work schedules of speciality salespeople vary wide by depending on what they sell. Although those who sell high cost capital equipment, such as machine tools, and those who sell stationery supplies to offices both set out to obtain orders, there will be a marked difference in the way they operate. The former, selling equipment which may cost £200 000 or more, will have far fewer prospective customers than the latter. To obtain an order he or she will have a series of meetings, possibly extending over many months, with not one but several different executives in the prospect's firm. He or she may have to make presentations to committees and will probably have to arrange visits to existing installations of his or her company's equipment. It is likely that he or she will be technically qualified; he or she will certainly be liaising closely with technical experts of his or her own company as well as those with the prospect's company. There will be a great deal of paperwork involved in completing recommendations, detailing specifications, and other data required by the prospect. Those who sell high cost capital equipment will make fewer calls on a range of different companies than most speciality salespeople, but they will spend far more time with each prospect, provided the prospect is interested in purchasing. They need to spend much time on research, paperwork and investigation.

Salespeople who sell office stationery may make twelve to thirty, or even more, calls a day. The number will depend on the area in which they are working and the number of interviews they obtain. Most will be 'cold' rather than by appointment. The prospect field is vast and the office stationery sales executive will spend little time on 'research', which is not justified by the value of individual orders. Deep research on a prospect's background and scale of operation is economic only when there is the possibility of a substantial order.

The subject of time allocation to prospect research is an interesting one. Salespeople should find out as much as possible about the prospects they call upon but how much close attention it is necessary to allocate to research depends on the type of product or service being sold. An order for the supply of a large installation cannot be achieved without acquiring a great deal of data both before and during the negotiations. A sales executive who sells inexpensive photocopiers to small businesses will on the other hand need to judge how much time to spend obtaining information about a new prospect before calling upon that prospect for the first time. What he or she needs to know is whether the firm could use a photocopier, and the name of the executive to see. Failing prior knowledge, this information can often be obtained when the call is made.

There is much variety in the working lives of salespeople. The pattern of visits varies from day to day. Some need to use the telephone frequently and others do not. Although the great majority are free to allocate their time as they think best they are never masters of their own time. They can be kept waiting in foyers and reception areas. Appointments may be cancelled by customers and prospects at the last minute. Some of the calls they make will involve lengthy interviews; in other instances the sales interview may be concluded quickly.

TRAINING

In contrast to the selling skill speciality salespeople are expected to acquire, and the large sums of money involved in their remuneration, travelling and administrative expenses, is the shortage of time devoted to their formal sales training.

Some companies provide extensive training to new recruits. They also run well-organized refresher courses and retraining programmes for established members of the sales force. The word 'extensive', however, needs qualification. Companies which have the time, resources and the intention of doing all they reasonably can to invest in training may devote several months to the day-to-day training of new recruits to their sales forces, but such companies are in a minority. In many organizations the initial formal training period may not extend beyond two or three weeks before recruits are sent out on their first calls, usually accompanied for a brief period by an experienced colleague. Even when a new sales executive is fortunate enough to join a company which has a thorough training programme the amount of training will be minute compared to the years of training received by doctors, architects, accountants, solicitors and members of other professions.

It is easy for people to complain about this absence of thorough initial training. What is not taken into sufficient consideration is the financial factor. Most of the young men and women who are to become members of a profession requiring qualifications which are recognised by the public at large are funded, to a considerable extent, by officially supplied grants. Salespeople – at least in the UK – do not spend several years at universities for the purpose of obtaining a degree in selling.

Companies have, for the most part, to finance their own sales training programmes. They have no guarantee that those they train will remain for any length of time in their employ. Nor, in spite of providing sound training, do they know in advance what the results will be, although in this respect, selecting the right people for training enables an employer to reduce greatly a wastage of sales training effort.

A new recruit to selling can have a high IQ, can be honest and may pay close attention to the instruction received on the sales training course but all this is no guarantee that he or she will become a good sales executive. Although he or she may have absorbed all the information provided on the training course and possess an admirable amount of product knowledge, a sales executive will not sell if he or she does not want to sell.

Although insufficient time is devoted to 'in-house' training courses salespeople will, if working for a well-run company, receive much advice and help throughout their careers from their sales managers. Ambitious salespeople can do much to educate themselves by reading and by analysing and benefiting from their experiences. Experience by itself will not necessarily improve competence. It is possible to acquire years of experience of doing things the wrong way. Sales managers, field sales managers and 'sales trainers' must encourage, motivate and enthuse members of the sales force. Their leadership plays a vital role in the effectiveness of the sales force. Speciality salespeople, although of an independent nature, constantly need to have their efforts recognized and appreciated.

One of the disadvantages of selling is the need to work alone so much of the time. A barrister in court has the benefit of observing other barristers at work. The same applies to an actor. Professional sportsmen watch other professionals perform. Once established on his or her own territory the sales executive is making calls alone and any errors are very unlikely to be pointed out by customers and prospects. There will probably be occasions when he or she is accompanied by a field sales manager but otherwise the sales executive works alone. This can lead to developing habitual errors and remaining unaware of them. In these circumstances it is only the most thoughtful and perceptive salespeople who capitalize fully on experience.

In recent years there has been a marked increase in the number of sales training companies to which clients send their salesforce for training courses. Alternatively, a sales training organization may design a custom-built in-house course for a client which is conducted on the client's premises. The expansion of this activity is the result of companies realizing the need to supplement and enhance their own training programmes.

SELECTION

The quality of sales force performance depends on the quality of the individuals selected to be its members. An error in selection will prove costly to the employer. Because newly selected recruits to the sales force will require time to prove their worth, their value – or potential value – to the company cannot be determined rapidly.

Several weeks or months will have to pass before an error of judgement in selection can be finally established. Should a mistake have occurrred, time and money will have been spent on training and financing an individual whose performance in the field falls woefully short of expectations. Small companies tend to have a higher percentage of selection errors than large companies whose resources enable them to avoid making hasty decisions.

Selection is never an easy process because the employer is looking for people of character as well as existing or potential selling ability. In the case of applicants with no previous selling experience there will always be an element of acceptable risk. There have been many instances where young people are selected who do not immediately create the impression they will be particularly effective in selling but who, after they have received sympathetic and encouraging guidance, become enthusiastic and efficient producers of orders.

MOTIVATING

Executives responsible for the direction and training of the sales force can do much to motivate individual salespeople by example, encouragement and practical advice. Sales contests certainly stimulate activity, providing they are fair and do not make the losers, who are trying hard, feel inadequate. Sales competitions, though, are not the most effective motivator because their energizing effect tends to be transitory.

The strongest motivation is the sales person's own desire to sell: those who want to sell will sell. Although the desire to sell is the strongest motivation it will itself have been created by one or more contributory motivations.

But why do people want to sell? It is often suggested that it is because they believe that success will lead to a high income. This belief assumes that a new entrant to selling does so for the sole purpose of achieving a large income. However, most people who apply for a sales vacancy do so with only a vague idea of what the work involves and what the rewards will be. They think selling could be a 'good job' and one which will be of interest, allow them a degree of independence and offer career opportunities. Few of them, before they go for their employment interview, feel committed to a long-term future in selling.

The desire to sell will develop quickly with some new entrants and more slowly with others. There will also be new recruits to selling who, after a short exposure to its realities, decide that it is an occupation with little or no attraction for them and look for another form of employment.

There are some high-earning salespeople, and they include some of the finest exponents of personal selling, who have never been motivated by money: those who sell for selling's sake. They love selling; they become leading producers of business and the 'big money' comes to them because of their high standard of accomplishment. A comparison can be made, in this respect, with leading artists who did not, in the first place, become artists, for the purpose of making money, but because they had a passion for painting or sculpture.

There are salespeople whose motivation is based on competitiveness. It is their nature to want to win, to show that they are better than their colleagues. They want to prove to themselves and to others that they are people of merit. There are those who wish to climb the executive ladder and realize that success in selling will help them do so.

Then, too, there are salespeople who are motivated by the determination to earn large sums of money, for the power, possessions and sense of security money can bring. Whilst it may be fashionable in some quarters to scoff at materialism, those who are selling because of an intense desire for wealth will become professionally competent. They know that to acquire a high income they need to be effective in their work.

Sales directors, sales managers and sales trainers can do much to motivate salespeople by their own leadership and positive, attitudes. They have the responsibility for providing sound advice and practical assistance and for showing that they care for the well-being of individual members of the sales force. Creating and maintaining high morale in the sales force is important. When morale is low the strength of motivation slackens.

Good sales managers continuously strive with tact, to assist salespeople to extend their capabilities. They realize that practically every sales executive in their companies has the latent ability to improve performance.

THE COMPANY PERSON

Every sales force will include what could be termed its 'stars'. These are the big producers of orders and they are very good indeed. They have two distinct assets which commend them to their employers: the lucrative orders they are responsible for, and the standards of sales performance they set, which the more sensible of their colleagues attempt to emulate. The stars show what can be achieved.

They are not, necessarily, their company's most valuable salespeople in the field, on a long-term basis. There is little permanence to them because they may be offered and accept a sales management position, be lured to go to another company or become self-employed. Furthermore, some of them have difficult temperaments.

A company's most valuable people are the steady, unspectacular types who month after month can be relied upon to bring in a supply of acceptable orders at a profit. They are loyal, settled and hard working but not brilliant exponents of selling. They are apt to stay with their companies as long as they consider they are receiving fair treatment and that their contribution to the company's welfare is recognized. The highly skilled, knowledgeable dilettante will always, over a period of time, be outsold by a less gifted colleague who is conscientious in carrying out his or her work. To secure orders it is not necessary to be an exceptionally talented salesperson; rather, it involves consistent application in telling the right sales story, in its correct sequence, to sufficient relevant prospects. A gifted salesperson who makes a few calls and who cares little about self-discipline cannot be relied upon to produce sufficient business.

One of the difficulties of selling relates to the time to be allocated to thought and to action. To occupy oneself in frenzied activity making call after call without sufficient thought about what one is doing and how it should be done is a waste of physical energy. On the other hand, hours spent just thinking about selling, planning whom to see, becoming involved in extensive but unnecessary research work – and then not going out to sell – result in a waste of mental energy. In all types of specialist selling thought and action need to be co-ordinated. A desk in a comfortable office can act as a magnet to a sales executive. The desks to be sitting alongside are those of customers and prospects. Salespeople need to acquire and use judgement in how they allocate their working time. Neither thought without action nor action without thought produces orders.

LONELINESS

Speciality selling can induce a strong feeling of personal loneliness during working hours. Salespeople out making their calls are not in continuous friendly working association with colleagues. Instead, they are seeing strangers or business acquaintances. They may spend much time driving and will be alone during most lunch hours. They are not in frequent contact with the sales director or sales manager for any length of time, unless they work directly from head office. If they work from home, as many do, communication with the sales director, sales manager and sales office will for the most part be by report, letter, memo or telephone.

The closest that speciality salespeople come to daily contact with colleagues is when they work from an office to which members of the sales force come in the morning and return to in the late afternoon after making their calls.

BELIEF

The most important of all selling assets is belief. Salespeople need to believe in the value of what they sell in relation to its price, and to believe that they will sell. They should be sustained by the belief that the work they do is worth doing. As they are selling the benefits of a product or service they should sincerely believe in the reality and value of those benefits.

Salespeople are commercial 'missionaries' and to succeed in their mission they must believe in its merit. Their objective is to secure orders influencing potential buyers as to the desirability and relevance of what is being sold. Unless they themselves 'believe' the likelihood of them being able to transmit belief to others is remote. Enthusiasm, a quality held in such high esteem, cannot exist without a strong foundation of belief.

APPEALING TO REASON

During the course of a year company executives, especially purchasing officers, buyers and executives responsible for passing buying requirements and requests to their company's buying department will meet and talk to many salespeople of varying calibre. They hope, but do not necessarily expect, that those they talk to will present sensible reasons for the products or services thay are selling. They also hope that the salespeople will be reasonable. A display of enthusiasm, will be of little avail to the salesperson who makes statements which sound unreasonable. Exaggerations, unsubstantiated generalities, 'clever-clever' remarks, inaccurate statements of fact, are quickly detected and result in a sales executive being considered unreasonable. When this opinion is formed the chances of making a sale evaporate because what he or she says will not convey the impression of a reasonable person with whom to do business.

THERE ARE NO BORN SALESPEOPLE

'He or she's a born salesman/woman' is a statement one sometimes hears about a person who sells with exceptional ability. There are no born salespeople any more than there are born barristers or ballet dancers. What *is* true is that because of their temperaments, family environment, youthful interests and other circumstances, certain individuals develop attributes and interests which are particularly suited to lead them to, and assist them, in selling.

Salespeople 'make' themselves. They can and do receive useful guidance, help and practical advice but their development, their forward progress and the amount they learn about their work, are dependent on themselves.

ATTITUDES AND TECHNIQUE

Salespeople are frequently and rightly advised by books and articles on selling, and verbally by sales managers and sales trainers, of the need for a positive attitude to their work. This statement can be illustrated by comparing the attitudes of two salespeople of equivalent intelligence and erudition. The first, A, when considering calling on a prospect, thinks of all the possible reasons why that prospect could be influenced to become a customer. The other, B, dwells on reasons why the prospect will not buy. A proceeds positively contacting the prospect in order to secure business. B may not even attempt to see the prospect, having concluded, as a result of negative thinking, that the prospect will not buy.

A progressive positive attitude leads to the acquisition and *use* of techniques which enable a sales executive to sell productively. An individual with a negative attitude may complete the training course having absorbed all the information that was supplied, but this information will not be put to effective use if his or her attitude to selling is defeatist.

Attitudes are all-important in speciality selling. Fortunately, negative attitudes can be eliminated. Attitudes do change. 'I've changed my attitude', 'I see things differently now', 'My viewpoint's changed', are comments quite often heard in daily life.

One of the main contributions made by people responsible for training salespeople is that, in many instances, thay have with tact, patience and skill been successful in assisting trainees to change their attitudes from negative to positive, from hesitancy to action.

THE INDIVIDUALISTS

This chapter has referred to the desirable qualities needed by salespeople: regrettably there are those who are deficient in them.

There are whingers, malcontents and idlers in sales forces, just as in other forms of employment. There are those who can sell but make little effort to do so; those who start late, finish early and take extended lunch hours. There are some who fail to render reports on time and whose ideas about 'expenses' are in marked contrast to those of their companies. Where insufficient care is paid to selection, a sales force is particularly likely to include these types.

In what could be termed a 'good' sales force a degree of licence may reluctantly be given by management to the idler who, nevertheless, brings in an acceptable amount of business due to skill. Similar tolerance may be shown to salespeople who delay in rendering reports but whose orders are sufficiently valueable to compensate for the inconvenience they cause.

What should not be permitted in a sales force is the malicious trouble maker, however good his or her sales figures may be. It is dangerous to employ such people because their destructive attitude can affect colleagues. The same applies to anyone who verges on being dishonest. If one individual is allowed to get away with manipulating petty cash and expenses, it is a sad reflection on the company which employs him or her.

SO WHO SHOULD BE EMPLOYED TO SELL?

A sensibly run company will not look for super-salespeople. It will not be dazzled by charismatic 'chancers'. When deciding whether an applicant is suitable, the company should not be looking for someone with the 'gift of the gab' or who appears to be wrapped in a cloak of self-satisfaction.

A company will want to be represented in the field by people who will do the job with dignity, sincerity, loyalty, capability and controlled enthusiasm. It needs people with stamina to keep on keeping on, who plan their work and work their plan. Selling is an unsuitable career for individuals who lack courage, 'guts', and determination.

The employer, therefore needs salespeople who can combine personal initiative with an acceptance of the need to conform to company policy.

A sales executive with these attributes who tells a relevant, straightforward sales story clearly and understandably to a sufficient number of appropriate prospects will obtain orders. The number of orders in relation to the number of calls made, and the value of those orders, will depend on the level of ability to influence. The transition from being a salesperson of moderate ability to one of outstanding merit is due to the acquisition of greatly increased skill in influencing people to want to buy.

Some salespeople become discouraged by the thought that they lack the capacity to make progress as producers of business. Exceptional achievement is beyond their mental horizon. They are handicapped because they do not appreciate that the journey to eminence consists of progressive steps forward. The practical solution is to concentrate, in the immediate months ahead, on improving their sales figures by a modest percentage which represents a realistic target. Having succeeded in this, they then set themsleves another objective which they know can be reached with determination. By advancing step by step they can attain a standard of performance which, at one time, they presumed was beyond their capacity.

If a salesperson is in good health there are few limitations to the progress he or she can make other than limitations which are self-imposed. Speciality selling is a creative activity. Good salespeople create orders – they are not given them as presents.

38

The art of negotiation

John Lidstone

Negotiation, the art of bargaining used by two people or two parties to reach an agreement on a particular matter acceptable to both is, like selling, as old as the history of mankind. But whereas selling and the techniques associated with it have been the subject of endless studies, books and films, negotiation has not until relatively recently had the same close examination.

There has been a dearth of reference material available and little in the way of practical guidelines to help today's sales negotiators to develop their knowledge, skill and expertise.

Yet throughout our lives from childhood to old age, in our social, family and working groups, we regularly find ourselves negotiating. When we are children, precious possessions take on a precise negotiable value as we trade them with friends for something they have and which we desperately want; a penknife with scissors attachment is traded for a chaffinch's egg; a set of 1935 Empire stamps for a peacock butterfly; and so on.

As adults we face negotiations all the time: buying and selling a car, for instance, or – the most complex as well as the biggest negotiation for most people – buying and selling a house or flat. But it is in our business lives that most of us negotiate the largest sums of money and conduct negotiations most frequently; and in business the ability to negotiate skilfully has never been more important then now.

THE NATURE OF NEGOTIATION

What is negotiation?

Many supplier/buyer situations which we have traditionally viewed as 'selling' relationships have changed significantly over the last twenty years or so.

During that time many major customers and leading agencies have developed their own expertise and their own commercial strategies, and are just as sophisticated as the big manufacturers. Some of them, perhaps, are even more advanced; certainly some are more powerful. There has been a considerable and growing concentration of buying power into a few hands.

These two developments have meant that there is an increased amount of interdependence between suppliers and customers. Although the two sides still occasionally make independent warlike noises, there is a large amount of tacit agreement that both sides need each other if they are to achieve their individual objectives.

Occasionally local situations change this balance of need:

1 the manufacturer's need to supply often rises at the end of profit accounting periods;
2 sometimes a buyer has a heightened need to purchase from a supplier to combat competitive activity, or to meet seasonal, or in some countries political, objectives.

For most buyers and sellers most of the time, the need to buy and the need to sell are more or less equal. This in turn means less and less emphasis on 'selling' and more and more on negotiation. To understand the difference between the two techniques let us start by looking at selling, and then go on to examine the important ways in which negotiating differs from it.

The nature of sales technique

Traditionally 'selling' is seen as the art and skill of persuading someone who at the outset of a sales interview is reluctant to buy that he or she should do so. To achieve this sales objective, the sales executive uses a

657

repertoire of techniques to raise the customer's perception of the need to buy to a point where he or she acts upon that need.

There are many different approaches to the structuring of sales techniques; some of the most simple approaches used by salespeople tell us about the seller's needs, for example:

1   opening questions or statements about a customer's needs, designed to pinpoint need or raise perception of it;
2   presentation of benefits based on identified needs, designed to raise desire in the customer's mind for these benefits;
3   handling and overcoming objections raised by the customer, designed to remove obstacles that could prevent the customer from buying, and
4   closing the sale, designed to get the customer to say 'yes' and buy.

Other approaches tell us more about the customer's needs, for example:

1   I am important and want to be respected;
2   consider my needs;
3   will your ideas help me?
4   what are the facts?
5   what are the snags?
6   what shall I do? and
7   I approve.

Whatever the approach, the objective in terms of the end result is to increase the customer's need for the sales executive's products, services or ideas to a level where, to satisfy that need, he or she states the decision to buy. If you examine the movement of the two parties involved (seller and buyer) in these sales approaches, you can see that the seller's need to sell is much greater than the buyer's need to buy. Indeed, he or she uses selling as a process of inducing the buyer to move to a position where the buyer's need for the product or service coincides with the seller's need to sell. Although the seller frequently goes physically to see a buyer to sell to him or her, the proposition is often inflexible. The sales executive in this sense does not move, but uses selling as a means of inducing or 'motivating' the buyer to *move* (see Figure 38.1).

What is selling?
Selling is the relationship between supplier and buyer (or potential buyer) in which the need to supply significantly exceeds the need to buy.

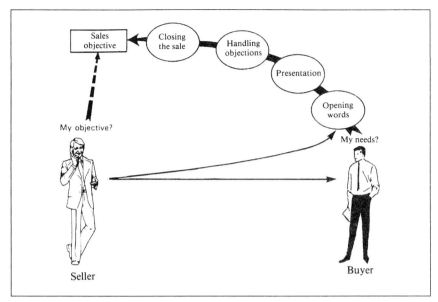

Figure 38.1   Stepping stones in a sale

Thus selling is the *persuasive* process by which a supplier aims to convince a buyer of his or her need for the supplier's product or service and the buyer acts upon that need.

Strength of a company's need to sell
In a good many companies, the persuasive sales approach is always used. Sometimes this is not only understandable but appropriate. For example, a new, unknown company, starting out in business to market a product or a service which may be original or a duplicate of a product or service already available, must make known its existence and then use all its powers of persuasion to get people to buy its products or use its services.

Strength of a sales executive's need to sell

Another and less defensible reason for maintaining the persuasive sales approach is that in some businesses where, in terms of results achieved over a period of years, it has been highly successful, the sales executive's need to sell, to persuade, to win is invariably high. This need has usually been present to a marked degree in the individual members of the sales force when they were recruited. Indeed, the presence of this need was an essential ingredient for sales success, heightened by skilfully structured sales training. But to pursue this approach to business development without assessing its relevance can be dangerous because it may lead to salespeople making general assumptions about the customer's low need to buy which are not true. They assume that the customer avoids buying decisions wherever possible by deploying supposedly unreal objections. One highly successful international group pioneered the development of photocopying, created excellent products and built up a formidable market share through aggressive selling. When its photocopying machine patents came to an end, other companies entered this lucrative market offering identical or improved versions of the pioneer's successful machines. So success in pioneering a market led to others entering it with the loss of product superiority which in the past had provided effective answers to the question: 'Why should I buy from you?'

To continue to use a traditional sales approach in such a situation, when the buyer's need to buy can almost be taken for granted, would not only be inappropriate but, when dealing with a sharp buyer, very costly. It could be said that a good product or service and the application of sustained sales technique together produce a position where the buyer no longer needs convincing of whether to buy but rather has to consider *on what basis to buy*. This is the stage at which negotiation takes over from selling and presents a quite different challenge to the traditionally trained sales executive. This is the stage when the heightened need 'to sell', often expressed in the adoption of simple objectives for the sale situation, can be counter-productive: for example, the sales executive plans to secure an order at every call, on the assumption that to do so indicates success and not to secure an order would be classified as failure.

When the relationship between buyer and seller becomes one of *negotiating* and not selling, it will either blossom or deteriorate, depending on the sales executive's capacity or incapacity to perceive that this selling situation is different from the past. This is where the temptation to fall back on yesterday's training or experiences to find satisfactory solutions to today's customer behaviour is understandable but ineffective. The sales executive is no longer engaging in a persuasive tug-of-war with the customer in which one of them wins; and so far as the sales executive is concerned, the evidence of victory is an order whatever the cost to get it. In negotiation there are no losers – both win.

The circumstances surrounding negotiation

Successful sales technique is not negotiation, but it creates the basis for negotiation. By sales techniques customers are moved to a position where, in order to satisfy their now heightened perception of their need, *they must consider the purchase decision.*

They then turn their attention to the *terms and conditions* surrounding sale and purchase. Having been satisfied in the selling process that they can actively consider purchasing, they will now be seeking the best possible deal in a number of detailed areas, including the following.

1 *Actual price*
   - What is the final price?
   - What discounts?
   - What further reductions/bonuses?
   - At what price will I have to buy to satisfy my criteria?
   - What is the resultant saving/loss?
   - When will I have to pay and in what currency?
2 *Product*
   - What precise specification?
   - Exactly what type of packaging?
3 *Allied services*
   - When do I want it delivered?
   - Where do I want it delivered?
   - At what rate do I want it delivered?
   - Should I collect or should they deliver?
   - How much distributive cost can I avoid?
   - What technical support will I need in using the product?
   - How can I avoid paying extra for it?
   - What additional help can I get at no extra cost in purchasing this product?
     - Training?
     - Technical literature?
     - Competitive leverage?
     - Financing?
     - Credit?

Based, therefore, on the platform of a common need to buy and supply created by the sales process, negotiation is *the give and take process whereby the final, detailed terms and conditions surrounding the purchase/supply decision are agreed.*

In this negotiation phase the supplier is tailoring the detail of the marketing mix (product, price, presentation) to fit the local, immediate needs of one particular customer.

Because of this both the supplier and the purchaser are involved in *controlled compromise.*

This element of controlled compromise (which is recognized by experienced negotiators) often clashes with the essentially uncompromising nature of the sales process which is accentuated by much sales training.

The arithmetic

A vital aspect of negotiation is the arithmetic, what the deal adds up to. The ability to understand the financial position of the buyer's company is essential, as is the ability to calculate the financial implications of any changes made to the 'package' during the negotiation. A good sales negotiator must understand balance sheets, profit and loss accounts and cash flow forecasts.

CONSTRUCTING NEGOTIATION STRATEGIES

What are the main elements of negotiation?

Actual stances
Given the underlying mutual needs, the strategy of negotiation is concerned with the actual and stated magnitude of those needs on both sides.

At the start of a negotiation there will usually be a gap of terms and conditions between what the buyer says he or she wants and what the supplier is prepared to offer.

The main strategic task of the sales negotiator is to measure accurately the *actual* gap that exists and to distinguish between that and the *stated* gap. The initial strategic ploy in negotiation is for both sides to *exaggerate* the distance between them.

Initial stances

Sometimes (not always) buyers will open up negotiations by deliberately (or automatically) exaggerating their stance; for example:

1 'Before we start, if you're thinking of offering me a deal on product X, forget it, because your competitors have already agreed the next supply contract with us.'
2 'There's no point talking to me about increased availability. We do not have any increase in demand this quarter.'

Or they may attempt to suggest that they are not likely to come to an agreement because of other negative factors which they raise at the beginning of the interview.

If (as is often the case) this is a strategic ploy, they will, if allowed to save face while doing so, move from this initial stance to an actual stance quite quickly and with a little encouragement. They may say, for example: 'All right, lets talk about it, but I warn you, the deal will have to be a good one for me even to consider it.'

We must be clear about the reasons for this initial stance. It is done purely to pull the supplier out of position. Thus, the first task is to establish by discussion the *actual* gap which exists between supplier and buyer. This is invariably achieved by an examination of the needs and covering benefits on both sides, but the supplier must ensure that *he or she* restricts the loss of position that this manoeuvring entails for both parties. (the supplier is usually more anxious to sell than the buyer to buy.)

Usually the parties will take up their actual stances with ritualistic face-saving comments, which are important if the fabric is to be preserved. These factors suggest that two research activities are maintained at any time of negotiation of contract.

1 We must have information on the buyer, his or her situation, applications, availability of funds, limits of authority and so on.
2 We must have clear, up-to-date information on the competition, the relative technical, financial, delivery, and pricing action they can take: the need they have for this order – the business and marketing success they are experiencing elsewhere – and the restraints present in their production facilities.

We should ask ourselves questions about markets, company and competition.

The key questions

1 What proportion of existing and prospective customers expect to negotiate the conditions of purchase?
2 What proportion of different categories of customer expect to negotiate?
3 What percentage of present sales volume do they represent?
4 What percentage of present profits is produced by sales to these customers?
5 What proportion of cases involves;
   - a group decision?
   - a decision made by one person alone or with the advice of others?
   - informed professional purchasing?
   - first time purchase or repurchase?
6 How strong are the buyers – what is the strength of their need to buy relative to our need to sell?
7 What proportion of negotiations involve contractual agreements?
8 How can a planned and skilled negotiation strategy help to service the market?

The company

1 What are the company's commercial and marketing objectives?
2 How does existing negotiated business aid or conflict with these?
3 What strengths and weaknesses are highlighted?
4 Are any changes necessary in the ways in which we negotiate business? Looking at past cases honestly, on which sides of the points of need balance did we conclude business?
5 Who is currently responsible for selling to whom and at what levels? Is too much or too little responsibility being given/taken? How is it being used? Does the level of contact meet the real needs of the market?
6 What levels of negotiating skills and authority are needed – and what levels exist?
7 What commercial and marketing benefits could result from better negotiation, or from applying negotiation skills to a wider level of sales activities?
   Are we satisfied with present margins from negotiated business?
   Are we sure that we are obtaining the optimum share of volume?
8 How can a planned and skilled negotiation strategy help the company?

The competition

1 Do we know how well our competitors perform in negotiating business?
2 What are their apparent strengths and weaknesses in negotiation?
   Look at, for example: speed of decision, range of authority (for example, in respect of price), product range, promotions, service, distribution, prices, capacity, cost and volume.
3 To what extent do they appear to strengthen or weaken the market?
4 What relationship can be perceived between the answer to 3 and correlation of their volume to their profitability?
5 What are their main concessions?
6 How do our plans compare with theirs?
7 How can we minimize their impact when we are negotiating with the buyer?

First offer

There are only two basic negotiating strategies which can be adopted if we want to gain the order:

• Quick kill (or final offer first)
• Holdback

If we are indifferent to the result then we may wish to adopt strategies which enhance any future negotiation and weaken competition.

We must determine, from our research into the client, whether we have a dominant or subordinate position to him or her, in relation to single supply sourcing, technical merit, delivery capability.

In terms of technical merit, the client *must* perceive the advantage. In many negotiations the client negotiating team may have insufficient knowledge or concern for technical performance. In some situations the supplier overestimates the technical advantage.

If we are in the process of tendering to a buyer not known to indulge in post-tender negotiations we can adopt only a quick kill strategy. However, when we know some discussion and bargaining is expected we can submit an offer which includes a defined negotiating margin, either in the main pricing, or in non-specific reservations on terms and conditions. We are then able to adopt a strategy which gives time to establish more clearly the negotiating position.

In dealing for the first time with a known 'bargainer' beware of the common delusion that he or she will recognize a 'fair' competitive offer and deal with it as such. Part of the satisfaction in the deal may well come from his or her enjoyment of the negotiation process itself. See the appendix for a checklist of points on 'Preparation for negotiation'.

THE TACTICS OF NEGOTIATION

We are now concerned with reaching, from the actual points of difference between the parties, a mutually acceptable agreement. We can see in this stage that the essence of negotiation is *compromise*, actual or apparent.

This discussion now proceeds in a highly structured way, each side reducing the gap by a series of mutual *concessions*.

At this stage the skilful negotiator *trades* a concession which in fact costs little, but which has a real or implied value which brings a relatively more valuable concession from the other party. (See the appendix for a checklist of factors to consider.)

Enhancing the cost and value of concessions

A great deal of skill is required on the part of suppliers in raising the apparent *cost to them and value to the buyer* of a concession they are trading. Remember that if there is no apparent cost to you then you are really conceding nothing.

Concessions from supplier to the buyer.
With these concessions we must credibly *raise* the value to the buyer of the concession we are offering by applying the benefits of the concession to his or her needs. We can reinforce this value by stressing credibly the high cost of the concession to us.

'You will understand that guaranteeing the special stock support is not something I could agree to easily, considering the cost and the existing commitments of my limited budget.'

Concessions from the buyer to supplier
Similarly, the buyer will magnify the cost to him or her and the value to

us of his or her concessions. You must attempt to minimize the value to
you of those concessions.

Matching and trading concessions

Concessions must be traded carefully. That is to say you must not take
your hands off your concession until the buyer has agreed on what he or
she will do in return ('I will do this if you do that').

If you continually talk about your concessions alone, the buyer will
accept them without reciprocation.

Maintaining the fabric of the negotiation

In many repects, negotiation is a vital game played for real consequences. Any unduly early attempt by either side to 'dig in their heels' by
being genuinely inflexible will be met by reciprocal inflexibility from the
other side, and the negotiation will break down.

Certainly the conclusion of the negotiation may be that both sides
agree that they cannot reasonably bridge the gap between them at this
stage, or in this instance. That conclusion leaves open the possibility of
further negotiation on the same subject, or new negotiations in another
area.

A breakdown in negotiation caused by the *unreasonable* inflexibility
of one party will not leave those possibilities so open for the future. At
all times, even when we have reached a point beyond which we are not
prepared to go, we must appear to be reasonable.

- Remember that you are playing a ritual game which is firmly based in
  hard financial reality.
- For many buyers much of their sense of achievement comes from
  'playing the game well'.

There is also a point in a negotiation when the amount of time invested
makes the deal harder to call off. In other words if the buyer declared
stalemate, or that he or she has reached the point of no return, and you
have been negotiating for several hours, you will both be losing a
considerable 'time' investment in the deal, apart from other considerations. At this stage it is worth pointing this out and suggesting another

look through all the aspects of the proposed deal before admitting defeat. Equally, it is important to bear in mind, and perhaps make use of the fact, that the pressure to come to an agreement rises as the negotiation proceeds, as a consequence of increased time investment.

The definition of a successful negotiation from the supplier's side is one which ends on *your side* of the point of need balance, but where the *buyer believes that the deal favours him or her*.

The steps and methods to be used in achieving a successful outcome are as follows.

1 Allow the buyer to do most of the talking in the early stages. Try to get him or her to declare all the points he or she wants to discuss before dealing with any of them, but don't frustrate the buyer by refusing to answer his or her questions, for example:

> *Johnson (buyer)*: Well, for one, finance. Take the recommended parts stock you've got down here. Now I understand why it's higher in volume and value than for a standard machine, but – so far as we're concerned – it still represents a higher financial commitment than we're prepared to accept. So I think we should start by discussing ways and means of reducing that commitment.
> *Edmonds (sales negotiator)*: Yes, we can certainly talk about that.
> *Johnson*: Never mind them for the moment. I'd like your suggestions on the recommended parts stock. After all, you were the one who brought up the importance of coming to a decision today. Let's get the parts stock recommendation out of the way and we can steam ahead.
> *Edmonds*: All right, if that's what you insist on.

2 Move the discussion from opening stances to a clear statement of actual stances taking care to restrict the losses on both sides. It is your responsibility to 'save face' for the buyer. If the buyer first presents his or her stance; you can,

   • accept it and persuade him or her that the negatives are greater than the positives
   • accept it and go back to the initial problem with alternatives
   • ignore it and take your own stance
   • take the opposite stance
   • accept it and use the 'suppose' technique

668

If you present your stance first, you can:

- take an exaggerated view
- take an actual stance, when strong
- 'give' buyer his or her stance, by seeming to accept the initial position
- place both stances in the current environment; in other words a summary of both positions

An example of the buyer's opening stance and the seller's counter:

Johnson: Oh, I see no reason at all why we shouldn't reach agreement today. All you and I have to talk over are a few points concerning the total package. Matters like getting the machines in, developing the staff and so on. The areas, in other words where your company – I'll say frankly – is a little weak as compared to some competitive quotes.

Edmonds: You needn't tell me. We know how worried our competitors are!

3   Avoid taking a premature stance on any point which might result in reaching a point of no return too early in the negotiation. Remember it is easier for the buyer to walk away than for you in most circumstances.

4   Make a trial close on a clear statement of the actual gaps between you, for example: 'So what you're saying is that assuming we can resolve these points [*give details*] we have a deal?'

5   Trade any concessions one at a time ensuring that you raise the value of your concessions above their cost to you. Make a small move on your part seem large to the buyer.

6   Devalue the cost to the buyer, and therefore downgrade the value to you of any concessions that he or she offers, for instance:

- treat it as given (assumption) that there is no real concession
- competitors always expect it (or more)
- there is benefit to the buyer in agreeing
- 'We've got the benefits anyway'
- 'We don't want the benefit'
- 'You'd incur the cost anyway'

7   Upgrade the value and cost of any concessions that you give to the buyer. Imply that you cannot really give it, for example:

Edmonds: What you're asking me to agree to is ... well it's a serious policy question. So serious I'd really have to take advice on it from our machine scheduling people.

Refer to problems that will be solved by the concession.
Refer to savings gained by the buyer, for example:

Johnson: Now, in order to pay them that kind of money, I imagine you'd be quite prepared to make some form of reduction in the course fee per head?
Edmonds: I know what. Instead of bringing them in on Saturday and Sunday – let's make it Friday and Saturday. That reduces your overtime costs by half – and the overtime it does leave you paying we could discount by knocking 20 percent off the training fees.

Calculate the financial results of the concession, for example:

Johnson: How would that help me? I'd be just cutting down your costs.
Edmonds: Not necessarily. Suppose, for instance, that you collected the 787s; in that case we could completely remove the delivery charge from our quote. I think that's about 0.7 per cent – but it could be as much as 1 per cent.

Refer to loss if concession not given.
Refer to past gains from similar concessions.
Imply loss that you will incur by giving concession, for example:

Johnson: Twenty per cent? Hardly seems enough
Edmonds: I think it is if you remember that we also wouldn't be passing on to you the extra costs we'd incur by having *our* staff in on a Saturday.

Build up notional cost or opportunity cost of giving the concession. Start by implying you are going to give a small concession then give a large one or enlarge the small concession. Mention the fact that it is not normal practice: 'competitors don't do it'.

8 Be positive and not defensive when the buyer asks for a concession you cannot give, by;

- building cost of giving the concession
- minimizing the importance to the buyer of the concession
- 'persuading' the buyer that the benefits of the deal without the concession still justify acceptance

670

- offering an alternative concession
- summarizing the problem area and offering alternative concessions, or a choice of solutions
- showing the concession would put the buyer at a disadvantage

9   Have facts and figures fluently to hand (but not 'pat' or 'glib' ones).

10 Avoid emotional reactions – but satisfy the buyer's emotional needs. The good buyer/negotiator will try to put you under emotional pressure, for example:

Johnson: Obviously, I'm disappointed you find yourself unable to offer me the facility of a buy back guarantee – but equally obviously, that is something it might be unfair to expect you to commit yourselves to.

11 Allow the buyer to save face in giving you a concession.

12 Ensure that the buyer is given the 'value satisfaction' he or she needs, and that you confirm it.

A set of points on 'Face-to-face negotiation' and a list of 'Key points of negotiating technique' are set out in the appendix.

SUMMARY

Negotiation relies on accurately identifying at the preparation stage:

1   the buyer's needs;
2   our needs;
3   the point of balance;
4   the value of our concessions to the buyer;
5   the benefits to the buyer of our concessions, which will increase their value;
6   the concessions the buyer will give, and how their 'cost' to him or her can be minimized;
7   the 'buyer's likely initial stance;
8   how we can move the buyer from his or her initial stance to the point of balance.

We are then in a position to meet the buyer without fear of conceding points for no reason.

We shall be able to reach a point of balance where the buyer is satisfied, and we have achieved our objectives.

THE FOUR NEGOTIATING COMMANDMENTS

1 Aim high.
2 Get the other person's shopping list before you start arguing.
3 Keep the whole package in mind all the time.
4 Keep searching for variables.

APPENDIX: CHECKLISTS

Preparation for negotiation

1 Have a total plan.
2 Beware any overt or known contact with competition.
3 The fewer the negotiators the quicker the agreement.
4 Make small concessions on arrangements for the meeting.
5 Always negotiate in your native language.
6 Know the needs of the other side.
7 Don't plan promises you are not convinced you can fulfil.
8 Don't ask for promises the other side cannot meet.
9 Avoid long sessions – plan to break them up.
10 Arrange to be able to leave the negotiation table and confer with your associates in private.
11 See that your staff respect your privacy if the meeting is at your offices.
12 Plan clearly what the next steps are after the meeting.

Factors to consider when negotiating

1 Price.
2 Currency in which bidder is willing to accept payment.
3 Facilities for reciprocal trading.
4 Ability to make offset arrangements.
5 Credit terms which can be offered.

6   Availability of government-to-government loan.
7   Delivery, including reputation for keeping delivery promises.
8   Risk of territory in which manufacture taking place being subject to industrial disputes.
9   Conformity with mandatory sepcifications.
10 Reliability of product.
11 Quality of product.
12 Ease of maintenance and level of running costs.
13 Standardization with purchaser's existing plant/system.
14 Ability to comply with performance guarantees.
15 Design and technical merit of product.
16 Capability of plant/system for expansion to meet purchaser's future requirements.
17 After-sales service.
18 Availability and price of spares.
19 Willingness to accept purchaser's commercial terms of contract.
20 Reputation on commercial negotiations of being 'hard' or 'soft'.

Face-to-face negotiation

1   Negotiate only with those in authority.
2   Be prepared to trade.
3   Be calm.
4   Don't compromise your objectives.
5   Don't oversell.
6   Don't show your thoughts on your face.
7   Don't underestimate your opponents.
8   Always appear reasonable.
9   Keep the meeting to your plan.
10 Be courteous and don't rush the other side.
11 When the mission is accomplished – leave.
12 Don't drink – it influences your judgement and speed of thought.
13 Tell it like it is and say clearly what you mean.
14 Distinguish between major points and details.
15 Appear relaxed and enjoy yourself.
16 Listen carefully to all the other side say, and to the way they say it. Read any documents they give you.
17 In multi-person negotiations, stay with your individual roles.

18 If the agreement is not right for you, get up from the table.

Ten key points of negotiating technique

(As shown at the end of Part II of the film *Negotiating Profitable Sales.)*

1 Never give a concession. Trade it reluctantly.
2 Leave the other person feeling he or she has done a good deal too.
3 Watch for the danger phrases. 'A few small details', 'One little point and we're in business', 'It's in your interest', 'Fairer to both sides'.
4 Once you've started backing down, it's quite a job to climb up again.
5 You must maintain neutrality in those early stages.
6 Absorb an attack by making notes.
7 If you want time to think, read over your notes or make a phone call.
8 Never make an offer till you've got the cost-list of everything the other person intends to argue with you about.
9 There hasn't been a deadline in history that wasn't negotiable.
10 Anything the other side accepts as a constant can nearly always be made into a variable.

FURTHER READING

Atkinson, G. (1977), *The Effective Negotiator*, 2nd edn, Quest Research Publications, London.
Lidstone, J. (1977), *Negotiating Profitable Sales*, Gower Aldershot. (Paperback (1986), *Profitable Selling*, Wildwood House, Gower, Aldershot.)
Vare, D. (1929), *The Handbook of the Perfect Diplomat*, published privately.

Film and audio material

Lidstone, J. (1985), *Making Effective Presentations* (audio manual), Gower, Aldershot.

Video Arts Ltd, *Negotiating Profitable Sales*, Part I 'The preparation';
Part II 'The negotiation', film based on Lidstone (1977). This chapter
is based on material prepared to accompany the film, for which the
author was technical adviser.

39

Telephone marketing

Bernard Katz

We mostly take the telephone for granted. It is always there. But used efficiently, as part of a planned marketing campaign, the telephone can be an extremely cost-effective marketing tool. It has many uses in business. They fall into four distinct categories:

1   *Generating new business*

- Prospecting for new customers
- Selling
- Order taking
- Prospecting for repeat business
- Converting enquiries into orders

2   *Customer service*

- Generating good PR
- Answering the phone efficiently
- Dealing with complaints and with angry customers
- Dealing with enquiries
- Debt collection

3   *Communication*

- Transmitting and receiving messages

- Transmitting and receiving telex and fax messages (through a modem and appropriate equipment)

4 *Research*

- Collecting data
- Linking with a viewdata system (via a modem and computer terminal or micro computer),

This chapter provides practical techniques, in the form of checklists, examples, and sets of rules for what to do and what to avoid, for prospecting action within category 1. It provides also a constructive approach towards achieving effective customer service from category 2. Other marketing applications of the telephone are beyond the scope of this chapter.

GENERATING NEW BUSINESS

When prospecting for new business there are a number of questions to be answered: Who to telephone? How to find names and numbers of potential customers? What is it that the prospects really need? What is the best way of telephoning? What is the best time of day to telephone? What records should be kept? How frequently should calls be made? How does the caller get better at telephoning?

The answers to all these questions are incorporated in a set of rules, the 'operating rules for prospecting by telephone'.

Rule 1: Identify the existing principal categories of customer. Select a spectrum of potential customers from within these categories

Cold canvass in selling is the process of starting at a given point, and making contact with every consecutive prospect. The starting point is the beginning of a road, the top of an office building, or the top of a page in a directory. Cold canvass generates some successes. But it involves much wasted effort, because contacts are made that have no chance of success. By restricting telephone calls to potential customers similar to those with whom business is already transacted, the opportunities for failure are restricted.

If five or six categories of customer are selected – and there is no magic

Prospective customer categories					
1	2	3	4	5	6
Prospective customer needs					
1	2	3	4	5	6

Figure 39.1 Customer control grid

number – the distribution of calls should be weighted in accordance with the volume of business received from each category. For example, ten prospecting calls made by a print shop might be made to:

- local retailers – 3
- insurance companies – 3
- professional firms – 1
- transport companies – 1
- local manufacturers – 2

It is productive to prepare a simple prospective customer control grid. An example is illustrated in Figure 39.1.

Rule 2: Compile a prospecting file of names and addresses of potential customers falling within the major customer classifications

Most businesses advertise themselves, if only by a one-line entry in a directory. If they are anonymous to the extent that their name does not appear in any published form it is unlikely that they qualify as a potential customer. The names of companies also appear in journals, magazines or newspapers.

A useful directory giving much detailed information is *Kompass* (Kompass Publishers Ltd, Windsor Court, East Grinstead House, East Grinstead, West Sussex RH19 1XD). It segments its data against many criteria – product type, distribution channels, turnover, resources employed, geographical locations and so on. Another useful and readily available directory is *Yellow Pages*, providing a general company classification of industry and trades. If the prospective customer is a private person his or her name and address are to be found in the electoral rolls. All persons living at an address are recorded, and there is therefore an indication of the size of a family in any dwelling. But no other information is provided. Information about private persons must be gathered from announcements and classified advertisements in the national and local press.

Rule 3: Identify the main needs of the different prospective customer categories

Customers are rarely motivated to buy unless their needs are satisfied. Occasionally a purchase decision is made on impulse because the product or service is wanted. Generally the seller must identify and match the buyer's needs. At the telephone there is little time for research – after one or possibly two questions there is a danger that the interest of the person spoken to begins to wane. So the seller's call must talk from the outset about matters likely to interest the customer. The second column of Figure 39.1 is headed 'prospective customer needs'. The grid is a planning document, from which the caller prepares to make the prospecting call.

Rule 4: Set objectives for the prospecting call

It is essential to be aware of what must be achieved. Does the caller want to take an order? Advertising space can be sold at the telephone, as can office equipment, spare parts or a number of personal services. In such cases, the caller must plan in advance the procedures to be adopted: a telex or letter is to be sent by the buyer, a deposit or the full cost of the product or service is to be paid into an account, or sent to the caller, or made available on delivery of the product. But with some products or services it is not possible to take an order from a cold prospecting call. Jewellery cannot be sold, or houses or life insurance. No one will buy a car without an opportunity for inspection and a test drive.

This does not mean that sellers of these products or services should not make prospecting calls. The level of communication in the prospecting call is inadequate. The objective is different. A meeting is necessary to allow further information to be provided to the customer. The customer must be in a situation where the benefit messages received from the salesperson are reinforced by seeing, touching, hearing or tasting the product. So the objective is to make an appointment.

Taking an order, or making a firm appointment, are the prime objectives of the prospecting call. But there is a secondary objective too. It is to create the opportunity to have a second attempt at success when the first attempt is seen to be failing. The person spoken to is manipulated. A particular effort must be made because if there was interest, the original prospecting call would not be failing.

'Mr/Ms Prospect. I am sorry you do not see how our product can increase your company profits. However, what I will do is put our company literature in the post to you. I never send it cold, because I imagine you are bombarded with unwanted literature. Is that right?'

'Yes, I do get a lot of junk mail.'

'The literature sets out clearly the specification and benefits of our equipment. I will phone you again in three or four days' time to answer any queries that arise. Thank you Mr/Mrs Prospect. Goodbye.'

The prospective customer is *not* asked whether literature may be sent *or* if the caller may telephone back. The natural tendency of courteous people is to ask rather than tell. Such questions invite a 'no' response. The action which will be taken is stated briskly and the call closed. The caller has then created a marginally favourable opportunity for a second chance. It is a better situation than attempting to speak again following an emphatic and possibly hostile initial rejection.

Rule 5: Write the script for the prospecting call, incorporating the 'golden rules for speaking at the telephone'

A script is always used for the prospecting call. Many salespeople and business executives with track records of success reject the suggestion of using a script. After all, they know their business thoroughly. But the script is of immense help in preventing the caller moving off at a tangent to the call objective. Unless controlled, this frequently happens whenever a detailed aspect of the product or service is being discussed.

The prospecting script is a planned pathway from the initial intrusion into the prospective customer's space up to the closing of the objective. Responses are projected in advance to the probing and persuasive questions to be asked by the caller. The first question is worded so that the response is 'yes' or 'no'. This type of question is called a 'neutral closed question'. Different follow-up questions are prepared, to be used depending on whether a 'yes' or 'no' answer is received. The prospecting script is an algorithm or flowchart of stimulus and reaction. Figure 39.2 illustrates a script in block format. The person telephoned is being led carefully and efficiently along a pre-planned path. He or she is unaware that this is happening. The caller must not sound as though the call is being read.

Getting the script right takes time. And different scripts are necessary for different categories of customer because the needs and the product or service benefits are different. A script is written and used. One or two calls soon disclose topic areas or customer objections that have not been considered. So the script is then adapted to accommodate the different responses.

'Golden rules' influence and guide the telephone prospecting script.

Golden rule 1: Always smile when speaking to the prospective customer

Smiling is relaxing. Smile inhibits aggression and tension. An effort should be made to adopt the habit of smiling every time the telephone is picked up. Even at the end of a long tiring day, a conscious smile helps to impart a friendly courteous manner.

Golden rule 2: Involve the customer in conversation as early as possible

On no account should the caller talk *at* the customer. If the telephone has to be held at arm's length to avoid the torrent of words pouring out, the objective will never be reached.

681

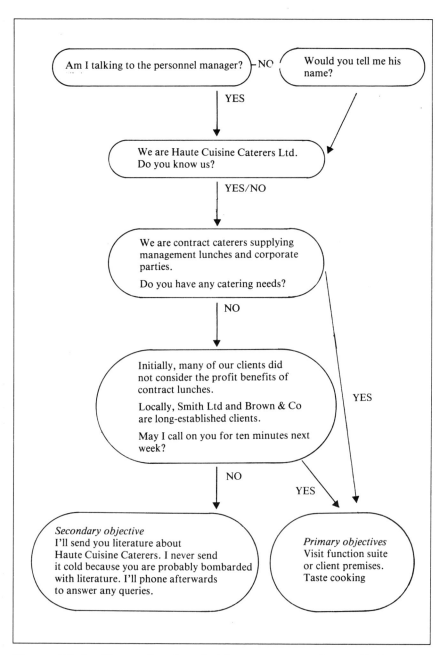

Figure 39.2 Example of script for a prospecting call showing 'block' format within the conversation

Golden rule 3: Ask frequent questions

Asking questions brings the person who has been telephoned into the conversation. It is a reinforcement of Golden rule 2. But in its own right, asking questions is the method of obtaining information. It is the way to 'qualify' the customer's needs, to ensure that the call is with the right person – one who has the authority to make decisions – and to establish that there are no identifiable constraints against the objective being achieved. Examples would include the lack of any remaining budget allocation preventing purchases being made currently, or absence on holiday or a business trip preventing appointments being arranged.

Golden rule 4: The prospective customer listens only as long as he or she is interested

Most people are courteous, and will not abruptly tell a caller to go away. But this is not licence for the caller to ramble. The prospective customer does not necessarily want to receive a stranger's views on the weather or the performance of the local cricket team, or even a detailed description of the caller's company and successes.

The objective of the prospecting call can be reached only when the caller has the full attention of the other person. That attention may be held when the customer's needs and wants are being discussed. The caller's product or service can be the best in the world but if it does not satisfy the prospective customer's needs or wants, it will not be of interest.

Golden rule 5: Always aim at achieving the objective

A pleasant easy conversation is no guarantee that the caller will achieve the objective. At all times the caller must remain aware of the set task. He or she must steer the conversation in the right direction.

Golden rule 6: When the prospective customer says 'no', start selling

A person with limited selling experience is disheartened by a 'no'. Most of us want to be liked. If we persist in selling to a prospective customer after being told 'no', any friendly relations established during the conversation are likely to be extinguished. Furthermore, the other person may become resentful and irritated or, worse, hostile. Withdrawal, with apologies for any disturbance caused is one option. But a pleasant conversation is not in itself productive – it does not increase profits in either the short or medium term. Another option for the caller is to treat the 'no' as an objection – an objection to be countered. The objection may take the form of:

- Not now . . .
- Next time we buy . . .
- Too much stock . . .
- Business is bad . . .
- No money . . .

The objections might be a smoke screen. They may be product criticism , or there may be a lack of product information. 'No' is a signal for the caller to redouble his or her efforts to identify the real needs of the customer in order to match them with appropriate benefits

WRITING THE SCRIPT

The script is written to deal with all the different stages of the prospecting call.

1   Contact is established with the correct person.
2   A reason for calling is provided.
3   The prospective customer is qualified to make sure that it is worth while to proceed.
4   Benefit messages are given to satisfy the needs of the customer.
5   A trial close is made.
6   If the close is unsuccessful, customer objections are identified and countered.
7   Additional benefit messages are given.
8   Close for the prime objective.
9   If unsuccessful close for the second objective.

Example of a script

Haut Cuisine Caterers Ltd supplies management lunches in house, or at its own elegant premises. The company caters for business functions and parties of all kinds. The greater part of its business comes from existing customers. New business is found through telephone prospecting calls to potential customers falling within existing customer categories.

Caller: Hello. I want to speak to the person who deals with company catering please, but before you put me through, would you please tell me the name?

Customer: Pardon? We don't have a company caterer. Who do you want to speak to?

Caller: Oh. In that case I'll speak to the personnel manager. What is the name, first, please?

Customer: We don't have a personnel manager. What is the call about?

Caller: My name is Peter Renwick of Haute Cuisine Caterers Ltd. Please put through to your managing director.

The opening moments of a prospecting call are often not straightforward. In bigger companies there is a catering manager. In some companies the catering function is looked after the personnel department. Sometimes there is neither a catering manager nor a personnel manager, but this information is not known until contact is made. The opening question is designed to establish the name of the potential contact before speaking. On occasion the telephonist ignores this request. At other times the telephonist compounds the problem by putting the call through to someone having no possible interest in catering, or the authority to take decisions.

Getting past the employees protecting the decision-makers requires confident authority. Often there is a direct question: 'What is the call about?' Such questions are ignored. The caller persists in trying to establish a convenient time to call back to speak to the person concerned.

If it is just not possible to get through, the best way to deal with the matter is to say authoritatively and courteously, 'Well, I'll call back at 4.30. Please advise that Peter Renwick is calling at that time. Thank you. Goodbye.'

Customer: Deborah Long.

Caller: Ms Long? Am I talking to the managing director?

Customer: Yes. I am the managing director.

Caller Ms Long. My name is Peter Renwick of Haute Cuisine Caterers Ltd. Do you know us?

People like to hear their own name mentioned – so 'Ms Long' is repeated. 'Do you know us' immediately brings the potential customer into the conversation.

Customer: No. I am afraid I can't say that I know the name.

Caller: Haute Cuisine Caterers is a local firm specializing in contract catering for management lunches and company functions. Do you employ your own catering staff?

Customer: No. Apart from a few kettles we have no cooking facilities.

Caller: We have a lot of experience in delivering a varied luncheon menu to customers' premises on a daily basis: as well as catering dinners and parties of up to seventy guests in our own elegant suites. We know that we are extremely competitive. Will you come and see us, one day next week, to sample our cooking and discuss how our service may be of benefit to your company.

Product information is given with implied benefits, and the first trial close is made.

Customer: Thank you for that invitation. It is kind of you to offer. But we have no plans for catering activities at the moment.

Caller: I understand. One question please. What arrangements do your management team make for their daily lunches?

Customer: My colleagues and I use a pub or restuarant or bring sandwiches – whatever is appropriate. Thinking about lunchtime has low priority in this company.

The customer is losing interest and is closing the caller out. The caller must offer significant benefits immediately to rescue any opportunity of doing business

Caller: Ms Long, I get that reply from many of the successful companies I talk to. Happily, a number of them are now our customers. Haute Cuisine lunches take away the need to think about finding restaurants and pubs. There is only one cuisine standard, and that is excellence. May I call and see you for ten minutes next week? Our services are designed to help busy companies restrict their non-productive activities to a minimum.

Customer: Thank you again for your offer. But I am sorry such discussions are not appropriate at the moment. Goodbye.

Caller Ms Long. I'll tell you what I will do. I'll put our literature in the post describing the range of services, and how they contribute to customer profits. I never send out literature cold, because I imagine you are bombarded with unwanted mail. Is that right?

Customer: It certainly is.

Contact name	Company name	Telephone number	Prospect address	Action

Figure 39.3   Format for index card system

Caller: OK. I'll phone you a few days after you receive the literature to answer any queries that arise. Goodbye Ms Long.

Rule 6: Prepare and maintain a simple records system for all prospecting calls made, particularly to show the *action* result of the initial call

Leads gathered at the outset of a telephone prospecting campaign appear great in number. If a call is abortive because of difficulties in getting through to the right person, it is tempting to shrug and move on to the next on the list. This temptation is to be resisted. There is a finite number of leads, even from unused directories.

Every prospective customer lead is valuable. If a prospective customer is called and he or she is not in, the call must be made again, later. If the person answering says that Mr Smith or Ms Jones will be available on Tuesday at lunchtime, that is when the second call is to be made.

Figure 39.3 illustrates an effective format for an index card system. Alternatively, the columns can be drawn into an exercise book. Before every call each column should be completed. The action column is completed afterwards. Even though the task is tedious, records must be kept. Memory is unreliable and is not a substitute for keeping records.

Every day the records are looked through to see which calls back must be made. When a decision is made that a prospective customer does not warrant further effort the name should be scored through. It should not be erased or obliterated. When the lists are checked later it is necessary to know which companies have already been contacted.

Rule 7: Establish by trial and error the best time of day to telephone different customer categories

The time of day at which to make a prospecting call varies with different industries. It is also a function of the caller's own work schedule. Currently it is much more expensive to telephone before 1.00 pm than after. Even so, at any time of day the prospecting phone call can be considerably more cost-effective than a personal visit.

There is no best time to call applicable to all customers. If there is a valid reason to call – call. The worst that can happen is that the receiver is slammed down in anger. But one is circumspect, so that whatever the time of the call, the 'worst' situation is never reached. Winning business by telephone is a combination of courtesy and the persistence, despite customer resistance, to identify and match the customer's real needs.

Rule 8: Establish the pace of a telephone prospecting campaign with an initial one-week trial period

A serious pitfall of a telephone selling campaign is excessive enthusiasm. When the great potential of the telephone as a marketing tool is accepted, it is dangerous to dispense with all other approaches to securing business. Prospecting by telephone works, but if too much is expected there is failure, and with failure telephone selling is rejected in its entirety.

For the novice caller, it is helpful to send a prospecting letter first. The caller then telephones and asks if the person has received the letter. In this way, there is no basis for apprehension. The caller is talking about something that is known.

Telephoning cold is difficult and fearsome for most people at the outset. With practice the difficulties and fears are overcome. Some, even with considerable success in face-to-face selling, find the idea of selling at the telephone daunting. If the secretarial resources and the cost of these resources are available, telephoning as a follow-up to the prospecting letter is an excellent method of self-training to use the telephone for prospecting and selling. With practice one is weaned off the prospecting letter.

To establish a benchmark for prospecting activities, make use of the initial week's programme as a trial. Establish the number of prospecting calls it is realistic to make, taking into consideration all other prospecting and selling activities. For half the calls, arrange to send a prospecting letter in advance of the call. Prepare a target grid as illustrated in Figure 39.4. Identify the number of successes from the calls made cold, and from those following a prospecting letter.

When the trial period is over decide:

1   a realistic target number of calls to be made each week;
2   a realistic number of prospecting letters to precede the telephone calls, until total confidence in using the telephone by itself is achieved.

Rule 9: Periodically monitor prospecting call performance by recording calls on a tape recorder and evaluating against an analysis grid

Prospecting at the telephone can work for everyone. If the results are not good, or not good enough, something is wrong. Is the call deviating from the script? Is the principal customer need identified? Have the 'Golden rules' been followed? Figure 39.5 gives a checklist of likely faults.

To record a call on a tape recorder, an inexpensive microphone is required. It is obtainable from most reputable audio equipment shops. The recorded call is then carefully analysed against the checklist of faults, using the analysis grid illustrated in Figure 39.6.

CUSTOMER SERVICE

The telephone has an important contributory role to play in the provision of efficient customer service. In many cases expectation of service is itself a factor of the purchase decision process. The buyer of a car, a computer or a photocopier needs reassurance that operating service is available promptly, whenever there is machine downtime. So important is service in marketing terms that it is helpful to upgrade the concept of the marketing mix – the variables in the control of marketing management – from four Ps to four Ps and an S (product, price, place, promotion and service).

The telephone call often provides the first contact with a company.

Target dates	Number of prospecting calls	Objectives reached	Number of prospecting letter/calls	Objectives reached	Total successes
target					
actual					
target					
actual					

Figure 39.4 Target record grid

	Yes	No
Is the prospective customer brought into the conversation early enough?	☐	☐
Is the prime customer need identified?	☐	☐
Are the objections identified?	☐	☐
Are correct benefit messages given in relation to the customer needs?	☐	☐
Is the close effective?	☐	☐
Is the script amended each time after analysis of an unsatisfactory call?	☐	☐
Is the call allowed to deviate from the script?	☐	☐
Are the prospective customer categories realistic?	☐	☐
Are the calls made at the right time of day?	☐	☐
Have the 'Golden rules' been followed?	☐	☐
Are the follow-up *action* requirements scrupulously observed?	☐	☐
Is the call continued after the customer says 'no'?	☐	☐

Figure 39.5   Checklist of faults

There is an immediate example of customer service. Many companies fail to observe when levels of service drop because of everyday familiarity. So an audit of telephone performance, periodically arranged through a third party, is an indicator for management of the image perceived by customers. A telephone effectiveness audit checklist is set out below. A simple evaluation scale (*inadequate – acceptable – good*) is sufficient to identify problem areas.

Checklist

1 How quickly is the telephone answered when the company is called?
2 How efficiently is the telephone answered, during lunchtimes and at the beginning and end of the day?
3 How reliably are messages transmitted?

Early prospective customer involvement			Frequent questions asked			Attainment of objectives					Interest sustained		Termination of call			Objections handled		Benefits messages	
Correct	Too early	Late	Correct	Too many	Too few	Sale demos		Literature			Tes	No	Correct	Early	Late	Well	Badly	Correct	Incorrect/insufficient
						Yes	No	Yes	No										

Figure 39.6   Telephone prospecting analysis grid

4 How patient is the person answering when there is sound distortion, or a message given is disrupted?

5 How supportive is the person answering when the command of the English language is limited?

6 How efficient is the giving of advance warning when delays in a service call visit occur?

7 How frequently is a contact name given to a customer with a service requirement, to help when making contact again?

8 How competently are customer complaints handled?

9 How effectively are customer enquiries converted into orders?

The courtesy call

The courtesy telephone call has an important role. Its value is disproportionately greater than the effort required to make the call.

'Hello Ms Gordon. It is John Weston of Patchwork Products Ltd. We have now made the delivery of all goods against your order xb223. Everything matches the specification given, and the delivery was made on the due date. I am just phoning to make sure that you are satisfied?'

'Yes. As far as I know.'

'Good. We have built our business by making sure that our customers are always supplied with what they ask for. Many thanks. Goodbye.'

FURTHER READING

Katz, B. (1983), *How to Win More Business by Phone*, Business Books, London.

Katz, B. (1987), *How to Manage Customer Service*, Gower, Aldershot.

Katz, B. (1987), *How to Win More Business by Phone, Telex and Fax*, Century Hutchinson, London.

40

Exhibitions

David Waterhouse

This chapter examines briefly the opportunities and pitfalls involved in the marketing of products or services by means of public or private exhibitions.

WHY EXHIBIT?

For most companies the prime reason for participation in exhibitions is to enable the sales staff of the exhibiting company to meet the buyers of potential client companies – on ground conducive to building a good relationship.

The success of an exhibition is not necessarily measured in terms of sales contracts signed and sealed on the stand. Rather, it should be measured in terms of new potential clients met and introduced to your products or services.

A stand at a public exhibition has an element of 'neutral ground' about it. Neither buyer nor seller is on 'home ground' so neither feels at a disadvantage. Nevertheless the seller, the exhibitor, does have the advantage of being able to prepare the exhibition stand carefully in a manner which will enhance the chance of achieving every objective.

If, in your business, you need to meet people there are few, if any, better ways than by participation in a carefully selected and appropriate national or international exhibiton. Such exhibitions, however, are expensive and should never be undertaken without careful consideration of the comparative cost of achieving the same objectives by alternative means.

Comparative costs

Regular exhibitors should have a fair knowledge of the cost of achieving their objectives by means of exhibitions compared with other means. Newcomers to exhibitions, though, are at a disadvantage as it is extremely difficult to draw comparisons until the costs and results of at least a few exhibitions have been recorded.

Even if it is not possible to draw comparisons based on real experience it is still possible to base the budget for participation in an exhibition on the cost of achieving your chosen objectives by other means. For example; if your sole objective is to achieve sales to a specified value you will know either how much it would normally cost you to achieve that value of sales or how much you can afford to spend without adversely affecting your profit margin. Whatever this figure is can be regarded as an absolute maximum hypothetical budget for the exhibition. Obviously you should not spend up to that budget, not least because you have no guarantee you will achieve your sales target.

The extent to which you can use this hypothetical budget will vary with the degree of certainty you can place on achieving your exhibition sales target.

The ideal situation is well represented by many of the boat-building companies which exhibit annually at the International Boat Show in Earls Court, London. This one ten-day exhibition is their most important marketing operation of the year. During the exhibition they take sufficient orders to keep their yards working to capacity for the coming year. They have no need for sales representatives and can restrict press advertising to a programme building gently through to the next Boat Show. Furthermore, exhibiting yachts does not call for elaborate and expensive stand construction; the yachts themselves being a sufficient draw.

Before you attempt to reach any decision it is as well to set down your objectives. These will be particular to your own business but could include some or all of the following:

• Display a selected range of your products
• Launch one or more new products

695

- Meet and entertain existing clients
- Make contact with new clients
- Distribute company literature
- Attract the attention of the press
- Take orders from old and new clients
- Increase awareness of your company within your industry

If you decide that these objectives, or such others as you select, can best and most economically be achieved in an exhibition, then, subject to the selection of the right event and to tight control over expenditure, go ahead, join the family of exhibitors.

If you are uncertain of the cost-effectiveness of exhibitions for your purposes you would be wise to seek professional advice. Several companies in the field of market research undertake special reports on the viability of named exhibitions for selected businesses. One in particular, Exhibition Surveys of Melton Mowbray, Leicestershire, offers a number of standard surveys, tailor-made to suit new exhibitors at very modest cost. Its BASE survey costs about £100. You are asked to name the exhibitions which interest you, state your proposed maximum expenditure, specify the type of people you wish to meet and describe the products or services you will be offering. In return you will receive a recommendation, based on an analysis of potential visitors to your stand, as to whether or not you should attend each suggested exhibition. In the case of favourable reports you will be given an optimum budget based on your potential audience at the event and the current cost (to best performers in your field) of meeting an interested visitor. In addition you will be advised on the optimum size of stand and number of staff required to run it. What the company cannot tell you is how successful you will be with the visitors on your stand.

Public or private exhibitions

If participation in one of the big national or international exhibitions is not appropriate to your company, for whatever reasons, it is possible that a private exhibition, staged in a hotel or public hall or even on your own premises, may be the answer. Private exhibitions can be well worth while but they require just as tight control over planning and expenditure as public exhibitions. In particular, timing is of the supreme importance.

Table 40.1 Advantages and disadvantages of public and private exhibitions

Public exhibitions	Private exhibitions
You are not responsible for attendance or publicity.	All publicity and the issue of invitations is in your hands.
You are in competition for attention with adjoining stands and with your direct competitors throughout the show.	There are no distractions of any sort. Visitors are entirely in your hands.
Press representatives attending the event have their attention divided many ways.	When members of the press attend their attention is solely on your products or services.
A product launch can be placed in the shade by other events at the show.	You have total control over a new product launch.
Total strangers to your company may be attracted by your displays.	It is difficult to get people you do not already know to attend a private exhibition.
More attractive or expensive stands may distract attention.	You set the level of display expenditure.
The timing of the event is beyond your control.	You can time the event to suit the convenience of your clients and yourself.

A private exhibition planned without due regard to the timing of other similar events, both private and public, could be disastrous.

Advantages and disadvantages

Table 40.1 lists some of the main advantages and disadvantages of public and private exhibitions. It is, of course, possible to draw many more parallels of a similar nature, selecting them as appropriate to your own business. Consideration of these and other points will help you to decide whether private exhibitions may be best for you.

CONTROL COSTS

All costs relating to an exhibition can be divided into two areas; those of a *direct* nature involving book expenditure, and those of an *indirect* nature involving staff time and petty cash expenditure. Each can be equally difficult to control, particularly as many people in business seem to consider that exhibition expenditure will inevitably run wild.

697

Direct costs

A full list of direct costs will depend on what you plan to do at the exhibition. The following, however, is fairly typical for a national exhibition:

- Space rental
- Advertising your presence
- Printing exhibition literature
- Stand design and working drawings
- Stand construction
- Electric mains connection
- Electrical rental and installation
- Telephone rental
- Carpet rental
- Furniture rental
- Mounting your products
- Graphic design
- Graphic production
- Stand cleaning
- Stand photography
- Allowance for site extras

If you wish to serve refreshments on your stand you will need to add some of the following:

- Water and waste services
- Coffee-making facilities
- Rental of a refrigerator
- Other catering equipment and staff

If you will be exhibiting heavy equipment and expect to have exhibits operating on your stand you may need:

- Crane or fork lift truck facilities
- A compressed air supply
- A 'clean' electrical mains
- Access to radio or TV aerials

All these items involve direct costs and must be allowed for in your exhibition budget. Some of them are easy to ascertain in advance: stand rental is a set figure, related to your space; electrical mains connection, water and waste, furniture and carpet rental and so on are all list items and easily prejudged; advertising costs and literature production are within the sphere of normal company experience. Stand design and construction and graphic design and production are the danger areas.

There is no 'rule of thumb' method of dividing the exhibition budget between the various areas of expenditure – there are too many variables. If the space you have booked is an area of exhibition floor on which you are to build a stand, the bulk of your budget, probably about two-thirds, will need to be spent on construction. Design of the stand is likely to cost about 10 per cent of the cost of construction. The production of graphics could cost a similar amount and the balance would be needed for other expenditure.

If you have booked what is known as a 'shell scheme' stand, or a 'booth' in American parlance, the cost of space will be a bigger proportion of your total budget, design will be negligible but graphic production will remain at a similar level.

Indirect costs

Indirect costs are even more difficult to assess then direct costs. An added complexity is that many indirect costs, although validly attributable to an exhibition, would be incurred even if you were not exhibiting. In the following list you might choose to ignore some items, while there may be others you ought to include:

- Management time in advance of the event
- Meeting expenses during planning stages
- Travel and subsistence visiting site and contractors
- Development costs related to exhibits
- Special finishing for exhibits
- Packaging and transporting exhibits
- Extending insurances to cover exhibition risks
- Staff and management time at the event
- Travel to and from the exhibition
- Hotel bookings during the exhibition
- Expenses and subsistence at the exhibition
- Client entertainment at the exhibition
- Telephone calls to and from the stand

There is really only one way to keep control over all the cost areas associated with exhibitions. Appoint one person with sole responsibility for all exhibition expenditure. Give that person a clearly defined budget and a clear statement of everything which is to be covered by that budget. Then inform all concerned that that one person has sole authority over all exhibition expenditure.

BOOKING EXHIBITION SPACE

There are two types of exhibition space available at most events – shell scheme space and free build space. Whichever type you choose to book, be certain to obtain copies of all the regulations governing the exhibition and read all the small print before you sign anything. Though the majority of exhibition organizers are honest and fair, 'fly by night' companies do enter the field from time to time.

In any case it is wise to read all the regulations every time you participate in an exhibition as they frequently vary between events, and certainly vary between different organizers. The regulations will tell you what you may or may not exhibit, will control the extent of freedom of design on your stand and will supply a schedule covering all the dates of payments and information required by the organizers. They will also lay down the conditions applicable in the event of cancellation of either the event or your participation in it.

Shell scheme space

A 'shell scheme' stand should take the form of three pre-finished walls with a muslin ceiling, floor covering and basic lighting. Over the front of the stand, and included in its cost, the name of your company should be clearly designated. Sometimes standard desks, chairs and coffee tables may be available as optional extras. To book a shell scheme stand is normally the most economical way of entering an exhibition, if such a stand is appropriate to your objectives.

Free build space

If you wish to design and build your own stand at an exhibition you must book 'free build' space. This will cost less per square metre than shell scheme space, but in the long run as much as you are willing to spend. Free build space is no more than chalk marks on the floor of the exhibition hall. Everything from those marks in and up is at your expense and, despite the term 'free build', is tightly controlled by the organizers' regulations and the safety standards laid down by local public authorities.

PLANNING FOR AN EXHIBITION

Space at an exhibition generally needs to be booked well in advance, sometimes even years before the event. However early the space is booked, planning for the exhibition should start as soon as your application has been accepted and the site plan and regulations issued. Together with the regulations you will normally receive a set of forms, each bearing the date by which it must be returned to the organizer of the event. The dates on these forms are excellent key dates round which to build your own exhibition progress schedule. The forms will cover a number of items such as the style of your company name to appear above your stand, electrical mains, telephone and stand cleaning requiements, your free entry in the exhibition catalogue and so on. The rest of your preparations can be divided into four clearly distinct areas, each of which requires a schedule.

Schedule 1: Design and construction of the stand and the preparation of graphic panels and stand literature

This schedule involves the selection of a designer and, eventually, a design for submission, first, to the organizers for approval and then to two or more contractors for competitive estimates. You should do likewise for the graphic panels and any special stand literature you require. Ample time should be allowed for each stage, not least for obtaining the approval of your own senior management at both design and final estimate stages.

All orders arising from this schedule must be placed a minimum of one month but preferably three months before the event. In the case of elaborate or double-decker stands an even longer lead time should be allowed. The deadline for completion of the stand in every respect should be set for twenty-four hours before the show opens or before press day, whichever is the earlier.

Schedule 2: Advertising and public relations

Only too often advertising and public relations for an exhibition are either overlooked altogether or treated separately from the company's normal activities. This should never be so. All advertising and PR activities relating to exhibitions should be integrated with normal company activities. To do otherwise risks both duplication of effort (and consequently expenditure) and missing opportunities to promote the company's exhibition activities on the back of standard advertising. The advertising and PR schedule needs be no more than diary notes to attend company publicity meetings.

Schedule 3: Products for display

It is easy to overlook just how much work needs to be done to ensure that all the products you wish to display will be available on the stand, at the right time and in perfect display condition.

The products schedule must start with giving the necessary orders to the production department, stipulating display standard, for delivery in ample time for any essential product mounting to be carried out by the exhibition stand contractor. In the case of goods intended for display in operation, a trial testing period must be allowed for. Arrangements must also be made for any necessary safety conditions demanded by the organizers or local authorities to be compiled with. In the case of heavy goods, arrangements must be made for handling within the exhibition hall and attention paid to allowable floor loadings both on your stand and along the route to it.

If the exhibition is overseas time must be allowed for obtaining carnets and shipping documents.

Schedule 4: Staff

The whole exhibition is a waste of time if your stand is not staffed by the right people with the right training. At a very early date the stand staff must be selected and warned to be available. They should be your best sales staff backed up by both technicians and top management. Any questions or complaints visitors make on your stand must be met with efficiency by appropriate staff, at any time throughout the opening hours of the show.

The question of the appearance of staff on your stand must also be considered early. Visitors must be able to recognize staff easily and if you are lucky enough to have a busy stand a simple badge will not be effective. So many people at exhibitions wear badges for various purposes that they are seldom of value other than for showing the name of the wearer.

If you decide that all stand staff should wear uniforms, or some matching item of clothing, measurements must be taken in good time to allow for the purchase.

In setting up the schedules for an exhibition always remember that the object is to make diary entries which will alert you to all necessary decisions and actions during the build-up period to the event, allowing you, in between such activities, to get on with your normal company functions.

STAND MANAGEMENT

An exhibition stand is a small part of your own premises. Every member of your staff on the stand is in the public eye and may be approached by any visitor. They will be in a position to give a good or bad first impression of your company; there is nothing to prevent the managing director of a potentially important new client company approaching the most junior member of your staff for information on your latest product or even your financial status.

There is a dramatic difference between a well-managed stand with carefully selected and briefed staff and a stand where little or no attention has been paid to such matters.

The stand manager

Appointing a good stand manager is one of the first priorities. The stand manager should be fully aware of the company's objectives, should have an important say in the selection of stand staff and should be held solely responsible for all activities on the stand during the event.

The person appointed to be stand manager must have management and personnel handling skills, a highly developed planning ability and an active mind capable of making spot decisions as problems arise. Sales ability and technical knowledge are secondary as the stand manager should never become involved with visitors unless all other staff are busy.

When on the stand the stand manager should be allowed absolute control, not only over the stand and the appointed staff but also over all other members of the company visiting the stand, of whatever seniority. Even the managing director should report to the stand manager upon arrival and take advice regarding stand activities.

Other stand staff

Irrespective of the nature of your business, the remaining staff will fall into four categories.

1 *Sales*: A sufficient number of your best salespeople to ensure that the stand will always be adequately manned, including during normal meal breaks.
2 *Technical*: If appropriate to your products, one or more of your best technical experts should be available on the stand at all times. If this is not practical an arrangement should be made for them to be available by telephone throughout the opening hours of the event, every day. This should include late evenings and weekends if needed.
3 *Public relations*: If you employ PR staff one or more should be in attendance at all times to deal with the press and with any problems brought to the stand by existing or past clients. If you have no regular PR staff a senior member of your company should be appointed to take PR responsibilities on the stand and all other stand staff should be instructed to pass all such matters on to that person.
4 *Miscellaneous*: These include all other staff you might need on the stand such as interpreters, receptionists, catering staff or cleaners.

In deciding the number of staff you require on the stand take into account the length of the day, whether full weekends are worked and the

704

need for all staff to take meal breaks. A day on duty on an exhibition stand is very tiring and, if everyone is to remain at that peak of peformance worthy of the cost of getting them there, it is worth while making sure they have enough time off. It takes stamina (particularly for those not used to it) to remain on one's feet all day, from nine in the morning till seven in the evening, not unusual hours for an exhibition.

Briefing stand staff

Exhibitions cost a lot of money so don't begrudge that little extra involved in arranging to brief all the stand staff in a manner compatible with the importance and cost of the event.

At the briefing the full objectives of the company at the exhibition should be clearly defined. Any new products or services to be launched should be displayed and explained. The current situation regarding deliveries and prices should be clarified. Copies of any new brochures or relevant advertisements should be distributed. Accommodation, travel arrangements and duty rosters should be announced and, finally, detailed plans for operating the exhibition stand should be discussed in depth.

Remember, everyone on the stand is going to be part of an interdependent team, so include even your most junior stand staff in the briefing and, what's more, don't let the most senior opt out because 'they know it all'.

Unless your company normally operates in a manner akin to the retail trade your staff will not be used to standing on their feet all day, waiting for potential clients to come to them. Only too frequently you come across exhibition stands on which a group of sales staff are sitting around an overflowing ashtray and a pile of dirty plastic cups, looking bored; or perhaps standing with their backs to the gangway, reading newspapers. Such behaviour is inexcusable and will do your company a great deal of harm. The stand and its staff must look clean and businesslike at all times.

Seats on the stand are for the benefit of visitors and for use by staff when discussing business with clients. If there are no visitors the attention of staff should be fully turned to making contacts. Obviously it would look ridiculous if a row of staff lined the edge of the gangway, as if to repel boarders. Under such conditions the stand manager should

705

take control, despatching some staff to walk around the hall, looking out for people they know or for people who have just left stands in the same line of business with a view to striking up a conversation and arousing their interest. Others could mingle with passers-by in the gangways, watching out for anybody showing any interest in the stand and encouraging them to step on board.

Staff briefcases, coats, umbrellas and other similar items should never be visible on the stand. They are better left in cars or hotel rooms or, if they must be brought to the exhibition hall, placed in the public cloakrooms. Offices and entertainment areas on your stand should never become a dumping ground for such items. Smoking by staff should also be banned from the stand except with clients in an entertainment area. If staff bring sandwiches to the stand for lunch make quite sure they eat them elsewhere.

Stand instructions

Everyone at the briefing meeting should be given a prapared set of stand instructions. They should be marked as confidential and should contain the following information.

1 Company information relevant to the exhibition with particular reference to products to be exhibited, new products and any products being discontinued.
2 Stand information, including the stand number and opening times and a plan of the stand indicating the main exhibits and features. Also the stand telephone number.
3 Exhibition venue information, including location of the hall, access points and a plan of the hall showing the position of your stand and any other features of note such as location of competitors' stands, toilets, restaurants and the organizer's office.
4 Cost of entry to the exhibition, availability of free tickets for clients, details of passes and tickets to be issued to staff.
5 Duty rosters.
6 Particulars of any papers to be presented by the company at any conference associated with the exhibition.
7 Standards of dress, availability of company ties, badges and the like.

8 Hotel information with lists of staff staying at each hotel and duration of their stay.

9 Catering and hospitality information. Details of any hospitality suite reserved for the company and particulars of any refreshments to be served on the stand. Also details of any plans for other client hospitality outside the exhibition hall.

10 List of other exhibitors.

11 List of literature to be available on the stand.

12 Details of any PR activities during the exhibition.

13 Details and, if possible, copies of any advertisements to appear immediately before or during the event.

14 Particulars of any special forms to be provided for recording information on visitors to the stand, or of any other method of recording such information as is to be used.

15 List of staff attending the exhibition together with particulars of the responsibilities of each.

16 List of technical staff to remain available on company premises together with details of their specialities and their telephone numbers.

It is well worth while producing the stand instructions in the form of a well-presented bound document, complete with index. The better it is produced the more notice will be taken of it by all concerned.

Stand housekeeping

The stand manager is also responsible for seeing that all the necessary housekeeping duties on the stand are carried out regularly and efficiently. The following duties should be delegated to members of the stand staff, either for the run of the exhibition or on a rota basis.

1 Check and dust all exhibits each morning. Although a stand cleaning company will probably be employed for general cleaning this does not normally include exhibits.

2 Check and replenish all displayed literature, removing any dog-eared copies or copies on which visitors have jotted notes. This should be done first thing each morning, at specified times during the day, and as necessary.

3 Check reserve stocks of literature; arrange for additional stocks to be delivered as necessary.

4 Check the supply of note pads, exhibition enquiry forms, pens and so on, and arrange for additional stocks if needed.
5 Check that you have an adequate day's supply of catering requisites.
6 Check that all messages taken on the previous day have been transmitted to the company.
7 Lastly, the duty of the stand manager in person is to check the structure, decoration, lighting and any other features of the stand regularly and to keep in touch with the various contractors to ensure that any necessary repairs are carried out promptly. In addition, the stand manager must see that all other stand housekeeping duties are carried out regularly and efficiently.

SECURITY

There are two aspects of security on an exhibition stand: company security, or the protection of confidential information; and security against theft and damage.

Company security

Company security can be assured only by vigilance during the opening hours of the exhibition and by the removal of sensitive paperwork from the stand at night. In addition, any products on display which would be a 'company security' risk if stolen should be removed from the stand at night. Most exhibition halls provide a 'secure room' service.

Theft and damage security

Theft and damage are even more difficult to protect against as you cannot clear the stand every night. Small goods of high value must be removed to safe storage. Larger items of comparatively high value can be efficiently protected by the method of exhibit mounting used. An item secured to a bulky plinth in such a manner that it cannot easily or quickly be detached is relatively safe.

Stands serving drinks should always keep the amount left on the stand to a minimum overnight and during any weekend closing. Rooms on stands used to store drink or cigarettes are best left unlocked at weekends as the damage caused by a break-in can far exceed the cost of any small quantity of drink which might be stolen.

The risk of damage to the stand itself and to displays on the stand is at its greatest during the last night before opening day – when extra staff are often working in the hall in an attempt to complete late stands. Companies with valuable exhibits would be well advised to employ a security guard to spend that night on the stand. During the run of the show the overnight risk is much less.

ASSESSING RESULTS

While reaching your decision to exhibit you will have considered all the objectives you would wish to achieve. These objectives would certainly include a specified minimum level of business but would also include such less quantifiable objectives as improvement in public awareness of the company and its products or services.

To assess the value of an exhibition after the event, it is necessary to estimate the cost to your company of achieving all your exhibition objectives by other means. Given that figure you can compare it with the total cost of mounting the exhibition and the degree of success you have achieved in reaching the named objectives.

In all likelihood the answers will be inconclusive as so many of the factors involved are difficult to quantify or value. If the answers are inconclusive it is probably worth trying again; at a second or third exhibition you will be better prepared to record your objectives and results more accurately. If, however, the answers to these straightforward comparisons come down firmly on one side or the other you may well wish to act on them.

If the answers suggest 'no' to further exhibitions, don't be too quick to give up. Do a thorough examination of your costs and results. Did you spend too much on space or on construction? Were you too lavish in entertainment? How did your stand compare with that of competitors of similar standing? In retrospect, were your stand staff as efficient and alert as you would wish? Were you at the right exhibition? Did you show the right products? However successful your exhibition it is most unlikely that, if it was your first, you would get favourable answers to all those questions.

If the answers suggest 'yes' to further exhibitions, still ask yourself the same questions. Honest answers could well lead to an even better performance next time.

EXHIBITIONS ARE TO DO WITH MEETING PEOPLE

If your business relies on meeting people to achieve success, exhibitions can be the best and most economical method. If, after a sensible period of trial with careful assessment of results, your exhibition programme achieves a level of return, which after accounting for all associated expenditure, is in excess of the return achieved by other sales methods, you should give careful consideration to redistributing your promotional budget, in favour of exhibitions.

To reach such conclusions, however, takes time and recorded experience. The picture can become clear only after you have participated in a series of well-chosen events, having kept clear records of apparent results. For many companies exhibitions are the most economical means of achieving the bulk of their annual sales. To discover whether this can be true for your company will take accurate and intelligent cost accounting over a reasonable period of time.

41

Countertrading

Stan Paliwoda

'Countertrade' is a new generic term for a multiplicity of trading arrangements incorporating payment wholly or in part in goods or services as well as currency which may be either convertible or inconvertible. Barter, which is itself relatively rare today, is only one of these many variants, and thus is not the generic term for what we are about to explore.

DEFINING COUNTERTRADE

There is no common agreement on either the terms used or what is held to constitute countertrade. However, after an exhaustive study of existing definitions, Asiwaju and Paliwoda (1987) offer the following definition of countertrade:

> Any contractual agreement, conditionally linking Western exports directly or indirectly to activities which accommodate the agreed needs of the importing nation (for example, hard currency cash flow, technology transfer and know-how, export market development, goodwill and so on) with transactions settled on a mutually agreed basis within a short- to long-term period.

Figure 41.1 shows Horwitz's model for countertrade, or offset, and Table 41.1 classifies its 'principal actions'.

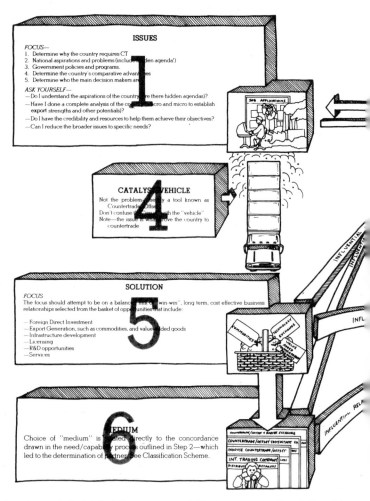

ISSUES

FOCUS—
1. Determine why the country requires CT
2. National aspirations and problems (includes 'hidden agenda')
3. Government policies and programs.
4. Determine the country's comparative advantages
5. Determine who the main decision makers are

ASK YOURSELF—
— Do I understand the aspirations of the country (are there hidden agendas)?
— Have I done a complete analysis of the country macro and micro to establish export strengths and other potentials?
— Do I have the credibility and resources to help them achieve their objectives?
— Can I reduce the broader issues to specific needs?

CATALYST/VEHICLE

Not the problem merely a tool known as Countertrade/Offset
Don't confuse the issue with the "vehicle"
Note—the issue is what drove the country to countertrade

SOLUTION

FOCUS
The focus should attempt to be on a balanced mix of a "win-win", long term, cost effective business relationships selected from the basket of opportunities that include:

— Foreign Direct Investment
— Export Generation, such as commodities, and value added goods
— Infrastructure development
— Licensing
— R&D opportunities
— Services

MEDIUM

Choice of "medium" is related directly to the concordance drawn in the need/capability process outlined in Step 2—which led to the determination of partner. See Classification Scheme.

Step 1. Evaluation of a countertrade/offset situation begins with understanding the "issues" involved in why the country is requiring countertrade/offset, such as industrial development or balance of payments considerations.

Step 2. The "need/capability identification" is a translation of the country's issues into specific needs (such as creating employment by upgrading an industry in a particular region), and,

Step 3. Drawing a concordance between those needs and the capabilities of the company. The shortfall that remains, if any, is an indication to the company of the type of "partner" needed to satisfy the countertrade/offset obligation.

Step 4. There is a tendency for a company faced with a countertrade/offset situation to view the obligation as the starting point, or issue. It is very important that the firm recognize that the countertrade/offset requirement is not the issue, merely the "vehicle" or "catalyst" that the nation is using to achieve some objective.

Step 5. After studying the issues and the need/capability identification, a basket of opportunities that can be applied to the country is

Source: Countertrade and Barter Quarterly, Autumn 1984, p. 42–3.

Figure 41.1   Horwitz's countertrade/offset model

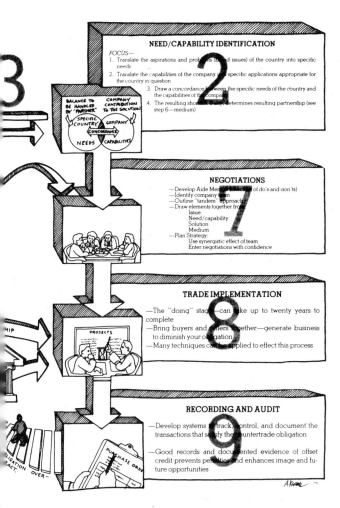

NEED/CAPABILITY IDENTIFICATION

FOCUS—
1. Translate the aspirations and problems (and issues) of the country into specific needs
2. Translate the capabilities of the company into specific applications appropriate for the country in question
3. Draw a concordance between the specific needs of the country and the capabilities of the company
4. The resulting shortlist determines resulting partnership (see step 6—medium)

NEGOTIATIONS

—Develop Aide Memoire (list of do's and don'ts)
—Identify company team
—Outline "tandem" approach
—Draw elements together from
  Issue
  Need/capability
  Solution
  Medium
—Plan Strategy:
  Use synergistic effect of team
  Enter negotiations with confidence

TRADE IMPLEMENTATION

—The "doing" stage—can take up to twenty years to complete
—Bring buyers and sellers together—generate business to diminish your obligation
—Many techniques can be applied to effect this process

RECORDING AND AUDIT

—Develop systems to track, control, and document the transactions that satisfy the countertrade obligation

—Good records and documented evidence of offset credit prevents penalties and enhances image and future opportunities

veloped, and becomes the basis for the olution".

Step 6. The "medium" is the "machinery" or "partner" that the company uses to diminish the obligation.

Step 7. At this point, all the inputs are coordinated, comprehensive strategy developed by the countertrade/offset team and the negotiations are entered into, with the company now prepared to commit to contract terms; while attempting to maintain maximum flexibility.

Step 8. Trade implementation serves two purposes. First, it satisfies the countertrade/offset contract. The goal is long-term, mutually beneficial, cost-effective projects that enhance both country and company. Second, of equal importance, is the goodwill that is created by effective implementation, entrenching the company in the local market. The company's reputation for successful implementation of countertrade/offset contributes to increased international business.

Step 9. The maintenance of auditable and accurate records is vital to avoiding disputes and potential penalties over the life of the contract.

713

Table 41.1   Horwitz's classification scheme of the principal actors in countertrade (CT)/offset

Who (are the actors)	How (do they do it)	What (do they trade)	Strengths	Weaknesses
Banks	Export trading company countertrade department	Financial instruments / Usually commodities / Broker/facilitator/ some take positions / Bundle of services	Broad international base / Good country knowledge / 'Confidence' factor / Experience in structuring complex deals	Discomfort with non-financial trading environment / Difference between banking and trading cultures / Reluctance to take a position (changing?)
Trading houses	In-house CT department / trading specialty sections	Commodities / Manufactured products / Strong on taking position	Flexibility / Good international knowledge base / Negotiating skills / Taking position	Generally specialized (for example commodities vs. manufactured products) / Reluctance to long-term industrial co-operation (changing?) / Earn revenue from seller (usually)
MNEs* seller (usually)	In-house CT department or trading company subsidiary / Consultants / Barter/CT exchanges / Trading houses / Banks etc.	Selected in-house use of foreign purchases / Move products to third parties	Purchasing power / Experienced purchasing culture / Easily relate 'sales' / Reputation / Continuity willing to undertake long-term involvement	Buyers not experienced in international trade (usually) / Often decentralized purchasing / Reluctance to displace existing suppliers / CT: a distraction from principal business / Unfamiliar with trading culture (excluding trading subsidiary)
Host government buyers (usually)	Impose CT obligation / Offer barter arrangement	Range of products and services		
Industry advisers or consultants			Good understanding of issues / Good negotiating skills / Long on 'advice'	Do not take a position / Want money up front / Lack of continuity
Barter/CT exchanges (concept still evolving)	Electronic communication / Databases	Exchange information on all products and services	Bring buyer and seller together	Offers 'leads' rather than 'deals' / Weak on 'personal' contact / Usually only rudimentary information provided – lacks depth

Note: Countertrade/offset is a dynamic and evolving industry. The reader should recognize that there are overlaps and changes occurring in the services provided.

*MNE = multinational enterprise

Source: *Countertrade and Barter Quarterly*, Autumn 1984

WHY COUNTERTRADE?

As a result of low economic growth, shrinking export markets, industrial over-capacity and the contraction of international credit, countertrade has grown in importance in its percentage of world trade and has therefore drawn many new users into its fold. Drawing upon the reasons cited by Welt (1984) and adding to them, we can point to the following:

1   For Third World and many socialist countries with a significant lack of convertible currency to pay for imports, countertrade may be the only means of trading.
2   The instability of energy prices since 1974 has badly affected the developing countries as both consumers and producers.
3   Declining confidence in principal world currencies such as the dollar, due among other reasons to the growing US deficit.
4   Use of countertrade has been made mandatory by countries in Latin America as well as by Indonesia and Romania (Verzariu, 1985).
5   Resource-rich but cash-poor countries such as China have specifically cited countertrade as a means of paying for industrialization programmes with commodities and raw materials.
6   Countertrade is an excellent method for working within import restrictions where these have been imposed by governments to cut the foreign currency drain.
7   Due to poor marketing channels and poor marketing expertise, many developing and socialist countries have a great need to develop export markets.
8   The severe debt problems of countries such as Brazil, Venezuela and Poland means that they are having to spend an ever-increasing percentage of their foreign currency earnings on interest charges relating to foreign debts without repaying capital or being able to undertake new loans.
9   Intense competition between Western suppliers forces companies to consider alternative forms of trading.
10 There is the philanthropic and political appeal of bilateralism.

COUNTERTRADE – A TEMPORARY PROBLEM?

Countertrade is not an *ad hoc* or transitory adjustment to a persistent

715

problem; it fulfils a vital marketing function in facilitating the exchange process between buyer and seller. Estimates of its importance as a percentage of world trade vary but hover around 30 per cent. (These estimates vary. For example: *Business Week*, 19 July 1982 – 25 to 30 per cent; Bracher (1984) – 10 to 30 per cent; JETRO (Japan External Trade Research Organization) – 30 per cent; UNECE (United Nations Economic Commission for Europe) – 30 per cent (East–West trade, 50 per cent); Weit, (1984) – 33 per cent.)

Despite this commanding position, countertrade is not liked by institutions such as the IMF and GATT (Liebman, 1984), which view it as regressive, inconsistent with the principles of a multilateral system of trade and payments, and a return to restrictive trade practices and what the French countertrading association ACECO (Association pour la Compensation des Echanges Commerciaux) refers to as the 'sulphurous fires of bilateralism'.

The GATT's restrictive trade provisions tend to be strictly construed. Thus, if put to the test, a form of restrictive trade practice not expressly covered by the GATT may not end up being proscribed. The relative ease in obtaining waivers under GATT Article XXV or in obtaining tacit waivers (for example in the area of interim regional arrangements) is also an important practical consideration in challenging countertrade under GATT. Finally, historically there has not been a strict application of the GATT rules or any rigid resort to the GATT panel procedure for adjudicating violations. Hence, even if no waivers were available, there is the final practical consideration of how a potentially real violation of the GATT can be pursued and remedied.

ACECO views countertrade as a palliative but a legitimate way of finding a favourable balance between diminishing exports and inevitable imports. Despite contravening the Treaty of Rome, EEC member states such as France, Belgium, Denmark and Greece have all imposed 100 per cent countertrade obligations on fellow EEC members. Whereas in 1975 there were perhaps only ten nations involved in countertrade, mainly those in the CMEA (Comecon) bloc, the figure now exceeds ninety (Paliwoda, 1986, p. 128).

A BANKING VIEWPOINT

Irrespective of how we may view countertrade, we must acknowledge that it provides a spectrum of trading possibilities presenting opportunities for creative marketing. From a trade policy viewpoint it may be second best but, as Bracher (1984, pp. 69–71) points out, for bankers the decision whether or not to develop a countertrade capability to provide strategic support for corporate and sovereign clients engaged in it should be based on a strict commercial assessment rather than on any prejudice against an 'inferior' form of trade. Bracher sees the role of the bank in countertrade as support for companies which have no countertrade experience and complementary to those which have acquired extensive in-house expertise. Pointing to the need for partnership, Bracher notes that traders would prefer to have the banks act as contract drafters, undertaking transactions which required only the injection of trading skills to become viable. The relatively low proportion of countertrade propositions which come to fruition, the ancillary services the bank provides and the large client base which it can bring to the trader, make for a sensible liaison. Further arguments for a bank to develop such a capability include:

1 Every form of countertrade except pure barter involved an actual or a nominal transfer of money.
2 Few of a bank's clients involved in international trade or overseas projects will not have to consider and/or engage in countertrade at some time.
3 The attractive element of a countertrade package is the often trade financing opportunity thereby generated.
4 Countertrade services can generate fee income in addition to risk-based earnings.
5 If countertrade helps a bank's clients to win export orders, it will strengthen the bank's relationship with the client in other areas.
6 When a bank is requested to process or finance an already structured countertrade transaction, it is as well to be able to apply a critical and constructive eve to the transaction.

POINTS TO NOTE

Paliwoda (1981, p. 7) lists the following points to consider in relation to countertrade.

1 Is the profit margin sufficient to justify the transaction?
2 Does compensation carry elements of risk? If so, how can these risks be analysed and integrated?

3   Are the countertrade obligations transferable? Is it possible to nominate a third party?
4   What percentage of your sales must you buy in goods?
5   Which goods? Can these goods be used within the company? If not, are these goods:
    • manufactures of merchantable quality for Western markets?
    • manufactures not of merchantable quality for Western markets?
    • commodities and raw materials?
6   What price? Discounts are necessary for manufactures because of parts and service considerations
7   Is re-export of countertraded goods permissible?
8   Does the countertrade deal have any intrinsic difficulties? What can be done to overcome them?
9   How can the above points be negotiated? Who is responsible for conducting negotiations?
10 Which local laws, particularly in banking, are applicable to financing, loans and so on?

CORPORATE COSTS AND BENEFITS OF COUNTERTRADE

Approximately one in ten countertrade proposals leads to a transaction (Rouse, 1986). Companies involve themselves in countertrade for three main reasons:

1   to overcome the competition factor;
2   to stretch the hard currency reserves of state foreign trade enterprises;
3   to uncover items which are 'good buys'.

King (1977) maintains that in the absence of these three criteria it would be unwise to enter into countertrade. Countertrade incurs special costs such as *disagio*, or subsidy, being commission payable by an exporter to an intermediary who handles a countertrade obligation on his or her behalf. Where exporters agree to countertrade goods which they use in their own production facility the cost of transferring the goods to a third party will be saved. According to ACECO (1985, p. 39), *disagio* on countertrade goods should be payable only when the third party can prove that the exporter no longer has any countertrade obligation to fulfil.

Non-performance penalties can be high. In Poland, for example, these usually range between 10 and 20 per cent but can be as high as 30 per cent. Unlike the situation in the past, when penalties were much lower at around 5 per cent, payment of the penalty is no longer viable due to the high levels now demanded and the fact that some countries do not regard payment of the penalty as discharging the obligation. Countertrade has become a very serious business.

The costs of countertrade are classified below in ascending order. The latter stages are more costly as intermediaries must be used.

1   Direct compensation (or buyback) where the counterdeliveries result from and are related to the original export. This may involve the design, commissioning, construction and equipping of an industrial plant.
2   Indirect compensation (or counterpurchase) where the counterdeliveries are not derived from or related to the original export. The British government requires North Sea operators to place 70 per cent of development contracts, for example drilling platforms, with British manufacturers. This is known as a form of countertrade linkage.
3   Reverse countertrade (or 'junktim') where anticipatory purchases by an exporter are contractually qualified for credit to be offset against his subsequent sales. Such credits can be made transferable to third parties.

Figure 41.2 shows the relative difficulty of various countertrade transactions.

FORMS OF COUNTERTRADE

There is much inconsistency in defining forms of countertrade due to the lack of commonly accepted terms and definitions. However, we will review the various forms using the definitions of Asiwaju and Paliwoda (1987).

Barter

Barter is the simplest to define, yet one of the most commonly misunderstood terms:

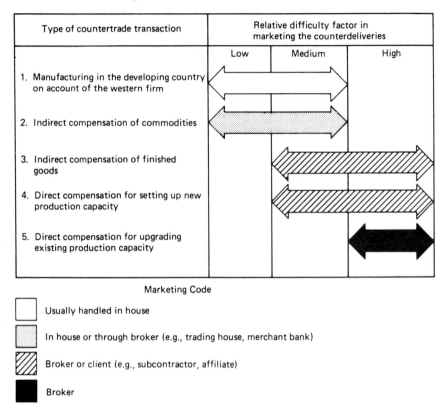

Type of countertrade transaction	Relative difficulty factor in marketing the counterdeliveries		
	Low	Medium	High
1. Manufacturing in the developing country on account of the western firm			
2. Indirect compensation of commodities			
3. Indirect compensation of finished goods			
4. Direct compensation for setting up new production capacity			
5. Direct compensation for upgrading existing production capacity			

Marketing Code

☐ Usually handled in house

▨ In house or through broker (e.g., trading house, merchant bank)

▨ Broker or client (e.g., subcontractor, affiliate)

■ Broker

Source: Pompiliu Verzariu, *Countertrade, Barter, Offsets*, McGraw-Hill, New York, 1985, p. 76.

Figure 41.2 Expected difficulty in marketing countertrade goods

Any direct or simultaneous exchange of goods and/or services of equal value without any monetary and third party involvement.

Barter carries specific risks, including the non-availability or non-delivery of compensation products (a list of restricted goods), the possibility of forfeiting part of the *disagio* to the countertrade company or outside partner on handing over the compensation products should the export sales side of the transaction be broken. These risks can be covered by private insurance (ACECO, 1985, p. 28).

Compensation trading

Compensation trading involves part payment in cash and part in goods. The goods available under the terms of this type of transaction are restricted mainly to categories of goods which are not of a quality or standard to make them normally saleable on Western markets. This has two consequences: first, the goods themselves will have to be substantially discounted, which will offend the seller; second, the services of a specialist countertrade specialist will be required to find a market for these unwanted goods to convert them into cash: this affects both buyer and seller. There is a relatively high risk in this type of transaction as the buyer will receive the goods before full payment has been made to the seller, and the costs of effecting this sale of compensation goods through an intermediary not only involve commission (*disagio*) and the discount agreed with the seller, but also possible cash flow problems for the exporter due to the delays in effecting the sale.

Escrow trading and account

An arrangement involving a third party, whereby exports are made only when sufficient funds have been raised from the sales of goods on behalf of the initial buyer and payment has been made against the usual shipping documents, from a blocked or trust account.

Escrow accounts remain probably the most popular security device, particular in forward countertrade. The trust account has certain advantages over the escrow account. First it is protected against all attachment; second, the funds are irrevocably assigned to the beneficiary without the need for the additional legal step of a formal pledge, which must be negotiated

Counterpurchase or parallel trading

Counterpurchase is one of the most widely practised transactions, particularly in key industrial sectors such as chemicals and engineering. It is defined as:

Any export settled with cash, but linked conditionally to a transferable, separate import contract of non-resultant good(s) and/or services from a designated market, and up to an agreed value in favour of the first buyer's (for example importer's or nation's) interest, and on a short-term basis.

The essential features of this type of contract are that two separate contracts are signed which have been negotiated together but are executed separately. Although the two transactions do not need to be synchronized, the transaction is complete only when the two contracts have been fulfilled. With counterpurchase, the seller agrees to become a purchaser, often of unrelated goods, to a fixed percentage of the original contract price. Prices quoted in both contracts are in convertible currency. The goods need not be related to the original contract, and therefore purchasers may select those goods which they may use or resell most easily at least cost. The seller of the counterpurchase goods has at least recouped some of the cost of the original contract through the export of some domestic goods. The term 'parallel trade' conveys quite appropriately the concept of two contracts being exchanged separately but simultaneously and being interdependent.

Evidence trading and account

Although usually classified as a form of countertrade in most reports, evidence trading is more a way of monitoring compliance with governmental countertrade regulations. It is defined as:

> A contractual commercial agreement between a key (Western) supplier and an importing market in which trade flows are recorded separately, settled multilaterally, and any partner with an import surplus will have it periodically remedied via direct or indirect trade reciprocation with any global market of mutual agreement.

Over a period of one to three years the two-way trade between the Western firm, and other parties designated by it, and the commercial organizations of the importing country should balance. Individual transactions do not need to be offset but cumulative balances at the end of the agreed period need to balance. Transactions are settled in cash, and all trade flows are monitored through the importing country's foreign trade bank and a bank specified by the Western signatory to the agreement (Verzariu, 1985, p. 43).

Buyback

Buyback has been defined as:

> An international long-term arrangement in which the Western exporter, a creditor, an authorized body, accepts future output from the transferred technology, know-how, licences, services and so on as full or part payment, which may exceed 100 per cent, to cover project interest charges.

The features to note here are that it offers the possibility of self-financing large projects, allowing the importing nation to acquire modern technology and achieve exports of the resulting products through the distribution channels of the Western company. For the Western company, buyback offers the opportunity of possibly low-cost sourcing of products manufactured under its own licence and designs from what is often a new purpose-built plant in which it has not invested any capital. Large projects, known as industrial co-operation agreements (or ICAs), which have incorporated buyback have also included a 'market health' clause so that buyback need be taken only when there is the capacity to consume this extra production on world markets, otherwise the obligation remains in existence but is postponed (Paliwoda, 1981).

Bilateral trading

> The exchange of goods and services usually between LDCs (less developed countries) to a predetermined value over a fixed period of years with payments in a nominated inconvertible currency with no surpluses or deficits being entertained.

So this creates opportunities for intermediaries and gives rise to switch trade. Bilateral agreements specify the type and volume of products to be exchanged over a fixed duration. More specific conditions relating to quality, price and transportation are dealt with in individual supply contracts. Exporters in either country are paid by local banks in local currency. The importer credits the exporter's account at a designated bank in a clearing currency that can be used only to buy goods in the importer's country. The agreement requires that all trade exchanges stop beyond a maximum specified trade imbalance or 'swing' – usually 30 per cent of the agreed annual trade volume (Verzariu, 1985, p. 33). Further trade can take place only when any imbalance has been corrected. Under bilateral agreements neither surpluses nor deficits are allowed, yet although it may be politically attractive for LDCs to engage in bilateral trading agreements, for two LDCs at similar stages of economic achievement there will be little opportunity for natural trade.

Switch trading or triangular trade

A Western corporate entity (or exporter) acting as a third party being paid from (or purchases) the surplus arising from the bilateral and/or evidence trading arrangement between two nations.

Switch transactions will therefore involve three or more parties and are based on the limitations prevailing within bilateral trading agreements. As noted above, there is an obligation to eliminate imbalances in bilateral trade, and these agreements contain provisions which allow a nation with a surplus in its bilateral trade to make all or part of it available to a third party. The third party, which acquires the right to the clearing account surplus, is able to purchase goods from the trading partner with the clearing account deficit. These third parties are usually specialist trading houses trading either in commodities or in geographical markets and so the prevailing qualities, quantities and market prices which these goods will fetch on an open market are relatively well estimated.

Swap trading

An arrangement between two suppliers of similar products but located at a distance from each other, in which one party makes deliveries to a third party located in a closer market in return for the other party reciprocating such deliveries to any market closer to it to the interest of the first partner.

The concept behind swaps is clear: products from different locations are traded to save transport costs. This is particularly suited to commodities such as sugar, metals, crude and chemicals (Welt, 1984, p. 46). An example is the 1983 swap of Soviet oil bound for Cuba and Venezuelan oil bound for West Germany. The Soviets supplied oil to Venezuela's customers in West Germany and Venezuela supplied oil to Cuba, both countries saving considerable transport costs. One essential feature of swap transactions is that the differences in quality of the goods being substituted must be clearly defined in contractual terms.

Offset trading

Compensatory transactions involving military trade and certain civil procurements such as sales of commercial aircraft are known as offsets (Verzariu, 1985, p. 43). Taking two examples priced in 1984 US dollars, twenty F-20 aircraft manufactured by Northrop cost $315 million and twenty F-16s manufactured by General Dynamics $382 million. A good offset programme may tip the balance toward buying the more expensive model (Harben, 1984). The British government decided to adopt the Boeing AWACS aircraft because of an offset programme amounting to 130 per cent or $1.5 billion worth of British goods. Note that although the US National Foreign Trade Council reported in 1983 that only 8 per cent of US exports were subject to countertrade obligations, 47 per cent of this figure was constituted by the American aerospace industry. Offsets may be defined as:

Exporter's direct commitment to incorporate certain materials or components into its final products sourced from within the importing country, or exports tied to a promise to assist an LDC to earn hard currency and ease the cost of hard currency exports.

Offsets may be grouped into different sets of arrangements, as shown in Table 41.2.

Table 41.2   One definition of offsets

A. Coproduction:	Overseas production based upon government-to-government agreement that permits a foreign government or producer to acquire the technical information and know-how to manufacture all or part of an item of US equipment. It includes government-to-government licensed production. It excludes licensed production based upon direct commercial arrangements by US manufacturers.
B. Direct licensed production:	Overseas production of all or part of an item of US equipment based upon transfer of technical information and know-how under direct commercial arrangements between a US manufacturer and a foreign government or producer.
C. Subcontractor production:	Overseas production of a part or an item of US equipment. The subcontract does not involve license of technical information, and is usually a direct commercial arrangement between the US manufacturer and a foreign producer.
D. Overseas investment:	Investment arising from the offset agreement, taking the form of capital invested to establish or expand a subsidiary or joint venture in the foreign country.
E. Technology transfer: (other than licensed production and coproduction):	Transfer of technology that occurs as a result of an offset agreement and that may take the form of: E.1 Research and development conducted abroad. E.2 Technical assistance provided to the subsidiary or joint venture of overseas investment (see D above). E.3 Other activities under direct commercial arrangement between the US manufacturer and a foreign entity.
F. Countertrade:	Purchase of goods and services from the buyer country as a condition of the offset agreement, excluding purchases under codes A, B, and C above. These purchases may be made by the US government, the US contractor, the contractor's suppliers, or by third parties with whom the contractor acts as middleman. The purchase may involve products for defence or civil use. *Countertrade subtypes* F.1 Defence purchases by US government. F.2 Civil purchases by US government. F.3 Defence purchases by the company. F.4 Civil purchases by the company. F.5 Defence purchases by suppliers or subcontractors. F.6 Civil purchases by suppliers or subcontractors. F.7 Defence purchases by third parties arranged by a company. F.8 Civil purchases by third parties arranged by a company.

Though the terms of the offset on individual contracts may vary substantially, and a contract may call for more than one kind of offset, offsets can generally be grouped into the types shown above.

Coproduction and licensed production are commonly grouped by industry because of their similarity. Likewise, the subtypes of technology transfer and countertrade may be aggregated.

These types of offsets differ in several crucial ways. First, while coproduction, licensed production, technology transfer, and in some cases foreign investment, explicitly entail the imparting of know-how to the recipient, subcontracting and countertrade may not. Therefore, the latter two are perhaps less likely to encourge the technological advancement of the recipient. (All offsets undeniably benefit the recipient in generalized economic ways, and the contracts with which they are associated benefit the seller, but the transfer of technology may have specific longer-term effects for buyer and seller.)

Table 41.2 concluded

Source: Offset/Coproduction Requirements In Aerospace And Electronics Trade: Report of a Survey of Industry, Dept. of the Treasury in co-operation with the Aerospace Industries Association and the Electronic Industries Association, Washington DC, 24 May 1983. This definition refers to 'US government', 'US contractor', and so on, but can be applied in general.

COUNTERTRADE AND INTERNATIONAL TRADING CERTIFICATES

The international trading certificate (ITC) was developed in 1985 by General Foods and First National Bank of Boston as a negotiable transferable instrument issued by the exporter of goods from a countertrading country in favour of the importer of those goods, which carries an endorsement or acceptance noted by the central bank (or designated commercial bank) of the country granting the importer or the bearer of the ITC the irrevocable right to export goods or services to the endorsing or accepting country under the conditions stipulated in the ITC and guaranteeing payment of the export value in hard currency. Figure 41.3 provides a flowchart for an ITC.

By granting a potential importer in the USA or any other developed country the exclusive rights to import specific products (Venezuelan sisal for instance) and to counter-export other goods back to Venezuela (for example wheat) ITCs are also valuable bargaining chips for firms interested in boosting their exports to developing countries.

The central bank or designated institution may restrict the ITC in its counter-export value, type of product, time for making the export and so on. However, the more the restrictions noted in the ITC the less value it will have for the importer or third party buyer. The issuing country's irrevocable assurance that exporters will be paid both in hard currency and on time strengthens its ability to import. ITC's also provide it with a useful method of establishing priorities for imports and exports.

Hector Caram-Andruet, president of General Foods, which originated the idea has said:

If the concept of ITCs takes off as we expect it to, it could do for countertrade what letters of credit did several decades ago for the international trade market.

727

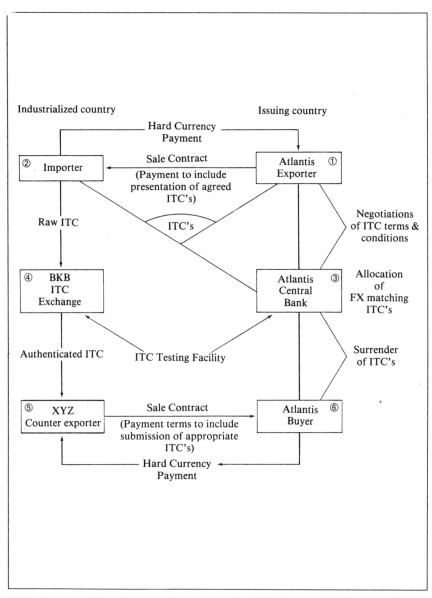

In this flow chart, 1 (foreign exporter) agrees to sell to 2 (a US importer) if 3 (a central bank or appropriate financial institution) issues an ITC. If 2 does not wish to use the ITC, it is sold through 4 (the exchange) to 5 (counter-exporter). When 5 supplies the shipping documents to 6 (foreign importer) the ITC is included, guaranteeing that 3 will provide the foreign exchange on the date payment is due to 5.

Figure 41.3   International trading certificate flowchart

Counter-exporters would be willing to pay a premium for the certificates because the ITC enables their customers to obtain an import licence in the issuing country and assures them that hard currency will be available for their products at maturity on a preferential basis. The tradeable value of ITCs will reflect the degree of difficulty in trading in a particular market, exisiting import restrictions and their ability to generate more credit. The more valuable the ITC the greater the incentive to buyers.

A key point is that ITCs carry the ability to make trade more multilateral. A transaction could cover the entire face value of the ITC or the ITC could be divided into tranches to support several smaller transactions over a period of time. The registration and control of the transfer of ITCs would be handled by the Bank of Boston for particular countries and customers.

As an example, an ITC could be issued by an African government to a US importer of chocolate, developing this industry as a hard currency earner. The American company could then sell the ITC (through the Bank of Boston's marketing system) at a premium to a French company wanting to sell the Africans goods specified on the ITC.

The concept of ITCs has so far been favourably received by government officials in China, Mexico, Colombia, Argentina, Peru and some Central American markets. Czechoslavakia has adopted the scheme and a number of Eastern bloc countries have also shown some interest.

The ITC shifts the funding of developing country export incentives offshore to the exporters who want to sell into the developing country. The launching of the ITC into the international market will accomplish many things.

1 For international traders the ITC will:
   • Promote exports by facilitating and expediting countertrade operations
   • Link the countertrade parties on a documentary basis, much like and/or as a part of letters of credit
   • Confirm the execution and payment of counter-export rights Facilitate the participation of banks as disciplined countertrade intermediaries
   • Enable trade intermediaries to manage a greater number of transactions with smaller organizations linked to an open market where the offer and demand for ITCs will take place

- Multilateralize countertrade, contributing to the standardization of norms and procedures

2   For the countertrading country authority it will:
- Promote exports and introduce an instrument of trade policy enabling the application of both quantitiative and qualitative import guidelines
- Add international liquidity to foster world trade via a new negotiable instrument
- Expand East–West trade through the transferability of ITCs beyond the importing countries
- Reduce the cost of countertrade through trade and organizational efficiencies.

LIKELY FUTURE DEVELOPMENTS IN COUNTERTRADE

Looking at the current position, particularly in the light of the recent developments, it is probable that the short to medium term will see some or all of the following.

1   Countertrade will expand within East–West trade and on a global scale. The USA predicts a 50 per cent increase by 1990.
2   As it expands, the countertrade market will become more ordered, introducing new negotiable forms of trading based on countertrade, similar to the ITC.
3   The ITC is likely to have only limited success and be based on those areas such as Latin America and Eastern Europe where indebtedness forces nations towards financial innovation.
4   New variants of countertrade will arise.
5   The profile of parties to countertrade will change with time and it is likely that smaller companies will become involved; local authorities may also involve themselves in the financial markets connected with countertrade.
6   Countertrade will never replace convertible currency as the preferred medium of exchange.
7   Further innovation will take place in the insurance of commercial risks connected with countertrade as the total market increases in size.

REFERENCES AND FURTHER READING

ACECO (1985), *Practical Guide to Countertrade*, Metal Bulletin Inc, London.

Asiwaju, G. O. A. and Paliwoda, S. J. (1987), 'Countertrade in the North-South context', unpublished paper, University of Manchester Insititute of Science and Technology, July.

Bracher, R. N. (1984), 'If countertrade is inevitable make the best of it', *The Banker*, May, pp. 69–71.

Cookson, D. S. (1984), 'Can ITCs get trade flowing?', *Euromoney Trade Finance*, December.

Cookson, D. S. (1985), 'International trading certificates – a multilateral trading system', *Export*, July/August.

Cookson, D. S. (1986), 'ITCs: a financial instrument whose time has come', *Export Today*, Spring.

Harben, P. (1984), 'Offset overview', *Countertrade and Barter Quarterly*, Autumn, p. 29.

King, J. A. (1977), 'Barter, compensation, parallel trade, switch deals', paper to the London Chamber of Commerce and Industry seminar 'Contra-trade with Eastern Europe', 19 September; cited in Paliwoda (1981a).

Liebman, H. M. (1984), 'Comment: GATT and countertrade requirements', *Journal of World Trade Law*, Vol. 18, No. 3, May/June, pp. 252–259.

Paliwoda, S. J. (1981), *Joint East-West Marketing and Production Ventures*, Gower, Aldershot.

Paliwoda, S. J. (1981a) 'East-West countertrade arrangements: barter, compensation, buyback and counterpurchase or "parallel" trade', *UMIST occasional paper 8105*, March.

Paliwoda, S. J, (1986), *International Marketing*, Heinemann, London, p. 128.

Rouse, W. (1986), 'Countertrade as a Third World strategy of development', *Third World Quarterly*, January, pp. 177–204.

Verzariu, P. (1985), *Countertrade, Barter, Offsets*, McGraw-Hill, New York.

Welt, L. (1984), 'Countertrade – business practices in today's world markets', *Countertrade and Barter Quarterly*, May. pp. 41–46.

42

Customer service/customer care

Michael J. Thomas and W. G. Donaldson

The epitome of the marketing concept in action is the approach an organization takes to the management of customer service. An effective approach reflects an understanding of user needs and the provision of adequate customer care and satisfaction. Customer service is not open-ended and there is always a finite level to such service since the cost of providing it must be controlled, even in non-profit organizations. It is important therefore that any enterprise understands and defines the various benefits, real or perceived, a prospect attaches to customer service and also how to manage and assess this function. Customer service is a boundary-spanning activity, an image, a cost, a revenue, a crucial element in the buyer's decision in both risk reduction and in post-purchase satisfaction.

THE IMPORTANCE OF CUSTOMER CARE

In this chapter the management of customer service will be considered on three levels – the strategic level, the systems or organizational level and the people or operational level. According to Albrecht and Zemke (1985) customers rate a service throughout its performance. They hold a kind of mental 'report card' and assess the company for all the types of contacts they have with it (for example telephone enquiries, sale, after

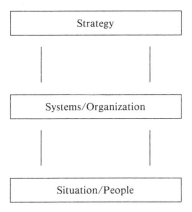

Figure 42.1   Concepts of customer care

sale and so on). These mental report cards are the main constituents of a company's image. Customer service relates to the identification and management of the 'moments of truth' (Normann, 1984) when customers come into contact with the organization and form their impressions of its quality and service.

Customer service is often considered to apply only to service industries which have higher levels of customer contact and personal involvement. This usually means greater emphasis on what constitutes customer service. However, this emphasis is the result of a focus on the people and situational factors (the operational level) which offers only a partial solution, ignoring the strategic and organizational problems (see Figure 42.1).

For this reason the term 'customer care' will be adopted here to avoid limiting the discussion to service industries, although the terms can be interchangeable. The characteristics of service marketing such as intangibility, inseparability, heterogeneity and perishability (Parasuraman *et al*, 1985a, 1985b) and the direct contact and social interaction in services mean a higher profile for customer care in the service sector. However, the artificial nature of the product/service dichotomy is clearly shown in situations where the physical product has a high service element, such as design services, delivery performance and after sales service. There are a variety of diverse and unpredictable 'moments of truth' in such situations. For example, a company in double glazing (or any home improvement) may be selling a product but also operates a service where product qualities cannot be tested in advance and where the customer is usually present. There are many situational and product-specific aspects which will affect the resources allocated to customer care. These factors inhibit a universal approach to customer care but may apply equally well to product or service marketing situations. Albrecht and Zemke (1985) suggest therefore a continuum of these moments of truth. This continuum will move over time as motivational and hygiene factors vary in importance. Customer care involves different aspects of a firm's offering and different time spans. Central to this theme is recognition of individual customers (bespoke rather than mass marketing), of expert help when needed prior, during and following the purchase and efficiency in execution of the product (delivery) or service (moment of truth). Customer care incorporates core and peripheral activities and in increasingly competitive environments it is the number and quality of these peripherals rather than the core benefit which provide the competitive advantage and differentiation. Many professional buyers will continue to favour an existing supplier despite objective product or price disadvantages, at least in the short term. This inertia is a reflection of various dimensions of continuing customer care and attention. Customer care is therefore important in differentiating between suppliers in competitive environments but is not an absolute. The level of service will always be affected by situational factors. What applies in personal computers is inappropriate for steel tubes, what is appropriate for crude oil not so for domestic soap powders and what is the norm in Nigeria will be different from that required in Japan. Where competition is intense, buyers' perceived level of customer service will vary. An additional complication is that the dynamic nature of many markets means that customers' views on acceptable service change over time. While it can be observed that the general level of the service component is increasing for most products in most markets, companies can penetrate niche markets with an alternative product, price and service mix. The implications of this are that constant re-evaluation of customer service must take place and trade-offs against, first, the demands of the market and, second, the relative position of competitors are essential. Customer care is not only a source of patronage and a revenue generator but a cost whose limits must be carefully monitored – no service is free though some elements of service are more cost-effective than others. These cost aspects of service can be identified internally and estimated with accuracy. Many organizations have concentrated on minimizing or strictly controlling these costs, and this can be myopic. Revenue arising from customer care is much more difficult to assess. Successful companies will allocate resources to this measurement problem and modify their customer care programmes.

INFLUENCES ON CARE LEVELS AND POSSIBLE BENEFITS

A variety of factors, both internally and externally generated, contribute to the growing importance of careful planning of customer care. First, as organizations increase in size there is a problem of a lack of understanding of customers' wants and needs and the real benefits offered by an organization's product/service capability. Second, as economies are achieved by standardization and increased scale of production, it becomes difficult to meet individual customer needs at a reasonable cost. Third, where personal contact is important there is variable quality. Fourth, communications from salespeople or advertising can lead to differences in expectations of what was expected and can be delivered. Pressures on sales and profits exacerbate these problems.

Externally generated reasons for careful planning of customer care may be even more compelling. Increasingly consumers seek higher-order benefits; Maslow's self-actualization needs begin to predominate as lower order needs are satisfied. Consumers are more demanding and more sophisticated. At the same time more is on offer from other suppliers, home and overseas, competing for disposable income. Yesterday's luxuries are today's necessities. Some service features which were considered as a plus or as motivational factors at the point of purchase may become mere hygiene factors as customers get used to them. Punctuality, which was Scandinavian Airline System's selling proposition in 1982, is not listed in the customers' choice criteria any more. Today, punctuality must be offered by airlines as a minmum level of quality and is not an incentive for customers to choose one particular airline over the others. Legal reasons, consumerism, environmental changes and international competition are all contributing factors to changing standards. Successful companies in the future will anticipate such trends, welcome the raising of standards and reap the benefits from providing real customer satisfactions and improving the quality of life.

Other reasons why the customer care movement should be welcomed are the benefits which accrue. First, there is the rather altruistic benefit of higher levels of customer satisfaction. This becomes a highly practical reason since greater satisfaction leads to customer loyalty commensurate with greater sales stability, more effective planning and lower levels of uncertainty. A second benefit is employee satisfaction and loyalty, enhancing job satisfaction and reducing employee turnover. Customer care also provides a competitive advantage not always easily imitated, usually highly cost-effective. Superior customer care can form the basis of promotional themes (for example British Airways). Effective customer care results in positive word-of-mouth communication from existing to potential customers. This is a most potent means of advertising, which contributes greatly to a company's improved image and reflects itself in improved sales and enhanced profitability. This is the most compelling of all reasons for a competitive enterprise – higher sales and profits and the achievement of corporate objectives.

A CONCEPTUAL MODEL OF CUSTOMER CARE

To reflect the importance of customer care and translate this to effective management it may be useful to model the three levels – strategic, organizational and operational – and consider the interfaces such a system may create. This is shown in Figure 42.2. The interfaces depicted by the model are labelled A to E. These are discussed below.

The management–customer interface (A)

Management does not often come into contact with most customers. However, when dealing with key accounts there is contact. Such accounts are normally the sole prerogative of top management. The logic of such a system, whereby a company distinguishes between customers, comes from Pareto's rule, which suggests that 80 per cent of a company's business comes from 20 per cent of its customers. While these percentages vary from one company to another, the general rule that the bulk of a company's business comes from a small number of customers still applies. By taking responsibility for key acounts, top management can control the bulk of the business.

The low level of contact which management has with customers calls for an efficient feedback system. The external component of this

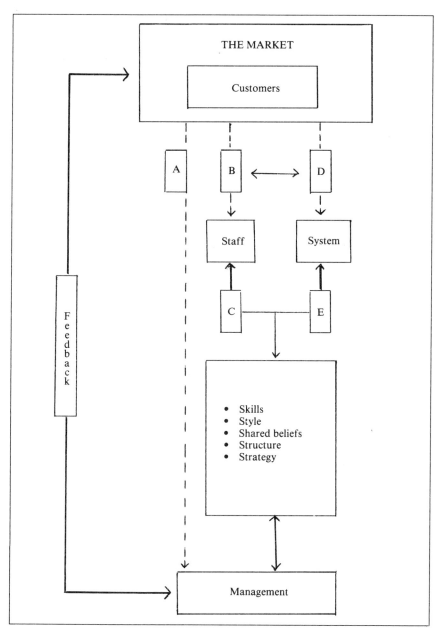

Source: 'Customer Care', a research report by Michael J. Thomas *et al.*, University of Lancaster, 1986.

Figure 42.2   The customer care model

737

involves the operation of a carefully planned market research programme. This is the most effective way of determining the customer's
'service report card' referred to earlier. To ensure customer satisfaction
top management clearly needs to know the elements of the report card.
The internal aspect of the feedback system involves the monitoring of
customer complaints. From this management can develop complaint
profiles. These will help to identify areas of weakness within the
organization enabling the adoption of corrective measures.

Management needs to create a service strategy which distinguishes the
company's service offer from that of competitors. This needs to be
clearly communicated to both the employees and the customer. Furthermore, the service strategy needs to highlight the critical importance of
the customers.

Management must ensure that the organization structure is customer
orientated. To achieve this the primacy of the marketing department
must be acknowledged, especially in the case of service organizations. In
a product organization the marketing department's role can be clearly
distinguished from the production process. However, in the provision of
a service, the customer is involved in the process. As a result of this the
customer is seen both as a consumer and as a producer – a 'prosumer'. It
is for this reason that marketing cannot be something done only by a
marketing department. The marketing department needs to have
control over the sales force and have considerable control over all
employees who influence the provision of the service. To ensure this the
marketing department needs to have a line as opposed to staff function.
Unfortunately, this is not the case with many organizations.

The staff–customer interface (B)

Undoubtedly, the front-line staff have most contact with customers.
The staff should be aware and understand the customer needs and
expectations on an individual basis. Customers will assess the company's service on the basis of the staff they come into contact with. The
staff are the ambassadors of the company and should reflect the
'managed image'. As such they need to display a high degree of skill.
This includes a professional approach, good interpersonal skills, ability
to communicate, a positive attitude, good product knowledge and an
ability to sustain this image even under pressure.

The staff who do not come into direct contact with customers need to realize that they are supporting those who do. The staff themselves can therefore be viewed as customers. This highlights the need for a team spirit among the staff. Clearly this will ensure flexibility in their performance. The staff need to understand the system and know how to use it to meet customer requirements. Since they make daily use of the system and know its strengths and weaknesses they could contribute significantly to its improvement.

The management-staff interface (C)

The quality of the service offered by a service company is only as good as the calibre of its staff. Staffing and recruitment, evaluation of performance, the operation of a welfare policy, feedback and shared beliefs or culture are vital.

Given that the service industry is people-intensive, management needs to understand people. This underlines the need for management to adopt a participative stance. To demonstrate its commitment, management needs to adopt a high visibility profile. This can be achieved by the adoption of an MBWA (manage by walking around) style.

It is the responsibility of management to see to the training of the staff. Training enhances the skills held by the staff and their confidence in dealing with customers. Furthermore, the staff would feel that management cares and this maintains their enthusiasm.

The customer-system interface (D)

The service strategy must extend to the system in use. This needs to be user-friendly. The design of the system must therefore take into account how the customer will use it. It must not be designed primarily to suit the company. However, to ensure a consistent service any system needs to maintain standards.

The management-system interface (E)

Management must continuously seek to make improvements in the system. This can be effected through O and M department studies aimed at streamlining the system. Identifying the elements of the task which must be performed in the customer's presence will ensure that non-essential elements are carried out away from the customer. Furthermore, the staff who are the main system users need to be involved.

Management should provide for breakdowns and for the maintenance of the system. To ensure continuity of service, adequate back-up/standby systems need to be available.

The layout of the premises has a profound effect on the atmosphere which is created within the service organization. It should create a comfortable atmosphere for its customers. As Winston Churchill once noted: 'We shape our buildings, and afterwards our buildings shape us.' The layout influences the image which a company can build. The clearing banks spend considerable sums of money to change their interiors to move away from their traditional image. Previously they were perceived as imposing, rather unfriendly institutions. Now they are moving towards a user-friendly stance.

THE COMPONENTS OF CUSTOMER CARE

Marketing research in customer care lags behind product and advertising research yet is as fundamental to a company's long-term success. Further, even where identification of these service components is well made, translation into operational measures may suffer distortion. Since customer care is aimed at the individual rather than the market, individual channel members or disparate members of a buying-decision unit may have quite different perceptions and expectations of what is required in terms of the service component. The organization has no real alternative to identifying the most important sources of power and influence in the purchase decision and giving these priority. Again, the higher the absolute standard of service the less the problem in customer terms, subject to cost constraints.

Identification of the components of customer care has been made using the classification shown in Figure 42.3. These are grouped as discussed below.

Buyer risk reduction

In some countries this element is partly covered by legal obligation but

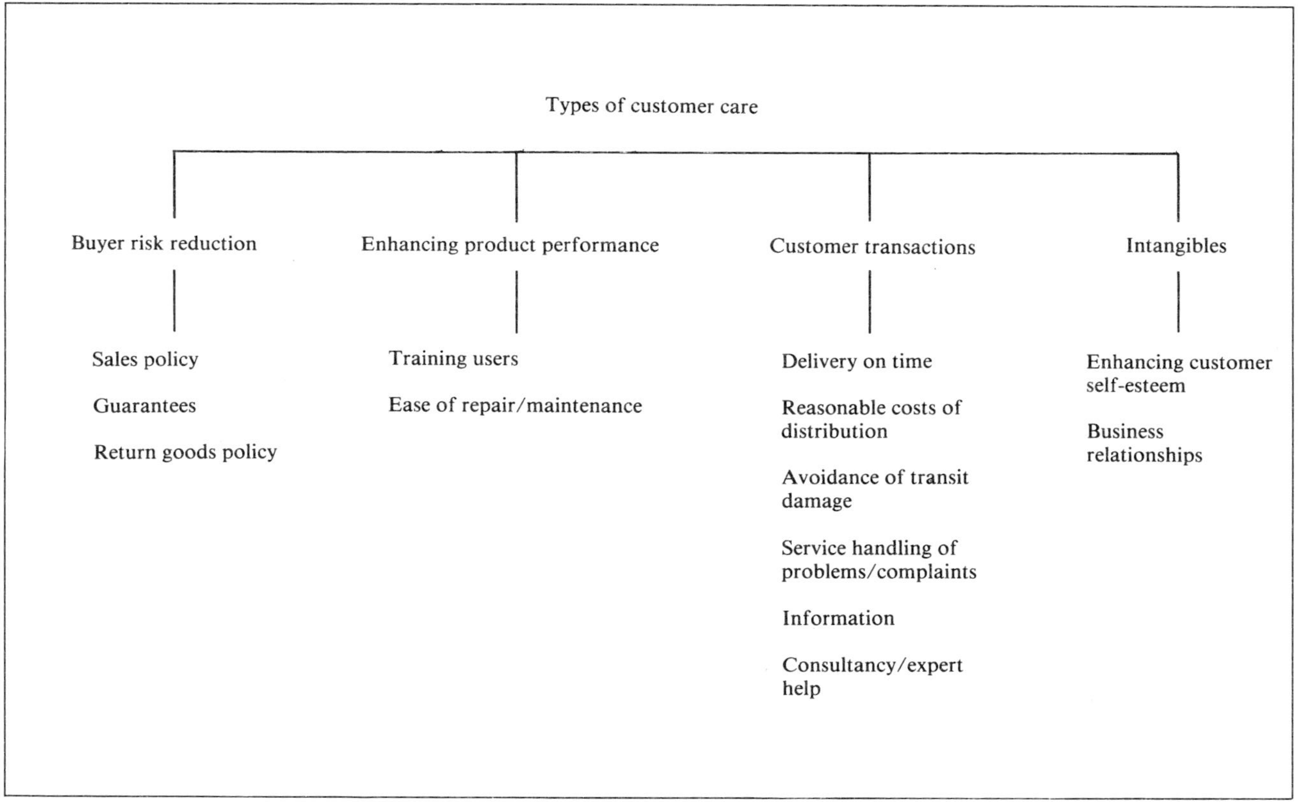

Figure 42.3 A classification of the components of customer care

Types of customer care

Buyer risk reduction

Sales policy
Guarantees
Return goods policy

Enhancing product performance

Training users
Ease of repair/maintenance

Customer transactions

Delivery on time
Reasonable costs of distribution
Avoidance of transit damage
Service handling of problems/complaints
Information
Consultancy/expert help

Intangibles

Enhancing customer self-esteem
Business relationships

companies which believe in their product's viability can offer extended periods of warranty. Companies which promote this service dimension must be aware of the costs of excessive claims and consumers must be confident that the warranty promise will be honoured. Some companies establish a service reputation by a declaration of their returned goods policy – UK retailer Marks and Spencer is an obvious example. Such policies contribute to the source effect in a company's reputation. Price guarantees such as 'if you can buy cheaper we will refund the difference' are also examples of an added service dimension.

Enhancing product performance

Various service components can be built on to the physical product which improve the benefits customers derive from the purchase. Easily repaired or maintained equipment with minimum downtime for users may be preferred to alternative products. Companies which offer training for users or temporary support staff may gain significant competitive advantage far outweighing the cost. Some computer suppliers who have made available such services find a new market demand for support staff as an optional extra. In addition to enhancing reputation such service becomes a profit-generating centre.

Customer transactions

In the customer transaction category are the traditional dimensions of customer service in terms of order processing and the physical distribution function (Christopher *et al*, 1979). Again, these elements vary with different situational factors affecting the exchange process. The premise here is that well-managed organizations will take a cost-effective, proactive approach to these elements and will have as part of their marketing plans written expectations on:

- delivery time and reliability
- a competitive cost of distribution to sales
- a responsibility for minimum damage in transit and handling
- speedy handling of enquiries, queries and delivery problems
- information on out-of-stock items or unfulfilled orders

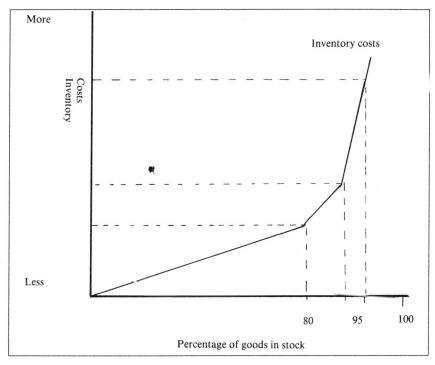

Figure 42.4   Cost of stockholding and service levels

- translation of order and product service levels into operational standards.

Some companies offer too high a level of service, increasing costs and reducing the distributor's stockholding function. The net effect may be that the service level to the end-user is unaffected while the cost of increased service has been transferred between channel members. Companies may use percentage figures for product service levels (out-of-stock items) or order service levels (number of orders incomplete). The cost of maintaining such levels is a crucial dimension of business efficiency (see Figure 42.4).

Customer care is perceived at a lower level where delivery is slow, a product is out-of-stock or an order incomplete. However, it is the speed, efficiency and courteous manner in dealing with such problems which impress a customer and achieve a higher score on his or her 'mental report card'. If the customer is ill-treated, antagonized or inconvenienced at least two outcomes are possible. One, the customer is

743

dissatisfied and the business is lost with the supply company often unaware of this outcome, or two, the customer takes the trouble to complain and the problem is corrected. One study suggests those who do complain are more likely to remain customers in the future (Priest, 1984). The moral must surely be that it is incumbent upon suppliers to identify levels of satisfaction or dissatisfaction among existing, potential and previous customers using a variety of marketing research techniques such as attitude surveys, lost order analysis and some form of customer service audit. Many firms such as Procter and Gamble, Hasbro Toys and Kellogg's are now encouraging customer comments rather than merely reacting to complaints.

Intangibles

A factor often suggested as discriminating between product and service marketing is the intangibility of services *vis-à-vis* products. This intangibility extends to services which enhance products. These provide the buyer with greater self-respect and self-esteem – the so-called higher order needs. An example would be new machinery which exposes buyer ignorance, reduces self-esteem and lost orders result. This feature is recognized in the reluctance of certain groups to adopt new products. Suppliers who offer guidance and training and 'free' expertise enhance potential buyers' confidence in new products, perhaps enabling them to 'sell the idea' to other members of the buying organization.

An extension of buyer confidence is the long-term business relationships which are built up between organizations and between individuals. Such relationships are vital in the exchange process over the longer term.

THE MANAGEMENT OF CUSTOMER CARE

The management of the customer care function within an organization requires consideration across the three dimensions – strategy, systems and people – referred to in Figure 42.1 and the interfaces in Figure 42.2. If this function does not achieve separate status, inter-functional co-operation and co-ordination are required. Does the customer have a number of contacts in different functions at different levels and is 'the story' the same? If there is just one point of contact, is this person a

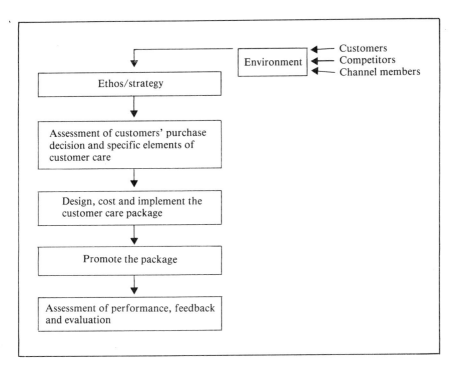

Figure 42.5   The process of managing customer care

specialist in product knowledge, in production and stock control or distribution methods or technical information and advice? Customer care programmes require effective management and therefore a planned approach is advocated. This is outlined in Figure 42.5.

Stage 1: The strategy of customer care

The starting point for any customer care plan is the ethos of the organization, usually established by the founder, the chief executive or the board of directors' consensus. In some cases this ethos is formally stated, while in others no formal statement exists but the ethos is understood via operational measures. These measures can either be implicit – high capability, advanced technology, integration of activities, highly qualified, trained and motivated staff – or explicit, such as product service, distribution standards, goods returns policy. In today's environment the customer care concept is typified by what is called 'new culture companies' (Normann, 1984). Characteristics of such organizations are:

1 An orientation towards quality and excellence.
2 Customer orientation.
3 Investment in people orientation.
4 Small is beautiful on a large scale.
5 Strong focus but broad perspectives.

Customer care is a policy, not a concept. Great attention needs to be paid to this aspect since overstating the level of customer care may lead to dissatisfaction at unfulfilled expectations, while understatement clearly misses a selling feature. Customer care is difficult to define, is usually intangible, and difficult even with sophisticated research technique to evaluate in customer terms. If our definition of customer care is too wide it will be ineffective, too narrow it will be restrictive.

Evaluation of customer care can be more easily established by operational measures such as quality control levels, items out of stock or the number of complaints, but also needs evaluation by senior management as to what they say, what they do and the price attached to care levels. This is more than a slogan such as 'the people who care', 'happy to help' or 'technology you can trust' but such slogans are a useful expression of this ethos. As Alan Sugar of Amstrad is quoted as saying, 'Pan-Am takes good care of you, Marks and Spencer loves you, Securicor cares ... At Amstrad: we want your money.' A word of warning, however, is that what successful people say they do is not necessarily what they do in reality. The result may be higher or lower service levels than those claimed. At Amstrad, for example, the first hint of any dissatisfaction or customer problem is dealt with very speedily – and the net effect is to 'make money'.

Ethos is such an important part of corporate strategy that it may require elaboration or a separate statement. This ethos or business logic has then to be translated into a corporate core benefit or unique selling proposition which provides the enterprise with its identity in relation to its markets and by comparison with the competition. It is also a means of creating shared values throughout the organization, a unifying direction for management and service priorities for staff. Although ethos can be expressed as a slogan, strategy requires a careful analysis of environmental factors matched with company resources (see Figure 42.6).

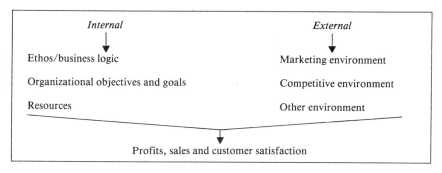

Figure 42.6   The strategy balance

Part of the difficulty with this strategic process is controlling both systems and people to implement the strategic role. Consistency with other elements such as product quality, advertising and personal selling is crucial and the integrated effect most important. There is also a tendency with customer care to consider levels as absolute when in fact they are relative. That is, levels of care will change over time and change in particular in relation to competitor activity. To some extent these organizational and situational factors may be more crucial.

Stage 2: Assessment of the customer's purchase decision and definition of the specific elements of customer care

Purely quantitative measures such as sales volume, growth or profit are the intended result of increased levels of care but, as indicated in the conceptual model, this statement is too simplistic. Part of the problem is shown in Figure 42.7 – sales and profits may be increasing in the short run as a result of a superior product or growth market. Yet customer care ratings are low, affecting not only what could be achieved but threatening long-term survival as existing customers are lost to new entrants.

Information regarding service-related purchasing criteria is vital to effective management of the customer care function. This information can be collected in different ways from a variety of sources. The following three are most commonly used.

1   *Unsolicited customer response.* The difficulty of using such response is that it can be particularly biased and unrepresentative. Usually those complaints which reach the chief executive get the most

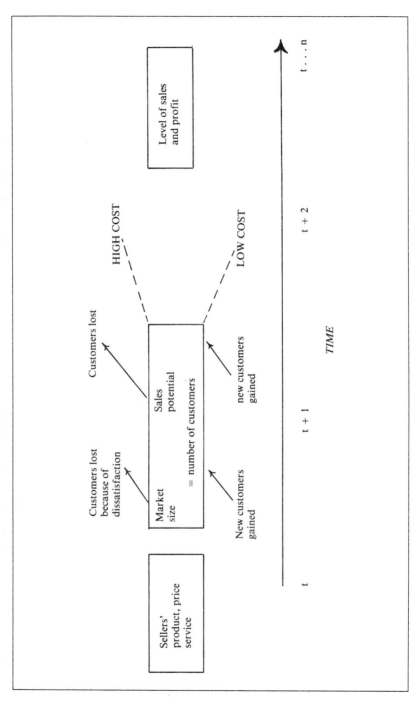

Figure 42.7 The hidden costs of poor customer care

attention irrespective of their worth. Such corrective action is also after the event and therefore treats the symptoms not the cause. However, formal recording of any negative feedback can identify possible problems at the earliest stage so that corrective action can be quickly implemented.

2 *Solicited customer response.* Having identified customer service to be important it is necessary to manage service effectively. For this to be achieved feedback is required from customers, members of the distribution channel and those people in the organization such as salespeople who are in contact with customers. The difficulty in using these sources is the lack of objectivity in their responses. Salespeople, for example, may report customers' views inaccurately so that they are seen not to have failed in their persuasive skills. Other salespeople may exaggerate customer service problems as an excuse for poor selling effort. Distributors too may exaggerate customer problems or use competitors as a source of blackmail to force manufacturers to increase their service and costs for their own ends. To be too generous in improving service may create additional problems. Customers are clearly desirable souces of information but, again, how objective and representative are their comments at one point in time for a given situation?

3 *Marketing research surveys.* The use of research is necessary to assess accurately the need for customer service and to measure existing performance *vis-à-vis* competitors. Such surveys can take a variety of forms. Where possible outside agencies should be used to maintain objectivity although qualified in-house personnel can also be considered. Such surveys cannot be one-off exercises and if not necessarily continuous should at least be regularly updated. These surveys should reveal:
   - a rating for the level of service provided by the organization
   - a comparative position with competitors
   - the relative importance of different service elements
   - the possibility of additional improvements in service.

Stage 3: Design, cost and implement the customer care package

Armed with an organizational philosophy, an understanding of buyers' decision processes and marketing research input, management must design, cost and implement the service elements. This is the systems or organizational level and is similar to that applying for product or promotional decisions – a subsection of marketing activity. The quality of the package will be most effective using a combination of marketing research, trading flair, customer contact and innovation. Also required are adequate information systems, efficient order processing facilities and clear communication. This may mean investment in computing capability, technical facilities and trained people and a policy of after-sales service. Recruitment, training and motivation of staff are essential, backed by top management involvement.

Improved service and customer care do not necessarily increase costs. For example, better quality control, formal reporting procedures and increased automation may both improve customer care and reduce costs. The implication of service both as a cost and a revenue must be carefully assessed. If the costs of improved service levels become excessive, leading to a comparative cost and price disadvantage, some compromise will be required. Some diminishing returns to increased service levels will result. Trade-offs must be made between more and better levels of service and other customer benefits. A separate issue, although one which can be evaluated at the same time, is the competitive advantage which does or does not accrue from the service package.

Stage 4: Promoting the package

The efforts to obtain an advantage in terms of customers through care programmes must be fully exploited in promotional and selling effort. Any marketing advantage must be confidently and repeatedly sold to the buyer.

Stage 5: Performance evaluation

Figure 42.8 outlines the process of service performance evaluation and feedback. As stated in stage 2, the establishment of standards for service performance is often quite challenging. This is because it requires the

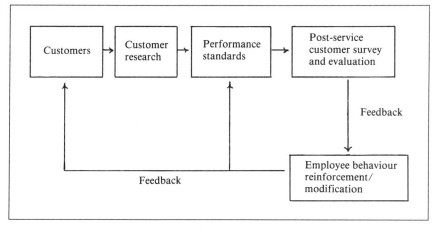

Figure 42.8 Service performance evaluation and feedback process

involvement of the customers in the production process. Preliminary market research is, therefore, mandatory because the evaluation factors that customers use for rating the service performance must be identified. This is a basic step in the customer research process.

The service performance standards are then established on the basis of the identified evaluation factors. These are incorporated in the service strategy and communicated to the front-line people.

The measurement of performance is done via post-service survey through customer and attitude tracking. Such research can be both continuous or discrete. Results obtained will indicate to management how customers view the organization's service performance. British Telecom is doing this via its Telecare programmes and British Airways uses customer surveys.   Post-service research provides feedback to management. This will be used to evaluate the performance of employees. If the feedback is positive management will consolidate its performance standards and engage in employee behaviour reinforcement. If the feedback is negative the company would review its performance standards and engage in employee behaviour modification. Feedback would also entail informing the customers of significant improvements undertaken by the organization to enhance service performance standards. A company which follows the service performance evaluation procedure described above would be one that responds proactively to its environment.

Stage 6: Operations and people

It is imperative that the customer care training programme has the support of top management. This will ensure their involvement and that the necessary resources are made available. Lower-level management and staff must know that their performance will be judged by their superiors. This ensures a motivating climate. Otherwise nothing is likely to result no matter how hard the personnel department tries. It is a feature of companies which have undertaken customer care programmes that the instigators have in fact been top executives. At SAS the strong personality of the president, Ian Carlzon, was instrumental in injecting a service culture to the organization. He ensured he talked to everyone and clearly put forward his commitment to service. The same can be said for British Airways. The new programme of 'putting people first' came about with the arrival at British Airways of Colin Marshall as chief executive. He was the prime mover, setting new objectives and ensuring that the service culture penetrated to all levels of the organization. Top management commitment was underlined to employees by Marshall making an appearance at the end of each course in the retraining programme. As Sasser and Arbeit (1976) note: 'the successful service company must first sell the job to employees before it can sell its services to customers'. This in effect involves an internal marketing exercise with the objective of ensuring motivated and customer-conscious personnel.

Effective management support can come about only if management has a means of receiving feedback from employees. The importance of operating a feedback system has been recognized at American Express, where staff at all levels report to management about problems they have encountered with their jobs and in dealing with customers. Another method aimed at obtaining feedback with a view to taking corrective action has been the setting up of quality circles. A number of companies, among them British Airways, have made use of these. Quality circles are groups of genuine volunteers whose task is to examine ways to better customer services. Quality circle programmes are based on the assumption that employee participation leads to valued outcomes, such as intrinsic satisfaction and recognition and that it also results in changes which enhance productivity and satisfaction. Management is also responsible for establishing standards of quality.

The result of customer care programmes ultimately depends on the attitude and motivation of the employees. Individuals must be aware of the company philosophy, trained in interpersonal skills and in providing expert help. In some cases personnel may be high in engineering skills and technical ability but are different from customers in temperament, lack a sense of shared values with the corporate ethos or simply do not understand the extended role they must perform. Role ambiguity may be exhibited where individuals do not know or care about what is expected when dealing with customers. It is as crucial that the management–subordinate interface is managed on the basis of consistency and clarity of role, as well as the company–customer interface.

REFERENCES AND FURTHER READING

Albrecht. K. and Zemke R., (1985), *Service America! Doing business in the new economy*, Dow Jones–Irwin, New York.

Christopher, M., Schary, P. and Skjott-Larsen, T. (1979), *Customer Service and Distribution Strategy*, Associated Business Press, London.

Normann, R. (1984), *Service Management: Strategy and Leadership in Service Business*, Wiley, Chichester.

Parasuraman, A. *et al*, (1985a), 'Problems and strategies in service marketing', *Journal of Marketing*, Vol.49, No.2, Spring, pp. 33–46.

Parasuraman, A. *et al* (1985b), 'A conceptual model of service quality and its implications for future research', *Journal of Marketing*, Vol.49, No.4, Fall, pp. 41–50.

Priest, A. A. (1984), 'Service departments become marketing adjuncts when they're used to field more than complaints', *Marketing News*, 7 December, p. 10.

Sasser, W. E. and Arbeit, S. P. (1976), 'Selling jobs in the service sector', *Business Horizons*, Vol. 19, pp. 61-65.

43

The legal framework

M. J. C. G. Carlisle

This chapter summarizes the very wide range of legal factors affecting the marketing of a company's products. Of necessity it is a considerable simplification, but its value should lie in making the broad principles clear and in providing a pointer for more detailed reference. The chapter is divided into sections covering business rights in products, contractual obligations, responsibility for product quality and performance, codes of practice and a short section on miscellaneous legal requirements.

PROTECTING YOUR INDUSTRIAL PROPERTY RIGHTS AND RESPECTING THOSE BELONGING TO OTHERS

Patents

Before launching a new product consider whether there are any original aspects which may be patentable. Patents are in essence a limited monopoly granted by a government to an inventor (or to that inventor's employer) in return for making an invention (whether it be a product or the process by which that product is made) public by publishing its specification at the Patent Office. Ownership of a patent in the UK prevents others from copying your invention for a period of twenty years.

The UK law on patents was revised by the Patents Act 1977. It provides that inventions may be patentable if you can show that they are original (that is, are not obvious to a person reasonably skilled in the field of the particular invention) and have not previously been made public either in the UK or elsewhere in the world.

In particular, it will not be possible to obtain a patent if you have used, sold, distributed or otherwise publicized your invention in virtually any country prior to applying for a patent. However, an improvement to an existing formualtion, product or manufacturing process or a novel use for a well-known substance may be patentable.

Registered designs

Your new product or its packaging may have a particularly unusual and interesting appearance. The features of the shape, configuration, pattern or ornament of that appearance may be sufficiently original to be registered, thus granting you a monopoly of its use for up to fifteen years. Once registered no one may use the same design and you can stop anyone from doing so even if their imitation of your design was inadvertent. If you wish to register a design in the UK you must apply to do so before using the design publicly (for example by sale or advertisement) in the UK. However, the law at present allows you to register a design in the UK which has already been publicized in another country but not in the UK. As mentioned below, your industrial designs may also be protected by copyright owned by you in them. However, the advantage of a registered design is that, unlike infringement of copyright, you can stop even unintentional and innocent imitation of your design.

Copyright

Copyright is a protection granted automatically, without the need for any registration, to prevent the deliberate copying of artistic works. It may cover films, photographs, drawings, music, and the written word, although in the latter case there must be something more substantial than just a brief advertising slogan such as 'Guinness is good for you' for copyright to exist. Clearly where you are having such artistic work done for you, for example pack designs, television advertising copy, or advertising photography, you should make sure that the copyright is

755

given to your company. In particular your advertising agents should automatically assign to you any copyright in their work for you.

Copyrights are often extremely complex. For example, there may be rights belonging to different persons in the same work. In the case of a pop song copyright in the sheet music and in the recorded version of that music may belong to separate people. Similarly, different people may own the copyright to the same artistic work in different countries. Thus, if you buy the right to use a copyright, it is essential to investigate very carefully that the seller really owns what he or she is offering to sell.

Copyright may also exist in industrial designs, for instance in engineering drawings, or in the external appearance of a product.

The copyright in artistic works lasts fifty years from the death of the author, whilst that in industrial designs lasts fifteen years from the first industrial application. To stop others from infringing your copyright you must show that they were deliberately or recklessly copying it, since it is always possible that two 'artists' may independently create the same thing. Compare this to design registration where proof of copying is not required.

Trademarks

Trademarks consist of words, symbols or devices used to distinguish your products from those of another company – for example 'Ford', 'Schweppes', 'Terry's' or 'Ajax'. They should not be confused with generic words which simply describe things – for example 'motor car', 'tonic water', 'chocolate' or 'scouring powder'.

Good trademarks can be of immense value and it is important not to use them in a way that simply turns them into generic words. Aspirin, linoleum, petrol and kerosene all used to be trademarks, the exclusive property of their originators, but are now everyday words.

If you treat them properly you should always be able to stop others using your trademarks on products. A few basic rules are:

1 Use a trademark as an adjective and try to make it stand out, rather than using it on its own. For example, refer to our 'Double Dealer' calculators and 'Easy Money' abacuses.
2 Try not to change the spelling of trademarks or use them to make

new words and do not play around with a trademark design, for example by altering it to fit in with your advertising.

3   It is often useful to identify trademarks on packaging, for example by printing a note: 'Double Dealer' and 'Easy Money' – trademarks.

As in most countries, many trademarks in the UK may be registered. Registration is available for marks which are invented words, are not descriptive or laudatory of the goods concerned and do not have surname or geographical significance. The main advantage of registration is that it enables you to stop other people from using that trademark (or one confusingly similar to it) on the goods for which it is registered. By contrast if you do (or cannot) register your trademark you can stop others from using it only if you prove that you have a public reputation in that trademark and that your competitor was 'passing-off' his or her goods as yours.

Remember that trademarks are designed to distinguish a particular trader's goods from another's. Suppose company A makes a variety of calculating machines, and owns the trademarks 'Double Dealer', 'Four Flusher' and 'Easy Money' in respect of calculators and the like. That does not mean it can stop a competitor from using the same or similar words on quite different products for which Company A's trademarks are not registered and for which products it has no reputation. Thus company A could not prevent Company B from marketing its 'Double Dealer' egg timer.

Other people's rights

Obviously it is possible for your competitors to have industrial property rights which could be infringed by your marketing activities. Accordingly it is essential that you discuss with your legal department at the earliest possible stage what precautionary measures should be taken to avoid a new product launch being interrupted by a writ from a competitor. For example, it may be necessary to carry out patent and registered design searches before introducing a product. If a new trademark is to be used it is necessary to search the Trademark Registry to try to ensure no one has already registered it. If possible a company should complete its own registration before using the trademark. Thus it could cost our imaginary company £20 000 to buy itself out of the difficulty encountered through ignoring Fagin Computers Ltd's registration of 'Easy Money' for adding machines when launching the 'Easy Money' abacus. Remember that it can take many months to 'clear' a new product for sale.

Passing-off

This is an old-established legal remedy designed to stop one manufacturer capitalizing on the reputation of another. To give an example of how far this remedy can go, there was a string of cases in which the champagne producers of the Champagne area of France successfully stopped Spanish producers from describing their sparkling wine as 'Champagne' and thus benefiting from the reputation of the French product.

The law of passing-off exists to protect a trader's property in his or her good will and reputation. Passing-off may occur where there is a representation made by a trader in the course of business to potential customers which injures or causes loss to another trader's goodwill or business – for instance by attracting business away from you – by deceiving other people into buying his or her goods, believing them to be yours.

Thus you must always be sure that in name or appearance your product and advertising is not so close to a competitor's product as to be likely to confuse people into thinking that your product is made by your competitor so that you benefit from his or her reputation. You should examine the competition closely to avoid such confusion.

CONTRACTUAL OBLIGATIONS

In the course of your marketing activities you will be involved in a variety of contracts. These will range from agreements for outside manufacture, special promotions, sale of products through distributors to the provision of refreshments for the weekly marketing management meeting. A basic outline of contract law is therefore necessary.

Formation of contracts

Contracts are formed by a definite offer by one party being firmly accepted by another. It is not enough to respond to an offer by a counter-offer: that may be part of the negotiations leading to a contract, but it is not the contract itself. It is also necessary to distinguish between 'offers' and 'invitations to treat', that is, invitations to others to make an offer which you may accept. For example, advertisements of goods for sale or displays of goods in shops are normally invitations to treat; in such a case the contract occurs when the actual sale agreement is made. The shopkeeper accepts your offer to buy – it's not vice versa.

Once an offer is accepted it must be clear that the parties intended it to be a legally binding arrangement. This will normally be the case between businesses, or between a business and its clients. However, between private persons agreements are often purely social arrangements, binding in honour only, and there is no intention that they be subject to the court's jurisdiction.

Normally a contract must be supported by consideration or value on both sides. In other words apart from the agreement itself, there must be a quid pro quo for all parties – as where goods are exchanged for money. Unlike some countries the UK courts will not enforce an agreement where one party promised to do something for nothing. The exception to this rule is when a contract is executed under seal: in such cases a gratuitous promise can be made legally binding.

The terms of a contract

A contract will consist of a number of terms. Where the contrast is wholly in writing these will be easily ascertained. Where it is wholly or partly verbal, there may be argument as to what the exact terms are. It is most important to remember that legally binding contracts can be made either in writing or verbally. The lack of a written document has no effect (except in special cases) on the validity of a contract; it only makes it more difficult sometimes to find out what the contract is about. Try not to lose sight of this fact during any negotiations. It is often useful in correspondence during such negotiations to refer to the fact that agreement is 'subject to contract', that is, that a binding agreement will exist only when a written contract is completed.

Apart from express terms (which are those specifically agreed by the parties) there may in addition be other terms, which were not specifically

759

included, but which are implied in the contract. Sometimes such terms are implied in order to make business sense of the contract. In other cases terms may be implied by statute, and in particular you should note in this context the Sale of Goods Act 1979 and the Unfair Contract Terms Act 1977.

Performance of a contract

Contracts will hold obligations for all parties to them. When each party has fully performed his or her obligations the contract is said to be discharged and is at an end. However, a party who fails properly to perform his or her obligations may be exposed to an action by the other parties to force him or her to do so or to compensate them for the non-performance. In such a case, the parties can also reach a fresh agreement which allows the defaulting party to discharge his or her obligations by doing something different from what was orginally agreed.

In practice the day-to-day performance of contracts will often differ from the strict contractual terms, and the parties will tacitly agree to this. However, do not underestimate the value of a carefully drafted written contract in the event of a dispute arising. Remember that if matters go wrong the defaulting party can be exposed to an action for damages (monetary compensation) or performance of the contract. For instance, it might be possible to insist on the supply of components under a fixed price contract long after inflation has made that price uneconomic to our suppliers and very attractive to ourselves.

Advertising agencies

Finally it may be useful to remind you of the unusual position of advertising agents in English law. Historically, they were the agents of the media – hence their name. Although the word agent implies that they are the servants of their clients, the companies which engage them, and act only within the bounds of the authority given them by their clients, the fact is that by custom and practice advertising agents are presumed in England to act as principals unless the contrary is stated. Thus, without specific authority from their clients, advertising agents can enter freely (but at their own risk) into whatever arrangements they feel are best for their clients. If you wish to ensure that your agency does not act in this way, but is limited in part or whole in the action it can take without your specific authority, it is important to make this clear in your contract with your advertising agency.

HAVING REGARD FOR THE CONSUMER

The law has shown increasing regard for the rights of the consumer over recent years and this trend is likely to continue for a while to come.

Negligence and product liability

English law imposes a duty on everyone to take all reasonable care to avoid doing something which he or she can forsee may injure those whom he or she can reasonably anticipate being affected by his or her action. This, in essence, is the principle established in the well-known case of Donoghue *v.* Stevenson, when a young lady recovered damages from the manufacturers of a bottle of ginger beer which she had drunk and which contained a decomposed snail.

The practical consequence of this principle is that companies such as ourselves must do everything reasonably possible to avoid harm coming to those whom we can forsee using our products. This involves safety testing and the issuing of any instructions and warnings necessary for the safe use of our products.

In common with other European countries, England has looked at the question of introducing strict liability of manufacturers for damage caused by defects in their products. This would mean a consumer would be entitled to compensation from a manufacturer or supplier for any loss or damage shown to be caused by a product, whether unforeseeable or not, and whether or not the manufacturer or supplier had been negligent. Such a system was recommended by a Royal Commission in 1978.

After some twelve years' labour, the EEC Product Liability Directive (85/374/EEC) was published in 1985, and must be implemented by member states by August 1988. In the UK the Directive has been brought into effect by means of the Consumer Protection Act 1987.

The Act makes producers of products strictly liable for death, personal injury or damage to property (over about £300) caused to consumers by defects in their products.

'Producer' is widely defined and includes manufacturers of raw materials, components and finished products; any person who puts his or her name or trademark on the product; the person who first imports the product into the EEC; and if no other 'producer' can be identified, the supplier of the product.

'Product' means all moveable property, but not land or buildings or primary agricultural produce or gain. A product is defective if it does not provide the safety which a person is entitled to expect in all the circumstances.

The Act provides an option of a 'development risk' defence – that is, producers would not be liable for defects which they can prove could not have been detected given the state of scientific and technical knowledge at the time of the product was put into circulation.

In this context of product liability remember that in 1977 the Unfair Contract Terms Act rendered invalid all notices or terms of contracts which attempted to exclude liability for death or personal injury resulting from negligence. It also provided that liability towards consumers for damage to their property caused by negligence can be excluded by a notice or contract term only in so far as to do so is reasonable. One should not, therefore, take too much notice of the absolute disclaimer for liability printed at the entrance to many cloakrooms disclaiming all responsibility for loss or damage to property left there.

Sale of Goods Act 1979

This Act consolidates the original 1893 Act and subsequent amendments. Its main purpose is to give purchasers certain implied warranties as to the quality of goods bought by them. Those warranties include the assurance that the goods must match their description – a gold watch must be gold and not gold plate; that they must be reasonably fit for their purpose – a lawn mower must be capable of cutting grass. Products must also be of merchantable quality, in other words they must be of the quality reasonable buyers would expect having regard to the nature of the goods and the price paid.

By virtue of the Unfair Contract Terms Act 1977 it is not possible to exclude these warranties when dealing with a consumer, and they may be excluded *vis-à-vis* another business entity only in so far as it is reasonable to do so.

Trade Descriptions Act 1968

The fundamental purpose of this Act was to protect the consumer from misleading statements about products or services. If, in the course of trade or business, a false indication as to certain matters (including size, weight, origin, nature, performance or composition) is applied to any goods otherwise than by mistake or accident, the person applying that indication is guilty of an offence. The false indication must be such as is likely materially to mislead an ordinary person. Similar provisions apply to false indications about services.

The Trade Descriptions Act pays particular attention to indications of price and specifically makes it an offence to indicate a price in such a way that suggests a product costs less than it actually does.

Retail prices and bargain offers

For many years it has been unlawful to impose minimum retail prices. However, it is still lawful to impose maximum retail prices and to recommend retail prices. Indeed manufacturers' recommended retail prices are often the only practicable as well as legally acceptable benchmark for bargain price offers, such as '10p off RRP'. Most industries are free to use recommended prices as the basis for such offers. However, the Bargain Offers Order 1979, as well as attempting to regulate the way in which bargain offers are made so as to reduce any risk of consumer confusion, also prohibited certain industries from basing bargain offers on recommended prices.

The Consumer Protection Act 1987 amends both the Trade Descriptions Act 1968 (by repealing section 11 – false or misleading indications as to price of goods) and by repealing the Bargain Offers Order. The new provisions prohibit misleading indications as to the price of goods, services, facilities and certain accommodation. A code of Practice for Traders has also been issued to provide guidelines as to what is or is not misleading. The Code will have a status close to that of law itself. A court will be obliged to take into account any transgression of the Code, and though this will not be conclusive it will be strong evidence that a trader is guilty of making a misleading price indication.

Consumer Credit Act 1974

This Act codifies the law on credit and hire purchase. It regulates virtually all credit business up to a specified limit (currently £5 000) and requires every business offering credit to hire facilities to consumers to obtain a licence from the Director General of Fair Trading. Ancillary businesses such as debt collectors and mortgage brokers are also required to be licensed.

Weights and Measures Act 1979

The law affecting the declaration of weight or volume of goods in the UK was largely revised by the 1979 Act to give effect to EEC law on the subject. Whereas before 1980 any declaration of contents had to amount to a guarantee of minimum contents to the consumer, with effect from 1 January 1980 it is generally sufficient to show only that batches of product contain on average not less than their declared weight or volume. There are, of course, provisions to ensure that no one package has too great a deficiency.

Fair Trading Act 1973

This Act aimed principally to promote increased economic efficiency and to protect consumers against unfair trading practices. The first part of this objective was dealt with by reconstituting the Monopolies Commission into the Monopolies and Mergers Commission and revising its powers to control monopolies and mergers in industry. The second objective was met by creating the office of Director General of Fair Trading and the Consumer Advisory Protection Committee, as well as giving the government power to make statutory orders on a wide range of consumer trade practices.

The government has now passed a new Competition Act which further enhances the investigatory and regulatory powers of the Director General and the Monopolies and Mergers Commission in the interests of ensuring competition between businesses is not restricted.

CODES OF PRACTICE

In addition to law, this country is noted for its tradition of self-regulation in industry. The centre of the system is the Advertising Standards Authority, an independent body financed by a levy on advertising expenditure. The authority has a Code of Advertising Practice Committee which is responsible for producing the British Code of Advertising Practice, the so-called CAP Code. This code contains guidance on a large range of general and specialist fields of advertising and seeks to balance the needs of industry, consumers, society and fair business practice. A subcommittee also produces the British Code of Sales Promotion Practice which deals specifically with the way in which competitions, premium offers and other sales promotions should be conducted. The sanction for infringing these codes is non-acceptance of advertisements and promotions by the media which adhere to the codes. However, on a day-to-day basis, the ASA is normally able to persuade advertisers voluntarily to comply with the codes.

The Independent Television Companies Association also publishes and enforces its own code for television advertising, and its sanction is to refuse to accept a particular commercial. Finally, the International Chamber of Commerce also produces codes on advertising and sales promotion practice.

The Code of Practice for Traders mentioned above will become an important feature of consumer protection.

MISCELLANEOUS

Limitations prevent coverage in detail of all the laws relevant to marketing activities. However, one or two special legal controls should be mentioned very briefly.

The Medicines Act 1968 introduced government control by licensing of all manufacture, import and sale of medicines in the UK, as well as controlling the promotion and advertising of medicines.

Food manufacture was one of the earliest industries to be controlled by law. The Food and Drugs Act 1955 and regulations made under it regulate the whole food industry.

Cosmetic products are controlled by the Cosmetic Products Regulations 1978 which enact EEC law on the subject in the UK.

The impact of EEC law will be clear to you from the above information and marketers should anticipate a steady increase in EEC law in pursuance of the EEC objective to harmonize the laws affecting trade and competition throughout the EEC.

44

Using new information technology

Alan Melkman

There is an inevitability about the ever-increasing rate of advance of new technology. New silicon-chip-based products ranging from compact discs to what appear to be intelligent video learning packages, appear almost daily. Similarly, computer products ranging from hand-held products like the Psion Organizer to lap-top portable machines, to new generations of microcomputers such as the IBM PS/2 system, rush in ever-increasing volumes into the marketplace. Telecommunications have evolved a long way since the voice telephone, telegraph and telex of the 1960s and now includes a whole range of sophisticated applications ranging from facsimile to videotex, mobile telephones to video conferencing. This trend will continue and accelerate.

Two significant challenges present themselves to the marketing professional.

1 To try to predict the changing situation.
2 How to use the changes to gain competitive advantage from information technology (IT).

It is salutary to recall that until recently marketing and sales executives had very little help in managing their information-handling requirements. In many organizations computers were used mainly for order processing, accounting, stock control and other administrative functions. The information received by the marketing department was generally a spin-off from the main administrative system. Many marketing managers have tried with varying degrees of success to get the computer to produce information more specific to their needs, and found it a lengthy and frustrating process.

This situation has now changed in many companies, and there is increasing use of personal computers and telecommunications links by marketing secretaries, support staff and even some marketing managers and directors. Although this is only one manifestation of the use of new technology, it is nevertheless significant in encouraging marketing management to become involved with new technology, thus reducing any fears they might have and making it fit in more naturally with their work. However, this type of response must go further and a deeper insight into the IT trends and changes is needed.

CHANGES IN INFORMATION TECHNOLOGY

New technology enables some functions to be carried out more easily or at less cost, or allows some things to be done which were not previously possible. In this sense, information technology is amongst the most enabling innovations in the history of man. Its building blocks are the ubiquitous chip (this is the cornerstone), software, optical fibres and telecommunications. An understanding of each of these technologies is helpful to understanding the future.

The chip

The history of the chip has been characterized by dramatic increases in its power and reductions in both its physical size and price. These trends will continue with new devices such as Josephson junctions and new materials such as superconductors, providing extra impetus. Projections for the year 2000 suggest at least a tenfold reduction in price and a similar increase in speed.

The direct impact of this is the continual increase of computer power at relatively low cost. Good systems are now available at well under £1000, while systems costing between £5000 and £10 000 provide power equivalent to that of a large mainframe computer of a decade ago. Typically such systems provide a wide range of functions including spreadsheets, database, graphics and word processing.

However, the basic way computers work today is little changed since the 1950s, with a central control unit which performs tasks allocated to it sequentially, in steps. New architectures are now evolving which allow many instructions to be performed at the same time. This further reduces the time taken to execute programs, as well as facilitating running several programs simultaneously. An early example of such chips is the Inmos transputer.

Software

While the falling cost of chips has reduced the price of computer hardware, the labour-intensive business of writing and maintaining programs to make the hardware of practical use has increased significantly as a proportion of the total cost of providing systems. However, a number of developments are addressing, slowing down and possibly halting the rate of increase. The first is the result of the large installed population of computers which allows software developers to create standard programs with potential sales of over 100 000 packages. Thus, the high development costs can be written off over a large number of unit sales, creating a relatively low-price product. Typical of these packages are Symphonie, Dbase III, Lotus 1-2-3 and DR Graph.

The second development which reduces the cost of software is systems engineering, where the computer itself assists in programming through pieces of software such as program generators.

The third development is yet to come. The next generation of computers, the fifth, will significantly improve the way the users interrelate with the machine through voice entry of instructions. This will be but one feature of a machine which will also give advice, produce films and video and translate the spoken word – and which anyone will be able to use.

The manner in which computers give advice is through a software technique which has become known as an expert system. Initial applications have included medical diagnosis and the identification of machinery malfunctions. They have also been applied in marketing to help sales staff prepare for negotiations.

Optical fibre and telecommunications

The traditional carrier of speech and data has been electricity through copper wires. This is able to carry only a limited amount of information and the signal must be boosted every few miles as it loses strength. A much better carrier is light, which can carry vast amounts of information, using the media of optical fibre. This carries not just data and voice but text and images also.

The linked development of chips and optical fibres is the basis of the next revolution. New telecommunications products and services are appearing at an enormous rate, as shown in Figure 44.1. The traditional telephone is now but one product among many, and has added functions including automatic redial, memory and call-cost monitoring. Increasingly there is a convergence of computing and telecommunication.

Over the next ten years ISDN, integrated services digital network, will completely replace the traditional copper network with electromechanical switches and exchanges. This will enable all telecommunications services to move down one cable into the office, factory, hospital, library or home, replacing the multiplicity of channels currently needed.

The possibilities these developments open up to the marketer in terms of how the marketing operation is run and how he or she communicates with the market are enormous. These developments can and will fundamently affect the way the marketer performs his or her job.

A FRAMEWORK FOR IT APPLICATIONS

The multiplicity of possible applications for IT in the marketing (and most other business) functions makes it useful to have a frame of reference. Such a framework will give insights that marketing managers can then apply to their own companies and individual situations.

Four broad areas of IT application can be identified as shown in Figure 44.2. The first quadrant covers those marketing activities which are already carried out in one form or another within the company. Typically, these include maintenance of customer records, budgeting, preparing and making presentations and analysing sales statistics, scheduling meetings and so on. The speed and effectiveness with which these types of functions can be carried out can be significantly enhanced by use of information technology.

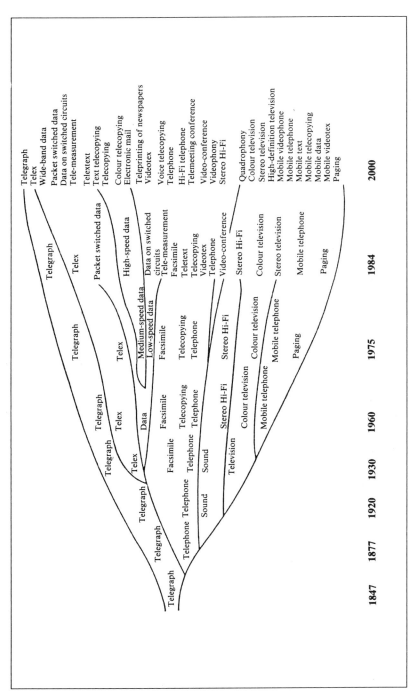

Figure 44.1 The evolution of telecommunications services

Source: NEDO, *IT Futures – IT can work.*
Reproduced with the permission of the Controller of Her Majesty's Stationery Office.

		Marketing activities	
		existing	new
Focus of activity	Internal	1 Enhancing operating efficiency	2 Changed methods
	External	3 Enhancing customer service	4 Marketing innovation

Figure 44.2 An IT applications framework

Customer records can be computerized and stored on a database. Presentations can be greatly enhanced using computer graphics to prepare slides, and by using desk-top publishing systems. Spreadsheets can be used to analyse sales statistics and assist in budgeting, while diary systems make it easier to fix meetings where the availability of several people needs to be established. Information technology therefore enhances the operating efficiency and productivity of the marketing function in carrying out its existing tasks.

The second quadrant goes further in enabling the marketing department to carry out internal functions which were not possible before. This often comes about through extending the applications developed for the first quadrant. For example, the customer database can be analysed further for segmentation purposes, for identifying prime prospects for particular products and establishing improved salesforce journey plans. Spreadsheets used for sales analysis and budgeting can be further developed to enable alternative pricing discount levels to be tested and to conduct routine reforecasting exercises. Contact with the sales force can be significantly extended through the use of mobile cellular telephones, computer-based messaging systems, direct link microterminals and paging systems. Videoconferencing enables meetings to take place between individuals and groups at different locations, while teleconferencing allows similar voice-only communications.

These types of applications tend to increase the scope of activity, by enabling marketers to do what could not be done before because it was too time consuming, cost too much or was impossible due to physical constraints.

The third quadrant concentrates on marketing activities which are directed externally at the customer, resulting in enhanced services to customers. For example, based on its customer purchase records the computer can automatically signal when a customer is likely to be interested in purchasing again, and then print out a personalized letter to encourage the customer to do so. These types of systems are used by financial services organizations such as credit card and life assurance companies and many others.

Another example is telephone interviewing, which has become increasingly important as a market research method. Now the responses to questions can be entered direct into the computer, eliminating the need to take a large amount of information from the interview form, edit it, code it and punch it on to cards. These steps are now eliminated when telephone interviewing is used. The questionnaire is set up on a VDU in front of the telephone interviewer, who types the respondent's reply to each question directly into the computer as it is given. The reply is automatically edited and if incorrect or illogical it will be highlighted instantly so that the question can be asked again.

All these applications increase the effectiveness and efficiency with which marketers relate to their marketplace.

The fourth quadrant is concerned both with extending the applications from existing marketing activities and creating genuinely new external applications. An example is the use of video cassettes in the home, office or retail outlet to demonstrate the usage of particular products or services. This makes it easier for potential customers to see the products in action in the real environment and thus increases their confidence. Another example is the development of large on-line databases of market information such as Data Scan, Information Line and Dialog, covering almost every conceivable product and market. Services such as Pinpoint and ACORN contain the names and addresses of UK householders classified by neighbourhood, which data provide marketers with the facility to target their customer communications at particular segments. For the business-to-business marketer, services such as those provided by Market Locations give names, addresses and maps showing the location of target customers.

Other new external applications include products ranging from video discs to robots, and systems such as home banking and home shopping.

Existing products and services can be substantially upgraded in ways which were not previously possible. London's underground system, for example, now displays information at each station showing when the next train is due. This removes one of the greatest sources of traveller frustration and annoyance.

The applications in this fourth quadrant are perhaps the most exciting of all. They can, and do, alter the very nature of particular markets and the basis on which suppliers compete.

MAKING IT A PART OF MARKET STRATEGY

There are three significant questions which senior marketing and general management should consider in the light of the applications framework outlined in the previous section.

1 Can technology be used to make a significant change in the way business is done so that the company can gain significant advantage over the competition (quadrant 4)?
2 Can the organization significantly improve its impact in the market-place using new technology so as to increase its market share (quadrant 3)?
3 Can IT improve internal operations by significantly lowering costs and enhancing productivity to enable a low cost strategy to be implemented (quadrants 1 and 2)?

An affirmative answer to any of these questions suggests that opportunities exist to gain competitive advantage that will generate improved profitability and enhanced market share.

For example, the use of computer-aided design led car manufacturers to concentrate on the aerodynamics of vehicles. This has led to the highlighting of a particular measure, drag coefficient, with which vehicle purchasers were previously totally unfamiliar. The message is simple; the lower the drag coefficient the better since it leads to enhanced fuel economy. The German car manufacturer Audi was among the first to choose to compete on this basis thereby adding a significant variable into the purchaser's decision-making process. Audi's early decision to concentrate on drag coefficient has helped it maintain a strong position over its competitors.

Metpath, a large US clinical laboratory, competes in a tough commodity business where low differentiation of service had led to a lack of customer loyalty and frequent price discounting. Doctors send specimens to the laboratories for processing, and timely test results are often critical for diagnosis and treatment. Metpath has enhanced its customer service by installing computer terminals and linking them to its laboratory computers so that, for a small monthly fee, physicians can retrieve test results as soon as they are known.

From a purely technical point of view, this is an on-line database application. Strategically, however, Metpath is consciously using this information system as a competitive weapon in two ways: to build barriers against new and existing competitors by raising the information system ante; and to gain advantage over other laboratories by differentiating an otherwise standard service by keeping records of patient data on file and by offering a financial processing service through invoicing and accounts payable applications. This differentiation is intended to secure the loyalty of physicians who normally have a tendency to switch laboratories in search of lower costs.

Another example is provided by the Bank of Scotland through its home banking system on Prestel. Using the power of computers and telecommunications customers manage their money effectively by checking account balances, paying bills, transferring money between accounts, checking transactions and so on, as frequently as they wish. This creates a totally new service which cannot be easily emulated by the traditional high street branch banks, but at the same time puts significant pressure on them to enhance their offerings to the innovative, higher-income customer segments who are attracted by home banking. Thus, in an attempt to compete they have introduced asset management services, encouraged branch managers to visit their business customers and automated some functions such as cash dispensing. New technology has therefore driven the basis on which banks compete.

An example of the way suppliers can significantly increase their impact on the market is the way in which the large pharmaceutical wholesalers such as Vestric and Unichem have used direct order entry systems with retail chemists, hospitals and dispensing doctors. The wholesaler supplies the retailer with a VDU terminal, allowing the retailer to order at any time. There are many advantages for the wholesaler as it reduces the number of staff needed to take orders, speeds up order processing, reduces errors and allows orders to be received outside normal working hours. There are also many advantages for the retail pharmacist who now has a terminal which can perform other functions such as printing drug labels, analysing sales and keeping records of various kinds. The key strategic factor is, however, that each terminal is compatible only with the supplier's system, thus strongly tying the retailer to the particular wholesaler. A barrier to entry is created against the competition who will find it difficult to convince the pharmacist to give room to an additional terminal providing few, if any, additional benefits.

USING IT IN MARKETING

There is virtually no limit to the applications to which technology can be put in marketing. The only constraint is that imposed by the marketer's vision. In this chapter it is possible to look at only a few marketing applications in outline.

Internal activities

Marketing database
Without speedy information on the market and the company's performance in it, marketing managers cannot do their job effectively. Managers generally receive statistical reports, from the computer or compiled manually, containing information on company sales in the preceding period, revenue received, discounts given and so on. Information is also received from the sales force on the numbers of calls made, by area, and the numbers of orders obtained as well as reports on competitor activity and other market information. In addition, information on the total market may be received from government or trade bodies and from market research.

In total this represents a tremendous volume of information of which only a fraction is generally used. The reason so much is wasted is that the task of analysing, collating and presenting the rest in a meaningful form can be extremely time-consuming. The dullness of the task often blunts the keenness of the intellect. Thus, although professional marketing managers would very often like additional information before making decisions, they know that the trouble involved in obtaining the information would not repay the benefit derived. For example, a decision may need to be taken on eliminating a product from the range. To help make this decision the manager would like the following information:

1 What have been the volume and value sales of the product over the last three years, in total and as a percentage of the product group?

2 What has been the average precentage change in sales per year for the last five years for the product?

3 Who are the five largest customers for the product, how much do they buy and what would be the effect on their turnover?

4 How much profit has the product contributed over the last three years?

All this information is likely to be available somewhere in the company. The difficulty lies in obtaining it, sorting through it, doing the analysis and calculations and presenting it in a form that is easy to understand.

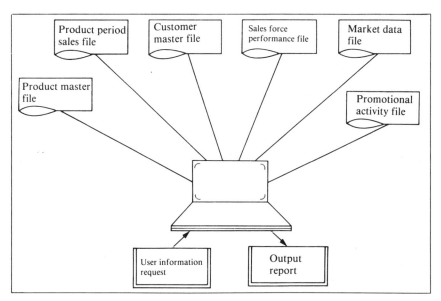

Figure 44.3   Marketing database

This problem can be solved by setting up a marketing database on computer. For all but the most complex of marketing information needs, a microcomputer or small minicomputer can be used.

Typically these systems operate as shown in Figure 44.3. The basic information is stored in a number of files on magnetic disk. Users enter their information requests via a keyboard and the relevant items of information are extracted from the appropriate files, analysed and an output report produced. The way the files are set up is crucial to the success of the system and considerable care must be taken.

The ease of use and flexibility of these types of systems vary. For example, if a product manager wishes to obtain a listing of all trade promotions on his or her product range costing more than £1000, the date of commencement of each promotion and the additional sales achieved, the instruction to be entered might read:

List Proms by buy-in sales cost where cost GT 1000.

The product manager would then receive a chronological list of all promotions.

Although the simple instructions are written in English, they obey special syntax rules and a two- or three-day training programme is needed if the user is to able to write such programs. To overcome this possible problem, specific marketing database packages have been designed which are very simple to use. For example, the promotions information would be requested by answering a series of questions from the computer:

Which products do you want to consider?
What is the earliest buy-in period?
What is the latest buy-in period?
What is the minimum promotion cost?
What is the maximum promotion cost?
Which of the following do you wish printed out (Enter Y/N):

- Product code?
- Product name?
- Pack size?
- Volume sold?
- Buy-in date?
- End date?
- Promotion cost?

Each question would be asked and answered in turn. The computer is, therefore being used to help the marketing manager utilize the considerable amount of available information and in turn improve the quality of the decisions made. Such systems dramatically reduce the vast amount of paper the manager receives and ensure he or she receives only what is wanted, when it is wanted. It is significant that the marketer needs no knowledge of how computers work or complicated languages to operate these systems.

Although some companies will want to develop complete marketing databases, others may wish to set up one aspect at a time. For example, they may first set up a database for market information, then for sales performance and so on, gradually linking them together.

A system originally designed to run on mainframes, pc Express, has been adapted for IBM-compatible micros. It is a database system, responding to simple commands like 'total sales RPQ', meaning 'show total sales by volume, per region and per quarter'; output information is displayed in the form of graphs, pie charts and bar charts as well as in numbers.

Price list updating

The process of regularly updating their price lists is, for many companies, a long and tedious process. Each new price must be calculated, appropriate discounts considered and the resulting price judged against that of other products in the range to ensure differentials are maintained. During inflationary times price lists must be updated frequently and organizations such as retailers, wholesalers and other distributors often update monthly.

The computer is used to carry out the necessary calculations and quickly produces the new price list. The logic of a typical system is shown in Figure 44.4 which gives users the facility to update all, or just part, of their price list, on either an individual, percentage or absolute basis. Having calculated the new prices users can vet them and change any which are unacceptable before the new price list is printed. The system can be extended to show the effect on sales value at budgeted (or any other) volume of sales, and even the impact on gross and net margins and profit at a variety of different prices.

This application can be modelled on a spreadsheet, which takes the drudgery out of a time-consuming task and greatly speeds it up. It can then be extended to give management additional useful information to help decide on the most appropriate price levels.

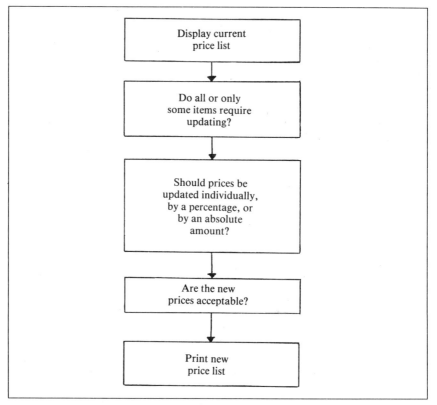

Figure 44.4 Updating a price list

Planning, budgeting and forecasting

Some time before the end of their financial year, most companies go through the process of trying to forecast their sales and costs for thefollowing year and drawing up plans and budgets. The amount of 'number crunching' to be carried out is enormous and there is rarely the opportunity (or the inclination) to try a number of possible projections to assess the most desirable. The computer can take a lot of the hard work out of preparing budgets, make them much easier to revise and greatly speed up the process.

The starting point for the budget is the sales forecast which is prepared by using statistical techniques and/or by getting sales staff and marketing management to 'guesstimate' future sales. A number of good forecasting packages exist, using statistical methods such as exponential smoothing, classical decomposition, generalized adaptive filtering and

Box-Jenkins. One particular program, 'Sibyl Runner', helps the users to choose which of the available statistical forecasting methods are suitable for their data and then runs the appropriate method. This enables marketers to run a number of methods and the computer will work out which is the most accurate. They can then choose the most appropriate to use for their forecasts.

The user needs to know very little about the actual statistics and even less about computers. The programs are 'user-friendly' and all the user need do is answer a series of questions. For example:

xxxSIA time share servicexxx
xinteractive forecasting packagex

Good morning

Need help – (yes/no/recover/change)
? yes

Help: The interactive forecasting system is divided into two segments. The first segment, referred to as 'Sibyl' analyses data, suggests appropriate forecasting methods. The second, 'Runner', can be used alone or after 'Sibyl'. It runs any forecasting methods, stores the results on a file and compares different methods. However, you can run the programs individually too.

Do you want to use:

a   Program data (40 obs)?
b   Your own data, in file?
c   Your own data, to be typed in at a terminal?
d   Data generated by the program?
?b   What is the name of your data file?
?   Tony

Communicating with the salesforce
Prestel can also be used to send information to the salesforce in their

homes. This can be done via a facility called a 'closed user group'. Only users with special adaptors on their TV sets and knowledge of special passwords can get into a closed user loop. If, for example, only first-line sales managers have this facility then information on, say, their sales teams' performance can be transmitted to them at the end of each day in the knowledge that no one else will be able to gain access to it (see Figure 44.5).

Typically, the sales manager wants to know the number of calls made, orders obtained, particular product sales, particular account sales and so on. The information can be analysed and presented by the computer in the form most useful to the managers. The basic information on the salesforce's performance is obtained from the salespeople themselves who enter it direct into their company's computer using remote entry microterminals. The keypads are not too dissimilar from the Prestel keypads and link directly into the telephone lines.

The main advantages of the system are that it speeds up the transmission of orders from the customer, hence expediting cash flow and getting information to sales management quickly. This in turn enables managers to take action promptly to overcome problems and redirect sales effort.

Sales force reporting and control

To keep their management informed salespeople usually do a lot of paperwork. Typically this includes daily and weekly reports, order forms, customer records and so on. These reports are then analysed to ensure that the sales executive is directing his or her effort appropriately, and identifying any significant problems. This analysis can be done using a computer as shown in Figure 44.6

The input may be either from the sales executive's daily report or directly from a microterminal used by him or her to enter orders. The system can, therefore, be either separate or a spin-off from the order processing system. The output can be sent in tabular printout form or via Prestel to sales management.

ICL has over the last five years developed and launched a sales manager system which provides a wide range of functions and is particularly easy to use by means of 'pull down' menus. Colour monitors show information in graphics form which facilitates interpretation of the output.

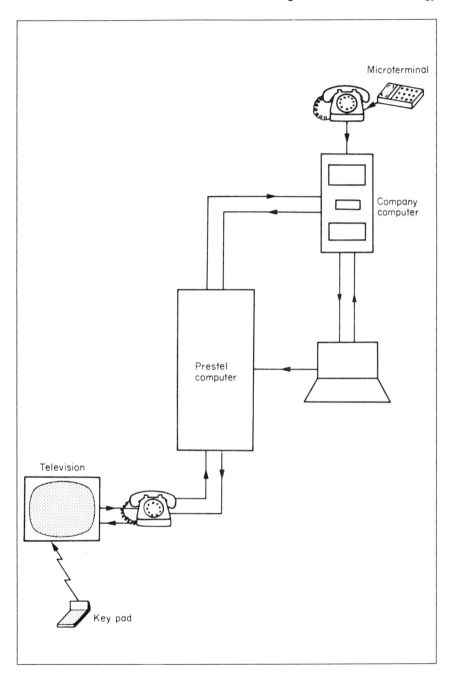

Figure 44.5   A closed user group

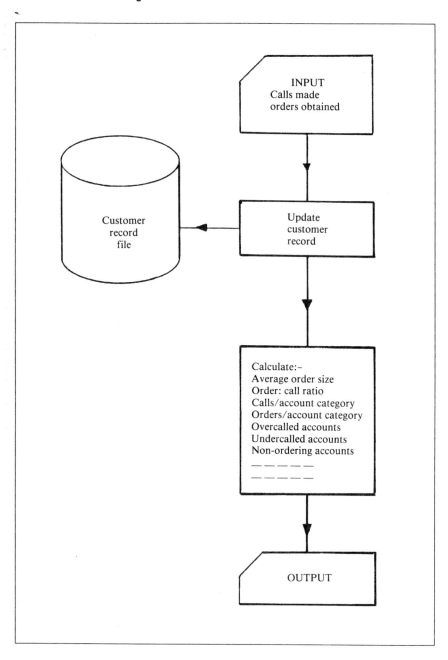

Figure 44.6   Reporting and control system

External activities

Direct mail/Database marketing

Whether on a selective product offer, or to announce a general price increase, most companies use direct mail to communicate with the market. By storing names and addresses on computer, the laborious job of typing them out can be eliminated.

In many instances the message the marketer wishes to communicate will be of interest only to a segment of the total list. For example, a car dealer may want to mail all customers who purchased new cars of less than 1600 cc from him three to five years ago with invitations to test drive new 2000 cc models. Or a manufacturer of agricultural equipment may wish to notify all diary farmers with a herd of more than 100 cows of a particular new bolt-on attachment for their milking parlours.

The facility to access sub-segments of the total list saves both time and money, as well as improving response rates. Word processing saves more time in compiling personalized letters to each potential customer.

This type of application is very straightforward and numerous well-tried packages are on the market. Generally they can be run on an inexpensive microcomputer, although a good quality daisy or laser printer is needed to produce well-typed letters.

Communicating with the market

Prestel/Viewdata provides a means of bringing the home or business directly into contact with an almost limitless range of information. This public service, operated by BT, has information stored in the form of a database on a network of computers, which can be accessed through an adapted TV set via the telephone network. The user accesses the system by using a keypad rather like an electronic calculator.

Someone who wants to buy a washing machine, for example, could use Prestel to help her. She would first want to get some impartial advice on the machines available and would, therefore, summon the consumer advice magazine *Which?*. The relevant sections would be displayed on the screen and the buyer would decide which she felt were worth further consideration. She would then want to know who stocked the machines and their cost, and would summon Comet Warehouses, Curry's and so on, each of which would have their latest price lists on display. She could then choose which supplier offered the best deal and even, in some cases, make a purchase by entering her credit card number. The supplier would then check her credit status and arrange delivery.

It is significant that so far the customer need not have left her armchair. Prestel, therefore, provides an additional communication and purchasing channel to the consumer which must be carefully considered by the supplier. It gives the consumer added information and the facility to compare alternative offerings, while giving the supplier direct contact with the customer when that customer is actually making up his or her mind as to what to buy.

Information technology as a sales tool

The sales executive carries out many tasks which can be carried out even more effectively using a computer. A number of examples will serve to illustrate the point.

1 *Selling the benefits.* When selling to a distributor or industrial buyer, many salespeople will try to convince the buyer that their particular product or service will save costs and/or generate more profit. This happens in many markets from oil to capital plant, from toilet tissues to vending machines. The sales executive will often present a typical situation to the buyer, showing how under a particular set of circumstances the product produces a certain cost saving or level of profit. Unfortunately, the particular example is usually a generalized one and each customer's particular situation is invariably slightly different. The computer can help the sales executive in such a case to present his or her arguments even better.

For example, a person selling filtration equipment for lubricating oils to be used in machine shops will want to justify the purchase of his or her products by showing how they can extend the usable life of machine oil and thus save money. He or she needs merely to make a note of the particular customer's method of operation, recording such details as number of machine tools of each type, workload, value of lubricating oil used, type of oil storage facility and so on. This information is sent back to head office where the computer works out the most economical solution to the customer's problem. On his next visit the sales executive will be able to show the customer how much better off he or she will be and how much money will be saved.

2 *Reducing routine work.* Many salespeople selling to retail outlets spend much of their time merchandising the shelves. With bulky

products such as toys, soft drinks, paper products and so on, making an attractive display can be extremely time-consuming. The sales executive must take into account the particular products stocked by the outlet, the dimensions of the shelving and the actual rate of sale in the store. These factors vary from outlet to outlet and generalized planograms of displays are often of little relevance.

By feeding the appropriate information into the computer, it can design the most suitable display and print a simple plan of which items should be put where and how many there should be. It can also list the cost of the display and the profit it produces. By getting a second computer printout for a display, say, two feet longer, the effective sales executive can show the store manager how much extra profit will be made by giving his or her products more shelf space, and thereby obtain more facings.

3 *Customer support packages*. Companies such as Ford and General Motors, which sell their products through distributors, support their distributors and help them manage their businesses more efficiently. They often help to install specific management systems and give the distributor regular management information produced on their own computer. Systems also show model and spare part availability using the Prestel network. In this way the distributor becomes more successful, sells more products, and is a better credit risk for the supplier.

CAPITALIZING ON NEW TECHNOLOGY

This chapter has given some examples of how information technology is being used in marketing. IT is potentially one of the most powerful tools available to the marketing manager. However, applications for IT are not always obvious. Before embarking on any programme, therefore, the marketing executive should carry out an opportunity audit to identify and rank the opportunities. The audit should examine the following matters.

Establishing trends

1 How will the market develop over the next ten years and how is the buying process going to change?

2 How will the cost structure change over the next ten years?
3 What actions are competitors likely to take?
4 What elements of the marketing mix are likely to change and in what manner?

Using information technology

In the light of the trends, what actual and potential applications are there?

1 How and where can value be added to the product/service, or how can it be differentiated?
2 Are there a lot of data which are currently not effectively used, and if so where?
3 Where is there paperwork which could be computerized?
4 What analyses are carried out which require a great deal of time to produce?
5 What information would it be useful to obtain but which does not warrant the additional paperwork currently required?
6 Where would speeding up the flow of information improve the quality of decision-making and/or save money?
7 Where can the offering to customers be tailored to meet their needs even better and increase the likelihood of getting the sale?
8 What decisions are taken on a trial and error basis which can be improved by a systematic approach?
9 Where are customers using IT techniques and how should the supplier react?

After conducting a systematic audit, all the possible applications should be identified and ranked. A strategy for implementing IT in the marketing department can then be formulated, concentrating most effort on applications that give strategic advantage over competitors.

SUMMARY

This chapter has examined the main new developments in technology, how they can be used in marketing and how the marketer should capitalize on the opportunity they represent. Because of its breadth of application, information technology is probably one of the most powerful and exciting tools marketers have at their disposal.

Those companies that exploit the opportunities, adopting a planned and controlled approach, will achieve an advantage over their less innovative competitors in the marketplace.

FURTHER READING

Benjamin, R. I., Rockart, J. E., Scott Morton, M. S. and Wyman, J. (1984), 'Information technology: a strategic opportunity', *Sloan Management Review*, Spring, pp. 27–34.

Forester, T. (1985), *The Information Technology Revolution*, Blackwell, Oxford.

Judkins, P. (ed) (1985), *Networking in Organizations: The Rank Xerox Experiment*, Gower, Aldershot.

NEDO (1987), *IT Futures – IT can work*, HMSO, London.

Stonier, T. (1983), *The Wealth of Information: A Profile of the Post Industrial Economy*, Thames Methuen, London.

Wiseman, C. and MacMillan, I. C. (1984), 'Creating competitive weapons from information systems', *The Journal of Business Strategy*, Vol. 5, No. 2, pp. 42–50.

Index